Dimensions
of
Learning Disability

Dimensions
of
Learning Disability

Edited by

Bob Gates

MSc, BEd, Dip Nurs(Lond), Cert Ed, RNT, RNMH, RMN

*Lecturer in Nursing, Institute of Nursing Studies, University
of Hull and Head of Profession for Learning Disability
Nursing, Hull and Holderness NHS Community Trust*

and

Colin Beacock

RNMH, RGN, Cert Ed, MA

*Professional Officer, Royal College of Nursing, Sheffield,
formerly Senior Education Manager in Learning Disability
Studies at Rampton Hospital*

Baillière Tindall
PUBLISHED IN ASSOCIATION WITH THE RCN

London   Philadelphia   Toronto   Sydney   Tokyo

Baillière Tindall   24–28 Oval Road
London NW1 7DX

The Curtis Center
Independence Square West
Philadelphia, PA 19106-3399, USA

Harcourt Brace & Company
55 Horner Avenue
Toronto, Ontario, M8Z 4X6, Canada

Harcourt Brace & Company, Australia
30–52 Smidmore Street
Marrickville
NSW 2204, Australia

Harcourt Brace & Company, Japan
Ichibancho Central Building
22-1 Ichibancho
Chiyoda-ku, Tokyo 102, Japan

A catalogue record for this book is available from the British Library

ISBN 0-7020-1916-X

Typeset by Paston Press Ltd, Loddon, Norfolk
Printed and bound in Great Britain by The Bath Press, Bath

Contents

Contributors

Janet Allen, RNMH, BA (Hons), Research and Development Co-ordinator, Hull and Holderness Community Health, Hull.

Sam Ayer, PhD, BSc (Hons), RNMH, RMN, Cert Ed, RNT, FRSH, Principal Lecturer and Head of Research and Development, University of Hull, East Riding Campus, East Yorkshire.

Colin Beacock, RNMH, RGN, Cert Ed, MA, Professional Officer, Royal College of Nursing, Sheffield, formerly Senior Education Manager in Learning Disability Studies at Rampton Hospital.

Jan Brown, Cert Ed. Pre-School Support Teacher, Pre-School Support Service, Debdale Management Service, Mansfield, Nottinghamshire.

Norman Daniels, BArch RIBA, Poplars Church Leader/Architect, Poplars Church Office, Worksop, Nottinghamshire.

Andrew Ferguson, RNMH, Care Manager, Horizon Trust, Hertfordshire.

Bob Gates, MSc, BEd, Dip Nurs(Lond), Cert Ed, RNT, RNMH, RMN, Lecturer in Nursing, Institute of Nursing Studies, University of Hull and Head of Profession for Learning Disability Nursing, Hull and Holderness NHS Community Trust.

David Hall, RNMH, Staff Nurse – Challenging Behaviour, 'Newhaven Unit', Huddersfield NHS Trust.

Rachel Jacklin, Special-needs Care Assistant/Community Worker, Brasov, Romania.

Susan Joseph, MBBS, DPM, MRCPsych, Consultant Psychiatrist, Hull and Holderness Community Health Trust, Tilworth Grange Hospital, Hull.

David Lewis, RNMH, RNT, Cert Ed (FE) Cert Ed (Special Needs) Counselling Cert, CSLA, Found Cert (Art), Senior Lecturer, University of Hertfordshire, Hatfield Campus, Hatfield, Herts.

Susan Merrylees, RNMH, Cert Ed, MA, Nurse Lecturer, School of Nursing, Faculty of Medicine, University of Sheffield, Sheffield.

Aru Narayanasamy, BA, MSc, RGN, RMN, Cert Ed, RNT, Lecturer/Honorary Adviser in Transcultural Health Care (Queens Medical Centre, Nottingham), School of Nursing & Midwifery, University of Nottingham.

Adrienne Regan, MBBS, DCH, FRCPsych, Consultant in Psychiatry of Learning Disabilities, Eric Short House, Harrow Hospital, Harrow, Middlesex.

Marilyn Robinson, SROT, MAOT, Senior Occupational Therapist, Retford Hospital, Nottinghamshire.

Tom Tait, MA, RNMH, RCNT, RNT, Cert Ed, MHSM, Lecturer in Nursing Studies, University of Bradford School of Health Studies, Bradford.

Carl Thompson, RGN, BA (Hons), Research Associate, Centre for Health and Advanced Nursing Studies/North Durham Community Health Care, University of Durham, Co. Durham.

Deborah Vernon, BSc (Hons), RGN, RNMH, Graduate Teaching Assistant, Institute of Nursing Studies, University of Hull, Hull.

Eileen Wake, RNMH, RGN, RSCN, BA (Hons), Paediatric Nurse Lecturer, School of Health, University of Hull, East Riding Campus, Willerby, East Yorkshire.

Foreword

Bob Gates and Colin Beacock are knowledgeable and respected members of their profession. So, I felt delighted to be asked to join them and their colleagues in making a contribution, however small, to this timely publication.

1996 marks the 25th anniversary of the Government White Paper, 'Better Services for the Mentally Handicapped'. It is therefore a time to take stock of achievements, especially those of people with learning disabilities themselves. It also prompts thinking about progress we need to make. As service models have come and gone, we can recognise some enduring themes: the challenge for all of us is to hold on to a vision of life for people with learning disabilities in which they feel they belong to the communities in which they live.

We also need to aim for a future in which we are confident of our own part in enabling this to happen. This book will provide ample opportunity for this, whether you are embarking on your journey in this field of work or whether you are a more experienced traveller. As a nurse and a health professional, my experience and education has taught me the value of health in people's lives. Health is a resource for us to draw upon to get the most out of life. In choosing health as the major theme for this book, Bob and Colin have earned my strongest approval.

Describing the elements of good health is relatively simple. What we need to do to bring it about is not so easy. What has become abundantly clear to me is that things are made so much easier when people recognise the part they can play and work together. The ideas and examples that follow will go a long way to giving us the will and the ways to harness all our talents.

John Turnbull RNMH, BA, MSc
Nursing Officer (Learning Disabilities)
Department of Health, London

Preface

This book has been written for those people who care for, and work with, people with learning disabilities. The primary audience is intended to be students of nursing studying at undergraduate or diplomate level, although it is hoped that other disciplines such as social workers, occupational therapists, special education teachers or students of psychology may find some aspects of the text useful.

Central to this book is the idea that one way of understanding learning disabilities is to portray it as a complex state of health comprising a number of dimensions of being:

- **educational**
- **spiritual**
- **cultural**
- **psychological**
- **biological**

In this book these dimensions are located within a context of national and international issues and on going research.

Each part of this book explores one or more of these dimensions of being. Part One explores the nature of learning disabilities from a number of differing theoretical perspectives. One of the theoretical orientations is concerned with the health

Figure 1 Learning disability as a state of health.

perspective and the role of the nurse in bringing about health maintenance and/or gain that has been advocated by others (Baldwin and Birchenell, 1993). Part Two discusses the concept of health and applies this to people with learning disabilities who may encounter challenges in achieving optimum health. In Part Three the educational dimension outlines the contribution of educational theory to learning disabilities and explores the concept of learning for life.

In Part Four the biological dimension of learning disabilities is explored. This part explains the causation and manifestation of learning disabilities and demonstrates how the various manifestations of learning disabilities may lead to changes to the health status of this group of people. Part Five explores the psychosocial dimensions of learning disability. This is achieved by tracing the practical application of normalist theory in learning disabilities. It is anticipated that this chapter will enable the reader to assess the relevance of such theory in relation to the life style of people with learning disabilities.

In Part Six, the cultural and spiritual dimensions of learning disabilities are explored. Part Seven analyses the economic and political dimensions of learning disabilities.

The penultimate part, Part Eight, provides three case histories from the UK, Sweden and Romania which highlight two mature services along with a country that is in the process of setting up services.

The final part of the book provides an overview and analysis of recent research in the field of learning disabilities that relates to each dimension of being explored within the book. Consistently throughout each part of the book the contributors contextualize how health, in its widest sense, may be affected by challenges to each dimension of being.

The NHS and Community Care Act (1990) gave local authorities the lead role in providing social care; some would argue that this has led to health providers and purchasers abdicating their responsibility in caring for people with learning disabilities (Waddington, 1995). This is clearly a book that attempts to place learning disabilities firmly back on the agenda of health. Learning disabilities, in spite of recent legislation, cannot simply be located into the separate arenas of either health or social-care provision. To talk of health and social care as mutually exclusive concepts, whilst politically convenient, is both dangerous and inaccurate. Dangerous, because the clearer this false distinction becomes, the greater the gap will develop for people to fall in between services, and subsequently fail to receive any services. Inaccurate, because health by all contemporary definitions is concerned with the wholeness of well being, and not simply the absence of disease or illness. The book contains case histories, reader activities and authentic examples from practice, which will enhance the reader's knowledge and understanding of learning disabilities. The book attempts to make sense of learning disabilities by providing an authoritative account that encompasses theoretical elements, yet remains practical enough to be used to enhance the lives and health of people with learning disabilities.

Bob Gates and Colin Beacock
Lincoln, January 1996

References

DOH (1990) NHS and Community Care Act. London: HMSO.

Baldwin, S. and Birchenell, M. (1993) The nurse's role in caring for people with learning disabilities. *British Journal of Nursing* **2**(7): 850–855.

Waddington, P. (1995) Joint commissioning of services for people with learning disabilities: A review of the principles and the practice. *British Journal of Learning Disabilities* **23**: 2–10.

Part One: Learning Disability

1   The Nature of Learning Disability   3

Bob Gates

The first part of *Dimensions of Learning Disability*, Chapter 1, provides an overview of the nature of learning disabilities. Bob Gates outlines the various ways in which learning disabilities have been defined throughout recent history. A temporal account is given of the ways in which they have been understood and the subsequent models of service provision that have been provided for people with learning disabilities. The chapter explores its subject by adopting a number of differing theoretical approaches. These approaches include sociological, psychological, medical, anthropological and health perspectives. These various contributions have helped to illuminate and provide valuable insights into our understanding of the nature of learning disabilities. At the level of formal theory such approaches are fascinating; however, problematic with single theoretical approaches is that they often fail to adequately account for the complexity of the phenomenon. In this chapter it is advocated that learning disabilities may more usefully be understood as a complex state of being. It is suggested that this state of being comprises a number of dimensions that include educational, spiritual and cultural, social and biological characteristics. Further, these dimensions may act for or against the lifestyle, opportunities and health of people with learning disabilities. The chapter outlines the nurse's role in bringing about health maintenance and/or gain for such people. This role is pivotal in enhancing the health of this group of people who sometimes need access to a learning disabilities nurse practitioner who is able to work with them and enable them to live healthy lives. The chapter seeks to provide a conceptual base for the remainder of the text so that the reader may understand health as a more complex state of being than merely being concerned with either the absence or presence of disease.

Chapter 1: The nature of learning disability
Bob Gates

1.1 Introduction and Defining Learning Disability

This chapter introduces the nature of learning disability, and outlines a number of different theoretical approaches that will help the reader understand the term learning disability. It includes the assertion that learning disability may also be understood as a complex state of being. Such a concept demands the presence of a number of dimensions that may act for or against the individual's life style, opportunities and health.

Health has been defined by Beck *et al.* (1988) whose definition included dimensions of being such as biological, educational, spiritual, cultural and social; it is these dimensions that provide a framework for the remainder of this book. They have stated that:

> Holistic health philosophy includes a primary focus on health promotion, or health as a positive process, rather than the absence of disease, it is a dynamic active process of continual striving to reach ones own balance and highest potential. Health involves working towards optimal functioning in all areas. The process varies among people and even within individuals as they move among people and even within individuals as they move from one situation and life stage to another, and is contingent on personal needs, imbalances and individual perceptions of reality. (Beck *et al.*, 1988, p.26)

It is the case that the health status of an individual with a learning disability, along with all people, is susceptible to:

- **Health loss.** This is experienced when there is a negative impact upon the physical, psychological, emotional, intellectual and or spiritual well being of an individual. It is likely that such a state may require the intervention of professional carers in order to bring about equilibrium to an individual's state of being.

- **Health gain.** This is experienced when the dimensions of physical, psychological, emotional, intellectual and/or spiritual well being are in harmony, and do not compromise the life style and/or opportunities of an individual. In this state there is often a positive effect not only upon the individual, but on significant others in that person's life.

- **Health maintenance.** This refers to a state of being when an individual may not be able to achieve a state of health gain, but rather they live within the limitations of a range of difficulties but do not experience health loss. It is the case, in learning disability, that some people achieve a state of health maintenance, and this should be perceived as a positive outcome of health. Some people with a learning disability require the sustained interventions of professional carers to achieve this state.

Gostin (1985) has estimated that there are 110 000 people with severe learning disability and more than 350 000 with a mild learning disability in England. This clearly represents a significant section of society who are entitled to access the resource of skilled professionals, who are able to meet their health needs.

The role of the professional and lay carer, in enabling people with a learning disability to reach their own 'balance and highest potential' of health, is vitally important to the well being of people with a learning disability. This issue is explored later in this chapter in the section that deals with differing theoretical approaches to understanding learning disability, and in particular focuses upon the role of the learning disability nurse in helping people with a learning disability lead valued life styles within their optimal health potential. The first part of this chapter explores what learning disability means. This is followed by an attempt to define it. It has to be said that this is much easier to say than it is to achieve. For clarity, understanding any concept, idea or phenomenon requires access to a prescribed language that expresses acceptable meanings. This is necessary for the development of all knowledge to bring about clarity as to what is being referred to, and learning disability is no exception. Herein lies a problem, this is because the term 'learning disability' means many different things to many different people.

Reader Activity 1.1
Consider Case Study 1.1 and then answer the following questions based on your existing knowledge of learning disability:

- **Do you think Vera has a learning disability?**
- **Identify those factors that led you to arrive at the conclusion as to whether Vera has or has not learning disability.**

It may have been the case that some difficulty was experienced in deciding whether Vera has a learning disability. How one decides whether an individual has a learning disability is not easy. It is in fact quite complex. For example, what criteria should be used in deciding whether someone has a learning disability? Is it not the case that arriving at such a decision cannot be arbitrary, with wide variance as to when one should conclude that a person has, or not, a learning disability? In order to be able to identify whether someone has a learning disability suggests a need for a reliable criterion or criteria, against which individuals could be measured, and then compared to the general population. The most common criteria for identifying learning disability comprise the following:

- **intellectual ability**
- **legislative definitions**
- **social competence.**

Each of these criteria is now discussed separately.

Intellectual Ability

Some would argue that intelligence is an obvious criterion upon which to judge whether someone has a learning disability. An immediate problem with

this is being able to decide just what intelligence is. This chapter does not have sufficient space to explore this issue in any great depth, but it is assumed that intelligence is something to do with the ability to solve problems and that this ability, or the absence of it, can be measured. One way of measuring intelligence is by using intelligence tests. These tests have been used since the turn of the century, they serve the purpose of enabling one to compare the intellectual ability of one individual to complete a range of standardized tests, against a large representative sample of the general population. The sample that an individual is compared with will be of a similar chronological age. The score that an individual attains, on completion of tests, can then be converted into a percentile, in order that one may understand how this individual compares with others in the general population. Normally the percentile is converted to an intelligence quotient (IQ) that has been, and still is, used as means for identifying learning disability. The intelligence test seeks to compare the mental age of an individual against their chronological age. This is achieved by using the following formula:

$$\frac{\text{Mental age}}{\text{Chronological age}} \times 100 = IQ$$

In the above formula, chronological age refers to the actual age of an individual and mental age refers to the developmental stage that an individual has reached, in comparison to others of a similar age. If the sum of the number reached by dividing mental age by chronological age is multiplied by 100 then one arrives at the IQ. Clearly, given the nature of this formula, if one was to continue using it throughout an individual's life then IQ would progressively diminish, therefore the formula is only of use until the chronological age of around 18 years. For the student who wishes to study both the concept and history of IQ, Gross (1991) is recommended. Given that intelligence is present in the population, and is evenly distributed, it is possible to measure how far an individual moves away from what constitutes 'normal'. This so-called normal distribution of intelligence can be demonstrated diagramatically by the normal distribution curve of intelligence. In such diagrams it can be seen that some individuals will have an IQ above the normal and some below the normal.

Intelligence tests were extensively used during the 1960s and 1970s; however, recognition by psychologists of the many limitations of their use has made them less popular today. These limitations include cultural bias, poor predictive ability, and an uncomprehensive relevance for the identification of learning disability. Despite the range of criticisms constructed against the use of intelligence tests, if used appropriately and by properly trained technicians then they do provide a relatively objective measure of the intellectual ability of an individual. In addition, if such a measure is used in conjunction with other criterion, such as social competence, this may be helpful in identifying whether an individual has a learning disability.

Legislative Definitions of Learning Disability

It is the case that legislators, both within the UK and in other countries, have for centuries attempted to use the law to define learning disability. This may in part be explained by the conflation of learning disability with mental illness; this 'clumping' together of two states of being has resulted in people with a learning disability being the subject of much unnecessary legislation. This brief exploration only considers legislation this century, and in particular focuses upon mental health legislation. For an overview of other related legislation and social policy refer to Appendix 1.

The Mental Deficiency Act of 1913 said:

Mental defectiveness means a condition of arrested or incomplete development of mind existing before the age of eighteen years, whether arising from inherent causes or induced by disease or injury.

The Act categorized four different types of learning disability:

- **idiot**
- **imbecile**
- **feeble minded**
- **moral defective.**

This Act followed the Radnor Commission of 1908, and introduced the compulsory certification of 'defectives'. In a sense, this Act reflected the strong eugenics movement of the time; not surprisingly the Act required that 'defectives' be identified and then segregated from the rest of society. By 1959 terminology, and perhaps attitudes, had changed and the Mental Health Act of (1959) introduced the terms listed in Box 1.1.

This Act required local authorities to make day service and residential provision for people with a 'mental subnormality'. Clearly, this Act placed new emphasis on the reintegration of people with 'mental subnormality' into being a part of the communities to which they belonged. However, this

---

Box 1.1 Classifications of the 1959 Mental Health Act

- **Subnormality** – A state of arrested or incomplete development of mind, not amounting to severe subnormality, which includes subnormality of intelligence, and is of a nature or degree which requires, or is susceptible to, medical treatment or other special care or training of the patient.
- **Severe subnormality** – A state of arrested or incomplete development of mind which includes subnormality of intelligence and is of such a nature or degree that the patient is incapable of living an independent life or guarding himself/herself against serious exploitation, or will be so incapable when of an age to do so.
- **Psychopathic disorder** – A persistent disorder or disability of mind, whether or not including subnormality of intelligence, which results in abnormally aggressive or seriously irresponsible conduct, on the part of the patient and requires, or is susceptible to, medical treatment.

Act must be seen in context, and it should be remembered that it followed the implementation of the NHS Act (1948). The consequential medicalization of 'mental subnormality' following the NHS Act is clearly reflected in the Mental Health Act of 1959, and therefore the definitions that it offered reflected this. Note the strong emphasis, in the definitions, that was placed on treatment. In addition, the Act made extensive reference to the Responsible Medical Officer. It is at this point in the history of mental health legislation that the influence of medicine in defining the nature of learning disability exerted its greatest impact. As a result of continued social reform and pressure from a range of lobby groups, mental health legislation was again reformed in 1983; the old Act of 1959 was replaced with the 1983 Mental Health Act; once again old terminology was changed and replaced with the terms exhibited in Box 1.2.

It can be seen that the nature of these definitions excluded the large majority of people with learning disability; that is, unless learning disability (mental or severe mental impairment) coexisted with aggressive or seriously irresponsible behaviour, then they were not subject to this new piece of legislation. This Act represented a major shift in the perception of people with a learning disability in mental health legislation; for the first time learning disability and mental illness were separated by law.

Social Competence

The final criterion, in this chapter, that is used for identifying learning disability is that of social competence. Mittler (1979) has suggested that most countries have used criteria based on social competence that include the ability of an individual to adapt to the changing demands made by the society in which that individual lives. Of course this sounds relatively straightforward; that is, one simply identifies people who are socially incompetent, and who do not respond well to changing societal demands. On the basis of an individual performing significantly below what might be considered as 'normal', one presumably may say that they might have a learning disability. However, there are a number of problematic issues to consider in relation to the criterion of social competence. First, social incompetence is to be found in a wide cross-section of people; and not just those with a learning disability. Consider, for example, people with chronic mental health problems as well as non-conformists to societal norms. Alternatively, there may be problems of communication, hearing and vision that could also be the cause of social incompetence, and may not necessarily involve a learning disability.

Second, there is an issue here of expectation and the notion of a self-fulfilling prophecy. Assume, momentarily, that an individual is identified as having a learning disability, on the basis of measured social incompetence. Is it the case that this individual genuinely has a learning disability, or is the social incompetence merely an artefact of the hospital setting in which this individual spent their formative years? Such a finding is not beyond the realms of credibility. It is only relatively recently that the large learning disability hospitals have been closing. It is the case that thousands of people with

---

Box 1.2 Classifications of the 1983 Mental Health Act

- **Severe mental impairment** – A state of arrested or incomplete development of mind which includes severe impairment of intelligence and social functioning and is associated with abnormally aggressive or seriously irresponsible conduct of the person concerned.
- **Mental impairment** – A state of arrested or incomplete development of mind (not amounting to severe mental impairment) which includes significant impairment of intelligence and social functioning and is associated with abnormally aggressive or seriously irresponsible conduct on the part of the person concerned.

a learning disability were segregated from society, and led very devalued life styles. Opportunities for the development of social competence were few and far between; even when opportunities did arise they were often perverted attempts to create some kind of social reality within an institutional setting. There have been numerous studies undertaken on the effects of people who are deprived of normal environments. Dennis (1973) found that institutionalized children were delayed in basic competencies such as sitting, standing and walking, and reported that they had no opportunity to practise these skills. It was also noted that with the additional lack of stimulation there was also significant delay in language acquisition, social skill development and emotional expression:

> . . . as babies they lay on their backs in their cribs throughout the first year and often for much of the second year . . . Many objects available to most children did not exist . . . There were no building blocks, no sandboxes, no scooters, no tricycles, no climbing apparatus, no swings. There were no pets or other animals of any sort . . . they had no opportunities to learn what these objects were. They never saw persons who lived in the outside world, except for rather rare visitors. (Dennis, 1973, pp. 22–23)

In short, the expectations of people in these environments were low, and therefore it is not unreasonable to assume that their ability to develop social competence in such environments was reduced. Despite the criticisms made in this section, the use of social competence as means for the identification of a learning disability remains a globally used criterion.

Reader Activity 1.2
Reflect on these criteria and then decide which one offers the greatest utility in identifying learning disabilities, or whether a combination of the three is more useful.

Box 1.3 Terms used to describe people with a learning disability

- **Learning disability**
- **Learning difficulty**
- **Mentally impaired**
- **Imbecile**
- **Moron**
- **Cretin**
- **Benny**
- **Spastic**
- **Idiot**
- **Mentally subnormal**
- **Mentally retarded**
- **Intellectual disability**
- **Morally defective**
- **Educationally subnormal**
- **Ineducable**

A General Discussion on Terminology

It should be pointed out that the term 'learning disability' is relatively new. It is used in the UK to describe a group of people with significant developmental delay that results in arrested or incomplete achievement of the 'normal' milestones of human development. These milestones relate to intellectual, emotional, spiritual and social aspects of development. Significant delays in one or more of these areas may lead to a person being described, defined or categorized as having a learning disability. The causes of learning disability are multifactorial and some causes are described in some depth in Chapter 6. Despite wide usage in the UK it should be remembered that the term is not one that is used internationally, nor is it a term that has been used for very long in this country. Until recently the term 'mental handicap' was much more frequently used but was replaced, because it was felt that it portrayed negative imagery concerning people with disability. Interestingly, a relatively recent study by Nursey *et al.* (1990) demonstrated that parents and doctors had preferences in the words that they chose to use when referring to people with learning disability. The study was conducted using a questionnaire and established that both parents and doctors preferred the term 'mental handicap' or 'learning difficulties'. However, the doctors were more inclined to accept the words dull, backward and developmentally delayed.

Reader Activity 1.3

Perhaps it might be worth spending some time to consider Box 1.3, which identifies a range of terms that are commonly used to describe people with a learning disability. Are you aware of other terms that have general usage? Which of these terms do you think is the most acceptable to people in general? Do you think that any of the terms used are capable of creating negative imagery concerning this group of people?

In the USA the term 'mental retardation' is widely used for the classification of learning disability. This system is based upon the ICD-10 Classification of Mental and Behavioural Disorders, World Health Organization 10th revision (1993). This uses the term 'mental retardation' to refer to:

a condition of arrested or incomplete development of the mind, which is especially characterised by impairment skills manifested during the developmental period which contribute to the overall level of intelligence, i.e. cognitive, language, motor and social abilities.

The World Health Organization have organized the degree of disability (retardation) according to how far an individual moves away from the normal distribution of IQ for the general population, as has been discussed previously. Using this system, an individual who consistently scores below 2 standard deviations of an IQ test, that is – a measured IQ of less than 70, would be said to be mentally retarded. Those individuals whose IQ is in the range 50–69 are generally identified as having a mild learning disability (F70), and those with an IQ of between 71 and 84 are said to be on the borderline of intellectual functioning. Moderate learning disability (F71) is identified when the IQ is in the range of 35–49; severe mental retardation (F72) is identified when the IQ is in the range of 20–34, and finally the term profound mental retardation (F73) is reserved for people whose IQ is estimated below 20. There is one final category that can be used and is known as F78 (other mental retardation) and this is reserved for people whose complex additional disabilities, for example sensory, physical or behavioural, makes the measurement of IQ difficult. Of course the use of all these labels, with the exception of F78, relies on the use of standardized tests that offer high validity and reliability.

It is becoming increasingly common for professional carers not to use these categories. This is because they represent static measures that tell us nothing of the needs of each individual person; these needs will vary considerably between people, even if their measured IQ is an exact match with another. In learning disability, one of the problems in deciding which term to use is the possibility that the term may become used as a label that conjures up negative imagery. The use of labels for people with a learning disability has in the past served as a way of segregating this group from society at large. For further information concerning the history of labelling in learning disability the reader should refer to Williams (1978), Ryan and Thomas (1987) and Hastings and Remington (1993). Clearly, the sustained use of a label, coupled with any subsequent negative imagery, has the potential to bring about a move from being a devalued group to being perceived as deviant. Wolfensberger (1972) has demonstrated what may happen when a group becomes marginalized as deviants. He described eight social role perceptions of people with a learning disability. These are:

- **Subhuman.** Throughout history and in different cultures it has often been the case that people with a learning disability have been viewed as subhuman. One does not have to search very far back in literature for evidence of this belief; for example in relation to absolute, complete or profound idiocy, Tredgold and Soddy (1956) said 'In this condition we see humanity reduced to its lowest possible expression. Although these unfortunate creatures are, indeed, the veritable offspring of *Homo sapiens*, the depth of their degeneration is such that existence – for it can hardly be called life – is on a lower plane than that of even the beasts of the field, and in most respects may be described as vegetative (Tredgold, 1956, p. 147).

- **Holy innocent.** Once again a consistent perception, throughout history, of people with a learning disability is that they are innocent from original sin, and somehow enjoy some form of special relationship with the deity, perhaps as recompense for their disability.
- **Sick.** With the development of the National Health Service (NHS), in the latter half of this century, came the inevitable medicalization of learning disability. This resulted in hospital provision being seen as the most appropriate way to care for people with a learning disability. A natural consequence was the development of a whole 'adult' nursing oriented approach to caring for people that was based upon the medical model of care.
- **Eternal child.** This is probably the most commonly encountered perception of people with a learning disability. In a sense, such a perception has the ability to prevent people with a learning disability from being allowed to 'grow up'. This often manifests itself by carers not allowing adults with a learning disability to take risks, make their own choices. In addition, it is sometimes the case that they are given childlike clothes or toys that are not appropriate to their age.
- **Object of ridicule.** There is some evidence that people with a learning disability were used as 'fools' and jesters in court entertainment

(Williams, 1985). Such a perception of people who are in some way stupid, thick, or incompetent is still prevalent in our own society; and it is often thought appropriate to ridicule such individuals.

- **Object of pity and burden of charity.** Because people with a learning disability are perceived as not enjoying the 'normalcy' of being human, it is common to find people who feel pity for them. This pity is experienced with such intensity that it is thought that they need charity or to be looked after. In some countries there is an historical involvement of the church in the care of people with a learning disability; and this is evidenced by charitable homes caring for them.
- **Menace.** It is the case that even today people with learning disability are perceived as a menace. It is common to find community initiatives for the relocation of people with a learning disability from hospital to community settings beset with problems of neighbour complaints. These complaints typically concern a drop in the value of their own property or people 'wandering around' who may get into trouble with the police.
- **Object of dread.** Because of the perception of learning disability, it is the case, that when a child is either born or diagnosed as having a learning disability, that it is regarded as a punishment. Prospective parents view the possibility of having a child with learning disability with dread. As Bannerman and Lindsay (1994) have said, 'A family's investment in and expectation of their children is often very high and the arrival of a child with a disability may be the end of dearly held dreams about what that child would achieve in life'.

It is, perhaps, evident that people with a learning disability are not perceived in the same way as other citizens within society, and this may be partly accounted for by the images and attitudes that society holds toward this group of people; and this in part is brought about by the effects of labelling and the creation of a deviant group. As human beings, we still have a long way to go before we arrive at the unconditional valuing of all human life, regardless of the level of disability.

1.2 Brief Historical Overview of Learning Disability

Tracing the origins of learning disability is actually quite difficult; this is because in centuries past learning disability has been conflated with problems of mental health. Indeed, prior to the nineteenth century people with a learning disability were often cared for in the same institutions as those who were mentally ill.

Early History of Learning Disability

Text books offering historical accounts of learning disability often contradict one another as to how learning disability has been viewed throughout history. For example, it has been suggested that in ancient times people with a learning disability were thought to be a gift from the gods, and were therefore generally treated with much kindness (Gilbert, 1985). However, an alternative account is provided by Rosen *et al.* (1976) who stated that in ancient Greek and Roman times:

the mentally handicapped were treated as objects of scorn and persecution. There was no role for the handicapped in Plato's republic, and in ancient Rome it is alleged that children who were blind or deaf or mentally dull were thrown into the Tiber by their parents to relieve themselves of the burden of support. (Rosen *et al.*, 1976, p. xiii)

It is highly likely, and here there is a consensus in the literature, that with the dawn of Christianity emerged a compassion and concern for those who had a learning disability. That part of history that covered the dark ages once again brought about a period of disinterest and lack of compassion for people with a learning disability. During this whole period of early history it is clear that people with a learning disability, even in relative periods of enlightenment, were treated with suspicion. It is worthy of note that during the reign of Edward II an Act of Parliament, *De Praerogativa Regis*, made a distinction between having a mental illness (a lunatic) or having a learning disability (idiot). This is indeed an important distinction and demonstrates the beginnings of an attempt to understand learning disability, or more likely to understand that a distinction should be made between a mental illness and an 'idiot'. A popular belief, to be found, in early history concerning the nature of learning disability was that of the changeling. Essentially, folklore led people to believe that babies were stolen from their cots and were replaced with a changeling – a child with a learning disability. Further, people believed that if they ill treated the changeling then the fairies would ill treat their own child who had been stolen. There are numerous citings to be found in both primary and secondary historical sources of this belief, for example in Shakespeare's 'A Midsummer Night's Dream' Puck said:

Because that she, as her attendant, hath
A lovely boy, stol'n from an Indian king;
She never had so sweet a changeling:
And jealous Oberon would have the child
Knight of his train, to trace the forests wild:
But she perforce withholds the loved boy,
Crowns him with flowers, and makes him all her joy.
Act II, Scene I, 21–27.

The Nineteenth Century

In 1869, Galton wrote his first important piece of work on eugenics (Galton, 1874). He had studied the families of eminent people and had concluded that it would be possible to produce a gifted race of men, by manipulating marriages through several consecutive generations. Galton made a distinction between positive and negative eugenics. Positive eugenics are the means adopted to ensure the promotion of offspring with 'good genes', whilst negative eugenics are those means adopted to bring about a decrease to offspring who have bad genes. Bannerman and Lindsay (1994) provide discussion on the eugenics movement of the latter half of the last century where segregation and the search for a prevention in the deterioration of the human race were seen as very important. As Mittler (1979) has pointed out:

> The late Victorians were so haunted by the spectre of a declining national intelligence that they pursued a ruthless segregationist policy which led to many thousands of people being identified as mentally handicapped and incarcerated in asylums and colonies. The fact that their names were later changed to hospitals does not alter the fact that they were sited and designed to meet the needs of the time to segregate the handicapped from the rest of society and to do everything possible to prevent them from multiplying.

The Twentieth Century

This section provides a brief overview of the history of learning disability during this century. In Chapter 13 the nature of more recent legislation is considered in greater depth to provide context and meaning to the more recent legislative and social policy reforms. The eugenics movement of the nineteenth century, previously discussed, can be traced through to this century. For example, evidence of the attempts to be rid of people with a learning disability can be found in the history of Nazi Germany.

> Defective people must be prevented from propagating equally defective offspring. For, if necessary, the incurably sick will be pitilessly segregated – a barbaric measure for the unfortunate who is struck by it, but a blessing for his fellow men and posterity. (Independent Television Corporation, 1993)

This was even reinforced in school material for children. Consider the following mental arithmetic problem that was set for German children in 1936:

> A mentally defective person costs the republic 4 Reichmarks per day, a cripple 5.50 Reichmarks … 300 000 persons are being cared for in public mental institutions. How many marriage loans at 1000 Reichmarks per couple could be annually financed from the funds allocated to these institutions? (Independent Television Corporation, 1993)

Kobsell (1993) has suggested that the popularity of eugenics has always been connected to economic situations, fiscal considerations and the dominant political ideology of the time. In 1939, a programme called Vernichtung lebensunwerten Lebens (Destruction of life not worth living) was prosecuted. The scale of this eugenics movement is frightening; Kobsell (1993) has estimated that 400 000 people were sterilized and 100 000, mostly disabled, people were murdered. In 1904, a Royal Commission was established to advise on the needs of the 'mentally defective' population. Bannerman and Lindsay (1994) have distilled the four major recommendations from this commission. These were that:

- **People who were mentally defective needed protection from society and indeed themselves.**
- **All mentally defective people should be identified and brought into contact with caring agencies.**
- **Mentally defective people should not be condemned because of their condition.**
- **A central organizing body should be established to work with the local caring agencies who would be responsible for the care of individual people.**

This commission resulted in the Mental Deficiency Act (1913). This Act introduced compulsory certification of 'defectives' admitted to institutions.

Clearly, this Act served to segregate people with a learning disability from the society at large. This desire to segregate people with a learning disability from the rest of society resulted in large numbers of institutions being built. Despite the issue of segregation in the 1913 Act, it is possible to find something positive. This Act brought about the demarcation of learning disability from mental illness. It was during the last part of the nineteenth century that a number of asylums and/or colonies were established. As detailed earlier in the chapter, up until this time people with mental health problems and learning disabilities were often cared for in the same institutions. It is interesting to note that the Act placed the management and responsibility for the care of people with a learning disability with the local authorities. The asylums that developed during the end of the last and beginning of this century did not become hospitals as we know them today until the emergence of the NHS in 1948. In a sense the NHS as major providers of care for people with a learning disability, occurred almost by chance. This shift in responsibility and the subsequent medical model of care has led to continuing argument as to the most appropriate agency and model for care provision; namely a social or health model of care.

Following the 1913 Act, the next major piece of mental health legislation to affect people with a learning disability was the 1959 Mental Health Act. This Act replaced previously used terminology with the terms 'mental subnormality', 'severe mental subnormality' and 'mental or psychopathic disorder'. This Act required local authorities to provide both day and residential care for people with a learning disability. The Act also made provision for the voluntary attendance at a hospital rather than compulsory certification. However, this Act, whilst providing new definitions, still perpetuated the apparent need for mental health legislation required for people with a learning disability.

During the 1960s, a series of scandals was reported concerning the care of people with a learning disability in the large hospitals. In 1971 the then Labour government published an extremely significant document in the history of learning disability known as *Better Services for the Mentally Handicapped* (DHSS, 1971). This document promoted a model of community care with a significant reduction in the provision of hospital beds to a corresponding increase in local authority provision. This shift in the responsibility for the provision of care resulted in the Griffiths Report (1988), the *Caring for People* (DOH, 1989a) and the *Working for Patients* (DOH, 1989b) documents and the National Health Service and Community Care Act (DOH, 1990).

This series of reports, White Papers and subsequent legislation enabled the final move from hospital care to the provision of community care, for people with a learning disability. The National Health Service and Community Care Act (1990) also made the local authorities responsible for acting as lead in the provision of the acquisition of care packages for people with a learning disability. For a comprehensive analysis of current legislation and its impact on the ways in which care is provided, consult Malin (1994). For readers with a special interest in the historical study of learning disability, Lazerson (1975) presents a fascinating histiography of learning disability in the USA. A comprehensive review of the history of learning disability in the UK can be found in Bannerman and Lindsay (1994).

Reader Activity 1.4
When time permits, identify an individual who is able to remember the type of care offered to people with learning disabilities from at least three decades ago, and then compare this account to your own experiences.

1.3 Theoretical Approaches to Understanding Learning Disability

Clarke (1986) has said that:

learning disability has been a source of speculation, fear, scientific enquiry for hundreds of years. It has been regarded in turn as an administrative, medical, eugenic, educational and social problem.

The manner in which learning disability has been catered for throughout history has, to some extent, reflected the dominant theoretical perspective that has been used at any one time in order to understand it. This next section provides a brief overview of five different theoretical perspectives that are commonly associated with learning disability.

A Sociological Perspective

Sociology has been defined as 'the science or study of society' (Seymour-Smith, 1986, p. 263). Sociology concerns itself with the study of the social phenomena of modern industrial societies, and employs methods of analysis and investigation to understand the component parts of society, and how these parts relate to one another. Sociological theory can be divided into two traditions: structuralist and interpretive approaches. Reid (1978) has said that *structuralist sociology* is concerned with understanding man as a receiver of and responder to society, as opposed to *interpretive sociology*, which perceives man as a manipulator and creator of society. Within this section an approach to understanding sociology from the structuralist viewpoint is explored. For further guidance and/or information in this area, refer to Bennett (1992).

Kurtz (1981) has provided a short, but none the less powerful, chapter on a sociological approach to understanding learning disability. He suggested that individuals within any society are incumbents of the status that is attached to the role that they occupy in that society. He cited Guskin (1963) who had noted that people with a learning disability play a very generalized role. This role, it is suggested, emphasized the inability of a person with a learning disability to adequately undertake functional activities. The functional activities referred to were everyday experience for most people, such as going to work, taking care of one's self, behaving in an acceptable way, or managing one's own finances. It was suggested that the person with a learning disability could not adequately perform these activities. Of particular interest to this approach was the question as to whether one could identify the causation of such inability. Simply, was the inability caused by the learning disability, or a consequence of behaving in the ways that people expected them to? Guskin (1963) suggested that:

. . . one could hypothesise non achievement orientation, dependency behaviour, and rebelliousness as patterns of behaviour determined by previous and present interactions with people who have role concepts of the defective emphasising inability, helplessness, and lack of control, respectively.

Kurtz (1981) argued that because of the ways in which learning disability had been perceived, two important images emerged of such individuals in the USA. These images were:

- **The person with a learning disability as a sick person.**
- **The person with a learning disability as a developing person.**

He suggested that the first of these images was chiefly held by medical personnel, whilst the second was held by educators, psychologists and, possibly, parents.

In conclusion, this sociological approach to learning disability focuses on the role of this group of people within society. It is suggested that because of the images that society holds toward them, expectations for their role are limited. Dexter (1958) has argued that it is in this sense that learning disability was a creation of society. The student who wishes to pursue this perspective should refer to a basic text by Petrie (1994).

A Psychological Perspective

Psychology is concerned with the study of human behaviour and as some human behaviour is deemed abnormal, a branch of study has developed known as abnormal psychology. This branch of psychology is concerned specifically with the study of abnormal behaviour. Paradoxically, like learning disability, abnormal behaviour is difficult to define, so there is a need to identify criteria in order to distinguish abnormal from normal behaviour (Atkinson *et al.*, 1990). In general, abnormal behaviour is identified by the following criteria:

- **deviation from statistical norms**
- **deviation from social norms**
- **maladaptive behaviour**
- **personal distress.**

This chapter has already outlined how IQ tests are used to establish whether people deviate from

---

Case Study 1.1 A woman with mild learning disabilities

Vera was born in 1963, following a normal pregnancy and labour. She was the younger of two sisters. It soon became apparent, to the family, that she was not reaching the normal developmental milestones. Therefore she was referred to a paediatrician at her local general hospital who diagnosed her as 'suffering' from a mild mental handicap. The paediatrician advised the parents to 'take her home, give her plenty of love but do not expect too much from her'. During her childhood Vera found it difficult to mix with other children. Her slowness and very distinctive delay in speech caused much teasing and bullying. Her parents decided that it would be better for Vera if she attended a 'special school'. It was apparent that Vera responded well to this environment; she learnt, within a short space of time to read, write and was able to undertake basic calculations in mathematics. At sixteen, she attended a boarding school for two years where she completed a basic catering course, that was designed to prepare her for future employment.

However, when Vera returned home a number of problems arose. She had become a confident, assertive young woman at the boarding school; but her mother still wanted the 'old' Vera. Her mother demonstrated this by encouraging Vera to stay in her room to do jigsaw puzzles, colour picture books and play her collection of pop tapes. It was not long before Vera developed aggressive outbursts that escalated over a period of time into vicious attacks on members of her family. Her mother sought the advice of their general practitioner who referred them to a community learning disability team. After a series of visits from a community learning disability nurse, Vera articulated a desire to leave home. With the reluctant support of her parents she left home and moved into a small community home for people with learning disabilities. Vera now lives in a four-bedroomed house that is run by her local authority; she shares the home with three other people who also have a learning disability. She now attends a local resource centre (social education centre) run by the local authority from Monday to Friday. She also attends further education college once a week to update the skills that she learnt on her catering course; she hopes this will enable her to leave the resource centre as she wants to find a full-time job in a restaurant. In addition, she now has a full social life, a boy friend and visits her family about once a month at her old home.

Case Study 1.2 A child with septo-optic dysplasia

Colin is a little, two and a half-year-old boy with winning ways; he has an infectious smile and laugh, dark blue eyes and is a little shy. His teenage mother reports a normal and uneventful pregnancy, as well as normal delivery without any complications. His development was always slow, and at about the age of one he was diagnosed as having a rare condition known as septo-optic dysplasia. This disorder has resulted in blindness, cerebral palsy and epilepsy that is manifested by partial seizures (Benner *et al.*, 1990, Yukizane *et al.*, 1990). The epilepsy appears to be reasonably well controlled although he does still have seizures; he is currently receiving two anticonvulsants that are being administered on a regular daily basis. He has some muscle control and can stand on his own feet for a few seconds. He is unable to feed, dress, toilet himself and, as yet, demonstrates no signs of developing any competence in these areas. His sleep pattern is very irregular and he will sometimes go for long periods without sleeping properly at all. This causes a great strain on his mother. In addition to the many and complex needs of Colin he is also a poor feeder and has not yet been weaned from a milk diet to more substantive foodstuffs. Because of his poor feeding he frequently has problems with constipation, and when weighed and measured by his health visitor it is apparent that he has not physically developed within the normal percentile ranges. It is known that with this condition there is pituitary insufficiency and this has implications for the release of growth hormone.

statistical norms, in relation to their measured intelligence. Concerning this deviation from social norms along with maladaptive behaviour and personal distress, consider Case Studies 1.1 and 1.2 and identify whether these three criteria may be said to be evident.

Within the USA, a category system has been used for the identification of abnormality. This is known as the *Diagnostic and Statistical Manual of Mental Disorders*, 3rd edn, which approximates the international system of the World Health Organization identified earlier in this chapter. The system comprises a number of diagnostic categories that are themselves comprised of subclassifications. Using this system, an individual is evaluated against a number of dimensions from which developmental disorders, such as learning disability, can be identified.

Within such a large academic discipline as psychology it is not surprising to find different theoretical explanations for learning disability. In behavioural psychology, for example, the major focus of interest is on the systematic observation of behaviour. The behavioural approach can be traced back to the earlier work of Skinner (1974) and is concerned with what people do, rather than what they feel or think. In short, behavioural psychology is concerned with observable behaviour rather than hypothetical constructs. It is concerned with individual problems and the identification of clear objectives for enhancing an individual's ability to perform behaviours that he or she is currently unable to do. It is thus an interventionist approach. Schwartz and Goldiamond (1975) have emphasized that it is not only observable behaviour that is important but also environmental aspects, such as thoughts and feelings. Alternatively, Bijou (1992) has reviewed and evaluated a range of concepts in learning disability within the scientific discipline of psychology. His review concluded that the 'restricted developmental' approach to understanding learning disability was the most advanced and defensible. He also argued its superiority to other approaches because it was an integral component of empirically based behaviour theory of human development. Waitman and Conboy-Hill (1992) have provided an overview of psychotherapeutic themes related to learning disability; along with other theoretical approaches, this demonstrates that psychology offers varied and valuable insights into the nature of, and practical approaches to enhance the lives of, people with a learning disability.

A Medical Perspective

Brechin *et al.* (1980) have provided a useful and comprehensive analysis of this approach to understanding learning disability. It is the case that cure, alleviation and prevention of disease, along with restoring and preserving health, are the central tenets of medicine. The practice of Western medicine rests upon the so-called positivistic paradigm; that is, it is concerned with the establishment of hypotheses and the acceptance or refutation of their predictions. Therefore, the medical model uses a deductive approach that follows a diagnostic path in search of an explanation for disease, often referred to as the cause–effect relationship. The whole point of Western medicine is to identify disease or disorders, and to determine their cause in order that the disease or disorder can be prevented and/or ameliorated. Illsley (1977) has identified four central assumptions of the medical model:

- **Illness is thought of as being the result of a physical cause.**
- **Physicians are seen as the key players in health care.**
- **Hospitals are seen as the repository and treatment centres of the sick.**
- **Advances in health care are viewed as developing from improved medical technology.**

It was noted earlier in this chapter that services for people with a learning disability transferred to the NHS following its genesis in the 1940s and that with the absorption of learning disability services by the NHS came the medicalization of learning disability, which unfortunately carried the corollary of viewing learning disability and mental illness as one and the same. Therefore, the tremendous advances made in mental health, especially pharmacological advances, were extrapolated to people with a learning disability. For example, the development of the phenothiazines, used in the treatment of people with psychotic mental health problems, became 'treatments of choice' for people with a learning disability with behavioural problems! It is fair to say that the medical model in learning disability has been extremely influential since this time. Some have argued that this approach to understanding learning disability has been unhelpful. Hattersley *et al.* (1987) has said:

> The emergence of treatment for mental illness was seen in the 1950s, and of the developmental change that took place within the psychiatric services there is no doubt. The revolution that was brought about, particularly by the introduction of phenothiazines (major tranquillizers), changed the world of psychiatric institutions. Unfortunately, the same model of providing services was bestowed on mentally handicapped people as well – but drugs do not cure mental handicap. (Hattersley *et al.*, 1987, p.101)

It may be the case that the medical approach to understanding learning disability has not always served the best interests of this group of people. However, the medical approach has contributed to our understanding of some of the more biological dimensions of learning disability, and therefore the contribution of medicine to people with a learning disability remains as valid as ever.

An Anthropological Perspective

Anthropology has been defined as 'the study of man and his work' (Pelto, 1965, p. 1). Anthropology may be divided into two separate but related branches:

- **Physical anthropology.** Physical anthropology is concerned with the examination of evidence for the evolution of man from 'lower' forms of life. This branch of anthropology is also concerned with the study of the variations of the population *Homo sapiens* that includes, for example, Mongoloid, Negroid and Caucasoid. More recently, physical anthropology has become concerned with aspects of human growth and constitution, in particular body builds. This has brought anthropology closer to a number of other academic disciplines, for example the study of medicine and physiology.

- **Cultural (social) anthropology.** A distinguishing feature of the behaviour of man is that it is pervasively cultural (Pelto, 1965). There are many different dimensions to human culture that include, for example, history, social structures and language. One area of particular interest to anthropologists is that of ethnology – the study of peoples and/or races. Of particular interest is the study of the varieties of human behaviour that can be observed across a range of peoples in different cultures. This study is undertaken by the anthropologist living with a particular group of people in order to observe their patterns of behaviour. This is usually undertaken by the anthropologist assuming the role of participant observer. Their study attempts to bring understanding and meaning to the different patterns of behaviour observed.

It is the second of these two branches of anthropology, that this section, on theoretical perspectives, concentrates upon.

Edgerton (1975) identified that learning disability was a culturally defined phenomenon. He provided fascinating insights as to how cultural differences make terms like 'learning disability' very deceptive. Consider the following:

Not only do games fail to interest them, they are almost completely unable to participate in most activities. They could not be taught to whistle, sing or even hum a simple tune. I wrote: 1111 2222 3– – – – –4 – 55– on a sheet of paper and asked a number of eight year olds who had never been to school to fill in the missing numbers. They could not. Nor were they able to draw a circle, a square, raise their right arms, raise their left arms, extend their fingers, or spell their names. (Gazaway, 1969)

These children probably did not have a learning disability at all; rather the children all lived in a very deprived area of the USA where such 'levels of attainment' were considered not unusual within that culture. Edgerton (1975) has said:

Most of us, myself included, are sometimes guilty of writing (and perhaps believing) that the mentally retarded and their lives are simpler than they really are. Granted, writers about any aspect of human reality could be similarly accused, but the charge here may not be entirely gratuitous since the retarded are by definition 'simple' and our accounts of them cannot be praised for their efforts to discover complexity. (Edgerton, 1975, p. 139)

More recently new and sensitive life-history accounts of people with a learning disability appear to be emerging within the literature. These accounts provide fascinating and in-depth accounts of the experience of living with a learning disability and are clearly contextualized within the cultural fabric of the communities and societies to which these people belong. An excellent example of this approach is offered by Bogdan and Taylor (1994), based upon an earlier edition. In this book they have provided biographies of two people with a learning disability – Patti and Ed. Another fascinating account that offered emotional depth as to the nature of learning disability is the autobiography of Deacon (1974). This story is compulsory reading for those who really wish to begin to understand some of the temporal and historical dimensions to learning disability as it affected the life of this man. Such biographical and/or autobiographical accounts, along with other anthropological methods, have the potential to provide both professional carers and the general public with valuable insights into the nature of learning disability.

Reader Activity 1.5
Spend some time reflecting on these differing theoretical approaches to learning disabilities. Which, if any, of these approaches offers the most insight into the nature of learning disabilities? You may find it helpful to pursue some of the references for further information.

Figure 1.1 Learning disability as a state of health.

A Health Perspective

An alternative way of understanding learning disability is to conceptualize it as a state of health comprising a number of dimensions of being. Figure 1.1 portrays learning disability as this complex state, which incorporates a number of dimensions. The model also depicts these dimensions in a context. This context is the national and international platforms of agendas of social policy, legislation and research that affect the lives of people, and their families, with a learning disability. It can be seen that each of these dimensions has the potential to affect health, and may result in health loss, gain or maintenance. These dimensions are now plotted in Boxes 1.4 and 1.5 to demonstrate how health loss may be manifested, and health gain brought about by therapeutic intervention. First consider the short case history concerning John (Case Study 1.3), then compare this with Boxes 1.4 and 1.5.

The Department of Health (DOH, 1995) has recently published a strategy for people with learning disabilities that relates this segment of society to the *Health of the Nation* targets (Smith and Jacob-

---

Case Study 1.3 A man with profound learning disabilities

John is a 45-year-old man. He has a profound learning disability and presents with a range of challenges to his parents, and the community learning disability nurse, who has just received a referral from the family's social worker to visit the family home. The visit is to establish what the community learning disability team (CTLD) can offer to support this man in his home. The challenges that John presents include: physical dependence upon his parents; cerebral palsy with spastic quadriplegia; epilepsy; no speech or apparent communication mode; double incontinence; repeated bouts of chest infections and urinary tract infections; and low body weight. He does not attend any day service provision and is cared for, at his home, by his elderly parents who believe that John is still 'our little lad'.

Box 1.4 Possible manifestation of health loss for John and his parents

Educational	Psychosocial	Biological	Spiritual
Poorly developed knowledge and skills	Disordered, delayed speech and failure to acquire social maturity	Repeated bouts of illness including urinary and respiratory infections	Little or no access to opportunities to meet spiritual needs
No opportunity to attend day service provision	Social isolation of John and his parents	Epileptic seizures	Little or no opportunity to acquire moral development
No opportunity of an education for life	No opportunity to develop friendships	Poor nutritional uptake	The eternal child
No opportunity to acquire a method for communicating	Negative social role	Poor body posture	Parental grieving in anticipation of the loss of their son when they die
No opportunity to learn how to move and/or exercise	Dysfunctional family life	Problems with constipation	Little opportunity to achieve harmony in the life of John or his parents

son, 1988). These *Health of the Nation* targets were concerned with:

- **coronary heart disease and stroke**
- **cancers**
- **HIV/AIDS and sexual health**
- **accidents**
- **mental illness.**

The Department of Health (1995) document, concerning learning disability, identified nine health problems that are common in people with a learning disability; these being:

- **communication problems**
- **hearing problems**
- **eyesight problems**
- **obesity, and poor cardiovascular fitness**
- **behaviour problems**
- **epilepsy**
- **psychiatric illness**
- **respiratory problems**

- **orthopaedic problems and other problems of mobility.**

Some of these problems are discussed in Chapter 4 in detail. In addition, an overview of research in the area of health is provided in Chapter 16.

It is the case that people with a learning disability should have access to the same range of health services as their fellow citizens; if only this was the case. Howells (1986) identified that a number of medical problems remain undetected in people with a learning disability. This study looked at the health of 151 people who attended a social education centre, it was found that circulatory, respiratory, nervous and metabolic disorders, as well as poor management of hearing and visual difficulties, were all detected by the researchers, yet none of them were being treated. The theoretical perspectives outlined earlier, whilst useful in understanding learning disability at a formal level of theory, do not help people understand learning disability at the more substantive level. The perspective of health

Box 1.5 Possible interventions bringing about health maintenance and/or gain for John and his parents			
Educational	Psychosocial	Biological	Spiritual
Develop simple self-help programmes for parents to follow	Enable access to speech therapist for assessment	Promote health surveillance and monitoring	Introduce family to local community groups, e.g. Church support groups
Enable access, following assessment to a resource centre (social education centre)	Enable access to a variety of social support groups	Ensure regular anticonvulsant monitoring	Ensure John is enabled to access relationships beyond the home
Ensure John has access to educational opportunities	Introduce John, with parents' permission, to a citizen advocate	Promote nutritional uptake, monitoring, regular weighing and referral to dietician	Promote age-appropriate life style for John
Following assessment by communication therapist, ensure methods recommended are implemented	Undertake to enhance the social role of John	Seek assessment by physiotherapist	Seek clinical psychology input for family support and/or therapy
Following assessment by physiotherapist, ensure methods recommended are implemented	Provide CTLD input Community Learning Disabilities	Monitor bowel function and promote high-fibre diet	Attempt to normalize family life to bring about harmony

provides a framework of inclusiveness for understanding the various dimensions of being, that the unidimensional perspectives such as the medical and sociological models, do not; namely they perhaps exclude a wider understanding of the phenomenon of learning disability.

Reader Activity 1.6
Consider the Case Study 1.2 and identify what the health needs of Colin might be. Do not just focus in on the obvious physical manifestations of his being, important though they may be. Consider the wider implications of attempting to maintain health, prevent health loss and/or bring about health gain.

1.4 Incidence and Prevalence of Learning Disability

Calculating the incidence of learning disability is extremely problematic. This is because there is no way of detecting the vast majority of infants who have a learning disability at birth. It is only the obvious manifestations of learning disability that can be detected at birth; for example Down's syndrome. In this example, the physical characteristics of Down's syndrome enable an early diagnosis and the ability to calculate incidence of this disorder. Where there is no obvious physical manifestation, one must wait for delay in a child's development in order to ascertain whether they have a learning disability. Therefore it is more common in learning disability to talk about the prevalence. Prevalence is concerned with an estimation of the number of people with a condition, disorder or disease as a proportion to the general population. If one uses IQ as an indicator of learning disability then one is able to calculate that 2–3% of the population have an IQ below 70. This represents a large segment of society. Given that a large number of people with such an estimated IQ never come into contact with a caring agency, it is more common to refer to the 'administrative prevalence'. Administrative prevalence refers to the number of people that are provided with some form of service from caring agencies. It is on this basis that there is a general consensus that the overall prevalence of moderate and severe learning disability is approximately 3–4 persons per 1000 of the general population (see, e.g. Open University, 1987; DOH, 1992). Such prevalence would appear to be universally common. For example, Craft (1985) has suggested that international studies have identified a prevalence for severe and moderate learning disability as 3.7 per 1000 population. The Department of Health have suggested that the prevalence of mild learning disability is actually quite common; it is estimated to be in the region of 20 persons per 1000 of the general population. In the UK it has been further calculated that of the 3–4 persons per 1000 population with a learning disability, approximately 30% will present with severe or profound learning disability. Within this group it is not uncommon to find multiple disability that includes physical and/or sensory disability as well as behavioural difficulties. It is this group of people that require life-long support in order for them to achieve and maintain a valued life style.

Earlier in the chapter it was said that people use different criteria, or bench marks, as to what constitutes learning disability. This different use of terminology has implications for calculating incidence and prevalence. It should be acknowledged that there is some controversy associated with being able to identify accurately the incidence and prevalence of learning disability. Some would argue that not being able to calculate prevalence accurately is unimportant, as the epidemiological study of learning disability creates labelling, and that this perpetuates inappropriate models of care that are developed outside the ordinary services that are available for ordinary people. One problem, amongst many others, with this line of argument is that without careful epidemiological studies in this area, it is inherently difficult to know how best to target resources for those who may need them. It has oft and long been complained that people with a learning disability are not afforded the same rights as other citizens. Careful measurement of prevalence provides one way of ensuring that people with specialist needs are provided with specialist resources when they are required.

1.5 Conclusion

This chapter sets out to introduce the nature of learning disabilities and provide an overview of learning disability. A range of issues has been explored that included: the nature of learning disability; a brief historical overview of learning disability; a range of theoretical approaches to understanding learning disability; and finally the incidence and prevalence of learning disability. Central to this chapter, and the book, has been the promotion of understanding learning disability as a state of health. It is anticipated that Chapter 1 will have provided the necessary, though not necessarily the sufficient, knowledge base to explore the remainder of this text, which has been organized to reflect the dimensions of learning disability outlined in this chapter.

Discussion Questions
Having read the brief historical overview of learning disabilities, do you think that society's attitudes have changed through history toward people with learning disabilities?

Given that some causes of learning disabilities can now be detected in the uterus, prior to birth, and a mother offered a therapeutic abortion, does this imply that people with learning disabilities are in some way less valued than others?

How do you think that learning disabilities should be defined, if at all?

In what ways do you think our understanding of learning disabilities is helped by conceptualizing it as a state of health that comprises a number of dimensions of being?

References

Atkinson, R.L., Atkinson, R.C., Smith, E.E., Bem, D.J. and Hilgard, E.R. (1990) *Introduction to Psychology*, 10th edn. London: Harcourt Brace Jovanovich.

Bannerman, M. and Lindsay, M. (1994) Evolution of services. *In* Shanley, E. and Starrs, T. (Eds) *Learning Disabilities: A handbook of care*, pp. 19–39. Edinburgh: Churchill Livingstone.

Beck, C.M., Rawlins, R.D. and Williams, S.R. (1988) *Mental Health Psychiatric Nursing – A holistic life cycle approach.* London: C.V. Mosby.

Benner, J.D., Preslan, M.W., Gratz, E., Joslyn, J., Schwartz, M. and Kelman, S. (1990) Septo-optic dysplasia in two siblings. *American Journal of Opthalmology* **109**: 632–637.

Bennett, K. (1992) The sociological self. *In* Kenworthy, N., Snowley, G. and Gilling, C. (Eds) *Common Foundation Studies in Nursing*, pp. 59–74. Edinburgh: Churchill Livingstone.

Bijou, S.W. (1992) Concepts of mental retardation. *Psychological Record* **42**: 305–322.

Bogdan, R. and Taylor, S. (1994) *The Social Meaning of Mental Retardation.* London: Teachers College Press.

Brechin, A., Hall, D. and Polnay, L. (1980) *The Medical Approach to Handicap. Block 2: This way or that.* Milton Keynes: Open University Press.

Clarke, D. (1986) *Mentally Handicapped People: Living and learning.* London: Baillière Tindall.

Craft, M. (1985) Classification, criteria, epidemiology and causation. *In* Craft, M., Bicknell, J. and Hollins, S. (Eds) *Mental Handicap: A multidisciplinary approach*, pp. 75–88. London: Baillière Tindall.

Deacon, J.J. (1974) *Tongue Tied: Fifty years of friendship in a subnormality hospital.* London: MENCAP.

Dennis, W. (1973) *Children of the Creche.* New York: Appleton Century-Crofts.

Department of Health and Social Security (DHSS) (1971) *Better Services for the Mentally Handicapped.* London: HMSO.

Department of Health (DOH) (1989a) *Caring for People: Community care in the next decade and beyond.* Cm. 849. London: HMSO.

Department of Health (DOH) (1989b) *Working for Patients.* CM. 555. London: HMSO.

Department of Health (DOH) (1990) *NHS and Community Care Act.* London: HMSO.

Department of Health (DOH) (1992) *Social Care for Adults with Learning Disabilities* (Mental Handicap LAC (92) 15). London: HMSO.

Department of Health (DOH) (1995) *The Health of the Nation: A strategy for people with a learning disability.* London: HMSO.

Dexter, L. (1958) A social theory of mental deficiency. *American Journal of Mental Deficiency* **62**: 920–928.

Edgerton, R. (1975) Issues relating to the quality of life among mentally retarded persons. *In* Begab, M. and Richardson, S. (Eds) *The Mentally Retarded and Society: A social science perspective*, pp. 127–140. Baltimore: University Park Press.

Galton, F. (1874) *English Men of Science, their Nature and Nurture.* London: Macmillan.

Gazaway, R. (1969) *The Longest Mile.* Garden City New York: Doubleday.

Gilbert, P. (1985) *Mental Handicap: A practical guide for social workers.* Surrey: Business Press International.

Gostin, L. (1985) The law relating to mental handicap in England and Wales. *In* Craft, M., Bicknell, J. and Hollins, S. (Eds) *Mental Handicap: A multidisciplinary approach*, p. 58. London: Baillière Tindall.

Griffiths, R. (1988) *Community Care: Agenda for action.* London: HMSO.

Gross, R.D. (1991) *Psychology: The science of mind and behaviour.* London: Hodder & Stoughton.

Guskin, S. (1963) Social psychologies of mental deficiency. *In* Ellis, N. (Ed.) *Handbook of Mental Deficiency*, pp. 325–352. New York: McGraw-Hill.

Hastings, R.P. and Remington, S. (1993) Connotations of labels for mental handicap and challenging behaviour: A review and research evaluation. *Mental Handicap Research* **6**(3): 237–249.

Hattersley, J., Hoskin, G.P., Morrow, D. and Myers, M. (1987) *People with a Mental Handicap: Perspectives on intellectual disability.* London: Faber & Faber.

Howells, G. (1986) Are the medical needs of mentally handicapped people being met? *Journal of the Royal College of General Practitioners* **36**: 449–453.

Illsley, R. (1977) Health and social policy – priorities for research. SSRC report of advisory panel to research initiatives board.

Independent Telelevision Corporation (1993) *Fuhere: Seduction of a Nation.* London: Independent Television Corporation.

Kobsell, S. (1993) Testing, testing the new eugenics? *Disability, Pregnancy and Parenthood International* **4** (October).

Kurtz, R. (1981) The sociological approach to mental retardation. *In* Brechin, A., Liddiard, P. and Swain, J. (Eds) *Handicap in a Social World*, pp. 14–23. Suffolk: Hodder & Stoughton in association with The Open University Press.

Lazerson, M. (1975) Educational institutions and mental subnormality: Notes on writing a history. *In* Begab, M. and Richardson, S.A. (Eds) *The Mentally Retarded and Society: A social science perspective*, pp. 33–52. Baltimore: University Park Press.

Malin, N. (1994) Development of community care. *In* Malin, N. (Ed.) *Implementing Community Care*, pp. 3–30. Buckingham: Open University Press.

Mental Deficiency Act (1913) London: HMSO.

Mental Health Act (1959) London: HMSO.

Mental Health Act (1983) London: HMSO.

Mittler, P. (1979) *People not Patients: Problems and policies in mental handicap.* London: Methuen.

Ministry of Health (MOH) (1946) *The National Health Service Act.* London: HMSO.

Nursey, N., Rhode, J. and Farmer, R. (1990) Words used to refer to people with mental handicaps. *Mental Handicap* **18**(1): 30–32.

Pelto, P. (1965) *The Study of Anthropology.* Ohio: Charles E. Merrill.

Petrie, G. (1994) Social causes. *In* Shanley, E. and Starrs, T. (Eds) *Learning Disabilities: A handbook of care*, pp. 83–91. Edinburgh: Churchill Livingstone.

Reid, I. (1978) *Sociological Perspectives on School and Education.* London: Open Books.

Rosen, M., Clark, G.R. and Kivitz, M. (1976) *The History of Mental Retardation. Collected Papers*, Vol. 1. Baltimore: University Park Press.

Ryan, J. and Thomas, F. (1987) *The Politics of Mental Handicap.* London: Free Association Books.

Schwartz, A. and Goldiamond, I. (1975) *Social Casework: A behavioural approach.* New York: Columbia University Press.

Seymour-Smith, C. (1986) *Macmillan Dictionary of Anthropology.* London: Macmillan.

Skinner, B.F. (1974) *About Behaviourism.* London: Jonathan Cape.

Smith, A. and Jacobson, B. (1988) *The Nation's Health: A strategy for the 1990s.* London: King Edwards Hospital Fund for London.

The Open University (1987) *Mental Handicap: Patterns for living.* Milton Keynes: Open University Press.

Tredgold, R.F. and Soddy, K. (1956) *A Text Book of Mental Deficiency*, 9th edn. London: Baillière Tindall.

Waitman, A. and Conboy-Hill, S. (1992) *Psychotherapy and Mental Handicap.* London: Sage.

WHO (1993) *Describing Developmental Disability: Guidelines for a multiaxial scheme for mental retardation (learning disability)*, 10th revision. Geneva: World Health Organization.

Williams, P. (1978) *Our Mutual Handicap: Attitudes and perceptions of others by mentally handicapped people.* New York: Campaign for Mentally Handicapped People.

Williams, P. (1985) The nature and foundations of the concept of normalisation. *In* Kracos, E. (Ed.) *Current Issues in Clinical Psychology. Clinical Psychology* **2**. New York: Plenum.

Wolfensberger, W. (1972) *The Principle of Normalisation in Human Management Services.* Toronto: National Institute of Mental Retardation.

Yukizane, S., Kimura, Y., Matsuishi, T., Horikawa, H., Ando, H. and Yamashita, F. (1990) Growth hormone deficiency of hypothalmic origin in septo-optic dysplasia. *European Journal of Paediatrics* **150**: 30–33.

Further Reading

Alaszewski, A. (1986) *Institutional Care and the Mentally Handicapped: The mental handicap hospital.* London: Croom Helm.

Audit Commission for Local Authorities England and Wales (1986) *Making a Reality of Community Care: A report by the audit commission.* London: HMSO.

Ayer, A. and Alaszewski, A. (1984) *Community Care and the Mentally Handicapped Services for Mothers and Their Mentally Handicapped Children.* London: Croom Helm.

Barber, P. (Ed.) (1987) Using nursing models series. *Mental handicap: Facilitating holistic care.* London: Hodder & Stoughton.

Blunden, R. and Allen, D. (Eds) (1987) *Facing the Challenge: An ordinary life for people with learning difficulties and challenging behaviour.* London: Kings Fund Centre.

Department of Health and Social Security (1984a) *Helping Mentally Handicapped People with Special Problems.* London: HMSO.

Department of Health and Social Security (1984b) *Mental Handicap: Progress, problems and priorities.* (Cmnd 4663). London: HMSO.

Department of Health and Social Security (1985) *The Role of the Nurse for People with a Mental Handicap.* (Ref. CNO 855). London: HMSO.

English National Board for Nursing Midwifery and Health Visiting (1985) *Caring for People with a Mental Handicap: A learning package for nurses.* London: ENB.

Malin, N. (Ed.) (1994) Implementing Community Care. Buckingham: Open University Press.

Owens, G. and Birchenall, P. (1979) *Mental Handicap – The social dimensions.* London: Pitman.

Reid, A. (1982) *The Psychiatry of Mental Handicap.* Oxford: Blackwell Scientific.

Rutter, M. (1995) *The Roots of Mental Handicap*, pp. 20–23. London: Medical Research Council News.

Shanley, E. and Starrs, T. (Eds) (1994) *Learning Disabilities: A handbook of care.* Edinburgh: Churchill Livingstone.

Sines, D. (1988) *Towards Integration: Residential care for people with a mental handicap in the community.* London: Harper and Row.

Todd, M. and Gilbert, T. (1995) *Learning Disabilities: Practice issues in health settings.* London: Routledge.

Wright, K., Haycox, A. and Leedham, I. (1994) *Evaluating Community Care: Services for people with learning difficulty.* Buckingham: Open University Press.

Part Two: Health and Learning Disability

Part Two of *Dimensions of Learning Disability* considers how a state of physical and mental health is established and maintained as part of our ordinary life pattern. From this baseline the authors extend their analysis to consider common factors affecting the health status of people with a learning disability and how these factors are addressed.

In Chapter 2, 'Defining Health', Deborah Vernon considers the concept of health and examines the relationship between human needs and the health status of the individual. By reflecting upon mental health issues in people with learning disabilities and how a person's health status influences their ability to cope with problems, 'health' is considered as part of a complex process of balancing of human functions.

Eileen Wake looks at overcoming common health problems associated with people who have learning disabilities within Chapter 3, 'Health Loss, Gain and Maintenance in Learning Disability'. The means of achieving improved health states from the perspective of direct interventions is considered. The outcome is a practical, clinical approach to tackling the problems involved.

Part Two of this book acts as a guide to health and the fundamental influence it has upon the life styles of all people. Furthermore, the clinical approaches that are described serve to illustrate how the maintenance and promotion of health in people with a learning disability is an elemental issue which must be addressed as part of any individual programme of care and development.

Chapter 2: Defining health
Deborah Vernon

2.1 Introduction

Health is a basic concept in the discipline and profession of nursing. The search for a definition of health pervades the literature. Philosophers, economists, health educators, psychologists and sociologists have all written about health from their own perspective. Hence, definitions of health are varied and contrasting. Understanding of the term 'health' varies between individuals and cultures, depending on the meaning and importance people give to it.

Box 2.1 Key terms

- **Coping behaviour**   Any behaviour that assists an individual in tolerating stress and relieving unpleasant feelings.
- **Health**   Being in an optimal state of homeostasis.
- **Hierarchy of needs**   Maslow's ascending rank of needs, primary or physical at the bottom and secondary or non-physiological at the top.
- **Holistic health**   Optimal functioning of all body parts including psychological components.
- **Homeostasis**   The tendency of all living organisms to restore and maintain itself in a condition of equilibrium.
- **Need**   That which is necessary or required for optimal functioning.
- **Self-actualization**   The maximizing of ones potential through goal-directed behaviour, reflecting personal growth and productive living.

The versatility of the word 'health' has led to vagueness and ambiguity. Thus, the concept of health is a complex one, with no immediate point of focus. The following discussion examines some of the principal ways in which health can be conceptualized in an effort to promote clarity. Specifically, this chapter seeks to provide:

- a historical review of the concept of health
- a philosophical analysis of health in relation to human needs
- an overview of health from a physical perspective
- a discussion of the notion of mental health and coping behaviours.

In so doing, it highlights that health is a balance of human function and much more than the absence of disease.

Historical Review

The origins of the word 'health' provide a context for examining the philosophical, physical and mental dimensions of health. The word 'health', as it is commonly used today, did not appear in writing until AD1000. It is derived from the old English word 'hoelth' meaning *safe* or *sound* and *whole of body* (Sorochan, 1970).

Historically, physical wholeness was of major importance for societal acceptance. The presence of 'disease' marked the person as 'unclean'. People born with a congenital malformation were ostracized from society. No attempt was made to address the psychological, social, educational or spiritual aspects of the individual. Similarly, individuals who exhibited unpredictable or hostile behaviour were labelled 'lunatics' and ostracized in much the same way as those whose stigma derived from physical appearance.

Reader Activity 2.1
Does society still ostracize these people but by a more subtle means?

With the advent of scientific technology and medical advances, more attention was directed towards disease and the disease process. In this context, health was viewed to be a disease-free state. This notion was extremely popular for the first half of the twentieth century and was recognized by many as *the* definition of health (Wylie, 1970). It was not until the World Health Organization (WHO, 1946) proposed a broader definition of health that aspects other than the absence of disease were addressed. The WHO definition proposes that health is:

> a state of complete physical, mental and social
> well-being and not merely the absence of disease
> (World Health Organization, 1946)

Unquestionably, this definition remains the most quoted and criticized, but enduring, definition of health. Although the WHO definition presents a simplistic portrayal of health as an unattainable state, it does make two important points: first, that health is to do with well being and about feeling good about oneself; second, it highlights the interdependence of physical, mental and social aspects of health. The notion of interdependence between all aspects of health underpins the remainder of this chapter, thus highlighting health as a *balance of human functions*.

2.2 What is Health?

At the end of this section it will be seen that:

- **Health is more than the absence of disease.**
- **Health is composed of many dimensions.**
- **Health is inextricably linked to personal needs.**
- **Needs must be fulfilled if an individual is to embrace health.**
- **Health involves maximizing individual abilities and potential.**

'Health' has become one of the buzz-words of the latter half of the twentieth century. It is constantly alluded to in daily conversation and pervades all aspects of twentieth-century living. People may now choose to buy their food from a health shop, attend a health centre, health farm or contribute to a private health insurance scheme. In addition, there are a vast array of magazines that devote themselves entirely to the subject of health. Is health, then, purely a commodity to be bought and sold? The philosopher, Seedhouse (1987) asked this and other related questions in a very influential paper:

> What is health? Is it a commodity to be possessed? A state which enables normal functioning? A reserve of strength? An ability? A resilient spirit? A means? An end? Or both? Is health some combination of these elements? Or is it a word which presents an intractable puzzle of a baffling maze of human creation within which we are destined to stumble forever?

It can be seen that health is both an abstract and complex concept. Attempts to unravel its meaning, by turning to everyday usage of the term give rise to tensions between the varied contexts in which it is used. Yet, all these different uses of the term 'health' demonstrate that 'it is an idea that usefully communicates about an important aspect of life' (Dines and Cribb, 1993).

To facilitate an understanding of the notion of health, researchers have constructed different theoretical models. Each of these models enables us to view health from differing perspectives. Some models are health oriented, whilst others are disease oriented. Tamm (1993) has identified six perspectives. These are:

- **religious**
- **biomedical**
- **psychosomatic**
- **humanistic**
- **existential**
- **transpersonal.**

Each of these models is briefly described. Particular emphasis is placed upon those models which have influenced pervasive in the field of learning disability. That is, the *biomedical* model of health and the *humanistic* model.

The Religious Model

The religious model is primarily a model of health. From this perspective, health is perceived as 'a correct way of living and not just as a state of being free of disease' (Tamm, 1993). To be healthy, the individual must be in harmony with nature, with others and with their god. Morality assumes central significance. Disease arises when harmonious living is violated.

The Psychosomatic Model

The psychosomatic model of health and disease was first developed by Flanders Dunbar (1935, 1943, 1947). According to this model, there are no somatic diseases without emotional and/or social antecedents. Diseases are developed through a continual interplay between physical and mental factors. Positive attitudes in combination with stress-reducing techniques are considered to have a strong influence on the individual and aid the restoration of balance, which is defined as health (Pelletier, 1977; Capra, 1982).

The Existential Model

In the existential model, emphasis is placed on subjectivity. A central belief is that human beings must work out how they wish to conduct their lives. For example, if he/she wishes to be fit, then, he/she can to some extent choose health. Conversely, he/she can to some extent, consciously or subconsciously, choose illness (May, 1985). Health is achieved when individuals work through their concerns and the conscious and unconscious fears and motives spawned by each (Hall and Lindzey, 1978; May, 1985).

The Transpersonal Model

This model incorporates aspects of Eastern religion. It is concerned with transcendental experiences; that is, experiences transcending the individual, time and space. The transpersonal model is primarily a health model. The individual is considered to have health in the sense of well being. Insight and mindfulness are the primary healthy factors. The unhealthy factors are agitation and worry, which create a state of anxiety – the central feature of most mental disorders (Hall and Lindzey, 1978; Wilber, 1978). According to this model, a state of absolute health is achieved by practising meditation. Through different meditative techniques, the individual develops powers of self-healing.

The Biomedical Model

Many people think of health in terms of disease. This view is rooted in the strongly scientific tradition of medicine. According to this perspective, health is viewed as the polar opposite of illness. Thus, 'health is defined negatively' (Aggleton, 1990). This idea of health is illustrated in Figure 2.1.

Figure 2.1 Health–illness continuum.

On this basis, it is assumed that an individual in whom no trace of disease can be detected is healthy. Conversely, if one or more disease states become apparent, then the individual becomes unhealthy to a corresponding degree. At first sight, this view of health holds considerable appeal. Indeed, research into lay health beliefs supports the idea that many people do in fact, conceive of health like this (Williams, 1983; Blaxter, 1987; Calnan, 1987).

Unfortunately, there are considerable drawbacks to this model. One problem occurs when we consider the example of a person who has a 'disease' but to whom we might also wish to apply the label 'healthy'. A man who has cerebral palsy, who has come to terms with his condition and is leading a full and productive life, within certain limitations, might be viewed by some, including himself, as healthy. Similarly, Schneider and Conrad (1981) writing about epilepsy have shown that strictly medical concepts and definitions are insufficient if we are to understand the way in which individuals conceive of health and illness and how this understanding shapes their behaviour. It seems, therefore, that the biomedical view would label some people as unhealthy whom we might wish to label as healthy. Another objection lies in the fact that the biomedical model operates at the level of the individual organism and thereby ignores the social, cultural, educational and spiritual aspects of health. Indeed, the pervasive influence of the medical model in the field of learning disability has resulted in 'issues of health' being 'among the least discussed aspects of care' (Darbyshire, 1991). Another problem with this model is that it makes those who are experts on disease the sole arbiters of health. Consequently, the views and experiences in relation to health, of people with a learning disability are disqualified.

The biomedical model, therefore, has many weaknesses. Its use in the field of learning disability is limited. In fact, health is much more than the absence of disease. Rather, health has cultural, educational, social, spiritual and psychological dimensions. These broader aspects of health can be explained more closely, by examining the humanistic model.

The Humanistic Model

The humanistic model of health is holistic. That is, health is viewed as the totality of a person's existence. The philosophy of holistic health emphasizes the 'ongoing interaction of mind, body and spirit' (Bermosk and Porter, 1979). Such a view recognizes the inter-relatedness of the physical, psychological, emotional, social, spiritual and environmental factors that contribute to the overall quality of an individual's life. It highlights that health is:

> more than the absence of disease, it is a dynamic active process of continually striving to reach one's own balance and highest potentials. Health involves working towards optimal functioning in all areas. This process varies among people and often within individuals as they move from one situation and life stage to another, and is contingent on personal needs, imbalances and individual perceptions of reality. (Beck *et al.*, 1983, p. 26)

This definition of health is comprehensive and takes a wide view of health. Beck *et al.* (1988) are careful to define health in terms of the individual's specific potentials. Health is thus an individualized notion whose emphasis changes from person to person and in relation to life stage and situation. At the same time, this definition acknowledges that health is dependent upon personal needs and infers that needs must be met if one is to embrace health. In this light, it is clear that we must address the notion of 'need' if we are to move closer to an understanding of the concept of health.

Reader Activity 2.3
Consider periods of illness from which you may have suffered. Do any of the models identified by Tamm (1993) apply to you in that period of illness?

2.3 The Notion of Need

Basic needs unite people. People are 'bonded to one another because they share the same needs' (Sorensen and Luckmann, 1986). It follows, therefore, that the needs of people with a learning disability are similar to many other members of the society within which they live.

The psychologist, Maslow (1954) developed one of the earlier theories based on human needs. His *hierarchy of human needs* focused on five areas which can be seen in Box 2.2.

Maslow portrayed human needs as a hierarchy in order to emphasize the relationship between them. He highlighted that people must fulfil physiological needs before attempting to address safety needs. Likewise, safety needs must be satisfied before a person can fulfil love needs. Several years after Maslow first described this theory, Kalish (1982) adapted it by adding another level (Figure 2.2).

This additional level fits in between the physiological and safety needs. It includes sexual needs and the need for activity, exploration, manipulation and novelty. In the view of both Maslow and Kalish, a healthy person was one who was striving to be self-actualized. The state of self-actualization can only be achieved when basic needs have been met through 'goal-directed behaviour, competent self-care and satisfying relationships with others' (Pender, 1987).

Similarly, O'Brien and Lyle (1987) allude to self-actualization in their identification of five key concepts that promote the achievement of health. They suggest that if the health of people with a learning disability was to be upheld, developed and respected then the following criteria must be adhered to:

- **choice for individuals**
- **opportunities for integration into the community**
- **opportunities for active participation in the community**
- **the ability to form and maintain relationships with others**
- **the acquisition of competence and skill.**

Box 2.2 Maslow's hierarchy of human needs

Physiological needs:
- food
- water
- air
- temperature
- elimination
- rest
- pain avoidance.

Safety needs:
- security
- safety
- protection and freedom from fear, anxiety and chaos.

Belongingness and love needs:
- closeness
- belonging.

Esteem needs:
- self-esteem
- esteem of others.

Self-actualization:
- the process of maximizing ones abilities and potential.

If these criteria are to be met, then it is vital that people with a learning disability are viewed from a holistic perspective. Moreover, it is essential that basic needs are met so that the individual might achieve self-actualization. It is the task of carers to ensure that opportunities are presented to people with a learning disability that facilitate the acquisition of skills. By maximizing abilities and potential, the individual is empowered to embrace health.

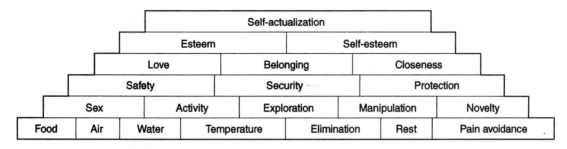

Figure 2.2 A hierarchy of human needs, after Maslow and Kalish.

2.4 A Physical Perspective of Health

The holistic view of health described in the last section is useful in highlighting the interactive nature of the constituent parts of health. Holism also alludes to a balance between these various parts (Dines and Cribb, 1993). This stresses the importance of equilibrium in life. The following discussion highlights that physical imbalance can affect other aspects of health. More specifically, this section demonstrates that:

● **Health is a balance of human functions.**
● **Balance or equilibrium is central to maintenance of health.**
● **To maintain this balance, physiological needs must be met.**
● **Imbalance may affect all dimensions of health.**
● **People who have a learning disability may require assistance to maintain or restore a balance of health.**

Health as a Balance

As was demonstrated in the last section, health is a dynamic process of continually striving to reach one's own *balance* and potential. The idea of health as a balance is a resonating pattern in the literature. For example, McMurray (1990, p. 6) suggests that health is:

> a state of equilibrium which derives from a balance between the striving for self-actualization and the compromises demanded by the physical, psychological, cultural and social environment.

Neuman (1982) has defined health as:

> a condition in which all subsystems are in balance and harmony with the whole individual.

Roy (1980, p. 179) has also ascribed to a balance-based definition of health. She views health as:

> a state of being and becoming an integrated whole person, that is, the condition in which needs are met and integrity is maintained because of adaptation.

Hence, health may be equated with balance or *equilibrium*. Conversely, disequilibrium leads to a health loss. The impetus for these balance-based definitions of health derives from the physiological concept of *homeostasis*. Homeostasis concerns the physiological processes by which the internal systems of the body are maintained at equilibrium, despite variations in the external conditions.

Homeostasis then, refers to a regulatory subsystem within the body whose aim is self-preservation. To illustrate this idea, consider maintenance of body temperature. For healthy adults the range of normal temperature is 36–37.5°C. Maintenance of a constant body temperature is essential for the numerous chemical processes occurring continually in the body. In cold conditions, homeostatic mechanisms maintain this temperature by causing the constriction of blood capillaries, shivering and the erection of bodily hair. Such homeostatic mechanisms within the body operate effectively only within narrow limits. That is, the homeostatic system is unable to supply compensatory adjustments in some situations. Consequently if the balance is lost – the individual may suffer a health loss. For example, if body temperature drops to an extremely low level, as in the case of hypothermia, homeostatic mechanisms break down and the body begins to show indications of malfunction or disorder – unless assistance is sought. From this example, you can see that homeostatic limits define the healthy state.

Of course, homeostatic mechanisms control functions other than temperature maintenance. Indeed, homeostatic processes encompass the:

- **maintenance of an adequate intake of oxygen**
- **elimination of waste products and toxic substances**
- **maintenance of intact defence mechanisms**
- **rest and sleep**
- **maintenance of normal posture and movement**
- **maintenance of normal water balance, electrolyte and hydrogen ion concentration.**

When these physiological requirements are satisfied a balance is achieved. Conversely any departure from homeostatic limits can have a widespread adverse effect on homeostasis and result in a health loss. Since health is composed of many dimensions it follows that a loss of homeostatic balance will affect all dimensions of health.

To illustrate this notion in relation to learning disability consider the following case history.

Case Study 2.1

Paul is 20 years old and has Down's syndrome. He is in a temporary state of psychophysiological balance and, therefore, healthy (see Figure 2.3). Because Paul's needs for food and fluid intake are met, the need for elimination is met. The need for adequate nutrition, fluid and electrolyte balance and healthy elimination are thus in equilibrium. Moreover, Paul is fortunate in that he is meeting his needs for sleep and rest. Because Paul's basic needs have been met he may now progress to addressing the need for self-actualization. However, because Down's syndrome is associated with mouth breathing (Craft *et al.*, 1985), Paul has a reduced capacity to combat infection as a result of poor immunological response. Consequently, he develops a respiratory infection. Hence the homeostatic mechanism responsible for maintenance of an intact defence mechanism is disrupted. Because of difficulty in breathing, Paul finds it difficult to sleep at night. He loses his appetite and feels unable to attend his workplace whilst he is ill. As a result, his relations with others are temporarily affected. Consequently, the need for self-actualization is halted. These manifestations have compromised his need for adequate oxygen, nutrition and sleep. Paul is in a state of psychophysiological imbalance (see Figure 2.4) and has, therefore, suffered a health loss. If assistance is not sought, then Paul's health will not be restored. This example clearly illustrates that health loss deriving from a homeostatic imbalance may give rise to disequilibrium or imbalance in all areas of life. This example also serves to highlight that the concept of homeostasis has far wider applications than simply physiological processes. In view of this, the next section further explores the concept of health as a balance by considering the concept of mental health.

2.5 A Psychological Perspective of Health

Physical health cannot be seen in isolation from mental health. Mental health encompasses thoughts, feelings and responses to life and is closely related to physical health. Because of this inter-relationship, actions aimed at promoting mental equilibrium may also help alleviate physical imbalance. Similarly, when physical equilibrium is achieved, mental health is likely to be improved. Thus, mental health, like physical health is a multi-

dimensional human state. This section focuses upon some basic mental health concepts in relation to learning disability. In particular, after reading the following discussion you will be able to:

- **identify aspects of positive mental health**
- **explore the relationship between learning disability and mental health**
- **discuss the concept of effective coping**
- **consider how effective coping may be achieved.**

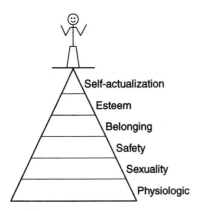

Figure 2.3 Psychophysiologic balance.

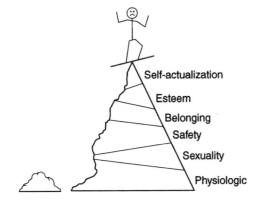

Figure 2.4 Psychophysiologic imbalance.

Traditional Definitions of Mental Health

As indicated in the last section, many theorists have applied the concept of homeostasis to psychological processes. The degree of psychological equilibrium experienced by the individual is central to the mental health of that person. Not surprisingly though, the concept of 'mental health' is as abstract and complex as that of 'health'. Terms such as 'mental disorder', 'mental illness' and 'psychiatric disorder' have been used loosely and sometimes interchangeably (Naylor and Clifton, 1993) when referring to issues of mental health. That is, many definitions simply redefine mental health in terms of mental illness (Newnes, 1994). Definitions of positive mental health are rare. One of those rare definitions was proposed by Jahoda (1956). Despite its age, it remains a classic account upon which to base an understanding of positive mental health. Box 2.3 illustrates the six cardinal aspects that he suggested constituted positive mental health.

Reader Activity 2.5
If you are able to accept the definition offered by Jahoda (1956) is it possible to prioritize the six

aspects which he identifies from the perspective of your own mental health?

Box 2.3 The six essential components that constitute mental health (Jahoda, 1956)

- **Attitude of the individual toward self.**   This refers the individual's feelings about his or her self-identity. A mentally healthy person has a realistic self-identity which is characterized by synthesizing life experiences.
- **Self-actualization.**   This term derives from the work of Maslow (1954) in relation to human needs. The term is also a commonly used phrase in mental health. A mentally healthy person demonstrates self-actualization in as much as he or she strives towards personal growth and productive living through goal-directed behaviour.
- **Integration.**   Jahoda suggests that in mental health terms, integration is a synthesis of attitudes towards self and the self-actualizing tendency. The outcome of such integration is a relative resistance to stress. An integrated person is rational and balanced.
- **Autonomy.**   According to Jahoda, autonomy means the ability to make decisions upon which an individual will base independent actions. The individual uses judgement and selectivity to accept or reject environmental factors.
- **Adequate perception of reality.**   That is, the mentally healthy person accepts reality as it is without fitting it into his or her own wishes. The individual is able to account for the opinions of others. Another's different perception does not evoke feelings of anxiety or inadequacy.
- **Mastery (control) of the situation.**   The mentally healthy person is able to master their environment in accordance with his/her own needs. Mastery of the situation involves adaptation to changing situations as well as manipulation of the environment when it is detrimental.

Modern Definitions of Mental Health

More recent definitions have built upon Jahoda's original work. For example, Haber *et al.* (1992) define mental health as:

a dynamic process in which a person's physical, cognitive, affective, behavioural and social dimensions interact functionally with one another and the environment . . . mental health permits persons to pursue life goals and culminates in the fulfilment of their own life purpose.

The emphasis placed upon the interaction between the individual and the environment is also highlighted by Sugden *et al.* (1986) who suggested that a mentally healthy person:

has the capacity to adapt, or to change to his environment.

They add that, in general terms, a mentally healthy person is:

recognizable as average, participates effectively in social interaction, is able to respond to and where necessary modify his environment and experiences a general sense of well-being as a consequence of satisfaction with the business of everyday life.

Typically then, a person who is in a state of mental health or emotional balance has:

- a stable physical environment – a safe and comfortable living situation with adequate food
- life experiences that are consistent with the individual's self-concept or self-image
- healthy relationships – close and supportive relations with significant others
- work or study that is interesting and fulfilling – a sense of interdependence with others
- good physical health
- adequate economic means
- enjoyable, creative and recreational outlets
- a sense of hope for the future. (Sorensen and Luckmann, 1986)

The concept of mental health encapsulates the notion of needs satisfaction as an outcome of the individual's inter-relationship with the environment.

It is important to acknowledge that learning disability is sometimes associated with mental health problems. There are of course, people with learning disabilities who do not suffer from a mental health problem (or psychological disequilibrium) and 'are in far better shape emotionally than some people without disabilities' (Sinason, 1992). Nevertheless, recent government reports (Department of Health, 1989, 1993) and other publications (Russell, 1991; Naylor and Clifton, 1993) have highlighted the need for health care professionals to address mental health issues in relation to learning disability. If the health-care worker is to effectively assist in the restoration or maintenance of mental health in relation to the individual with a learning disability, then the factors that contribute to psychological imbalance must be addressed.

2.6 Mental Health and Learning Disability

Research evidence indicates that the incidence rates of mental ill health is higher amongst people with a learning disability than for the rest of the population (Corbett, 1979; Lund, 1985; Jacobson and Ackerman, 1988). Reasons for this are relatively unknown due to a lack of research in this area. Theories have been put forward suggesting that mental health problems are related to underlying abnormalities of brain structure and function or the effects of epilepsy (Holland and Murphy, 1990). In many other cases, however, emotional and behavioural disturbances can be attributed to social and psychological factors. These factors have been described by Russell (1991) in terms of 'burdens'.

Russell identified three psychosocial burdens that may be summarized as:

(1) Not being sufficiently skilled to be able to adapt quickly to the world of work and the social demands of other people.
(2) The burden of living in a society which fails to provide resources for those who are disabled and in which social attitudes to disability encourage rejection, segregation and isolation.
(3) The burden of being aware that one has a learning disability and the self-doubt that this can generate.

These burdens expose the individual with a learning disability to *psychological stress* and to the possible development of a mental health problem. Identifying those who may be at risk and providing them with psychological support is, therefore, an important task for people working with individuals who have a learning disability.

2.7 Coping Behaviour

Because of the anxiety and physiological arousal created by psychological disequilibrium, the individual is motivated to do something to alleviate the discomfort. The process by which an individual attempts to manage psychological stress is called *coping*. How well a person copes is central to psychological well being. Furthermore, the way in which people cope with psychological disharmony is inextricably entwined with the quality of life that an individual experiences.

A Definition of Coping

Most definitions of coping incorporate the notion of attempting to restore equilibrium in response to stress (Weisman and Wordern, 1976; Pearlin and Schooler, 1978; Monat and Lazarus, 1985). According to Bailey and Clarke (1989), coping includes all attempts by the individual to reduce the impact of perceived threat or demand upon him or herself whether or not they are successful in reducing demand. It is important, however, that in attempting to define coping, we do not lose sight of the complexity of the concept. Rather than a static one-off event, coping is a 'complex constellation of processes' (McHaffie, 1992). The concept of coping is 'a product of the actions an individual takes in attempting to maintain personal control and psychological equilibrium within the duration of the life-span' (Skodol-Wilson and Ren-Kneisl, 1992).

The Process of Coping

Coping efforts operate in one of three ways: directed towards the environment, towards the self, or in both directions (Lazarus and Launier, 1978). How people cope is determined by their own interpretation – or cognitive appraisal – of events in the light of available resources such as social support networks, physical health or spiritual security. An individual can cope on different levels, including the physical, social, cognitive and emotional levels. Generally speaking though, an individual's attempts to cope take two major forms. One focuses on the problem; the individual evaluates the stressful situation and does something to change it. The other focuses on the emotional response to the problem; the individual tries to reduce anxiety without dealing directly with the anxiety-producing situation. The former is referred to as problem-focused coping and the latter as emotion-focused coping (Lazarus and Folkman, 1984).

Problem-focused coping may involve: 'defining the problem; generating alternative solutions; weighing the alternatives in terms of costs and benefits ... and implementing the selected alternative' (Atkinson *et al*, 1990). The effectiveness of these strategies depends upon the individual's past experience, level of intellect and self-control. According to Lazarus and Folkman (1984), problem-focused coping strategies are more likely to occur when a person is experiencing stress which is appraised as changeable.

Emotion-focused forms of coping, on the other hand, are more probable when a person is experiencing a high level of stress and perceives that nothing can be done to minimize the threat. Emotion-focused strategies may be behavioural or cognitive.

Suppose you have not studied for an important examination. You may decide that the examination is not worth worrying about. This indicates that you have redefined the problem to make it less of a threat. This is a cognitive form of emotion-focused coping. Alternatively, you may seek the comfort and support of friends or you may decide to decrease your anxiety by drinking alcohol. These strategies are behavioural. Each individual copes with stressful situations in a unique way. Most commonly though, a combination of problem-focused and emotion-focused strategies are employed in order to minimize psychological stress.

Personal Control

Successful coping hinges in no small degree upon the amount of personal control an individual experiences (Bailey and Clarke, 1989; McHaffie, 1992). That is, 'personal control as an outcome of effective coping is often experienced by the individual in terms of a return to psychobiological equilibrium' (Bailey and Clarke, 1989). This notion is summarized in Figure 2.5.

Conversely, individuals who feel a personal lack of control to overcome threats to psychological well being are likely to show more stress-related prob-

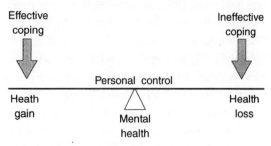

Figure 2.5 The relationship between personal control and psychological equilibrium.

lems such as anxiety and depression. This is particularly relevant to people with learning disabilities whose mechanisms for successful coping may be compromised by a primary impairment or by psychosocial factors. To illustrate this point, consider the function of communication. Communication, turning to a comforting person or talking through problems, are everyday ways of coping with stress. Indeed, Zeimer (1982) found that over 50% of his study sample reported that their preferred method of coping was to talk to someone. Clearly, this has profound implications for those individuals whose verbal communication is limited. Moreover, coping mechanisms operate within the limitations of the individual's genetic make-up, physical condition and level of intelligence. It follows, therefore, that some people may find it difficult to cope with stress successfully. Such knowledge must be put to good effect. Carers must strive to enable personal control, thereby assisting the individual to cope with stressful events. In so doing the carer will be facilitating the restoration or maintenance of psychobiological equilibrium.

2.8 Conclusion

This chapter began by recognizing the difficulty of trying to define a concept as complex as health. While it may not be possible to formulate a wholly definitive theory of health, 'it is important to examine competing definitions for the contribution they are able to make to our understanding' (Sim, 1990, p. 7). A number of perspectives have been considered. Specifically, health has been examined from a philosophical, physical and psychological perspective. The interactive nature of the constituent parts of health has highlighted that health is a balance of human functions. To maintain this balance, the physiological, psychological, social, cultural and spiritual needs of the individual must be met. Recognizing that health is a balance of human functions will contribute to the enhancement and maintenance of an individual's health and in the

process significantly contribute to the advancement of services provided for people with a learning disability.

Discussion Questions

1 **What does being healthy mean to you?**

2 **Health has many dimensions: physical, psychological, spiritual, cultural, environmental and social. Which of these dimensions is the most important to you?**

3 **Identify a client with whom you have worked. Consider how you would enable this individual to strive towards self-actualization.**

4 **What do you think being healthy may mean to someone who has a learning disability?**

5 **Consider the last time you were in a stressful situation. Recall how you responded to the situation. Identify the coping strategies that you employed.**

6 **Explore how you would enable a person who has a learning disability to exercise personal control.**

7 **What life-style issues affect the balance of our daily patterns of living in our society and does coping with these issues influence how we live?**

References

Aggleton, P. (1990) *Health*. London: Routledge.

Atkinson, R.L., Atkinson, R.C., Smith, E.E. and Bem, D.J. (1990) *Introduction to Psychology*. London: Harcourt Brace Jovanovich.

Bailey, R. and Clarke, M. (1989) *Stress and Coping in Nursing*. London: Chapman & Hall.

Beck, C.M., Rawlins, R.D. and Williams, S.R. (1988) *Mental Health Psychiatric Nursing – A holistic lifecycle approach*. London: C.V. Mosby.

Bermosk, L.S. and Porter, S.E. (1979) *Women's Health and Human Wholeness*. New York: Appleton-Century-Crofts.

Blaxter, M. (1987) Attitudes to health. *In* Blaxter, M., Cox, B. and Buckle, A.L.J. (Eds) *The Health and Lifestyle Survey*, p. 15. London: Health Promotion Trust.

Calnan, M. (1987) *Health and Illness: The lay perspective.* London: Tavistock.

Capra, F. (1982) *The Turning Point: Science, Society and the Rising Culture.* London: Wildwood House.

Corbett, J.A. (1979) Psychiatric morbidity and mental retardation. *In* James, F.E. and Snaith, R.P. (Eds) *Psychiatric Illness and Mental Handicap*, pp. 11–25. London: Royal College of General Practitioners.

Craft, M., Bicknell, L. and Hollins, S. (1985) *Mental Handicap – A multi-disciplinary approach.* London: Baillière-Tindall.

Darbyshire, P. (Ed.) (1991) *Cited In* Roth, S. and Brown, M. (Eds) Advocates for health. *Nursing Times* **87**(21): 62–64.

Department of Health (1989) *Needs and Responses: Services for Adults with Mental Handicap Who are Mentally Ill, Who Have Behaviour Problems or Who Offend.* London: HMSO.

Department of Health (1993) *Services for People with Learning Disabilities and Challenging Behaviour or Mental Health Needs (the Mansell Report).* London: HMSO.

Dines, A. and Cribb, A. (1993) *Health Promotion Concepts and Practice.* London: Blackwell Scientific.

Dunbar, H.F. (1935) *Emotions and Bodily Changes: A Survey of Literature on Psychosomatic Interrelationships 1910–1933.* Columbia: Columbia University Press.

Dunbar, H.F. (1943) *Psychosomatic Diagnosis.* New York: Paul B. Hoeber.

Dunbar, H.F. (1947) *Mind and Body: Psychosomatic medicine.* New York: Random House.

Haber, J., McMahon, A.L., Price-Hoskins, P. and Sideleau, B.F. (1992) *Comprehensive Psychiatric Nursing.* London: Mosby Year Book.

Hall, C. and Lindzey, G. (1978) *Theories of Personality.* New York: Wiley.

Holland, T. and Murphy, G. (1990) Behavioural and psychiatric disorders in adults with mild learning difficulties. *International Review of Psychiatry* **2**: 117.

Jacobson, J.W. and Ackerman, L.J. (1988) An appraisal of services for persons with mental retardation and psychiatric impairments. *Mental Retardation* **26**(6): 377–380.

Jahoda, M. (1956) *Current Concepts of Positive Mental Health – A Report to the Staff Directorate.* New York: Basic Books.

Kalish, R.A. (1982) *The Psychology of Human Behaviour.* Monterey, CA: Brooks/Cole.

Lazarus, R.S. and Folkman, S. (1984) *Stress, Appraisal and Coping.* New York: Springer.

Lazarus, R.S. and Launier, R. (1978) Stress-related transactions between person and environment. *In* Pervin, C.L.A. and Lewis, M. (Eds) *Perspectives in Interactional Psychology*, p. 287. New York: Plenum Press.

Lund, J. (1985) The prevalence of psychiatric morbidity in mentally retarded adults. *Acta Psychiatrica Scandanavia* **72**: 563.

McHaffie, H.E. (1992) Coping: an essential element of nursing. *Journal of Advanced Nursing* **17**: 933–940.

McMurray, A. (1990) *Community Health Nursing – Primary Health Care in Practice.* London: Churchill Livingstone.

Maslow, A.H. (1954) *Motivation and Personality.* New York: Harper & Row.

May, R. (1985) *The Discovery of Being: Writings in existential psychology.* New York: Norton.

Monat, A. and Lazarus, R.S. (1985) *Stress and Coping: An anthology.* New York: Columbia University Press.

Naylor, V. and Clifton, M. (1993) People with learning disabilities – meeting complex needs. *Health and Social Care* **1**(6): 343–353.

Neuman, B. (1982) *The Neuman Systems Model.* Norwalk: Appleton-Century-Crofts.

Newnes, C. (1994) Defining Mental Health? *Nursing Times* **90**(19): 46.

O'Brien, J. and Lyle, C. (1987) *Framework for Accomplishment.* Georgia: Responsive Services Associates.

Pearlin, L.I. and Schooler, C. (1978) The structure of coping. *Journal of Health and Social Behaviour* **19**: 2–21.

Pelletier, K. (1977) *Mind as Healer, Mind as Slayer: A Holistic Approach to Preventing Stress Disorders.* New York: Dell.

Pender, N.J. (1987) *Health promotion in Nursing Practice.* California: Appleton & Lange.

Roy, C. (1980) The Roy Adaptation Model. *In* Roy, C. and Riehl, J. (Eds) *Conceptual Models for Nursing Practice* p. 179. New York: Appleton-Century-Crofts.

Russell, O. (1991) Presentation of psychiatric illness in the mentally handicapped. *Medicine International* **95**(2): 3975–3977.

Schneider, J.W. and Conrad, P. (1981) Medical and sociological typologies: the case of epilepsy. *Social Science and Medicine* **15**(3): 211.

Seedhouse, D. (1987) The need for a philosophy of health. *In* Lamb, D., Davies, T. and Roberts, M. (Eds) *Explorations in Medicine,* Vol. 1, pp. 123–198. Avebury: Aldershot.

Sim, J. (1990) The concept of health. *Physiotherapy* **76**(7): 423–428.

Sinason, V. (1992) *Mental Handicap and the Human Condition – New approaches from Tavistock.* London: Free Association Books.

Skodol Wilson, H. and Ren Kneisl, C. (1992) *Psychiatric Nursing,* 4th edn. California: Benjamin Cummings.

Sorensen, K.C. and Luckmann, J. (1986) *Basis Nursing: A psycho-physiologic approach.* London: W.B. Saunders.

Sorochan, W. (1970) Health concepts as a basis for orthobiosis. *In* Hart, E. and Sechrist, W. (Eds) *The Dynamics of Wellness,* pp. 211–219. California: Wadsworth.

Sugden, J., Bessant, A., Eastland, M. and Field, R. (1986) *A Handbook for Psychiatric Nurses.* London: Harper & Row.

Tamm, M.E. (1993) Models of health and disease. *British Journal of Medical Psychology* **66**: 213–228.

Weisman, A.D. and Worden, J.W. (1976) The existential plight in cancer: significance of the first 100 days. *International Journal of Psychiatry in Medicine* **7**: 1.

Wilber, K. (1978) *Up from Eden: A Transpersonal View of Human Evolution.* New York: Anchor Press.

Williams, R. (1983) Concepts of health; an analysis of lay logic. *Sociology* **17**: 185.

World Health Organization (1946) *Constitution.* New York: World Health Organization.

Wylie, C.M. (1970) The definition and measurement of health and disease. *Public Health* **85**: 100.

Zeimer, M.M. (1982) Coping behaviour; a response to stress. *Clinical Nurse* **2**(4): 8.

Further Reading

Dines, A. (1993) *Fundamental Skills and Concepts in Patient Care.* London: Chapman & Hall.

Hinchcliff, S. and Montague, S. (1988) *Physiology for Nursing Practice.* London: Baillière-Tindall.

Keller, M.J. (1981) Towards a definition of health. *Advances in Nursing Science* **4**(1): 43.

McHaffie, H.E. (1992) Coping; an essential element of nursing. *Journal of Advanced nursing* **17**: 933. Primarily written for nurses, this article provides a detailed account of coping as a multifaceted concept. Identifies the functions of coping, coping behaviours and implications for nursing practice.

Naylor, V. and Clifton, M. (1993) People with learning disabilities: meeting complex needs. *Health and Social Care* **1**(6): 343. This paper discusses how the needs of people who have a learning disability which is associated with a mental health problem may be met.

Simmons, S.J. (1989) Health: a concept analysis. *International Journal of Nursing Studies* **26**(2): 155.

Tamm, M.E. (1993) Models of health and disease. *British Journal of Medical Psychology* **66**: 213. This paper provides a comprehensive useful critique of six models of health and disease.

Chapter 3: Health loss, gain and maintenance in learning disability
Eileen Wake

3.1 Introduction

This chapter further develops Chapter 2 and reflects upon the meaning of health for people in their everyday lives. The emphasis is placed upon choices, experiences, or the lack of them that may restrict the person with a learning disability in maintaining their own health. This chapter also explores how health is defined for the individual with a learning disability and by whom. Health is regarded in terms of how we maintain our health, how we as individuals cope with illness/injury (health loss) and how we can improve our own health. This delicate balance, previously explored in Chapter 2, is termed 'homeostasis'.

Homeostasis is something that everyone strives for even if they have never heard of the actual term. It includes wanting to feel healthy physically and emotionally in everyday life – at work, in relationships with others and at leisure. However, there are many constraints on our attempt to maintain this homeostasis. These include external influences such as social, economic and environmental factors, as well as internal influences, for instance feelings, worries and fears as well as aspirations for one's life. The expectations of others also affect feelings of self worth and value. For the person with learning disability goals to be achieved are often dictated by able-bodied people.

The right to realistic life-goal planning, informed choices regarding one's life style and issues such as health education and health promotion for people with learning disabilities is therefore of importance. As is the right to adequate resources to enable the above to occur. Attitudes of able-bodied people towards people with a learning disability are also important when considering health and people with learning disabilities. It is an important issue to consider as it affects health-care delivery by professionals for and to people with learning disabilities. Health care tends to focus upon the short-term physical needs of the individual with a learning disability rather than a holistic approach including, for example, preventive health work and the impact of social, cultural and environmental aspects of that person's life and life style.

Legislation must also encompass the holistic (all aspects of what it means to be a human being) approach, for example the *Health of the Nation* document (DOH, 1991) cites that a key target provision area is:

> . . . where there is clear scope for improvement . . . rehabilitation services for people with a physical disability. (DOH, 1991, p. 9)

There are no specific additional key targets in terms of the health issues for people with learning disabilities, but it is argued that all of the key targets, that is, coronary heart disease, healthy living issues such as smoking, diet and alcohol, refer to everyone (Department of Health 1995). This chapter seeks to encompass them where appropriate. It is not possible to consider health as merely a physical concept, there are many dimensions and perceptions around health which are reflected in the definition of health offered by Sarafino (1990).

> . . . a positive state of physical, mental and social well being . . . that varies over time . . .
>
> (Sarafino, 1990, p. 5)

As stated earlier there are also external factors that can directly affect the individual's actual state of health.

For the person with a learning disability, the issue of access to services can influence health in terms of access to preventative health support and also accessing specialist help where appropriate. Howells (1986) argued that people with learning disabilities consult their general practitioner (GP) less than the general community population despite having a wide range of health needs. Wing and Gould (1979) have argued that this was mainly due to communication problems experienced by people with learning disabilities, as well as difficulties understanding the surgery appointment system.

It is a common misconception that social role valorization (see Chapter 8) means exclusively using local services 'because that is what we all do'. This denies the right of the individual with a learning disability to seek specialist help, in epilepsy management when required, for example. Everyone should have the right to seek the best care possible. This is particularly pertinent in that it has been argued that GPs may lack experience in co-ordinating the care for people with learning disabilities and they may feel that this responsibility lies with a consultant. A lack of liaison between professionals involved in the care of people with learning disabilities was seen to be linked to this (Howells, 1986). This was despite the fact that over 60% of people with learning disabilities living in the community required ongoing medical support for chronic physical and/or mental health problems (Mininhan and Dean, 1990).

Service providers need to be able to offer a range of services that are enabling rather than purely prescriptive. This includes reflecting upon the ways in which health care is delivered, and the jargon that is used by health professionals. Many people feel disempowered by the language that health professionals use and feel unable to articulate their needs and feelings. This is a common experience that people have encountered at some time or another.

> . . . a common feature of communication between doctor and patient is a discrepancy between their labelling of significant symptoms. The medical dilemma is that of discerning the 'presenting' symptoms of clinically significant disorders; the patient's concern is with the normalisation of her [*sic*] subjective experience of discomfort. (Oakley, 1992, p. 173)

Economic Impacts on Health

This is an important area in terms of health-care provision for people with learning disabilities. It is recognized that there is an inherent poverty 'trap' within western societies that has a domino effect on all aspects of people's lives, not just health. The Black Report (Black *et al.*, 1980) acknowledged the overall impact of having a disability by stating that the aims of services for people with disabilities should include:

> . . . to reduce the risk of early death, to improve the quality of life whether in the community or in institutions, and as far as possible to reduce the need for the latter. (Black *et al.*, 1992, p. 237)

Although the report is somewhat dated and institutions are thankfully reducing in size and number, the report was also useful in that it highlighted the links between poverty and ill health within the UK. This included the effects of overcrowding on health in terms of, for example, the increased likelihood of respiratory illnesses and more injuries due to home accidents. It is therefore important to acknowledge that many adults with learning disabilities enter the cycle of poverty and dependence on the benefits system for support. This is especially true in times of high unemployment as is currently being experienced in the UK. This results in even less meaningful employment, with decent wages, for the individual with a learning disability (Pfeiffer, 1990).

Carers may also be drawn into this spiral of dependency because there are limited day-care facilities for adults with profound learning disabilities. Carers therefore have to be at home more and thus have less opportunities to seek employment. This is more problematic with regards day-care provision for adults who also have 'challenging behaviours', which is currently very limited. This all contributes to varying levels of carer 'burnout' and health problems that can in turn affect the health of the whole family. The economic dimension of health is further explored in Chapter 12.

Environmental Factors

The environment has a significant impact on one's overall well being. Perhaps one of the main issues facing the person with a learning disability, relating their environment to their health, is where the person lives. It is acknowledged that institutional care can have a profound impact on an individual's mental health, for example in terms of belief in self worth and individuality. Goffman (1961) highlighted the impact of institutionalization on the individual. It should be remembered by carers of people with learning disabilities that those currently residing in small group homes may have spent a significant part of their lives in large institutions. Therefore a lot of time will have to be invested when caring for that person in encouraging him or her to feel empowered with decisions regarding health. It is important to avoid always giving advice and 'telling the person what is best for them' rather than using empathy and congruence skills (Rogers, 1961). The latter approach can help to empower the person to participate in his own care to the best of his *a*bilities, rather than focus on *dis*abilities.

Reader Activity 3.2

A person with a learning disability need not have had the experience of living in an institution to feel disempowered. Messages of dependency and negative views of self worth are constantly being unconsciously transmitted by able-bodied people.
Consider the following conversation between two people:

Claire, a young friend of Jane was watching her holding a baby with severe learning disability and they were talking about what Claire, who had learning and physical disabilities, would like to do when she left school:
'I'd really like to do what you do, you know, look after babies with problems because I know what it's like'
then there was a silence and her head bowed down:

'... but they won't let me do that 'coz I'm disabled you see...'

The question to raise here is who is disabling who? Disability can be perceived in terms of lack of access to opportunities to grow as an individual, be it in terms of education or employment. It is interesting to note that the World Health Organization cited in its 'Health for all' document (WHO, 1985) that:

by the year 2000, disabled persons should have the physical, social and economic opportunities that allow at least for a socially and economically fulfilling and mentally creative life. (WHO, 1985, p. 30)

3.2 Specific Health-Care Needs

This chapter is essentially about conditions that commonly affect people with learning disabilities. However, it is important to point out that although some conditions are perhaps encountered more amongst people with learning disabilities than in other groups, it would be wrong to medicalize all aspects of care for people with learning disabilities just as one wouldn't for any other group of individuals. What it does mean, however, is that, for people with learning disabilities who do require ongoing health care or monitoring of chronic health problems, they are entitled to the level of health care they need as individuals, regardless of whether they have a learning disability or not. This includes the right to access specialist health-care provision, where appropriate, as well as the skills of a primary health-care team.

Some of the common conditions that are encountered when caring for people with learning disabilities are chronic, ongoing health needs. It is important to state that a list of 'common conditions' could be endless due to the fact that individuals are unique. Each with their own genetic make-up, health needs, life styles and experiences. Illness and health problems generally depend on an individual's own perception of what illness is, and the extent of the impact of that condition on everyday life. It is the same for people with learning disabilities; however, the impact of health problems on the person with a learning disability may also depend on whether the person requires the help of carer(s) and the extent and intensity of input from those carer(s). The carer's perception of health and chronic health problems as well as the environment in which the person with a learning disability is being cared for, will also have an impact. Perhaps most importantly of all, the level of communication skills that a person has and the extent of any physical disabilities may greatly influence how his or her health needs are interpreted.

Reader Activity 3.3
Imagine that you are the person with a learning disability. You have very limited movement and are dependent on others for all daily needs, and reliant on basic sign language to express your needs and feelings. You have had a headache all morning and would like it to be relieved, you try to let your carer know. How would you do this?

Knowledge about a person on an individual level is vital when caring for a person who has additional needs in terms of physical disabilities. If he or she is being cared for in a group home, for example, the allocation of a named main carer and associate carer(s) is essential to ensure that care is holistic and unfragmented. A working knowledge of the communication system used by the person is very important, as well as a commitment to ensuring that the person who is reliant on non-verbal communication has the opportunity to learn and be able to use the most appropriate communication methods that will enable expression of all his or her needs.

There is a wide range of communication systems currently available to aid the person who is unable to communicate effectively verbally or is totally reliant on non-verbal communication techniques. This includes an eye pointing, picture or symbol systems on boards which can be used by eye point-

ing or touch, various computer-based aides such as Alpha Talker's which are picture and/or symbol boards with voice synthesizers that are touch activated, to an all-inclusive sign vocabularies such as Makaton, an adapted form of the British Sign Language. Makaton is widely used by people with learning disabilities as it has stages of single signs that can be learnt dependent on ability. Each sign represents frequently used words/actions/occasions and phrases such as 'toilet', 'dinner', 'time' and 'bed'. It is important, however, that whenever a sign system is used, that verbal language is also used simultaneously by, for example, carers.

This chapter covers mainly physical conditions which commonly result in health loss for the person with a learning disability. Remedies, treatments and interventions which promote health gain in people affected by these conditions are described throughout. The conditions that are outlined in this chapter are:

- **epilepsy**
- **oral health issues**
- **vision impairment**
- **hearing impairment**
- **problems linked with continence**
- **nutrition and feeding issues**
- **cardiac (heart) problems**
- **respiratory problems**
- **problems linked with immobility.**

Reader Activity 3.4
Are there any more conditions/health needs which may be added to this list? Is there any single source from which a person may gain information relevant to the care of someone who has such health needs?

3.3 Epilepsy

Epilepsy is perhaps one of the most misunderstood chronic health problems. It is bounded by centuries of beliefs around its origin and causes, many based on religious beliefs, for example, that the person who had epilepsy had evil spirits inside or was 'mad'.

Box 3.1 Common anticonvulsant medications used in the treatment of epilepsy		
Drug	Used for	Common side effects
Sodium valproate (Epilim)	Generalized seizures	Gastrointestinal problems, weight gain, mild alopecia
Carbamazepine (Tegretol)	Partial seizures	Nausea, tonic–clonic seizures, dizziness, drowsiness and ataxia with high doses
Phenytoin (Epanutin)	All types of seizures	Nausea, vomiting, ataxia, drowsiness, gum hypertrophy can be problem in long-term use
Ethosuximide (Zarontin)	Absence seizures	Gastrointestinal problems, drowsiness, dizziness, ataxia
Phenobarbitone	All types, except absence seizures	Drowsiness, lethargy, depression in adults
Lamotrigine (Lamictal)	In addition to other medication – for partial generalized seizures	Skin rash, headaches, drowsiness, tiredness
Vigabatrin (Sabril)	Partial and generalized seizures	Drowsiness, fatigue, nervousness

Even today many assumptions are made about a person with epilepsy (Hoare, 1990), perhaps related to the unpredictability of onset of seizures and the range of ways in which epilepsy is experienced.

The incidence of epilepsy is argued to increase with the severity of learning disability (Chevrie, 1991). This increased prevalence could also be argued to be due to often being part of the many syndromes/conditions that are associated with learning disabilities in the first instance, such as: tuberous sclerosis; phenylketonuria and similar metabolic conditions; Lennox–Gestaut syndrome; rubella; cytomegalovirus; toxoplasmosis; West syndrome; and is often associated with cerebral palsy (Gram, 1990; Wallace, 1990).

What is Epilepsy?

Normal nerve cell function in the brain involves the discharge of small electrical waves in a stable manner. In epilepsy, bursts of uncontrolled large electrical waves occur. These can occur in one area (termed as localized activity) or may be more widespread throughout large areas of the brain. The latter often being related to idiopathic epilepsy.

What Causes can be Identified?

Whilst there are specific conditions linked with learning disability that are associated with epilepsy, it is important to remember that a person with a learning disability can also have epilepsy for the same reasons as any other person.

Almost any type of neurological problem could be seen as a possible cause of seizures and the development of epilepsy, including a major head injury in which there is resultant raised intercranial pressure or haemorrhage, or an intercranial space occupying lesion which can itself be linked with epilepsy. It may also occur after surgery to remove such lesions. Cerebral oedema and infections such as meningitis and encephalitis are also causes of seizures. There are many general conditions which can cause seizures and resultant epilepsy including, for example, hypoxia (lack of oxygen supplied to the brain). This is particularly so in terms of both acute and/or chronic hypoxia for the baby whilst in the uterus, during labour and also in the neonatal period. High fever, especially in young children, is cited in some text books as being a potential cause of epilepsy, but it should be remembered that many toddlers experience these episodes which are termed 'febrile convulsions' without going on to develop epilepsy. Other medical conditions which can cause seizures include conditions such as renal insufficiency (uraemia, in which there is a build up in the bloodstream of the body's waste products which are thus toxic), hypoglycaemia (low blood sugar), and chemical poisoning, for example due to lead, although this is less common nowadays due to the removal of lead piping from most homes. Toxaemia of pregnancy can also cause seizures.

How is Epilepsy Diagnosed?

It is important to rule out any underlying medical condition such as those listed above before a diagnosis of epilepsy can be considered. If a person with a learning disability and/or his or her carer(s) are concerned about their health, then the first contact should be the person's GP to seek medical advice. The GP will usually arrange for the referral to an appropriate specialist for further investigation of the presenting signs and symptoms.

Diagnosis will involve a detailed medical history. This is taken with regards the individual and family (the latter details are taken to try and identify whether there is a hereditary link). A comprehensive history of what happens to the person just before, during and just after a seizure is a key part of diagnosis especially in cases of idiopathic epilepsy. Information is usually taken from the person concerned and any eyewitnesses who may be able to give a more complete history of what has happened, particularly if the person is unable to recollect what has happened, which can often occur. It is often useful to have kept a diary of the episodes that have occurred to ensure a more accurate medical history can be collated. (This will also prove a useful baseline if epilepsy is diagnosed, to measure the effectiveness of any treatment commenced.)

A thorough medical examination should be carried out including:

- **detailed brain scan – known as a CAT scan (computerized axial tomography)**
- **an electroencephalogram (EEG) which uses a machine to measure the brain wave patterns.**

A range of blood tests is also carried out; full blood count (to rule out infection or chemical poisoning), blood glucose levels, and urea and electrolyte levels.

From the above tests other causes of the seizures can be identified or ruled out. The EEG in particular is very useful as it may highlight specific forms of epilepsy by the brain wave patterns recorded, although most diagnosis of epilepsy is based on the clinical information collated during the detailed medical history. Where a specific cause has been identified, medical treatment is organized to treat the specific cause. If epilepsy occurs as a result of a head injury, then the cause is treated as and when appropriate and the person may also commence treatment for epilepsy, which will be described in the following pages.

Types of Epilepsy

When epilepsy is diagnosed either as a condition on its own, or as part of an underlying medical problem, it manifests in many different ways. Seizures vary in type, frequency and duration depending on the part(s) of the brain affected by the outburst(s) of increased electrical activity. Movement, consciousness and behaviour can all be affected, in isolation or at the same time. Varying sensations in terms of

---

Box 3.2 Epilepsy: defining causes

- When a specific cause for the epilepsy is ascertained this is known as *symptomatic* or *secondary* epilepsy.
- However, for the majority of people with epilepsy no specific cause can be identified, thus their epilepsy is classed as *idiopathic* or *primary* epilepsy, even if there may be inherited predisposition for epilepsy identified in the family history.

auditory and/or visual experiences can also occur. An individual may experience many different forms of seizures throughout his or her life.

Partial Seizures

In epilepsy the frontal, temporal and parietal lobes in the cerebral cortex of the brain are the most often affected. These seizures can cause difficulties because people may not understand that the behaviours observed in the individual are due to the epilepsy.

Simple Partial Seizures

These tend to occur more frequently whilst asleep and are cited to be more common in childhood.

Complex partial seizures (psychomotor seizures)

These are considered to mainly evolve from the temporal lobe region of the brain and are perhaps more difficult to recognize and control. They are usually identified as periods of altered behaviour where the person does not respond to his or her immediate environment. The person may appear confused and he or she may have experienced unusual sensations immediately beforehand (known as *auras*) and may be seen doing what appear to be repetitive and aimless behaviours, for example, lip smacking or inappropriately laughing. These are known as *automatisms*. The person does not usually lose consciousness during this type of seizure.

Reader Activity 3.5
Imagine you have a friend who has a learning disability and complex partial seizures. Often without warning she will laugh very loudly and flap her hands for no apparent reason. Think about the social implications, for example embarrassment for her when she is in a large busy shop and the seizure occurs. Do you think the general public knows enough about epilepsy to understand that you do not have to 'convulse' to have epilepsy?

Seizures Affecting Both Hemispheres of the Brain

Absence Seizures

The person appears to suddenly stop what they are doing and is very briefly unconscious, which is accompanied by a minor (if any) loss of muscle tone. They will usually then carry on with the activity they were doing, unaware of the experience. The problem with this type of seizure is that it is often not noticed by others due to the very short time factor, although one may notice that the individual has perhaps dropped an object he or she was holding. It can occur many times throughout the day, thus interfering with everyday activities due to the effect, for example, on attention span. This can cause problems in itself such as ability to complete tasks, learning, and can affect everyday living activities and indeed may make certain activities such as cooking a potentially hazardous scenario. Absence seizures can be precipitated by many factors such as stress, low blood sugar, and extreme tiredness. Often this type of seizure ceases in adolescence, although some people may then develop tonic–clonic seizures.

Atonic Seizures

This type of seizure is more commonly known as 'drop attacks' due to its nature. It involves a very brief loss of muscle tone, and can result in the person falling to the floor without any warning. This could present problems in terms of the risk of injury to the individual although atonic seizures are considered to be more common on waking.

Myoclonic Seizures

With this type of seizure the person experiences brief unexpected contracture(s) of muscle/muscle group, but does not lose consciousness.

Tonic–clonic seizures

This is the best-known form of epilepsy and can cause much apprehension for onlookers if they are not familiar with this type. The seizure usually manifests itself in two stages: the tonic then the clonic stage. For some people, this is often preceded by an aura. This can manifest itself in many ways such as: unexplained irritability; headaches; ringing sound in ears; strange taste in one's mouth (e.g. a creosote-type taste); 'butterfly' sensations in the stomach; or visual sensations such as flashing or very bright lights. Auras can serve a very useful purpose even though they may be unpleasant in that they help to warn the person of the impending seizure. However, many people with this type of epilepsy also experience the tonic–clonic seizure without any warning in the form of an aura.

In the *tonic stage* of the seizure, the individual's eyes will 'roll'; this occurs just prior to losing consciousness. The person's arms often then will flex, and the head, neck and legs will go into a state of extension. This stage usually tends to last around 20 seconds, but it is difficult often to be exact about the time unless the whole seizure is observed.

The next stage of the seizure is termed the *clonic stage*. This usually involves the rhythmic relaxation and contraction of limbs and neck muscles and can last from 30 seconds up to a few minutes, depending on the individual. The person may develop urinary incontinence although faecal incontinence is not a common occurrence. Some people bite their tongue during the seizure.

This is followed by what is termed the *post ictal phase*. This is a time when the individual has stopped convulsing and appears difficult to rouse but does wake up gradually, although is still very drowsy. The person may then fall asleep. This period can last for up to a couple of hours, sometimes longer; every individual who has this type of epilepsy will have a different recovery time. Some individuals, understandably, have a headache and/or aching muscles after the seizure. Most people who have this type of epilepsy will not remember having the seizure. It is very important to know how long the individual usually experiences the tonic and clonic stage of the seizure, and how long he or she usually takes to recover as there may be occasions when the recovery is much slower than usual, the seizure is prolonged, or indeed the seizure is followed by another seizure (or more).

This latter situation is known as *status epilepticus*. In these situations prompt medical advice will need to be sought. Some people with epilepsy are prescribed a medicine that is given rectally by another adult/carer who has to be taught by a health professional to do this. The medicine is called diazepam (Stesolid), which comes in a special tube to be used only for giving via the rectum. If carers have been shown how to give this medicine, it should be promptly administered. One may find that the giving of this medicine actually stops the seizures; however, it is still prudent to seek medical advice in case the seizures recommence again that day. The person's GP and/or consultant should always be informed of the times when rectal diazepam has had to be used as it may be an indicator that current drug therapy requires reviewing or that the person is generally unwell. Other causes of this situation includes non-compliance with treatment, so it is important that all medicines for epilepsy are regularly taken as prescribed.

What Should you do if Someone is Having an Epileptic Seizure?

Don't panic!

- **Try to lie the person in the recovery position, ensuring that his or her airway is clear.**
- **Never put anything into the person's mouth during the seizure.**
- **Move objects in the immediate vicinity out of the way to prevent the person injuring themself.**
- **Never leave the person unattended.**
- **Gently rest person's head on, for example, a pillow or jumper to protect his or her head from the floor.**
- **Loosen tight clothing.**
- **Try and observe the length of time the person is in the tonic–clonic stage of seizure (if appropriate).**

- When person is in post ictal phase, ensure he or she has an opportunity to rest and recover.
- If at all concerned about the person's health, medical advice should be sought.

Reader Activity 3.6
You are a parent of a young person (teenager) with a mild learning disability who has epilepsy. He frequently has generalized seizures. He wants to go out riding his bicycle on his own with his friends. Would you let him go? Would you be worried and if so, why?

Treatment of Epilepsy

Drugs, known as anticonvulsants, are the treatment of choice for epilepsy, although special dietary regimes are also used for some people in addition or instead of drug therapy.

Why are Drugs Used?

Anticonvulsant medicines help reduce the responsiveness of the neurons in the brain to the sudden large bursts of nerve impulses that occur in epilepsy. Complete control is almost impossible. The aim is to achieve a level of control of the epilepsy as to ensure minimal interference by the condition on the person's everyday life.

Compliance with the therapy is essential. It is important for carers as well as the individual who has a learning disability to receive appropriate information and advice on all aspects of epilepsy, including potential side-effects of the drugs. The most commonly used drugs are described in Box 3.1.

Taking the Anticonvulsant Medication

The individual with epilepsy must never stop taking the medicines unless advised to do so by a doctor, therefore it is important that he or she should always seek to ensure they have sufficient supplies of the prescription (or that if the person is unable to ensure this himself or herself then a named person

should be responsible for this if the person is, for example living in adult assisted housing). It is important that he or she has a well-balanced diet, including foods rich in vitamin D and folic acid. If the individual and/or the carer feels that there is perhaps some untoward reactions to the medication, medical advice should be sought. If the person with a learning disability is in one of the various forms of independent living schemes, it may be difficult to ensure drug compliance, thus use of various memory aids may be helpful. Daily tablet dispensers may be utilized, for example, with supervision by family/carers. If the person has severe learning disabilities and receives varying levels of 24-hour care, the family/carer(s) should be aware that the medicines do come usually in a liquid form and/or crushable tablets which could be used if the person has difficulty swallowing tablets or capsules. Advice should be sought from an appropriate health professional such as the GP if the person is experiencing difficulty taking the prescribed medicines, as this may mean that he or she is not receiving the correct dose of the anticonvulsant medication prescribed.

Life Style Issues for People with Epilepsy

Photosensitivity

The British Epilepsy Association, in its excellent leaflet entitled *Photosensitive Epilepsy*, cites that 3–5% of people with epilepsy are sensitive to flickering light mainly from artificial light sources such as television and computer games. The association advises that if someone has epilepsy, he or she should sit in a well-lit room at least 2.5 m from the screen and avoid frequently switching channels. Polarized sunglasses are recommended when outdoors on sunny days to minimize the effect of, for example, sunlight reflecting off objects. The association also recommends that if the person experiences photosensitivity, discos, etc. where flashing lights are used, should be avoided. If the person inadvertently finds himself or herself in a place where there are unexpected flashing lights, they should cover one eye using their hand.

Swimming

The issue of 'risk-taking' worries many families and carers. However, as long as the person with a learning disability who has epilepsy does not swim alone and uses a pool that has a life-guard, then there is no reason not to go swimming. Practising basic life saving is a good idea for everyone, not just carers of people with a learning disability who have epilepsy. Information regarding this can be obtained from any local swimming pool. The British Epilepsy Association produces a leaflet regarding swimming and epilepsy.

There has been much concern voiced around the safety regarding bathing and epilepsy. It can be embarrassing for the individual if the family/carer insist on supervising bathing, but it is an important issue. For the person with severe epilepsy it may be prudent to suggest that the bathroom door is closed but not locked during bathing or that showers may be a better option.

Alcohol

Many, if not all, of the anticonvulsant drugs can cause dizziness and drowsiness. Alcohol therefore potentiates the effects of the drugs and thus enhances the possible side-effects. Alcohol can make the drugs less effective. So although the occasional drink is considered not to be harmful, the British Epilepsy Association advises that 'binges' are to be avoided, and that the medication should not be omitted. Also consuming large amounts of alcohol can be detrimental if the individual is taking an anticonvulsant known as carbamazepine (Tegretol). This drug is cited to potentially cause fluid retention and consequent water intoxication and thus may increase seizures if large quantities of alcohol are consumed.

For families/carers of people with learning disabilities who have epilepsy it is important that time is invested in empowering the individual, to the best of their abilities, with a practical understanding of epilepsy. Use of age-appropriate educational material, such as those produced by the British Epilepsy

Association, is very useful. It is worth contacting the health professional(s) usually involved in the person's epilepsy management, for example the GP, hospital staff or community nurse for further information and help.

3.4 Oral Health Care

This is an area of health care that is not given enough attention. It has been argued that it is an area of low priority amongst all the other problems involved in caring for people with profound learning and physical disabilities (Griffiths and Boyle, 1993). However, tooth decay does not have to be inevitable.

General reasons why dental services may not be sought include:

- **Mobility.** It may be difficult for the person to access the dental surgery physically, although most National Health Service (NHS) dentists will do home visits.
- **Economic.** The individual/family may worry about the cost of the treatments although if the individual is in receipt of benefits then much (if not all) of the costs will be borne via the State.
- **'Challenging behaviour'.** If the individual with learning disabilities also exhibits 'challenging behaviours' then it may be very difficult to obtain consultation with a dentist or the consultation may become extremely difficult to carry out. Specialist dental services may need to be sought as well as help from the community nurse (learning disabilities) in behaviour management techniques.

Problems Experienced

Dribbling

This can create many problems for the person with a learning disability. Causation may include poor swallowing reflex and/or poor head control. Weakness of facial and/or jaw muscles can also cause dribbling. The effect on the individual's appearance and his or her perception of self image must be acknowledged. This is perhaps especially poignant for a young adult with a learning disability who is already dealing with many issues around adulthood as well as coping with his disability (or more to the point coping with the attitudes of others towards his disability).

It may cause the individual to have difficulties in terms of personal relationships, for example kissing and clothes being wet due to the dribbling. For an adult with this problem, where medication is not felt to be appropriate or suitable, clothing may need to be protected.

Reader Activity 3.7
If you were an adult with learning disabilities and had this problem, how would you like carers to act? Do you think it could affect your personal relationships, for example, being held whilst your clothes are wet from the dribbling? What about kissing, how would you feel?

The use of bibs should be avoided as they are not age appropriate for adults. Clothing can be protected by age-appropriate interchangeable fashionable scarves for women or even perhaps cravats for men. *It should not be brushed aside as an insignificant problem.* The constant dribbling can have physical effects, for example, a sore chin. The use of appropriate, unperfumed, barrier creams may be useful to prevent such skin problems. Medication is sometimes used to help reduce salivation such as hyoscine (Scopolamine), a drug usually used for motion (travel) sickness. When used to reduce excess salivation, this drug is used in the form of an impregnated skin patch worn behind the person's ear. The amount of drug given can be gradually titred until the benefits are felt by the amount of the patch worn. The patch is changed every 72 hours. This drug has to be carefully monitored by a medical practitioner and precautions taken when handling the patches. For further advice, including informa-

tion with regards any specific side-effects when using the hyoscine patches, the person's GP or medical consultant should be contacted.

For People with Down's Syndrome

People with Down's syndrome are considered to have an increased susceptibility to peridontal disease due to possibly having abnormal teeth and jaw development. Mouth breathing, a common problem for people with Down's syndrome can cause gum dryness and halitosis (bad breath). Varying degrees of '... immunodeficiency may be a major contributory factor ...' to oral health problems (Griffiths and Boyle, 1993, p. 156). Cardiac problems are also considered to be highly prevalent in people who have Down's syndrome. Up to a third of children with Down's syndrome are reported to have congenital heart defects of varying severity (Malone, 1988; Burns and Gunn, 1993), although it has been argued that there is even up to a 50% chance of such problems occurring (Lane and Stratford, 1985). Thus the individual must have antibiotic cover before and after any dental treatment, including teeth scaling. This is because the bacteria that are normally present in the mouth may enter the individual's bloodstream and cause endocarditis (inflammation of the lining of the heart).

Also, some individuals with Down's syndrome may have what is termed 'atlanto axial' (cervical) instability, thus their necks must not be extended too far as there is a risk (however rare) of dislocation. It is important that the dentist is informed if there is any risk of this type of orthopaedic problem.

For People with Learning Disabilities and also Epilepsy

It should be remembered that some medications such as certain anticonvulsants can affect dental health, especially phenytoin (Epanutin), which can cause a condition known as gingival hyperplasia. In this condition the gums become very sensitive and tender, and eventually significantly enlarge, which results in bleeding. Specific dental care regimes to help reduce the incidence of gum problems including regular teeth cleaning, flossing and frequent dental check-ups are advised. It is always prudent to ensure that the dentist is informed of any medication an individual is taking. Dental problems can occur due to trauma, considered to be a potential risk during tonic–clonic seizures, often due to inappropriate first aid by onlookers, for example, placing an object in the person's mouth during the seizure thinking it will help maintain the person's airway.

For People with Learning Disabilities who also have Cerebral Palsy

There are several issues regarding dental health for people who have cerebral palsy and learning difficulties. Bruxism (persistent teeth grinding) can cause teeth irregularities; however, it should be remembered that not all bruxism is habitual – it may be an indication of dental pain and should always be investigated to rule out any underlying dental problems.

A problem known as malocclusion, due to irregular teeth, can cause a problem especially as it makes teeth cleaning more difficult. Food and therefore plaque can build up due to this, which can then cause enamel erosion to occur. Another area of concern is when oral hygiene is made difficult due to poor swallowing and 'gag' reflexes as well as general difficulty in chewing foods as there is potential for enamel erosion to occur, especially when small amounts of food end up being left in the mouth as a result of the above problems.

Some Ideas to Aid Good Oral Hygiene

- Make oral hygiene skills part of overall self help skills development.
- Ensure that the person sees the dentist at least every 6 months, or more frequently if need be. Dental hygienists are usually employed within the dental surgery and can give useful advice regarding general dental hygiene techniques, for example plaque disclosure tablets. Use of

the tablets may enable the individual with a learning disability who is able to self care, to have a better understanding of how much to brush his or her teeth.
- Modified toothbrushes may be necessary and the dentist in conjunction with the individual's occupational therapist will advise.
- Teeth cleaning has to be a relaxed and unhurried event, especially for the person who also has cerebral palsy who may have an exaggerated bite reflex. Use of desensitization is important, gently stroking the person's mouth and lips and gradual introduction of the toothbrush into the person's mouth is essential.
- Avoidance of medication that has a high sugar content, especially if the person is on a long-term drug regime. The individual's GP can advise with regards this; however, medication should never be stopped without such advice from the GP or the person's medical consultant.
- Remember the need for antibiotic cover if the person has a heart condition. This also applies for individuals who have shunts *in situ* for hydrocephalus.
- A well-balanced diet is important. Plenty of fluids will be helpful, especially if the individual mouth breathes as well. It can be helpful to use/offer lipsalve to be regularly applied to lips to minimize potential lip cracking which can be painful.

3.5 Vision

The ability to see is important to everyone.

Sight is the most accurate and far reaching of our senses . . . No other sense can tell us anything like so much about the world around us. (Klemz, 1991, p. 9)

This could be argued to be particularly so in terms of sensory stimulation as well as a method of non-verbal communication. This is especially true for the individual who has severe learning and physical disabilities, whose eyes may be the main source of communication, and who may use eye pointing for expression. Thus one of the aims/priorities in caring for such individuals must include the preservation and promotion of good ophthalmic health wherever possible, including prompt treatment of any related medical problems. This will include regular appointments with an optician and/or ophthalmologist where appropriate.

There are too many eye conditions to consider in this short chapter, thus it is stressed that if the individual and/or the carer has concern with regards to the individual's eye health, advice should be promptly sought, initially via the person's GP.

Common Conditions

Three common eye conditions are myopia (short sightedness), hypermetropia (long sightedness) and presbyopia (far sightedness). All are treatable, to varying degrees, via the wearing of spectacles with the appropriate lens prescription(s) prescribed by an optician. Regular eye tests are recommended with an optician – the frequency is according to the needs of the individual. Obviously if there are other eye problems present, the degree of corrected vision will be affected.

In *myopia* the person has difficulty focusing on distant objects, although the person can often see close up objects without any difficulties. In this condition the light rays from the object in the distance focuses in front of the retina, hence the retina only receives a blurred image of the object in question. Spectacles using concave lenses are prescribed.

In *hypermetropia*, the person is unable to focus on nearby objects as the light from objects in the distance focuses well behind the retina. Focusing on near objects can also be problematic if untreated. Spectacles using convex lenses are prescribed.

In *presbyopia*, the lenses of the eyes 'lose' their elasticity and thus the eyes cannot alter in shape as

well as they could. This results in the person holding items further away than he would usually, for example in order to read. Spectacles are prescribed based on the needs of the individual (Scarr, 1991).

Two conditions that are not as common as the above but would appear to have a higher incidence in people with learning disabilities include:

(1) *Hemianopia*. This is a condition in which the optical tracts that carry the visual fibres to the visual cortex in the brain are damaged. The visual cortex is where visual images formed on the retina are interpreted. There is no specific treatment available, and care is aimed at encouraging the individual to remember and visualize all aspects of self and the environment. For example, for the person with severe learning and physical disabilities this would include placing objects at the person's 'affected' side so that they have to reach over, thus acknowledging the visual field which would not have been considered had they not reached over.

(2) *Coloboma*. In this condition the person's eyes will appear pear shaped. There is not usually much affect on vision. However, if the optic disc is involved, then vision will be poor. Coloboma can occur as part of a syndrome, for example *Charge Association* – a rare syndrome which is also linked with learning disabilities in which there are a range of congenital physical problems such as heart and renal defects as well as orthopaedic problems such as talipes. Choanal atresia is also present at birth and requires surgical repair of this defect involving the nasopharyngeal septum.

Other Visual Health Problems

Cataracts

Cataracts may be defined as 'a clouding of the crystalline lens, resulting in opacity' (Watson and Royle, 1987: p. 1072). Cataracts can be present from birth, for example due to an inborn error of metabolism or due to maternal infection such as rubella. Up to 50% of people with Down's syndrome are reported to have cataracts (Lane and Stratford, 1985). Cataracts, however, often do not become apparent until adolescence and the most common type of cataracts in people often are not noticeable until over the age of 50 years. Treatment involves the wearing of spectacles to help in counteracting the loss of distant vision, but the cataracts will increase and surgery is the main option for most people.

Diabetes Mellitus

Eye care of the individual with learning disabilities who has diabetes mellitus, whether insulin dependent or not, is very important. This is due to the increased risk of retinal haemorrhages. Thus frequent reassessment of the person's eyes are essential; this is usually under consultant medical supervision. Prompt treatment of any eye problems must be ensured.

Eye Conditions Associated with People with Down's Syndrome

Many people with Down's syndrome encounter the problem of *abnormal tear production*. Usually tears ensure that the eyes are bathed and that any debris that is on the eye such as grit or dust is washed away. For people with Down's syndrome, tear production is characteristically abnormal, containing a lot of protein, which is usually only seen in infants up to a few weeks old. This results in the eyelash follicles becoming irritated causing the eyelids to become red and inflamed. This results in chronic eye infections involving the hair follicles. This chronic infection is known as *blepharitis*. Therefore eye care is very important. If infection is suspected, medical advice should be sought as antibiotics to be applied to the eye area may be required, such as chloramphenicol.

If an infection is present strict hygiene methods must be used to prevent the spread of the infection to the person's other eye or indeed to the carer's eyes. Advice on the most appropriate method, known as an aseptic technique, and advice regarding

hand hygiene can be obtained via the GP or practice nurse.

Medication and Eye Care

A range of medicines can cause blurred vision as a side effect. It can be very distressing and also a concern in terms of the individual's physical safety. Medical advice should be sought whenever this symptom is experienced, especially if it persists.

Deficiencies in certain vitamins and minerals can cause problems with eye health as detailed in Box 3.3.

The Impact of Visual Impairment

Visual problems need to be recognized as a common problem within learning disability. Indeed it is argued that over 70% of children with cerebral palsy have varying degrees of visual impairment (Black, 1980). It must be acknowledged that, whatever the degree of visual impairment a person

---

Box 3.3 Deficiencies in minerals and vitamins leading to poor eye health

- **Vitamin A** – a lack of which can cause eye dryness. In extreme vitamin A deficiency there is decreased production of the retinal pigment known as rhodopsin, which can cause night blindness.
- **Vitamin B** – if there is an extreme lack of this vitamin the person may develop changes in the retina. It is important to note that most people will take in adequate amounts of vitamins and minerals in their diet and supplements are not usually necessary. Indeed *vitamin A* supplements should only be taken under medical supervision in women of child-bearing age due to the risk of foetal problems it can cause. If the carer is concerned that the individual with a learning disability is not receiving a balanced diet, advice can be obtained from the GP.

experiences, it will have an impact on many aspects of his or her life. For the person with severe learning and visual impairment the carer (where appropriate) should recognize that the person will not have the same visual clues regarding the environment and about people around them. Intensive support is required to help them continue to experience new skills and situations. The person as a child may have found gross motor skills, for example, quite difficult due to the lack of visual clues; toys will not have been visible to attempt to reach out for. This situation can persist into adulthood if carers/families are not aware of the need to use other senses such as hearing and smell to promote development. It is important to remember that severe visual impairment does not usually mean that there is no sight, many people can see very bright lights and can distinguish between light and darkness. These are individual assets to be built upon. The avoidance of self-stimulatory behaviour that is inappropriate must also be acknowledged. Behaviours that may be considered in this way may include 'rocking, light gazing, exaggerated finger play' (Moller, 1993). Thus activities should be age appropriate and designed to offer enjoyment and pleasure. It is difficult to stop the person enacting repetitive self-stimulatory behaviour, therefore advice should be sought from the person's community (learning disabilities) nurse and the local visual impairment service, in order to seek ways in which such behaviour can be minimized. Help and advice is also available through the Royal National Institute for the Blind (RNIB) for general and specific information, including information on aids and adaptations. Help is also available regarding aids and adaptations, such as low-vision aids and audio aids, book scanners for example, from occupational therapists.

3.6 Hearing

In an overall four centre longitudinal study for the National Study of Hearing, it was highlighted that approximately 16.1% of the adult population in the UK had some degree of hearing impairment (Davis, 1989). It has been suggested that 1 in 10 people with a learning disability also have varying degrees of hearing impairment (Ball, 1991).

Causes of Hearing Impairment/Loss

Hearing impairment is usually termed conductive or sensorineural hearing loss.

Conductive Hearing Impairment

Conductive hearing problems occur when the mechanical transmission of auditory stimuli, and usually the external and/or middle ear, is affected. Ball (1993) described conductive hearing loss as 'anything that impedes the transmission of sound entering the ear while on its journey to the nerve endings in the cochlea'. One of the most common causes for this is a condition known as 'glue ear' (serous otitis media), where fluid (normally present in the ear) accumulates in large amounts in the middle ear section behind the ear drum. Other causes of conductive hearing impairment include ear wax, or cerumen, in the external ear canal, and thickening of the tympanic membrane due to infection or trauma, for example a severe skull fracture.

What Causes 'Glue Ear'?

Watson and Royle (1987), stated that it is caused, for example, by ear infections which are not responsive to the usual medical treatment such as antibiotics, recurrent ear infections and enlarged adenoids. Indeed, Lane and Stratford (1985), have suggested that people with Down's syndrome are particularly prone to developing this condition due to their susceptibility to recurrent upper respiratory tract infections. It is important to note also that, despite the introduction of antibiotic therapies for ear infections or otitis media, it is argued that there has not been a reduction of chronic ear infections and the resultant impairment of hearing (Nadol, 1993).

Treatment of 'Glue Ear'

This is achieved by the prompt identification and treatment of the main source of the problem. If an ear infection is diagnosed appropriate antibiotics are commenced. Analgesia is also required, as ear ache or otalgia, one of the main symptoms of an ear infection, can be very painful and distressing for the individual. It should be remembered that an acute ear infection can cause a temporary loss of hearing in itself. Enlarged adenoids can be another reason why 'glue ear' occurs and an adenoidectomy may be required. Treatment of 'glue ear' itself involves drainage of the excess fluid in the ear performed under general anaesthesia. Grommets are inserted in the middle ear to allow drainage of the excessive fluid. This operation is known as a myringotomy.

Sensorineural (Perceptive) Hearing Loss

Usually auditory information is transformed from a mechanical signal from the external and middle ear to a neurally conducted electrical impulse by hair cells and neurons in the inner ear. There are then transmitted via the eighth cranial nerve to the part of the brain which is responsible for hearing known as the temporal lobe. Sensorineural hearing impairment thus occurs as a result of damage to the hair cells in the inner ear. Aminoglycoside antibiotics such as gentamycin, neomycin and streptomycin can damage hair cells. Aspirin and other salicylates can also cause damage to the hair cells. Maternal infection such as rubella, cytomegalovirus and herpes zoster can cause damage to the foetus' hearing whilst in the womb. However, it is argued that the classic links with common illnesses, such as mumps and measles in childhood, and hearing impairment has not yet been sufficiently proven (Morrison, 1993). It is essential to acknowledge that meningitis is still recognized as a significant causative factor in the development of hearing impairment, another reason why prompt identification and treatment of meningitis is so important.

Possibly the main cause of hearing impairment is argued to have a genetic link (Nadol, 1993),

although Hotchkiss (1989) argued that genetic disorders only account for 13% of profound hearing impairment in childhood with 50% of profound hearing impairment having an unknown cause. Hotchkiss (1989), acknowledged that of this 50% many incidences of such severe hearing loss could perhaps be attributed to some genetic predisposition. Prematurity, neonatal jaundice and cerebral palsy, particularly athetoid cerebral palsy, are all linked with varying degrees of potential hearing impairment. Hearing impairment is also strongly linked with syndromes such as charge association, a rare syndrome described earlier in the chapter.

Individuals with severe hearing impairment utilize sign language and/or oral speech. For the person with a severe learning disability who has a hearing loss, a simplified form of the British Sign Language is available, known as Makaton, as described earlier in the chapter. However, the use of signing, even Makaton, may be difficult for people with additional physical disabilities, thus they may

---

Box 3.4 How to help people with hearing loss

- Don't shout!
- Face the person when talking to them.
- Don't exaggerate your lip movements or speak slower.
- Be aware of the impact of background noise.
- Don't all talk at once if in a crowd.
- Don't assume that the person can't hear at all, sounds are often interpreted albeit sometimes in a distorted manner, but that distorted manner of sounds will give the same clues. A telephone ringing may sound completely different but the person will still know that the telephone is ringing.
- Everyone is an individual, don't assume all levels of deafness are the same.
- Don't assume being deaf means that the person can't make their own decisions, even if they have a learning disability.
- Ensure the person has access to resources that will enhance everyday living.

use a 'touch talker', an electronic communication device that is individually tailored in terms of its functions. A simple single buzzer activated by a platform switch can be very useful for the individual with severe learning and physical disabilities, allowing the person to at least attract attention or press the buzzer when the carer asks the right question; for example, using the buzzer to say yes when asked if hungry. Symbol systems as well as sign systems are available, though both of these systems are culturally dependent.

Examples of symbol systems include the Paget Gorman Sign System, which is based on 21 hand postures and also includes iconic symbols, and Blissymbolics, which is based on approximately 400 symbols which can be combined to create additional vocabulary. If the person has difficulty with visual perception and/or understanding of symbols such as arrows, Blissymbolics may be difficult to use. The Rebus System uses symbols including letters of the alphabet as well as icons. Symbol systems can be very effective as they allow the individual to make a fuller use of the English language, including grammar. However, they can be difficult for individuals with severe learning disabilities to use. Also the symbols may prove difficult to use socially as only a limited amount of people actually know what any of the symbols mean.

Reader Activity 3.8
You are in charge of a group home for young adults with visual, hearing and learning disabilities. John, one of the young adults has started head banging and rocking a lot, which is stopping him participating in everyday leisure activities. What do you think is causing his behaviour? How are you going to help? Who would you turn to for advice?

3.7 Continence

This is an aspect of our lives that many people take for granted, yet loss or lack of continence is a real issue that can cause distress and embarrassment. It is a problem for many people with learning disabilities. However, it should not be assumed that incontinence is part of having a learning disability and other causes should be explored and ruled out first. The majority of children achieve continence by the age of 5 years; for the child with learning disabilities this may be difficult to achieve as the child may, for example, not have the ability to communicate verbally or indicate non-verbally. The child may have severe physical disabilities and/or be unaware of passing urine/defecating due to having a neurological condition where there is no sensation when going to the toilet, such as spina bifida.

It is important to offer the child the opportunities to develop continence, including toileting the child regularly and praising the child whenever the child successfully uses the toilet. It may take a long time to achieve, but it is achievable for many children who have a learning disability. The skills of the community nurse can be invaluable in toilet-training. Various approaches can be utilized, offering positive reinforcement, rewarding the child when successful, as cited above, in ways in which the child feels good about himself or herself. Consistency of approach is a key element. However, even with intensive toilet training regimes where appropriate, some children still will not achieve continence. It is important to identify whether this is due to an underlying medical condition. For adults with learning disabilities who have continued to be incontinent into adulthood, the possibility of underlying conditions can still exist. Urinary incontinence can be caused by urinary infections (especially if the person frequently has such infections) and hypersensitivity of the bladder can also be a common cause. A weak external urethral sphincter and/or structural problems within the kidney, bladder or urethra can also cause urinary incontinence. Faecal incontinence can be caused by many problems such as bowel diseases and haemorrhoids. Various investigations may be used to rule out such potential problems. These include for urinary incontinence renal function tests and/or urodynamic tests to observe the flow of urine and bladder function.

For people with learning disabilities for whom there is no specific cause for the incontinence and toilet training is not appropriate/achievable, continence aids will then be required. These are provided via the local health trusts through the continence advisory service. For further details contact the person's GP, health visitor or community nurse. There is a large range of aids available and these are usually available to children from the age of 3 years.

Promoting Continence – The Key Issues

The individual with a learning disability has the right to access the skills and expertise of a continence advisor who will be able to advise and supply appropriate continence aids. It is important that carers ensure that there are sufficient supplies of the continence aids for the individual as the aids such as pads must be changed frequently to prevent soreness and discomfort. There may be times when the person will require the use of more continence aids than usual, for example during illness, especially gastrointestinal problems, thus an adequate supply of the relevant continence aids is essential. Personal hygiene is essential for everyone, especially for the person who is incontinent. Regular toileting is very important as is the need to ensure that the person's dignity and privacy is maintained at all times during such intimate care. It is important to ensure that the person either washes their bottom or has this done for them at each continence pad or nappy change in order to prevent skin breakdown. Barrier creams may be useful to protect the individual's skin.

There are many myths around how to reduce incontinence, one of which is the limitation of fluids. However, the opposite is in fact true and it is important that the individual has a good fluid intake, especially if he or she is prone to urinary tract infections. If the person is on specialist feeds, for example specialist enteral feeds, it is important to seek the advice of the dietician regarding whether additional fluids may be required to be offered, especially during illness and/or hot weather. If carers are not sure how much fluid to give the individual, it is important to seek the advice of an appropriate health professional such as the individual's GP as there may be times when fluid intake is carefully monitored, for example in chronic renal failure. A well-balanced diet, high in fibre, is important especially in achieving faecal continence and the avoidance of constipation. People with severe learning and physical disabilities do seem to have a tendency towards constipation mainly due perhaps to an inadequate diet, not having enough fluids and immobility. Constipation can be very distressing for the individual and carers need to be aware of the importance of discreetly monitoring the person's bowel movement pattern, when the individual is reliant on a high level of carer support. It may mean that, if the person does not have a bowel movement for approximately 3 days or more (depending on the individual's usual bowel habits), the advice of the GP is sought. Aperients such as a stool-softener medicine or bulk-forming laxatives may need to be prescribed. As a final option, suppositories or even a Microlax enema may have to be used to alleviate the discomfort and feeling of being unwell that constipation can cause for the individual.

Urine infections can become a chronic problem and cause the individual to frequently be unwell. Medical advice should be sought if it is suspected that the individual has a urine infection, especially if he or she has a history of such infections. Maintenance antibiotic therapies are often used when the person has frequent urine infections and regular urinalysis is performed to assess the effectiveness of such treatments. The use of cranberry juice as a regular drink is considered useful for people who have frequent urine infections as it is considered to help reduce the bacteria in the urine which cause the urinary infection.

The impact of dependency with regards continence and self-care for the person with severe learning and physical disabilities should not be underestimated.

Reader Activity 3.9
Consider how it feels to wear continence aids yourself:

the noise that waterproof pants make, the increased sweating from wearing plastic coated pants which causes itching and discomfort in summer and cold and uncomfortable sensation in winter. (Ryan Woolley, 1987)

How would you like to be cared for if you were incontinent?

3.8 Nutritional and Feeding Issues

There have been many campaigns both nationally and on a local level aimed at encouraging 'healthy eating', including central government directives via organizations such as the National Advisory Committee on Nutritional Education (NACNE) and the Department of Health: Committee on Medical Aspects of Food (COMA). Both provide guidelines such as the *Report of the Working Group on Weaning Diet* (DOH, 1994a) and the *Report on Nutritional Aspects of Cardiovascular Disease* (DOH, 1994b). For many people with learning disabilities choice about what they eat is usually made by the family/carers. It is important to seek ways in which individuals can be enabled, to the best of their abilities, to make decisions regarding the food and drink they consume. However, health education material that families/carers may wish to use on the whole are inadequate in that they focus on children or articulate adults. It is difficult to obtain resources that are clear and easy to use that are age appropriate although this is beginning to be addressed by local health educationalists and by organizations such as 'People First'. There are several other issues which need to be considered briefly in terms of nutritional issues.

Individuals with Difficulties Eating/Swallowing who Require Maximum Assistance

It is important that carers carefully consider how much a person with a severe learning disability actually is able to eat. He or she may only be able to manage small amounts more frequently rather than 'three set meals a day'. If the carer is concerned that the individual is not receiving an adequately balanced diet, the person's GP should be contacted so that a referral can be made for a dietician to review the individual's dietary and fluid needs. Meal supplements such as Ensure or Fortisip may be suggested. However, any specialist feeds used must be under the direction of the dietician as products are prescribed based on individual need. Certainly in the case of children, especially for infants under the age of 1 year, food supplements should never be offered without medical and dietetic advice and ongoing supervision. Indeed, if parents are finding that their child is having feeding difficulties, even in infancy, it is important that medical advice is sought as persistent feeding problems can be an indicator of disability (Davies, 1986).

Meal times for the individual with cerebral palsy can be difficult. Head extension and also 'tongue thrusting' can make eating and drinking difficult. It is important that meal times are relaxed and therefore pleasurable for both the carer and the individual who is being fed or having help to feed himself or herself. Seating position is very important; the person needs to be sitting upright with good head support where necessary, especially if they experience exaggerated extensor movements. Avoidance of the person's head arching back when he or she is being fed will help reduce the risk of aspiration. Seating systems are provided via the person's occupational therapist. There are many different types available and the seating system must be tailored to the needs of the individual. Desensitization techniques may be needed to enable the individual with facial and oral hypersensitivity to be able to eat. This involves positively stroking the individual's face whilst quietly and gently talking to them. It is important that carers inform the individual of what they are doing, as sudden movements can make the situation worse by causing the person's mouth to 'clamp down', due to exaggerated bite reflex, on the fork or spoon for example.

It is important that all foods offered to the individual who has feeding difficulties is of the right consistency and temperature; this may involve food being chopped finely or even pureed. If foods require to be pureed, each food type should be individually pureed so that the individual will be able to taste the different flavours, rather than be served the full meal in one whole pureed portion. There are plates available that enable food to be kept hot if the person requires to be fed very slowly. Equipment such as 'stay warm' dishes, non-slip dycem mats, specialist cups such as 'doidy' or sloping cups or cups with two handles and a spout, specially shaped cutlery and plates with sloping sides such as manoy dishes and plate guards to enable the person with a severe learning disability to feed themselves wherever possible is available via the occupational therapist. There is a wide range of such equipment; all are usually available in a range of styles to ensure that they are age and ability appropriate.

Care of the Individual who has Swallowing Difficulties

It is particularly important to seek advice from the speech therapist and medical practitioner when the individual has swallowing and/or chewing difficulties due to the potential risk of aspiration, which is when food and/or drink is inhaled. This can be very serious as it can cause aspiration pneumonia. If a carer feels that the individual has aspirated, medical advice should be sought. Certainly if the individual frequently 'chokes' on being fed, medical advice is required.

Indeed, some individuals have such difficulties with oral feeding that they require alternate feeding methods to be used. A nasogastric tube (a thin tube passed through the nose and going into the stomach) may be utilized on a short-term basis with a gastrostomy (a tube, which is usually inserted via a procedure known as endoscopy, that actually goes straight from the stomach to the outside of the abdomen) being the most appropriate long-term feeding method for people unable to tolerate oral feeds or unable to manage adequate levels of food and drink orally. If the person is fed in this way it should always be under the supervision of a medical practitioner and the dietician. Guidelines and ongoing support in using nasogastric and gastrostomy feeding are usually provided via a specialist nurse and/or through trained nursing staff within the local hospital or respite care unit. Some people can continue to have food orally with the specialist method of tube feeding used to 'top up' their daily needs; however, some individuals with profound learning and physical disabilities may have little or no swallowing reflex, thus all their drinks and food are given via the nasogastric tube or gastrostomy and they may not be able to have anything orally. If the latter is the situation, the person's mouth will become very dry and they may experience some discomfort. Thus regular mouth care must be offered including lip salve to prevent dry and cracked lips. Some individuals may also use artificial saliva in the form of an aerosol mouth spray that is available on prescription, such as glandosane (Dylade). If the individual has a poor swallowing and/or a 'gag' reflex, carers may be shown how to utilize a suction machine which enables excess secretions to be removed from the individual's mouth, especially prior to meal times. This must always be under the guidance and supervision of medical/trained nursing personnel and is often taught to carers so that such equipment can be used within the home.

Nutritional Needs and Life Skills

Eating and drinking is often seen as a social event and consideration therefore needs to be given to the needs of the person who has a learning disability to enjoy the social benefits of eating and drinking with others. For example, drinking alcohol is a valued adult social activity but there are boundaries in terms of safe amounts and the physical effects of drinking alcohol which adults are expected to know about. However, for the person with a learning disability, time may not have been spent with them in social skills development relating to socially acceptable behaviour and alcohol consumption, including pacing out the number of drinks taken especially if they are on long-term medication, and what low alcohol alternatives are available (Lindsay *et al.*, 1991).

The problems of under/overeating are relevant to all individuals. They should not be ignored as irrelevant to people with learning disabilities. Body image is important to one's self-esteem and learning disabilities does not mean that you do not have feelings. Thus anorexia and bulimia can be very real problems and if they are experienced then the individual has the right to the range of support and therapies available – through support groups and also the community mental health teams.

However, the problem of being underweight due to other reasons must be acknowledged. It may be that the person has difficulty swallowing (as discussed above); has frequent muscle spasms; is taking medication which depresses appetite or increases one's metabolism; or simply may not be able to communicate when hungry (Perry, 1992). Overeating generally is not a unique problem for anyone; it is argued that it is a common problem for adults with learning disabilities (Perry, 1992). The person with a mild learning disability may need help in terms of making healthy choices with regards to shopping, cooking and eating habits. Exercise should be encouraged appropriate to the person's needs and abilities. If dieting is being attempted, this should include exercise and also the time to build on the person's self-esteem with the support of the community nurse. Weight targets (if used) should be realistic and achievable.

3.9 Cardiac (Heart) Problems

Coronary heart disease, as mentioned in the previous section, is an area where much work is needed to encourage 'preventative measures', for example healthy eating, exercise and generally encouraging people to take control of their own lives in terms of limiting the potential impact of this disease. Indeed, coronary heart disease is considered to be one of the main causes of death of adults in the Western world.

What is Coronary Heart Disease?

It is where there is a build up of fatty substances (as an example) on the lining of the main arteries, particularly those around the heart. Thus the arteries become narrower and this means that the flow of blood to the heart is reduced. If the fatty deposits build up it may cause a blockage of the arteries involved in the blood flow to the heart and cause what is known as a myocardial infarction (heart attack) or, if some of the deposits enter the blood flow supplying the brain and cause a blockage in that aspect of the overall bloodflow, the person may have a cerebral vascular accident (a stroke). So the potential impact of coronary heart disease is serious for everyone, there are no exceptions, thus people with learning disabilities have the right to advice and support, and care where appropriate, which will help minimize this problem.

Helping the Person with Learning Disability and their Carers

Awareness of the impact of diet and being overweight, including avoidance of foods high in saturated fats, is important. A well-balanced diet should be encouraged. When the individual has a mild learning disability and shops for their own food, with or without assistance, they should be encouraged to make healthy choices. The 'traffic light' system used by the British Diabetic Association, for example grouping foods, including 'fast food' in three groups – green for foods that can be eaten freely, orange for foods only to be eaten in moderation, and red for foods to be avoided when possible, could be adapted to meet the particular needs of the individual. If the individual has a family history of heart problems it would be useful to consult with the GP to check his cholesterol levels. This can be done within the current 'MOTs for adults' available at GP surgeries. This usually also includes blood pressure monitoring and careful consideration of the person's needs for lowering the risk of heart disease.

Community nurses (for people with learning disabilities) can be very helpful in adapting health education material to meet the needs of the individual with a learning disability. This could include ways to stop smoking where appropriate and acknowledgement that people with learning disabilities experience stress like everyone else and therefore appropriate advice and support to help the individual reduce their stress, including the use of regular exercise, is required. Exercise should be encouraged. Even if the only exercise a person can do is passive exercises done by the carer, the individual's physiotherapist usually can advise on a range of passive exercises that can be undertaken. It is important that a programme of exercise should not commence if the person has additional health problems without first being discussed with the individual's GP, especially if the person has not exercised before.

Congenital Heart Problems

Up to 3% of the general population have such problems (Chilman and Thomas, 1983). It is argued that up to a third of people with Down's syndrome have congenital heart problems (Gunn, 1993). For the majority of these defects, surgery is indicated and performed. It is felt that current advances in medical and surgical care have increased the overall survival rate of people with Down's syndrome with heart problems (Malone, 1988). It would be difficult in this chapter to consider the full range of con-

genital heart problems (of which there are many); readers are advised to consult more specialist texts. There are various support groups nationally who may be of some help and a source of contact is cited at the end of this chapter.

3.10 Respiratory Problems

The range of respiratory conditions to consider would complete a chapter in itself, thus only a brief resume is possible here.

Whilst it could be stated that people with learning disabilities are no more at risk of developing respiratory problems than the general public, it is true that there are certain individuals who would be more at risk. This includes people with additional severe physical disabilities who have difficulty in mobilizing or are completely dependent on carers to change position physically. There are some people for whom sitting up, even completely supported, is very difficult to achieve. If the person has additional health problems this can also mean a higher risk of development of respiratory problems. For example, if they are unable or do not understand the need to expectorate excess secretions (they may not have an adequate cough reflex in the first instance, or even a 'gag' reflex), they may be dependent on carers to utilize equipment such as a suction machine to remove excess secretions throughout each day. The frequency of need for nasal and/or oral suction is dependent on the individual. Suction will be more frequently required if the individual has a respiratory infection. Regular daily intensive physiotherapy is usually also needed, such as postural drainage. Poor swallowing skills, as discussed earlier in the chapter, will also mean that the person is more at risk of respiratory problems.

Specific conditions/syndromes related to learning disability are linked with respiratory problems, for example San Filippo syndrome, Down's syndrome and Goldenhar syndrome. If there is a family history of respiratory problems such as asthma linked with allergy problems, including hayfever and eczema, this may result in the person also developing associated allergies and/or respiratory problems. The person's own medical history is particularly important especially if the individual was born prematurely and required prolonged ventilation (life support). Children with learning disabilities who have required intensive ventilatory support as neonates are considered more at risk of developing a long-term predisposition to respiratory problems, indeed some develop bronchopulmonary dysplasia as neonates and may have required continuous low flow oxygen therapy over a significant part of their infanthood. This is a result of immature lung function and resultant high pressure ventilation as a neonate. Fortunately, drugs known as surfactants are considered to be reducing the incidence of need for such high pressure ventilation for some neonates.

A Brief Guide to Asthma

Asthma is the most common respiratory problem. There is no set definition of asthma, indeed it is felt that trying to define asthma in one single sentence may limit understanding of the condition due to the different types and causes of the condition (Pearson, 1990). There is no single cause cited in any text with regards asthma. Whiteside (1991) relates it as being where the bronchial tubes in the lungs, which are soft and kept open by muscles, become constricted due to certain trigger factors such as dust, thus a narrowing of the person's breathing tubes (airways) occurs and the person hence finds breathing difficult. Causes vary from person to person and includes allergy, respiratory infection, pollution (i.e. traffic fumes), and exercise.

Treatment of Asthma

This is divided into two mean areas: *prevention* and *relief* of symptoms

Prevention

This is a very important aspect of asthma management. Prevention therapy is aimed at ensuring that the person is able to live with as little affect from asthma as possible and also at preventing exacerbation of the asthma and the potential for respiratory distress to occur, as an asthma attack can cause respiratory arrest if severe enough. Drugs utilized in the preventive aspect of asthma management include, for example, beclamethasone (Becotide), sodium cromoglycate (Intal), budesonide (Pulmicort), nedocromil sodium (Tilade). Drugs used for prevention should not be stopped except on medical advice, even if the person does not experience any current asthma symptoms.

Relief of Acute Symptoms

During an asthmatic episode certain drugs, known as bronchodilators, are used that 'open the airways'. Drugs that are quick acting in this way are, for example, salbutamol (Ventolin) and terbutaline (Bricanyl). These drugs are usually able to relieve the symptoms of an asthma attack; however, there may be times when the drugs do not provide the level of relief needed and additional medication such as prednisilone may be required for a short time, usually for 48–72 hours. In addition to this (or instead of), bronchodilator medication may be given in a larger dose via a nebulizer as described below. Therefore it is very important that if the individual with a learning disability and/or their carers feel that the individual is not gaining relief by using their usual bronchodilator therapy that medical advice is sought.

Drugs used for asthma come in a variety of delivery methods depending on an individual's needs and their ability to use the devices. For people with learning disabilities, it is important that the method of delivery used is based on their individual abilities to use the medicines appropriately and effectively. Meter dose inhalers are most frequently used by adults with asthma, but they require an ability to co-ordinate breathing and activating the device at the same time, a difficult feat for anyone, especially when breathless. Alternatives may thus be used, for example, spacer devices, disc inhalers or breath-actuated devices such as the Aerolin autoinhaler. However, even these alternative devices would be extremely difficult to use with a person with a severe learning disability especially if they also have physical disabilities, therefore a nebulizer may be used which is electrically operated, and allows the medication delivered via a mask system over the mouth and nose, rather like wearing an oxygen mask.

The individual's GP may have an asthma clinic at the surgery which is worth utilizing. All aspects of asthma management must be co-ordinated via a medical practitioner. If complementary therapies are being considered, these should be discussed with the individual and the GP and/or chest physician.

3.11 Mobility Problems

Physical disabilities are encountered by people with learning disabilities just as with any other individual. The focus of the section is to consider the impact of physical disabilities, such as cerebral palsy, in relation to people with severe learning disabilities, particularly the implications of immobility. For the individuals encountering these problems there are many aspects of care to consider.

Muscle Atrophy

If the person is immobile, muscles in the limbs are not being used, hence the risk of muscles losing their strength and atrophy can occur.

Contractures

If the person is laid in the same position for long periods of time, the joints begin to atrophy and also because the muscles are not receiving enough oxygen they eventually begin to be shorter in size. As more and more of the muscle fibres contract the actual joints become increasingly stiffer and have a tendency to stay in one position, and the ability to move the joint becomes less possible even with intensive physiotherapy.

However, it is argued that deformities are more likely to occur in people with profound learning and physical disabilities despite high levels of physiotherapy, particularly hip subluxation or dislocation. People with Down's syndrome are also considered to be at risk of the development of hip deformities. Surgery is usually required to correct the problem as the individual will experience pain in the hips as he or she grows older (McKinlay and Holland, 1986). The decision to utilize orthopaedic surgery is always well thought out as even surgery may not permanently rectify the situation as the cause is long standing as a result of 'an interaction between several forces: neurological, postural and gravitational' (Galasko, 1986). Therefore the underlying cause of the hip problems cannot be eradicated, but it can be relieved by regular limb physiotherapy and may be helped by the use of medication in the form of a muscle relaxant such as baclofen (Lioresal).

Problems with the person's Achilles tendons as well as scoliosis are also considered to be common and require orthopaedic management.

Pressure Sores (Decubitus Ulcers)

When the person is unable to change position without the help of carers there is always the potential for pressure sore development. When the person is laid in the same position for a long time (NB: for some individuals lying in the same position for an hour is enough for a pressure sore to develop), pressure is created which affects the integrity of the skin and can cause skin breakdown. This skin breakdown can be so severe it can create a significant loss of layers of skin tissue with the inherent resultant risk of infection developing. Pressure sores can usually be prevented by a range of measures that include ensuring that the individual has a well-balanced diet and fluids and regular changes of position unaided or with help. If the individual is considered to be prone to pressure-sore development, for example due to their physical disabilities, there is a vast range of pressure relieving equipment available including wheelchair seats and mattresses for beds, as well as, for example, dressings such as Opsite or Tagaderm which act as a 'second skin' to protect any areas of the person's body which has a tendency to become very reddened. Bony prominences such as the person's elbows, heels, shoulders and hips are the areas most at risk of pressure-sore development. If the person develops a pressure sore, it is important to seek prompt medical advice in order for the correct treatment to be instigated. A hydrocolloid dressing such as Granuflex to promote wound healing and protect the person's skin from further breakdown may be required. It is essential that the person is in an optimal nutritional state as far as possible to promote good wound healing. Additional food supplements, especially those that are protein enriched, may therefore be prescribed. Systemic antibiotics may also be prescribed if it is felt that the pressure sore is infected.

How Can Carers Help?

It is important that the individual is regularly reviewed by a medical practitioner. Many people with the above types of problems are cared for by a medical consultant in conjunction with an orthopaedic specialist and physiotherapist as well as the primary health-care team. On a day to day basis it is essential that the individual is always positioned correctly in their wheelchair, where appropriate. Specialist seating is usually provided under the supervision of the occupational therapist. All equipment for use for the individual is designed to be used every day, thus if the person goes to school/day centre/respite care it is important that all relevant equipment (which is tailor made for the individual), accompanies them. It is also important that they have a regular change of position so to prevent discomfort and the development of pressure sores. The physiotherapist and occupational therapist do explain and demonstrate ways in which carers can carry out regimes which help prevent muscle atrophy and contractures. Carers need to be willing to carry out the appropriate regime on a daily basis and should inform the relevant health professional if they are having difficulty in following the physiotherapy regimen. Aids such as orthosis or splints are often used to protect weak muscles, stabilize joints and aim to prevent/limit deformities. It is therefore important that they are used correctly according to the therapist's advice (Footner, 1987). Such equipment must be put on properly if it is to be of any use. If carers are in any doubt with regards how to apply the orthosis, prompt advice from the physiotherapist should be sought and the orthosis not applied until the physiotherapist has reviewed the overall problem.

There is much to consider in terms of mobility issues that cannot be included in a short section. Mobility is such an important area and prevention of discomfort and limb difficulties must be a priority. It is therefore important that all individuals with physical disabilities have the option of being reviewed by a physiotherapist and occupational therapist as frequently as needed by the individual.

Discussion Question

This chapter has described how factors influencing the health state of a person with a learning disability can be overcome. When considering the interventions involved consider the role of the carer in respect of the following three factors:

- **their skills**
- **their knowledge**
- **their attitudes.**

Can any single practitioner or carer provide all of the factors involved?

3.12 Useful Addresses and Publications

Epilepsy

British Epilepsy Association,
Anstey House,
40 Hanover Street,
Leeds LS3 1BE

Tel: (01532 439393) National helpline (charged at local rate) (0345) 089599

The National Society for Epilepsy,
The Chalfont Centre for Epilepsy,
Chalfont St Peter,
Gerrards Cross,
Buckinghamshire LS9 0RJ
Tel: (012407) 3991

Visual Impairment

Royal National Institute for the Blind,
224 Portland Street,
London W1N 6AA
Tel: 0171 388 1266

Optical Information Council,
57A Old Woking Road,
West Byfleet,
Weybridge,
Surrey KT14 6LF

SENSE,
The National Deaf–Blind and Rubella Association,
311 Grays Inn Road,
London WC1X 8PT
Tel: 0171 278 1005

Hearing Impairment

Royal Association in aid of Deaf People,
27 Old Oak Road,
Acton,
London W3 7HN
Tel: 0181 743 6187

Royal National Institute for the Deaf,
105 Gower Street,
London WC1E 6AH
Tel: 0171 387 8033

Heart Problems

Rees, P. *et al.* (1989) *Heart Children: A practical handbook for parents.* London: Heart Line Association/The Hospital for Sick Children, Great Ormond Street.

Support Groups Regarding a Full Range of Conditions

Contact a Family,
16 Strutton Ground,
London SW1P 2HP
Tel: 0171 222 2695

Asthma

Pearson, R. (1990) *Asthma: Management in primary care.* Oxford: Radcliffe Medical Press. (Aimed at health professionals)

Whiteside, M. (1991) *Childhood Asthma: A doctor's complete treatment plan.* London: Thorsons. (Good for families to use)

Support/advice

National Asthma Campaign,
Providence House,
Providence Place,
London N1 0NT
Tel: 0171 226 2260

References

Ball, B. (1993) Helping with multiple handicap. *In* Shanley, E. and Starrs, T.A. (Eds) *Learning Disabilities. A handbook of care*, pp. 229–268. Cited on p. 232. Edinburgh: Churchill Livingstone.

Black, P.D. (1980) *Cited in* Stanley, E. and Starrs, T.A. (Eds) (1993) *Learning Disabilities. A handbook of care*, 2nd edn. Edinburgh: Churchill Livingstone.

Black, N. *et al.* (1992) *Black Report 1980. In* Black, N., Boswell, D., Gray, A., Murphy, S. and Popay, J. (Eds) *Health and Disease. A reader*, p. 237. Buckingham: Open University Press.

British Epilepsy Association Leaflets: 1. Photosensitive Epilepsy. 2. Swimming and Epilepsy. 3. Epilepsy and Alcohol. Published by British Epilepsy Association. Leeds. No date given.

Burns, Y. and Gunn, P. (Eds) (1993) *Down's Syndrome. Moving through Life.* London: Chapman and Hall.

Chilman, A.M. and Thomas, M. (Eds) (1983) *Understanding Nursing Care*, 2nd edn. Edinburgh: Churchill Livingstone.

Chevrie, J.J. (1991) Epileptic seizures and epilepsies in childhood. *In* Dam, M. (Ed.) *A Practical Approach to Epilepsy.* Oxford: Pergamon Press Inc.

Davies, E. (1986) *Cited in* Davies, E. and Gordon, N. (1986) Children with delayed development of speech and language. *In* Gordon, N. and McKinlay, I. (Eds) *Neurologically Handicapped Children: Treatment and Management.* Oxford: Blackwell Scientific.

Department of Health (DOH) (1991) *Health of the Nation. A summary of the Government's proposals.* London: HMSO.

Department of Health (DOH) (1994a) *Report of the Working Group on Weaning Diet, of the Committee of Medical Aspects of Food Policy. Weaning and the Weaning Diet.* London: HMSO.

Department of Health (DOH) (1994b) *COMA. Report on Nutritional Aspects of Cardiovascular Disease.* London: HMSO.

DOH, Health of the Nation. *A Strategy for People with Learning Disabilities.* London: HMSO.

Footner, A. (1987) *Orthopaedic Nursing.* London: Baillière Tindall.

Galasko, C. (1986) Orthopaedic management of children with neurological disorders. *In* Gordon, N. and McKinlay, I. (Eds) *Neurologically Handicapped Children: Treatment and Management*, pp. 109–147. Oxford: Blackwell Scientific.

Goffman, E. (1982) *Asylums.* Essays on the social situation of mental patients and other inmates. Middlesex: Pelican Books.

Gram, L. (1990) Epileptic seizures and syndromes. *The Lancet* July 21, pp. 161–163.

Griffiths, J. and Boyle, S. (1993) *Colour Guide to Holistic Oral Care. A practical approach.* London: Mosby Year Book.

Gunn, P. (1993) Characteristics of Down's syndrome. *In* Burns, Y. and Gunn, P. (Eds) *Down's Syndrome. Moving through life*, pp. 1–17. London: Chapman and Hall.

Hoare, P. (1990) Psychological consequences of epilepsy. *Update* July 15, pp. 87–88.

Hotchkiss, D. (1989) *Demographic Aspects of Hearing Impairment: Questions and Answers*, 2nd edn. Washington, DC: Gallaudet University Press.

Howells, G. (1992) *In* Cumella, S. Corbett, J.A., Clarke, D. and Smith, B. *Primary Health Care for People with a Learning Disability*, pp. 123–125. *Mental Handicap* **20**. Bristol: BIMH.

Klemz, A. (1991) *Blind and partial sight.* Cambridge: Woodhead–Faulkner.

Lane, D. and Stratford, B. (Eds) (1985) *Current Approaches to Down's Syndrome.* East Sussex: Holt, Rinehart & Winston.

Lindsay, W.R., Allen, R., Walker, P., Lawrenson, H. and Smith, A.H.W. (1991) An alcohol education service for people with learning difficulties. *Mental Handicap* **19**: 96–100. Bristol: BIMH.

Malone, Q. (1988) *Cited in* Gunn, P. (1993) Characteristics of Down's Syndrome. *In* Burns, Y. and Gunn, P. (Eds) *Down's Syndrome. Moving through life*, London: Chapman & Hall.

McKinlay, I. and Holland, J. (1986) *In* Gordon, N. and McKinlay, I. (Eds) *Neurologically Handicapped Children: Treatment and Management*, pp. 27–59. Oxford: Blackwell Scientific.

Minihan, P.M. and Dean, D.H. (1990) *Cited in* Cumella, S., Corbett, J.A., Clarke, D. and Smith, B. (1992) *Primary Health Care for People with a Learning Disability*, pp. 123–125. *Mental Handicap* **20**. Bristol: BIMH.

Moller, M.A. (1993) Working with visually impaired children and their families. Pediatric opthalmology. *Pediatric Clinics of North America* **40**(4): 881–890.

Morrison, A.W. (1993) Sensorineural deafness due to infections. *In* Ballantyne, J., Martin, M.C., and Martin, T. *Deafness*, Chapter 14, pp. 191–195. London: Whurr Publications Ltd.

Nadol, J.B. (1993) Medical progress: hearing loss. *The New England Journal of Medicine* **329**(15): 1092–1102.

Oakley, A. (1992) Doctor knows best. *In* Black, N., Boswell, D., Gray, A., Murphy, S. and Popay, J. (Eds) *Health and Disease. A Reader*, p. 173. Buckingham: Open University Press.

Pearson, R. (1990) *Asthma. Management in primary care.* Oxford: Radcliffe Medical Press.

Perry, M. (1992) Learning disabilities: community nutrition. *Nursing Standard* **7**(11) Dec 2–8: 38–40.

Pfeiffer, D. (1990) The influence of the socio-economic characteristics of disabled people on their employment status and income. *Disability, Handicap and Society* **6**(2): 103–113.

Richardson, N. (1993) Fit for the future. How a healthy lifestyles' programme benefited a group of people with learning disabilities. *Nursing Times* **89**(44) Nov. 3–9: 36–38.

Rogers, C.R. (1961) *A Therapist's view of psychotherapy. On becoming a person.* London: Constable.

Ryan Woolley, B. (1987) *Aids for the Management of Incontinence. A critical review.* London: Kings Fund Centre.

Sarafino, E.P. (1990) *Health Psychology: Biopsychosocial Interactions.* New York: Wiley.

Scarr, V. (1991) Helping nature. Refractive errors and their correction. *In* Hawker, M. and Davis, M. (Eds) *Visual Handicap. A distance learning package for physiotherapists, occupational therapists and other health professionals.* London: Disabled Living Foundation. pp. 95–105.

Wallace, S.J. (1990) Childhood epileptic syndromes. *The Lancet* July 21, pp. 486–488.

Watson, J.E. and Royle, J.A. (1987) *Watson's Medical – Surgical nursing and related physiology*, 3rd edn. London: Baillière Tindall.

Whiteside, M. (1991) *Childhood Asthma. A doctor's complete treatment plan.* London: Thorsons.

Wing, L. and Gould, J. (1979) *Cited in* Cumella, S., Corbett, J.A., Clarke, D. and Smith, B. (Eds) (1992) *Primary Health Care for People with a Learning Disability*, pp. 123–125. *Mental Handicap* **20**. Bristol: BIMH.

World Health Organization (WHO) (1985) *Targets for health for all.* Targets in support of the European regional strategy for health for all. Geneva: World Health Organization.

Further Reading

Bornat, J., Pereira, C., Pilgrim, D. and Williams, F. (Eds) (1993) *Community care: a reader.* Hampshire: Macmillan Press Ltd.

Craft, A. and Craft, M. (1983) *Sex Education and Counselling for Mentally Handicapped People.* Tunbridge Wells: Costello.

Dale, N. (1996) *Working with families of children with special needs. Partnership and practice.* London: Routledge.

Goldhart, J., Warner, J. and Mount, H. (1994) *The development of early communication and feeding for people who have profound and multiple disabilities.* Mencap. PIMD section. Manchester.

Gordon, N. and McKinlay, I. (Eds) (1986) *Neurologically Handicapped Children: Treatment and Management.* Oxford: Blackwell Scientific.

Hawker, M. and Davis, M. (Eds) (1991) *Visual Handicap. A distance learning package for physiotherapists, occupational therapists and other health professionals.* London: Disabled Living Foundation.

Kay, B., Rose, S. and Turnbull, J. (1995) *Continuing the commitment. The report of the Learning Disability Nursing Project.* Dept. of Health. London.

Sarafino, E.P. (1990) *Health Psychology: Biopsychosocial interactions.* New York: Wiley.

Swain, J., Finkelstein, V., French, S. and Oliver, M. (1993) *Disabling barriers – Enabling environments.* London: Sage Publications Ltd.

Thompson, T. and Mathias, P. (1992) *Standards and Mental Handicap: Keys to competence.* London: Baillière Tindall.

Readers are advised to consult journal articles as their main source of information to ensure that any guidelines related to care reflects current theory and practice. There is a vast array of journals available which may interest readers for further reading, these include, for example:

- British Journal of Learning Disabilities

- British Journal of Social Psychology

- Community Care

- Developmental medicine and child neurology

- Disability, Handicap and Society

- Mental Handicap Research

Part Three: Educational Dimensions of Learning Disability

The very term 'learning disability' illustrates how significant the acts of teaching and learning are to the client group around whom this book is written. Part Three of *Dimensions of Learning Disability* is concerned with the process of education and the manner in which the developmental needs of people with learning disabilities are met; or otherwise!

In Chapter 4, 'Educational Theory and Curriculum Issues' Colin Beacock offers a perspective of life-long learning which challenges the established principles of a school-based system in which the student is a passive recipient of education. Rather than presenting an overview of existing works on learning theories, the author seeks to establish principles against which to evaluate and establish educational processes.

David Lewis continues this theme in Chapter 5 'Learning Throughout Life'. He examines the nature of learning and concentrates his view upon the creation of learning opportunities for people with learning disabilities. Central to this theory is the creation of an educational culture and a learning environment which addresses the needs of the client. Once more, the author challenges stereotypical approaches to teaching and learning and offers a model of shared and action-led learning in which teacher and student have equity of power and parity of status.

Chapter 4: Educational theory and curriculum issues
Colin Beacock

4.1 Introduction

What and how people learn is the subject of considerable research and debate. The very fact that people with learning disabilities were identified by the Education Act (1983) as pupils with 'special needs' indicates that the services they require will need to be somehow different from those of their peers in society. A further issue is the title by which such people are identified within society. 'Learning disability' or 'learning difficulty' each hold their own social connotation. Their relative values depend upon the philosophical and cultural bias of the person evaluating them. Of greater relevance, perhaps, is a comparison not with each other, but with the titles and descriptors they have come to replace. 'Mental handicap', 'mental deficiency' or 'mental subnormality' indicate a state of irredeemable imperfection rather than a prevailing develop-

mental delay. Such terms have arisen from societal norms which have been led by medical, rather than educational, perceptions of the potential of individual needs.

It is against such a background that any analysis of the educational dimension of learning disability should be undertaken. The societal context of services for people with a learning disability has more influence over what and how a person learns than scientific theories of education and learning.

It is not the intention within this chapter to examine sociological and psychological theories of learning as they apply to services for people with a learning disability. Rather, the chapter seeks to examine how societal features affect the education of people with a learning disability, their carers and concerned others. The outcome will be a model for structuring services around the concept of life-long learning.

4.2 Educational Theory

The means by which humankind gains greater knowledge and understanding depends upon our individual and collective capacity to learn. Child (1986) considers that:

> ... learning is a very necessary activity for living things. Their survival depends upon it. For humans, the versatility of their adaptation to diverse environments and the joys of abstraction in art and science are founded on their phenomenal learning capacity ... learning occurs whenever one adopts new, or modifies existing, behavior patterns in a way which has some effect on future performance or attitudes.

The compulsion for humans to learn would appear to be generated by their fundamental need to survive. It is suggested that our capacity to learn has led to the development of our appreciation of artistic and scientific features within our environment. This capacity for learning would account for the major differential between ourselves and other species and assists in establishing the cruciality of a learning disability in the life pattern of any human being.

Societies strive to organize the need of individuals to learn into systems of education. Whether that education be offered in the form of a primitive hunter teaching their successive generation to catch their food and establish sound shelter or the lecturer addressing a class of undergraduate students, the minimum long-term outcome of such a process must be the continued evolution of their society. The long-term outcomes will vary according to the sophistication of life styles within that society.

Modern, capitalist societies such as the UK have developed systems of education which encourage the principles of societal survival at a very high level of sophistication.

The gross national product (GNP) of our society depends heavily upon the skills and knowledge of the work-force within it. In such societies, the generation of wealth underpins the provision of welfare and the continued financial and economic well being of society drives the educational system. Increasingly, the products of the educational system are being measured in terms of the national capacity to compete with their peer group in international 'markets'. In such a society the focus for learning lies predominantly with the major source of education – the school. Society can therefore control and influence the rate and nature of learning of individual pupils within the educational systems it develops. One analysis of the outcomes of such a system is offered by Illich (1973) who suggested that:

> Many students, especially those who are poor, intuitively know what the schools do for them. They school them to confuse process and substance. Once these have become blurred a new logic is assumed: the more treatment there is, the better the results; or escalation leads to success. The pupil is therefore 'schooled' to confuse teaching with learning, grade advancement with education, a diploma with competence and fluency with the ability to say something new.

Reader Activity 4.1
To what degree does Illich summarize your own experiences of 'school'?

Illich considers that 'schooling' in itself is insufficient and corrupts the learning of an individual as much, if not more, than it promotes it. If Illich's reference to the poor is translated to include those people with greatest need of education, then it might be taken to encompass people with learning disabilities. As individuals with a clear disadvantage in terms of their reduced capacity to learn, they are susceptible to an increased dependency upon the formal systems of education available to them. Although the intensity of their need is indicated by the label which society attaches to them, people with a learning disability may be seen as offering little to the GNP of society and any education they receive is vulnerable to the effects of centralized policy.

A further consideration of how society's view of the relevance of education has come to bear upon people with a learning disability is offered by Tossell and Webb (1986) who considered that:

> ... People with learning difficulties are marginalized in our society primarily because of their inability to learn as quickly or as comprehensively as others. This negatively affects how they perform everyday living tasks and correspondingly increases their dependence on other people. Their full social integration is further hampered by the predominance of myths and demeaning stereotypes concerning people with learning difficulties.

The vulnerability of this group of people and their susceptibility to variance in educational policy at local and central governmental level makes them a barometer for the effects of change.

Downey and Kelly (1986) explained how:

> Decisions of educational policy ... some of them of a far-reaching kind, have been made either under the urgings of some ideological view promulgated by whatever political faction happens to be in power, as has been the case with the comprehensivization of secondary education, or on the basis of evidence culled from some other field of knowledge which can have only a partial contribution to make to any educational issue, as was the case with the establishment of selective forms of secondary education.

In this description the authors have offered examples of how macro issues of policy and political ideology can impact upon the educational system and its structures. Downey and Kelly (1986) go on to illustrate how at a micro level:

> ... the decisions made by the individual teacher in relation to the education of his or her own pupils are still too often made on the basis of a less than adequate appreciation of the significance and

implications of alternative approaches which might be more productive.

The nature of the relationship between teacher and pupil is therefore crucial to the rate and volume of learning which results from the educational process. The resource offered in the form of the knowledge, skills and attitudes of the teacher are as crucial a component of the process of learning as the same characteristics in the pupil. Where the pupil has an identified learning disability the resources of the teacher must be of even greater relevance.

Theories of learning are not, in themselves, sufficient to guide the process of education in a complex society. They represent a scientific means by which to describe and explain the process of learning. As such, they are insufficient to explain the complexities of the overall process of individual and collective education with its susceptibility to macro and micro influences. Whereas learning theories are an essential component in assisting to design and monitor the process of education, they are but one of a number of such components. Downey and Kelly (1986) described three features which they considered were the constituent components of an educational theory. These were:

(1) A means by which to denote a range of problems, most particularly those problems which teachers and others concerned with the practice of education need to give thought to and make decisions about.
(2) Some set or sets of views which may help decide the directions in which decisions might take the overall process.
(3) A proper and rigorous scientific basis to ensure that decisions are theoretically sound and consistent with whatever evidence is available.

4.3 Educational Approaches

Whilst learning theories are of use in determining the decisions illustrated by Downey and Kelly (1986), the teaching methods applied to people with learning disability have tended to be dominated by the perception that the learner is forever a child. That is, no matter what the chronological age of the learner, the developmental delays they have encountered have appeared to cloud the perceptions of the educator leading them to view and treat the learner as a child. The term 'educator' is not given to indicate any specific individual involved in the process of learning. This person may be the carer, parent, practitioner or teacher.

The dilemma of approaching learners in a manner which is inappropriate to their stage of chronological and social development is an acknowledged feature of educational practice. Life-long learning is a concept which contemporary society has only recently begun to recognize. Knowles (1970) stated that:

> ... the main reason why adult education has not achieved the impact upon our civilization of which it is capable is that most teachers of adults have only known how to teach adults as if they were children.

The teaching of adults is based in a process of 'androgogy'. The process by which children are educated is known as 'pedagogy'. Knowles (1980) further analysed the implications of these processes and described four main areas of variance as shown in Box 4.1.

Reader Activity 4.2
Does Knowles (1980) describe your experience of adult education in his definitions of 'androgogy'. If not, why not?

4.4 Education and Culture

The matter of how educators and carers approach people with learning disabilities and the ways in which society views and values their needs is indicative of the culture which prevails in respect of their care. Given the susceptibility of services for people with a learning disability to social and political

---

Box 4.1 Variance in learning

- **The Learner.** In pedagogy, Knowles suggested that the learner is viewed as being dependent and the teacher directs the whole process of learning including what, when and how subjects are taught. The teacher also tests what has been learned. In androgogy the learner is progressing towards greater independence and is self-directing. The role of the teacher is to encourage and nurture the learning process.

- **The Learner's Experience.** Teaching methods in pedagogy are didactic and the learner's experience is of little worth, whereas in androgogy this is taken to be a rich resource for learning and the teaching methods involve discussion and problem solving.

- **Readiness to Learn.** The standardization of the curriculum is a reflection of the fact that society dictates what students are expected to learn in a pedagogical process. By contrast, androgogy provides opportunity for the student to learn what they need to know and learning programmes are organized around the student's life style.

- **Orientation to Learning.** In pedagogy the curriculum is organized around subjects and the student is driven to acquire subject matter. The androgogical approach indicates that the curriculum should be organized around problems since people are performance centered in their learning.

---

change, the culture of care within which they exist is crucial in determining how they are educated, both collectively and as individuals. Deal and Kennedy (1988) sought to account for the complexity of culture and to offer a more viable working description of what culture is and does. They explained that:

> ... Culture as *Webster's New Collegiate Dictionary* defines it is 'the integrated pattern of human behaviour that includes thought, speech, notion and artifacts and depends on man's capacity for learning and transmitting knowledge to successive

generations' . . . Martin Bower . . . offered a more informal definition – he described the informal cultural elements of business as 'the way we do things around here'.

Reader Activity 4.3
Have you ever shared a home with someone? Was their way of 'the way we do things round here' the same as yours?

4.5 Culture and Curriculum

If educational provision is to be organized and effective there must be a method of planning at school or service level which ensures these outcomes. This is the province of the 'curriculum'. What then is a curriculum and how can it reflect the richness and variety of culture? Brennan (1985) in describing a curriculum for people with special needs said that:

> . . . A curriculum may be regarded as a course of study to be followed in the process of acquiring education, a concept which goes back to the earliest meaning of the word . . .

From this definition it would appear that the educational curriculum is entirely geared to formal, classroom-based learning. By such a definition there appears to be no means by which the curriculum can allow for cultural and individual variances and 'the way that we do things around here' would be dominated by the formal process of teacher-led learning. Brennan (1985) recognized these deficiencies and went on to say that:

> . . . This notion of a curriculum is of limited value. It is useful only where concern is for the knowledge acquired by pupils, in particular knowledge in a form which may be tested through written examinations or checklists. Once concern goes beyond what the pupils 'know' and becomes involved in the kind of

persons they are, or are becoming, broader aspects of curriculum assume importance . . .

Where a student has an identified developmental delay then this may result in any number of outcomes of a personal and intellectual nature. That is to say, the person with a learning disability will encounter impairment of far more than their cognitive development. Their intellectual development may not be as severely delayed as their social skills development, depending upon the causes of their learning disability. This is most especially so in people whose learning disability results in social deprivation. There are others whose predisposing medical diagnosis may have led to social labelling and stereotyping of their potential when, in fact, their intellectual and cognitive development is at or beyond normal attainment levels. Cerebral Palsy is one such condition and Professor Stephen Hawkins and Christy Brown offer specific examples of people whose potential was significantly underestimated because of society's response to their overlying medical condition. In the case of each of these individuals their early life learning patterns were not dominated by the application of a formal, teacher-led curriculum yet they achieved significant levels of intellectual understanding. In such circumstances the application of examination-type assessment of their levels of cognitive development would have proved to be of little significance without the resource of new technology. None the less, the recognition of their potential in each of these individuals offered them opportunities for greater social interaction and subsequent enhanced personal development.

Brennan (1985) goes on to describe how the educational curriculum can reflect the subtlety of individual and cultural differences and remain an effective means by which to plan and manage the process of learning:

> . . . A modern concept of curriculum retains the idea of knowledge to be acquired by the learner but sets it in the framework of cognitive development . . . In the curriculum process there must be the flexibility to

allow for the development of unique individuals who differ in personality, potential and background; at the same time, common experiences must enable the individuals to relate, both to each other within the shared society of the school and to those aspects of development common to all.

From this perspective, learning is seen as something greater than the simple acquisition of sets of intellectual understandings. Learning is given to include elements of personal and social development which equip each of us to survive in and contribute to our immediate social group and society as a whole.

The flexibility and responsive nature of curriculum, as described by Brennan (1985) would appear to be the means for ensuring that cultural aspects of the educational system can be promoted and sustained at the school or service level. This should indicate that the curriculum has the potential to promote group and individual development of culture without threatening the integrity of society's overlying educational policy.

This potential is further recognized in the work of Kelly (1986) who considered that:

> ... The link between education and culture is very close ... Furthermore it would be difficult to argue that the connection is not merely contingent but also necessary, that a concept of education which did not embrace some notion of cultural transmission is no concept of education at all.

That a curriculum might be nothing more than a means by which to organize and manage the formal system and process of education would appear to be a wasted opportunity. Whereas the prevailing educational policies might guide and influence the educational provision of a school or service, the curriculum represents the means by which to ensure that the products of the educational system are to the continuing benefit of all involved in that process. Kelly (1986) goes on to consider this application of the curriculum further when he states that:

> ... the transmission of a society's culture is always a major part, and in some cases the whole, of the educational process. In primitive societies for example ... systems of education ... have as their prime and perhaps only function, the handing on to the next generation of not only the skills and knowledge but also the values and ways of life of the present generation. Thus do societies renew themselves through successive generations ...

Emerging from this description is an indication of both positive and negative implications of transmission of cultural features from one generation to the next. Having identified the fact that people with learning disabilities are marginalized within modern societies, the potential for this situation to be continued within successive generations of society is evident. What also emerges, however, is an opportunity for curriculum planners and the participants in the process of education to tackle this issue from the perspective of the learner, the service user and society as a whole.

Reader Activity 4.4
Have you witnessed or experienced the effects of negative stereotypes regarding people with learning disabilities being transferred from one generation to the next?

In recognizing that systems of education offer a means by which to address the transmission of negative cultural features across successive generations, educational planners can facilitate the most appropriate forms of education for people with learning disabilities and those involved in their care. However, the potential corruption of this process by factors external to the school itself is realized within the work of Williams and Young (1985) who wrote that:

> If the ordinary curriculum has been a secret garden, then in special education it has been not only secret, but neglected, too. The hard-pressed professionals working with children with special needs have had to

be more concerned with extending scarce facilities for the children than with the content offered by those facilities.

This predicament for professionals is typical of problems faced by individuals who must apply the products of societal and political policies which conflict with the philosophy and intent of their immediate organization or service. Historically, such dilemmas have characterized the role of practitioners within services for people with learning disabilities. The situation within the context of the educational process is further complicated by the potentially detrimental effect which can be produced by the practitioner adopting the pedagogical stance as educator. By affirming their personal role as enacting the policy of society, the professional, however overworked, can be seen as perpetuating the marginalization of the individuals they have been seeking to educate. Williams and Young (1985) go on to describe the difficulties which have arisen:

> ... All too often, where to place a child has taken priority over what is actually taught. The purposes of special education were rarely explored and formulated: the school for speech problems was presumed to specialize in teaching communication skills; the unit for maladjusted children was meant to 'adjust' them – but few had thought through what those deceptively simple aims might imply for the curriculum.

What Williams and Young (1985) describe as 'deceptively simple aims' are fundamental to society's view of the purpose of 'special' education. The very notion that people with learning disabilities are special and therefore need a special form of education can be seen as a reflection of a society which is fully aware of and accommodating to those needs. In reality, what had emerged was a system of education which segregated and further marginalized such people and their families. Throughout the 1980s and 1990s, the decreasing relevance of the medical model of services for people with a learning disabil-

ity has been reflected in the educational service as well as the residential and care services. The outcome is captured by Williams and Young (1985) who go on to say that:

> ... Now that the special educational service has grown, now that we increasingly appreciate that the education of our children matters at least as much as their medical care, our attention is turning to what is after all the key question in special education – what shall we teach?

4.6 Conclusions: Towards a Model for Life-long Learning in People with Learning Disability

If the activity of learning is intended to equip us with the abilities to survive and develop then the rate of that learning must be at least equivalent to the rate of change in our environment. If we failed to do so, human kind would fail to thrive and ultimately perish. The same could be said to apply to individuals. When one considers the rate of change in the environment of a person with learning disabilities, then the volume and rate of change in the environments and organization of their lives in contemporary services has been dramatic over the last 30 years.

Homans (1951) described three 'environments' which related to the context of all organizations. These environments are shown in Box 4.2.

If that organization were to be the overall service and support for people with a learning disability and those individuals who are involved in the process of their care and development, then the task of describing 'what to teach' can be made somewhat clearer. A model for curriculum planning is therefore emerging. If the intention of a system of eduction for people with learning disabilities is to enable them to maximize their individual potential and if the intention is that all those persons involved in providing that system should learn in partnership with the 'student', then the outcome should be a curriculum

---

Box 4.2 Environments

- The *physical* environment. Whereby Homans considered the issues of terrain, geography, climate and layout of the physical element of an organization.
- The *technological* environment. Whereby Homans included the mechanical plant and the knowledge and skills of the relevant workforce and operatives within an organization.
- The *cultural* environment. Whereby Homans considered the norms, attitudes and values which pertained to an organization.

---

of constant evolutionary change. Given that the student is a person whose developmental delays will probably mean that their learning disability is never entirely overcome, then the need for a life-long programme of learning would appear to be automatically established. In such a model of care, the concept of life-planning is replaced by the concept of life-long learning and the curriculum of each individual could be taken to be equivalent to an individual programme plan or whatever form of system management is in use. From an extended interpretation of education, the direction of service and policy development can be geared to establishing a culture of growth and enablement in which the overall process is dominated by individual, group and societal learning based upon partnership and shared responsibilities.

Discussion Questions

1 Educational provision is driven and guided by a number of established theories. Practitioners and educators in services for people with learning disabilities have tended to study each in isolation. As a means of further inquiry, consider the three points raised by Downey and Kelly (1986) in respect of the purpose and value of learning theories. From these points, try to evaluate the theories such as those propounded by:

- Pavlov
- Skinner
- Piaget

2 The emergent theme is one of learning in partnership and of equality of status for student and teacher. When examined against theories of 'empowerment' and 'normalization' the androgogical process of learning has a great deal in common with these other humanistic perspectives on care practice. Can education for children with learning disabilities gain from the work of Knowles and, if so, how might it apply?

3 Where a system is susceptible to so many external influences, can the provision of education for people with a learning disability be controlled through national and local policy to such a degree that 'the way we do things around here' is obscured and lost? Is individual identity necessary or merely desirable in a state educational system?

References

Brennan, W. (1985) *Curriculum for Special Needs.* Milton Keynes: Open University Press.

Child, D. (1986) *Psychology and the Teacher*, 4th edn. London: Cassell.

Deal, P. and Kennedy, S. (1988) *Corporate Cultures.* London: Penguin.

Downey, M.E. and Kelly, A.V. (1986) *Theory and Practice of Education*, 3rd revised edn. London: P. Chapman.

Homans, G. (1951) *The Human Group.* London: Routledge.

Illich, I. (1973) *Deschooling Society.* London: Penguin.

Kelly, A.V. (1986) *Knowledge and Curriculum Planning.* London: Harper & Row.

Knowles, M.S. (1970) *The Adult Learner. A neglected species.* Houston: Gulf Press.

Knowles, M.S. (1980) *The Modern Practice of Adult Education.* Chicago: Association Press.

Tossell, D. and Webb, R. (1986) *Inside the Caring Services*. London: Edward Arnold.

Williams, P. and Young, P. (1985) *In* Brennan, W. (Ed.) *Curriculum for Special Needs*. Milton Keynes: Open University Press.

Further Reading

In respect of psychological theories the recommended further reading is:

Child, D. (1986) *Applications of Psychology for the Teacher*. London: Cassell.

For sociological theory the recommended further reading is:

Meighen, R. (1986) *A Sociology of Educating*. London: Holt Reinhart & Winston.

For further analysis of curriculum studies:

Brennan, W. (1986) *Curriculum for Special Needs*. Milton Keynes: Open University Press.

Chapter 5: Learning throughout life
David Lewis

5.1 Introduction

The chapter heading offers the reader the notion that these two independent activities, 'living' and 'learning', are closely inter-related and best considered as one. Learning might be seen as occurring each and every day of our lives, deliberately, spontaneously and often unplanned. Learning occurs any time, and not necessarily at set times and with set people (Brudenell, 1986). It is the result of a life-long process. Brudenell (1986) goes further, to consider it more intensely as a day-long process, a path constantly travelled with encounters and changes occurring both in time and environments:

A journey of discovery, exploration growth and development, a widening of horizons and experiences. (Brudenell, 1986)

Gagne (1983) defines learning as a 'change in human disposition or capability, which persists over a period of time, and which is not simply ascribable to the process of growth' (Gagne, 1983).

Learning can be defined as a change in behaviour as a result of experience. From this perspective one of the most important concepts in the development of a person who has a learning disability, might be that of experience. Experience consists of the situations, events, environments and interactions that an individual encounters actively or seeks out for themselves. Whether intended or accidental, experiences have an effect upon the learning process of an individual.

Also related to this concept of experience, is the notion of opportunity. Limiting the range of experiences an individual undergoes throughout their lives is bound to be detrimental to their development. Where the opportunity for experience has not been recognized as important by those responsible for its creation, then an individual's experiences are not only restricted but subtly controlled, and a 'denial of rights' occurs.

Reader Activity 5.1
Reflect on examples you could give of how control is exerted over the rights of a person with a learning disability. Who exerts that control?

Theories of learning attempt to explain the process whereby an individual acquires the skills, knowledge and attitudes which will equip them with regard to their development and coping strategies throughout their life span.

The aim of this chapter is to examine learning opportunities themselves and reflect upon how they might best be manipulated to provide the maximum benefit for the person in need of support and care.

It must also be recognized that the person with a learning disability is foremost an individual, unique in history and time, and as with all individuals their modes of learning will differ with the variations of environments, interactions, influences, previous learning and experiences, and emotional climates. It would be impossible to offer, describe or even apply an approach without first knowing the person as an individual with personal preferences, abilities, needs and social networks.

The question therefore 'why isn't the person with a learning disability learning?' needs to be addressed by analysing the processes involved.

5.2 Emerging Educational Perspectives

Many new and innovative approaches to teaching people with learning disabilities have emerged in recent years, often offering valuable advice towards improving the learning process. Gentle teaching and goal planning are good examples which emphasize that 'methodical and consistent teacher–client interaction' is central to the learning process. These new approaches seek to improve, update and replace the outdated approaches utilized throughout the late 1960s, 1970s and early 1980s. Then, 'integration' and 'social valorization' were merely futuristic ideals expounded by unknown Scandinavians whose names were often difficult to remember, and extremely unfamiliar. Names such as Grunewald, Nirje and Bank-Mikkelson are now far more well known to us and their principles and philosophies have now emerged as practical realities in systems of care.

The irony is perhaps that these new approaches and applied ideals are not really about the learning processes for people with learning disabilities (although learning is often a successful outcome), but are actually about care providers, care services and the methodologies and processes adopted in care provision. In particular the attitudes, consistencies and opportunities created by those directly involved with delivering a service, and those responsible for the management of that service.

The arguments of the service user have remained unaltered throughout this period and still today centre around devalued social roles, being unaccepted as a person and having a life style that is still so dissimilar from the 'norm'.

Often the focus of new innovations and approaches has been those people with a learning disability who present with a more serious set of behaviours which inhibit learning. These behaviours more often reflected service deficiencies, and were not representative of the vast majority of people with learning disabilities whose problems centred around slow or impaired learning.

'Normalization' principles (Wolfensberger and Glenn, 1982) were introduced to challenge a service which had lost sight of the individual, but have still emerged as focusing on care providers, and are not sufficiently client-centred. Although there has been considerable change achieved by their introduction, the clients themselves remain the recipients of the principles rather than becoming the means by which they are developed.

However, in relating normalization to learning there is one feature that is common throughout their various theories. That is the belief that learning needs to be an enjoyable experience, creating in turn the desire to re-experience, memorize and recall the event with pleasure and satisfaction. The learning environment should support not only the abilities of the clients, but should consider their state of mind, factors and traumas which affect the emotional climate with the same degree of unpredictability as experienced by everyone struggling and striving throughout their lives.

For people with a learning disability – a term in itself non-specific and minimally descriptive of an individual's abilities – learning has more often meant conforming to a vague and bland set of social norms. Although these norms may act as a mean indication as to that person's degree of normal behaviour, they reflect the abilities of an illusory character invoking sympathy and laughter, but lacking social credibility and acceptance.

Do we all in reality butter our bread in exactly the same way, make tea identically and dress in the same manner? Yet too often this is the sort of criteria by which we judge the performance of a person with a learning disability.

Wolfensberger and Glenn (1982) include in Programme Analysis of Service Systems (PASS) a criteria which considers the physical appearance of a person with a learning disability. It asks the person (carer) completing it to judge whether the individual 'looks and dresses in a way which is appropriate to their age'? But what does that mean? Is there a particular image at certain ages we all strive for? One needs to consider what does looking 'age-appropriate' actually mean? It is likely that different carers asked to judge this may well have differing expectations in relation to such a statement.

There is also an overall expectation that happiness and contentment will be attained once all the criteria within such documents are met by:

- **a comfortable, but shared, home**
- **social interaction, often with other learning disabled**
- **meaningful daytime activities, often for little financial reward.**

These reflect the goals to be met and in reality can only be described as utterly trivial. A quality life has a pivotal concept relating to self-esteem. Where does one consider how the individual sees their life going? Where are the aspirations that are comparable to most normal people?

- **I want to be rich and famous**
- **I want to win the lottery**
- **I want to look good and have a face-lift.**

Wanting more! Wanting to better oneself, achieve personal contentment and life satisfaction – a concept that requires closer examination.

5.3 Individuality and Personal Differences

Should people with a learning disability be content with 'sameness' and a run-of-the-mill ordinariness? It is a sad fact that at least when people with learning disabilities were segregated they retained their differences, they were identifiable.

They faced challenges, albeit uphill, but this at least gave their lives some purpose.

The direction and facilitation which supports it has tended to create a boring and unadventurous life style for people with learning disabilities which is more often monitored and controlled by non-disabled people throughout their entire existence. If sameness and mundaneness appear to be the goals for care, then this is likely to be reflected in the learning opportunities also. The criteria within the range of assessment formats available seem to support this view. Their differences are minimal and their application a template for a set of uninspiring competencies often too simplistic and child-like. Some even exclude the client from participating other than in a recipient role, such as Skills Teaching and Educational Programme Planning (STEP's) Community Living Skills Assessment, which although based upon the principles of normalization in terms of its philosophical background, actually instructs the staff on how to complete it – the clients themselves still considered not able enough to adopt a more positive role in the process. With assessment formats pursuing this predictable outcome from the client, and the assessment being used in a similar way to the old IQ test as a predictor of behaviours and the means by which to determine priorities for intervention, the care providers have in a sense created a 'cartel' for care provision. They retain the responsibility and exclude not only the client but more often family, relatives and advocates, too.

Although an unwritten rule, no-one steps outside the parameters determined by these processes, rigidly determined through care plans which are not only similar in nature to all others, but also retain their uninspiring and unadventurous formats. They are certainly far from 'individualized'.

Individuality as a concept has become smothered and, in striving for this now vague concept, it has become confused with and often replaced by conformity.

To include dreams, which do not exist for people with learning disabilities, and riches and fame,

which cannot be handled by them, may seem wasteful to purchasers of services.

When a person with a learning disability actually emerges into the public limelight, it is only for a short period. They evoke a temporary spell of sympathy more often related to their disability rather than the contact of their achievement. Examples of this are in television programmes where learning disabled people appear, but only as learning disabled people. Where an individual gains public acclaim, such as the individual person who was awarded an MBE for his involvement in Special Olympics – was it a token gesture or a genuine achievement? It received minimal media coverage despite its significance for the image of people with learning disabilities.

Reader Activity 5.2
Can you recall images of people with learning disability in the local or national media? Were they predominantly positive or negative?

Such publicity can result in a more positive image of people with a learning disability, but where are their individual identities? They retain their learning disability labels, as though their unique personalities do not exist.

In acting, non-disabled people might portray a person with a disability, such as 'Walter' and 'Rain Man'; yet when do disabled people have the opportunity to reverse this and portray non-disabled people? Black actors have portrayed white men, and white men played black. Why then is it so difficult for a person with a learning disability to portray anything other than themselves? It must indicate that they are confined to these roles as a result of our expectations inhibiting their aspirations. We have created perhaps a perfect self-fulfilling prophecy in that they will never be any different to what we tell them they are, teach them to be, and in reality actually allow them to be.

Learning opportunities have been refined and limited to such a degree that until there is a radical change in attitude and approach, it is almost possible to predict the entire range of behaviours that will be presented in almost every person with a learning disability throughout every stage of their life span.

Integration is not just about using the same facilities, resources and opportunities. Not only is it more complex, it requires far greater societal involvement regarding being a part, sharing this with others regardless of outcome and in a climate of equity. Failing, having faults, being imperfect and showing human responses which are both good and bad towards life's traumas do actually make us real, and should not be regarded as setbacks in progress. It is not essential that one is able to do everything. We all have limitations on what we do well, and we all have the choice to try, good or not. Failure should be seen as a commonly accepted outcome for us all, including those with learning disabilities, whose developmental pathway seems to be directed only towards competency and achievement. For people with a learning disability non-achievement, inability and failure are seen as major weaknesses and are often used as reasons to maintain non-integrative life styles and continued control. Even the term 'learning disability' focuses on what they cannot do, rather than what they can and like doing.

Every individual has a range of strengths that compensate for areas where they do not achieve, which allows them to come back and try again when success is not achieved, for example the driving test.

5.4 The Public Image

People with learning disabilities are seen as being 'different'. With this in mind, the images presented need to be radically reviewed, if this is the consequence of our approaches, both historically and currently. It is sad that the differences that people with learning disabilities have are not celebrated like so many other differences in modern society with its varying cultures, religions and languages. Our attempts to hide these differences have reflected an insecurity on the part of carers to advocate for the disabled person's right to be different.

The result is often confusion over the role of the staff. Conflict occurs between care or control. The end product of an applied care process seems to be of more importance than the process itself. The public are expected to tolerate only those who reach the goal of care and meet a set of criteria that is deemed acceptable, but acceptable to whom?

Case Study 5.1 Teignmouth – The 1970s Experience

In the mid-1970s this beautiful Devon town created national media headlines when it either courageously or foolishly, depending on one's viewpoint, placed restrictions on the number of learning disability groups taking collective holidays in its locality.

Typical of a number of seaside towns, Teignmouth was used by a range of institutions to send whole wards of clients chaperoned by a few staff for their annual holiday, primarily because a number of 'hotels' were offering special provisions and were turned into small institutions for the week. This offered an easy option for providing clients with an annual break away from their usual setting. However, this particular town felt it had had enough of 'crocodiles' of people within its streets, massed beach groups and total monopolization of its cafes and other holiday facilities.

The populace themselves did not feel any sympathy but argued that the care and supervision so obviously required by these groups meant that their impact was being felt by those people living there and those on holiday themselves. They felt that such clients needed to be controlled and in massed settings and therefore could not freely interact at a level the ordinary person would have readily accepted.

Reader Activity 5.3
What do you think could or should have been done to resolve the issue raised by the people of Teignmouth?

Might it not be beneficial for the general public to grow to understand, accept and even assist with the process itself? Their exclusion results in those same features which Smith and Brown (1992) highlighted. Their attitudes towards people with learning disabilities result from fear, ignorance and mistrust.

Blunden and Allen (1987) define challenging behaviour as being the challenge presented to a service provider, and in the case of a holiday town, the service providers here were ill-equipped to meet such a challenge. Interactionist skills are taught to the professional carer, yet the layman is expected to readily interact without these specialist skills, and without the supportive education and understanding and need.

The professional may have an expectation that the community will readily take on its expected role, failing to recognize that this expectation has been transferred to the professional as a result of the inabilities of community members who face their own life-challenges and do not see the disabled as their primary concern. The stand undertaken by the town did not endear them in the eye of the socially minded members of society, but one might consider that as many of these feelings are still prevalent today, they were supported by the less vocal, often silent, majority of the population.

Is it possible that the change in attitude to annual holidays, with smaller groups adopting a more integrative approach towards a trip out, was a result of the media explosion which resulted from this incident?

5.5 A Higher Profile – Society and Client Group Learning Together

Like anyone else, the person with a learning disability wants very much to be part of a community. This is reflected in the many outcomes from self-advocacy conferences where disabled individuals themselves expressed this preference regarding their life style. As with all people, they are aware that they are different, just as someone small can see they are not as tall as others, someone with one arm recognizes their difficulties, and someone fat knows they are overweight. How they cope with this is primarily a personal thing, but it is also a societal responsibility. We can all help to make things easier for people with a variety of differences – ramps for those confined to a wheelchair will aid access, diets and dietitians help people to lose weight, and a more patient and tolerant populace can aid the individual who is slower to learn. They can help them to cope, but only if:

- **they are encouraged to do so through a greater awareness of this group of people who are different**
- **the people with learning disabilities themselves are available to be helped by the public, and not 'controlled', 'restricted' or 'limited' in their interactions by staff fearful of something going wrong.**

A 'First World' country such as the UK should be judged on its ability to care for its less-able members. Many of our less-able citizens still find themselves alienated due to their inability to contribute productively to the growing wealth of the country. This reflects a need to re-examine values within our society towards the individual. The problems may arise from *what* rather than *how* people with learning disabilities are taught. Furthermore *who* is considered best equipped to support the process of learning for the person with learning problems?

Recent publications demonstrate that confusion regarding the roles of caregivers and educators persists into the 1990s.

> Nursing is a profession with a considerable history of providing care and nurturing to those who have some kind of medical need; social work, on the other hand, is seen as coping with problems both possessed by and caused by certain groups within society. (Bannerman and Lindsay, 1993, p. 34, cited in Shanley and Starrs, 1993)

Neither role has been fully described. This is extended further with the notion that:

> nursing-based personnel will tend to write a report which specifies medical history, definition of the particular type of disability, analysis of skills and recommendations based on the individual needs and potential of the person concerned . . . little attention may be paid to the family background or social systems surrounding the person. (Bannerman and Lindsay, 1993, p. 34, cited in Shanley and Starrs, 1993)

Comments of this nature certainly reflect the fear and caution of carers from within differing caring organizations and agencies. Rogers (1983) recognized the dangers that resulted from the professionals seeing themselves as the experts, the consequence being that the person with a learning disability became an 'object' that was guarded and protected from the other organizations, each 'profession' developing its own style of service delivery and continually finding fault with all the others.

Brudenell (1986), in introducing the role of an educator with people with learning disabilities, has recognized the major problem as a commonly held belief that education for people with learning disabilities is something very specialized:

> Belonging to special schools . . . to colleges of further education, in effect that special education is special . . . nothing could be further from the truth. (Brudenell, 1986, cited in Parrish, 1987, p. 47)

The implications here are that the learning process is the responsibility of all those who come into contact or affect the individual with a learning disability. Brudenell (1986) adds further:

> Teachers do not have the monopoly of the educational process. (cited in Parrish, 1987, p. 47)

This could be further extended to include professional caregivers. Thus an unco-ordinated and jealously guarded professional service still ignores the issue of *what* to teach, continuing to focus upon the issue of *how?*

It is commonly accepted that people with learning disabilities are slow to develop. Whelan and Speake (1984) highlight the primary characteristic of learning disability as being a slowness to learn, and the terms mild, moderate, severe and profound can then be described as four different speed settings in relation to the learning process. They mean little else. In addition, Whelan and Speake (1984) recognized that the basic learning process experienced by 'mentally handicapped' people is the same which we all experience . . .

> most of us learn as a result of everyday experience. (Whelan and Speake, 1984, p. 38)

This seems to indicate that *how* a person is taught is not the main issue, as the *how?* will be the same as is applied to all of society; in fact, it asks us to consider *why* is there a slowness to learn?

Professionals tend to agree that the process is likely to be longer than one would expect for normal people, but there exists a wide range of factors which affect the learning of *all* individuals in society, and even where learning activities are similarly experienced by individuals determined to be 'normal' there are still varying outcomes with respect to the learning itself. Therefore the term 'slow' cannot be so readily applied to this particular client group, for the issue is not quite that simple. One cannot offer a given length of time with respect to learning disability, for as individuals, and as with all society, there exists a wide variation in the responses to 'learning situations'.

In certain situations and with certain skills it is possible for persons with a learning disability to learn quicker than a number of 'normal' members of society. A multiplicity of factors influence learning: strength; previous experience; height and weight; mood; motivation; who is helping, supporting or facilitating; with or without friends; whether it is perceived as necessary; whether it is liked, or, more importantly, enjoyed.

It is possible to offer only a hypothetical comparison whereby if two people, A and B, identical in background, mood, physical ability, and current environmental influences were subjected to identical learning situations, their only difference being that of an intellectual/cognitive nature in that person A is deemed as 'normal' and person B is described with the label 'learning disability', then one could suggest that the learning activity being undertaken would be perceived, assimilated and acquired quicker by person A. Even so there could be no absolute on this.

It is likely that as characteristics are so readily applied to learning disability so, too, are expectations which in consequence become the responsibility of the caregiver to achieve, for they are the experts.

Imagine spending one's entire life being compared to hundreds of 'target areas' for every aspect of one's life. This approach is generally only applied when the functioning of an individual is considered impaired. If this is the only means by which the community will accept members already part of it, whose only significant difference is their intellectual abilities, then it may be too high a price to pay. It means forfeiting one's independency and autonomy, and the freedom to choose one's own destiny to come under the control of one of the many organizations operating within this disjointed service network.

The term 'control' is used for it aptly describes the position of the care-deliverer in relation to the care-receiver. MacKay (1986) notes that:

> matching the learner to the desired goal and the reinforcement may be difficult (cited in Shanley and Starrs, 1993, p. 127)

reflecting the modern directive role applied by the caregiver. This view is further supported by MacKay (1986) when he described how:

> in formal education and in health care, the behaviours to be strengthened are usually chosen for the learner, so deciding how best to reinforce them can often be a delicate art. (cited in Shanley and Starrs, 1993, p. 127)

This approach, although well-meaning, reflects a pattern that has emerged over time. Although this has improved the life styles and living environments for the clientele, it shows little attitudinal change other than that the power and coercion are now far more subtly and carefully applied.

5.6 The Influence of Societal Factors in the Learning Environment

Historically, the disabled individual's differences could not be accommodated and the consequence was a 'separatist' approach which segregated the deviant from the norm. The reasons for this were that society was not able to recognize the most appropriate life style or mode of functioning for these groups, and was also ill-equipped to do anything about them. There was little commitment in relation to provision of opportunity to enable the deviant to adopt an autonomous life style. If they deviated outside of the 'normal' boundaries, they were excluded from society, and this was applied to all deviance, not just learning disability. In 1914, people were imprisoned for not wanting to fight and kill in the Great War. Failure to adopt the old lie: 'dulce et decorem est pro patria mori' (it is sweet and glorious to die for one's country) (Wilfred Owen,

1915) resulted in rejection and hostility from the main body of society.

One is not surprised by society's rejection of its learning disabled populace, considering the response to other social problems at the time.

Reader Activity 5.4

What do you consider to be the major social problems of today and how do they influence care provision for people with learning disabilities?

What value was placed upon learning in society where infant mortality was high, disease, hunger and starvation common amongst an extremely poor working class? With squalid living conditions prevalent, lacking in hygiene and sanitation; children under 10 years working in mines and factories; limited availability of school education; harsh sentences for minor crimes; deportation; poverty; minimal land ownership for ordinary people; and women's roles reduced to house slavery, not even able to vote – the learning disabled were not rejected but protected, in comparison to a large proportion of the population. Their life style was at the time far better with regular food, clothing and warmth, and with the individual in society – owing to massive social class distinction – particularly vulnerable and unprotected, the learning disabled person at least was afforded some protection despite their personhood not being recognized.

The problem once again is that as society changed, the approaches to care did not. In relation to educators, Rogers (1983) considers that too often the approach is static and fails to recognize the need to create a flexible learner able to adapt. Whereas such flexibility would have been of limited value in Victorian society it is now a prerequisite for life-long learning.

In comparison with today, institutionalized learning was poor but in the context of society at the time it represented a fair standard. The fact that care providers protected their expertise and failed to change along with society consequently resulted in this particular client group becoming forgotten, left in a time warp, as other major welfare changes took precedence. Had learning disability the advocate support that other groups had, such as Elizabeth Fry, Lord Shaftesbury and later Nye Bevan, they, too, would have experienced a more radical change. It was not until the emergence of the Scandinavian philosophy that learning disability would see any major change in care provision but, even with this, the question as to what the person with a learning disability should learn still remained an enigma.

Concentration upon the structure of the service became the priority, to such an extent that even today confusion between normalization principles and the process of social role valorization still persists.

Chisholm (1993) stated 'the simple answer is that there is no difference, they are one and the same theory and principle' (cited in Shanley and Starrs, 1993, p. 53). How can it be that having a valued social role is the same as being subjected to a set of principles applied to the service being supplied to you? This is further complicated by Chisholm (1993) when he offers a major criticism of the social role valorization perspective in that it expects too much of the people being supported, which seems to imply it, too, is about service provision. Being accepted for who and what you are is having a valued social role. Society is comprised of a multitude of varying social roles each seemingly unimportant yet significant in their own way.

As the isolationist approaches faded, so too, emerged a new approach disguised as a more integrative one, yet reflecting an even greater subordinate role that the client group were now expected to undertake.

The 'new wave' of carers now empowered with professional qualifications were even more eager to sustain their status and imposed an even greater set of expectations upon people with learning disabilities. These expectations not only affected people with learning disabilities but were to have impact upon the public, too, who despite protests and expressed fears could do little to change the practices of service organizations legitimized through their discourses, which the non-professional would not be able to challenge. How can the unskilled be expected to change those processes implemented by the ones who know best? Their inability to successfully challenge the experts further enhanced the 'power' exercised by service providers.

The consequence was a socially constructed image of learning disability in which the experts were seen as essential to the processes, and the disabled individual was perceived in total as *not* being able to meet societal norms. The fact was that society had developed a more materialistic approach to life as a result of its adopted capitalist economic policies which excluded this disabled group, who were not only different but were also costly to maintain, time-consuming and unproductive.

The lack of challenge and failure to come forward as advocates who might question the newly implemented processes and policies led to the application of learning provision aimed at meeting 'normal' targets to be applied throughout the entire service provision. Today, the similarities in documentation processes, plans and formats throughout the entire service provision enable caregivers to move freely and easily into a multitude of roles in almost any organization. The service provision is so predictable in that the activities experienced by all learning disability client groups are almost identical through the mass adoption of these processes, all targeted at the society to enable an eventual acceptance of the planned client in terms of their targeted normal functioning.

It appears that a proviso has been applied which insists the differences expressed by people with learning disabilities will be minimal, to such an extent that one would be shocked to see a 'punk' with Down's syndrome, or accept that a women with cerebral palsy enjoys a variety of sexual partners. The predictability of outcome is such a reality now that individual needs and care-planning have become philosophical misnomers.

Occasionally isolated pockets of resistance emerge to challenge these processes but these are,

unfortunately, short-lived. Control and power remain in the hands of the bureaucracies which run service provision. They eradicate variations in care by withdrawing funding due to the cost implications of initiatives. Alternatively, they might enlist their own managers who initially support and eventually bring the deviation back into line, by enveloping them into existing care networks whose influence is too great to be withstood, as the rules and policies gradually introduced eliminate the possibility of continued or further variation.

The person with a learning disability is also the victim here in that they, too, fail to challenge the discourses of the professional organizations. They conform to the imposed expectations which at best only guarantee them second class citizenship – a social underclass tolerated, sympathized with and often ridiculed. The activities and learning opportunities do not empower the individual, neither do they encourage enterprise, adventure or risk. They fail to result in ownership and autonomy and what is significantly absent is the creative and spontaneous approach which Whelan and Speake (1984) stress when indicating that most of us learn as a result of everyday experiences. What has resulted is a dull 'blanket' application of unimaginative and predictable care process formats. These fail to produce any real-life successes with people with learning disability to become rich and famous, influential or businesslike. There are no corporates or companies enjoying financial booms, and the public continue to see the socially constructed image of inability.

Why is this approach perpetuated, and a possible variation from 'norms' seen as a fantasy? It might be that to consider new sets of norms inclusive of the variation in human behaviour that learning disability is known for, might be an answer. Concepts such as age-appropriate and normalization perhaps need to view the variations in normality before they are applied to the care processes for people with learning disability. What we teach is an area of concern in that it is the expectations of non-disabled people rather than the result of having listened to people with learning disabilities and having accepted them for who they actually are.

5.7 Creating the Appropriate Learning Environment

Learning environments, like any other environments, should be reflective of the people who use them. An environment is a space which has its own culture, image and philosophy and should be specific in its aim to reflect this. A bedroom that contains a dishwasher or is lacking in a bed would be particularly inappropriate, although should not be considered to be unacceptable. Likewise, a classroom that contains a teacher but not a blackboard should not be judged as lacking in resources. A public bar that omits to create a culture, for example for the young or the local community, may state that it has a multifaceted audience, although arguably lacks an identity for the people wishing to consume its beverages and partake in its social activities.

Learning environments are not confined to educational establishments such as schools, colleges or universities, but are available in any given situation, whether at home or at church or within the context of a relationship, whether painful or pleasurable.

The community within the environment should not be seen in isolation. It forms part of the environment, not only by its numbers but by the affect it brings to the overall dynamics of the experience. Whether these people are carers, parents, siblings, facilitators or others who require a similar environment, they should not be seen in isolation, but in the context of the whole picture. Those participating within this environment should be made aware of the impact on each other and on the culture within. The 'community' should be involved in the making of the environment, the politics, the norms, the boundaries and the experiences.

In the process of designing or unfreezing an environment to create a healthy community to enable or facilitate the process of learning, professionals should concern themselves with the inclusion of new opportunities, experiences and, most importantly, involvement – not just as passengers – but all participants taking their turn in a role or roles which may include roles of driver, nurturer, clown, deceiver, etc.

Reader Activity 5.5
Have you ever taken 'risks' to promote the needs of people in your care? What were they and what did they achieve?

The facilitation of people adopting changing roles requires courage on the part of the enabler, the courage to take risks, to manage outcomes and to support the same. All of us adopt roles to match given situations, roles we feel comfortable in and roles we must adopt to achieve goals. People with a learning disability usually have no such demands placed upon them other than that of complier, or predictor; a person with a learning disability who adopts a role outside of this description is often termed 'demanding' or 'challenging'.

All of us have met people who fit these latter descriptions, yet it is unlikely that these people were administered medication or sent to another environment. A friend who becomes challenging or unreasonable is accepted as the same; they remain a friend and are often unconditionally regarded, and more often are given the opportunity to act out their behaviour, to speak about it and to shout about it.

The designer of this environment or experience should consider the non-adaptation of this activity to meet the norms of society, its organization and its structure, but seriously considering adapting society to the experience. An example of this would be the Disabled Olympics, or the adaptation of buildings to ensure that access to disabled people is more viable or, more overtly, by moving groups of people from institutions to individual homes, flats, houses, etc. For all of the events described previously, the strides take time, interventions by acts of law or substantial pressure from groups of people.

An environment needs to be cultivated; this skill should not be underestimated. Social scientists have been studying this for years – changing, adapting or moulding these environments requires careful planning. The argument is, of course, that behavioural change often precedes cultural change, since culture is an adaptive learning process that responds to the needs of the people.

Resourcing an environment usually creates a whole range of problems, such as appropriateness, safety and cost. Much time is spent on the subject of appropriate materials with regard to age and safety when in fact the time should be spent on what the ideal outcome should be, and what this environment should enable people to achieve, learn and experience.

The risk at this stage is to consider assessing the individual, gleaning information from the baseline to enable carers to demonstrate development, when the assessment should ideally incorporate 'what do you want to achieve?'. It is possible that service-users wish to achieve goals that, as service-providers, we do not see the benefit of, or we have not prioritized as essential to the service-user's goals. A good example of this is a service-user who may wish to acquire the skills of betting in a bookmaker's. The service-provider will consider this unsafe and will justify the reasoning behind this by using their value judgements and imposing them upon the service-user, thus ensuring that the goals achieved are of a desirable nature, for example Jonathan can now independently use the washing machine. The service-user – however adept at using the washing machine – has conceded to the predictable plan arranged for him, and remains dissatisfied by having never entered a bookmaker's.

5.8 Care Planning as a Means of Enriching the Learning Experience

Using a life plan or care plan as a resource to facilitate learning and development for people with a learning disability is usually implemented by applying comprehensive documents and processes, without which an individual's needs could more often be forgotten or ignored. This planning process is usually completed by service-providers to document/prove and justify the service-user's development. If implemented with creativity, ingenuity and entrepreneurialism, such planning can ensure that an individual's life plan is neither boring nor predictable. The constraints that service-providers face are those enforced by the organization, society and its own culture. To enable life planning that is meaningful and valued would require the service-provider with the service-user to lobby the external forces, and then account and justify why this action is taken. To challenge one's own culture and judgement would require great inner strength and the support of others in the process of this achievement.

In terms of the right learning environment, the notions of service accomplishments developed by O'Brien and Tyne (1981) enabled the caregiver to perceive the aspect of individual choice as 'a central position in normalisation' (Emerson, 1991, p. 14) which as Emerson (1991) points out differentiated them from some other theories in that they were devoid of the sociological trappings.

The service accomplishments are uncomplicated and generally well known, and a number of variations have appeared based upon them which indicate the impact they have had upon the services themselves. Brandon and Brandon (1988) created an even simpler set of principles based upon ordinary living which create an even more central role for the person with a learning disability and, more importantly, ask the caregiver to consider more carefully their role and the organization in which they work. The introduction of concepts such as 'deviancy magnification' (Brandon and Brandon, 1989) enables the carer to pursue a life style for the person which is shared far more with members of the public when considering aspects such as being 'judged by the company they keep' (Brandon and Brandon, 1989, p. 8), and by the environments that are frequented.

Imagery and the dynamics associated with it have resulted in attitudes prevalent in service facilities and surrounding localities:

Physically moving people into locally based facilities does not ensure people with learning disabilities will interact. (Chisholm, 1993, cited in Shanley and Starrs, 1993, p. 44)

In order to provide the most appropriate learning environment, it is important to recognize the local community as the most essential teaching resource, and create a 'day-long' learning process (Brudenell, 1986).

O'Brien and Tyne (1981) offer five main areas which help us to consider what should be taught. These are displayed in Box 5.1

Development of skills in an individual will increase that person's overall competency but those skills should not only reflect personal preference but also should assist in the development of their own identity. They should promote a set of personal characteristics that enable the individual to feel a valued member of society. It is not abnormal to have individual idiosyncrasies, if anything, it is abnormal not to have them. By promoting the opportunities to enable people with learning disabilities to participate in life's activities, the consequence of whether they fail or achieve is more likely to be that of respect from others but, more importantly, for themselves. It is important to create 'memories' which in turn offer the person with a learning disability the chance to express these, share them and increase the significance of their interaction. It

is a commonly held belief that most people's friendships are based upon a sharing of some form of experience. If people with learning disabilities are to be afforded the chance to really mix with others – non-disabled or not – then it is essential that they share similar experiences, good or bad, risky or not, weird or dull, in order to be able to develop common interests and overcome discrimination.

5.9 Carer or Controller – Cared for, Cared by or Caring With?

In considering the educative role of the carer one's initial urge is to provide a description of a multifunctional individual equipped to provide a range of learning activities for people with learning disabilities. It is tempting to provide the reader with an image of an individual with expertise planning and co-ordinating care activities for their client group. Do the carers need reminding to congratulate success at any level, bearing in mind that some people are unable to cope with too much praise, or that we must have methods of recording and evaluation of pressure which adhere to local policies and guidelines? A number of books and articles exist which provide the carer with the necessary information pertaining to these matters.

It is important to address the attitudinal domain when considering learning for people with learning disabilities. Consideration of the process outside of the limitations and expectations currently available is essential.

Being real and seeing clients/students/people with learning disabilities as real requires a change in the current modes of thinking which tend to negate the wide range of learning activities which exist outside of planned regimes. Rogers (1983) stated that:

professional training and experience has resulted in a conditioning where one thinks of oneself as the expert, the information giver, the keeper of order, the evaluator of products, the one who formulates that goal. (Rogers, 1983, p. 2)

Box 5.1 Teaching: five key areas

- **Ensuring a presence within a community**
- **Utilizing fully what is available through the exercising of individual choice**
- **Remembering that choices are important**
- **Undertaking the options and consequences**
- **Minimizing the 'influence' we are able to exercise over another's choice**

Believing that one would be destroyed if they allowed themselves to emerge as human – not just the 'expert' they appear to be – with good and bad days and with times when 'I don't know' is the only response some professionals are able to offer.

Too often the carer finds it difficult to acknowledge their own human failing, which limits their flexibility to create learning situations. More appropriate and less rigid regimes will create a joy of learning in an individual rather than a specific outcome.

Society is obsessed with improving our ability to instruct, impart knowledge and skills, to show, direct or even guide. Rogers (1983) notes that for too long, too many people have been guided and directed without being really sure of what it is they should actually know. Too often we teach things which quickly change or are inappropriate in a different context. Nothing stays the same and therefore the goal of education should be the facilitation of change and learning (Rogers, 1983), especially for people with learning disabilities who face disrupted life styles on such a consistent basis.

There is a need to break free from the existing almost stereotypic approaches and create:

> a freedom – freedom with responsibility, a freedom in which the excitement of significant learning flourishes. (Rogers, 1983, p. 2)

When one considers the formats, programmes and schedules so consistently applied one is reminded of an aphorism attributed to W. H. Auden who said that 'the lecturer is someone who talks in someone else's sleep'. This seems to adequately reflect the approaches so often adopted with learning today. Mullawney (1983) cites a 1969 Education report which noted that:

> there are children leaving national schools who in all their time there have scarcely ever opened a book other than a textbook, or who have never been encouraged to develop their natural interest in living creatures, who have never been asked to listen to a piece of music, and who have never made anything

with their hands apart from the plasticine figurines which they made in infant class. (Mullawney, 1983, p. 83)

This quote seems to echo the concerns felt when teachers fail to recognize the many learning opportunities that occur outside of their planned activities, and in consequence create the predicted planned 'individual' who totally lacks any individuality. There is a tendency to turn learning into a challenge with its reward and punishment procedures, whereas:

> when you move out into the real world and find learning and punishment brought into everyday relationships, it appears disgusting. (Mullawney, 1983, p. 30)

Hence there is no need to create situations which in effect inhibit learning through creating a fear of not achieving, and in turn creating failure identities.

Learning is not meant to be abstract – it is a real positive and all-embracing activity from conception to death. Education of a formal nature is only part of the process of becoming a whole person.

Rogers (1983) sees teaching as vastly over-rated. He sees the initiation of learning as not dependent upon:

- **teaching skills**
- **scholarly knowledge of the field**
- **curriculum planning**
- **audiovisual aids**
- **programmed learning used**
- **lectures and presentation**
- **an abundance of books.**

Although these can each be utilized at some time as important learning resources, Rogers sees that the:

> facilitation of significant learning rests upon certain attitudinal qualities that exist in the personal relationship between the facilitator and the learner. (Rogers, 1938, p. 121)

The qualities which are seen as essential are related to being human, showing acceptance, valuing another person, placing trust and being able to empathize (Rogers, 1983). Hence learning needs to be exciting, fun-filled and experienced in an atmosphere which encourages the learner to want to learn more.

It is not our professional expertise that will enable learning to occur, but our ability to develop a meaningful relationship with the person with a learning disability where trust is present and sharing occurs. The rewards for an excellent facilitation are different from those of a brilliant teacher:

> People might remember vividly the brilliant teachers they had, but they may not remember what they had learned from them, but it is possible that they might remember in detail the learning experience they had themselves initiated. (Rogers, 1983, p. 40)

This leads us to consider the importance of shared activities where cues are taken from both the learner and the environment. Where the valuing of individuals is present and sharing occurs, the opportunities to learn seem to escalate. In recent years staff have had the opportunity to accompany people away from their homes and places of residence:

> Friendships have also had an opportunity to develop strongly through the week-long attendance at national events where the emphasis is not only on sport but on being away together. Other skills have developed . . . with the opportunity for social interaction. Individuals have grown in stature, their self-esteem greatly enriched by the opportunities offered. Through participation they have become more accomplished, been successful and enjoyed themselves – a true measure of success. (Lewis, 1990)

Although opportunities such as these do not occur frequently they can provide a template for the way in which the relationship between teacher and student should be viewed. Taking greater responsibility for the learning experience will create the individual who is able to adapt and willing to learn from whatever opportunity may occur whether planned or not.

A further example of this occurred where retreats were utilized with students of nursing (Lewis and Bedford, 1996) where the opportunity was created to enable the students to accept a degree of responsibility for the learning process and, at the same time, to develop greater intimacy between teacher and students, the result being memorable learning experiences, unlikely to be forgotten.

> The informality and involvement of living together almost always ensures that barriers are broken down and facades lifted. For better or worse most individuals will come out of their shell, and find the strength to be themselves. (Lewis and Bedford, 1996)

Could this be the answer to learning with people with learning disabilities? Spontaneous exploitation of the moment, true valuing of the individuals, shared experience coupled with intimacy and honesty? Too often we not only underestimate the ability of people with learning disabilities but their thinking, too. How often do we really consider their aspirations and hopes?

> Life is where you find it. I'm really a mature girl. I dream of happier things to come in my life.
> (Women's Groups William Bruson Centre, cited in Atkinson and Williams, 1990)

Discussion Questions

1 **What events are the most vivid in your experience as:**

   (a) a child at school?

   (b) an adult learner?

2 **Why is this?**

3 **How can routine activities of care be adapted to create learning opportunities?**

4 **How can the need to create a learning environment be reflected in the life style of a person with a learning disability?**

References

Atkinson, D. and Williams, F. (1990) *Know Me As I Am. An anthology of prose, poetry and art by people with learning difficulties.* London: Open University/Hodder & Stoughton.

Blunden, R. (1989) *Facing the Challenge,* Blunden, R. and Allen, D. (Eds). London: Kings Fund.

Brandon, D. and Brandon, A. (1989) *Putting People First – A handbook on the practical application of ordinary living principles.* Hamilton Press/Hexagon Publishing.

Brown, H. and Smith, H. (Eds) (1992) *Normalisation: A reader for the nineties.* London: Routledge.

Brudenell, P. (1986) *The Other Side of Profound Handicap.* London: Macmillan Education.

Curzon, L.B. (1990) *Teaching in Further Education: An outline of principles and practices,* 4th edn. London: Cassell.

Emerson, E. (1991) *Evaluating the Challenge.* London: Kings Fund.

Lewis, D. and Bedford, R. (1996) Retreat – the benefits to nurse education. *Professional Nurse* **11**(5): 293–294.

Lewis, D. (1990) Sporting life. *Nursing Times* **86**(45): 33–35.

Mackay, G. (1986) *Early Communication Skills.* London: Routledge.

Mullawney, M. (1983) *Anything School Can Do, You Can Do Better,* Fontana, (2nd edn, 1985).

O'Brien, J. and Tyne, A. (1981) *The Principle of Normalisation: A foundation for effective services.* London: CMH.

Parrish, A. (Ed.) (1982) *Mental Handicap.* MacMillan.

Parrish, A. (1987) *Mental Handicap (essentials of nursing).* Houndmills: Macmillan.

Rogers, C. (1983) *Freedom to Learn.* New York: Merrill.

Shanley, E. and Starrs, T. (Eds) (1993) *Learning Disabilities – A handbook of care,* 2nd edn. Edinburgh: Churchill Livingstone.

Whelan, E. and Speake, B. (1980) *Learning to Cope.* London: Souvenir Press.

Whelan, E. and Speake, B. (1984) *Learning to Cope.* Human Horizon series. London: Souvenir Press.

Wolfensberger, W. and Glenn, L. (1982) *Programme Analysis of Service Systems (PASS). A method for the quantitative evaluation of human services.* Ontario: York University.

Part Four: Biological Dimension of Learning Disability

In understanding the relationship between the phenomenon of learning disabilities and health, it is important to have knowledge of both causation and the various manifestations of learning disabilities. Within the field, academics have for some time appeared almost exclusively preoccupied with a particular agenda, for example social policy and issues of shared training. This has resulted in the study of and available literature on some of the dimensions of learning disabilities being neglected. This part of the book does not represent a re-emergence of the medical model, rather it is an attempt to portray the complexities of how certain conditions may be caused and the particular challenges to health caused by their particular manifestations. Some might argue that understanding the causation and manifestations of learning disabilities is unimportant. This is not the case, the people concerned are whole people; just as the educational and psycho-social dimensions of learning disabilities impact on the lives of people with learning disabilities, so too does the biological dimension. In Chapter 6, Susan Joseph provides an authoritative account of the various causes of learning disabilities. She traces various aetiological factors and provides a clear account of pre-, peri-, and post-natal causes. The reader is presented with an account of malformations of the central nervous system, chromosomal disorders and primary genetic disorders. She concludes with a section that outlines the performance targets of the World Health Organisation concerning the prevention of conditions that limit intellectual development. In Chapter 7, Adrienne Regan and Bob Gates use a case history approach to depict some manifestations of different disorders found in learning disability. This chapter develops the exploration of their causation and links it to the sometimes unique challenges to health that the people affected face. It will be demonstrated in this chapter that there is a clear correlation between some disorders and the health of the individuals concerned. It is imperative that nurses and other professional carers understand the relationship between causation, manifestation and the health of people; such an understanding has the potential to positively affect the knowledge and skills of carers that will impact on the health of people with learning disabilities.

Chapter 6: Causation of learning disability
Susan Joseph

6.1 Introduction

The prolonged gestationary period of 9 months, between conception and birth, makes the human brain particularly vulnerable to pathological processes. The developing embryo and the fetus may be affected by a number of adverse factors that may cause major structural abnormalities of the brain and subsequent dysfunction, that could result in learning disabilities. The developing brain may be affected by genetic factors, including chromosomal and genetic aberrations, as well as by adverse environmental factors that include infective agents and environmental toxins such as alcohol or lead. Depending on the site and the developmental period at which the damage was sustained, and the nature of the pathological process concerned, a wide variety of brain functions may be affected, with particularly disastrous effects on the development of motor, sensory and intellectual function. This chapter provides a broad overview of a number of causes of learning disability.

6.2 Aetiological Factors

Generally speaking, learning disability may be caused by hereditary or environmental factors or a combination of both. It may be determined by a single abnormal gene or a combination of genes or by various harmful external factors affecting the brain early or late in embryonic, fetal or postnatal life. Two different but overlapping varieties of learning disability can be identified (Box 6.1).

> **Box 6.1 Two different, but overlapping varieties of learning disabilities**
>
> - The subcultural form, in which a combination of genetic and environmental factors conspire together.
> - The pathological group in which genetic, chromosomal, infective, toxic or traumatic factors are responsible for producing the severe degree of learning disability.

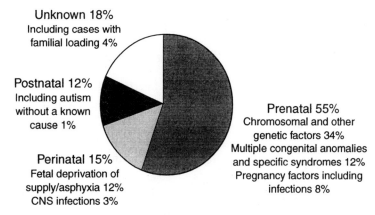

Figure 6.1 The aetiological panorama of severe mental retardation (adapted from Hagberg and Kyllerman, 1983).

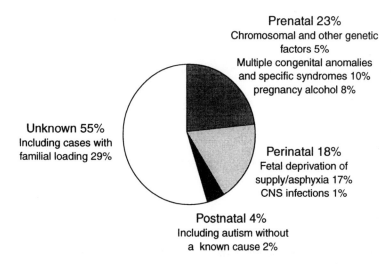

Figure 6.2 The aetiological panorama of mild mental retardation (adapted from Hagberg and Kyllerman, 1983).

It can be seen in Figure 6.1 that in the case of severe learning disability, prenatal causes account for 55% of the total cases, with chromosomal and genetic factors being predominant. Perinatal and postnatal factors contribute to 15% and 12% respectively with aetiology remaining unknown in the remaining 18%.

On the other hand (see Figure 6.2) in the cases of mild learning disability, prenatal factors account for only 23% of cases, with perinatal and postnatal factors contributing to 18% and 4% respectively, the aetiology remaining unknown in 55% (Hagberg and Kyllerman, 1983).

Severe Learning Disability

The aetiology of severe learning disability can often be established accurately. Chromosomal abnormalities and enzyme deficiencies due to single-gene, or in some cases multiple-gene, defects account for most cases. In some cases the aetiology cannot be established with certainty but a plausible cause can be inferred as in the case of perinatal asphyxia, infections and disorders due to environmental toxins including alcohol poisoning or environmental lead. Hagberg and Kyllerman (1983) in their study of aetiology of severe learning disability in Sweden found a definite, or highly probable, cause in just over 80% of cases, two-thirds of which were of prenatal origin and the remainder of perinatal or postnatal origin.

Chromosomal disorders particularly Down's syndrome (trisomy 21) accounted for more than half the cases among the prenatal factors and in a further 20% multiple congenital anomalies were present in the absence of chromosomal abnormalities. Neonatal infections accounted for 13% of the cases, while clear genetic disorders without chromosomal abnormalities accounted for less than 10%. The perinatal factors were accounted for by fetal deprivation and asphyxia in most cases with perinatal infections of the central nervous system in a minority of cases. Postnatal factors were variable.

Mild Learning Disability

It is more difficult to arrive at correct aetiological diagnosis in mild learning disability, and, as shown by a study by Hagberg and Kyllerman (1983), a definite or highly probable cause was found in just under 45% of the cases.

More than half of the known or probable causes were of prenatal origin with a very different pattern from that seen in severe learning disabilities. One-third of the prenatal causes were accounted for by fetal alcohol exposure and identifiable chromosomal abnormalities were much less common in people with severe learning disability. However, several cases of multiple congenital anomalies were found to be relatively common in this group. The perinatal factors were relatively common and almost all of these were associated with fetal deprivation and asphyxia. Postnatal factors were a rare cause for mild learning disability and of the 55% of mild learning disability cases without a known or probable cause, more than half showed familial clustering.

6.3 Prenatal Causes

Infectious Diseases

Infectious diseases in the fetus result in two main types of consequences. If the infection occurs early in pregnancy, tissue damage disturbs the subsequent brain development thus resulting in brain malformations. Infections in the later gestational stages cause inflammatory and destructive changes with subsequent gross tissue necrosis and calcification of the brain. Calcification of the brain in a newborn infant strongly points towards an infectious, rather than a genetic, cause. Fetal infections may result in abortion or still birth at one extreme, while at the other end, the infection may not be apparent at birth and can only be detected with blood tests or it may result in delayed complications such as hearing loss, microcephaly, learning disability or ocular lesions that may only become obvious after the passage of several years.

Brain malformations induced by infections depend on the time of action of the teratogen and the type of infection, with the first trimester being the most dangerous period and congenital malformations becoming less common during the second trimester.

Most embryonic and fetal infections are due to the action of viruses and most are transmitted to the fetus via the placenta, with the exception of late bacterial disorders. The invading virus may result in the death of fetal cells or in their reduction or arrest of cell growth with some viral infections persisting for months or years in the affected individual.

The most important infections that affect the fetal brain include toxoplasmosis, cytomegalic inclusion disease, rubella, syphilis, herpes simplex virus infection and human immunodeficiency virus infection; each of these are now discussed.

Congenital Toxoplasmosis

Congenital toxoplasmosis is caused by *toxoplasma gondii*, which is a protozoan parasite whose usual host is the domestic cat. The disease is transmitted by ingestion of the tissue cyst. Transmission to the fetus occurs across the placenta, usually after the second month of gestation from the mother who more commonly shows a subclinical infection. The infection is most common during the third trimester and usually results in occular disease. The placental infection precedes fetal infection.

Cerebral lesions of toxoplasmosis include areas of necrosis and calcification and inflammation of the inner lining of the ventricles in the brain, resulting in blockage of the aqueducts and subsequent hydrocephalus. The parasite may be seen in recent lesions. Hydrocephalus resulting from aqueductal stenosis is often associated with severe brain damage, learning disabilities and epilepsy. Inflammation of the choroid and retinal layers of the eye is found in up to 85% of the cases. *Toxoplasma gondii* can be isolated from the abnormal cerebrospinal fluid. In some cases, toxoplasmosis may manifest itself in the first few months of life and produces a less severe disease form with choroido retinitis being the most frequent feature with accompanying microcephaly, intracranial calcification and various neurological symptoms and signs.

Subclinical infection is the most common form of congenital toxoplasmosis and results from late contamination. Its diagnosis rests on systematic serological tests that permit prenatal diagnosis. It may remain asymptomatic or may be complicated by the late appearance of choroido retinitis.

The diagnosis is usually made by tests measuring the immunoglobulin G (IGG) or immunoglobulin M (IGM) specific antibodies. Maternally transmitted IGG antibody may persist beyond 6 months of age. Neonatal diagnosis can be suspected when maternal infection occurs early in pregnancy. It is the case that 95% of fetuses do not become infected as shown by testing the cord blood. Ultrasound examination would be helpful for the assessment of lesions in prenatal and postnatal periods but a computerized axial tomographic scan (CAT scan) would be more precise.

Treatment

Most infections caused by *toxoplasma gondii* are self-limiting and do not require specific therapy. However, treatment is essential for those infants who are immunosuppressed and those with eye involvement. Treatment of choice is a combination of pyrimethamine and sulphadiazine given for several weeks. Treatment should be monitored by serial blood counts and possible bone marrow depression can be prevented by folinic acid 5–10 mg per day orally or parenterally. Treatment appears to reduce the risk of secondary choroiditis and may limit brain damage. Neurosurgery may be indicated for active hydrocephalus.

Prevention

Prevention is based on systematic serological diagnosis of maternal infections. Spiramycin has little effect on severe brain damage in the first trimester infections. Neonatal blood sampling may rule out infection and thus avoid termination in up to 95% of cases. Avoiding undercooked meat and contact with cat faeces is effective.

Congenital Rubella

Infection with the rubella virus, during infection, frequently affects the central nervous system in addition to heart and blood vessels of the fetus. The frequency of congenital rubella following maternal infection is over 80% during the first 12 weeks of pregnancy, and over 50% during the weeks 13–14 and 25% at the end of the second trimester. Severe malformations occur in virtually all fetuses infected before the 12th week. One-third of those infected during the 13th to 16th week show deafness and infants infected during the second trimester tend to show delayed mental development and disorders of communication. Intrauterine growth retardation is commonly seen. Intrauterine infection has also been seen following immunization with rubella vaccine which should not be given to women who may be pregnant. The virus may remain persistent several months after birth in the infant and may be reactivated by postnatal stress.

Prognosis

Prognosis of congenital rubella is severe, most children are deaf and a significant proportion also show low visual acuity or blindness due to cataracts or choroido retinitis.

Treatment

There is no effective treatment for rubella.

Prevention

The disease has become rare in developed countries since the vaccination of prepubescent girls has become routine.

Cytomegalovirus (CMV) Infection

CMV infection is a common viral disease known to be transmitted *in utero* and to affect the central nervous system. Incidence of infection ranges from 0.2 to 2.2% of all live births. Fewer than 10% of infected infants show symptoms at birth and 5–10% of asymptomatic infants are at risk of developing neurological complications within the first 2 years of life. Maternal disease is transmitted to the fetus across the placenta. Sensory–neural hearing loss is the most common clinical manifestation and the risk of severe disease seems greater when infection is acquired during the first 4–24 weeks of pregnancy. Virus reactivation and spread can take place despite maternal immunity and infection can also occur at birth through contact with an infected cervix. Transfusions of unscreened blood can result in infection of preterm infants.

Clinical manifestations of CMV infection, which may appear during the neonatal period or early infancy, include enlargement of the liver and spleen, microcephaly, hyperbilirubinaemia and thrombocytopenia with petechial haemorrhages. Infected infants are occasionally preterm and small for gestational age. Among infants who are symptomatic at birth there is a high risk of death and 90% of survivors have sequelae in the form of learning disabilities, seizures, microcephaly and choroido retinitis.

Further, 5–15% of infected asymptomatic newborns develop sensory–motor hearing loss that is bilateral in half the cases and may be progressive; hydrocephalus is only rarely present.

Treatment

Treatment of symptomatic CMV infection by antiviral drugs, Ganciclovir or Foscarnet, is effective but brain damage is usually extensive by the time of birth.

Prevention

Prevention is not feasible at present but female employees in their reproductive years should be informed of the potential risk and strict hygienic measures enforced.

Herpes Simplex Virus (HSV) Infection

This is much less common than CMV infection. Primary maternal infection with HSV appears to carry a significant risk to the fetus both early in pregnancy and at term. In the first 20 weeks of pregnancy primary infection is associated with an increased frequency of spontaneous abortions and still birth (Robb *et al.,* 1986). Severe brain abnormalities may occur including instances of choroido retinitis, microcephaly and microphthalmia. Recurrent infection is the most common form of infection during gestation but more often infection is acquired during labour and vaginal delivery. Symptoms most commonly appear in the first week but may occur in the ensuing 3 weeks of the neonatal period. If maternal herpetic lesions are present at the onset of labour, Caesarian section is often recommended. Prophylactic administration of the antiviral drug, Acyclovir, to women with genital herpes at delivery or to asymptomatic babies is not now indicated.

Treatment

HSV is susceptible to Idoxuridine and Acyclovir. Most infections resolve spontaneously.

Prevention

Acyclovir does not eradicate HSV from posterior root ganglia and recurrent attacks and therefore it cannot be prevented.

Varicella Zoster Virus Infection

These infections rarely occur during pregnancy and transmission to the fetus occurs in around a quarter of cases, although no significant adverse consequences follow. A few fetuses infected before 20 weeks gestation show hypoplasia of the limbs, skin lesions and occular abnormalities. Of 27 such infants studied (Paryani and Arvin, 1986) half were small for their gestational age, 11 had motor or sensory disturbances of the limbs and 10 had choroido retinitis and brain damage. Varicella occurring during the last few days of pregnancy can produce severe neonatal disease and when varicella occurs during the last 5 days, preventive administration of specific gammaglobulin and Acyclovir to the infant has been advised.

Treatment

No treatment is required in the majority of patients. Acyclovir may be used in immunocompromised patients.

Prevention

Human antivaricella gammaglobulin (zoster immune globulin) may be given to immunocompromised children who have been in contact with chicken pox.

Other Viruses

No consistent pattern of malformation or fetal disease has been found with smallpox, influenza A and B, measles or hepatitis virus, though cases of aqueductal stenosis have been reported following maternal mumps.

Box 6.2 Human immunodeficiency virus (HIV) infection

Human Immunodeficiency Virus (HIV) Infection

HIV infection of mothers is transmitted to the foetus in approximately 30% of the cases. Most mothers are seropositive but do not show symptoms of the disease during pregnancy. HIV can be transmitted as early as 15 weeks gestation but perinatal or postnatal infection can also take place as demonstrated by the presence of the virus in cervical secretions and breast milk. Infected neonates are severely affected and about 20% die by 18 months. Infants of HIV-positive mothers have been found to be smaller at birth than uninfected controls and some investigators have described a dysmorphic syndrome including prenatal growth retardation and abnormalities of the cranium and craniofacial abnormalities.

Diagnosis in the new born is difficult because passively transmitted antibodies are present in the infant's blood. The detection of proviral sequences of HIV may be promising for the early diagnosis of HIV infection.

Treatment

There is no specific therapy for HIV infection. Certain antiviral drugs such as Zidovudine can suppress the virus.

Prevention

No vaccine is yet available. Prevention of transmission of infection depends on:

- modification of sexual practices
- screening of donated blood and blood products for HIV antibody
- counselling of persons found to be antibody positive.

Congenital Syphilis

Infection by *Treponema pallidum* can be transmitted from mother to fetus at any time in pregnancy. Neurosyphilis can result in meningeal thickening and inflammatory exudates resulting in hydrocephalus. It can also result in diffuse degeneration of the cerebrum and the cerebellum.

Active fetal infection may result in spontaneous abortion or still birth. Infected infants show enlargement of the liver and spleen, chronic haemorrhagic inflammation of the nasal membranes and inflammation of the bones resulting in osteochondritis. During the first few months of life syphilitic meningitis results in irritability, vomiting and paralysis of the cranial nerves and chronic hydrocephalus.

Tertiary syphilis is now extremely rare and juvenile paralysis only develops many years after birth with marked progressive mental deterioration, disturbed behaviour, spasticity and cerebellar signs. In addition, optic atrophy and deafness may be present. The spinal cord may be occasionally affected. Diagnosis of congenital syphilis is by serological tests. The classical tests (Venereal Disease Research Laboratory and Wasserman) are positive as also the *Treponema palladium* immobilization test and the fluorescent treponemal antibody absorption test. Treatment of neurosyphilis is with aqueous penicillin G 30–60 mg per kilogram per day for 14 days. In cases of penicillin allergy, erythromycin and tetracycline 5–8 mg per kilogram per day every 6 h for 10 days may be used but they are said to be less effective. Negative serological tests should be maintained by 2 years of age and cerebrospinal fluid (CSF) should be re-examined 1 year after completion of treatment.

Circulatory and Vascular Disorders Affecting the Fetus

Disturbances of fetal circulation to the brain, from whatever cause, are a major cause of cerebral damage in the embryo and subsequent neurological disorders and learning disabilities. It is not always possible to separate the damage that occurs prenatally from that sustained during the perinatal and immediate postnatal periods. There is considerable evidence that prenatal factors play the most important role in the genesis of central nervous system (CNS) damage and impairment (Nelson and Ellenberg, 1981; Freeman, 1985).

Fetal circulatory disturbances may result from either maternal anaemia, maternal hypertension and toxaemia of pregnancy, repeated seizures during the second trimester of pregnancy, or from the direct result of trauma to the abdomen of the expected mother. They may also arise from factors related to the fetus such as twins, especially when one twin is macerated, prenatal occlusion of the arteries, blood dyscrasias and haemolytic disease of the new born with or without Rhesus incompatibility.

Abnormalities of the placenta such as chronic placental insufficiency, abrupt separation of the placenta, or knotting of the cord may also give rise to fetal circulatory disturbances. Virtually any type of brain damage may result from fetal circulatory disturbances, depending on the precise nature of the insult, and the gestational age at which it occurs. Circulatory disturbances in general tend to affect the periventricular white matter in preterm babies and the cortex in term infants, while infectious fetal disorders can directly damage the neurons or glial cells by directly inducing circulatory failure.

Although the placenta constitutes an effective barrier, certain therapeutic agents or drugs cross the placental barrier resulting in serious damage to the developing fetus. The Thalidomide disaster has alerted the world to the potential adverse effects of drugs on the developing fetus, when administered to pregnant women. Anticonvulsant drugs such as phenytoin, barbiturates, carbamazepine and sodium valproate can all produce adverse effects on the fetus resulting in fetal malformation, intrauterine growth retardation, facial dysmorphism, congenital heart disease as well as behavioural and cognitive changes in postnatal life (Yerbi, 1988). Some studies have revealed the rate of abnormalities to be as high as 58% among children of women who have received a combination of carbamazepine, phenobarbitone and sodium valproate during pregnancy.

Narcotics like heroin, codeine, methadone, amphetamines and cocaine may all produce fetal growth retardation and a small head, as well as withdrawal symptoms in the newborn. Cocaine can induce abrupt separation of the placenta and fetal death, also it may be responsible for skull and brain malformations.

Inhalation of toluene may result in microcephaly, anomalies of the limbs and other minor craniofacial anomalies.

Tobacco smoking in pregnancy has been known to result in low birth weight infants.

Excessive consumption of alcohol during pregnancy, particularly in excess of 80 ml of alcohol, may result in full blown fetal alcohol syndrome (FAS). Consumption of alcohol throughout pregnancy or during the second and third trimesters is said to result in increased frequency of growth retardation and morphological abnormalities. It is important to note that the occasional 'binge' may also result in the fetal alcohol syndrome. Fetal alcohol syndrome results in intrauterine growth retardation, abnormalities of the face and brain malformations with excess neuronal migration and other CNS defects. The affected infants are short and have a small head circumference and mild degree of learning disability is extremely frequent, being seen in up to 85% of cases.

Toxic Factors

Maternal Phenylketonuria and Hyperphenylalaninaemia

Children born to mothers with untreated phenylketonuria may show microcephaly, intrauterine growth retardation, neurological abnormalities such as cerebral palsy, seizures, or abnormalities of the vertebral column and ribs. The affected children may also be born to asymptomatic phenylketonuric mothers, or to women who have been previously treated for phenylketonuria. A strict diet of low phenylalanine regime should be strictly followed before the onset of pregnancy and blood levels of phenylalanine should be regularly monitored and maintained below 10 mg/dl (Pueschel *et al.*, 1977; Lenke and Levy, 1980).

Diabetes Mellitus

The main problems seen in infants of diabetic mothers are macrosomia and congenital malformations, particularly of the brain and the lower end of the vertebral column. Macrosomia usually develops late in pregnancy, but ultrasonic examination earlier in pregnancy reveals fetal growth delay which is associated with an increased risk of congenital malformations. It is possible to prevent the congenital malformations in the fetus by careful control of diabetes, especially during the first 7–8 weeks of pregnancy when such defects appear.

Intrauterine Growth Retardation and Preterm Birth

Infants whose weight is below the tenth percentile are generally regarded as being growth retarded. Two major subgroups can be identified. Symmetrical growth retardation affects equally body length and weight as well as head circumference and it may be due to chromosomal abnormalities in the fetus or to fetal deprivation from early on in pregnancy. In asymmetrical growth retardation, weight is affected more than length and head growth may be normal. It is mainly seen in fetuses deprived during the later part of gestation as seen in toxaemia of pregnancy. Fetuses with intrauterine growth retardation have malformations or dysmorphic syndromes and approximately 2% of chromosomal abnormalities and less than 3% may have suffered intrauterine viral infections (Lindhal and Michelsson, 1986). In the asymmetrical group maternal haemorrhage, hypertension, renal disease, diabetes, malnutrition, smoking and cardiac disease are all important factors.

Rapid head growth after birth is a favourable prognosis, while infants whose head growth is insufficient at age 2 years have an unfavourable developmental outlook.

Preterm Birth

Preterm birth and a low birth weight are the ultimate consequences of preconceptual, prenatal and perinatal influences. They are more frequently seen in lower socioeconomic groups and with complicated pregnancies. A high proportion of children of very low birth weight (less than 1500 g) have learning disabilities, visual problems or frank cerebral palsy. Regular antenatal medical examination of vulnerable groups of pregnant women along with appropriate medical and social interventions could lessen the burden of preterm birth and consequent neurodevelopmental difficulties.

Reader Activity 6.1
Make reference to other texts on the causation of learning disabilities and see if you are able to identify a range of other prenatal causes of learning disabilities.

6.4 Perinatal Causes

It is not always possible to strictly separate perinatal from prenatal disorders and further the separation is often arbitrary. Prenatal factors, such as intrauterine growth retardation or prenatal hypoxia at preterm birth, may have an important role in the development of subsequent perinatal disorders. The perinatal period is conventionally limited to 28 postnatal days. Two major pathological conditions seen in the perinatal period, giving rise to severe learning disability are as a result of intracranial haemorrhage and postasphyxial encephalopathy. These two conditions can coexist and may be provoked by the same precipitating factors, such as hypoxia and ischaemia.

Intracranial Haemorrhage in the Neonatal Period

While the incidence of traumatic haemorrhage, mainly subdural haemorrhage, has decreased as a result of better obstetric practice, the frequency of intraventricular haemorrhages has increased because they are mainly a disorder of preterm infants, and many more such babies survive now than before. Better imaging techniques have made it possible to make an *in vivo* diagnosis of intraventricular and subarachnoid haemorrhage with great degrees of precision.

Subdural haemorrhages are mainly of traumatic origin and occur in full term often high birth weight babies, whereas intraventricular haemorrhages are at least in part related to asphyxia and predominate in preterm babies (Leblanc and O'Gorman, 1980).

The most frequent type of intracranial haemorrhage in the neonate is the periventricular–intraventricular type of haemorrhage (PIVH). Intraventricular haemorrhage is predominantly seen in preterm infants, though occasionally it may be seen in full-term babies. The incidence is particularly high in very small preterm infants. The possible aetiological factors include deficiency of vascular support and haemodynamic factors, such as changes in arterial pressure being passively transmitted to cerebral vessels of preterm infants who lack autoregulation of brain blood vessels. Increases in blood pressure have been seen to occur in preterm infants during crying, feeding or suctioning and may precipitate bleeding. Asphyxia (hypoxia with hypercapnia) is another important aetiological factor. It aggravates the circulatory disorders by increasing blood flow and disturbs autoregulation. Other aetiological factors include abnormalities of coagulation and use of agents such as alcohol and heparin for flushing catheters.

Prognosis

The cause may be rapidly lethal if the haemorrhage is large and the mortality rate may be as high as 81% (Volpe, 1989). Currently the recovery rate is close to 70%. Hydrocephalus may appear immediately after haemorrhage due to a large obstructing blood clot or may develop progressively within the next 3 weeks following haemorrhage. The incidence of posthaemorrhagic hydrocephalus is less than 10% after mild haemorrhage, 15–20% after a moderate haemorrhage and 65–100% after severe bleeding (Hill and Volpe, 1981).

Prevention

The recognition of the importance of fluctuations of cerebral blood flow in the aetiology of periventricular haemorrhage has led to special precautions being taken to avoid factors which affect systemic blood pressure during labour and delivery and during routine neonatal procedures such as suctioning of infants with respiratory distress. Preventive strategies include simple measures such as early intubation of infants with respiratory distress syndrome, avoiding rapid volume infusions and minimal handling of infants as well as pharmacological interventions such as the curarization of infants to reduce the incidence of bleeding by eliminating fluctuation of blood flow.

Hypoxic Ischaemic Encephalopathy (HIE)

Hypoxic ischaemic encephalopathy (HIE) occurs in 1.5–6 per 1000 live births. The deficit in oxygen supply that leads to HIE can result from hypoxaemia (i.e. a reduced supply of oxygen in the blood) and ischaemia, reduced perfusion of the brain. In most cases both hypoxaemia and ischaemia are due to asphyxia; that is, hypoxia associated with hypercapnia. The prognosis of HIE in term infants depends mainly on the severity of clinical picture during the first days of life. Neurodevelopmental sequelae due to hypoxia are not observed in the absence of clinical manifestations of HIE in the neonatal period. Prognosis for mild HIE is favourable, but the prognosis for severe HIE is poor. No treatment has proved effective in treating HIE and utmost attention should be paid to disturbances in the functioning of other organs such as kidney and heart and immediate correction of metabolic derangements is essential. Control of seizures may increase the chance of a favourable outcome.

The prevention of hypoxic ischaemic brain damage is a major issue that requires the co-operation of obstetricians, paediatricians, child neurologists and neonatologists.

Metabolic Factors in the Neonatal Period

Neonatal Hypoglycaemia

In neonatal hypoglycaemia the blood sugar level is usually found to be less than 20 mg/dl (1.5 mmol/l), although some infants with higher blood sugar levels of 30–40 mg/dl, may show signs of hypoglycaemia, while yet others may not show any symptoms when the blood sugar level is well below 20 mg/dl. Transient hypoglycaemia may be found in up to 11% in new borns during the first hours following birth before oral feeding is commenced. This is especially seen in infants with intrauterine growth retardation or those who have suffered hypoxia at birth or in infants of mothers with diabetes or toxaemia of pregnancy. In addition to the level of blood glucose, the rate of fall of glucose is also important. Neonatal hypoglycaemia essentially seems to result from an imbalance between the demands of a relatively large brain, mainly dependent on glucose as its primary source of energy, and the capacity of a small liver depleted of glycogen reserves. This is especially important in infants who are small for gestational age and may be related to the fact that the brain of the new born infant can use ketone bodies and other fatty acids for its energy supply in addition to glucose.

Up to 50% of infants with neonatal hypoglycaemia are said to show serious mental or motor sequelae, while only 6% of infants without any symptoms later showed neurodevelopmental abnormalities. Lucas *et al.* (1988) found children who had prolonged biochemical hypoglycaemia to be about 13–14 points behind children with normal blood sugar levels when tested on the Bailey's developmental scale.

Neonatal hypoglycaemia is treated by intravenous administration of 25% glucose solution.

Disturbances of Electrolyte Metabolism

In neonatal hypocalcaemia the blood calcium level falls below 1.75 mmol/l (7 mg/dl) and this is often associated with hypomagnesaemia (blood magnesium levels below 0.6 mmol/l (1.5 mg/dl). Early hypocalcaemia occurs mainly in preterm infants, infants who are small for gestational age and infants of diabetic mothers and usually occurs before 48 h of age, whereas late hypocalcaemia develops between 5 and 10 days of life, particularly in infants fed on cows' milk formulae with a high phosphorus content. Late hypocalcaemia may also be seen in infants born to mothers with hyperparathyroidism and may also be seen in the Di George syndrome where seizures may appear before manifestations of immune deficiency.

Hypomagnesaemia may result from malabsorption or with malnutrition and may respond to magnesium supplementation.

Hypercalcaemia and Hypermagnesaemia

Fat necrosis in new born infants may produce hypercalcaemia and it is also seen following intravenous infusion of calcium gluconate and rarely in patients with a defect of intestinal transport of the amino acid tryptophan.

Hypermagnesaemia occurs following administration of large doses of magnesium sulphate to pregnant mothers during treatment of toxaemia of pregnancy.

6.5 Malformations of the Central Nervous System

It is now possible to diagnose many different types of CNS malformations, with the help of CT scan and magnetic resonance imaging. The prenatal diagnosis of genetically determined CNS malformation allows the possibility of genetic counselling and the choice for parents as to whether to prevent the birth of such affected infants, although this raises considerable ethical dilemmas.

Considering the complexity of the processes during the development of the human brain, it is hardly surprising that it is vulnerable to a number of factors that can disturb its normal course of development. Morphological abnormalities of the CNS may arise either during the embryonic or the fetal period of development and may be due to transmission of faulty genetic information, or due to interference with the harmonious development of correct genetic information. Alternatively, malformation may result from damage to normally formed structures as a result of faulty repair and this type usually occurs late in pregnancy.

It is suggested that up to 25% of conceptuses may be affected by disturbances of CNS development and this may account for a high percentage of fetal deaths (Warkany, 1981; Kalter and Warkany, 1983; Freeman, 1985). Evrard *et al.* (1989) have estimated that up to 40% of deaths in the first year of life are related in some way to CNS malformations and a study by Nelson and Ellenberg (1986) indicated that many neurological problems such as cerebral palsy are more frequently of prenatal than postnatal origin and that a significant number of prenatal cases are due to malformations. It is believed that the timing of an insult to the fetus is more important than the nature of the insult in determining the type of resulting malformations as the same noxious agent operating at different periods of development can produce different types of malformations. It has been estimated that about 5% of congenital malformations may result from environmental causes, such as infectious or toxic agents or X-rays or exposure to toluene gas and alcohol. It is held that around 6% of malformations may be due to chromosomal abnormalities and single gene defects may account for another 7.5%, while polygenic inheritance is said to be the cause in 20% of the cases where there is an interaction between environmental and genetic factors. In about 60% of CNS malformations, the cause remains unknown.

Malformations that occur during the first 5 months of pregnancy affect the proliferation and migration of neurones leading to defective cortical genesis, whereas malformations that arise during the latter months of gestation are the result of destructive processes such as ischaemia or infection (Laroche, 1986).

Many CNS malformations may be associated with malformations of the heart or other organs of the body and there is also an association between CNS malformations and more general disturbances in development, the abnormalities being 2.5 times more frequent in people with intrauterine growth retardation than the general population (Khoury *et al*, 1988).

Neural Tube Defects

Failure of the neural tube to fuse completely may result from anencephaly or sacral myelomenigocele or agenesis of the sacrum. Genetic factors seem to be important in the causation of neural tube defects, though usually they are due to polygenic or multi-factorial causes.

A young maternal age and low socioeconomic status and deficiency of the folic acid vitamin have all been associated with neural tube defects. The administration of multivitamin preparations containing folic acid during the first 6 weeks of gestation have shown a significant reduction in the incidence of new cases. The incidence of neural tube defects varies widely in different parts of the world, being low in Japan and reaching up to 3% in the British Isles. Currently there is a sharp decrease in frequency of neural tube defects in western countries.

Prenatal diagnosis of neural tube defects is by the use of ultrasonography and determination of the level of alpha-fetoprotein in the amniotic fluid obtained by amniocentesis. Alpha-fetoprotein accounts for 90% of total serum globulins in the fetus and in open tube defects it leaks into the amniotic fluid and hence into the maternal blood.

The determination of alpha-fetoprotein levels from the amniotic fluid at 16–28 weeks gestation by amniocentesis allows for the detection of 99% of fetuses with neural tube defects. Alpha-fetoprotein levels may also be used as a screening test for neural tube defects at 13–16 weeks of gestation.

Microcephaly/micrencephaly

These conditions result from abnormalities in cellular proliferation that normally takes place throughout the fetal period, although at differing rates. The most active part of proliferation occurs during the first half of pregnancy but it may continue to the end of the first year of life. Proliferation and migration are highly inter-related processes and disturbance of one may invariably affect the other.

Children with a head circumference below the third percentile are referred to as having microcephaly, whereas micrencephaly refers to a small brain. There is an increased prevalence of mild microcephaly among children with learning disability (Smith, 1981) and learning disability may be more common when a small head is associated with growth retardation. The causation of microcephaly is insufficiently understood, disturbances in cellular proliferation being only one of the mechanisms while excessive embryo fetal cell death, or later destruction may be other contributory factors. Primary microcephaly is present by the seventh month of intrauterine life, whereas secondary microcephaly occurs after the seventh month of gestation.

Microcephalia vera refers to a genetic type of microcephaly where the degree of microcephaly is at least 5 or 6 standard deviations below the normal. The brain weight may be as little as 500 g in the adult. Recessive inheritance is said to be more common, though dominant and X-linked transmission have also been recorded. Microcephaly is a feature of a large number of chromosomal abnormalities and dysmorphic syndromes with learning disability.

The non-genetic type of microcephaly may result from a whole host of factors occurring throughout gestation or even in postnatal life, including exposure to X-rays, drugs, noxious chemical agents, severe malnutrition and circulatory insufficiencies. Acquired microcephalies usually show a moderate degree of microcephaly with severe learning disabilities and evidence of destructive changes on the CT scan. The prognosis of microcephaly is variable, some children having relatively good intellectual potential, while others may require special schooling.

Macrocephaly and Megalencephaly

The term macrocephaly like microcephaly is usually defined by reference to head circumference and is applied when 2 standard deviations above the mean occur. Macrocephaly must be distinguished from hydrocephalus or pericerebral collections of fluid because these conditions require immediate treatment. In this condition males outnumber females by 4:1, and 50% of the affected people have a family history of microcephaly.

Megalencephaly

Megalencephaly implies an increased brain weight and it refers to excessive brain weight combined with various developmental anomalies with an increase in both neuronal cells and glial cells. This is often associated with disturbances of migration and organization and sometimes giant abnormal neurones may be present. Brain weight in some cases may be twice as much expected for the age. Learning disability is present in virtually all cases and many of them show diffuse neurological abnormalities and seizures in addition.

6.6 Chromosomal Disorders

Abnormalities of specific chromosomes have been found to be associated with recognized clinical syndromes in man. It has been estimated that 1 in every 200 live-born babies shows a gross abnormality of chromosome number or structure. This figure does not reflect the frequency with which chromosomal anomalies occur in aborted products of conception. Many of these chromosomal abnormalities are rarely found in live-born babies, presumably as they are not compatible with life and hence responsible for a significant number of early abortions. A considerable number of fetuses with chromosomal abnormalities still reach full term and are born with major congenital malformations. Neurological abnormalities, especially impaired intellectual functioning, are extremely common in people with chromosomal anomalies. Chromosomal anomalies can involve either the autosomal chromosomes or the sex chromosomes and most live-born children with structural abnormality involving a pair of autosomal chromosomes will show severe learning disabilities. If alterations of the chromosomes occur in regions of the chromosome where there is little genetic material of importance then the resulting changes are not clinically significant.

As stated above, chromosomal abnormalities can affect either the autosomes or the sex chromosomes and these abnormalities may affect either the number or the structure of the chromosomes. Aneuploidy results when one or more chromosomes are either lost or gained, whereas polyploidy occurs when a whole set of chromosomes is gained and the latter condition is lethal in man. The term monosomy refers to a condition when a whole autosome is lost and this is again lethal in man, whereas the addition of an extra chromosome resulting in three chromosomes instead of two gives rise to trisomy (e.g. trisomy 21, Down's syndrome) which is compatible with survival and near normal life expectancy.

Structural abnormalities of the chromosomes result in deletions when chromosomal breakage takes place and the fragment is lost or gives rise to partial trisomies when there is an extra piece of chromosome, either in the short or long arm of another chromosome.

Ring chromosomes occur when deletions take place at both ends of the chromosomes which then join together to form a ring and inversions occur when the broken section of a chromosome is reinserted the wrong way around.

Isochromosomes consisting of either the two long or the two short arms of the chromosomes may result when during cell division the division takes place horizontally across the centromere instead of longitudinally. Normally, during the meiotic cell division, like chromosomes pair together and exchange material, but when this exchange takes place between non-identical or non-homologous chromosomes a translocation results. Translocation is said to be balanced when the amount of genetic material that is rearranged is identical to that found in the normal cell. Unbalanced rearrangements are clinically significant and result in greater or lesser degree of learning disabilities, whereas balanced rearrangements do not usually produce clinically significant changes.

Disorders of Autosomal Chromosomes

Down's Syndrome (Trisomy 21)

Trisomy 21 is the single most common cause of learning disabilities and the condition occurs on average in about 1 in 650 live births. The frequency varies with maternal age and in mothers aged 45 years or more the frequency is about 1 in 54 births. A high incidence is also observed in infants of very young mothers (Smith and Berg, 1976).

It is the case that 90% of Down's syndrome cases are due to the presence of an extra chromosome 21, whereas 8% of cases may be due to translocation of chromosome 21 to another chromosome. About 1% of Down's syndrome are mosaics; that is, they possess two different cell lines, one of which has a normal chromosome constitution and the other an extra chromosome 21. The clinical picture may often be considerably modified in these cases.

The brain in Down's syndrome is found to be small correlating with a small head circumference of the patient. The cerebellum is found to be disproportionately small and is easily detectable by mag-

netic resonance imaging (MRI) scans. The brains of people with Down's syndrome show the premature development of senile plaques and fibrillary tangles similar to that found in Alzheimer's disease and these plaques are visible from the age of 30 years onwards and show a significant correlation with the development of dementia that occurs in at least one-third of people with Down's syndrome from the age of 40 years onwards.

The birth weight of infants with Down's syndrome is low, about a quarter of them weighing less than 2500 g. The dysmorphic features of Down's syndrome are easily recognizable, even in new-born infants. The face is usually flat with widely spaced and upward slanting eyes; the skull is brachycephalic with a flattened occiput; the ears are simple and malformed with a narrow external auditory meatus; the neck is short and the mouth open with large protruding fissured tongue. The eyes show brushfield spots, a collection of fibrous material on the iris which itself is poorly developed. Keratoconus and cataracts may develop leading to blindness in 8% of cases. Congenital heart lesions, such as ventricular septal defects, atrial septal defects or patent ductus arteriosus is found in 50% of the cases. A transverse palmar crease is seen in about half the patients with characteristic dermatoglyphics (Smith and Berg, 1976). Abnormalities of the gastrointestinal system, such as duodenal stenosis, may be present and umbilical hernias are common. The genitalia are usually underdeveloped and males are usually sterile and although females can reproduce, it is rare. On average, half their offspring is normal and half has Down's syndrome.

Children with Down's syndrome show an increased sensitivity to infection and have an increased risk of autoimmune diseases and leukaemia.

Most people with Down's syndrome show a severe degree of learning disability with the average IQ being around 40–50. Mosaic patients may have higher IQ levels and higher verbal perceptual skills (Fishler *et al*, 1976). Epilepsy may occur in 5–6% of patients and reflex seizures may be more common than other types. Hearing loss is common in children with Down's syndrome and is usually due to the conductive type of deafness.

Antenatal diagnosis can be made by amniotic fluid cell culture or trophoblast biopsy and is indicated in pregnant women older than 35 years and in younger mothers who already have had an affected child. The main medical conditions requiring treatment in Down's syndrome are dementia resulting from hypothyroidism and Alzheimer's disease, neurological complications related to instability of the atlanto-axial joint, repeated respiratory infections and visual and hearing defects (see Chapter 7).

Reader Activity 6.2
In the section that has dealt with Down's syndrome, a number of terms have been used to describe various abnormalities of chromosomal structure. Spend some time ensuring that you understand these terms before progressing with the chapter. Use the glossary at the end of the text to help you understand any terms that you have not encountered before.

Other Trisomy Syndromes

Trisomy 13 (Patau syndrome) probably occurs in about 1 in 4000 to 1 in 10 000 births, the risk increasing with increasing maternal age. The birth weight of infants is around 2400 g and the affected children show a profound degree of learning disability. Characteristic clinical features include microcephaly, severe facial abnormalities, severe bilateral cleft lip and palate, and a small chin. Occular abnormalities are common with eyes being absent in some or others showing small eyes with cataracts and defects of the iris. Congenital defects such as ventricular septal defects or patent ductus arteriosus or transposition of the heart are seen. Dextra position of the heart is seen in 80% of the cases, with renal abnormalities being present in 30–50%. Severe neurological abnormalities are found in most people affected and often infants die before their first birthday with only 5% surviving beyond 3 years of age. Parents should be advised that the

recurrence risks are small, but if the affected patient has an unbalanced translocation, parental examination is essential. If the parent shows a balanced translocation the recurrence rate is high enough to warrant amniocentesis.

Trisomy 18 (Edward's Syndrome)

The incidence of trisomy 18 is around 1 per 8000 births and there is a 4 : 1 female preponderance with increasing maternal age. The mean birth weight is around 2000 g and affected children have a long and narrow skull with a prominent occiput, a small mandible and low-set ears. Major malformations of the brain may be present including partial agenesis of the corpus callosum, anomalies of the cerebellum, and visceral malformations including congenital heart disease, horse shoe shaped kidneys, hydronephrosis and diaphragmatic hernia are common. Cryptorchidism is constant in males. The degree of learning disability is severe and epilepsy is frequently present. Only half survive beyond 2 months and 10% beyond the first years of life.

Other Autosomal Anomalies

Severe learning disability, neurological abnormalities and dysmorphic features are seen in a number of conditions with autosomal chromosomal abnormalities other than trisomies. Some of these associated syndromes show microscopically detectable chromosomal abnormalities which may be partial as well as other types of abnormalities of the autosomal chromosomes such as monosomy, ring chromosomes or interstitial deletions. Molecular studies using deoxyribonucleic acid (DNA) analysis with appropriate DNA probes (Ledbetter *et al.*, 1989) detected abnormalities that were not apparent by cytogenetic studies, for example, Prader–Willi syndrome, Angelman syndrome (see Chapter 7). The small, submicroscopic deletions are associated with a mild form of a particular syndrome whereas large deletions result in severe forms with other associated abnormalities. To be visible, a small deletion must involve at least 2 million base pairs or 40–50 genes (Punnett and Zackai, 1990).

These techniques have revealed that many multi-system disorders are due to involvement of closely spaced genes which are not related through their function, but by their proximity – the contiguous gene syndromes. Other syndromes that may be due to small deletions are William, Rubinstein–Taybi and Cornelia de Lange syndromes.

Prader–Willi Syndrome

Prader–Willi syndrome is relatively frequent and is associated in approximately half the patients with interstitial deletions of chromosome 15q, 11–13 and the deletion in virtually all cases is of paternal origin. New-born infants are generally born at term but are small for gestational age and present with severe hypotonia, severe feeding difficulties that may necessitate tube feeding and some fail to thrive. The muscle tone improves later on and the striking features are the development of hyperphagia and obesity in later childhood. Other dysmorphic features include almond-shaped eyes, small hands and feet and hypogenitalism with crypt orchidism in males. The affected patients usually show a moderate degree of learning disability but occasionally a severe degree of learning disability may be seen as well as normal intelligence. Treatment aims at preventing the development of obesity and providing specialized education.

Angelman Syndrome

Angelman syndrome, formally known as Happy Puppet syndrome, is caused by deletion of chromosome 15, but unlike Prader–Willi syndrome the deletion is of maternal origin. Features consist of a severe degree of learning disability, ataxia with jerking movements of the limbs and trunk and persistently cheerful mood (Williams and Frias, 1982). The majority of affected children have tonic or atonic seizures. Walking is delayed until 5–6 years and is very abnormal, with legs wide apart. CAT scan and MRI do not show any specific change but the electroencephalogram (EEG) suggests a specific type of wave pattern.

Disorders of Sex Chromosomes

Sex chromosome abnormalities are frequent, the incidence being about 1 in 365 live male births and 1 in 661 live female births. The most common abnormalities are XXY (Klinefelter syndrome) and XYY syndrome in males and XXX and XO (Turner syndrome) in females.

The fragile X syndrome previously known as Martin Bell syndrome is the second most common cause of learning disability in the general population.

In general, the XO female will be of normal intelligence but in those with multiple X chromosomes there is an increased risk of learning disability. Learning disability is not a feature of Turner's syndrome and any child with severe learning disability whose chromosome analysis shows an XO pattern must be investigated for other causes of learning disability. The frequency is about 1 in 1000 live female births. About 14% of those aged between 4 and 8 years have an IQ about 25 points below the expected value and few will have IQs less than 70. No specific congenital malformations are associated with XXX females.

Klinefelter's Syndrome

Klinefelter's syndrome occurs in approximately 1 in 1000 live male births. The clinical features of Klinefelter's syndrome do not appear until puberty and sometimes may never occur. About 18% show one or more major congenital abnormalities, of which the most frequent is cleft palate. Development delays may be observed with more than half showing delay in speech development and one-third of them are below the borderline range of IQ. Klinefelter's syndrome is one of the commonest causes of hypogonadism and infertility in males. Most affected males remain infertile, except if they are mosaics. They usually tend to be of dull normal intelligence and seem to show problems with auditory perception as well as language difficulties. It is suggested that 50–75% will show breast enlargement and breast cancer occurs 20 times more frequently than in normal males.

Fragile X Syndrome

The fragile X syndrome is characterized by a morphological abnormality of the X-chromosome, the fragile site having been localized on the long arm of X chromosome involving the q27 or q28 bands. The fragility becomes apparent when a folate-deficient medium is used for culture. It has been estimated that approximately 1 in 1000 females are carriers and that 1 in 1300 males are affected (Blomquist and Gustavon, 1983). The fragile site is no more than a marker and its relationship to learning disabilities and associated anomalies remains unclear. This syndrome accounts for only part of the excess cases of learning disability found in boys, the remaining cases being due to several distinct types of X-linked learning disability, without the presence of non-chromosomal markers.

The recognition of the syndrome becomes easier after puberty. The most important features being a normal physical growth, normal or increased head circumference, a long face with a prominent jaw and macro-orchidism. Prepubescent children show a large head, large ears and high arched palate and other abnormalities include hyperextensibility of the joints and fingers and hyperelastic skin. The degree of learning disability may range from mild to moderate or severe in some adolescents and adults. Many of these people exhibit difficulties in speech, language, behaviour and social skills. Hyperactivity and attention deficit are commonly found and up to 23% may show autistic features. In women carriers, 28% may show facial stigmata, while 35% may have mild learning difficulties.

The diagnosis of fragile X syndrome is difficult, especially in prepubertal boys and in female carriers who do not show any physical findings. Sometimes macro-orchidism or large ears may be unassociated with a fragile site on the X-chromosome. A family history of learning disability is an important feature, but is only seen in two-thirds of cases. Routine

testing of the chromosome is not of much value and the definitive test is a karyo type on special culture medium showing the fragile site in more than a randomly expected proportion. Prenatal diagnosis of fragile X is possible on cultured amniotic cells and on chorionic villi cells. Ethical problems arise because only some carriers, especially among females, will be affected.

Dysmorphic Syndromes Without Chromosomal Abnormalities

Cornelia de Lange Syndrome

The patients affected by this syndrome show a peculiar facial appearance with the eyebrows growing together, a low hair line on neck and forehead, depressed bridge of the nose with upturned nostrils and long eye lashes. There is a moderate degree of microcephaly with short stature and delayed bone maturation. There is a severe degree of learning disability and most affected children never develop speech. About 20% of the patients develop seizures and 30% have congenital heart defects. De Lange's syndrome is thought to be dominantly inherited, virtually all cases being new mutations. A recurrence risk is said to be around 2–5%.

Rubinstein Taybi Syndrome

This syndrome is characterized by short stature, severe learning disability, big nose, broad tongue and toes, and squint. Palms of the hand show unusual dermatoglyphic patterns, suggestive of a chromosomal anomaly, although this has not been demonstrated by high resolution cytogenetics.

William's Syndrome

Individuals affected by this syndrome show supra-valvular aortic stenosis, multiple peripheral pulmonary arterial stenosis, elfin-like face, short stature and moderate to severe learning disability, characteristic dental malformations and infantile hypercalcaemia.

Fifty per cent may develop epilepsy and most show difficulties with motor co-ordination and cerebellar function. An autosomal dominant inheritance has been suggested, but the vast majority of cases appear to be sporadic.

Smith Lemli-Opitz Syndrome

Affected individuals present with peculiar faces with a high square forehead, antiverted nostrils, micrognathia and genital abnormalities in males, including crypt-orchidism or hypospadias and there is marked hypertonia and learning disability. Some patients develop seizures and mortality is high in the first year of life. This syndrome is said to be inherited as an autosomal recessive trait and the higher incidence in males is probably due to the fact that it is more easily diagnosed in males because of the obvious genital abnormalities.

Sotos Syndrome Cerebral Gigantism

The most striking feature of Sotos syndrome is the excessively rapid somatic growth that begins before birth and is associated with advanced bone maturation. The most affected people show learning disability which may range from profound to average IQ. Most cases of Sotos syndrome are said to be sporadic, although dominant transmission has been implicated in some cases.

Reader Activity 6.3
You have now been introduced to a range of different causes of learning disability. Before proceeding with the remaining sections of this chapter it might be worth jotting down those causes that you can remember along with the characteristics of the disorders outlined.

6.7 Primary Genetic Disorders

These disorders are due to defects of a single gene; that is, the primary error is in the DNA code and these are inherited in a simple fashion following Mendelian laws and the risk of the recurrence occurring in a family may be predicted on theoretical grounds making genetic counselling more straightforward. These disorders may be further classified according to the chromosome on which the abnormal or mutant gene is situated and also by the nature of the trait itself. Thus a trait which is determined by a gene situated on an autosome is said to be inherited as an autosomal trait and this may either be dominant or recessive. A trait determined by a gene situated on one of the sex chromosomes is said to be sex linked and this may also be either dominant or recessive.

Nearly 10% of people who have severe learning disability are found to have some genetic abnormality, dominant or recessive, that affects either an autosomal chromosome or a sex chromosome.

Autosomal Dominant Disorders

A single dominant gene of variable expression and penetrance is responsible for the manifestations of the disorder. In contrast to autosomal recessive disorders, it is difficult to point out a precise underlying metabolic disturbance with the exception of a few dominantly inherited conditions, such as porphyrias where the specific enzyme defects can be demonstrated. Some conditions may result from mutations in structural molecules of cell membranes and others are due to specific failures of regulatory processes. Recognition of autosomal dominant inheritance is essential for appropriate genetic counselling. Affected individuals have a 50% chance of transmitting the disorder to a child of either sex but the children of healthy individuals are not at risk. In some cases of tuberous sclerosis, myotonic dystrophy or Treacher Collins syndrome parents may only be mildly affected and the birth of a severely affected child is often the first indication for the parents to be examined. Where both parents are unaffected the most probable cause is a new mutation and there is only a rare chance it will recur in future children.

Some autosomal dominant disorders associated with severe learning disabilities are described below.

Apert's Syndrome

Common features of Apert's syndrome and related conditions, such as Carpenter's and Chotzen syndrome, are abnormalities of the skull, and fusion of the digits. Microcephaly or tower skull may be present in association with fusion of digits (acrocephalosyndactyly) or with extra digits in addition to fusion (acrocephalopolysyndactyly). Most varieties of acrocephalosyndactyly are autosomal dominant and occur equally among men and women. With Apert's syndrome there is lack of reproduction and it is assumed that many cases are due to fresh mutation. Increased paternal age has been implicated in some isolated cases. In Apert's syndrome the appearance of the skull is characteristic, with a high forehead and a flattened occiput with the apex at the anterior fonta giving a tower-like appearance. The mid-facial bones are poorly developed with the nose, chin and eyes appearing prominent. There is facial asymmetry and the eyes are wide apart and protuberant and have a downward slant. This may also be associated with abnormalities of the palate and teeth, the palate being high and cleft and the teeth often irregular. In type 1 acrocephalosyndactyly (i.e. Apert's syndrome), all the digits in the hand and foot are fused by the skin and sometimes even the bone cartilage and nails may be fused. Apert's syndrome is the most severe and most common type of craniocynostosis and because of the premature closure of cranial sutures the intracranial pressure may be increased giving rise to dilated ventricles and atrophy of the brain tissue. Surgical procedures are used to relieve the intracranial pressure but the benefit in terms of subsequent mental functioning remains uncertain.

Mandibulo Facial Dystosis (Treacher Collins Syndrome)

This condition is inherited as an autosomal dominant disorder and the expression of the gene varies within the family so that a severely affected child may be born to a mildly affected parent. The affected person shows under development of the mid-facial bones giving rise to the description of the face as having a pinched appearance. The eyes slant downwards and outwards and the normal nose and mouth appear large in contrast. Half of the affected individuals have only rudimentary ears that may in some cases be entirely absent. The teeth are often irregular and crowded with a cleft lip in some cases. A substantial number may show learning disability and the abnormalities of the external ear may be associated with defects in the inner ear giving rise to deafness. Skull X-rays show under-developed central skull bones that include facial bones and maxilla, zygoma and mandible, and middle ear bones.

Neurofibromatosis

Neurofibromatosis is not a single disorder, and two distinct forms are generally recognized: neurofibromatosis 1 – Von Recklinghausen's disease or peripheral neurofibromatosis; and type 2, central neurofibromatosis. These two types are two distinct conditions, the gene for neurofibromatosis 1 being located on the long arm of chromosome 17, while that for neurofibromatosis 2 is located on the long arm of chromosome 22. The two conditions show different clinical and pathological characteristics with learning disability being a feature of neurofibromatosis 1 with up to one-third of people being affected.

Type 1 neurofibromatosis accounts for at least 85% of all cases of neurofibromatosis and occurs in about 1 in 3000 individuals. About one-third of the new cases may be mutations. *Café au lait* spots are the hallmark of neurofibromatosis and are found in all cases. They may be present at birth and increase steadily during childhood and adolescence. Freckling is common in the axilla and may also develop in other intertriginous areas. The neurofibromas may be intracutaneous and of a soft consistency or they may be subcutaneous presenting as firm tumours along the trunk of peripheral nerves. They increase steadily in number with age, especially around puberty. Cutaneous and subcutaneous elements may fuse together to form tumours that may be continuous with intracranial or intraspinal tumours, giving rise to one of the more serious complications of neurofibromatosis 1. Tumours of the optic nerve may be present in 15% of the cases and may produce proptosis and diminished visual acuity. CT scan and MRI scan are of great diagnostic help in identifying the intracranial tumours.

Abnormalities of the skull are frequent in neurofibromatosis 1 and microcephaly occurs in 16–45% of affected people. Hydrocephalus may be present and in the majority of cases is the result of aqueductal stenosis. As stated earlier, up to 40% of the affected people may show learning disability. In neurofibromatosis 2, bilateral acoustic neuromas are the predominant feature occurring in about 90% of the cases and loss of hearing is the first symptom. These tumours develop mainly in adolescence and early adulthood and neurofibromatosis 2 is rarely found in children. Most patients do not show *café au lait* spots or other cutaneous manifestations. Intracranial tumours are frequently present, as also tumours of cranial nerves 5–12 which are frequently bilateral and multiple. A complete clinical ophthalmological and neurological examination is essential in the management of people with neurofibromatosis and for those with suspected brain tumours progressive CT scans or MRI scans may be required. Surgical treatment is indicated for invasive tumours and surgery may also be indicated for cosmetic deformities.

Tuberous Sclerosis

Tuberous sclerosis is a dominantly transmitted disorder with a variable expression and occurring in about 1 in 20 000 to 1 in 40 000 live births. A high incidence of new mutations have been recorded in up to 50–60% of cases. The gene responsible for tuberous sclerosis seems to be located on the long arm of chromosome 11 but possible linkage to chromosome 9 has also been considered. An abnormality of differentiation of embryonic cells with a tendency to tumour-like proliferation and the disturbance of the migrational process of CNS

cells has been implicated. The characteristic lesions found in the brains of people with tuberous sclerosis include cortical tubers, subependymal nodules and giant cell tumours. The cortical tubers may become calcified. Tumours may also be found in other parts of the body, including heart, kidneys, liver and also the retina. The skin lesions may include *café au lait* areas or a butterfly rash over the face that usually begins in the preschool years and consists essentially of hyperplastic vascular and connective tissue.

The clinical manifestations of tuberous sclerosis vary considerably with the extent of involvement and age of onset. In infants and children, seizures are the most common presenting complaint. They are generalized in about 85% of the cases with infantile spasms being most common in infancy. Clonic or atonic seizures may also be seen as well as partial complex seizures. Death is usually due to complications such as heart failure and pneumonia, though life expectancy is variable according to the severity of pathological features.

Tuberous sclerosis is said to account for almost up to 1% of the population of long-stay learning disability hospitals, and learning disability is said to be particularly common in hospital-based samples. Some studies have shown learning disability to be found only in people with seizures, especially if they occurred before the age of 2 years whereas others have found it to be a common feature in those with numerous physical abnormalities.

Reader Activity 6.4
Sometimes people with tuberous sclerosis experience an increase in the frequency and severity of seizures along with behavioural difficulties, how might these two phenomena be accounted for?

Autosomal Recessive Disorders

Autosomal recessive conditions giving rise to learning disability are invariably associated with metabolic disorders and evidence of metabolic disturbances before or after birth is found in the histories of many people with learning disability. There are a large number of metabolic abnormalities that may give rise to varying degrees of intellectual deficit but the presence of a particular abnormality does not necessarily imply a particular degree of intellectual impairment. In some cases, such as neuronal storage diseases, the biochemical abnormality may be the decisive factor where the deficiency of a single enzyme results in destruction of cells and progressive intellectual deterioration. Similarly in phenylketonuria, the metabolic abnormalities such as an inactive or absent enzyme are clearly related to the subsequent intellectual impairment but in many other cases of biochemical abnormalities such as amino-acid abnormality, it is difficult to demonstrate a causal relationship.

It is convenient to describe these metabolic disorders according to the nature of the metabolic abnormality; that is, disturbances of protein metabolism giving rise to hereditary amino-acid urias, disturbances of carbohydrate metabolism and disturbances of lipid metabolism.

Most of the disorders for which a clear biochemical basis has been identified show an autosomal recessive inheritance and most of these are proved to be enzymatic defects. Genetic counselling for families in which autosomal recessive disorder has occurred is important. There is a 1 in 4 risk of future siblings of an affected individual being similarly affected. Since both parents have to transmit an abnormal gene, the risk will be small for children of healthy siblings or if a parent remarries. Consanguinity, marriage between close relatives, is a particular feature of rare autosomal recessive disorders.

Disorders of Protein Metabolism – Hereditary Amino-acid Urias

A large number of autosomal recessive conditions are associated with severe learning disabilities and most of the in-born errors of metabolism are due to autosomal recessive genes. Each step in a metabolic process is said to be controlled by a particular enzyme that in turn is the product of a particular gene. Activities of most enzymes can be reduced to up to half the normal level before any serious harm ensues. As a result, an individual who is heterozygous for such a recessive gene has around half the normal enzyme activity and still will show no outward manifestations of the disorder and the decrease in enzyme activity can be used as a biochemical test for identifying unaffected heterozygous carriers.

Phenylketonuria

Phenylketonuria is the most important of the autosomal recessive conditions, occurring in about 1 in 10 000 live births. The affected children are deficient in the enzyme phenylalanine hydroxylase that converts phenylalanine to tyrosine, as a result of which phenylalanine tends to accumulate in the blood. Some of this may be diverted to form phenyl pyruvic acid that is then excreted in the urine. Screening tests for phenylketonuria depend on the detection of excess phenylalanine in the blood (Guthrie test) or phenyl pyruvic acid in the urine. Partial or transient deficiency of the enzyme may produce hyperphenylalanaemic states that may be detected by screening, but does not show clinical effects. There are cases of phenylketonuria that result from deficiency of related enzymes; that is, phenylalanine transaminase or dihydropteridine reductase. The heterozygote carriers can be identified by giving a high-phenylalanine protein diet that causes a temporary rise in plasma phenylalanine. More recently, more advanced techniques using DNA probes that are homologous for the phenylalanine hydroxylase have made prenatal diagnosis possible and also help in the identification of carriers in families with at least one affected child. Affected children, if treated early, can develop normally on a low phenylalanine diet. Many children homozygous for the defective gene develop into intellectually normal adults if given a low phenylalanine diet. Half of those who are untreated become microcephalic and show light colour of the skin and eyes. Eczema occurs in a third of untreated cases and the patients colour of the hair is often lighter than other members of the family. Some individuals abandon the low phenylalanine diet as they grow older without much harmful effect, but affected women who are contemplating becoming pregnant must avoid phenylalanine since high circulating phenylalanine levels can have toxic effects on the developing fetus. Untreated individuals show severe learning disability and many develop epilepsy. The level of phenylalanine has to be kept below 10 mg per 100 ml during the first year of life, but it is uncertain how long the dietary restriction has to be enforced in order to avoid severe learning disability. Children with phenylketonuria whose special diet was stopped at the age of 6 years fail to show increases in mean IQ, reading and spelling ability, whereas those who continued the diet until the age of 10 years improved on these measures.

All new-born infants in Britain are screened in the postnatal period using the Guthrie test or biochemical phenylalanine estimation on capillary blood. Diagnosis is confirmed by finding a blood phenylalanine level greater than 20 mg/dl and the presence of phenyl pyruvic acid in the urine. The diet has to be carefully controlled to avoid neurological damage that can occur even up to 7–10 years of age. However, a minimum of phenylalanine is essential for the diet and too little phenylalanine leads to weight loss, feeding difficulties and poor development, whereas too much phenylalanine leads to severe learning disability, microcephaly and growth retardation. While the risk of phenylketonuria in the offspring is small, affected women may have brain-damaged children as the result of transplacental passage of phenylalanine. If treatment is started before the age of 2 months and controlled well by regular blood phenylalanine development, normal mental and physical development may result.

Hartnup Disease

This is an autosomal recessive condition where the enzymatic defect results in large quantities of monocarboxylic acids being lost across the renal tubules and intestinal mucosa and as a result of the massive loss of all amino acids pellagra results. The affected people show a pellagra-type rash after exposure to sunlight, coincident attacks of cerebellar ataxia and mental changes and varying degrees of learning disability are also present. The severity of symptoms depends on the amount of protein consumed and can lead to dementia in later life. Twenty per cent of children are said to show a steady deterioration. The diagnosis is established by urinary chromatography showing a particular pattern of urinary amino acids and the treatment is by oral administration of nicotinamide together with a high-protein diet.

Homocystinuria

This is an autosomal recessive condition and most affected people have reduced or absent cyst athionine synthetase, an enzyme which is necessary for converting methionine to cystine. Fifty to sixty per cent of affected patients show the presence of a dislocated lens in the eye, malar flush, osteoporosis and varying degrees of learning disability. Some infants may be normal at birth but fail to thrive some months later. The affected people show long and slender limbs with stiff joints, with a narrow palate and mouth and crowded teeth and there is a marked tendency towards thrombotic episodes. Treatment with pyridoxine is said to be effective.

Disorders of Carbohydrate Metabolism

Galactosaemia

This is a recessive disorder in which the absence of galactose-1 phosphate uridyl transferase prevents the normal transformation of galactose to various glucose products. This disorder is inherited as an autosomal recessive abnormality, the incidence being about 1 in 30 000 live births in the UK. It is a rare condition where galactose accumulates in the blood owing to failure to convert into glucose because of the enzymatic defect. Galactosaemia presents during the first few weeks of life with failure to thrive and development of cataracts. Fatal septicaemia is frequent during the neonatal period and all untreated infants show enlargement of the liver, spleen and ascitis. Half of the affected infants develop jaundice during the first few weeks of life, anaemia and thrombosis resulting from sepsis of the feet. Most infants are lethargic and hypotonic, epilepsy is rare but most develop progressive deterioration in mental functioning resulting in severe degrees of learning disability.

Exclusion of galactose from the diet, provided this is done early, is said to prevent all clinical manifestations of the disease, including failure to thrive and learning disability. It is possible that the child may develop alternative pathways for metabolizing galactose and may be able to consume galactose without risk by the age of 5 or 6 years.

Disorders of Fat Metabolism (Lipidosis)

In this group of disorders lipid material is deposited in the cells of the CNS resulting in severe physical and mental abnormalities.

Gangliosidoses are a group of conditions where the main finding is the presence within neurones of lipid-soluble material in the cytoplasm with later disappearance of many neurones and the development of extensive gliosis. Perkinge cells in the cerebellum and neurones and brainstem nuclei are also affected.

Tay–Sachs disease is by far the most frequent form of gangliosidoses affecting 1 in 2000 persons among Ashkenazi Jewish populations of eastern Europe. Lipids accumulate throughout the CNS including in ganglion cells of the retina. The onset is between 3 and 9 months of age with loss of acquired milestones and of muscle tone following a period of normal initial development. Excessive startle response may proceed all other symptoms and persist for several months. Neurological symptoms progress rapidly and the child appears listless and weak with slow mental development. The initial hypertonia is followed by spastic tetraparesis and epileptic seizures occur later. After the first year of life the infants are helpless, blind and unresponsive and often develop a progressive macrocephaly. Death usually occurs before 3 years of age. Early in the course of the disease a cherry red spot is present in both macular areas, surrounded by a zone of

milky whitish retina. The whitish zone is due to lipid storage in the retinal ganglion cells whereas the red spot represents the normal macula which is devoid of ganglion cells, and appears abnormally red in contrast to the surrounding retina. Prenatal diagnosis is possible by amniocentesis or by trophoblast biopsy.

No effective treatment for the gangliosidosis is known. The process of ganglioside accumulation and consequent brain degeneration is already well established by mid-trimester of fetal life and so prospects of enzyme replacement do not appear favourable.

In the juvenile type of the disorder, the clinical picture may not be present until the child is of school age. Visual difficulties predominate and progressively impair both physical and mental development. Subsequently, ataxia, fits and blindness develop and death is usual before the age of 20 years. Both these conditions are characterized by cerebromacular degeneration and no specific treatment is available for either conditions.

Niemann–Pick Disease

Niemann–Pick disease is a group of heterogenous conditions characterized by accumulation of sphingomyelin in the reticuloendothelial system. It is transmitted as an autosomal recessive abnormality and is most common in Ashkenazi Jews. The hallmark of the condition is the presence in the reticuloendothelial system of large vacuolated cells. Foam cells and ballooned ganglion cells are found in the CNS. Biochemically, there is marked storage of sphingomyelin, a major component of normal myelin in association with cholesterol in the liver spleen and kidney. Storage may also be present in the brain.

The disease may develop at any time from early infancy to young school years. Both physical and mental abnormalities are present with hepatic and splenic enlargement causing prominence of the abdomen, anaemia and occasionally cherry red spots may be seen at the macular, similar to that seen in cerebromacular degenerations. The deterioration in mental functioning is commonly accompanied by epilepsy.

Gaucher's Disease (Cerebroside Lipidosis)

This is an autosomal recessively inherited condition caused by deficiency of glucocerebrosidase. It occurs in males and females with a particularly high incidence in Jewish populations. Type 1 Gaucher's disease is the most common form and is only occasionally seen in children. It is usually marked by hepatosplenomegaly and bone abnormalities and sometimes by hypersplenism and pulmonary manifestations. There is no CNS involvement. Glucocerebrosides accumulate throughout the reticuloendothelial system. The Gaucher cells are found in bone marrow, spleen, liver and lymph nodes.

In type 2 Gaucher's disease the clinical onset is at 3–5 months of age with muscle hypotonia and loss of interest in surroundings. Spasticity gradually sets in and bulbar paralysis follows resulting in marked feeding difficulties. Splenomegaly is usually pronounced and cherry red spots are sometimes present in the eyes. Death usually occurs before 2 years of age.

In type 3, Gaucher's disease or (juvenile Gaucher's disease) the disorder becomes apparent during the first decade of life, the major features being slowly progressive hepatosesplenomegaly and rapid progressive intellectual deficiency. Cerebellar ataxia and extrapyramidal signs frequently develop as well as myoclonic epilepsy. Replacement therapy with glucosecerebrosidase is said to be effective in type 1 cases and is being currently tried in a few type 3 cases.

Sulphatidosis (Metachromatic Leucodystrophy)

This group of conditions, known as progressive leucodystrophies, is related to the lipidosis and they comprise many syndromes in which the white matter of the brain degenerates in a diffuse symmetrical fashion. This is an autosomal recessive condition caused by deficiency of cerebrocide sulphatase. Onset may occur at any time from infancy onwards.

Inheritance is autosomal recessive except in certain types of the disorder, where an X-linked recessive gene is responsible. The leucodystrophies invariably have a bad prognosis and no treatment is available. Progressive mental and physical deterioration with ataxia, blindness, deafness and fits is the usual pattern of the illness; death is usual before 2 years of age.

Mucopolysaccharidoses (MPS)

The mucopolysaccharidoses (MPS) are inborn errors of metabolism caused by deficiency of a lysosomal glucosidase or sulphatase that leads to accumulation of mucopolysaccharides in the lysosomes.

Hurler's Disease (Gargoylism)

This disorder is usually due to an autosomal recessive gene, through X-linked transmission and has been reported in male subjects. There is accumulation of mucopolysaccharides and glycolipids in the brain and other organs and affected patients show a large head, corneal clouding, thickened long bones, hepatosplenomegaly and kyphosis. The head is large and CT scan and MRI scan show ventricular dilatation and hypodensity of hemispheral white matter. Death occurs before 20 years of age. Enzyme replacement by bone marrow transplant has been partially successful leading to disappearance of corneal clouding, but the effects on growth and neurological development have yet to be ascertained.

Hunter's Syndrome

This disorder is inherited as an X-linked trait and runs a more benign course than Hurler's syndrome with a minimal to moderate degree of learning disability. Neurological abnormalities include sensory neural deafness, retinitis pigmentosa and moderate hydrocephalus but corneal clouding is absent.

X-linked Disorders

There are several X-linked disorders associated with learning disability. Only males are affected with transmission being through healthy female carriers. Any female children of an affected male will all be carriers. Besides the fragile X syndrome, other X-linked disorders resulting in learning disability include Leschnyhan syndrome due to deficiency of the enzyme hypoxanthineguanine phosphoribosyl transferase. This leads to accumulation of uric acid in the blood and particularly affects the basal ganglia which are unduly sensitive to hyperuricaemia resulting in choreoathetosis. Self-mutilation is common as are spasms of the neck muscles. The face is usually normal, but severe lip biting in early childhood causes scarring and loss of tissue. The deposition of uric acid at the tips of the ears causes gouty tophi and may also result in gouty arthritis of the joints, and kidneys may show uric acid stones. The most affected people have a severe degree of learning disability as well as speech difficulties. Custom-made mouth guards and gloves are valuable in minimizing self-injurious behaviour.

Alphathalassaemia/Mental Retardation Syndrome (ATRX Syndrome)

The association of haemoglobin H (HbH) with learning disabilities was first reported in 1981. The most recent discovery has been that of alphathalassaemia associated with learning disabilities, where there is deletion on the short arm of chromosome 16. The HbH disease may be associated with a mild to moderate degree of learning disability but where there is non-deletion the HbH may be associated with a severe degree of learning disability. This condition is characterized by microcephaly, short stature, hypertelorism, convulsions, hypoplasia of the mid-face, and genital abnormalities.

All the patients showing non-deletion are chromosomally males and it is possible that a mutation on the X chromosome is responsible with a sex-linked recessive inheritance.

6.8 Prevention of Learning Disability

Reader Activity 6.5
If one accepts that people with learning disability have the same human value as everyone else, then how can such a belief be reconciled by those who advocate its prevention?

The World Health Organization (1985) has identified performance targets for the prevention of conditions causing limitations of intellectual development.

Low birth weight children brought up in deprived socioeconomic circumstances are likely to attain poor intellectual competence. Improved obstetric and neonatal care has substantially reduced the number of early deaths among low birth weight babies. The number of low birth weight, intellectually impaired babies who have survived their infancy remains constant. In the UK, the number of low birth weight babies as a proportion of all birth weights has remained constant in recent years, and it is around 7% per annum; that is, roughly double Swedish statistical data for this area. Even within the UK, there is a difference in distribution of light for date babies. They are more often found in areas of social disadvantage, although the precise relationship between environmental and biological factors is complex and is hard to elucidate. None the less, it may be the case that such a finding reinforces the promotion of understanding learning disability as a complex state of health comprising the range of dimensions that are explored in this book.

Antenatal Screening

The majority of cases of Down's syndrome are due to the random occurrence of chromosomal abnormalities, the probability of which increases as maternal age advances, it being nearly 20 times more frequent at age 40 years than at 20 years. A quarter of the total number of babies born with Down's syndrome were to mothers aged over 35 years.

Amniocentesis can often provide a positive diagnosis at around 18–20 weeks. It has the disadvantage that it is rather late for any couple who wishes to contemplate a termination of the pregnancy. Chorionic villi sampling enables a diagnosis to be made at about the 8th week of gestation, although the safety of this technique is still under scrutiny. Unusually low levels of alpha-feta protein in maternal blood are associated with Down's syndrome. Alpha-feta protein level screening is already undertaken in connection with neural tube defects and has played an important part in the declining incidence of neural tube defects over the last 10 years. Where there are high levels of serum alpha-feta protein, then one may wish to use diagnostic ultrasound that can detect open spina bifida and anencephaly with considerable accuracy. Preventive screening for fragile X syndrome has been proposed and prospective screening of all newly diagnosed children with learning disability where the cause is not known irrespective of age together with their families is now considered to be good clinical practice. Fragile X syndrome is the second most common cause of learning disability after Down's syndrome and one survey has demonstrated that about 1 in 544 school-girls in an English city were found to be carrying the fragile X mutation with a 1 in 2 risk that any of their sons could have learning disability and a 1 in 6 risk that any of their daughters might have learning disability. Retrospective screening of all learning-disabled children, young adults, together with their relatives may substantially help reduce the prevalence of learning disability in the community.

The prevention of conditions producing learning disability can be considered in four stages:

Preconceptual

- Rubella immunization.
- Genetic counselling.
- Health promotion for potential mothers including advice about diets, smoking and alcohol use.

- Appropriate treatment of medical conditions, including diabetes, hypertension, toxaemia of pregnancy.
- Availability of contraception and family planning advice to avoid unwanted pregnancies.

Prenatal

- Identification of at-risk groups and genetic counselling.
- Estimation of alpha-fetoprotein levels in maternal blood.
- Rubella screening.
- Screening for syphilitic infection.
- Rhesus incompatibility check.
- Awareness of maternal age at conception.
- Fetal cell screening for genetic and chromosomal abnormalities.
- Use of diagnostic ultrasound for diagnosis of growth retardation, microcephaly, hydrocephalus, neural tube defects, multiple births and placental abnormalities.
- Improved antenatal services with special reference to factors contributing to low birth weight babies and availability of services at local clinics.

Perinatal/Neonatal

- Improved obstetric and neonatal care with the aim of reducing hypoxia, hypoglycaemia and trauma.
- Neonatal screening and treatment for hypothyroidism and phenylketonuria.
- Prompt surgical treatment for hydrocephalus.
- Use of anti-D immunoglobulin in mothers at risk of future Rhesus incompatibility.

Postnatal

- Improved uptake of immunizations (e.g. measles) to reduce the incidence of encephalitis, meningitis.
- Prevention of further damage of impaired children, for example expert control of epilepsy, physiotherapy for the non-ambulant.

- Prevention of circumstances leading to child abuse, road traffic accidents and accidents at home.

Reader Activity 6.6
Attempt to locate a range of health promotion material aimed at the prevention of learning disability. Where did you find this material? Was it in a public place with ease of access? Was the material helpful and informative?

Discussion Questions
Why do you think that it is important, if at all, to understand the causes of learning disability?

How can parents and professional carers reconcile the dilemma of actively preventing learning disability, on the one hand, whilst on the other promoting people with learning disability as equal citizens in our society?

Do the various causes of learning disability outlined in this chapter have implications for the health of the person affected, and if so how may those implications be ameliorated?

References

Blomquist, H.K. and Gustavon, K.H. (1983) Fragile X syndrome in mildly retarded children in a north Swedish county. *Clinical Genetics* **24**: 393–398.

Evard, P., De Saint Georges, P., Kadhim, H. and Gadisseux, J.F. (1989) Pathology of prenatal encephalopathies – Child neurology and developmental disabilities, pp. 153–176.

Fishler, K., Koch, R. and Donnell, G.N. (1976) Comparison of mental development in individuals with mosaic and trisomy 21 Down's Syndrome. *Paediatrics* **58**: 744–748.

Freeman, J.M. (1985) *Prenatal and Perinatal Factors Associated with Brain Disorders*. NIH Publication: No. 85-1149. Washington, DC: National Institute of Child Health & Development.

Hagberg, B. and Kyllerman, M. (1983) Epidemiology of mental retardation – A Swedish survey. *Brain & Development* **5**: 441–449.

Hill, A. and Volpe, J.J. (1981) Seizures, hypoxic ischaemic brain injury and intraventricular haemorrhage in the new born. *Annals of Neurology* **10**: 109–121.

Kalter, H. and Warkany, J. (1983) Congenital malformations. Etiologic factors and their role in prevention. *New England Journal of Medicine* **308**: 424–431.

Khoury, M.J., Erikson, J.D., Cordero, J.F. and McCarthy, B.J. (1988) Congenital malformations. Intrauterine growth retardation. A population study. *Paediatrics* **82**: 83–90.

Laroche, J.C. (1986) Fetal encephalopathies of circulatory origin. *Biology of the Neonate* **50**: 61–74.

Leblanc, R. and O'Gorman, A.M. (1980) Neonatal intracranial haemorrhage. *Journal of Neurosurgery* **53**: 642–651.

Ledbetter, S.A., Van Tuinen, P. and Summers, K.M. (1989) Molecular dissection of a contiguous gene syndrome: frequent microscopic deletion. *Proceedings of the National Academy of Sciences USA* **86**: 5136–5140.

Lenke, R.R. and Levy, H.L. (1980) Maternal phenylketonuria and hyperphenyl alananemia. *New England Journal of Medicine* **303**: 1202–1208.

Lindhal, E. and Michelsson, K. (1986) Neurodevelopmental significance of minor and major congenital abnormalities in neonatal high risk children. *Neuropaediatrics* **17**: 86–93.

Lucas, A., Morley, R. and Cole, J.J. (1988) Adverse neurodevelopmental outcome of moderate neonatal hypoglycemia. *BMJ* **297**: 1304–1308.

Nelson, K.B. and Ellenberg, J.H. (1981) Apgar scores as predictors of chronic neurologic disability. *Paediatrics* **68**: 36–44.

Nelson, K.B. and Ellenberg, J.H. (1986) Antecedents of cerebral palsy, multivariate analysis of risk. *New England Journal of Medicine* **315**: 81–86.

Paryani, S.G. and Arvin, A.M. (1986) Intrauterine infection with varicellar zoster virus after maternal varicella. *New England Journal of Medicine* **314**: 1542–1546.

Pueschel, S.M., Hum, M.A. and Andrew, M. (1977) Nutritional management of the female with phenylketonuria during pregnancy. *American Journal of Clinical Nutrition* **30**: 1155–1161.

Punnett, H.H. and Zackai, E.H. (1990) Old syndromes and new cytogenetics. *Developmental Medicine & Child Neurology* **32**: 820–831.

Robb, J.A., Benirschke, K. and Barmeyer, R. (1986) Intrauterine latent herpes simplex virus infection – spontaneous abortion. *Human Pathology* **17**: 1196–1209.

Smith, R.D. (1981) Abnormal head circumference in learning disabled children. *Developmental Medicine & Child Neurology* **23**: 626–632.

Smith, G.F. and Berg, J.M. (1976) *Down's Anomaly*, 2nd edn. Edinburgh: Churchill Livingstone.

Volpe, J. (1989) Intraventricular haemorrhage in the premature infant. Current concepts, Part II. *Annals of Neurology* **25**: 109–121.

Warkany, J. (1981) *In* Warkany, J., Lemire, R.J. and Cohen, M.M. (Eds) *Microcephaly, Mental Retardation and Congenital Malformations of the CNS*, pp. 13–40. Chicago: Year Book.

Williams, C.A. and Frias, J.C. (1982) The angelman (happy puppet) syndrome. *American Journal of Medical Genetics* **11**: 453–460.

Yerbi, M. (1988) Telatogenicity of anti-epileptic drugs. *In* Pedley, T.A. and Meldrum, B.S. (Eds) *Recent Advances in Epilepsy*, Vol. 4, pp. 93–107. Edinburgh: Churchill Livingstone.

Further Reading

Aicardi, J. *Diseases of the Nervous System in Childhood.* Clinics in Developmental Medicine No. 115/118 MacKeith Press. Oxford: Blackwell Scientific Publication. Cambridge University Press, New York.

Brett, E.M. (Ed.) (1979) *Paediatric Neurology*, 2nd edn. Edinburgh: Churchill Livingstone.

Clarke, A.M., Clarke, A.D.B. and Berg, J.M. (Eds) *Mental Deficiency – The changing outlook*, 4th edn. London: Methuen.

Craft, M., Bricknell, J. and Hollins, S. (Eds) (1985) *Mental Handicap – A multidisciplinary approach.* London: Baillière Tindall.

Edwards, C.R.W. and Bouchier, I.A.D. (Eds) (1988) *Davidson's Principles and Practice of Medicine*, 16th edn. Edinburgh: Churchill Livingstone.

Kendell, R.E. and Zealley, A.K. (Eds) (1987) *Companion to Psychiatric Studies*, 5th edn. Edinburgh: Churchill Livingstone.

Modell, B. and Modell, M. (1992) *Towards a Healthy Baby: Congenital disorders and the new genetics in primary health care.* Oxford Medical Publications OUP

Roberts, J.A.F. and Pembrey, M.E. (1985) *An Introduction to Medical Genetics*, 8th edn. Oxford Medical Publications OUP

WHO (1985) *Targets for health for all.* Targets in support of the European regional strategy for health for all. Geneva: World Health Organization.

WHO (1994) *The ICD10 Classification of Mental and Behavioural Disorders.* Geneva: World Health Organization.

Chapter 7: Manifestations of learning disability
Adrienne Regan and Bob Gates

- Gilles de la Tourette syndrome with associated obsessional thinking

- Schizophrenia and mild learning disability

- Profound learning disability with screaming

- Mild learning disability with epilepsy and aggression

- Brain damage, emotional outbursts and sexual assault

7.1 Introduction

This chapter presents a number of case histories that depict some manifestations of different disorders found in learning disability. The usual approach for describing these manifestations is to present long lists of phenotypical characteristics. To provide more meaningful and realistic descriptions this chapter presents a series of case histories. For each case history a number of significant references are provided, concerning that particular disorder, and a full and further reading list is provided at the end of the chapter concerning a wider range of manifestations of learning disability. Understanding the presenting physical and psychological effects of different disorders in learning disability is important. This is because there is a clear correlation between the manifestation of some disorders in learning disability, and the health of the individual concerned (see Chapter 16 for an overview of research in the field of learning disability and health). Each case history presented clearly demonstrates the effects on health brought about by that particular clinical manifestation of learning disability.

7.2 Chromosomal Abnormalities

Case Study 7.1 Down's syndrome and Alzheimer's disease

Julie was the youngest of four children and born prematurely when her mother was 35 years old. Julie's condition was diagnosed soon after birth as she had typical facial features with epicanthic folds over her upper eye lids, a square-shaped head and square little hands with a single crease crossing each palm. She also had a heart murmur due to a congenital heart defect, and a small umbilical hernia. As a child she was cheerful, affectionate and mischievous. Teachers at her special school thought she was talking to an imaginary companion when it suddenly dawned on them that she was mimicking and impersonating others with heartless accuracy. Her parents doted on her and when she left school she went to work with them and stacked shelves in their corner shop. Over the years she had many eye, ear and chest infections that usually cleared with antibiotics. When she was 30 years old her father died and her mother did not allow her to attend the funeral as she wished to protect her from this. She became depressed and was prescribed a course of antidepressants as bereavement counselling was not available nor even considered by her family; she continued to live with her mother. Over the next few years she became slower and developed severe constipation. A community nurse who was asked to assess her, reported that she was wearing a heavy sweater in the summer and that her skin was dry and her voice was hoarse. Blood tests showed she had developed hypothyroidism, and after treatment with thyroxine her bowel function, voice and skin returned to normal. Her general practitioner (GP) continued to check her thyroid function and medication every year at her annual physical examination.

In her late 40s she gradually became more untidy and increasingly withdrawn and apathetic. There was a gradual weight loss and decline of self care skills and she appeared to age rapidly. When she was 50 years old she found it increasingly difficult to manage the stairs and walked with a bent posture and a broad-based gait. Her mother aged 85 years was adamant that she and her daughter planned to live together for as long as possible, even though both now had severe mobility problems. On assessment it was found that her physical and mental health had deteriorated when compared with previous records. She now had a form of myoclonic epilepsy shrugged off by mother as 'a few jerks'. She also hesitated when stepping off pavements and through doorways, had fewer interests and a much poorer memory. Psychometric testing was difficult to perform as she was unable to focus or concentrate and made a scribble when she could previously print her name. On neurological examination she had increased tone in her lower limbs whereas previously she had flexible joints and reduced muscle tone. It was clear that she was now suffering from Alzheimer's disease with parietal and temporal involvement confirmed by a computerized tomography (CT) brain scan. She was prescribed sodium valproate for her seizures which had become tonic–clonic as well as myoclonic in nature. When myoclonic seizures became very frequent ethosuximide was also prescribed; fortunately she was not sedated by either of these anticonvulsants. Adaptations were made to the house with extra railings and a lift that could be used by both women. A district nurse came to bathe Julie. The community learning disability nurse assisted with obtaining orthopaedic and psychiatric opinions and helped counsel both women in preparation for the possibility that one, or the other might need admission to hospital or a nursing home. Because of mother's fear of interference from professionals it was essential to hold regular multidisciplinary reviews so that services visiting the family could be co-ordinated, and professionals be clear about their roles. At one stage, mother had refused her own GP access to her home. Fortunately, the community learning disability nurse had developed a therapeutic relationship with both mother and daughter by gaining their trust over a period of time. This meant that she could regularly monitor the physical and mental state of both women and could call on the necessary help or alert specialist attention when it was needed.

Summary of Case Study 7.1

- Low nasal bridge, epicanthal folds, small ears, simian crease and cardiac defects.
- Variable degrees of learning disability, the majority in the moderate or severe range.
- Hypotonia, friendly but may be stubborn, language deficits.
- Approximately 94% due to extra chromosome no. 21, 6% due to mosaicism or translocation.

(Connolly, 1978; Piper and Ramsay, 1980; Smith, 1982)

Case Study 7.2 Fragile X syndrome

Michael has severe learning disability and has a sister with a mild learning disability. Chromosome testing of a blood sample from Michael revealed that 20% of his lymphocytes, cultured in a folate-deficient medium, showed a pale ragged constriction at the end of the long arm of the X chromosome (the fragile site Band Xq 27). Mother had an uncle who was very slow to learn and always lived with his parents, and possibly also had fragile X syndrome. When Michael was a very young child he would look away instantly on meeting strangers. At school he had special difficulty with arithmetic and dealing with any information given in sequence. He also seemed unable to play or initiate activities in the same way as other children of his age and ability. He was then prescribed folic acid because some research suggested that this vitamin could reduce hyperactive behaviour and increase the attention span in prepubertal children with this syndrome but little change was noticed.

Michael is tall with a long narrow face, long nose, large jaw and a high palate. He wears a baseball cap which rests on his prominent ears. Annual physical examination has shown he has had large testicular size since adolescence. He is shy and speaks in a high-pitched voice with a 'sing song' quality, and when nervous his speech becomes rapid, disorganized and cluttered. He dislikes prolonged eye contact and reacts defensively if he is touched. He will then fidget, flap his hands or bite his hand at the wrist. When he was 19 years old and in transition between school and college he suddenly became very aggressive, and refused to leave his bedroom. He had been behaving in an unusual way for a few weeks before this and had become withdrawn, suspicious and began talking to himself. His parents feared he may have had a nervous breakdown and felt quite unable to manage his behaviour, or his obvious distress. They requested an urgent psychiatric opinion. The psychiatrist who visited him at home saw that he was tense, agitated and depressed. With antipsychotics and antidepressant medication, and with the community learning disability nurse using a gentle teaching approach, he remained living with his family. The nurses were able to effect change in both Michael and his parents' response to him, by working through situations with them. They advised his parents not to confront him, but to reward any desired behaviour. They put great emphasis on support and counselling and for the parents to enhance their listening skills. The nurses monitored the effects of medication and assessed his behaviour on a day to day basis during the crisis period. By the end of the month he could again attend school and was sleeping better. Because he was vulnerable to a relapse of depression, in the first 6 months after this episode, his medication was continued and then withdrawn gradually after 6 months. His parents are now more confident as to how to manage Michael's behaviour and how to understand his feelings. They know who to contact if he is under any undue stress that might lead to a recurrence of his depression. They also know the behaviour he may show in the early stages of depression and are aware that such episodes can occasionally occur in people who have fragile X syndrome. The family prefer that neither Michael nor his sister know about the genetic nature of this syndrome. The community learning disability nurse has had to consider Michael's rights in this matter and has consulted with the Department of Genetics. It is unlikely that Michael will ever marry. However, if his sister should ever wish to marry and have children, she and her partner could be offered help with genetic counselling. In addition, antenatal diagnosis of fragile X can be made by sampling of chorionic villi or foetal blood. The geneticist has strongly recommended that his sister is tested.

Summary of Case Study 7.2

- **Increased growth rate in childhood, large ears, prominent jaw, thickened nasal bridge, macro-orchidism.**
- **Learning disabilities usually severe in males.**

- **Hyperactivity, mood swings, autistic behaviours, language delays**
- **Marker X chromosome [fragile site] at Xq27.**

(Howard-Peebles *et al.*, 1979; Turner *et al.*, 1980)

Case Study 7.3 Cri du chat

Jane was the youngest of three children and was born by a normal delivery, at full term, but had a birth weight of only 2.5 kg. In the first few months she vomited and failed to gain weight and had a peculiar cry. At 6 months she was unable to hold a rattle or hold up her head, or sit. She was predicted to have life-long severe learning disability when a chromosome test showed deletion of the short arm of chromosome 5 in all cells examined. She had a tiny head and mouth, a broad nose, flat lowset ears and was always very short for her age, she also had a cataract in one eye. However, both eyes were so deformed that an operation on the cataract would not have helped her vision. She would hit herself at meal times. She was unable to say how she felt at these times but a functional analysis of her behaviour indicated that these were the times when she had less individual attention. She also had a habit of bending over and regurgitating, and as a complication of this she developed sinusitis. As this was thought to be self-stimulatory behaviour, nurses encouraged other appropriate ways in which she could be happy and occupied. She was able to feed herself but was prone to pneumonia; this was thought to be the result of aspirating food. Nurses had to be very careful about the possibility of choking and sought advice from the speech therapist on feeding techniques.

At the age of 30 years, she developed increasing spasticity of her limbs and required extra physiotherapy and sensory stimulation. She could help dress herself but needed to be bathed. Her self-help skills were recorded carefully and skill-teaching programmes were set up to be followed in all settings. It was initially thought that she needed regular enemas but was found to have some sphincter control. When she was given extra fibre and fluids and regular toileting she was able to use a toilet. She had great character and stamina and despite all her physical problems she showed great enthusiasm for rhythm and dance and dressing up for parties.

Summary of Case Study 7.3

- Low birth weight, microcephaly, cat-like cry in infancy, round face, cardiac problems, micrognathia.
- Learning disability usually severe to profound.

- Hypotonia, marked speech deficits, self-stimulation, aggressiveness.
- Partial deletion of short arm of chromosome no. 5.

(Wilkins *et al.*, 1980; Smith, 1982)

Reader Activity 7.1
Reflect on Case Study 7.3. Identify those things that are proving detrimental to her achieving optimum health.

Case Study 7.4 Prader–Willi syndrome

   Shahzia was a premature floppy baby whose mother had difficulty feeding her. She quickly made up for this and developed such a voracious appetite that her mother had to put `padlocks' on the refrigerator and food cupboards. Her mother often despaired of understanding her daughter who was moody and self-centred, and easily shifted responsibility on to others. She attended a school for children with mild learning disability, where she learned to read. She developed diabetes at 11 years but this was well controlled by tablets and diet. She was always short for her age and had very little breast development or growth of body hair at puberty and never menstruated. She continued to have histrionic outbursts and regularly picked and scratched sores on her skin. All these physical and emotional features were characteristic of Prader–Willi syndrome, this was confirmed by karyography that showed a deletion at chromosome 15q12. She appeared quite unselfconscious when she quoted textbook summaries of her syndrome, which included descriptions of an egocentric personality and a pear-shaped body. As an older teenager she began to mimic epileptic seizures, having observed these at school. When these were recognized to be pseudoseizures she learned with the help of the community learning disability nurse alternative ways of obtaining attention, recognition and control of her own life. She learned to test her own glucose levels and became quite dogmatic about her diet. She later attended a local college and young peoples' clubs and enjoyed horse riding and swimming. She dressed in casual teenage clothes and would speak at great length, even when uninvited, at the Diabetic Association and the Prader–Willi Association meetings.

Summary of Case Study 7.4

- Short stature, small hands and feet, small penis, hypogonadism.
- Learning disability in most affected with an average IQ of 55.
- Hypotonia, feeding problems in infancy, excessive eating, obesity in early childhood, temper tantrums, moodiness, inappropriate behaviours.
- Frequently interstitial deletion of chromosome no. 15.

(Smith, 1982; Cassidy, 1984)

Case Study 7.5 Rett's syndrome

Emily was the youngest of six, and was born after a normal full-term pregnancy and delivery. She was breast fed for 9 months. She developed normally in her first year of life, and was described as an unusually 'good' baby who was perhaps more floppy in muscle tone than others. She sat at 9 months, fed herself with a spoon at 9 months and spoke several words at 15 months. She preferred to 'bottom shuffle' rather than try to walk, but nevertheless walked alone at 17 months. Soon after a smallpox vaccination at 18 months she became irritable, hard to console, screamed at night, rocked and appeared to regress. At 19 months she had lost her speech and began to pat or wring her hands persistently rather than using her hands to feed and drink or play. At this stage, severe learning disability was diagnosed by a paediatrician. Initially her parents wrongly attributed this to the smallpox vaccination as the real cause of her handicap was unsuspected at that stage. At 5 years she had convulsions and by the age of 8 years she was unable to stand unaided. By 13 years she had an obvious scoliosis, had progressive wasting of her muscles and poor balance. At 15 years, screaming spells began along with periods of hyperventilation. During these episodes she would look tense, would wring her hands, gnash her teeth, suck in air, and seemed to be alert and agitated. A plain X-ray of the abdomen showed a dilated intestine which was thought to be caused by air swallowing. She had an unusual electroencephalogram (EEG) which showed a diffuse abnormality but no epileptic foci. By 22 years she had screaming spells alternating with clusters of epileptic seizures. Eventually the attribution of her handicap to vaccination encephalitis was discounted when it was recognized that she had Rett's syndrome. She had the classic features of this syndrome in her appearance (a tiny woman with a small head and an alert facial expression) and her history (hand patting and cognitive and physical deterioration after a normal development in her first year of life). Her scoliosis became increasingly a problem so that she was bent double. To benefit her cosmetically and physically, her physiotherapist, her family and her orthopaedic surgeon decided to go ahead with a 'straightening' operation. Although this was a difficult procedure the family in retrospect consider it was worthwhile. She now has better posture, increased self-esteem and there are also the long-term prospects of her being mobile without needing a wheelchair and without having respiratory or cardiac embarrassment. She has regular hydrotherapy and physiotherapy and medical check-ups of her physical health. Her community learning disability nurse visits regularly and keeps an accurate record of her epileptic seizures, as an aid to prescribing, also a record of the hyperventilation episodes that are associated with this syndrome. When she attends the Rett's Syndrome Association meetings her mother comments that all these young girls and women are so similar with their bright faces and friendly smiles, their usually placid natures and their tiny arms and legs, that they look like sisters.

Summary of Case Study 7.5

- **A progressive degenerative disease affecting girls.**
- **Severely impaired receptive and expressive communication difficulties.**
- **Regression and loss of psychomotor and cognitive functioning.**
- **Stereotype hand movements, toe walking, breath holding and hyperventilation.**
- **Severe learning disability.**

(Hagberg *et al.*, 1985; Coleman *et al.*, 1988; Wood-yatt and Ozanne, 1992; Wehmeyer *et al.*, 1993)

Reader Activity 7.2
Reflect on Case Study 7.5. List those things that are proving detrimental to her achieving optimum health. Next identify a range of actions that you think could be taken, over and above what is currently being done with her, in order to improve her health.

Case Study 7.6 Down's syndrome and self-injury

Erol's birth was normal but as a neonate he was blue and slow to feed. He was diagnosed to have Down's syndrome shortly after birth, and this was confirmed by a chromosome study at 3 weeks. He had recurrent chest infections in early childhood. From the age of 7 years there have been a variety of behaviour problems developed mainly involving head banging, non-compliance and aggression occurring both at his special school and at home. One particular behaviour would be evident for a phase of 1–2 months at a time and would occur several times a day. His head banging would occur out of the blue, or when he was frustrated. He would either bang his head on an object or bang his head with his hand. His non-compliance was shown when he refused to go upstairs or to walk anywhere or to eat at a table. His aggression to others involved kicking and hair pulling; he also attacked furniture and threw things. He has smeared himself with faeces and has experimented with self-induced vomiting. Over the years he has caused such injury to his ear lobes and to his vision by head banging that he has required plastic surgery to his face and is now partially sighted. During very fierce head-banging sessions he needs to wear a helmet and ear protectors to prevent further damage. He needed to be provided with removable arm splints to protect himself, and others. He is able to feed himself and help dress himself and is continent with regular toileting and is dry at night. He is very particular about things being done in a predictable sequence. He has a full occupational programme involving music, swimming, horse riding and jacuzzi. He prefers activity involving movement and sound, but sometimes even refuses to participate in these. Ever since his school days he has responded best to loud, confident encouragement and staff who are firm but who are also sensitive when he needs to have his own space. There are times when one to one supervision appears to crowd him or overpower him. With the help of a clinical psychologist and community learning disability nurse, care staff are monitoring his mood, alertness, co-operation, need for prompting, behaviour incidents, use of splints, and the type of activity and the staff who are present at the time of any incident. If there is any marked increase in the incidents, in his social withdrawal and in mood disturbance, it may be helpful to consider an antidepressant or mood-stabilizing medication such as carbamazepine or lithium carbonate. The residential day staff, his parents and the community team work closely together to attempt to maximize his quality of life.

Summary of Case Study 7.6

- **See Case Study 7.1.**

(Gath and Gumley, 1986; Ghaziuddin *et al.*, 1992)

Reader Activity 7.3
Identify why it is important to monitor the serum levels of lithium carbonate and to undertake a liver and thyroid function test on a regular basis for Erol.

Case Study 7.7 Angelman syndrome (happy puppet syndrome)

After a difficult pregnancy, labour was induced after which there followed a prolonged forceps delivery. As a child, all of Helen's milestones were delayed and she had profound learning disability. As an adult she developed a broad grin, a happy disposition and walked with stiff legs and jerky movements. She has fair hair, blue eyes and a wide mouth with spaced teeth and a small face. She has no speech but babbles and makes noises when happy and grumbles when unhappy. She is constantly on the move and walks with her arms abducted and elbows flexed with an unsteady, broad-based gait usually directing herself with the purpose of picking up objects to chew or put in her mouth. She appears to understand complex emotional and verbal messages, and enjoys being cuddled. She will play with objects in a quite self-sufficient way. Chromosome testing shows an interstitial deletion of chromosome 15 (q11q13) close to the deletion site found in the Prader–Willi syndrome. Both of her parents have normal chromosomes and no balanced translocation was found.

The main risk to her health is that she stuffs food into her mouth and, if it is lying around, will stuff paper down her throat. As a result she develops an oesophageal obstruction although occasionally it involves the pharynx, so that she has a partial airway obstruction. If she has trouble breathing, her carer can open her mouth and clear away anything that can be removed with the fingers. If this fails, the Heimlich manoeuvre is carried out and usually works. If her oesophagus is blocked, water or lemonade sometimes loosens the obstruction, but only a small volume of these liquids is advised as otherwise she may regurgitate the liquid, aspirate and develop lung problems. Turning her upside down and banging her back has worked in the past; however, it is not a generally approved method as the obstruction may be dislodged even further down unless her head is well down, and her bottom is above her head. On one occasion when she was found disturbed and choking and unable to swallow small quantities of liquid, she was referred urgently by the GP to the casualty department where an abdominal X-ray revealed no foreign body, but an urgent endoscopy revealed impacted cotton wool in her oesophagus. The foreign body was removed and she was discharged from hospital the following day. Another problem can be her epilepsy. She has in the past developed status epilepticus, and during these episodes she is not unconscious but every few seconds blinks her eyes and has an altered level of consciousness. This is recognized when her behaviour changes and she is no longer active and smiling and socially interactive. Such a state usually responds within several days to an increase in sodium valproate, although on some occasions it can be abated by rectal diazepam. These episodes of status are sometimes precipitated by constipation. Serial EEGs have shown rhythmic high amplitude activity in all records with some discharges particularly over the occipital region, and are regarded by the neurologist as consistent with the diagnosis of Angelman syndrome.

Summary of Case Study 7.7

- **A rare condition characterized by a protruding lower jaw, prolonged paroxysms of laughter and widely spaced eyes.**

- **Bizzare physical and jerky movements in infancy.**
- **Numerous absence seizures.**

(Berg and Pakulza, 1972)

7.3 Genetic Abnormalities

Case Study 7.8 Tuberous sclerosis

At birth Karen's mother noticed white oval marks on her neck. She appeared to develop normally, but at 5 months she had odd movements and falls which were thought to be somehow associated with teething. She was not prescribed anticonvulsants until the collapses became severe and it was clear that she was actually suffering from infantile spasms. This was confirmed by a disorganized EEG showing a typical hypsarrhythmia pattern. By then it was also clear that her development was now delayed and she also had problem behaviour. By the age of 3 years she was thought to have severe learning disability with autistic traits. At 5 years, tiny flesh-coloured lumps developed around her nose and cheeks similar to a butterfly rash, that her mother also had from her early childhood. X-ray of her skull showed scattered calcified nodules and the paediatrician noticed *café au lait* skin depigmentation and a firm brown 'shagreen' patch over her lumbar spine. Because of all these features a diagnosis was made that she had tuberous sclerosis present from birth. Although her mother had no epilepsy, and only had a very mild learning disability, the paediatrician noted her facial rash and realized that she also had tuberous sclerosis. He was also able to advise these parents that the condition occurs in 1 in 10 000 births in the general population and is probably caused by a single dominant gene on the long arm of chromosome 9 and that inheritance is variable in each generation. He was able to advise these parents that there would be a 1 in 2 risk of another child being affected by this condition in any of its varying forms. However, it was also possible that early recognition and treatment of epilepsy in subsequent affected children could reduce the degree of learning disability. The parents accepted his offer to refer them to receive expert advice and counselling from a geneticist so that they could weigh up all the risks of a future pregnancy. Their daughter attended a special school and whilst her epilepsy was well controlled with anticonvulsant medication, she would still scream or hit out at strangers. She was overactive with a short attention span and teachers needed to keep her day as structured and predictable as possible. A behavioural assessment was carried out by the clinical psychologist and regular meetings were held so that parents, teachers and respite staff had a consistent approach in encouraging acceptable behaviour and activities she enjoyed. As a young adult a screening ultrasound showed up cysts and tumours in both kidneys. A CT scan confirmed that these tumours were benign angiomyolipomas associated with this syndrome. It was recommended that she now has a repeat ultrasound every 2 years to follow up their size so that there could be early detection of the much more rare carcinoma.

Summary of Case Study 7.8

- An autosomal dominant genetic disorder estimated birth frequency of 1 in 8000–12 000 births.
- Degree of learning disability variable, one study found that only 38% of people with tuberous sclerosis have learning disability.

- Epilepsy a common feature of this disorder, also hyperactive behaviour and sleep problems.
- Adenoma aebaceum, a particular characteristic, is a butterfly rash found on the face.
- Pigmented patches may be found on the skin.

(Connor, 1990; Hunt, 1993)

7.4 Learning Disability Caused by Maternal Infection

Case Study 7.9 Rubella syndrome

Linda's mother had German measles in the first 3 months of pregnancy. She was born with cataracts in both eyes and a loud cardiac murmur and was found to have a patent ductus arteriosus. She had operations on her heart and eyes in the first year of life but unfortunately remained almost totally blind and was only able to distinguish dark and light. She was admitted to a large mental handicap hospital at the age of 5 years because her mother had recurrent mental illness and could not cope with her and also because she was considered unsuitable for fostering. At that time she was still learning to stand and had a habit of rolling her head from side to side because she was scanning her environment for visual stimuli. She was deaf and unable to speak but nurses discovered she could distinguish between people by smell and that she was affectionate and ticklish and enjoyed rough and tumble games. Sometimes she would become agitated for periods of hours or days and this was always worse at night. She would calm down with the short term use of tranquillizing medication or creative methods of distracting and occupying her. When she was 19 years she had a tenotomy operation of her deformed toes. She had no contact from her parents when she was living in hospital as they had divorced and were now living abroad. Nursing staff who cared for her received post-registration education in the understanding of people who are deaf and blind. No medical cause was found for her periods of agitation which seemed to be her way of attracting attention. Nurses developed a structured programme whereby they redirected her to an alternative or appropriate activity and then consciously praised any desirable behaviour. As a young adult she was usually cheerful and responsive and particularly enjoyed activities involving movement or sensation such as massage, water play and cuddles. She eventually went to live in a special community project managed by SENSE (the national deaf, blind and rubella association) for people who had both a sensory handicap and severe learning disability. There are regular multidisciplinary reviews of her care and needs to ensure she continues to have an optimum quality of life. In this project special techniques are used to help people with such sensory deficits. She has learned to use 'objects of reference' which are objects that are identified by 'feel' and can also be used to symbolize activities so she can make choices. These objects can also be used to identify the environment she is about to enter.

The buildings where the residents live are designed as open-plan flats, and each has a 'quiet' room with a sprung floor. Residents are encouraged to hand-trail the walls so that they can navigate successfully round the building, identifying types of room by the decor. In the art and craft room, residents do pottery, collage and tactile paintings. In the cafeteria area they are taught to fill urns and make tea for others and later clear up. There is a snoozelum for relaxation. This has optokinetics equipment so that light sequences change with different temperatures, a machine can blow bubbles on to the face and soft music plays in sequences. There is a gymnasium with a sprung floor and trampoline, and here residents do obstacle courses to help them learn to problem solve and explore the environment.

She enjoys the outings and has been horseriding and ten-pin bowling. She has even gone ice skating with an ice tutor and loves the sound and feel of the ice and the rush of air when she gathers up speed on the rink.

Summary of Case Study 7.9

- If mother contracts rubella (German measles) during pregnancy this may adversely affect the fetus. Generally speaking, most prepubescent females are now vaccinated against rubella.

  If the fetus is affected the damage appears related to the severity of the infection, and the gestational period in which the mother contracted the disease.

- In affected infants cataracts are common, the liver and spleen are often enlarged, and deafness is also common.

  There is psychomotor as well as learning disability that may be severe.

(Leck, 1981; Fryers, 1986)

7.5 Learning Disability Caused by Metabolic Disorder

Case Study 7.10 Phenylketonuria

Rachel and her brother Paul are fair with blue eyes in contrast to their eight brothers and sisters who have dark eyes and hair. They live on a caravan site and move about the country with an itinerant extended family. Both have phenylketonuria (PKU) that was not diagnosed soon after birth because the family had moved on before the Guthrie test could be completed.

Because Rachel's condition was diagnosed when still an infant and she had early treatment she does not have such severe disabilities as many others with this condition. She was, nevertheless, in the top class of a school for children with severe learning disability but her attendance was sporadic. Paul attended a school for children with mild learning disability. The paediatrician advised a diet low in phenylalanine along with synthetic protein substitute and recommended that regular phenylalanine levels should be tested from blood taken by finger prick. The risk to Rachel, if she does not adhere to the diet, is the possibility she will develop epilepsy, tremors and neurological damage. There is an additional concern for Rachel as within her culture there is a pattern of early marriage and childbearing, and it is common practice to find a partner in the extended family. There would be a higher than even chance if she became pregnant that her baby could be damaged either by inheriting PKU genes or even if the baby does not have PKU, its brain and heart could be damaged by toxic chemicals crossing the placenta when Rachel is 'off the diet'. She would need to be admitted to hospital for most of her pregnancy and adhere to a very strict diet. The alternative practice of using contraception is a very contentious question as the family members have strong objections to contraception. Because a community learning disability nurse has formed a special supportive relationship with her, Rachel herself has agreed to have monthly finger pricks performed by her community nurse. She has also agreed to adhere partially to the diet when she is at school although she lapses at home as she dislikes such restrictions. Because her community learning disability nurse has given her careful information about her condition, that includes sensible dietary precautions and counselling about relationships and sexuality, she feels better able to choose her own course. At present she wants to go to college, and does not want to have a boyfriend yet, but she insists she does not want to keep to a strict diet. Her community learning disability nurse will monitor her health regularly and will try to keep track of her moves about the country, and consult with those doctors involved with her care. An account will always need to be taken of her own wishes, balancing this with any long-term risks to her health. Her nurse is very conscious of the importance of being non-judgemental about her client's life style and beliefs, but is also aware of the rights of an individual to have treatment and to understand as well as possible the effects expected of this treatment.

Reader Activity 7.4
Determine what the Guthrie test is, when it is carried out and why?

Summary of Case Study 7.10

- An inherited, autosomal recessive disorder of amino acid metabolism.
- High serum phenylalanine leads to irreversible brain damage and learning disabilities, usually severe.

- Behavioural difficulties, irrational behaviour.
- Microcephaly may be present, light-coloured hair and skin apparent, epilepsy common.

(Clarke and Yapa, 1991; Hoskin *et al.*, 1992)

7.6 Learning Disability of Mixed or Idiopathic Origin

Case Study 7.11 Cerebral palsy

Darren was born prematurely by emergency Caesarean section that was performed because of obstetric complications and foetal distress. He is now 25 years old but is the size of a 10-year-old boy. He is heavy to lift as he can make few movements of his own to assist. He has weakness of both arms and legs, and dislocation of both hips from early childhood. He has a small head and wears spectacles as he is very short sighted. A tendon-release operation for flexion contractures of his wrists has enabled him to perform some voluntary movement and also his appearance is less deformed. He has no speech but can show when he is uncomfortable. He will laugh and babble and clucks when he wants to be touched or have air blown gently on his face. He is learning to have better head control and balance when sitting. He has a deformed chest. Usually antibiotics are started as soon as he has a temperature as he is prone to pneumonia and such an infection could be rapidly fatal to him. He is also prone to choking and can be quite awkward if someone unfamiliar to him attempts to feed him, and when this happens he will take up to 1 h to eat a meal. Twice now, staff have prevented him from inhaling food and choking to death by using the Heimlich manoeuvre. An elective gastrostomy was considered because of his difficulty with swallowing, but with careful feeding techniques it has not been required. He has some bladder control and has been taught by nurses to use a bottle by day, but he still needs to be changed by nursing staff at night. He has no voluntary anal sphincter control and used to have problems with constipation that could only be recognized in the early stages when he developed nausea, discomfort or irritability. Sometimes he had soiling due to overflow when he was constipated and on one occasion his rectum was empty but a plain X-ray of his abdomen showed higher intestinal blockage. These episodes were managed by an oral stimulant laxative such as senna at night and a suppository or enema the following morning. Now there is planned regular evacuation using either suppositories or enemas twice a week and the consistency of his stools is deliberately kept compact rather than bulky, for his own comfort. At night he still needs to be turned regularly to prevent pressure sores developing. His Disability Living Allowance, at the higher mobility rate, helps with the purchase of wheelchairs and a custom-made commode. He enjoys going to the zoo and going on fun rides and has been up in a helicopter and down an artificial ski slope in a banana boat. He has tonic–clonic seizures approximately every 2 weeks but these occur more frequently when he is constipated or when his levels of anticonvulsant medication are low. His parents visit him regularly, particularly since he has moved out of a hospital ward to live closer to them in a staffed residential home. There he has visits from a physiotherapist, from community medical and nursing staff and his GP. One residential worker has taken on the responsibility of being the key contact person for receiving and giving out information about him, as such co-ordination is essential to the future care-planning of all his needs.

Summary of Case Study 7.11

- This condition was first described by Little in 1853.
- An acquired condition where there may be minimal cerebral dysfunction to severe cerebral dysfunction with varying degrees of learning disability. It is estimated that the incidence is approximately 1 in 400 births.
- It has been estimated that 55% of people with cerebral palsy will have an IQ of less than 70.

- There are a variety of forms of cerebral palsy that include spastic, athetoid, ataxia and mixed.
- In spastic cerebral palsy different parts of the body might be affected: hemiplegia, monoplegia, paraplegia, tetraplegia, quadraplegia and diplegia.

(Clarke, 1986)

Case Study 7.12 Autism

Zbigniew was born after a prolonged labour and as a baby appeared active and alert and had normal physical milestones. However, in infancy he did not play with other babies. In his second year of life he had no speech. He did not respond to toys in an imaginative way, and developed awkward behaviour. He was openly angry when pressed to eat, and would throw his food. He showed prolonged screaming and distress with strangers. There were times when his mother needed to chew his food first to persuade him to eat and she even resorted to tube feeding. He was obsessed with the plastic wheels of toys and over the next few years developed tantrums, slapping, head banging and butting and self pinching. He was dismissive of others apart from his mother. He preferred to climb or collect objects and hoard and twiddle them. His mother took him to many specialists and the diagnosis of autism was made because he had the cardinal features of this condition (impairment of social interaction, impairment in communication and lack of imaginative play in combination with a restricted repertoire of activities). As with most other children with autism, these features were recognized in him before the age of 3 years. Behavioural intervention by community nurses or psychologists was not available in his district at that time. When he was 8 years old he went to a residential school after his parents appealed to the education authorities concerning his special needs. In his second year there, he developed very disturbed behaviour. He pinched himself, pulled out tufts of his own hair and bit his wrist causing open sores. Physical investigations did not reveal any abnormality although he appeared to be in pain. Neither school teachers nor his mother could at first think of a life event or change which may have caused this distress. Eventually it was discovered that he was terrified of one of the night residential staff, who had a particularly firm and disciplinary approach directed towards him. This person forced him to eat by squeezing his nose then putting food in his open mouth. Another staff member heard her slap him, after he had soiled himself. Once she pushed his chair so that he fell to the floor, where he had to stay for 10 min as she refused to help him get up. A child protection investigation resulted in this person's suspension. A community learning disability nurse became involved as an advocate for him, and to give support to him and his parents throughout the child protection proceedings. He subsequently settled well in the school with only occasional bouts of minor self-injuries, particularly when there was any change to his routine.

When he reached his mid-teens he developed complex partial epileptic seizures that were well controlled by anticonvulsant medication. When he was very anxious he performed repetitive rituals that seemed to help him calm down and give him more control over his surroundings. He liked to stand and rock from side to side or sit and rock forwards and backwards, gently shaking his head. He would also compulsively straighten furniture and pluck off specks of dust. He could hum several tunes and showed interest in tuneful sound and touch and became especially relaxed in music therapy sessions where he could express himself by playing the drums. For dental procedures he needed a short-term anxiolytic to calm him but when he had long periods of very disturbed behaviour he seemed to be helped by a low dose of haloperidol which it was possible to reduce and stop completely when a behavioural approach was used in his home. A functional analysis of behaviour was carried out by a clinical nurse specialist who found that his behaviours were multifunctional and indicated his needs for escape or avoidance, for protest, attention and for demand. This nurse used an analogue recording of his behaviour with the help of the key worker in his staffed house. They recommended the creation of different situations and measured the change in behaviour in each situation over a period of time. Because of this knowledge, new activities and experiences could safely be planned for him. He has been hiking in Wales and goes swimming and sailing. He has drama and massage sessions and is constructing a bird table for the garden with the help of his key worker. He shows great interest in domestic activities such as hoovering, and helps to water plants and arrange flowers and can cook eggs on toast. His mother has recently died and has bequeathed him a large legacy that will be administered by the Court of Protection.

Summary of Case Study 7.12

- **Onset before the age of 30–36 months.**
- **Difficulty in developing reciprocal relationships with people.**
- **Difficulty in communicating both verbally and/or non-verbally with others.**
- **Difficulty in adjusting the repertoire of behaviour to changing circumstances.**
- **The above three characteristics are often referred to as the diagnostic triad.**

(Bagenholm and Gillberg, 1991; Gillberg, 1993)

Case Study 7.13 Gilles de la Tourette syndrome with associated obsessional thinking

Bill's parents realized his development was slower than his sisters by the time he was 5 years old, but they had hopes that with external private tuition he could keep up. He started in an ordinary school, but became very withdrawn and although his parents were reluctant to accept the decision, he eventually went to a school for children with mild learning disabilities. When he was 10 years old teachers commented on his mannerisms of hair flicking and throat clearing and the fact that he preferred to be on his own. This was initially attributed to his nervous disposition and his reaction to his family's expectation for him to achieve. At 14 years he started to swear loudly and make silly noises at home which shocked his parents who thought he was copying others from the school. He would touch objects repetitively and echo the speech and mannerisms of others. He appeared unaware he was doing this, and to have little control over such behaviour. At 18 years, after he had left school, he spent long periods alone in his bedroom dwelling on his own shortcomings and his desire to have a career in electronics or computers. Because of his checking and repetitive counting and rearranging, he achieved very little. He became depressed, was unable to concentrate, slept poorly and talked about death and illness. He had difficulties with impulse control and to his mother's great distress he began to physically attack her. He was prescribed antidepressants by a psychiatrist, who also noticed his involuntary swearing and mannerisms and made the additional diagnosis of Tourette's syndrome. He agreed to a trial of low dose antipsychotics commonly used for this condition. His tics and mannerisms were modified but his major concerns remained to be those of the mismatch between his expectations and his actual abilities. Over the next 2 years his community learning disability nurse helped him with practical problem solving, and introduced him to clubs and social activities which would enhance his self-esteem. He also joined a group for young people who met regularly to talk about ways of coming to terms with their learning disability. This also helped him in developing confidence and being independent from his family. This opportunity to discuss his problems made him less aware of his disability, in comparison with others, although he still admits that he would like to have his own job, family and home. He continued to need practical help and emotional support and monitoring of his mental health by his community nurse throughout his early adult life.

Summary of Case Study 7.13

- This disorder is characterized by a triad of symptoms that includes involuntary movements, involuntary utterances and obsessive thoughts.
- There is some evidence that this disorder is associated with self-injurious behaviour.
- A condition that manifests itself with neurological, psychological and psychiatric symptoms.

(Baron-Cohen *et al.*, 1994)

Case Study 7.14 Schizophrenia and mild learning disability

Peter came from a large family and attended a school for children with mild learning disability. In the last 2 years his attendance had dropped off, and he began to go to discos and clubs in the evening where he could obtain recreational drugs. On leaving school he started to help his father in the gardening trade, but this came to an abrupt halt when one day he was found standing stock still and mute. He was admitted to a psychiatric ward with a diagnosis of acute catatonia. He complained of hearing voices and had unusual religious and sexual preoccupations. These subsided with antipsychotic medication. Despite his doctor's advice he stopped taking this medication on discharge from hospital and needed to be readmitted 6 months later, after he attacked his mother whilst he was suffering a recurrence of the hallucinations and delusions. He was unable to participate in groups or in occupational therapy catering for adults recovering from a mental illness, but he eventually went to a sport and leisure centre with other young special school leavers. His community learning disability nurse visits his home once a month to supervise his depot injection and to recognize any early signs of relapse. This nurse has explained his illness to him and his family, and helped him with structuring his day. He has also had help with problem solving, independence skills and budgeting, which he had always found stressful. He is planning, in the future, to live in a staffed house or hostel with other young people with similar needs.

Summary of Case Study 7.14

- Thought disorder, disturbance of volition, delusions, emotional disturbances and hallucinations common.
- Some would suggest that this disorder is more common in people with learning disability than in the general population.
- A disorder that presents itself with different manifestations: simple, hebephrenic, catatonic and paranoid schizophrenia.
- Age at onset varies among the different types of schizophrenias. Diagnosis may be problematic because of difficulties of accessing a medium to identify thought disorder.

(Reid, 1982; Gostason and Akesson, 1986)

Case Study 7.15 Profound learning disability with screaming

It was a normal pregnancy, following birth Yee-Wah appeared to be a normal baby but all her developmental milestones were delayed. She sat and walked 6 months after the time expected, was unable to speak at 3 years, yet appeared to have normal hearing. The diagnosis of severe learning disability, of uncertain cause, was made. Because she began to attack her younger sister, and because of her screaming, she was eventually admitted as a child to a hospital for people with learning disability, as this was a common practice 25 years ago. Although the hospital was a long distance away, her family visited her regularly. She learnt to dress herself and use the toilet but needed help with bathing. She also had to learn how to use sanitary pads, and that masturbation was not socially acceptable in public places. She had screamed daily for many years and many theories were given for this. Reasons given included epilepsy, discomfort due to foreign bodies in her stomach, attention seeking, escape from demand, boredom, or that it was just a habit, yet there appeared no particular pattern to her screaming. Nursing staff thought she was not in pain, and sometimes found that her screaming would stop if it was ignored, although this was difficult for staff to do. When she moved from the hospital into a house in an ordinary street her screaming was so intolerable that an environmental officer was called by neighbours. Even when she was doing the things she enjoyed (such as eating, listening to pop videos, going in the minibus to cafes) her screaming would start. A multidisciplinary assessment was arranged by the community learning disability team in order to identify what practical help could or should be offered to her within her home. The strategies used were based on direct and video observation and an analogue assessment of her behaviour. First, there was the realization that her screaming was a method of communication that was entirely consistent with her prelinguistic developmental level. Second, the approach from all staff was to be a consistent one. Mild antidepressant anxiolytic medication was helpful for 2 months whilst staff concentrated on understanding and interpreting her other methods of communication (facial expression, posture, tone of voice, touch). The use of a hearing aid to magnify the sound of her own voice startled her and was a deterrent for a short time. Staff also encouraged her to interact with others in games of turn taking, and using eye contact. Sometimes stereo headphones were used to play for her a variety of music and sounds. One to one activities were carefully planned. Now she screams much less frequently, and any screaming appears to have the function of being more responsive and communicative. Only once a week is it prolonged, and occurs in specific circumstances such as when she is tired or when someone says 'No' to something she wants.

Summary of Case Study 7.15

- Causation of learning disability perhaps not known.
- Behavioural difficulties in people with profound learning disability can be very problematic to change.
- There is often a need to undertake a functional analysis of behaviour to adequately understand its complexities.
- With such complex needs it is often advisable to involve the total resource of the community learning disability team.

(Carr and Carlson, 1993; Peterson and Martens, 1995)

Case Study 7.16 Mild learning disability with epilepsy and aggression

Neil is now 35 years old and lives in a staffed house, having spent his childhood and young adulthood in various hospitals and centres for people with epilepsy. He had a normal birth and development until he had meningitis at 18 months; following this infection he was left with a left-sided paralysis, severe tremor, epileptic seizures and difficulty controlling his temper. Neil has had his intelligence measured using the Weschler Adult Intelligence Scale (WAIS) (Weschler, 1981) which indicated an IQ level of 60. He has learned to read, write and use public transport. He appears fluent and articulate, but he is emotionally immature and volatile. He is impatient towards others, yet is oversensitive himself, particularly about his own severe physical and performance difficulties. He usually feels rivalry towards men in authority and needs reassurance and explanation at a logical level that needs to be much simpler than would be expected from his apparent understanding. He can be irritable for days before an epileptic seizure and these occur every 1–2 weeks with occasional status epilepticus. His community learning disability nurse has trained certain residential staff in the use of rectal diazepam. Another health issue is that he is a high-risk hepatitis B carrier, having acquired this infection when living in close contact with another carrier at a time when vaccination was not readily available. Because of the risk of the transmission of the infection from cuts, injuries and blood contact, all residents and staff who were not already immune have received hepatitis B vaccination. He has threatened, and/or been physically aggressive to staff or his companions once every 2–3 months, and although he does not suffer from a mental health problem, he finds that in periods of stress he feels calmer if he takes a short course of antipsychotic medication. His frustration and aggression can be so severe that other residents have asked him to leave the house. Changes in the type of long-term anticonvulsant medication prescribed for him have been of some help to him in preventing his rapid mood swings. He has also had help with relaxation and stress management from a clinical psychologist, but still finds such techniques difficult to apply in the heat of the moment. Staff are now working with him by using a simple behavioural approach that allows him to feel in control as much as possible, whilst taking increasing responsibility for areas in which he can succeed. He values the special attention of regular chats on his own with staff along with a cup of coffee. With this daily feedback and praise for calm behaviour, the frequency of aggressive incidents has reduced. However, both he and the staff know that his problem is a long term one and that such incidents will probably recur. He needs continuing supervision, anticipation of stress and assessment of risk and very careful gearing of any emotional and practical demands on him so that he can manage with dignity.

Summary of Case Study 7.16

- **Learning diability may have minimal impact upon the individual's life.**
- **Epilepsy needs careful monitoring along with regular anticonvulsant monitoring.**
- **Mental health problems are as common, if not more so, in people with a learning disability, than in the general population.**

(Kaski *et al.*, 1991; Forceville *et al.*, 1992; Harris, 1993)

Case Study 7.17 Brain damage, emotional outbursts and sexual assault

Kevin's birth was by a difficult, premature breech delivery. He was a nervous emotional child and although he started at a normal school it soon became clear he was unable to cope with this, so his parents paid for a private school and eventually he went to a boarding school for maladjusted and educationally subnormal children. He never learned to read, but did develop road sense and could tell the time. He eventually returned home in adolescence because of his asthma and nervous vomiting. There is a family history of peptic ulcers, diabetes, asthma and ulcerative colitis, which are all physical disorders that can be exacerbated by anxiety. He himself has always had difficulty expressing his feelings and appears to convert any emotional discomfort into physical symptoms. Whenever he was challenged or confronted for his unacceptable behaviour, he has found that if he pleaded he had an upset stomach his teachers and parents were lenient with him. He developed into a courteous and conscientious young man who was easily embarrassed and volatile under stress. At home he would shout and bang doors if frustrated and unable to get his own way. The most testing time for him was in his mid-twenties when he most keenly felt that he wanted to have an ordinary job and an ordinary life. He was having work experience training in a day centre, hoping to work in a supermarket that would entail independent travel and good time-keeping. On several occasions over a period of 6 months he had touched female staff in his day centre on the breast or neck. This was sudden and unexpected to the women concerned, but appeared to be determined and intrusive in nature. When challenged, he claimed to have no knowledge of what he had done but said he had had an upset stomach. At the time of these attacks he appeared to be quite conscious and accurate in his target. However, because these attacks were unexpected and brief and always followed the same pattern, it was thought that they may be epileptic in nature. It was decided to observe him closely and his community learning disability nurse provided regular sex and relationship counselling as well as relaxation sessions. Because of the nature of previous attacks, another nurse who was experienced in behaviour techniques and risk reduction was present during these sessions. During the first session he physically attacked the community nurse and needed to be carefully physically restrained by the second nurse. At the start of subsequent sessions he was told that if an attack was attempted he would be restrained and the session terminated. No further attacks took place in following sessions. There were no aggressive or sexual incidents for another 6 months, then one day when he was travelling alone on a bus to the work experience placement he grabbed the throat and breast of a middle-aged woman who was sitting nearby. He was taken to the police station and charged with assault. His community learning disability nurse ensured that his solicitor was called and informed the psychiatrist who came quickly to assess his mental state and prepare a report for the court. His nurse remained with him throughout interviews with his solicitor and by the police and herself gave evidence in the magistrates' hearing. The court directed, as a condition of bail, that he could be admitted to hospital on Section 2 of the 1983 Mental Health Act for assessment because of his significant learning disability, and the possibility that he may have epilepsy or mental illness, hence he did not have to undergo a prison sentence that would have been inappropriate and extremely stressful for a man of his ability. The community nurse gave support to his family during and following the court hearing and liaised with hospital staff during the period of his admission to hospital. Whilst he was in hospital the use of antilibidinal hormones or antipsychotics was considered, but thought to be inappropriate as his attacks were not considered persistent and dangerous enough. Instead, he was prescribed carbamazepine to help with his mood swings and outbursts of poor control, in view of his history of probably anoxic brain damage at birth. This medication later was reduced to the lowest therapeutic level, as on higher doses he had a low white cell count. When he was discharged from hospital he again became easily frustrated and emotional and sensitive about being teased. He agreed to the overall policy that he would continue on a low dose of carbamazepine, and would accept counselling to help him with his relationship with his girlfriend. He rather reluctantly relinquished his ambitions of having regular paid work as he realized this would be too stressful for him at present. When he followed this course and took on more routine tasks at the day centre for fewer days of the working week he felt more confident and his difficult behaviour did not recur.

Summary of Case Study 7.17

- **Overall delay and arrest of development.**
- **Inappropriate sexual behaviour.**
- **Unable to deal with difficult situations.**
- **Poor social skills likely to bring about inevitable confrontation with the police.**

(Brown and Barrett, 1994; Clare and Gudjonsson, 1995)

Discussion Questions

What sorts of therapeutic interventions might professional carers make to bring about health maintenance and/or gain in the various case histories presented in this chapter?

A wide range of causes of learning disability can be detected *in utero*. Is it the case that such prevention is no more than a positive form of eugenics?

In people with Down's syndrome, cosmetic surgery has been used to reshape the epicanthic folds over the upper eye lids. Do you think such surgery is justifiable and would it assist in the maintenance and/or improvement of the health of such individuals?

References

Bagenholm, A. and Gillberg, C. (1991) Psychosocial effects on siblings of children with autism and mental retardation: a population-based study. *Journal of Mental Deficiency Research* **35**: 291–307.

Baron-Cohen, S., Cross, P., Crowson, M. and Robertson, M. (1994) Can children with Gilles de la Tourette syndrome edit their intentions? *Psychological Medicine* **24**(1): 29–40.

Berg, J.M. and Pakulza, Z. (1972) Angelman's (Happy Puppet) syndrome. *American Journal of Disability Child* **123**: 72.

Brown, H. and Barrett, S. (1994) Understanding and responding to difficult sexual behaviour. *In* Craft, A. (Ed.) *Practice Issues in Sexuality and Learning Disabilities*, pp. 50–80. London: Routledge.

Carr, E. and Carlson, J. (1993) Reduction of severe behaviour problems in the community using a multicomponent treatment approach. *Journal of Applied Behaviour Analysis* **26**(2): 157–172.

Clare, I. and Gudjonsson, G. (1995) The vulnerability of suspects with intellectual disabilities during police interviews: A review and experimental study of decision-making. *Mental Handicap Research* **8**(2): 110–128.

Clarke, D. (1986) *Mentally Handicapped People: Living and Learning.* London: Baillière Tindall.

Clarke, D. and Yapa, P. (1991) Phenylketonuria and anorexia nervosa. *Journal of Mental Deficiency Research* **35**: 165–170.

Coleman, M., Brubaker, J., Hunter, K. and Smith, G. (1988) Rett syndrome: A survey of North American patients. *Journal of Mental Deficiency Research* **32**: 117–124.

Connor, J.M. (1990) Epidemiology and genetic approaches in tuberous sclerosis. *In* Ishibashi, Y. and Hori, Y. (Eds) *Tuberous Sclerosis and Neurofibromatosis: Epidemiology, pathophysiology, biology and management.* Amsterdam: Elsevier Science.

Forceville, E., Dekker, M., Aldenkamp, A., Alpherts, W. and Schelvis, A. (1992) Subtest profiles of the WISC-R and WAIS in mentally retarded patients with epilepsy. *Journal of Intellectual Disability Research* **36**: 45–59.

Fryers, T. (1986) Factors affecting prevalence of severe mental retardation. *In* Berg, J. (Ed.) *Science and Service in Mental Retardation*, pp. 3–14. London: Methuen.

Gath, A. and Gumley, D. (1986) Behaviour problems in retarded children with special reference to Down's syndrome. *British Journal of Psychiatry* **149**: 156–161.

Ghaziuddin, M., Tsai, L. and Ghaziuddin, N. (1992) Autism in Down's syndrome: presentation and diagnosis. *Journal of Intellectual Research* **36**: 449–456.

Gillberg, C. (1993) Autism and related behaviours. *Journal of Intellectual Disability Research* **37**: 343–372.

Gostason, R. and Akesson, H. (1986) Epidemiological and psychiatric aspects of mental retardation: A Swedish population study. *In* Berg, J. (Ed.) *Science and Service in Mental Retardation*, pp. 111–123. London: Methuen.

Hagberg, B., Goutieres, F., Hanefield, F., Rett, A. and Wilson, J. (1985) Rett syndrome: Criteria for inclusion and exclusion. *Brain Development* **7**: 372–373.

Harris, P. (1993) The nature and extent of aggressive behaviour amongst people with learning difficulties (mental handicap) in a single health district. *Journal of Intellectual Disability Research* **37**: 221–242.

Hersh, J.H., Bloom, A.S., Zinnerman, A.W., Dinno, N.A., Greenstein, R.M., Weisskopf, B. and Reese, A.H. (1981) Behavioural correlates in the happy puppet syndrome: a characteristic profile. *Developmental Medicine and Child Neurology* **23**: 792–800.

Hoskin, R., Sasitharan, T. and Howard, R. (1992) The use of a low phenylalanine diet with amino acid supplement in the treatment of behavioural problems in a severely mentally retarded adult female with phenylketonuria. *Journal of Intellectual Disability Research* **36**: 183–191.

Hunt, A. (1993) Development, behaviour and seizures in 300 cases of tuberose sclerosis. *Journal of Intellectual Research* **37**: 41–51.

Kaski, M., Heinonen, E., Tuominen, J. and Anttila, M. (1991) Treatment of epilepsy in mentally retarded patients with a slow release carbamazine preparation. *Journal of Mental Deficiency Research* **35**: 231–239.

Leck, I. (1981) Insights into the causation of disorders of early life. *In* Davis, J. and Dobbing, J. (Eds) *Scientific Foundations of Paediatrics*, 2nd edn, pp. 947–979. London: Heinemann.

Peterson, F. and Martens, B. (1995) A comparison of behavioural interventions reported in treatment studies and programs for adults with developmental disabilities. *Research in Developmental Disabilities* **16**(1): 27–41.

Reid, A. (1982) *The Psychiatry of Mental Handicap*. Oxford: Blackwell Scientific.

Wehmeyer, M., Bourland, G. and Ingram, D. (1993) An analogue assessment of hand stereotypes in two cases of Rett syndrome. *Journal of Intellectual Research* **37**: 95–102.

Weschler, D. (1981) *Weschler Adult Intelligence Scale – Revised.* New York: The Psychological Corporation.

Woodyat, G. and Ozanne, A. (1992) Communication abilities in a case of Rett syndrome. *Journal of Intellectual Research* **36**: 83–92.

Further Reading

Bloom, A.S., Hersh, J.H., Podruch, P.E., Weisskopf, B., Topinka, C.W. and Reese, A. (1986). Developmental characteristics of recognizable patterns of human malformation. Berg, J.M. (Ed.) *Science and Service in Mental Retardation*, pp. 34–51. London: Methuen.

Cassidy, S.B. (1984) The Prader–Willi syndrome. *Current Problems in Paediatrics* **14**: 5–55.

Connolly, J.A. (1978) Developmental outcome in Down Syndrome. *American Journal of Mental Deficiency* **82**: 193–196.

Heaton-Ward, A. and Wiley, Y. (1984) *Mental Handicap*. Bristol: Wright.

Howard-Peebles, P.N., Stoddard, G.R. and Mims, M.G. (1979) Familial X linked mental retardation, verbal disability and chromosomes. *American Journal of Human Genetics* **31**: 214–222.

Lindsey, M. (1990) *Dictionary of Mental Handicap*. London: Routledge.

Little, W.J. (1862) On the influence of abnormal parturition, difficult labours, premature birth and asphyxia neonatorum on the physical condition of the child, especially in relation to deformities. *Obstetrical Transactions* **3**: 293.

Magalino, S.I. (1990) *Dictionary of Medical Syndromes,* 3rd edn. Philadelphia: Lippincott.

Oliver, C. and Holland, A.J. (1986) Down's syndrome and Alzheimer's disease – A review. *Psychological Medicine* **16**: 307–322.

Piper, M.L. and Ramsay, M.K. (1980) Developmental outcome in Down Syndrome. *American Journal of Mental Deficiency* **85**: 39–44.

Russell, O. (1985) *Mental Handicap.* Edinburgh: Churchill Livingstone.

Salmon, M. (1978) *Developmental Defects in Syndromes.* Aylesbury: HM and M.

Smith, D.W. (1982) *Recognizable Patterns of Human Malformation.* Philadelphia: Saunders.

Thapar, A., Gottesman, I.I., Owen, M.J., O'Donavan, M.C. and McGuffin, P. (1994) The genetics of mental retardation. *British Journal of Psychiatry* **164**: 747–758.

Turk, J. (1992) The fragile X syndrome. On the way to a behavioural phenotype. *British Journal of Psychiatry* **164**: 747–758.

Turner, G., Daniel, A. and Frost, M. (1980) X linked mental retardation, macro orchidism and the Xq27 fragile site. *Journal of Paediatrics* **96**: 837–841.

Wilkins, L.E., Brown, J.A. and Wolf, B. (1980) Psychomotor development in 65 home-reared children with Cri du Chat syndrome. *Journal of Paediatrics* **97**: 49–405.

Part Five: Psychosocial Dimensions of Learning Disability

8	**Leading a Normal Life**	**161**

Sue Merrylees and Bob Gates

Part Five of *Dimensions of Learning Disability* explores the ability of people with learning disabilities to lead normal lives. The impact of the introduction of the various concepts of normalization on the planning of services has been profound. Some commentators have stated that there cannot be a single service specification for people with learning disabilities that does not make reference to normalist theories. In this chapter, Sue Beacock and Bob Gates trace the context that provided the necessary conditions for the development of normalization, followed by an overview of the significant contributors to this field of study. It is suggested that normalization, whilst being a generic term, has meant and continues to mean different things to different people. It is further argued that the implementation of normalization occurs within the context of a continually changing social policy arena. Thus, the principles of normalization have to be mediated through this context into the practice dimension of caring for people with learning disabilities. The final section of the chapter briefly outlines this practice dimension and suggests how health (in its widest sense), well being and the quality of life may be enhanced by practice that is grounded in the principles of normalization.

Chapter 8: Leading a normal life
Sue Merrylees and Bob Gates

8.1 Introduction

Enshrined in the 1959 Mental Retardation Act of Denmark was the genesis of the various concepts of normalization. This Act said that the aim of services for people with learning disabilities was:

> to create an existence for the mentally retarded as close to normal living conditions as possible. (Bank-Mikkelson, 1980)

This chapter examines the various concepts of normalization and is contextualized in the experiences of people with learning disabilities, and those who share this experience with them. The chapter explores the relationship between policy and practice, and the effect of this relationship upon the lives of people with learning disabilities.

Normalization, in learning disability, has long held the floor of debate. The fundamental principles of an 'Ordinary Life' (Kings Fund, 1980) enabled us to understand the concepts of normalization within the context and culture of contemporary societies. However, much recent debate has focused on the reality of applying these principles in the arena of service delivery in the 1990s (Dalley, 1992; Ward, 1992), and there is evidence of a growing discontent with the premises of the normalist theories. A central aim of this chapter is to clarify and explore ideas that, although not new, offer the reader opportunity to define, and/or perhaps redefine their thinking concerning contemporary practice in the delivery of services to people with learning disabilities. The chapter addresses a range of issues that are grouped into two major themes.

The Policy Dimension

This theme examines policies that have had an impact on the implementation of the principles of normalization as well as those policies that have grown out of the concept. This theme also addresses the changing perception of client need, and the implications of this for the individual, the carer and providers of services.

The Practice Dimension

This second theme discusses the realities of attempting to apply the principles of normalization to the practices of everyday life. A case study approach is used, and the aim is to use examples of a range of issues that support normalization, and contrast these with the experience of individuals in their natural setting.

Before these themes are explored, the next section of the chapter provides a context for the development of normalist theories, followed by a brief overview of the various definitions of normalization.

8.2 A Context for the Development of Normalist Theories

In the early part of this century people with learning disabilities were classified under the legal definitions of the Mental Deficiency Act (1913). This Act predominantly used measures of social competence as a way of categorizing people with learning disabilities. The Act used the terms:

- **idiot**
- **imbecile**
- **feeble minded**
- **morally defective**

and clearly reflected the prevailing opinion that learning disability was a social, rather than a medical or health-related issue (see Chapter 1). It is therefore perhaps somewhat ironic that one of the most significant pieces of twentieth century legislation, the National Health Service Act (1946), served to confirm a growing move towards the clinical classification of people with learning disabilities. This had emerged from the increasing medicalization of institutions and treatments. This division of need of an individual as being either health oriented or socially oriented can be understood as a reflection of the origins and roots of service provision. As a result of such continued confusion over divisive policy, people with learning disabilities have consistently found themselves in receipt of services that have met one defined need; that is, social or medical need.

The medical model became prevalent throughout the 1920s and 1930s (see Chapter 1) as a result of the growth of the specialism of psychiatry. The closed world of the institutions enabled the development of medical treatments in the belief that a 'cure' could be found for the symptoms (if not the cause) of learning disability. The powerful effect of the medical view is one that continues to prevail and causes a great deal of confusion over the application of contemporary philosophies of care, and continues to contradict current thinking of the need for ordinary community-based services for people with learning disabilities. There is a fear that many of the present policies can be seen to be driving services back towards a medical model.

Another significant factor that enabled the emergence of the need for new ways to think about people with learning disability was the advent of community-based care programmes. As early as the 1950s, a Royal Commission (1954–1957) published a report that highlighted the need to end segregation, and place a greater emphasis on community care. Subsequent legislation from this commission, the Mental Health Act (1959), introduced the concept of 'informal status'. This lifted previous legal constraints of having to certify and detain people with learning disabilities in hospital, and began to reverse the trend of institutional care. This shift was more imagined than real, and it is only in the last few years that we have witnessed a significant move from institutional care. With trends reversing on both admission and discharge, the demise of the large institutions is almost upon us.

Changes in mental health legislation and the dominance of the medical approach towards learning disability were not the only factors that resulted in the development of the principles of normalization. Other issues, such as local, national and global factors, wove together to force a reappraisal of the treatment of devalued and disadvantaged groups. These factors are useful to examine as they further contextualize the application of views on normalization. The first factor was an increasing awareness of the needs and rights of people with disability. Various movements and campaigns concerning the rights of disabled people grew out of a cultural change, and recognition of the disabled as a priority group. Glennester and Korman (1985) for example, have highlighted that one of the reasons for this attitudinal shift was the discharge of ex-servicemen from the Vietnam conflict. In the mid-1960s, the then President of the USA J. F. Kennedy, made his infamous speech concerning the need to:

> retain in and return to the community the . . . mentally retarded. (cited in Scheerenberger, 1983)

In 1975, the United Nations made a declaration of human rights for the disabled person, among which was the right to:

> enjoy first and foremost a decent level of living, as normal as possible. (United Nations, 1975)

This international declaration brought disablement issues into sharp focus and highlighted the need for a change to care philosophies. Another important factor was the publicity surrounding the care and treatment of people in supported accommodation. The campaign for the mentally handicapped discussed in depth the implementation of the principles of normalization for people with learning disabilities (Shearer, 1972). Many adverse reports surfaced concerning learning disability services such as the Normansfield (DOH, 1969b) and Ely (DOH, 1969a) enquiries. These enquiries played a vital part in forcing providers of services for people with learning disabilities, as well as society at large, to address the appropriateness of care being based on a medically oriented model. This brief historical background provides a temporal analysis of some of the factors, albeit superficial, of a context of the necessary conditions that enabled the principles of normalization to emerge as an influential force of change in the UK.

8.3 The Normalist Theories Outlined

This section outlines some of the major contributions that have been made in attempting to define the concepts of normalization. These form the basis for a further discussion of the practical issues that face providers of care in operationalizing the concept(s). Normalization has developed over the last three decades and has had an undeniable effect upon helping to shape and define attitudes towards the needs of people with learning disabilities. The literature concerning normalization is vast. Brown and Smith (1992) provide one of the most authoritative and comprehensive overviews of normalization to be found. An alternative and very accessible account of normalization is given by Chisholm (1993).

In 1980, Nirje articulated the following definition of normalization:

> making available to all mentally retarded people (and those with a handicapping condition) patterns of life and conditions of everyday living which are as close as possible to the regular circumstances and ways of society. (Nirje, 1980)

Nirge's definition appears to be based upon a social welfare model that takes as its fundamental characteristics the *right* that all people have to services and provisions that would be acceptable to all people in society. At a problematic level, such an ideal would appear difficult to achieve due to lack of resource and also because some people with learning disabilities cannot speak for themselves, and require others to help them in making choices. Juul and Linton (1978) offered the following view of normalization:

> The normalisation principle simply implies that the handicapped ought to be able to live a life as equal as possible to a normal existence and with the same rights and obligations as other people. The handicapped are to be accepted for their exceptionalities where these cannot be remedied. (Juul and Linton, 1978)

Juul and Linton (1978) moved some way towards accepting that individuals with learning disabilities needed services that acknowledged their *uniqueness*. He discussed the acceptance of '*exceptionalities*' that moved the boundaries of accepting one single set of norms as standard. Juul and Linton (1978) also recognized the centrality of obligations and rights and how these two issues affect the lives of people with disabilities.

One fundamental issue when dealing with rights is the authority of caregivers to withdraw rights, based upon some loose assessment of the obligations of the individual. A prime example of this is the person whose behaviour challenges others and has to remain in institutional care, because their behaviour means they cannot or will not fulfil their obligations to the wider society. This element of the normalization principle is open to abuse and can be applied in a punitive manner. The question of right and responsibility is one that is based in philosophy and ethics.

Juul and Linton (1978) also used the language of '*ought*' rather than '*should*'; this unfortunately has been interpreted by some rather cynically. For example, participation in society is not defined as an automatic right, but becomes dependent on obligations and resource. Grunewald (1978) added to the debate by highlighting that:

> The validity of normalisation is not negated by the fact that the majority of handicapped individuals cannot become fully adjusted to society thus even the most severely handicapped can in one or more ways become normalised. (Grunewald, 1978)

Grunewald (1978) also drew upon Juul and Linton's (1978) notion of accepting the '*exceptional*' but reinforced this by arguing that if strengths were exploited then weaknesses became less pronounced. Grunewald's (1978) explanation of normalization enables services providers and carers to meet the specialist and complex needs of the individual with learning disabilities within a framework of the normalization principles. Grunewald (1978) accepted that there were resource and structural limitations to the application of normative practice.

Another exponent of the principle of normalization, and probably the best known, is that of Wolf Wolfensberger, who in (1972) said that normalization could be seen as:

> The use of culturally valued means in order to establish and/or maintain personal behaviours and characteristics which are likewise culturally valued. (Wolfensberger, 1972)

On an unproblematic level this definition of normalization would appear clear and achievable. Wolfensberger (1972) advocated using culturally valued means; however, this may be, and has been, interpreted in many ways. For example, regular ways of society could be interpreted as living in ordinary houses. Wolfensberger (1972) argued that exposure to these means would result in the establishment of personal behaviours that were as equally valued as others in society. Put simply, normalization could be interpreted as placing an individual in a normal situation, such as living in an ordinary house, following which the individual would begin to behave in a normal and culturally valued way.

There would appear to be problems in this literal interpretation of normalization. By addressing individual behaviour as a consequence of exposure, then structural issues such as support and skilled interventions become secondary considerations. The literal interpretation of this most commonly used statement negates many of the complex needs of the individual with learning disabilities and has, perhaps, resulted in policies that have questioned the worth of supported living and specialist services for people with learning disabilities. Another problem is that exposure is only part of the socialization process. Wolfensberger's emerging ideas on normalization were developed into existing sociological theory, which he believed to be universally applicable to all deviant and evaluated groups. This view of normalization advocated exposure to valued means as being the key to the development of personal worth and belonging.

Out of Wolfensberger's work grew the ideas of citizenship and belonging. From these ideas the concept of *social role valorization* was born. The principal difficulty with the concept of social role valorization lay in its highly theoretical nature. This related mainly to the difficulty that people with learning disabilities and those who work with them had in convincing others, in particular purchasers of care, of the value and meaning of this approach.

Because of the complexity and, some would argue, inaccessibility of Wolfensberger's definition of normalization, it has been the subject of misinterpretation by many. Despite this, Wolfensberger has remained influential in the development of normalization, and in 1980 produced two major papers that defined and explored the extent of the problems associated with the various ways in which the concepts of normalization had been interpreted.

The final writer to be examined in this brief overview is John O'Brien, who wrote extensively on normalization throughout the 1980s. His best-known work has become known as the five accomplishments (O'Brien and Tyne, 1981) shown in Box 8.1.

Box 8.1 The five service accomplishments (O'Brien and Tyne, 1981)

- **Community presence**
  This accomplishment requires that people with learning disabilities have a real presence in the community in which they live. This means using and being a part of ordinary neighbourhood facilities in the same way as others.
- **Making choices**
  Here there is a requirement for people with learning disabilities to be enabled to make their own choices. This means helping people with learning disabilities appreciate the context, options and consequences of decisions made.

  Competence
  This accomplishment is concerned with helping people with learning disabilities develop skills in order that they are less dependent upon others and are therefore perceived as being dependent.
- **Respect**
  This accomplishment requires that all media, concerning the ways in which people with learning disabilities, are perceived by others, should always promote them positively and with respect.
- **Participation**
  The last accomplishment requires that people with learning disabilities are supported in developing and maintaining their networks of friends and relatives. This network should be developed and enhanced where ever possible.

These five accomplishments were initially intended to improve the provision and development of services for people with learning disabilities. The service accomplishments of O'Brien and Tyne (1981) are very flexible and may be used as a basis for both service and client development. Many practitioners at an individual level, and service providers at a collective level, have built these tasks to be accomplished into either their individual models of care, or the way in which they provide services. O'Brien has offered a very functional approach that attempts to operationalize the centrality of rights, social role valorization and exceptionalities, into a framework from which to develop and measure services, rather than offering a prescriptive solution to service delivery problems.

Reader Activity 8.1

In order to explore some of the ideas outlined so far, this activity looks at valuing, as well as looking at the right to have an issue valued. Think of one aspect of your life that you value and then answer the following questions:

- **What right have you to this?**
- **What obligations do you fulfil in order to enjoy it?**

Now think of a person whom you know with learning disabilities and answer these questions again. Note any differences or similarities in the way in which these are viewed. For instance, you may have highlighted for yourself that you value spending time alone.

This section provides a brief overview of some of those who have contributed to the development of the different theories of normalization. These different approaches collectively encompass egalitarianism, rights, quality of life, exceptionalities, social role valorization and non-segregation. Issues of valuing and promoting the life styles of people with learning disabilities are a consistent theme in all of the different definitions explored. The next section explores three areas within social policy that have run alongside the concepts of normalization and perhaps challenge some of its philosophical premises, when contextualized in the 'cold climate' of purchasing and providing services for people with learning disabilities.

8.4 Leading a Normal Life: The Policy Dimension

This section commences with an exploration of some important social policy changes and traces their impact on the health of people with learning disabilities. The reasons for selecting these particular pieces of social policy is to examine how they have affected the status of people with learning disabilities. The policies examined are:

- **Working for Patients (1990) and The NHS and Community Care Act (1990)**
- *The Health of the Nation* **(DOH, 1992)**
- **The growth of charterism, 1990 onwards.**

Working for Patients (1990) and The NHS Community Care Act (1990)

Working for Patients (1990), like the Community Care Act (1990), is concerned with imposing an internal market on health care (see Chapter 11). This document enabled local authorities, general practitioner (GP) fundholders and district health authorities to become purchasers of services. Geographically, it would appear that the interpretation and implementation of this paper have been variable. For example, as the large learning disability hospitals have closed, purchasers of services in some parts of the country have sought the reprovision of services exclusively from the independent sector whilst other purchasers have relied solely on National Health Service (NHS) community trusts, or the very rare learning disability NHS trusts. In the case study that follows, a brief history of a learning disability hospital is traced and the destiny of the people who lived there is pursued. There follow reader activities that are designed to 'make real' the complexities of applying the principles of normalization within the current context of health and social care.

Case Study 8.1 A hospital service for people with learning disabilities

This case study involves a learning disability hospital service on the outskirts of a large industrial town. This service became part of a NHS community trust with diverse interests. Twenty-eight years ago the service was largely hospital based; however, it began to discharge clients into supported community living about 12 years ago. The NHS trust was formed in 1992 and has the following interests: community nursing, mental health services, care of the elderly, and learning disability. The priorities for the learning disability directorate were to continue with the move to the community and to develop a purpose-built care unit on the site of the existing hospital provision. The hospital has been successful in finding suitable community-based accommodation for most of the people who lived there. However, a number of people are left with complex and multiple needs and require purpose-built accommodation with specialist learning disability nurses to provide this care. A range of small specialist residential and day-care services are to be built on the old hospital site. There is considerable anger by a number of professionals concerning this development, because they feel that this group of people is being denied the opportunity of pursuing an ordinary life style in a home away from a hospital site. There is also a cynical view that as the trust is already in receipt of the hospital site then capital cost implications make the site preferable to purchasing land in a more expensive part of the town.

Reader Activity 8.2
In the section that dealt with the various interpretations of normalization it was clear that all promoted valuing and improving the life styles of people with learning disability. In addition, O'Brien identified five service accomplishments. How do you think a manager in this NHS trust would defend their decision to retain specialist services on the old hospital site?

- people with learning disabilities will be happier with their life styles
- that as a general rule people with learning disabilities will develop few new skills
- there will be little community presence
- there will be an increase in contact between staff and clients
- there will be an improvement in material standards of living

Assumptions have been made concerning the move of people with learning disability from hospital to community settings. A recent scholarly review of research in this area provides some very interesting insights. Following a review of a number of research studies, conducted between 1980 and 1993, of people with learning disability who had moved from hospitals to community settings, Emerson and Hatton (1994) identified that:

- **behavioural difficulties will continue in community settings and may worsen**

The NHS and Community Care Act (1990) sought to improve services of care in the community. It advocated a multi-agency approach to care that would require the statutory sectors to work alongside, and depend upon, a flourishing independent sector. The Act has heralded fundamental changes in the arrangements of funding and delivery of care for people with learning disabilities, with social service departments taking the lead role in the assessment and management of care. The NHS and Community Care Act (1990) made a clear distinction between care that was considered to be health, and that which was considered social care and this appears to have had a profound effect upon the types of services accessible to people with learning disabilities. Funding arrangements within this Act have caused problems; social services now control the budget for individual placements. It has been estimated that of this budget some 85% is required to maintain existing residential placements. Of the remaining 15%, approximately 12% has been spent on staff training and the administration necessary for implementation. This has left only 3% for the development and promotion of services as highlighted in Booth (1993). With such a scenario in funding arrangements, it is not difficult to envisage problems in prioritizing demand.

Lee (1993), for example, has described how in one division of a social services department, that operated in a largely working class community, the services for people with learning disabilities have been affected. Under new arrangements in this area a community care assessment team comprising one social worker, three assessment officers and one occupational therapist was established. The assessment officers are people from a caring service background who have undertaken three extra days training for their current role. On receipt of a referral the assessment officers are responsible for initial contact; if they feel it necessary, the person is then referred to the social worker. Once assessment has been completed, the subsequent 'care' plan has to be implemented within five working days or the person has right of redress. With the limited resource available there is already a backlog of assessments.

It is suggested that in the real world applying the principles of normalization in resource-led services is at best difficult and at worst impossible. Services often fail to meet the needs of the individual, and this means that a fundamental principle of normalization, that of treating the person as an individual, fails to be addressed.

Perhaps the principles of normalization will be severely compromised within a context of loss of priority for people with learning disabilities, as a result of the NHS and Community Care Act. This loss can be summarized by the following:

- **lack of resource**
- **confusion over implementation**
- **issues of equity.**

It can be seen from the above that community care and the principles of normalization are inexorably linked. Community care policies have been a significant factor in the development of the normalization philosophies. However, when normalization is placed within the context of current social policy, then its meaning to people with learning disability, their families and those who provide care for them, becomes problematic. Case Study 8.2 recounts another experience concerning the closure of a different hospital for people with learning disabilities and the fate of those people who used to live there.

Case Study 8.2 Closure of a hospital for people with learning disabilities

This hospital was built around an existing stately home that was purchased by a local health board in 1934. The hospital catered for around 150 male residents and was 8 km from the nearest town. The hospital was not on a bus route and had to rely on its own transport. A bus did come past the hospital on a Sunday that carried the residents' relatives from the city which was 27 km to the west of the hospital. When the local health boards were reorganized after the NHS Act the hospital became part of a group of three, the largest of which was in another rural location; 24 km north of the city this hospital housed 280 residents. The third was on the edge of the city, this catered for only female residents. As with most hospitals, rationalization began in the mid 1970s with the discharge of residents who, although institutionalized, could function independently in the community. Social services opened a hostel in a local village and several of the so-called 'high-grade lads' went there and came back to the hospital to work as porters, gardeners and domestic assistants. As the years progressed, the clients changed, the children were transferred to the largest hospital in the group in 1976, when a school was built to provide each of the children with an education. The profile of the needs of the residents changed and dependency considerably increased. The residents got older and a new unit was set up to cater for the elderly residents and the increasing health needs of others. Care plans and individual programme planning (IPP) were introduced in the very early 1980s; residents started going on holidays to places other than holiday camps; but the two constant factors of rural isolation and an all-male resident group remained a barrier to integration. As with many of these hospitals, the facade changed, fixtures and fittings improved and the principles of normalization, or at least what staff understood to be normalization, were applied within the constraints of the environment and resource available. The will to make the hospital a better place was there, but a range of factors was stacked against care staff making any real progress. In the end it was not the poor quality of care and indifference of the staff that caused the closure of this hospital, but the economic policies of the local health authority. The hospital closed in 1989 – what happened to the 80 residents who had lived there? They were discharged into the care of local private organizations. These arrangements varied from an ex-member of staff who 'adopted' three residents into her own home, to a private company who moved into the area and converted boarding hotels into 8–10-bedded residential homes that are registered with social services. The residents discharged into these private care homes left under the dowry scheme. This meant that the residents were 'kick started' with a lump sum equivalent to 1 year's care costs. The remaining residents were transferred, rather than discharged; the majority went to the largest of the three hospitals left.

Reader Activity 8.3
Having read this case study consider the following points:

- **Do you feel that the principles of normalization already outlined governed the approach to the reprovision of care for this group of people?**
- **Identify a range of people who were involved in the closure of a local learning disability hospital near you. Interview them and attempt to identify the model/s of reprovision that were pursued after the closure of the hospital. Attempt to find out where people now live, how many went to the private, independent, not for profit and, lastly, health or Social Service sectors. Also identify the size (number of beds) of the new alternative residential provision.**

To conclude, a major problem with the NHS and Community Care Act (1990) has been one of resource. Evidence from a series of articles published by Community Care (1995) points to a serious underfunding situation. When this is examined alongside the shifts in demographic changes in our society (i.e. an increasing older population that demands more of the resource) then people with learning disabilities must compete for services along with other groups. It is suggested that there is a certain inevitability that the vast proportion of the community care budget will not go to people with learning disabilities. Clearly, the people with learning disabilities will become a low priority, not because their needs are any less important but because there will be little other specialist provision available in the form of health services. This ultimately means that people with learning disabilities who live either in hospital or community settings, purchased by social services or provided by funding from the district health authorities, continue to be subjected to divisive policies. This conflicts directly with care that is based upon individual need, and the applications of philosophies of care based upon the principles of normalization.

The Health of the Nation (DOH, 1992)

The second policy document highlighted here is the *Health of the Nation.* This document was the British Government's response to the World Health Organization's (WHO) *Health for All – A strategy for health for the year 2000.* In a relatively recent publication *The Health of the Nation – The* BMJ *viewpoint,* the radical statistics group highlighted that the Government's document failed completely to address any question of inequalities in health. People with learning disabilities have always had problems in accessing the types of service provision they require. Moves during the late 1970s and the 1980s have gone some way to redress issues of equity. Health was highlighted in the Cullen Report (1987) *Caring for People in the Next Decade and Beyond* (*Mental Handicap Nursing*) by using the WHO's definition that concluded that health was a:

state of complete physical, mental and social well-being rather than solely an absence of disease or infirmity. (WHO, 1946)

This link between health as an issue and people with learning disabilities is important. This is because, despite people with learning disabilities falling into health-care categories, little attention

has previously been paid to health promotion and health enhancement for them. It is therefore somewhat strange to find that not only are issues of inequity in health ignored, but mention of people with learning disabilities in the original *Health of the Nation* document was absent. It could be argued that people with learning disabilities should have their health needs met in the same way as any other citizen, accessing the same range of ordinary services. It is, however, the case that without strong advocates these people have difficulty in accessing health services and their health needs remain largely unaddressed (see Chapters 1, 2 and 16). The Department of Health (DOH) has gone some way towards redressing this issue by releasing a recent publication entitled *The Health of the Nation – a Strategy for People with Learning Disabilities* (DOH, 1995a). However, what appears to be missing from this document is research evidence on the types of health conditions and the epidemiology of health issues affecting people with learning disabilities. It is worth turning our attention towards the practice of health promotion policy at this point.

Reductionism by some learning disability nurse practitioners has resulted in them interpreting health promotion as taking regular clinical measures of client health. This includes, for example, the monthly checking of urine of people who are fit, strong, healthy and holding down a full-time job. Clearly, this might be argued as inappropriate. It is unfortunate, but is often the case, that people with learning disabilities with a recognized need for health promotion end up being the subject of a medically oriented and clinical issue. Health promotion for people with learning disabilities should in itself be a specialism, based on objective evidence that recognizes the environment and situations in which people with learning disabilities live. There is a tremendous need to undertake work in a range of areas, for example examining the causes of accidents in people with learning disabilities, understanding issues of sexuality and health, and addressing the nutritional needs of people with learning disabilities from a specialist viewpoint. In its recent publication

Continuing the Commitment: the Learning Disabilities Project, the DOH (1995b) health surveillance was identified as one of the eight key areas needing to be addressed (see Chapters 1 and 2). It is necessary for all those who work with people with learning disabilities to examine their own practice and to do this within a framework that acknowledges the principles and philosophy of care based on normalization. However, it is important that this framework acknowledges the plurality of concepts of normalization, and therefore takes into account the exceptionalities of the people being cared for.

The Growth of Charterism (1990 onwards)

The last piece of social policy explored in this section *The Patient's Charter* (DOH, 1991) is of relevance to people with learning disabilities because the charter standards are of particular concern to the everyday services provided for people with learning disabilities in health care. Those standards of particular interest are:

- **that a named qualified nurse is responsible for every patient (DOH, 1991)**
- **that arrangements are made to ensure that everyone, including people with special needs, can use services (DOH, 1991).**

As with all charter standards a significant point is made in the introduction to the document that:

These are not legal rights but major and specific standards that the Government looks to the NHS to achieve as circumstances and resources allow. (DOH, 1991)

The language of *The Patient's Charter* is significant in that it is written in 'should' rather that 'will'. It could be argued that this somewhat negates the power of the document, and underlines the fact that some cynics might view this charter as an elaborate public relations exercise. The targets highlighted might be effectively achieved, but reference to resource demonstrates the practical problems

associated. For example, the concept of the named nurse does not identify a ceiling for the number of people that each nurse could be accountable for. To highlight this, consider an example of a community learning disabilities nurse with an active case load of 60 clients – do each of these clients receive a quality service as the result of having a named nurse? The second target that is highlighted here is again achievable, but once again limited by resource. Many facilities within NHS provision remain under-resourced and are used for purposes for which they were not designed. For example, the contraction of the NHS's ability to accommodate people with learning disabilities who have challenging behaviour, in residential care, has resulted in 'difficult to place' clients. Other standards within *The Patient's Charter* are relevant to the needs of people with learning disabilities in much the same way as they apply to all health-care users. However, *The Patient's Charter* appears not to mention standards that reflect the needs of those people who rely upon health service provision for their long-term care.

If we are to apply normal-life principles to people with learning disabilities, then the services they receive should reflect the charter standards that are offered to others within our society.

This brief analysis of *The Patient's Charter* attempts to demonstrate that people with learning disabilities often do not receive the same standard of care as others in our society, and that this means they may need to have someone advocate on their behalf.

The purpose of this section is to offer a view that there is conflict between some current social policy and the implementation of the principles of normalization.

The main issues that are identified are:

- That much current social policy relies on the introduction of the internal market into care provision.
- That current social policy will mean that professional interventions with people with learn-

ing disabilities need to be measurable in order to be 'bought' and 'sold'.

- The divisive measure of attempting to make a clear distinction between 'medical', 'health' and 'social care' may not be in the interests of people with learning disabilities.
- That normalization principles and practice, dependent upon the theoretical path one pursues, may be misused by service providers and purchasers. In other words to use ordinary services can be used as a perverse argument for not meeting the special and unique health needs of some people with learning disabilities.

Having provided three examples of social policy and their actual or potential impact upon the lives of people with learning disabilities, the final section of this chapter focuses on how the principles of normalization may be applied in everyday practice.

8.5 Leading a Normal Life: The Practice Dimension

The aim of this final section of the chapter is to briefly place the concepts of normalization within a framework of practice issues. This is done by examining an example of what is believed to be good practice that demonstrates how the principles of normalization can be incorporated into the different levels of the caring process; that is, from the heady abstractions of theory and social policy to care plans. This is best depicted in diagrammatic form as a practice model (see Figure 8.1).

Figure 8.1 depicts a model where theories and social policy are inexorably linked at all levels of the caring process. This means that theory has to be integrated into local and personal philosophical frameworks, which must then be translated into caring practices. These practices should reflect the positive elements of promoting a normal life style for people with learning disabilities.

This section briefly explores each stage of the model and uses examples from practice that demonstrate how nurse practitioners can work towards a

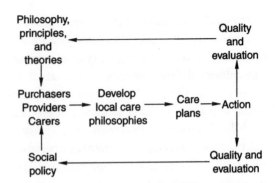

Figure 8.1 A practice model for implementing normalization.

person-oriented system of care delivery. This is achieved by describing one small community home for people with learning disabilities, and in particular the care of one woman who lives in this home whose name is Tina. Both the home and Tina are briefly introduced next before looking at some aspects of her care in more detail.

The Home

This small four-bedroomed home is located on a large private estate of houses in a large city. Four people with learning disabilities live there and they are supported in the home by a range of care staff that includes, a learning disability nurse, a social worker, and a recent graduate who has studied psychology. The people who live at the home all contribute to paying for the food, heating, lighting and other domestic bills. The levels of ability and disability between them is considerable but they support one another and for the most part get on extremely well. All four people moved to the home having been relocated when the large learning disability hospital closed. Relationships with neighbours and local community are extremely positive.

Tina

Tina is a 35-year-old woman who was originally admitted to hospital because she became very aggressive and attacked a fellow worker at a small laundry where her parents had found her a job. After this aggressive outburst her parents were reluctant to allow Tina to continue to live at home, and she was admitted to the local learning disability hospital. Tina is a woman with mild to moderate learning disabilities who has a history of losing her temper with those around her. When this happens she lashes out and has, on a number of occasions, physically hurt those around her. Following admission to the learning disability hospital time was spent on developing her communication skills and working with her on anger management. Care staff recognized her potential and therefore she was encouraged to develop as much independence as possible. Tina struggles with a weight problem and has epilepsy that in the main is well controlled but she does still experience an occasional seizure.

Developing Local Philosophies of Care

The Registered Homes Act (DOH, 1984) has had an effect on the development of community services, by encouraging a written philosophy to be available for registration purposes. This, along with the advent of an increasingly accountable service delivery, has resulted in a directive that most services should make explicit their care philosophies. The following is the written philosophy of care that was developed for this community home:

> We aim to provide a homely environment and to provide the people who live here with the opportunity to lead as normal a life as possible, and to develop new skills and maintain them. We aim to provide excellent standards of care.

Although this is a brief philosophy of care it perhaps demonstrates how in developing such a statement there is a need to take into account the people who will be working in the home, who ultimately will be responsible for operationalizing the philosophy. It is unfortunate but true that many complex claims about care philosophies tend to represent rhetoric that actually prevents the philosophies from being translated into practice. The philosophy of care

outlined above is known to be practised by the care staff, and is also understood by the people who live within the home.

Reader Activity 8.4
Over the next few months attempt to locate and analyse various philosophical statements from various day and residential services. Identify similarities and differences. Also look for evidence that what they say they will do is reflected in the care provided.

Being able to present a philosophy of care that seeks to promote normative life styles, still leaves two important questions that need to be addressed:

- **Do all of the staff working in this community home agree with the statement and believe that it can be transposed into practice?**
- **Assuming that one may answer the first question affirmatively, then how will they actually achieve this?**

Developing and implementing a local philosophy of care based upon the principles of normalization needs to be formulated and implemented by the team of people who will be working on the 'front line'. Most importantly, this philosophy must reflect something that one will aim for yet at the same time such a statement must be achievable. If identifying and articulating a philosophy of care becomes an exercise of manipulating words to present good sound bites, but without the substance of commitment, then the caring process will be compromised and, simply stated, care will not be based upon the principles of normalization.

Care Planning

There are many models and theories for the development of care planning activities. Some confine themselves to addressing nursing theory, some include other disciplines. This section examines how principles of normalization have been integrated into the practice of care planning for Tina, a young woman who lives in the community home already described. The IPP approach is a now familiar process in the field of learning disability and enables care staff, in partnership with people being cared for, to develop goal plans to address the total care needs of the individual. IPP systems have their strength in a multidisciplinary approach.

The following is taken from the IPP process that was used to construct Tina's care plan and demonstrates how such an approach can be used to support a person in developing a normative life style.

Tina is now living in a community home and has been attending a resource centre that is run by social services. Owing to pressure for places, Tina can only attend the centre for 2 days a week. Tina has expressed a wish that she would like a job. Tina's key worker (Jenny) a learning disability nurse practitioner has agreed with Tina to look into the possibility of some kind of employment opportunity. Jenny explored the following issues with Tina:

- **What sort of job would Tina like?**
- **How could Jenny best support and help Tina to apply for a job?**

Some time was spent by Jenny examining the issues and eventually she and Tina decided to hold an IPP meeting that Jenny organized. She invited Tina's mother and father as well as other staff from the home and the day centre. In addition to this, they invited the local pathways employment officer, who was responsible for helping people with special needs seek employment. At the IPP meeting Jenny and Tina presented their progress and difficulties that they had encountered. The following goals were set:

- **Tina would, with help from the pathways officer, seek part-time employment in a local cafe (this is where Tina had said she would like to work).**

- **Tina would, with the help of the day centre staff, develop her written skills in order to be able to complete any application forms.**
- **Tina would at home continue to practise a range of communication and self help skills that would help her in the cafe.**

Tina's mother and father expressed a concern that Tina would not cope in a work environment and that this might result in her developing behaviour difficulties, as had occurred on a previous occasion. However, following considerable discussion it was agreed that Tina had the right to seek out ordinary employment in the same way that anyone else would. To combat the parents' fears, reassurances were given about the importance of allowing Tina plenty of time to practise and develop the skills that she would need and everyone agreed to meet in 3 months' time to see how she had developed. It was also felt that Tina should apply for jobs and compete on her own merits rather than a job being 'set up' for her. All agreed that the pathways officer should help Tina with her applications and that Jenny should accompany her to interviews. Tina spent 3 months working hard on her communication and self-help skills as well as her appearance. She applied for two jobs but failed to get a response. Just before the review meeting, a third part-time job was advertised in a local food chain; Tina applied and was successful. She began work for 12 h a week at a local burger bar. At the review meeting, the parents and care staff agreed to continue to support Tina and further develop her skills in areas of time management and using public transport.

Clearly, the psychosocial value that work can bring to an individual is immeasurable, Tina merely was seeking to exercise her right to employment and enjoy the same types of opportunity as other citizens. IPPs are clearly an important mediator in addressing the psychosocial needs of an individual. However, it is advisable to consider using an overall framework that considers the wider dimensions of being, as advocated in this book. It is suggested that each of these dimensions should be reviewed within the context of the principles of normalization. The following areas should form an integral component of a planning care for an individual:

- **physical care**
- **psychosocial care**
- **skill development**
- **activities of daily living**
- **provision of an appropriate environment**
- **removal of constraints**
- **reduction in undesirable behaviour.**

Each of these areas are now outlined briefly.

Physical Care

This clearly should address the health care needs of the individual. In addition to the physical health care issues that are normally addressed, it may be necessary to explore other aspects of health in more detail. For example, special assessment may be necessary for the person with epilepsy. However, people with learning disabilities should be encouraged, wherever possible, to attend a 'well persons' clinic at their local health centre.

Psychosocial Care

This area should seek to examine activities that include employment and daytime activities, it should also examine how much time the individual person spends with others and how well the service allows their integration into everyday activities. This area is concerned with the psychosocial well being of the individual.

Skill Development

Enhancing the repertoire of skills that we all have increases the possibility of opportunities that as a subsequence open up to us. It is of the utmost importance to identify goals that are designed to meet any deficits in skills that have been highlighted. It should be remembered that skill development does not solely apply to people with learning disabilities. Skill development includes those areas

that either the service and/or carer need to develop to help bring about ordinary life opportunities.

Activities of Daily Living

It is important to consider in a broad sense the normal everyday activities of daily living in which we all engage. This can usefully be undertaken using a framework of activities after the Roper *et al.* (1986) model of nursing. This allows carers to assess the meeting of need within the overall principles of normalization. This model of nursing considers the following activities:

- **breathing**
- **eating**
- **sleeping**
- **eliminating**
- **activity**
- **rest**
- **playing**
- **spirituality**
- **sexuality and safety.**

Barber (1987) and Gates (1996) discuss the uses of this model of nursing in learning disability.

Provision of an Appropriate Environment

Our environment is of special importance to us all. It provides the medium through which we interact with others and to an extent determines the types of opportunities that are open to us for our development. It is important to ask questions about a person's environment from a variety of perspectives (e.g. did the person choose to live where they are – if not where would they prefer to be?). In addition to these questions about decoration, furnishings need to be considered so as to reflect the normalcy of our own environment.

Removal of Constraints

This section examines the interaction between the environment and the person with learning disabilities. It is important to examine attitudes towards an individual with learning disabilities. It should also consider other more tangible barriers to development, for example speech or communication problems.

Reduction in Undesirable Behaviour

If a person has behavioural difficulties then their ability to function independently will be impaired and the range of opportunities available to them become significantly reduced. This area requires carers to identify and reduce behaviour that is undesirable. A part of this process would require an acknowledgement that behaviour is a reflection of the unique interaction between the person and their environment. Therefore to understand undesirable behaviour may mean that carers' own behaviour is unacceptable and that it perpetuates the undesirable behaviour in the person with learning disabilities. In other words the location of that which is undesirable may not in fact rest with the person with learning disabilities.

This section attempts to demonstrate how one may apply the principles of normalization in a practice setting that will enhance the psychosocial well being of people with learning disabilities. Nurse practitioners should deliver nursing care based upon broad workable principles of normalization that transcend the arguments of social and health care.

Quality and Evaluation

Quality is not an absolute. One person's view of quality in a service (or product) will not necessarily be the same as that of another. Quality is about that which is perceived to be good or bad and is essentially subjective and value based. (Chisholm, 1993)

It would appear that deliverers of human services inevitably have to address two issues:

- **The measurement of customer and client satisfaction.**
- **The satisfaction of the agenda of the purchasers.**

The quality measures employed must ensure that they reflect the needs of the individual. *The Patients' Charter* and other initiatives profess to protect the consumer. As was discussed earlier, this is often not the case. It is vital that the person with learning disabilities has their voice heard when service quality is measured.

One common method is through a residents' committee. However, how do we measure the satisfaction of a person with a severe disability? One way is through using measures that acknowledge communication problems such as alternative communication systems. Also the testimony of others, (e.g. parents and volunteers) is a good way of verifying standards. With regard to purchasers of service, it is vital that feedback reflects the value of any approach. The need for clear and explicit outcome-based measurement is vital. Audit systems often measure the quantity but not the quality. Given that the focus of this chapter has been on the psychosocial dimension of learning disabilities and has used normalization as a means of exploring this dimension, it would be incomplete without outlining, albeit briefly, two important ways of measuring quality: namely program analysis of service systems (PASS) and program analysis of service systems implementation of normalization goals (PASSING). Both of these measures attempt to evaluate the quality of the service against the principles of normalization. Chisholm has said that:

PASS has 50 separate ratings and evaluates outcomes for service users using the principle of normalisation, other service-oriented ideologies and administrative considerations . . . PASSING has 42 ratings and is concerned only with issues relating to the normalisation principle. (Chisholm, 1993, p. 42)

Details concerning these particular approaches to measuring the quality of services offered to people with learning disabilities can be found in numerous texts; see for example Heron and Myers (1983) and Lindley and Wainwright (1992).

The political agenda is set, yet often purchasers need the advice of providers in seeking quality. Those who work at the 'coal face' often fear their purchasers, some do not even know who they are.

The responsibility lies with each practitioner to inform purchasers of the value in terms of life enhancement of an approach based on the theories and practice of normalization.

Reader Activity 8.5
Make arrangements to attend an IPP review and consider whether the review made reference to any of the principles of normalization.

8.6 Conclusion

This chapter set about to explore the development of normalization and to examine the major theories and philosophies, and the conclusion drawn from this was that the principles of normalization are complex. The philosophies and theories are linked to the development of practice and should acknowledge the development and the recognition of the need to develop the competence of people with learning disabilities. The aim of this analysis was to give an overview of what the principles mean and to enable the reader to draw their own conclusions on the continuing relevance of the principles of normalization to the care of people with learning disabilities.

The policy section demonstrated how current policies in the care sector have served to disempower individuals and negate the value of the principles of normalization to such an extent that many working in the care sector have begun to question their own base and practice and move towards that which is expected at a cost to the principles of normalization. The final section was designed to show how this is not the case and that adopting such principles can cut across divisive policies and enhance the quality of life of people with learning disabilities.

Discussion Questions
Reflect on the similarities and differences between the various definitions of normalization.

How does normalization differ conceptually from social role valorization?

Given that the context and social climate that exist in the 1990s are considerably different to those of the 1970s is there any future for normalization in human service systems?

References

Bank-Mikkelson, N. (1980) Denmark. *In* Flynn, R.J. and Nitsch, K.E. (Eds) *Normalisation, Social Integration and Community Services.* Austin, TX: Pro-Ed.

Barber, P. (Ed.) (1987) *Mental Handicap: Facilitating holistic care.* London: Hodder & Stoughton.

Booth, P. (1993) Community Care Act. Unpublished essay. Huddersfield University.

Brown, H. and Smith, H. (Eds) (1992) *Normalisation: A reader for the nineties.* London: Routledge.

Chisholm, A. (1993) Quality of care. *In* Shanley, E. and Starrs, T. (Eds) *Learning Disabilities: A handbook of care,* 3rd edn. Edinburgh: Churchill Livingstone.

Dalley, G. (1992) Social welfare ideologies and normalisation: links and conflicts. *In* Brown, H. and Smith, H. (Eds) *Normalisation: A reader for the nineties.* London: Routledge.

Department of Health (DOH) (1969a) *Report of the Committee of Enquiry into Ely Hospital, Cardiff.* London: HMSO.

Department of Health (DOH) (1969b) *Report of the Committee of Enquiry into Normansfield Hospital.* London: HMSO.

Department of Health (DOH) (1984) Registered Homes Act.

Department of Health (DOH) (1991) *The Patient's Charter.* London: HMSO.

Department of Health (DOH) (1992) *Health of the Nation: Strategy for people with learning disabilities.* London: HMSO.

Department of Health (DOH) (1995) *Continuing the Commitment. The Report of the Learning Disability Nursing Project.* London: HMSO.

Gates, B. (1996) Learning disability. *In* Kenworthy, N.K., Snowley, G. and Gilling, C. (Eds) *Common Foundation Studies in Nursing*, 2nd edn, pp. 453–467. Edinburgh: Churchill Livingstone.

Glennester, H. and Korman, S.K. (1985) *Planning for Priority Groups.* London: Robertson.

Grunewald, K. (1977) *Scandinavian Journal of Education Research* **21**(4).

Heron, A. and Myers, M. (1983) *Intellectual Impairment: The battle against handicap.* London: Academic Press.

Juul, K.D. and Linton, T. (1978) European approaches to the treatment of behaviour disordered children. *Behavioural Disorders* **3**(4): 232–249.

Kings Fund (1980) *An Ordinary Life. Comprehensive Locally Based Residential Services for Mentally Handicapped People.* London: Kingsfond Centre.

Lee (1993) Submission for Community Programme, Sheffield University (unpublished).

Lindley, P. and Wainwright, T. (1992) Normalisation training: Conversion or commitment. *In* Brown, H. and Smith, H. (Eds) *Normalisation. A reader for the nineties.* London: Routledge.

Mental Deficiency Act (1913) London: HMSO.

Mental Health Act (1959) London: HMSO.

Mental Retardation Act (1959) Denmark.

National Health Service Act (1946) London: HMSO.

Nirje, B. (1980) The normalisation principle. *In* Flynn, R.J. and Nitsch, K.E. (Eds) *Normalisation, Social Integration and Community Services.* Austin, TX: Pro-Ed.

O'Brien, J. and Tyne, A. (1981) *The Principle of Normalisation: A Foundation for Effective Services.* London: Campaign for the Mentally Handicapped.

Roper, N., Logan, W. and Tierney, A. (1986) Nursing Models: a process of construction and refinement. *In*

Kershaw, B. and Salvage, J. (Eds) *Models for Nursing*, p. 1. Chichester: Wiley.

Scheerenberger, R.C. (1983) *A History of Mental Retardation.* Baltimore: P. H. Brookes.

Shearer, A. (1972) *Normalisation? CMH Discussion Paper* **3**. London: Campaign for the Mentally Handicapped.

United Nations (1975) *Declaration of the Rights of the Disabled Person.* Geneva: UN.

Ward, L. (1992) Foreword. *In* Brown, H. and Smith, H. (Eds) *Normalisation: A reader for the nineties.* London: Routledge.

Wolfensberger, W. (1972) *The Principle of Normalisation in Human Management Services.* Toronto: National Institute of Mental Retardation.

World Health Organization (WHO) (1946) Constitution of the World Health Organization. *In* Caplan, A.L., Engelhardt, H.T. and McCartney, J.J. (Eds) *Concepts of Health and Disease: Interdisciplinary perspectives.* Reading: Addison-Wesley.

Further Reading

Chappell, A.L. (1992) Towards a sociological critique of the normalisation principle. *Disability, Handicap and Society* **7**(1): 35–51.

Couchman, W., Gray, B. and Kenny, B. (1987) Three steps to normalisation. *Senior Nurse* **6**: 11–12.

Day, P.R. (1987) Mind the gap: normalisation theory and practice. *Practice* **Summer**: 105–115.

Emerson, E. and McGill, P. (1989) Normalisation and applied behaviour analysis: Values and technology in services for people with learning difficulties. *Behavioural Psychotherapy* **17**: 10–17.

Glennerster, H. and Korman, N. (1990) Normalisation is not easy. *Community Care* **May**: 25–27.

MacKay, D.N., Mackey, T., McDonald, G. and Gollogly, J. (1988) Normalisation the impossible dream. *British Journal of Mental Subnormality* **34**: 75–77.

Mesibov, G.B. (1990) Normalisation and its relevance today. *Journal of Autism and Developmental Disorders* **September**: 379–390.

Part Six: The Cultural and Spiritual Dimensions of Learning Disability

The dimensions of ethnicity and spirituality are both able to affect the health of people with learning disabilities. In Chapter 9, Sam Ayer first defines and then explores aspects of the diversity of the multicultural composition of Britain. He then develops an argument that suggests that people with learning disabilities face discrimination in terms of employment, lack of appropriate services and access to public places that collectively conspire to cast them into negative social roles (see Chapter 1). Therefore, to be black and have a learning disability means a double level of discrimination. Sam argues that 'Black and ethnic minority people with learning disabilities are doubly stigmatized because of fear based on society's ignorance and unfamiliarity with both disability and race'. He recounts the experiences of people who have been in receipt of racist services. It is clear that such a situation will impact upon the health and well being of people with learning disabilities. The chapter concludes with a useful resource section that nurse practitioners might wish to access. In Chapter 10, Aru Narayanasamy traces the development of spirituality and relates this to people with learning disabilities. Health and well being, amongst other things, are dependent upon inner peace. Enabling the individual to develop their spiritual dimension can assist in their developing inner peace, and thereby contribute to their health and well being. The chapter explores how a nurse practitioner might foster a relationship for enabling spiritual growth. The chapter advocates the development of caring relationships that are based upon self awareness, communication (listening), trust building, giving hope and enabling spiritual growth and suggests that this provides the necessary conditions for providing care based on individual needs.

Chapter 9: Cultural diversity: issues of race and ethnicity in learning disability
Sam Ayer

9.1 Introduction

First, this chapter provides geographical detail of the human structure of the UK. This is followed by defining and exploring the terminology used when talking of ethnicity and/or minority groups. This provides an adequate framework to then explore the provision of services for people with a learning disability. It must be said at the outset that Britain is a multiracial, multilingual and multicultural society. The Policy Study Institute estimates that 4.6% of the total British population were born in the New Commonwealth and Pakistan. Over 43% of the black population is British born. Eighty per cent of young Afro-Caribbean adults are British born. Three per cent of the black population are of pensionable age. Twenty per cent of Afro-Caribbeans and 13% of Asians are over the age of 45 years. Fifty per cent of the population of some cities and boroughs are from black and ethnic minority communities (Brown, 1984).

In Britain, the black and ethnic minority people are disadvantaged and discriminated against in almost every aspect of their lives, for example in housing and employment (Brown, 1984); in education (DES, 1985); and health (Torkington, 1983; McNaught, 1984; Malmot *et al.*, 1984). They consistently receive less than their entitlement to benefits and services (Gohil, 1987; Baxter *et al.*, 1990).

In spite of the culturally diverse nature of society, the key literature on developing services for people with learning disabilities has largely ignored this fact (see e.g. Kings Fund Centre, 1980; Audit Commission, 1986).

Key 'progressive' concepts and principles that underpin service provision show a colour-blind, culture-free and ethnocentric approach in the manner in which they reflect white Anglo-Saxon protestant values. Three examples illustrate this point.

Program analysis of service systems (PASS) is a comprehensive system for evaluating the extent to which services are implementing normalization principles (see Wolfensberger and Glenn, 1975). *Program Analysis of Service Systems: Implementation of Normalization Goals* (PASSING) is similarly used to judge how well services are doing normalization wise, looking in particular at how a service supports devalued peoples' social image and their competence or abilities (see Wolfensberger and Thomas, 1983).

PASS and PASSING evaluations can be a powerful force for change in services. However, almost all the people trained to undertake PASS evaluation in this country are white. There is, therefore, a real risk that their assessment of the environment and life style of black and ethnic-minority clients who have a learning disability will inevitably reflect their own white Anglo-Saxon protestant values. Goals and standards that are culturally more appropriate and relevant for black and ethnic-minority service users are likely to be hard for them to formulate (Baxter *et al.*, 1990).

Individual programme planning (IPP) provides a systematic approach to support and care for people with learning disabilities. It is designed to enable people with learning disabilities to achieve short and longer term goals in their lives that are appropriate to their wishes, needs and circumstances (see Blunden *et al.*, 1987). As Baxter *et al.* (1990) have pointed out, in many ethnic minority communities the collective spirit of families and communities are more highly valued than the more self-centred individualism encouraged in white British society. For black and ethnic minority adults with learning disabilities, this difference in emphasis may be very important.

Another example concerns the assessment tools that are used for people with learning disabilities from the black and minority ethnic communities. Most assessment tools for people with a learning disability have been standardized on a predominantly indigenous white population. They reflect images that are based on white middle-class life styles and experiences. Thus, their 'norms' are inappropriate for black and minority ethnic respondents. The contents of tests also tend to have a strong cultural bias. These are questions on culture bound information (e.g. on English history); questions that the only correct answer reflects Western 'norms' of behaviour; and there are tasks that assume previous familiarity with such things as strip cartoon and jigsaw puzzles (see e.g. Anastasi, 1973). Worse, there may be items in a test that a particular ethnic group finds offensive. As a Moslem health visitor comments:

> in our religion the pig and the dog are not considered nice animals. We find it very offensive when our children are tested on their ability to recognise a pink plastic pig. It is even worse when they are expected to show affection to dogs. It is against our religion. I just don't use them. (Baxter *et al.*, 1990, p. 24)

This chapter explores issues of race and ethnicity and their impact on the life chances, and therefore health, of people from the black and ethnic minority community who have learning disabilities.

9.2 Definition and Terminology: Do We Mean What We Say?

This section attempts to clarify some of the terms that are used in discussions about cultural diversity in multicultural Britain. The use of some terms to describe different groups within this society is an extremely sensitive issue. It is the case that several terms are used to discuss issues of ethnicity and race.

Ethnicity and ethnic groups are elusive concepts; they are difficult to categorize and define (Obidinski, 1978; Peterson, 1980; Therstrom *et al.*, 1980). Each discipline concerned with ethnicity seems to have its own conceptual position on how the term is determined and measured. Ethnicity is obscured by multiple definitions and conceptual positions. Several writers have attempted to identify its major components. Factors that are used for determination of an individual's ethnicity are past origins, conceptions of sociocultural distinctiveness, subcultural social relations, territoriality, kinship and symbolic identification (see e.g. Abramson, 1980; Sorofman, 1986). Also, geographic origin, migratory status, race, language, religion, literature, food choices, settlement patterns, and political and social interests play a part in describing an individual's ethnicity (Therstrom *et al.*, 1980; Sorofman, 1986). Commonly used delineations of ethnic status are race, nationality, religion and geography. Race may be defined as a group of individuals related by common descent, blood or heredity. Nationality is largely determined by the geographic or social location of birth of the individual or the individual's ancestors (e.g. Danish or Ghanaian); that is, not necessarily limited to political boundaries. Religions such as Judaism and Islam may also provide categories for the subdivisions of ethnic groups that are not limited to geographic location.

Segments of a population form ethnic groups by virtue of sharing the combination of:

- **common descent**
- **a socially relevant cultural or physical characteristic**
- **a set of attitudes and behaviours (Kuper and Kuper, 1985).**

On the basis of this definition, people are usually born to an ethnic group rather than acquiring their ethnic status through some special act. Most people marry within, and remain part of, the ethnic group of their origin throughout their entire lives. Since ethnic group members are actually related to one another by blood ties, an ethnic group is a kind of superextended family.

Members of an ethnic group also share certain feelings, ideas and behaviours. To form a real ethnic group and not just an ethnic collection of people, people must, at least to some degree, perceive themselves as a distinctive social group ('we' and 'they' feelings), sense a common fate, interact more among themselves than with outsiders, and think and behave similarly (Smith, 1981; Kuper and Kuper, 1985).

Various political–civic connotations of ethnicity focus upon numerous groups integrated in terms of a sense of peoplehood, common ancestry or similar historical experience implicit in the Greek term 'ethos' meaning 'people' or 'nation' (Francis, 1947; Gordon, 1964).

Similarly, the term 'ethnic' is comparable to the German 'volk' referring to 'people', according to Shibutani and Kwan (1965) who defined the ethnic group as:

> people who conceive of themselves as being of a kind . . . united by emotional bonds . . . concerned with preservation of their type. (Shibutani and Kwan, 1965, pp. 41–44)

The term 'ethnic relations', refers to the interactions between ethnic groups, relations that are very often replete with intolerance, hostility and violence. The most common terms used to convey the troubled substance of ethnic relations are the social psychological concepts of prejudice and discrimination (Simpson and Yinger, 1972). Prejudice is a set of preconceived, rigid, beliefs, emotions and preferences of one ethnic group towards another (e.g. the idea that all blacks are lazy). Discrimination is a denial of equal treatment on ethnic grounds. It is thus assumed that if prejudice and discrimination were eliminated the relations between the ethnic groups would cease to be problematic (Ayer, 1988).

Nations with multicultural communities take steps to promote harmony in ethnic relations. In the field of education, Britain enacted The Race Relations Act in 1976. This Act made it unlawful to discriminate against a person in the field of education, as well as health and social care. This chapter now explains the legal concepts of racial discrimination and definitions under the Race Relations Act. Examples are given from legal cases in order to illustrate how the Act has been applied in specific settings.

Direct discrimination consists of treating a person, on racial grounds, less favourably than others are, or would be, treated in the same or similar circumstances. Racial grounds are grounds of race, colour, nationality – including citizenship or ethnic or national origins. Groups defined by reference to these grounds are referred to as racial groups. For example, by a decision of the Court of Appeal, gypsies are defined as a racial group (see CRE *vs* Dutton; Court of Appeal, 1988).

Possible examples are:

- **In education,** the operation of a computer program in the sorting of medical school applications that gave adverse weightings to ethnic minority candidates in such a way as to lower their chances of being admitted constituted direct discrimination (CRE, 1988).
- **In employment,** this case study is illustrative. Mrs Crawford, who is black, was employed in a hospital (Mrs Crawford *vs* Royal Hospital and Howe for incurables, a private hospital) for 5 years as a catering assistant. Her normal duties were washing pots and pans, sinks and floors. However, a supplier and catering officer instructed her to clean 6 m of high walls as well. The three white catering assistants were not required to do so. Mrs Crawford objected,

and following disciplinary action against her, took her case to an industrial tribunal. The tribunal found that she had been unlawfully discriminated against on racial grounds (CRE, 1983).

Indirect discrimination consists of applying in any circumstances covered by the Act a requirement or condition which, although applied equally to persons of all racial groups, is such that a considerably smaller proportion of a particular racial group can comply with it to their detriment, and cannot be shown to be justifiable on other than racial grounds. Possible examples are:

- **In education,** a clear example of indirect discrimination based on a case that went to the House of Lords is that of a requirement to wear a cap as part of a school uniform. Although this requirement was applied equally to all pupils, it had the effect of excluding Sikh boys, whose religion required them to wear a turban, and it was held not to be justifiable on educational grounds (Nandla *vs* Dowell Lee; House of Lords 1983).
- **In employment,** an employer who requires higher language standards than are needed, from an employee from a different racial group, for the safe and effective performance of the job.

This chapter uses the collective term 'black and ethnic minority'. People of African, Caribbean and Asian origin widely refer to themselves as 'black'. This term underlies a common experience of life in this country among people whose skin colour is not white, but who live in a white majority society. The term 'ethnic minority' (see Box 9.1) refers to the many people from minority communities who do not identify themselves as 'black' (e.g. Chinese) but who, because of their ethnic origin, language, cultural or religious differences, share a similar experience to 'black' people (DOH, 1992). These two groups are considered in this chapter.

Box 9.1. Definition of ethnic groups (from Jones, 1993)	
● **White**	White, white mixed, white–other
● **Afro-Caribbean**	White Indian/Guyanese, West Indian/Guyanese–white mixed, West Indian/Guyanese–other
● **African Asian**	South Asian/Indian, Pakistani or Bangladeshi
● **Indian**	Indian, Indian–white mixed, Pakistani–other
● **Pakistani**	Pakistani, Pakistani–white mixed, Pakistani–other
● **Bangladeshi**	Bangladeshi, Bangladeshi–white mixed, Bangladeshi–other
● **Chinese**	Chinese, Chinese–other
● **African**	African, African–white mixed, African–West Indian mixed, African–Asian mixed, African–other
● **Other/mixed**	Other, Arab, Mixed, other Asian–white mixed, Asian mixture, miscellaneous partly coloured, miscellaneous coloured, other Asian. Insufficient information
● **All ethnic minorities**	All groups except white

What is a minority group? A numerical category or social category? There are many definitions of social minorities which have been proposed by sociologists, political scientists, and others.

Wagley and Harris (1958, cited in Tajfel, 1987) in their book on racial and cultural minorities, defined social minorities in the following way:

- Minorities are subordinate segments of complex state societies.

- Minorities have special physical or cultural traits which are held in low esteem by the dominant segments of the society.
- Minorities are self-conscious units bound together by the special traits that their members share and by the special disabilities that these bring.
- Membership in a minority is transmitted by a rule of descent which is capable of affiliating succeeding generations even in the absence of readily apparent special cultural or physical traits.
- Minority peoples, by choice or necessity, tend to marry within the group (p. 233).

As Tajfel (1987) pointed out, it is interesting and important to see that numbers do not play much part in this definition of social minorities. Some numerical majorities, as, for example in preindependent South Africa, conform to all the five criteria, while some numerical minorities – such as Afrikaners in the same country – probably only conform to the fifth; they tend to marry within the group. Members of a women's liberation movement in Britain and elsewhere would argue that women are a 'minority' in the sense outlined above, although they would obviously not fit some of the criteria, and often are not a numerical minority.

The essence of the principle guiding the definition selected by Wagley and Harris (1958, cited in Tajfel, 1987) and other writers is not to be found in numbers but in the social position of the groups to which they refer as minorities (Tajfel, 1987). Groups such as people with learning disabilities who share certain kinds of handicaps (see e.g. World Health Organization (WHO) International Classification of Disease (ICD) based on the work of Wood's (1980), definition) may be considered as social minorities on the basis of the fact that they fit the majority of Wagley and Harris (1958, cited in Tajfel, 1987) criteria especially the first three.

Safilios-Rothchild (1976) has argued that people who are disabled can be conceptualized as a disadvantaged or minority group because they have a great deal in common with the old, blacks, women, the poor and other minorities. One reason is because they are treated and reacted to in a similar way – as a homogenous category of people.

Another reason for this similarity is the popular notion that disability, as well as old age, blackness of skin colour, poverty, and the female gender entails biological inferiority. Therefore disabled persons as well as other underprivileged and disadvantaged social and cultural minorities are often considered to be less intelligent, less able to make the right decisions, less realistic, less logical and less able to determine their own life than non-disabled persons.

There is an acknowledged paucity of direct information concerning the feelings, wishes and self-definitions of underprivileged minority groups. Safilios-Rothchild (1976) has argued that a professional or an expert in one specific area often makes important decisions about individuals in areas in which they may have no greater legitimate knowledge and expertise than those about whom he makes the decisions (see e.g. Flannery, 1981; Orzack, 1969). It is the case that doctors and nurses make clinical decisions for the disabled, the infirm and the old; lawyers, welfare experts, officials and human rights activists and liberals make decisions for blacks, women, the old, the infirm, the disabled and the poor.

Different professionals define the self-concepts, goals and inner motivations of underprivileged minority groups and determine their 'real' wishes and potential. They often do so either without asking the individuals about their problems, preferred solutions and alternatives, or by openly disregarding all information received from the individuals themselves about desirable goals and solutions (Safilios-Rothchild 1970, 1976).

Wagley and Harris (1958, cited in Tajfel, 1987) have offered a sensible approach to the problem of attempting to understand and deal with some of the implications behind the concept of ethnic minority. The social psychological perspective enables us to understand what happens to this category of people – called ethnic minorities. As Tajfel (1987) has

pointed out, it would be very difficult to adopt a meaningful frame of reference based on numbers. The social definition is more important, meaningful and much more flexible than a definition based on numbers.

The psychological criteria of referring to certain social groups as minorities is clearly stated by Wagley and Harris (1958, cited in Tajfel, 1987). They are 'self conscious units' of people who have in common certain similarities and certain social disadvantages. In the view of some writers, this psychological criterion is not as simple as it may appear.

Some sociological writers make a sharp distinction between what they call a 'social group' and a 'social category'. For example, Morris (1968) defined ethnic groups as 'a distinct category of the population in a larger society whose culture is usually different from its own'. He added that members of ethnic groups:

. . . are or feel themselves, or are thought to be bound together by common ties of race or nationality or culture. (Morris, 1968, p. 167)

This he distinguished from:

a mere category of the population, such as red-haired people, selected by a criterion that in the context is socially neutral and that does not prescribe uniform behaviour. (Morris, 1968, p. 168)

By contrast, a genuine group must consist of people:

recruited on clear principles, who are bound to one another by formal, institutionalised rules and characteristic uniform behaviour. (Morris, 1968, p. 168)

In addition, these groups must be organized for cohesion and persistence; that is, the rights and duties of membership must regulate internal order and relations with other groups. Having already once recognized the psychological criteria that people must 'feel themselves' or must be 'thought to be' similar to each other and distinct from others in certain ways in order to be considered as an ethnic group, Morris (1968) comes back to the 'internal' characteristics of an ethnic group and gives it a name (p. 168). These clear-cut distinctions can be very useful for thinking about some minorities, but they may present problems if one considers many fluid and changing social situations in which, for example, people with learning disabilities slowly acquire (in common) their beliefs, reactions, feelings and attitudes about their special status in a wider society.

The internal cohesion and structure of a minority group may sometimes develop as a result of this development of an awareness of being considered as different. Tajfel (1987) has argued that it is precisely this development of a special kind of awareness that some people within minorities are sometimes trying hard to achieve through social action and through initiating social and political movements.

9.3 Immigration, Race Relations and Inequality

The history of Britain contains many stories of immigration. Through the centuries Britain has been the destination for settlement of many groups of people from other countries. These have included the Romans, the Angles, Saxons, Danes, Normans, Dutch, Belgians, Irish, Jews and Eastern Europeans. As Foot (1965), Braham (1982) and Cashmore (1989) have observed, until 1948 there were relatively small numbers of non-white residents in Britain. A small number of Afro-Caribbeans who had come to Britain to fight in the Second World War stayed on after 1945 when their labour was desperately needed. Labour was also directly recruited from the Caribbean in the post-war years. From June 1948 until the early 1970s, when legislation restricted immigration, there was a steady influx of immigrants, at first from the Caribbean and later Asians from India, Pakistan, Bangladesh and African states. According to the 1981 census, the number of Asian immigrants numbered 750 000. By

the end of the 1980s, approximately 6% of the British population was non-white.

Writers such as Miles (1982), Castles and Kosack (1973) and Fryer (1984) have observed that increased immigration was encouraged by government and firms in the 1950s and 1960s to provide large quantities of cheap labour for the expanding post-war economy. They noted that discrimination and exploitation of black and ethnic minorities by employers was widespread. Earlier, Little (1947) and later, Petterson (1965) predicted that racial hostility from white workers would increase, particularly as economic crises generated competition for jobs and housing.

The urban riots of the 1980s, particularly in Bristol, Brixton, Toxteth and Handsworth, led many to examine the relationship between the black and ethnic minorities and government agents, notably the police, education, housing, health and the welfare services. Benyon and Solomons (1987) have observed that the main cause of the riots was a profound sense of injustice felt by inner-city residents. Rioters, not all black and ethnic minority people, believed themselves to be discriminated against, exploited and rejected by the establishment in Britain. Even the official report by Lord Scarman (1982) recognized that many black and ethnic-minority people experienced such a deep sense of alienation and rejection by society that they lashed out at the police and distrusted all representatives of the establishment. A number of studies have reported the pervasiveness of racial discrimination and inequality in Britain (see e.g. Braham, 1982; Deanley and Milner, 1984; Brown and Gay, 1986; Jones, 1993). In the first major study of racial discrimination in Britain, Daniel (1968) noted that:

there is racial discrimination varying in extent from massive to the substantial. (Daniels, 1968, p. 209)

Officially, attempts have been made by governments to outlaw racial discrimination through the Race Relations Acts of 1965, 1968 and 1976, yet research such as Smith (1977), Braham *et al.* (1981)

and Jones (1993) have continued to demonstrate the existence of widespread discrimination, particularly in employment opportunities. A Church of England Report, *Faith in the City* (Church of England, 1985) noted the appalling rate of unemployment and sense of hopelessness and alienation among the young black and ethnic minority population in British cities. The report laid much of the blame for this situation on the failings of the government and government agencies. Policy Studies Institute reports (see e.g. Brown, 1984; Jones, 1993) pointed out that even people from black and ethnic minority communities who are lucky enough to be economically active experience racial discrimination and disadvantage, particularly in terms of promotion at work and in the running of their business. Phizacklea and Miles (1987) observed that despite their proud record of supporting the British trade union movement – Afro-Caribbean women had high rates of trade union membership compared to women in other groups (Jones, 1993) – workers from black and ethnic minority communities had received little practical union support in the fight against racial discrimination and disadvantage.

As Ahmed *et al.* (1986) emphasized, it is important for all health and social welfare professionals working in the community to understand that racism bears hard on the lives of black and ethnic minority people. The authors noted that black and ethnic minorities experience racism from professional people, that in turn affects their behaviour towards all community practitioners whom they meet. Ahmed *et al.* (1986) noted that stereotyped beliefs about black and ethnic minority families even influenced the behaviour of health and social welfare workers. They pointed to incidents where social workers have prematurely intervened to remove children from black and ethnic minority families because of the mistaken view that the parents were over strict and unable to adapt to a changing environment. The authors pointed out that given the power of health and welfare professionals it is vital for community practitioners to attempt to obtain a detailed understanding of black

and ethnic minority peoples' cultures (see also Shaw, 1988; Cameron, 1989; McFarland *et al.*, 1989; CRE, 1990a, National Institute for Social Work, 1990; Eribo, 1991).

9.4 Disablement and Disability

There is a universal social stigma attached to disability because of the undesirability of illness and disease (Khan, 1985). It has been shown, beyond doubt, that illness and impairment are positively correlated with low socioeconomic status (Smith and Jacobson, 1988; Whitehead, 1988). The response to differences in society has produced many devalued and disenfranchised groups of people. People with learning disabilities form one such group. Societies emphasize good health, independence and intellectual capabilities, and can often view the person with disability as a burden. People with disabilities face discrimination in terms of employment, lack of appropriate services, access to public places and other peoples' attitudes as epitomized in the title of one of Radio Four's programmes 'Does he take sugar?' (Larbie *et al.*, 1987). Because of their intellectual impairment, people with learning disabilities find themselves cast into negative social roles. As Wolfensberger (1975) has argued, this produces a process of devaluation and discrimination that results in their being denied their full rights as citizens.

As with discrimination against people with learning difficulties, racism is also a form of devaluation and oppression. To be black and have a learning disability as well, therefore means double levels of discrimination. Black and ethnic minority people with learning disabilities are doubly stigmatized because of fear based on society's ignorance and unfamiliarity with both disability and race. For more information on the related terms of 'double discrimination' and 'double jeopardy' as they apply to black and ethnic minority people with disabilities (see National Urban League, 1964; Bengston, 1979;

Mays 1983; Baxter, 1989, 1992; Baxter *et al.*, 1990 and Blakemore and Boneham, 1994).

9.5 Cultural Diversity and Ethnicity

Provision of Services for People from Ethnic Minority Communities

One area of welfare where major issues relating to ethnicity – namely race, culture, religion, and linguistic background – are accepted as important prerequisites for good practice is in child care. The National Children's Bureau (NCB) accepted the view that one of the most contentious subjects in the area of adoption and fostering (see Smith and Berridge, 1993) is the question of appropriate placement for children who are black and are from the minority ethnic community, especially the debate over whether black children should be placed with white families. The issues involved are complex for social workers, health visitors and other interested agencies.

It is also a subject that attracts widespread media attention. Witness two relatively recent newspaper headlines: 'Black boy torn from White family's love' (*Daily Express*, 24 August, 1989). 'White family wins battle to keep a Black foster child' (*Daily Mail*, 12 December, 1990). The dramatic language used emphasizes winning and losing, black and white, separation and loss. Such headlines fuel a potent mix of emotion, heightened by conscious and unconscious attitudes to colour, ethnicity, religion and linguistic differences. Behind the attention-seeking headlines lie serious and very complex issues. In addressing their concern, the NCB decided to base their approach to adoption on a rigorous review of research evidence from the UK as well as from the USA.

Evidence on the effects of 'transracial' placements is complex, highly controversial and in many ways still inconclusive. Ahmed (1989) stressed that children in care separated from their parents and their community are at special risk. She argued that most black children in white society

are in danger of growing up in a devalued self-image. Black children separated from their families are much more vulnerable because they rarely have the opportunity to experience close and loving relationships with black adults. Other writers have articulated their field experience in a variety of ways (see e.g. Gill and Jackson, 1982; Maynard, 1988; Chambers, 1989; Mallows, 1989; Jarvis, 1990 and Charles *et al.*, 1992).

The concept of 'self-identity' is so complex and problematic that the plethora of literature emerging on the subject is inconclusive as to whether the placing of black children in white families is necessarily a negative experience. The personal experience of transracially fostered and adopted young people varies. Some young people report very positive experiences, others have different experiences. Tizard and Phoenix (1993) concluded from their studies that transracial placements were not necessarily psychologically damaging to black children. (Against similar conclusions see e.g. Black and In Care (1983) and Dominelli (1988)). The Commission for Racial Equality (CRE, 1990b) have argued that usually such reported outcomes mean that black children have been successfully indoctrinated into thinking they are white; that is, they have had to either repress or reject their identity and become colour blind reflecting the nature of white families into which they have been placed.

Payne (1983) has demonstrated that there are a number of dilemmas that are inherent in every child-placement decision. The first being supply and demand factors in the home-minding field. There is generally an imbalance between the resources available – that is, families – and the need of waiting children. Other problems include the length of time that a social worker can wait to place a child. There can also be the pressure from families wishing to offer a place and a suitable child being unavailable at the time. Supply-related factors have a much greater influence on the experience of children being looked after than we often think. For detailed discussions of these issues, see for example Beveridge and Cleaver (1987) and Ceaser *et al.* (1994).

Another issue is the resources available to cope with the demand for care in the relevant agency. Richford (1990) has cited the London Borough of Lambeth, with a population of 245 000, that had a team of 21 social workers and four team leaders who were attempting to find placements for children; compared to Rochdale with a population of 206 000 who employed only three people to find carers, even though Rochdale had proportionately more children in its care.

The success in placing black children within families of the same ethnic background also depends, to a considerable extent, on the commitment of the agency in allocating adequate resources of manpower and funding. Field workers must also have a detailed knowledge of the cultural, linguistic and religious background of the communities within which they work. The placing of children and young people with learning disabilities provides its own unique problems that require careful and sensitive approach. After a thorough review of the available evidence the NCB pointed out that the present state of knowledge does not support the case for absolute statements of policy regarding ethnic matching in the placement of children and young people. However, the evidence from available research and from self-reports by transracially adopted adults provides the basis for the NCB to support the position that black and minority ethnic children and young people should be placed with families with as similar an ethnic, religious and linguistic background as possible (Smith and Berridge, 1993).

In the last few years leading child care, health and social work organizations and agencies have also published policy statements and practice notes that reflect their concern 'that racism, both in its overt and in its covert manifestations, is an endemic feature of British Society affecting children and young people and their families' (Smith and Berridge, 1993). The British Agencies for Adoption and Fostering (BAAF), British Association of Social Workers (BASW) and the National Foster Care Association (NFCA) have taken on the issue of 'transracial placements'. BAAF believes that placement of choice for a black child is always a black family:

> Each child in care is an individual with both the moral and legal right to have a plan made for his or her future which takes into account that individual's specific needs and circumstances. (BAAF, 1989, 1992).

Hammond (1990) explained the rationale behind this approach in the following way. Black families can offer children an added dimension over and above a loving environment. Examples of 'added value' for black children in care include continuity of experience; contact with the relevant community; understanding of and pride in the child's particular inheritance; and skills and support in dealing with racism.

For children temporarily in care, the value to them and their families of a familiar environment should not be underestimated both in coping with the trauma of separation or in aiding the process of reuniting the family. BASW stated that a child has a right to a culturally matched placement. The first priority for authorities and agencies is to attempt to secure such a placement, having taken into account the child's own wishes and feelings, bearing in mind the individual situation of each child (BASW, 1988). NFCA believed that the placement of choice for all children and young people should be with carers who share the child's race, culture and religion. The well being of the child or young person must be the first consideration in a placement (NFCA, 1989).

The above statements reflect considerable differences of emphasis, but they illustrate the important areas of agreement between concerned organizations. The statements generally emphasize the following contextual issues: services for black and minority ethnic families should be accessible to all; and children and young people should not be in care because of a lack of suitable services

Box 9.2 Department of Health guidance on adoption (DOH, 1991)

It may be taken as a guiding principle of good practice that, other things being equal and in the great majority of cases, placement with a family of similar ethnic origin and religion is most likely to meet a child's needs as fully as possible and to safeguard his or her welfare more effectively. Such a family is most likely to be able to provide a child with continuity in life and care and an environment which the child will find familiar and sympathetic and in which opportunities will naturally arise to share fully in the culture and way of life of the ethnic group to which he belongs. Where the aim of a placement is to reunite the child with his or her own family, contact and work with the family will in most cases be more comfortable for all and carry a greater chance of success if the foster parents are of similar ethnic origin. Families of similar ethnic origin are also usually best placed to prepare children for life as members of an ethnic minority group in a multi-racial society, where they may meet with racial prejudice and discrimination, and to help them with their development towards independent living and adult life. (DOH, 1991)

sensitive to needs and customs of different ethnic groups. For those children and young persons who have to be looked after away from home, there should be a pool of possible adoptive and foster families available so that each individual person can be placed in a setting where he or she feels most 'at home'. The Department of Health guidance (DOH, 1991) gave cogent reasons for this position (Box 9.2).

The Children's Act 1989 prescribed format for a child-care plan stipulated that the plan should be recorded in writing and contain the child's and his or her family's social history and the child's identified needs including needs arising from race, culture, religion or language, special educational or health needs (DOH, 1991).

Provision and Delivery of Services: the Positive Approach

Families of children with learning disabilities are provided with inadequate help (see e.g. Hannam, 1980; Ayer, 1984; Ayer and Alaszewski, 1986; Seed, 1988; Ellahi and Hatfield, 1992; Gates and Wray, 1995). In the UK help is virtually non-existent for families who are from the black and ethnic minority communities who do not speak English (Davis and Choudhury, 1988). Powell and Perkins (1984) found that Asian families had limited understanding of their child's disability and inadequate knowledge of available services. A similar situation exists in the east end of London, where a very large Bangladeshi population makes very heavy demands upon the child health services (Watson, 1984). Gulliford (1984) found that Bangladeshi families with severe learning disabilities were more deprived and more socially isolated and lacking in social support than white families. It should be noted that people from the black and ethnic minority community tend not to take up readily the welfare services that are available such as aids and equipment, antenatal care, meals-on-wheels, rehabilitation and preventive medicine (GLAD, 1987). The uptake of benefits is also low (Baxter et al., 1990).

As French (1992) has pointed out, people from the black and ethnic minority communities are often blamed for this behaviour, but on close inspection it is not difficult to understand the reasons why. As mentioned above, a general lack of knowledge about what services exist has been found among some black and ethnic minority groups (see also CIO, 1987; Baxter et al., 1990). This included lack of awareness of statutory services, aids and equipment, disability organizations, community groups and benefits. There is also uncertainty, particularly among those who do not have British citizenship, regarding their rights and perhaps a fear of inquiring into such issues too deeply (French, 1992). An enormous barrier for many black and ethnic minority people is their inability to speak English very well and the inadequate response of service providers to this problem. The resulting lack of communication leads to many serious difficulties. Therapists such as speech therapists, psychotherapists and physiotherapists cannot communicate with their clients, and teachers and educational psychologists cannot communicate with parents and their children. Tomlinson (1990) and Baxter *et al.* (1990) pointed out that children whose mother tongue is not English are assessed using tests written in English and may be placed inappropriately in special schools as a result. Tomlinson (1990) found that parents of disabled children from black and ethnic minority communities do not understand the complex assessment and referral procedures, are confused by receiving conflicting advice from professionals, have problems with keeping in contact with special schools, and are dissatisfied with the ethnocentric nature of the curriculum.

Difficulty with the English language is only one aspect of the problem. There is also a lack of understanding among the indigenous population concerning the life style, social customs and religious practices of people from black and ethnic minority communities (Waller, 1991). This can lead to inappropriate service provision. As French (1992) has pointed out, hospitals, day centres and residential homes are unlikely to attract people from black and ethnic minority communities unless they provide suitable food, leisure activities, music and religious services. Health and social work professionals often believe that the lack of service uptake among people from black and ethnic minority communities reflects a greater family and social network than the majority population enjoys.

Recent reports have disputed this notion. CIO (1987), GLAD (1987) and Baxter (1990) believed that stereotyped beliefs that Afro-Caribbean disabled people are catered for by their families should be challenged. For example, GLAD (1987), reporting on a survey in Brent, revealed that 68% of elderly Afro-Caribbeans live alone. McColman (1990) studied Afro-Caribbean, Asian and Vietnamese/Chinese carers of old people in the London Borough of Southwark and found little evidence of

extended family network. McColman (1990) stated that individual carers take the main responsibility for the care of the elderly and disabled relatives, look after them for long hours, and undertake all the personal and basic household tasks (such as feeding, dressing, toileting, cooking and washing as well as baby sitting). This is a consistent pattern across the three communities studied. Minority ethnic carers care in the same way as white carers. There are recorded cases reporting community mental handicap teams' concern that many services are not being used by families from black and minority ethnic communities (see e.g. Horn, 1982; Gulliford, 1984; Powell and Perkins, 1984; Watson, 1984; Cunningham and Davis, 1985; Davis and Choudhury, 1988 and Ellahi and Hatfield, 1992).

Improvements in the desperate situation of these families have been recorded whenever community mental handicap teams take it upon themselves to act to make local services more applicable and accessible to clients. The example from Tower Hamlets child development team in the east end of London illustrates this approach. In their study of Asian families with a preschool child with learning disability, Powell and Perkins (1984) concluded that such families desperately needed a named person who spoke their own language. The Tower Hamlets child development team planned to provide comprehensive help to children with learning disabilities of Bangladeshi families in the east end of London. The team instituted the parent adviser scheme (Davis, 1985a,b). A full-time Bangladeshi parent adviser was employed. She was trained in counselling and child management skills before she began home-visiting working with families on an ongoing and regular basis. The help given by the parent adviser included providing the mother with someone to talk to who would listen; social and psychological support; information; someone to accompany her out of the house; child management and developmental advice; referral to professionals such as health visitors, physiotherapists and teachers; and social contacts outside the family. The parent adviser facilitated other professionals such as health visitors, physiotherapists and teachers, and social contacts outside the family. The parent adviser also facilitated other professionals' work with the family by interpreting and explaining on their behalf, and she mediated between family members.

As Davis and Choudhury (1988) have pointed out, such help brought enormous change in the circumstances of the families. Changes observed included, for example, improved ability to cope in many areas, such as managing and organizing the home; financial management, child care, communicating by learning English and general independence; improved general quality of life; increased family cohesion; improved social support; improved developmental progress and decreased behaviour problems in the children. Davis and Choudhury (1988) concluded that their study showed that the need for specialist medical, social, therapeutic and educational skills is very much secondary to the need to facilitate people's own resources, to provide them with general support, and to treat them with respect.

Provision of Services; the Nature of Racist Services

This section provides a few quoted examples of prejudiced remarks, reported by clients/carers and patients, which revealed negative professional perceptions of health and social care practitioners and managers towards black and ethnic minority people who have learning disabilities.

I often heard 'nicknames' and jokes with racist overtones being aimed at these clients who were usually very upset by these comments. One man who had a speech problem was made fun of because of this and was called a tribal sounding name by staff and clients alike. He was noticeably uncomfortable in this situation and deeply disliked being made fun of. (adult training centre (ATC) worker)

Other things overlooked at the centre were: dietary requirements of ethnic minority clients, music and just having positive images of black people around

the centre, . . . racist attitudes and comments were allowed to continue unchallenged; no black staff was employed in the centre. (ATC worker – quoted from Baxter, 1990)

I was miserable . . . it seemed every time I touched the baby they (nurses) thought I was doing it wrong and tried to tell me something different . . . but I couldn't understand what they were saying. In the end I was so desperate I phoned my husband to come and take me home . . . they got quite angry. (Chinese woman)

I was put in a ward with an Iranian woman and three Asian women. I heard a nurse say, 'I'm sure she will be more at home in there'. (Afro-Caribbean woman)

I tried several times to ask if I could see a lady doctor, but the midwife didn't understand me, or pretended not to. (Asian woman)

By mistake I took my wife to the wrong department for her scan appointment. The receptionist snapped at me, 'why can't you read English', which I can, and probably better than her. In fact it's a mistake lots of patients make because the appointment note isn't very clear. Two English patients turned up at the same time as me, having made the same mistake. She didn't snap at them. (Asian man)

Often when I was eating the food my family had brought in for me, nurses and white patients would open the windows and pull faces and make comments like 'what a smell!' (Asian woman)

The above examples quoted from Larbie et al. (1987) show what some black and ethnic minority clients and patients may experience: poor access to the maternity services, with limited communication and choices, that is not helped by racial discrimination (see e.g. Bhaat and Dickenson, 1992); poor-quality services that are not always appropriate to their needs and are sometimes dealt with insensitivity (see e.g. Fenton, 1993; Neile, 1995) and less than adequate services and the lack of provision for their specific needs and those of their babies. Many are still more likely to experience perinatal deaths and many of those who need benefits most will experience difficulties in claiming them (Beech, 1987; OPCS, 1990; Parkside CHC, 1992).

Reader Activity 9.1
Reflect on the various people you have cared for or worked with. Are you able to recollect any overt or covert discrimination based upon either disabilities or ethnic origin? It might be worth discussing this activity with a colleague or friend.

Improving Access to and Take Up of Services

Given the availability and range of service, a major issue for black and ethnic minority clients and their families is to devise ways of improving access to, and take up of, available services that are provided by both statutory and voluntary agencies. Other issues also important to these client groups include special diets, antiracist training for staff, the participation of black and minority community groups and associations in planning, and the recruitment of staff who reflect the racial mix of the local community.

The authors raised relevant issues that needed to be considered in the development of community care in order to make community care services accessible and appropriate to the black and ethnic minority community. They raised relevant issues when considering the development of community care that was accessible, appropriate, adequate and accountable to the black and ethnic minority community. Set out below are the main issues that were raised by the Race Equality Unit and the Griffith's Task Force for inclusion into the White Paper *Caring for People*. This White Paper:

(1) Made reference to equal opportunities and recognized the need for antiracist and antidiscriminatory strategies for providing services for black and minority ethnic populations.

(2) Clarified the statutory duties and legal responsibilities that community care planners, service providers, co-ordinators and assessors had for providing appropriate and adequate services to black and minority ethnic populations.

(3) Acknowledged the diverse and differing needs of black and minority ethnic populations as an essential prerequisite for providing different community care services as opposed to the 'same' approach adopted for white and majority ethnic populations.

(4) Validated the contributions made by black and minority ethnic voluntary organizations in providing community care services and strongly recommended support and resources from mainstream authorities and agencies to these organizations.

(5) Recommended positive action to negotiate with and award contracts to black and minority ethnic voluntary organizations and groups.

(6) Gave explicit guidance to local authorities about the allocations of budgets (care element of social security budget) for private and voluntary residential care establishments catering for black and minority ethnic communities.

(7) Made it a requirement for all community care planners, providers, co-ordinators and assessors to consult black and minority ethnic users, carers and service-providing groups in planning and resourcing community care to black and minority communities.

(8) Made it mandatory for statutory agencies to assess in their local profiles the demographic construction of black and minority ethnic communities in their areas and their present services access.

(9) Made specific recommendations for recruiting black and minority ethnic staff and antiracist training for all staff responsible for designing and delivering packages of care.

(10) Gave special attention to the criteria for assessment to be undertaken by people with appropriate awareness, understanding and knowledge of the needs of community care of

black and minority ethnic communities. This included the right of appeal.

(11) Prioritized both quantitative and qualitative monitoring of all community care services for black and minority ethnic communities as an essential part of community-care policies and practices, and recommended representation of black and minority ethnic users, carers and service providing groups in the monitoring process.

(12) Recognized the need for national guidance on the quantity and quality of community-care services that were able to respond to the needs of black and minority ethnic users and carers and recommended the establishment of a working group with black and minority ethnic involvement and representation.

However, the entry in the statutory documents; NHS and Community Care Act 1990 and Training for Community Care; A Joint Approach (DOH, 1989) was so bland as to bear no relationship to the reality of the needs of people from the black and ethnic minority community. The White Paper (DOH, 1990) stated:

> to develop effective anti discriminatory practices for all and to pay particular attention to the needs and perspectives of black and minority ethnic group community staff development, and training can play an important part in ensuring access to new and relevant services.

The failure of the NHS and Community Care Act 1990 to address many of the above recommendations has meant that the requirements for community care services to respond to the needs of the black and ethnic-minority community do not appear in the statute. What should be done? Racism, prejudice, discrimination and injustice are subtle, supple and usually covert. It is only by attacking them at the roots that people with learning disabilities from the black and ethnic-minority communities can take, with pride, their place in society merited by their individual talents as well as their

rights as citizens, to health, social and welfare provision. It is almost impossible to be entirely free of racist beliefs and attitudes when one is brought up in a racist society like our own (French, 1992). Some of these attitudes and behaviour patterns may be conscious, while others are submerged. In many ways the more subtle and submerged racism is the more difficult it is to deal with. Read (1988) and Tarpey (1984) believed that white people have to learn that although it is not their fault they are racist, however well intentioned they are, they can learn to change their behaviour.

Health and social workers are predominantly white and receive very little training concerning the needs and difficulties of people who have learning disabilities from black and ethnic minority communities. Baxter *et al.* (1990) believe that the training of health professionals in the learning-disability field fails to prepare them for work in a multiethnic society and that awareness of racism and inequality should be a prominent strand that runs through the curriculum (see also CCETSW (1990) and Larbie *et al.* (1986)). Johnson (1986) pointed out that it is no longer acceptable to treat people from the black and ethnic minority communities 'just like everyone else' or to take a 'why can't they be like us' approach as this fosters prejudice. The authors of *Double Bind* (CIO, 1987) have stated that true integration is recognizing that Asians with learning disability may have special needs. Treating everyone the same is not equality, because it does not take into account their special needs. Connelly (1988) put it succinctly when he said that policy makers and practitioners should at all times strive to alleviate problems of people from black and ethnic minority communities rather than compounding them.

9.6 Summary and Conclusion

This chapter discusses some issues relating to similarities between the experiences of people with learning disabilities and black and ethnic minority people. As has been pointed out in the text, these

---

Box 9.3 Recommendations

(1) Racism awareness training should form part of all professional training, to ensure that the services that are provided are appropriate to the needs and aspirations and cultural backgrounds of black and ethnic minorities disabled people. This training, when skilfully carried out by people from black and ethnic minorities may help professionals to be aware of their own attitudes and behaviour in a relaxed and non-threatening environment. Disability awareness training is needed and there is no shortage of skilful disabled people who are willing to run disability awareness workshops. Also, there needs to be a greater awareness and understanding of the cultural diversity to these differences when communicating with and treating them (also, see suggestions in Joseph, 1982; Sharron, 1984; Larbie *et al.* 1987; Dominelli, 1988).

(2) Equal opportunity policies should relate directly to the circumstances of black and ethnic minority people who have a learning disability. Principal elements of such policies as advocated for example by Baxter *et al.* (1990), Larbie *et al.* (1987), CCETSW (1991), Cunatatnam (1993) and Connelly (1993) include:

- A clear commitment to reject and challenge racism.
- A review of consultation with local black and other minority community groups of established policies, procedures and practices to identify how and where services are failing to meet the expressed needs of disabled people from black and ethnic minority communities.
- Drafting and implementation of strategies for change.
- Allocation of responsibility for the policies implementation to a senior manager.
- Monitoring and assessment of the impact of initiatives and changes that are implemented and designed to enhance the quality of life of people with learning disabilities from the black and ethnic minority communities.

are complex issues that need detailed and extensive study. A broad perspective is taken in looking at the issues that affect the life chances and circumstances of people from the black and ethnic minority communities who have learning disabilities. It is likely that this effect upon the life chances and circumstances of people with a learning disability from black and ethnic minority communities may well impact on the health of this segment of society. To conclude the chapter, it is felt appropriate to provide practical suggestions that will provide leadership and guidance for those who work with people with learning disabilities and their families. These practical suggestions are in two forms. First, recommendations for future action (Box 9.3) and, second, a list of resources that will provide a source of help to people with learning disability and their families.

Discussion Questions

1 **How do you think that discrimination can be removed from our practice in the field of learning disabilities?**

2 **Which of the recommendations, if any, listed for future action are already a feature of the organization/s that you are currently with?**

3 **Could it not be argued that discrimination is a feature of all societies, and that to attempt to remove it from human service provision is an attempt to change human nature?**

Resources

Association of Blind Asians
322 Upper Street, London N1 2XQ Tel. 0171 226 1950

The association organizes social and cultural events. It produces information in different Asian languages in large print and also a cassette magazine.

Barnardos

Tanners Lane, Barkingside, Essex IG6 1QG Tel. 0181 550 8822

It provides youth training, day care for young children, special education, adoption and fostering. Barnardos aims to help families find a better future.

Being White

A video in which white people from different backgrounds talk about their understanding of the roots of racism and how they take account of it in their daily lives and work situations. Available from Albany Productions.

Black and In Care

A video in which children talk about their experiences of being in care and how they have and are trying to overcome their difficulties. Available from: Black and In Care Steering Group, c/o Childrens Legal Centre, 20 Compton Terrace, London N12 W1 Tel. 0171 359 6251.

Chinese Community Centre

Arcadain Centre, Cathay Street, Unit B206 Tel. 0121 022 3003

It provides help and advice for Chinese people including translation and help with social security matters.

Confederation of Indian Organizations (CIO)

5–5a Westminster Bridge Road, London SE1 Tel. 0171 928 9889

The CIO has 53 affiliated organizations with a membership of 500 000. Major concerns include issues relating to equal opportunities.

Federation of Jewish Family Services

221 Golders Green Road, London NW11 9DW Tel. 0181 458 9820

The Federation provides a service for people with learning difficulties (Ravenswood) and for children (Norwood). It helps in contacting local Jewish support agencies such as the Jewish Welfare Board, Kosher, meals-on-wheels and homes for the aged and disabled.

Greater London Association of Disabled People (GLAD)

336 Brixton Road, London SW9 7AA Tel. 0171 274 0107

GLAD pioneered work in the field of race and disability and continues to support the development of groups of disabled people from all ethnic minority communities.

National Childrens' Bureau

8 Wakley Street, London EC1V 7QE Tel. 0171 278 9441

It promotes the interests of all children and young people and improves their status in a multicultural society.

The Islamic Centre

146 Park Road, London NW8 7RG Tel. 0171 724 3363

The centre caters for the religious, educational and social needs of the Moslem community.

References

Abramson, H.J. (1980) Assimilation and pluralism. *In* Therstrom, S. *et al.* (Eds) *Harvard Encyclopaedia of American Ethnic Groups*, pp. 150–160. Cambridge, MA: Harvard University Press.

Ahmed, S., Cheetham, J. and Small, J. (1986) *Social Work with Black Children.* London: Batsford.

Ahmed, S. (1989) The racial dimension in Social Work assessment. *In* Morgan S. and Righton P. (Eds) *Child Care: Concerns and Conflicts.* Milton Keynes: Open University.

Anastasi, A. (1973) *Psychological Testing*, 3rd edn. London: Macmillan.

Audit Commission (1986) *Making a Reality of Community Care.* London: HMSO.

Ayer, S. and Alaszewski, A. (1986) *Community Care and the Mentally Handicapped: Services for mothers and their mentally handicapped children.* London: Croom Helm.

Ayer, S. (1984) Community care: failure of professionals to meet family needs. *Care, Health and Development* **10**: 127–140.

Ayer, S. (1988) *Race Relations in a Prison Setting.* Report to the Home Secretary on HMP – Hull. Hull: Bov.

Baxter, C. (1989) Parallels between the social role perception of people with learning difficulties and black and ethnic minority people. *In* Brechin, A. and Walmsley, J. (Eds) *Making Connections. Reflections on the lives and experiences of people with learning difficulties.* London: Hodder & Stoughton.

Baxter, C. (1992) providing care in a multi-racial society. *In* Thompson, T. and Mathias, P. (Eds) *Standards and Mental Handicap: Keys to competence.* London: Baillière Tindall.

Baxter, C., Poonia, K., Ward, L. and Nadirshaw, Z. (1990) *Double Discrimination Issues and Services for People with Learning Difficulties from Black and Ethnic Minority Communities.* London: King's Fund Centre.

Bengston, V.L. (1979) Ethnicity and ageing: problems and issues in current social science enquiry. *In* Gelfand, D.E. and Kutzik, A.J. (Eds) *Ethnicity and Ageing.* New York: Springer.

Blakemore, K. and Boneham, M. (1994) *Age, Race and Ethnicity: A comparative approach.* Buckingham: Open University Press.

Beech, B.L. (1987) *Who's Having Your Baby?* London: Camden Press.

Benyon, J. and Soloman, J. (1987) *The Roots of Urban Unrest.* Oxford: Oxford University Press.

Beveridge, D. and Cleaver, H. (1987) *Foster Home Breakdown.* London: Basil Blackwell.

Bhaat, A. and Dickenson, R. (1992) An analysis of health education materials for minorities by cultural and linguistic groups. *Health Education Journal* **51**(2): 72–77.

Black and In Care (1983) *Evidence to the House of Commons Social Services Committee.* London: Association of Black Social Workers and Allied Professionals.

Blunden, R., Evans, G. and Humphreys, S. (1987) Planning with individuals: An outline guide. Cardiff: Mental Handicap in Wales, Applied Research Unit.

Braham, P., Rhodes, E. and Pearn, M. (Eds) (1981) *Discrimination and Disadvantage in Employment.* London: Harper & Row.

Braham, P. (1982) *Migration and Settlement in Britain: Ethnic Minorities and Community Relations.* Block 1, Unit 2, Open University.

British Agencies for Adoption and Fostering (BAAF) (1989) The placement needs of black children, amplified in a letter to the Minister of Health dated 25 September 1989.

British Agencies for Adoption and Fostering (BAAF) (1992) *Children Act 1989 – Children and their heritage: the importance of culture, race, religion and language in family placement.* London: BAAF.

British Association of Social Workers (BASW) (1988) *Practice Guide for Social Workers on the Placement of Black Children in Care.* London: BASW.

Brown, C. (1984) *Black and White Britain: The Third PSI Report.* London: Heinemann.

Brown, C. and Gay, P. (1986) *Racial Discrimination: 17 years after the Act.* London: PSI.

Cameron, E., Badger, F. and Evans, H. (1989) District Nursing; the disabled and the elderly: who are the black patients? *Journal of Advanced Nursing* **14**: 346–382.

Cashmore, E.E. (1984) *United Kingdom's Class, Race and Gender Since the War.* London: Allen & Unwin.

Cashmore, E.E. and Troyna, B. (1989) *Introduction to Race Relations.* London: Falmer Press.

Castles, S. and Kosack, G. (1973) *Immigrant Workers and the Class Structure in Western Europe,* 2nd edn. Oxford: Oxford University Press.

Ceaser, G., Parchment, M. and Beveridge, D. (1994) *Black Perspectives on Services for Children in Need.* London: Barnardos and NCB.

Central Council for Education and Training of Social Work (CCETSW) (1990) *One Small Step Towards Racial Justice.* London: CCETSW.

Chambers, H. (1989) Cutting through the dogma. *Social Work Today* **21**(6): 14–15.

Charles, M., Rashid, H. and Thuburn, J. (1992) The placement of black children in permanent new families. *Adoption and Fostering* **16**(3): 13–19.

Church of England (1985) *Faith in the City: The Report of the Archbishop of Canterbury's Commission on Urban Priority Areas.* London: Christian Action.

Commission for Racial Equality (CRE) (1983) *Ethnic Minority Hospital Staff.* London: CRE.

Commission for Racial Equality (CRE) (1988) *Medical School Admission: Report of a formal investigation into St George's Hospital Medical School.* London: CRE.

Commission for Racial Equality (CRE) (1990a) *Social Services and Race: Guidelines for social services/ social work department.* London: CRC.

Commission for Racial Equality (CRE) (1990b) *Adopting a Better Policy: Adoption and Fostering of Ethnic Minority Children.* London: CRE.

Confederation of Indian Organizations (CIO) (1987) *Double Bind: to be disabled and Asian.* London: CIO.

Connelly, N. (1988) Care in the multi-racial community. London: Policy Study Institute.

Court of Appeal (1988) *Commission for Racial Equality* vs *Dutton.* Court of Appeal.

Cunatatnam, Y. (1993) *Health and Race: A starting point for managers on improving services for black populations.* London: KFC.

Cunningham, C. and Davis, H. (1985) *Working with Parents: Frameworks for collaboration.* Milton Keynes: OVP.

Daniel, W.W. (1968) *Racial Discrimination in Britain.* Harmondsworth: Penguin.

Davis, H. (1985a) Developing the role of parent adviser in child health service. *In* Pugh, G. De'Ath, E. (Eds) *Working Together with Children with Special Need.* London: National Children's Bureau.

Davis, H. (1985b) Counselling parents of children who have intellectual disabilities. *Child Development and Care* **22**: 19–35.

Davis, H. and Choudhury, A. (1988) Helping Bangladeshi families: Tower Hamlets parent adviser scheme. *Mental Handicap* **16**: 48–51.

Dearnley, J. and Milner, J.W. (1984) *Ethnic Minority Development* (*Kirkless MDC.*) London: Social Services Inspectorate, DHSS.

Department of Education and Science (DES) (1985) *Education for All. The Report of the Committee of Enquiry into the Education of Children from Ethnic Minority Groups* (*The Swann Report*). London: HMSO.

Department of Health (DOH) (1989) *Caring for People: Community Care in the Next Decade and Beyond. CM849.* London: HMSO.

Department of Health (DOH) (1990) *Community Care in the Next Decade and Beyond.* London: DOH.

Department of Health (DOH) (1991) *The Children Act 1989. Guidance and regulations,* Vol. 3, *Family Placements,* paragraph 2.40. London: HMSO.

Department of Health (DOH) (1992) Health of black and ethnic minorities. *In DOH on the State of the Public Health for the Year 1991, The Annual Report of the Chief Medical Officer of the DOH to the Secretary of State for Health,* Chapter 3. London: HMSO.

Dominelli, L. (1988) *Anti-Racism Social Work.* London: Macmillan Education.

Dutt, R. (Ed.) (1989) *Community Care Race Diversion.* London: N1SW Race Equality Unit.

Ellahi, R. and Hatfield, C. (1992) Research into the needs of Asian families caring for someone with a mental handicap. *Mental Handicap* **20**: 134–136.

Eribo, L. (1991) *The Support You Need: Information for Carers of Afro-Caribbean People.* London: Kings Fund Centre.

Fenton, S. (1993) *The Sorrow in my Heart.* Bristol: CRC/ Bristol University.

Flannery, E. (1981) Ethnicity as a factor in the expression of pain. *Psychosomatics,* **22 January**: 39–50.

Foot, P. (1965) *Immigration and Race in British Politics.* Harmondsworth: Penguin.

Francis, E.K. (1947) The nature of the ethnic group. *American Journal of Sociology* **52**: 393–400.

French, S. (1992) Health care in a multi-ethnic society. *Physiotherapy* **March 19 78**(3): 174–180.

Fryer, P. (1984) *Staying Power: The history of black people in Britain.* London: Pluto Press.

Gates, B. and Wray, I. (1995) Support for carers of people with Learning Disabilities. *Nursing Times* **91**(46): 36–37.

Gill, O. and Jackson, B. (1982) Trans racial adoption in Britain. *Adoption and Fostering* **6**(3): 30–35.

Gohil, V. (1987) DHSS: Service delivery to ethnic minority claimants. *Leicester Rights Bulletin* **June/July**(32): 7–8.

Gordon, M. (1964) *Assimilation in American Life.* New York: Oxford University Press.

Greater London Association for Disabled People (GLAD) (1987) *Disability and Ethnic Minority Communities: A study in three London boroughs.* London: GLAD.

Gulliford, F. (1984) A comparison study of the experiences and service needs of Bangladeshi and white families with severely mentally handicapped children, (unpublished dissertation for the Diploma in Clinical Psychology). Leicester: British Psychological Society.

Hammond, C. (1990) BAAF and the placement needs of children from minority ethnic groups. *Adoption and Fostering* **14**(1): 52–53.

Hannam, C. (1980) *Parents and Mentally Handicapped Children.* Harmondsworth: Penguin.

Horn, E. (1982) A survey of referrals from Asian families to four social services area offices in Bradford. *In* Cheetham, J. (Ed.) *Social Work and Ethnicity.* London: Allen & Unwin.

House of Lords. (1983) Nandla *vs* Douwell Lee. London: House of Lords.

Jarvis, M. (1990) Balancing the damage. *Social Work Today* **21**(22): 16–17.

Johnson, M.R.D. (1986) Inner city residents, ethnic minorities and primary health care in the West Midlands. *In* Rathwell, T. and Phillips, D. (Eds) *Health, Race and Ethnicity.* London: Croom Helm.

Jones, T. (1993) Britain's ethnic minorities: An analysis of LFS. London: Policy Studies Institute.

Joseph, D. (1982) People and disability. Unpublished paper for Brunel University; BSc dissertation.

Khan, Y. (1985) Disability among Asian communities. *Contact,* **Summer 1985**: 21–22.

Kings Fund Centre (1980) *An Ordinary Life.* London: Kings Fund Centre.

Kuper, A. and Kuper, J. (Eds) (1985) *The Social Science Encyclopaedia.* London: RKP.

Larbie, J., Baxter, C. and Mares, P. (1986) *A Training Handbook for Multi-racial Health Care.* Cambridge: National Extension College.

Larbie, J., Baxter, C. and Mares, P. (1987) *Trainer's Handbook for Multi-racial Health Care.* Cambridge: National Extension College and Race.

Little, K. (1947) *Negroes in Britain.* London: Kegan Paul, Trench, Trubner.

McColman, J.A. (1990) *The Forgotten People – Carers in Three Minority Ethnic Communities in Southwark.* London: KFC/Help the Aged.

McNaught, A. (1984) *Race and Health Care in the United Kingdom.* London: Centre for Health Services Management Studies, Polytechnic of South Bank.

Mallows, M. (1989) Aftercare weekend: exploring the needs of trans racially adopted young people. *Adoption and Fostering* **13**(3): 34–36.

Malmot, A., Adelstein, A. and Bulusu, L. (1984) *Immigrant Mortality in England and Wales, 1970–1978. OPCS Studies of Medical and Population Subjects* **47**. London: HMSO.

Maynard, C. (1988) Am I Black or am I White? *Childright* **49**(15): 1988.

Mays, N. (1983) Elderly South Asians in Britain: a survey of the relevant literature and themes for future research. *Ageing and Society* **3**: 71–97.

McFarland, E., Dalton, M. and Walsh, D. (1989) Ethnic minority needs and service delivery: the barriers to access in a Glasgow inner-city area. *New Community* **15**(3): 405–415.

Miles, R. (1982) *Racism and Migrant Labour.* London: Routledge and Kegan Paul.

Morris, H. (1968) Ethnic groups. *In International Encyclopaedia of the Social Services,* Vol. 5, 167–172. New York: Macmillan/Free Press.

National Foster Care Association (NFCA) (1989) *Cultural and Racial Identity.* London: NFCA.

National Institute for Social Work (1990) *Black Community and Community Care.* London: Race Equality Unit NISW.

National Urban League (1964) *Double Jeopardy: The Older Negro in America Today.* New York: National Urban League.

Neile, E. (1995) The maternity needs of the Chinese community. *Nursing Times* **91**(1): 34–35.

Obidinski, E. (1978) Methodological considerations in the definition of ethnicity. *Ethnicity* **5**: 213–228.

Office of Population and Censuses (OPCS) (1990) National Audit Office: Series DS No 9. London: OPCS.

Orzack, L.H. (1969) Social changes, minorities and the mentally retarded. *Mental Retardation* **5**: 2–9.

Parkside Community Health Council (CHC) (1992) *Women Speak Out.* London: Parkside CHC.

Payne, S. (1983) *Long Term Placement for the Black Child in Care. Social Work Monograph* **15**. Social Work Today/University of East Anglia.

Petersen, W. (1980) Concepts of ethnicity. *In* Therstrom, S., Orlov, A. and Handlin, O. (Eds) *Harvard Encyclopaedia of American Ethnic Groups*, pp. 234–241. Cambridge: Harvard University Press.

Petterson, S. (1965) *Dark Strangers: A Study of West Indians in London.* Harmondsworth: Penguin.

Phizacklea, A. and Miles, R. (1987) The British Trade Union movement and racism. *In* Lee, G. and Loveridge, R. (Eds) *The Manufacture of Disadvantage*, pp. Milton Keynes: Open University Press.

Powell, M. and Perkins, E. (1984) Asian families with a pre-school handicapped child – a study. *Mental Handicap* **12**: 50–52.

Read, J. (1988) *The Equal Opportunities Book.* London: Inter-Change Books.

Richford, F. (1990) Out of the background. *Social Work Today* **21**(24): 8.

Safilios-Rothchild, C. (1970) *The Sociology and Social Psychology of Disability and Rehabilitation.* New York: Random House.

Safilios-Rothchild, C. (1976) Disabled persons' self-definitions and their implications for rehabilitation. *In* Albrecht, G.L. (Ed.) *The Sociology of Physical Disability and Rehabilitation*, pp. 39–46. Pittsburg: University of Pittsburg Press.

Scarman, L. (1982) *The Scarman Report.* Harmondsworth: Penguin.

Seed, P. (1988) *Children with Profound Handicaps: Parents' views and integration.* London: Falmer Press.

Sharron, H. (1984) Meeting the ethnic challenge. *Social Work Today* **6 August**, 9–11.

Shaw, A. (1988) *A Pakistani Community in Britain.* Oxford: Basil Blackwell.

Shibutani, T. and Kwan, K.M. (1965) *Ethnic Stratification.* New York: Macmillan.

Simpson, G.E. and Yinger, J.M. (1972) *Racial and Ethnic Minorities.* New York: Macmillan.

Smith, A. (1981) *The Ethnic Revival.* Cambridge: Cambridge University Press.

Smith, A. and Jacobson, B. (1988) *The Nation's Health.* London: Kings Fund Publishing Office.

Smith, D. (1977) *Racial Disadvantage in Britain: The PEP Report.* Harmondsworth: Penguin.

Smith, P.M. and Berridge, D. (1993) *Ethnicity and Child Care Placement.* London: NCB.

Sorofman, B. (1986) Research in cultural diversity: deriving diversity. *Western Journal of Nursing Research* **8**(1): 121–123.

Tajfel, H. (1987) The social psychology of minorities. *In* Husband, C. (Ed.) *'Race' in Britain: Continuity and change*, pp. 232–274. London: Hutchinson University Library/Open University.

Tarpey, M. (1984) *English Speakers Only.* Action Research Project. London: Islington Peoples' Rights.

Therstrom, S., Orlov, A. and Handlin, O. (1980) Introduction. *In* Therstrom, S., Orlov, A. and Handlin, O. (Eds) *Harvard Encyclopaedia of American Ethnic Groups*, pp. v–vi. Cambridge, MA: Harvard University Press.

Tizard, B. and Pheonix, A. (1993) Black identity and Transracial adoption. *Community Care* **15**(3): 427–437.

Tomlinson, S. (1990) Asian children with special needs, a broad perspective. *In* Orton, C. (Ed.) *Asian Culture and Special Needs: A report from Advisory Centre for Education.* London: ACE.

Torkington, N.P. (1983) *The Racial Politics of Health – A Liverpool Profile.* Liverpool: Merseyside Area Profile Group Department of Sociology, University of Liverpool.

Wagley, C. and Harris, M. (1958) *Minorities in the New World.* New York: Columbia University Press.

Waller, B. (1991) Nursing in a multi-cultural world. *Nursing Standard* **5**: 30–32.

Watson, E. (1984) Health of infants and use of health services by mothers of different ethnic groups in East London. *Community Medicine* **6**: 127–135.

Whitehead, M. (1988) *Inequalities in Health: The health divide.* Harmondsworth: Penguin.

Wolfensberger, W. (1975) *The Origins and Nature of our Institutional Models.* New York: Human Policy Press.

Wolfensberger, W. and Glenn, L. (1975) *Pass 3. Program Analysis for Service Systems – A method for the quantitative evaluation of human services.* Toronto: National Institute On Mental Retardation.

Wolfensberger, W. and Thomas, S. (1983) *Program Analysis of Service Systems: Implementation of normalisation goals.* Toronto: National Institute on Mental Retardation.

Wood, P.H.N. (1980) *International Classification of Impairments, Disabilities and Handicaps.* Geneva: WHO.

Further Reading List

Baxter, C. (1990) *Sharing Experiences to Challenge Assumptions. A Report of Two Workshops Around Services for Black People with Learning Difficulties.* London: CCETSW.

Baxter, C., Poonia, K., Ward, L. and Nadishaw, Z. (1990) *Double Discrimination: Issues and Services for People with Learning Disabilities from Black and Ethnic Minority Communities.* London: Kings Fund Centre.

Bhat, A., Carr-Hill, R. and Ohri, S. (Eds) (1988) *Britain's Black Population,* 2nd Edn. London: Gower.

Brown, C. (1985) *Black and White Britain: The Third PSI Survey.* London: Policy Studies Institute/Gower.

Cheetham, J. (1981) *Social and Community Work In Multi-Racial Society.* Milton Keynes: Harper and Row in association with the Open University Press.

Contact a Family (1989) *Reaching Black Families? A Study of Contact a Family in Lewisham and the Relevance of Services for Black Families who have children with Disabilities and Special Needs.* London: Contact a Family.

Ely, P. and Denny, D. (1987) *Social Work in a Multiracial Society.* London: Gower.

Shar, R. and Silent Minority (1992). *Children with Disabilities in Asian Families.* London: National Children Bureau.

Sing, J. (1992) *Black Families and Respite Care: A Study of Minority Ethnic Families who have Children with Learning Disabilities in South Glamorgan.* Cardiff: Barnardos.

Townsend, P., Davidson, N. and Whitehead, M. (1988) *Inequalities in Health: The Black Report and the Health Divide.* Harmondsworth: Penguin.

Chapter 10: Spiritual dimensions of learning disability
Aru Narayanasamy

10.1 Introduction

In the caring professions a focus on individuals as psychosocial–spiritual beings is gaining recognition, but there is little elaboration on what is meant by spirit. The term 'spirituality' is often misapplied and used synonymously to represent institutional religion; in the UK institutional religions, for example Protestantism, Catholicism and Judaism, are usually understood.

Secularism

In many secular societies the focus can be on things that are oriented to the present, materialism, and things that are tangible. Many people regard spirituality as something to do with religion, whilst others may attach very little importance to it. Concern for the spiritual aspects of a person (things that are sacred and eternal) is likely to receive less attention in our world that is dominated by technological advances and expectations of immediate results. Although we live in a secular society, the spiritual dimensions of individual's lives are beginning to emerge as significant. This spirituality is expressed in a variety of forms and some people find that religion acts as a medium for expressing it. Human life is governed by social, psychological, physical and spiritual influences.

Faith

Faith plays an important part in many individual's lives. It directs and governs them and it may feature as a powerful vehicle in the spiritual journey of a person. Faith is a prerequisite for spiritual growth to occur, especially in relation to a deity or transcendent. Faith motivates an individual to believe in a being who cannot be directly seen or heard. For some individuals a firm belief in faith is a gift from a supreme being. There is a developmental nature to faith in individuals in that it grows continuously in response to their life events.

Faith, spiritual belief and its practices are intertwined and permeate the life of a person, whether in health or illness. Certain spiritual needs tend to feature during our personal development and growth (this is expanded on later). The influence of spirituality and religion is commonly seen in the following aspects of a person's life: relationship with others; living style and habits; required and prohibited behaviours; and the general frame of reference for thinking about oneself and the world.

Britain is a complex, multicultural and multiracial society (see Chapter 9) with religions from across the world, and it is significant to note that 74% of its total population declared that they belong to a particular faith (Narayanasamy, 1991).

What is Spirituality?

The word spirituality is used widely in the caring context but despite its common usage there would not appear to be a single authoritative definition of it, although a variety of explanations are offered in the emerging literature on this subject. Often in the literature spirituality is explained from the following perspectives.

Theological

In the Christian theological context an individual is seen as made up of a body and spirit. This perspective is derived from the anthropology of the book of Genesis when God breathes into Adam's* nostrils to give him life. Carson (1989) illustrates a person's spirit as:

> . . . an animating, intangible principle that gives life to the physical organisms . . . [it] integrates and transcends all other dimension of person . . . The literal breath of life. (Carson, 1989, p. 6).

In the Christian theological context spirituality also represents prayer, worship and a range of other practices that are associated with the development of spiritual life.

Existential

According to the existentialists, humans have to make sense of their meaningless world; in other words, we are trapped in a completely meaningless world. We cannot escape, and therefore have to deal with 'existence' as well as having to make sense of it. Therefore, an individual becomes a spiritual person when one has made sense of the meaningless world, and has learned to be at home in the universe by deriving certain serenity and inward peace. It is implied that people in their endeavour to make sense of their world have developed this extra dimension; that is, spirituality.

Experiential

There is the claim that human capacity for spirituality probably stems from our potential for religious experience. In this context the numinuous and mystical states are said to be commonly responsible for the inducement of an individual's spirituality. The numinuous experience is when an individual experiences an awe-inspiring feeling that can also be fascinating as well. The word 'numinuous' is derived from the latin word *numen* meaning divinity or power implicit in a sacred place or object.

James (1982) regarded mysticism as a form of spiritual experience. Mysticism is the intimate feeling of being in touch with God or a transcendent to the exclusion of all other sensations. Some regard this as an experience of God-intoxication in which the individual becomes completely detached from self and the surrounding and in the process becomes aware of the highest and fullest truth.

Research studies have suggested that a significant number of people have undergone some form of religious experience (Hardy, 1979; Hay, 1987). Hay found that 42% of the population surveyed in his study had undergone some forms of religious experience. According to Hardy (1979) the characteristics of religious experiences are as follows:

- **A transcendent reality which frequently manifests itself in early childhood.**
- **A feeling that 'something other' than the self can actually be sensed.**
- **A desire to personalize this presence into a deity and a private I–thou relationship with 'it', communicating through prayer.**

In the health-care context, spirituality is gaining popularity as a holistic notion which means care of the body, mind and spirit. But the spiritual nature of the person is not given adequate consideration in the caring context because of a lack of real understanding of what spirituality is about and, as mentioned earlier, because it is used synonymously with religion. Expressions of religious needs are often likely to get attention; and this is especially so for people with a learning disability.

We need to understand the concept of spirituality if we are going to offer it as a component of holistic care to people with learning disabilities.

Box 10.1 Spirituality: related issues

For many, when they think about spirituality the following concepts may arise in their minds:

- **a belief in God**
- **a belief affecting your life and how it relates to others**
- **something not necessarily religious**
- **a belief/concept; purpose and meaning**
- **faith/peace with oneself**
- **a source of strength**
- **a feeling of security/to be loved**
- **a philosophy of life/death/religion**
- **self-esteem/inner self, inner strength**
- **searching/coping; hope**
- **an idealism, a striving to be good**
- **trusting relationship.**

Reader Activity 10.1.
Spend a few minutes to think about what is meant by the term 'spirituality'.

History suggests that since the origins of humanity, spirituality has prevailed in peoples' lives in some way or another. Spirituality is one of the fashionable words in health care, yet like so many useful and comprehensive terms, it is not easy to define. Murray and Zentner (1989) offered a definition that tried to embrace the various facets of spirituality. They defined spirituality as:

A quality that goes beyond religious affiliation, that strives for inspirations, reverence, awe, meaning and purpose, even in those who do not believe in any god. The spiritual dimension tries to be in harmony with the universe, strives for answers about the infinite, and comes into focus when the person faces emotional stress, physical illness or death. (Murray and Zentner, 1989, p. 259)

One assumption is that all individuals are spiritual beings and in this sense spirituality therefore applies equally to the needs of believer and non-believers and in contexts where religious beliefs may be varied. It is not uncommon for individuals with no firm religious allegiance to be able to relate to spiritual or natural forces beyond the physical and self.

Spirituality is seen as an 'inner thing' that is central to an individual's being and one that makes a person unique and 'tick over'. For example, I may see it as my being; my inner person; it is who I am, unique and alive. It is expressed through my body, thinking, my feelings, judgements, and my creativity. My spirituality motivates me to choose meaningful relationships and purpose in life; a sense of harmonious relationship (interconnectedness) with self and others, nature, an ultimate other, and other factors which are necessary for our integrity.

Model for Spirituality

Nursing theorists have proposed that the whole person consists of body, mind and spirit, and that these are inseparable. Stallwood (1981) developed a conceptual model to illustrate this inter-relationship (see Figure 10.1). The outermost circle represents the biological nature of an individual; the

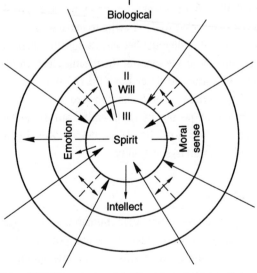

Figure 10.1 Conceptual model of the nature of a person (from Stallwood, 1981).

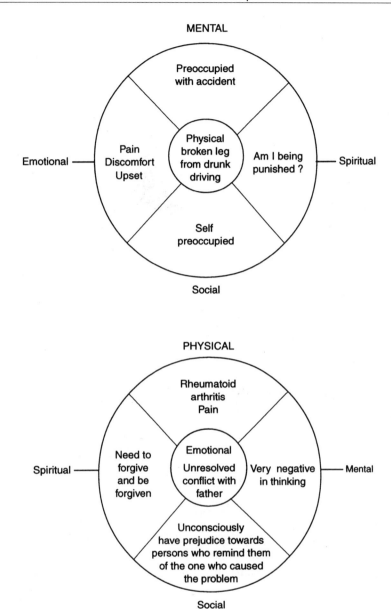

Figure 10.2 Five component person model (from Gorham, 1989).

middle circle depicts the mind as having four separate components – will, emotion, intellect and moral sense; the innermost circle represents the spiritual nature. Alteration to any of the three components affects the two other components, and ultimately, the whole person.

Unlike Stallwood, Gorham (1989) suggested a five-component person model. According to this model, a person is made up of five different aspects – the mental, the physical, the social, the emotional, and the spiritual. The interaction is so closely related that they are almost inseparable. The spiritual is the most difficult one to be recognized. The interaction of these five components is illustrated in Figure 10.2.

10.2 Development and Spirituality

Certain spiritual needs tend to feature at different times during an individual's development and growth. However, it is important to bear in mind that life may not develop in a logical and organized way as individuals, depending upon their learning capability, develop in their own individual way. All of us have the capacity to develop spiritually.

During infancy, trust is a major spiritual need, and during childhood individuals learn to understand concepts about religion from their parents and people close to them. In adolescence, there is a tendency to search for meaning and value in life.

Fearful expressions and behaviour can be regarded as clues to children's spiritual needs. Such fears may include sudden movements, loud voices, loss of support, pain, fear of strangers or strange objects, heights, or anticipated unpleasant situations. Unmet needs for love and relationship may manifest as those fears. So, meeting the infant's need for basic trust has an impact on spiritual development.

Childhood is a developmental period when one learns to understand religious concepts from parents and other people in his/her environment. Inquisitiveness may prevail when the child may ask questions about basic issues of life, for example, 'what is God?', 'Why doesn't Thomas have a Christmas Tree?' and 'why did granny go to heaven?'.

A child's spiritual needs include need for love and security. These provide a foundation for the development of a trusting relationship. We learn and internalize beliefs and values from people we trust during our childhood. So the child is likely to imitate their parent's faith, and some of their own concepts of faith may be based on fantasy.

In childhood, one learns to recognize what is 'good' or 'bad' from parents and other significant people. During a crisis, such as an emergency admission to hospital, the child often has a great difficulty in verbally expressing their spiritual concerns. The death of a loved one may make this even more of a problem. The child does not understand that death is universal, inevitable and irreversible.

In adolescence, the search for meaning and value may feature as a spiritual need. People around the individual are a useful source of help and support during this development. Adolescents may experience confusion and act in conflicting ways if they are not adequately supported to seek meaning and purpose during this crucial period of development. Also, peer groups may act as a useful source of strength and support for the adolescent. So a stable and supportive environment is required for the adolescent's need for the search for meaning and value, as part of their spiritual development.

During young adulthood, one seeks for trust, for love, for hope, and for forgiveness. There may be an experience of tension, expectation and spiritual struggle. It is also a transitional period in which restructuring of religious, moral and ethical values may take place. So this may be the period where reorientation and growth in the spiritual realm takes shape.

In middle years, the questioning of life precipitated by the death of parents or peers, children leaving home, plans for retirement, or an awareness of one's failings may feature. The four common spiritual needs in middle age are:

- **the need for meaning and purpose in life**
- **the need to be forgiven**
- **the need to receive love**
- **the need for hope and creativity.**

For many, in old age, taking stock of life's successes and failures is undertaken together with a renewal of religious faith and spiritual beliefs. Many people experience a more positive self-concept as a result of reassured feelings of accomplishment and worth. Some may find great social and spiritual fulfilment in having some kind of religious affiliation. Religious ceremonies, such as marriages, baptism and burials, may become significant. Religious expressions may be fulfilled by attendance at the church or place of worship. Church or religious affiliation promotes feelings of hope and purpose to life for many older people.

10.3 Spirituality and Learning Disability

Spirituality is part of the central concepts of 'normalization' and 'free will'. In the context of spirituality, Birchenall (1987) defines these concepts as set out in Box 10.2.

Box 10.2 Normalization and free will

- **Normalization**

    . . . being in a position to pursue those activities which together form part of normal existence, this includes all things spiritual and temporal. (Birchenall, 1987, p. 74)

- **Free will**

    . . . is a logical extension of normalisation, and should be seen in the context of representing an individual's right to self-determination. (Birchenall, 1987, p. 74)

Birchenall (1987) is emphatic that opportunities for spirituality should be embodied within the principles of normalization that includes preservation of an individual's right to worship, according to his/her faith.

As individuals, people with learning disabilities have the right to comprehensive care when in a state of health imbalance. By this, it is meant a state of disharmony between the body, mind and spirit. The person in this state needs to be helped to return to a state of spiritual well being. Spiritual well being is an important facet of health and is considered as

affirmation of our relationship with God/transcendent, self, community and environment that nurtures and keeps us as an integrated whole person. The following can be features of a client's spiritual well being:

- **the belief in God that is fostered through communication with a Supreme Being**
- **expression of love, concern, and forgiveness for others**
- **giving and accepting help**
- **accepting and valuing of self**
- **expressing life satisfaction.**

Furthermore, an individual's well being is usually demonstrated by their ability to find meaning and purpose in their present life situations and to search for meaning and purpose for the future. One can attain spiritual well being through a dynamic and integrative growth process that leads to a realization of the ultimate purpose and meaning in life.

Attitudes Towards Learning Disabilities: A Historical Perspective

History is full of evidence of the harsh treatment endured by people with learning disabilities due to other people's ignorance and to some extent in the name of religion. People with learning disabilities were often mistakenly associated with people with a mental illness (see Chapter 1). It is the case that the prevalent mood and attitude of the day determined the ways people with learning disabilities were cared for. Each generation reflected certain attitudes to learning disabilities by a variety of behavioural approaches. There was a stigma attached to people with learning disabilities that has not totally disappeared even today. The past has recorded historical evidence about people's ambivalent attitude towards people with learning disabilities.

Also, it was mistakenly thought that people with learning disabilities were possessed, and because of this they were chained up. Some saw them as a risk to the genetic purity of the race. Any association with learning disabilities was regarded as a recipe for generations of abnormal population. Therefore, all contact with learning disabilities people was avoided. On the other hand, some saw them as holy innocents requiring protection and at times they were referred to as 'God's children' or 'beloved of God'. Even now some people refer to these individuals in those terms. In the past, some people relegated them to the state of subhuman, unworthy of the most basic respect. All of this led societies to treat learning disabilities people as different; that is, different from the normal ones in society.

In the past, religion played an important part in the way communities treated people with learning disabilities. In Saxon times, people with learning disabilities were approached with a strange mix of pharmacy, superstition and castigation (Bannerman and Lindsay, 1993). Holy wells, assumed to be pre-Christian in origin, were rife throughout the British Isles. The order of the day for the treatment of learning disabilities was cold water from those wells. Some holy wells became famous for the treatment of lunacy and became the subject of many stories told as a testimony of miraculous cures. For example, Fillon's well in Perthshire, Scotland was well documented, where in the early eighteenth century about 200 people a year were treated. Bannerman and Lindsay (1993) give an account of this:

Patients were first made to walk three times round a cairn on which were placed offerings of flowers and clothing. They were then immersed three times in the pool and left overnight bound hand and foot in the nearby chapel. If found unbound next morning there was said to be a good chance of recovery. If still bound, the cure was in some doubt. It was stated in the same record that 'many were relieved by death of their troubles in the night'. (Bannerman and Lindsay, 1993, p. 20)

In addition to holy wells, other complicated and bizarre treatments prevailed. Detailed instructions and rituals were included in treatment guides and these had to be followed if effective treatment was to

be achieved. Bannerman and Lindsay (1993) give another example:

. . . a clove of wort to be tied round the lunatic's neck with a red thread when the moon is on the wane in the month April or in the early part of October and hell will be healed'. (Bannerman and Lindsay, 1993, p. 20).

Such prescriptions were complimented by religious ritual, prayers and incantations. Priests and monks became involved in the treatment; therefore, the church became linked with the practice of healing from earliest times.

Around those times many monasteries existed with extensive libraries and gardens full of medicinal herbs. The monks became the chief dispensers of medicine for local folk who often turned to them for assistance in matters concerning religious and secular aspects of life. Also, many at that time attributed mental disorders to demonic possessions. Consequently, the mentally disordered were subjected to harsh treatments. Typically, treatment was not considered a punishment but essential to drive out the devil. Commonly, treatment included potent doses of purgatives and emetics along with herbal baths, fomentations and poultices.

Mandrakes and periwinkle were noted as being powerful for this purpose in conjunction with holy incantation and exorcism. (Bannerman and Lindsay, 1993, p. 21)

The influence of church in the treatment of the mentally disordered remained until the dissolution of the monasteries in England by Henry VIII when all medical matters transferred to lay control. A number of hospitals began to emerge several years later, the most popularly known being Bethlehem (better known as Bedlam). Better services for the learning disabilities began to evolve as a result of further legislations and development of medical, nursing, social and allied professional involvement.

Thanks to changing attitudes and professionals' determined efforts to regard learning disability clients as individuals, caring has become a shared relationship; that is, a relationship embedded in partnership that means working with clients and their families. In a spiritual context parents/families and clients need support in re-establishing their spirituality, whether it has a religious or secular orientation. The learning disability person is capable of entering into a relationship with another person (Clegg, 1990). In a way this is sufficient to suggest that they can express spiritual or religious needs. Also, positive directions come from Birchenall and Birchenall (1986). They implied that people with learning disabilities are capable of following the general meanings, within a normal family-style

church service, of the Gospel of Christ. People with learning disabilities can experience spiritual growth in terms of their faith. In another source, Birchenall (1987) stated:

> ... even the more profoundly handicapped may understand far more than they are given credit for. This leads to the question of how far does having a normal intellectual level equate with the establishment of faith? (Birchenall, 1987, p. 74)

In the next section, the spiritual needs of a man with a learning disability are illustrated to demonstrate the points that have been made so far.

10.4 Spiritual Needs

Case Study 10.1

Steven, aged 38 years, a man with Down's syndrome, lives with his elderly parents. They are Christians who attend church every Sunday. Steven follows his parents to the church and appreciates church activities. He sometimes talks to himself about Jesus and his love for him. During week days he attends a social education centre. Steven's parents have decided to go on a short holiday and he is admitted to a residential respite care unit. On admission, Steven appears upset that his parents have gone without him but persistently mentions Jesus and his love for him.

The above case study and the section that follows are adapted from Narayanasamy (1994a).

Reader Activity 10.2.
You may wish to consider for a few minutes what Steven's spiritual needs are.

Many of us express our spiritual needs in a variety of ways and forms. For example, Steven's spiritual needs may emerge as something like these (see Case Study 10.1):

- **the need for meaning and purpose**
- **the need for love and harmonious relationship**
- **the need for forgiveness**

- **the need for a source of hope and strength**
- **the need for trust and security**
- **the need for expression of personal beliefs and values**
- **the need for spiritual practices, and expression of the concept of God.**

Meaning and Purpose

Many of us find ourselves wrestling with the meaning and purpose of life during a crisis, whether in health or illness. Steven had meaning and purpose through his relationship with his parents and the routine of his life. Whilst in care, although temporary, he is likely to be distressed through loss of meaning and purpose, because of his parents' absence and being estranged from his usual surrounding. In this situation the carer may have to act as a catalyst in helping Steven to find meaning and purpose whilst in care. This may mean helping him to talk about his concerns and distress. Keeping contact with his church may help him to regain some meaning and purpose. Such opportunities may help Steven to become less distressed spiritually.

Love and Harmonious Relationships

Steven's need for love and harmonious relationships goes hand in hand with a need for meaning and purpose. As Maslow (1968) has pointed out, the need for love is one of the fundamental human needs that last throughout life (from childhood to old age). Steven requires unconditional love; that is, love that has no strings attached. This is sometimes referred to as 'in spite of' love. The person is simply loved for the way he or she is, regardless of faults or ignorance or bad habits or deeds. The spiritually distressed person does not have to earn it by being good or attractive or wealthy. The caring environment of his residence, the church and the relationship he has with Jesus may meet Steven's need for love.

Forgiveness

A person who experiences spiritual distress expresses feelings of guilt and therefore requires the opportunity for forgiveness. Steven may feel guilty because he assumes that his parents have left him at the home because he has done something wrong. If he is unable to attend his church this may add to his distress. Guilt often emerges when people experience the feeling that they have failed to live up to standards set for them by their parents. We often contradict them and do the very things we are told not to do. Guilt breeds in us in the form of regrets, not only for the things we have done but for our failures in many things. Forgiveness may bring a feeling of joy, peace and elation, and a sense of renewed self-worth. Steven may achieve this if he is reassured and helped to feel that he is forgiven.

Hope and Strength

Hope is necessary for life and without it we may begin to give up. For many, a sense of hope can be a powerful motivator in enabling an open attitude toward new ways of coping. Steven may experience a feeling of hopelessness for being removed from his familiar environment. A caring and supporting environment, as well as his religious faith, may help him regain his hope and give him the strength to continue with a meaningful life. Hope is closely related to our need for a source of strength. A source of hope provides the strength that we may need. The main source of hope and strength is found by individuals who pray because of their faith in God or the transcendent.

Trust

We feel secure when we can establish a trusting relationship with others. In order to feel secure, Steven needs an environment that conveys a trusting relationship. Such an environment is one which demonstrates that carers make themselves accessible to him, both physically and emotionally. Trusting is the ability to place confidence in the trustworthiness of others and this is essential for spiritual health and to total well being. Learning to trust in an environment that is alien could be a daunting task and not an easy skill to accomplish.

Personal Beliefs and Values

The opportunity to express personal values and beliefs is a known spiritual need. In this sense spirituality refers to anything that a person considers to be of highest value in life. Steven may hold certain beliefs about Jesus and he needs the opportunity to express them freely. Personal values, that may be highly regarded by an individual include, for example, beliefs of a formalized religious path, whereas for others it may be, for example, a set of very personal philosophical statements, or perhaps a physical activity.

Spiritual Practices and Concept of God/Deity.

The opportunity to express our needs related to spiritual practices, the concept of God or deity, may present as a feature of spirituality. The concept of God or the image of Jesus Christ may be an important function in the personal life of Steven. The need to carry out spiritual practices concerning God may be too daunting for the person if an opportunity is not available or the environment is alien or unreceptive to this need. Steven should be provided with an opportunity to carry out spiritual practices if he seeks them.

10.5 Fostering a Relationship for Enabling Spiritual Growth

Carers can enable clients such as Steven to meet their spiritual needs by fostering a relationship that is facilitative and supportive. The following are suggested ways of enabling such a relationship to develop.

Self-awareness

As carers, individuals need to understand their own spirituality. This means an examination of one's personal beliefs and values. This is necessary if we are to be effective in fostering a relationship that enables a client to undergo spiritual growth. A carer who has a positive attitude to spiritual health is likely to be sensitive to any problem a client has concerning spirituality. A continuous and objective review of one's own personal and spiritual beliefs enables the carer to appreciate that everybody does not share the same faith. An awareness of their own prejudices and bias would ensure that carers do not impose their own values and beliefs on others,

especially spiritual doctrines. A good level of self-awareness would enable the carer to adopt a non-judgemental approach and avoid taking steps that would lead to the accusation that one is trying to proselytize. It is likely that a person who has developed self-awareness will show more tolerance, acceptance and respect for another person's spirituality regardless of the differences.

The benefits of self-awareness are stressed here, but these are more easily said than done. It is a skill that has to be acquired and continuously developed. In the following section (adapted from Narayanasamy, 1994b) self-awareness is explained with an outline of a method for developing it.

Self-awareness is an acknowledgement of our own feelings and behaviours, and accepting and understanding these. Self-awareness can be elaborated as an acknowledgement of our:

- **values, attitudes, prejudices, beliefs, assumptions and feelings**
- **personal motives and needs and the extent to which these are being met**
- **degree of attention to others**
- **genuineness and investment of self, and how the above might have an effect on others**
- **the intentional and unconscious use of self.**

It is widely acknowledged that training in self-awareness is a fundamental process before one can understand others. According to Burnard (1985), to become aware of, and to have deeper understanding of, ourselves is to have a sharper and clearer picture of what is happening to others. Limited awareness of ourselves may mean remaining blind to others. The first step to being self-aware is to examine oneself as outlined earlier. We can develop self-awareness by various means. However, the methods used for increasing our awareness must contain the facets of inner search and observations of others.

One simple method of enhancing our self-awareness is the process of noticing what we are doing; the process of self-monitoring. All that is involved here is staying conscious of what we are doing and what is happening to us. To put it another way, we 'stay awake' and develop the skill of keeping our attention focused on our actions, both verbal and non-verbal.

Assessment of our present understanding of knowledge, skills and the learning of new materials, skills and techniques will be heavily influenced by our degree of self-awareness. We are most likely to lose control of our self-development if we remain blind to the need to increase our self-awareness. Without self-awareness we cannot be in control of our own development:

- **We cannot identify key performance areas.**
- **We cannot analyse our performance, or identify concrete objectives.**
- **We cannot make action plans to help our development.**
- **We cannot monitor our progress.**

A greater self-awareness in us is not only the beginning of wisdom, but also the growth of our personal and professional effectiveness. We can foster an attitude to increase our self-awareness by evaluating ourselves by asking questions such as:

- **How much time do I invest in reflecting about myself?**
- **How reassured am I that I have a reasonable understanding of myself?**
- **How do I see myself, and how do I feel about myself?**
- **What are my significant strengths and weaknesses?**
- **Do I really face up to the truth about myself, or do I try to evade the truth about myself?**

Other methods of developing our self-awareness are through introspection, through experience and through feedback.

Introspection

Meditation and yoga can be a useful way of developing self-awareness using the introspection method. Simple breathing and meditation techniques are sufficient for this purpose. Meditation and yoga serve another useful purpose in that these techniques can be useful methods of dealing with job-related stress. Becoming aware of, and consciously noting, experiences are other means of introspection. Complementing these processes the following are useful: identifying past and present prejudices: and identifying past and present approaches to personal problem solving.

Experience

Self-awareness is also developed through experience. The experiential method is one useful method of learning through experience. Participation in experiential exercises brings the desirable increase in self-awareness.

Self-awareness Through Feedback

Self-awareness cannot be developed by adhering solely to the introspection and experiential methods alone. Introspection and experiential exercises will give us some understanding of ourselves, but complete self-awareness requires knowledge about behaviour too; for this we require the help of others: it takes two to know one fully:

> I am aware of my inner feelings (inner processes) but sometimes I cannot see my behaviour. Another person can see my behaviour, but is not aware of my inner feelings and experience. I can see the other person's behaviour, but not his inner experience.

For a complete self-awareness, then, we need to strengthen the knowledge gained by introspecting with knowledge obtained by feedback from others about our behaviour.

Self-disclosure is a fundamental part of self-awareness and has three characteristics. These are:

- **subjectively true**
- **personal statements about self**
- **intentionally revealed to another person.**

Self-disclosure involves the process of revealing information about oneself – ideas, values, feelings – that are similar to the ones experienced by those one is trying to help.

Clinical evidence has suggested that a carer's self-disclosure increases the likelihood of client's self-disclosure (Stuart and Sundeen, 1983). Self-disclosure results in successful therapeutic outcome. However, our self-disclosure must be handled judiciously, and this is determined by the quality, quantity and appropriateness of higher disclosures. We must handle our disclosure sensitively so that clients feel comfortable enough to produce their own self-disclosure. A limited self-disclosure from us may reduce client's willingness to disclose about self and conversely, too much may decrease the time available for client's disclosure or alienate the client.

Communication Skills

Good communication skills are essential for fostering a carer–client relationship that enables spiritual growth and development. Knowing the comprehension levels of your clients and their families would be a starting point in working out the right pitch and level of transactions that could take place for addressing spiritual concerns. Needless to say, the key communication skill in enabling clients and families to achieve spiritual wellness is active listening without being judgemental. The points about self-awareness outlined earlier are necessary for developing non-judgemental attitudes.

Non-judgemental means unconditional acceptance of a person. In other words, you have to have faith, trust and respect for another person despite his or her behaviour. This is often a difficult quality to achieve but with increasing self-awareness this can be developed. A non-judgemental approach is acceptance of an individual without any kind of judgement, without criticism, and without reservation. This also requires not only unconditional acceptance of a person but to respect him/her

without necessarily knowing what his/her previous behaviour has been.

The rudiments of being a good listener are as follows:

- The carer needs to create the right kind of climate in which individuals feel accepted and confident enough to talk about their spiritual thoughts and feelings. Clients need to feel the carer is listening to what they are saying and what they are feeling and not only listening, but accepting and understanding them. All this ties up with responding to people in ways that are helpful.
- Good listening is actually paying close attention to what someone is saying, and this is essential, but it is not easy. We need to suspend our thoughts and give the other person our complete attention.
- We can demonstrate understanding by reflecting the clients thoughts back, showing that we are listening hard, that we are making a real effort to understand what the client is thinking and feeling.
- Make the clients feel it is all right to go on talking, that feelings are being accepted. State that you are genuinely interested in what they are saying, and responding warmly.

Trust Building

Trust enables a feeling of security to develop and acts as a basis for relationship formation. It is necessary because confidence in therapeutic relationship is vital and, indeed, to the spiritual well being of the client. Trust grows over a period of time as the client tests the environment, risks self-disclosure, and observes the carer's adherence to commitment.

The following approach enhances initial trust:

- **listening attentively to client's feelings**
- **responding to client's feelings**

- **demonstrating consistently, especially keeping appointments and promises**
- **viewing situation from the client's perspectives**

As stated earlier, an increasing level of self-awareness of personal feelings, along the points outlined previously, on the part of the carer also enhances trust. It enables the client to unload uncomfortable, even forbidden feelings, in safety. The carer must continue to strengthen the trust gained earlier and this task can be achieved by being reliable. Reliability is a vital ingredient that strengthens and sustains a trusting relationship. Reliability is shown through our commitment to the spiritual needs of our clients and this means promises and adherence to care plans. In other words, carrying out care plans promptly and following them through. These should not be a convenient paper exercise.

Giving Hope

Hope is something that we cannot easily give to another, but every effort can be made to support and encourage the hoping abilities of a client. Health carers are often in ideal positions to foster or hinder hope. A caring relationship can be offered that permits, rather than stifles, the efforts of the client to develop hope. The carer can support individuals and their families who are testing their own beliefs or struggling with questions of fear and faith when faced with challenges to health well being. They can be encouraged and supported to talk about their fears. Helping them to relive their memory of good things is another way of facilitating hope. Memories of events when life's needs were met, when despair was overcome and when failure was defeated, can all be used to take on a fresh view and face the future with confidence as part of spiritual recovery.

Herth (1990) identified hope-fostering strategies that could be used as part of spiritual care. This author defines hope-fostering strategies as 'those sources that functioned to instil, support or restore hope by facilitating the hoping process in some way'.

The following can be utilized as hope-fostering strategies.

Interpersonal Connectedness

A meaningful and shared relationship with close ones and others (including carers) is said to be a feature of interpersonal connectedness. For example, a harmonious and supportive relationship within the family offers the client hope and strength which are fundamental parts of a person's spirituality. The willingness of a carer to share in a client's hope is a feature of this strategy.

Light Heartedness

Feelings of delight, joy or playfulness are all features of light heartedness and these are communicated verbally or non-verbally. The carer can foster lightheartedness among clients. The spirits of lightheartedness can be therapeutic in that it can provide a communication link between persons and a way of coping with deteriorations in body function and confused emotions. It can be cathartic; in other words, it can provide a sense of release from the present moment.

Personal Attributes

The carer can bring out the best from clients, especially enable them to maximize their attributes of determination, courage and serenity. A search for a sense of inner peace, harmony and calm is one way of enabling the client to achieve serenity.

Attainable Aims

Personal aims can be powerful means of achieving a sense of meaning and purpose and these often foster hope. The carer who helps clients to search for meaning and purpose in life actually fosters hope. Helping clients and their families rework their aims and challenging their thoughts on to events or significant others are useful means of achieving a sense of hope.

Spiritual Base

The presence of active spiritual beliefs (in God or a 'Higher being') and spiritual practices is a source of hope. This may enable clients to participate in specific practices and these may include praying, corporate worship, listening to spiritual music and spiritual programmes on the radio or television, religious activities, maintaining specific religious customs, and visiting members and leaders of the spiritual community.

10.6 Giving Spiritual Care

It may be the case that a systematic approach to the planning of care as used in nursing could be employed to assist in meeting the spiritual needs of clients. The following four stages are included in the process of delivering nursing care: assessment, planning, implementation and evaluation.

Reader Activity 10.3
Reflect again on Case History 10.1 and consider how you would plan Steven's care.

Assessment

Information obtained on religious needs alone is not enough for spiritual care. Such information does not allow us to go deeper into feelings about meaning and purpose of life; love and relationship; trust; hope and strength; forgiveness; and expressions of beliefs and values. Also, this approach may lead to the assumption that a person who does not belong to a formal religion has no spiritual needs. As indicated earlier, the unreligious may have spiritual needs. The person who does not express obvious religious beliefs may still struggle with guilt, or lack meaning and purpose, or with need for love and relationships. On the other hand, an individual who declares as belonging to a particular religion may not necessarily abide by the beliefs and practices of that religion. Assumptions or conclusions should not be drawn about spiritual needs on the basis of the client's religious status alone.

The carer must remain sensitive to verbal and non-verbal cues from clients when carrying out spiritual assessment. These cues might indicate a need to talk about spiritual problems.

Assessment of the client's physical functioning may also provide valuable information for understanding their spiritual component. Such obvious status about the client's ability to see, hear and move are important factors that may later determine the relevance of certain interventions. Also, psychosocial assessment data may serve a useful purpose in determining the client's thought patterns; content of speech, affect(mood), cultural orientation, and social relationships may all provide the basis for identifying a need, or planning appropriate care, in conjunction with spiritual intervention.

Reader Activity 10.4
Return, once again, to Steven's Case History (10.1) and consider what assessment procedure could be used before planning his spiritual care.

Tubesing (1980) has suggested a spiritual assessment procedure in which there are five questions to assess a person's spiritual outlook. Spiritual outlook embraces a person's goal, faith, value, commitments, and ability to let go and to receive forgiveness from self and others. Tubesing's assessment questions for spiritual outlook are listed in Box 10.3.

The presence of religious literature, for example the Bible or Koran, gives an indication of the client's concerns about spiritual matters. Objects such as

---

Box 10.3 Tubesing's assessment questions for spiritual outlook

- **What is the aim of life?**
- **What beliefs guide me?**
- **What is important to me?**
- **What do I choose to spend myself on?**
- **What am I willing to let go?**

religious needs, pins, or articles of clothing are symbolic of the client's spiritual expressions. Clients may keep religious statues or deities to carry out their religious rituals.

The following observation schedules can be used to carry out spiritual assessment by observations:

Non-verbal Behaviour

- Observe affect. Does the client's affect or attitude convey loneliness, depression, anger, agitation, or anxiety?
- Observe behaviour. Does the client pray during the day? Does the client rely on religious reading material or other literature for solace?

Verbal Behaviour

- Does the client seem to complain out of proportion to his illness?
- Does the client complain of sleeping difficulties?
- Does the client ask for unusually high doses of sedation?
- Does the client refer to God in any way?
- Does the client talk about prayer, faith, hope, or anything of a religious nature?
- Does the client talk about church functions that are part of his or her life?
- Does the client express concern over the meaning and direction of life?
- Does the client express concern over the impact of the illness on the meaning of life?

Interpersonal Relationships

- Does the client have visitors or does he or she spend visiting hours alone?
- Are the visitors supportive or do they seem to leave the client feeling upset?
- Does the client have visitors from his or her church?
- Does the client interact with staff and other clients?

Environment

- Does the client have a Bible or other religious reading material?
- Does the client wear religious medals or pins?
- Does the client use religious articles such as statues in observing religious practices?
- Has the client received religious get-well cards?
- Does the client use personal pictures, artwork, or music to keep his or her spirits up?

Observation of the ways in which an individual relates with people 'significant others' (people close to them, friends, and others who matter to them) may provide clues to spiritual needs. The quality of interpersonal relationships can be ascertained. Does the client welcome his or her visitors? Does their presence relax the client or cause distress? Does s/he get visitors from the church or religious community? Observations of these factors can lead to conclusions about their social support system. The social system enables the client to give and receive love and lack of such support may deprive the client of this need and leave him/her distressed. The client who has faith in God may feel estranged if s/he is cut off from his/her support network.

Observations of the client's environment and significant objects/symbols related to his/her religious practice may give evidence of his/her spirituality.

The other area of spiritual assessment includes attention to three factors: sense of meaning and purpose, means of forgiveness, and source of love and relationship. Observations and routine conversations with patients can lead to valuable information about each of those factors. Questions can be framed to include the following:

- **What is your source of meaning and purpose in life?**
- **Why do you go on living?**

Reader Activity 10.5
What observations could contribute to your understanding of a client's spiritual needs? List these.

Observations may include: how does the client deal with other clients? Does s/he ruminate over past behaviours or how s/he has been treated by other people? How does the client respond to criticisms? If the client responds with anger, hostility and blames others, these behaviours may suggest that s/he is unable to forgive himself/herself and that consequent inability to tolerate anything that resembles criticism.

The spiritual assessment must also look at the client's ability to feel loved, valued and respected by other people.

Planning

The planning of spiritual care requires careful attention. The data obtained from assessment must be interpreted in terms of spiritual needs, and a care plan should be designed to incorporate this information.

The planning of spiritual care should include respect for the client's individuality; willingness of the carer to get involved in the spirituality of client; use of therapeutic self; and the nurturing of the inner person, the spirit.

Assistance to meet spiritual needs should be given according to the indications of the individual, which may be unique and specific. If, for example, the client is part of a church or religious group, and this effect on him appears positive, the nurse can strengthen this contact. A client who is accustomed to practices such as meditating, praying, or reading the Bible or other religious books, should be given time and privacy. A visit by the client's religious agent (pastor, rabbi, or others) can be arranged.

The carer can make it easier for an individual to talk about spiritual beliefs and concerns, especially about how these relate to his or her illness, or state of health imbalance. The carer may need to help an individual in his/her struggle and search for meaning and purpose in life. On the other hand, if the client is trying to find a source of hope and strength, then it can be used in planning care.

Other aspects of the care plan may include comfort, support, warmth, self-awareness, empathy, non-judgemental listening and understanding. All these measures are the essence of a therapeutic relationship. An empathetic listener can do much to support a person who is spiritually distressed by being available when needed, especially those clients suffering from loneliness, and expressing doubts, fears and feelings of alienation. The presence of another empathetic person may have a healing effect.

A powerful source of spiritual care and comfort can be prayer, scripture and other religious reading. All these may alleviate spiritual distress. Prayers as a source of help would help a client develop a feeling of oneness with the universe or a better relationship with God, comfort the client, and help relieve spiritual distress. A particular prayer should be selected according to the client's own style of comfort and needs. Although a carer may not belong to the same faith as the patient, individuals can still be supported in carrying out their spiritual beliefs.

Meditation, both religious and secular, can play an important role in enabling clients to relax; clear the mind; achieve a feeling of oneness with a deity or the universe; promote acceptance of painful memories or decisions; and gather energy and hope that may help them to face spiritual distress.

The use of music gives an inspirational and calming effect. A wide variety of religious, inspirational and secular music may spiritually uplift a client.

Implementation

Implementation of spiritual care is a highly skilled activity. It requires education and experience in spiritual care. Sufficient information is provided in this guide to extend the carer's knowledge of spirituality. In carrying out nursing actions related to spiritual needs, it is imperative that carers observe the following:

- **Do not impose personal beliefs on the client or their family.**
- **Respond to the client's expression of need of a correct understanding of their background.**
- **Do not allow a detached scene to be used as an occasion to proselytize.**
- **Be sensitive to the client's signal for spiritual support.**

It is important that if a carer feels unable to respond to a particular situation of spiritual need, then he or she should enlist the services of an appropriate individual.

Interventions, by professional carers, should be based on an action that reflects caring for the individual. Caring signifies to the person that he or she is significant, and is worth someone taking the trouble to be concerned about. Caring requires actions of support and assistance in growing. It means adopting a non-judgemental approach and showing sensitivity to a person's cultural values, physical preference and social needs. It demands an attitude of helping, sharing, nurturing and loving. These actions fulfil the requirement of individual-ized spiritual care.

An understanding of the client's unique beliefs and values or religious views is paramount in spiritual care. The carer must respect and understand the need for a client's beliefs and practices, even if these are not in accord with the carer's faith. To allow a better understanding of the client's spiritual needs, the carer must establish a rapport and trust which facilitates the client to share those beliefs. The carer's own self-awareness of personal limitation in understanding these beliefs is paramount and he/ she must seek outside help if necessary.

It is the case that interventions of professional carers should be based on a relationship that encourages the person to express views, fears, anxieties, and new understanding through creative acts, writing, poetry, music or art. Time for quiet reflection and opportunities for religious practices would enable the client to develop a deeper understanding of life and a particular belief system.

The person who has no strong philosophical or religious belief may seek the opportunity to explore feelings, values and an understanding of life with another individual who is willing to give attention and time to discuss those areas of concern and share common human experiences. The carer is the person who is most immediately available and receptive to the client's thoughts and feelings for some of them. Certain clients may require their close friends, family or a religious person to share those thoughts and feelings. The carer must remain sensitive to these needs and make the necessary arrangements. However, it must be remembered that spiritual growth is a life-long process and the carer who initiates spiritual care would have been a catalyst in the client's goal to achieve eventual spiritual integrity and well being.

Evaluation

Evaluation is an activity that involves the process of making a judgement about outcomes of nursing intervention. There are many indicators of spiritual outcomes, one of which is spiritual integrity. The person who has attained spiritual integrity demonstrates this experience through a reality-based tranquillity or peace, or, through the development of meaningful, purposeful behaviour, displays a restored sense of integrity. O'Brien (1982) commented that the measure of spiritual care should establish the degree to which 'spiritual pain' was relieved. Another view offered by Kim *et al.* (1984) suggested that spiritual care may be measured as the disruption in the 'life principle' was restored. The contents of another's unique thoughts and feelings may also reflect spiritual growth, through a greater understanding of life or an acceptance and creativity within a particular context.

10.7 Summary

Clearly, there is no one single authoritative definition of spirituality, although some authors have attempted to define it in broad terms. Spirituality would appear to refer to a broader dimension that is sometimes beyond the realm of objective explanation. It is an inspirational expression as a reaction to a religious force or an abstract philosophy as defined by the individual. It is a quality that is present in believers, and even in atheist and agnostics, provided there is the opportunity to feel and express this inspirational experience according to the individual's understanding and meaning attached to this phenomenon.

Spirituality features as a significant dimension in many individual's lives and it is often expressed through their particular faith or religion. There is evidence to suggest that a significant number of people belong to a particular faith in the UK. Individual spiritual needs include the need for meaning and purpose; the need for love and harmonious relationships; the need for forgiveness; the need for a source of hope and strength; the need for trust; the need for expression of personal beliefs and values; the need for spiritual practice; the expression of concept of God or deity; and creativity. These are by no means exclusive, but are commonly recognized as being within the province of professional carers in learning disabilities to incorporate into care plans as part of the spiritual care of clients.

A caring relationship based on self-awareness, communication (listening), trust building, giving hope and enabling spiritual growth (client education) is an important prerequisite for spiritual care. This shared relationship, together with the previous introduction to the knowledge of spirituality, offers the reader a basis for providing spiritual care based on individual needs.

Effective spiritual care can therefore be given, for example through the systematic steps of the process of nursing. Appropriate assessment strategies and tools should be employed for the purpose of assessing an individual's spiritual needs. Data obtained from assessment strategies can be used for the planning of spiritual care.

Discussion Questions

1 From your experience do you think that the spiritual dimension of people with learning disabilities is largely ignored?

2 How can those who care for people with severe or profound learning disabilities be sure that they have spiritual needs?

3 Reflect on your own spiritual needs. Does this influence how you would meet those needs in others?

4 How would you argue, if at all, that failure to meet the spiritual dimension of our needs may result in health loss?

References

Bannerman, M. and Lindsay, M. (1993) Evolution of services. *In* Shanley, E. and Starrs, T.A. (Eds) *Learning Disabilities. A handbook of care*, pp. 19–39. Edinburgh: Churchill Livingstone.

Birchenall, P. (1987) The spiritual dimension. *In* Parrish, A. (Ed.) *Mental Handicap*, pp. 74–79. London: Macmillan.

Birchenall, P. and Birchenall, M. (1986) Caring for mentally handicapped people: The community and the church. *Professional Nurse* 1: 148–150.

Burnard, P. (1985) *Learning Human Skills.* London: Heinemann Nursing.

Carson, V.B. (1989) *Spiritual Dimensions of Nursing Practice.* London: W.B. Saunders.

Clegg, J. (1990) Interactions and relationships in adults with intellectual disability. Unpublished PhD thesis, the University of Nottingham.

Gorham, M. (1989) Spirituality and problem solving with seniors. *Perspectives* **13**(3): 13–16.

Hardy, Sir Alister (1979) *The Spiritual Nature of Man.* Oxford: Clarendon Press.

Hay, D. (1987) *Exploring Inner Space.* London: Mowbray.

Herth, K. (1990) Fostering hope in terminally ill people. *Journal of Advanced Nursing.* **15**: 1250–1257.

James, W. (1982) *The Varieties of Religious Experience.* Middlesex: Penguin.

Kim, M.J., McFarland, S.K. and McLane, A.M. (1984) *Pocket Guide to Nursing Diagnosis.* St Louis: C.V. Mosby.

Maslow, A.R. (1968) *Toward a Psychology of Being.* New York: Van Nostrand.

Murray, R.B. and Zentner, J.B. (1989) *Nursing Concepts for Health Promotion.* Englewood Cliffs: Prentice Hall.

Narayanasamy, A. (1991) *Spiritual Care: A practical guide for nurses.* Lancaster: Quay.

Narayanasamy, A. (1994a) Spirituality. *Journal of Mental Handicap Nurses Association* **11**(1): 20–23.

Narayanasamy, A. (1994b) Spirituality and mental health competence. *In* Thompson, A. and Mathias, P. (Eds) *Lyttle's Mental Health and Disorder,* pp. 367–384. London: Baillière Tindall.

O'Brien, M.E. (1982) Religious faith and adjustment to long-term haemodialysis. *Journal of Religious Health* **21**: 68.

Stallwood, J. (1981) Spiritual dimensions of nursing practice. *In* Beland, I.L. and Passos, J.Y. (Eds) *Clinical Nursing,* pp. 392–501. New York: Macmillan.

Stuart, G.W. and Sundeen, S.J. (1983) *Principles and Practice of Psychiatric Nursing.* St Louis: C.V. Mosby.

Tubesing, D.A. (1980) Stress: Spiritual outlook and health. *Specialised Pastoral Care Journal* **3**: 17.

Further Reading

Birchenall, P. (1987) The spiritual dimension. *In* Parrish, A. (Ed.) *Mental Handicap,* Chapter 10. London: Macmillan.

Carson, V.B. (1989) *Spiritual Dimensions of Nursing Practice.* London: W.B. Saunders.

Narayanasamy, A. (1991) *Spiritual Care: A practical guide for nurses.* Lancaster: Quay/BKT.

Sampson, C. (1982) *The Neglected Ethic: Religious and cultural factors in the care of patients.* London: McGraw-Hill.

Shelly, J.A. and Fish, S. (1988) *Spiritual Care: The nurses role.* Downers Grove, Illinois: Inter Varsity Press.

Part Seven: Political and Economic Dimensions of Learning Disability

Part Seven of *Dimensions of Learning Disability* considers how policy factors influence and affect services for people with a learning disability. The impacts that such factors bring to bear upon the life style of individuals involved in the provision and use of these services are also considered.

In Chapter 11, 'Political Dimensions of Learning Disability', Carl Thompson undertakes an analysis of the key issues and concepts involved in the politics of services for people with a learning disability. From this analysis, Carl considers how the status of 'citizen' can be utilized to promote the political dimension and illustrates how a political agenda might be established. The chapter emerges as a discussion paper which offers guidance in a more proactive approach towards influencing the policy dimension of services for people with a learning disability.

Colin Beacock and Tom Tait explain the basic principles of the study of economics as they apply to those involved in the care of people with a learning disability. In Chapter 12, 'The Economic Dimension of Learning Disabilities', the authors consider the study of health economics and the influence this has had upon prioritization of health-care interventions. Their examination of how economic theories influence the 'purchaser:provider' arrangements for provision of health and social care reflects contemporary approaches to policy developments in the UK.

Part Seven offers an opportunity for the reader to examine the relationship between politics and economics and to consider how the development of social policy has been influenced by these factors. Furthermore, the authors have sought to describe a means by which to evaluate how each of these dimensions has influenced services for people with a learning disability.

Chapter 11: Political dimensions of learning disability
Carl Thompson

Box 11.1 Political dimensions: key issues/concepts

- **Politics**
- **Values**
- **Policy and policy arenas**
- **Discourse**
- **Political, economic and professional contributions to disability**
- **Citizenship**
- **Rights**
- **Politicization**

11.1 Introduction

This chapter examines those features of what might be termed 'the politics of learning disability'. The term 'politics' is used in its broadest sense and does not merely refer to the processes of government, policy formation and the legislative functions of Parliament, although of course these enter the discussion. The intention is to take the discussion of politics in relation to learning disability away from the largely sterile areas of legislation and parliamentary function, and to steer it towards a recognition of the role of values, ideology and discourse in politics. This makes it necessary to incorporate relevant 'theory' in the chapter. One of the aims in examining the reality of legislation relating to people with a learning disability was to combat what some commentators have recognized as the lack of a theoretical framework for 'many of the reforms and solutions of the last thirty years' (Borsay, 1986). By examining the politics of learning disability from within an explicit theoretical framework the reader is given the opportunity to argue against the value stance of the author – a luxury that is often not afforded to those people with a learning disability, their carers and representative organizations. In this way the chapter encourages an active dialogue around, and increase awareness of, the politics of learning disability.

An understanding of the politics of learning disability is vital to all involved in empowering people with a learning disability. Depending on the viewpoint held, politics can be viewed as either the cause of a myriad of disabling labels or the saviour through which it may be possible to liberate individuals from the legacies of discrimination and stigma that characterize the lives of so many people with a learning disability. Whichever view one adopts, it is difficult to argue against the assertion that we owe it to those people with a learning disability to develop our knowledge of what is in effect both the fundamental challenge to, and one of the best means of, increased self-actualization for this group of people.

This chapter explores three of the key areas in the politics of learning disability:

- **A theoretical exploration of the concept of 'politics' in relation to learning disability.**
- **An exploration of the 'outcomes' of political decisions. In the form of the question, 'what do the politics of learning disability mean to people with a learning disability and for their status as citizens?'.**
- **Arguments for and against the politicization of services for people with a learning disability.**

11.2 Towards a Framework for the Politics of Learning Disability

Before examining the effects of political decisions on the lives of people with a learning disability it is necessary to develop an explanatory framework to outline some of the reasons why such decisions occur and, consequently, why the legal and policy frameworks within which we must all operate present themselves in the form that they do.

Deciding what constitutes 'politics' for people with a learning disability is not as straightforward as it might seem. Lay notions of politics often refer to the functions and processes of Parliament and government, such as debate, legislation, pressure group lobbying and the like. While such functions and processes are undoubtedly interesting they offer no real clue as to the true nature of politics itself. If politics were merely the variously stirred outcomes of a few key processes it would offer little attraction to groups who share similar experiences of disability but whose participation in the processes identified above is not always assured. Deutsch (1974) offers a more conceptual view:

[politics is] . . . the making of decisions by public means as opposed to the making of personal decisions privately by individuals and the making of economic decisions in response to such impersonal forces such as money, market conditions and resource scarcities.

Deutsch's definition, when applied to the reality of the British context, appears flawed. His view of politics neglects the reality that decision making by 'public' means can be stretched so that the processes of government do not always include public discussion. Governmental intervention which prevented debate of a Bill which would have given effective rights to antidiscrimination recourse for disabled people, and the consequent admission from Sir Nicholas Scott that he 'misled' Parliament and disguised the collusion of the Civil Service, all amount to a distortion of the term 'public' in relation to political decisions. That such issues should arise in 1995 illustrate how parliamentary processes are out of keeping with the politics of modern care provision.

Deutsch's definition also underplays the role of 'impersonal forces' in legitimatize political decisions. Impersonal forces such as budgets, management doctrine, and performance indicators, for example, reinforce governmental claims that resources available for health and social care are necessarily limited in some value-neutral way. The impact of impersonal forces, however, is not just a feature of national policy – they also permeate the lower levels of direct service provision. The quasi-markets in health and social care mean that budgets are limited on an annual basis and the effects of this

may be felt by consumers in the form of reduced access to services or a lowering of the standards previously delivered.

However, Deutsch recognizes that almost all aspects of life are affected by 'politics' and political decisions – an observation which is particularly applicable to those members of the population with a learning disability. Political decisions play a part in publicly allocated finance, the benefits system, employment, education and political participation itself. As these components constitute various 'life chances' then politics is also associated with the quality of an individual's life. In short, political decisions have the power to raise or lower the standards of living for individuals with a learning disability.

The value of politics to people with a learning disability and their carers, including professionals, is that it offers the chance to renegotiate that which is considered important or valuable to society, as well as providing the opportunity to explore what is actually real and true in social terms. 'Good' political decisions, according to this criteria, are those that contribute to a concern for 'truth', which in turn leads to the search for solutions, new discoveries, new ways of working together and the chance to decide (as far as is possible) one's own fate – that is, they empower. This view of politics provides a theoretical baseline for those political theorists who see politics as the 'art of the possible' (Eayres, 1961). This important perspective on politics has obvious attractions to those seeking to reverse the tide of discrimination against people with a learning disability, of which more is said later.

If we view politics as the allocation of value and worth, via decisions made on behalf of others, then it becomes clear that 'politics' in this sense applies not only at governmental (macro) level but also at the level of services and service providers themselves (the micro level). The Ely Hospital inquiry in the 1970s, and more latterly the Ashworth Special Hospital inquiry, demonstrated that defining worth, allocating value and controlling access to life chances is not only the preserve of government, but

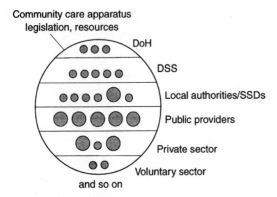

Community care apparatus
legislation, resources

DoH

DSS

Local authorities/SSDs

Public providers

Private sector

Voluntary sector

and so on

Figure 11.1 Examples of policy levels and arenas in community care. ● Arenas; —, levels, DOH, Department of Health; DSS, Department of Social Security; L. auth/S.D.D.s, Local Authority Social Services Departments.

also extends down to individual professionals within organizations. Fulcher (1989) provides an illuminating analytical model which not only helps explain the 'gaps' between policy rhetoric and the reality of service provision, but also the role of professionals and agencies in developing worth and value in policy for people with disabilities (Fig. 11.1) (the model has been adapted for the British context).

Within the model, the term 'levels' describes the stages at which policy is made rather than simply implemented. 'Arenas' comprise those forums within which issues are debated, struggles ensue, decisions are made and values allocated. In relation to people with a learning disability, Fulchers's model explains much of the apparent gap between the rhetoric of a policy such as Community Care, with its emphasis on 'choice', 'support' and 'participation', and the reality of 'care in the community' as experienced by people with a learning disability. The model represents the antithesis of the 'passive' dilution of policy which is often a feature of conventional 'top-down' policy analysis – instead it places professionals, and other participants in policy or service 'arenas', in an active policy-developmental role. This assertion reinforces Lipsky's (1980) observations about the methods and powers employed by 'street level bureaucrats' who have the power to absorb policy recommendations and actively interpret and distort

their values through the professional and administrative role in the delivery of services:

> In an impressive range of welfare state policies the residual discretion enjoyed by workers who interact with and make decisions about clients results in workers effectively 'making policy'. They effectively 'make policy' not in the sense that they articulate core objectives or develop mechanisms to achieve these objectives. Rather, they make policy in the sense that the aggregation of their separate discretionary and unsanctioned behaviours adds up to patterned agency behaviour overall. (Lipsky, 1980)

Reader Activity 11.1
Do you believe that, as a worker, you shape policy either in your role as practitioner or student? If so, how do you achieve this?

If one accepts this model has some worth in the context of current service structures for people with a learning disability then one might also accept the potential for practitioners to actively assist clients and their carers in shaping 'political' agendas which reflect *their* concerns and promote *their* values is definitely present. This potential is dependent on the acceptance of two key arguments:

- **that the values and concerns of people with a learning disability and their carers are worth promoting**
- **that altering the values promoted by policy, and therefore the democratic process, should be part of the professional's remit.**

That disabled people's views are of worth would seem to be beyond question, but the conscious or subconscious alteration of democratically formulated and sanctioned values in the form of official policy is altogether more tricky, perhaps even immoral. The developing model accounts for this moral hurdle by placing the formulation of policy within the context of a struggle between competing

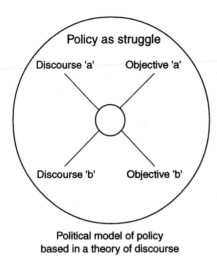

Political model of policy
based in a theory of discourse

Figure 11.2 The policy arena.

discourses in arenas and by avoiding making any value judgements on the desirability of professional's actively making policy. If we look at the term 'arenas' in more detail the 'political' approach to policy at all levels becomes clear (Fig. 11.2).

Within this model of policy development, based on competing and possibly conflicting discourses and objectives one can see the professional's role could be one of reconciliation of potentially divergent values and promotion of customer's own agendas. If the flip-side of this argument is adopted, however, you can also see that professional's own adopted discourses have the potential to swing the struggle in their favour. Any model based on unmitigated conflict necessarily means that the most powerful win and gain control of the agenda and the interests promoted. Currently, it is professional and policy making groups who hold the bulk of the power in the provision of services for people with learning disabilities.

11.3 The Role of Discourse and the Person with a Learning Disability

As has been seen, the predominant factor in this model is the concept of discourse. Discourse can be defined in various ways but for the purposes of this chapter a general notion of discourse is deployed. Hugman (1991) sees discourse as a means of:

> defining the concept of the client or patient (*sic*) by way of the control of language and knowledge.

Discourse is more than just language-based communication, it is a means for groups to achieve dominance in policy and service arenas. Language in discourse reproduces and communicates power (Hugman, 1991). The importance of discourse as a theoretical concept to a person with a learning disability should not be underestimated. Discourses articulate the world in certain ways, they 'identify' problems, perspectives on those problems and, most importantly, help generate solutions. An example of discourse in practice can be seen in the area of schooling for people with disabilities:

> . . . the notion that some children have handicaps divides the school population into those with and those without handicaps: it constructs the notion of normal and abnormal, of belonging here or elsewhere, it leads to the view that specialist teachers are necessary for some children and this view suggests or articulates a particular range of objectives for special education: such as identifying 'difference', separate career structures, a focus on disability and so on . . . this [is] a divisive discourse and is a close companion of professionalism . . . An alternative view comes from the discourse that children are firstly *pupils*: this provides a different theory and articulation: it unites the school population, it identifies what children share, it provides an objective of including all children in regular schools and directs us to a particular means for achieving that, it invites us to focus on pedagogy. This is an inclusive discourse. (Fulcher, 1989)

Discourse is often employed as a tactic in political arenas. Therefore, it is a useful tool for those wishing to promote certain policies and values. Potter and Collie (1989) imply that such a tactic can be seen in the development of Community Care. In their discussion of the findings of a study looking at societal perceptions of different, language-based, community-care scenarios they found that:

> ... [community care] policy, which for critics in some cases amounts to little more than privatisation of large areas of the health service, can be represented in the reassuring humanistic imagery of neighbourliness, close ties, social support and a life-style akin more to the village than the urban housing estate. For advocates, of course, this discourse is an effective and appropriate support for a policy which amounts to a dramatic enhancement of the quality of life of people with a mental handicap. (Potter and Collie, 1989)

If discourse is the essential unit of a political model of policy which operates at both macro and micro levels then what are the dominant discourses attached to learning diability? There are at least two major discourses in play relating to people with a learning disability, and disabilities generally:

- the individualistic or 'personal tragedy' approach
- the social approach.

11.4 Individualistic or 'Personal Tragedy' Discourse

The essential conflict between the two competing views and discourses on disability roughly equates with the classic distinction drawn by the sociologist C. Wright Mills in the 1950s, who argued the case for recognizing the distinction between 'personal troubles' and 'public issues':

> Troubles occur within the character of the individual and within the range of his immediate relations with others; they have to do with his self and with those limited areas of social life of which he is directly and personally aware. Accordingly, the statement and resolution of troubles properly lie within the individual as a biographical entity and within the scope of his immediate milieu – the social setting that is directly open to his personal experience and to some extent his wilful activity. Issues have to do with matters that

transcend these local environments of the individual and the range of his inner life. They have to do with the organisation of many such milieux into the institutions of a historical society as a whole, with the ways in which various milieux overlap and interpenetrate to form the larger structure of social and historical life. (Wright Mills, 1970)

An individualistic approach to learning disability promotes differentiation between people on the basis of different types of impairment, which are seen as occurring entirely within the individual. Applied to people with a learning disability this means that their primary classification in life is not as a person with a degree of impairment, but as a condition, with a degree of humanity attached almost as a postscript, for example the 'Down's' or 'Apert's' sufferer. Such an approach encourages the development of syndromes and classifications of biological deficiencies, even where the validity and prognoses attached to such classifications is questionable – not all people with Down's syndrome die of weak hearts or chest infections at the age of 50 years and there are significant degrees of functional ability within specific conditions. Such classifications are inherently weak as scientific tools and, more importantly, as indicators for social action. This approach to disability neglects the common economic, social and political dependencies which people with a learning disability share in everyday life. The approach encourages paternalistic and 'charitable' interventions in people's lives by virtue of the fact that their deviation from normality – as defined by the non-disabled – is judged as a personal and tragic loss. The overwhelming effect on people with disabilities of such a discourse is that they are expected to adapt themselves to society, as opposed to society adapting itself to cope adequately with people with a disability. This approach to disability has traditionally been the one which has been utilized by able-bodied academics and policy makers.

The discourse of individualistic tragedy has been challenged in recent years, most forcibly by people with disabilities themselves and their proponents and advocates in the social, policy and academic communities (Borsay, 1986; Oliver, 1986, 1990). An alternative view has emerged which addresses the issues from the disabled person's own perspective and which locates impairment in its social context.

11.5 A Social Discourse on Disability: Disability as Social Oppression

An alternative to the presentation of disability as an individualized 'trouble' is the idea that the category of disability has itself been constructed as a form of social problem. Albrecht and Levy (1981) sum up the crux of this particular discourse neatly, and in doing so highlight the importance of 'politics' in relation to people with learning disabilities:

> . . . disability definitions are not rationally determined but socially constructed. Despite the objective reality, what becomes a disability is determined by the social meanings individuals attach to particular physical and mental impairments. Certain disabilities become defined as social problems through the successful efforts of powerful groups to market their own self-interests. Consequently the so called 'objective' criteria of disability reflects the biases, self-interests and moral evaluations of those in a position to influence policy. (Albrecht and Levy, 1981).

This argument implies that the more powerful groups in society influence policy, by controlling the policy agenda and the definitions employed, to the detriment of those people with a disability. Given this implication, the social construction approach to learning disability can be used as a means of understanding the oppression that people with a learning disability endure as part of daily life. *The Oxford Concise Dictionary* (1985) defines the expression to oppress as:

> [to] . . . keep under by continual cruelty or injustice.

Commentators such as Oliver (1986) recognize this reality and describe the social construction

approach to disability as 'social oppression theory'. Within this approach, disability will be defined by social policies which are subject to the influence of ideologies. A simple way of thinking of ideology is as sets of shared values, which can positively or negatively impact on people's lives. This ideological component becomes increasingly evident when one examines the ways in which society creates and perpetuates 'disability' as a euphemistic term for dependence. The keys to understanding this creation can be found in the ideologies dominant in the areas of economics, politics and professionalized services.

Economic Contributions

Work is a fundamental component, either directly or indirectly, of every individual in industrialized societies. It provides material resources, social status and a means of establishing satisfactory social relationships (Oliver, 1990). The ideological frameworks of capitalism and economic rationality encompass all aspects of policy and leave few areas of daily life untouched in their influence. Industrial society has created hitherto unknown wealth for Britain as a whole but has created special problems for those with learning disabilities. Because neither ideology or 'disability' is fixed over time and/or between cultures it is important to understand the importance of these contexts to the development of the 'dependent' disabled person. Finklestein (1980) offers an explanation for the creation of dependence that acknowledges the roles of both ideology and economic progression. His thesis centres around the notion of three phases of industrial development in Britain:

- **Phase 1** represents Britain prior to the Industrial Revolution; a period within which Finklestein suggests the disabled were part of the general underclass and were assimilated into communities by way of participation in social roles such as 'beggar' or 'village idiot' (Oliver, 1990) and as workers who could contribute to the mainly agrarian or small industrial modes of production.

- **In phase 2,** the production process shifted from the home to the factory. Consequently, exclusion of disabled people from the new processes of production, and from the accompanying social relationships, became more pronounced. The disabled during this time became a segregated class of person and the asylum flourished as a means of separating those people with a learning disability from the rest of society. This was due, in part, to the rise of the medical profession's involvement in the lives of those people with a disability. During phase 2 of the development of the category of the disabled individual Finklestein identifies the emergence of the essential paradox in relation to those people with a disability, namely, that disability came to be seen as both individual impairment and social restriction.
- **In phase 3,** the utilization of new technologies and the identification of common goals for the disabled and professionals, coupled with the development of working relationships based on these common goals, marks the beginning of the end for segregative practices and liberation for the disabled.

Oliver (1986) highlights a number of flaws in this construct. First, the assertion that segregation of the disabled accompanied the industrial revolution (in phase 2) is essentially inaccurate. Section 1 of the 1601 Poor Law made provision for special facilities for the lame, infirm and blind and many hospitals, asylums and workhouses were segregating the 'handicapped' as early as the eighteenth and nineteenth centuries.

Second, Oliver (1986) suggests that it could have been the need to control the non-working population in the face of the transition from feudalism to capitalism that led to segregation rather than the rise of the hospital-based medical professional. Prior to the development of sophisticated medical diag-

nostic categories and tests, the segregated (whether they be physically disabled, mentally ill or people with a learning disability) only had one thing in common: an inability or unwillingness to exchange labour for wages in the factory. Segregation and medical specialization then becomes a function of an increasingly sophisticated mode of social control for the potentially disruptive.

Finally, the assumed liberation of the disabled through the introduction of new technologies can be questioned. Technology assumes an almost 'value neutral' face in Finklestein's analysis which does not bear up to close scrutiny. A social aetiology of learning disability recognizes that technology can be the cause of many disabilities as well as its saviour. Witness the preservation of severely handicapped babies and infants by the use of medical technology and the value neutrality implied in Finklestein's construct becomes difficult to accept. Further, there is little guarantee that any benefits that technology can offer will be spread equally across all social groups (Oliver, 1986) – technology costs money!

There are also at least three ways in which the development of the labour market (as the vehicle for the values attached to the economic explanation of disability) disadvantages the disabled person:

- Credentialism, or judging a person on the basis of 'paper' qualifications, as the dominant expression of assumed ability discriminates against those who, for whatever reason (e.g. age, interrupted or inadequate schooling) may not possess qualifications which mirror their abilities.
- Technological change, which opens up new opportunities for the young, devalues the experience of older employees. Also, their age makes retraining unattractive for employers.
- Employers often consider *all* disabled people as unreliable and a high risk group with an associated inability to reach normal productivity levels (Borsay, 1986).

If these arguments are accepted then it will be seen that the economic–political explanation of disability has much to offer the observer trying to understand the politics of learning disability. Indeed, the economics and politics of learning disability are closely intertwined.

Stone (1984) suggests that all societies operate a 'distributive principle' through which they can allocate goods and services. She suggests that this distributive principle recognizes that not everyone can or will work. There are two distribution systems operating in parallel: the work-based and the needs-based systems. In our society the allocation of goods and services is more heavily weighted in favour of the work-based system (e.g. tax concessions, national insurance principles, home ownership); consequently this means that it is better to be in work than in need. Within Stone's analysis the category of disability is one means of 'steering' individuals into either the work-based or needs-based systems. Therefore the parameters of what constitutes disability are a powerful force in shaping an individual's access to goods and services. Further, Stone argues:

> The assignment of citizens into the work-based or needs-based distributive systems is a highly political issue which is not readily resolved by the creation of formal administrative schedules or the delegation of decisions to the medical profession (or any other technical experts). (Stone, 1984)

Because of the political nature of this assignment into systems, and the social role of the category of disability, it follows that disability in this sense cannot be anything other than a social construct.

Political Contributions

Politics in this sense refers to the machinery of government, i.e. Parliament, legislation and policy making rather than the broader definition employed thus far. According to this perspective, policy (as the end result or outcome of the legislative process) can be seen as playing an important role in the development of the category of disability. Oliver (1990) points to the ability of legislation to perpetuate socially created images of the disabled as dependent and 'helpless'. He suggests that the Chronically Sick and Disabled Person's Act (1970) and the Disabled Person's (Services, Consultation and Representation) Act (1986) represent an extension of professional and administrative approaches to the *problem* of disability rather than an acknowledgement of disability as a human rights issue. The spirit of this idea – that learning disability inevitably involves dependency, and that the dependent individual and their family deserve professional or official help in choosing services, adaptive aids and providing opportunities – can be seen in the supposed 'new wave' of community-care legislation. In the White Paper *Caring for People* (HMSO Cmnd 849) one can see how the government subscribes to the view that disability should be explicitly linked to professional practice, administrative rationality and a secondary role for the disabled in processes such as assessment or service development. Some of the viewpoints espoused in this White Paper can be seen in Box 11.2.

Within these paragraphs in Box 11.2 there are a number of assumptions made or implied by government which can be questioned from a social discourse perspective. First, given the context of a declining hospital service, and the dominance of the social over the health-based model of 'care', quite what the 'important role' is in relation to mental handicap psychiatry is not clear. Is the government suggesting that both sets of values (the medical and the social) can coexist, or is the statement merely the result of concessions to powerfull professional groups?

Second, many people with a 'mental handicap' (*sic*) are not amenable to 'treatment'. It can be argued that the notion of disability is a human rather than a medical condition: a deviation from 'normal' perhaps, but not a sickness with cures, variable prognoses, and all the reliance on skills

---

Box 11.2 *Caring for People*: UK Government White Paper

'. . . there will continue to be an important role for those such as consultants in the psychiatry of mental handicap with particular knowledge and experience of treating patients with a mental handicap.' (para 2.16)

'. . . Nurses' skills and experience are highly valued and will continue to be needed as part of the new forms of service which will be increasingly the responsibility of local authorities. The Department of Health will be exploring with the professions, the Local Authority Associations (LAAs), and other interests how this can best be facilitated.' (para 2.17)

'The Government wishes to promote further progress within available resources and is exploring how this can best be done. In particular, it wishes to encourage the provision of services to individuals, developed from multi-disciplinary assessment of their needs and made with proper participation of the individuals concerned, their families and other carers.' (para 2.15)

---

and knowledge that the term implies. It is also interesting to note the Department of Health explored the changing role of the local authorities with the professional groups and the local authority associations (LAAs) and other 'interests' without specifying a role for representative groups in the process, or indeed, elaborating on what these other interests were (presumably the newly resurgent private sector of the 1980s). Similarly, the idea that there should be 'proper' participation of the individual with a learning disability in assessments is open to broad interpretation by service planners and puchasers alike. Such participation could take the form of purchaser/provider dominated meetings or protocols for access or involvement – all of which tend to favour the more powerful administrative and professional groups, a point recognized, in part, by the advocacy movement and the move to increase

the force of service user's views and opinions in services.

Reader Activity 11.2
What opportunities exist for the carer to act as advocate for their client in the services that you have encountered?

A further way in which 'politics' influences perceptions of dependency amongst those people with a learning disability is via the discourses used within policy and Parliament. Oliver (1990) suggests that Parliament often discusses disability in patronizing ways and that social policy analysts have by and large failed to examine critically the notion of 'disability'. This lack of attention to the ways in which one thinks of disability generally, and learning disability specifically (i.e. the personal tragedy approach is often employed), can be seen in the writings of the Audit Commission. In 1986 they suggested that community care implies 'looking after people' (Audit Commission, 1986). Similarly, in 1992 they link community care to the provision of services for 'the care of sick and dependent people' (Audit Commission, 1992). Given the influence of such bodies, and the narrow discourses and conceptions of the disabled employed, it appears that the influence of politics in this sense is far from positive, at least from the perspective of the person with a learning disability.

Professional Contributions

There are a number of ways in which professionals and professionalized services contribute to the dependent disabled.

First, following the footsteps of commentators such as Goffman (1961), it is clear that regimes inherent to many provider units have in the past encouraged dependence in their residents or clients via the process of institutionalization. Whilst acknowledging the shift from long-stay residential care towards a community-based model has done much to improve the lot of many people with a learning disability, it is still not clear that problems of inflexibility, limited choice and disproportionate allocation of power and control in professional's favour have been resolved. Community Care, as a means of empowering users and carers, still has its limitations. Many of the small community residences used as part of the 'mixed economy' of service provision still have a degree of reliance on fixed times for meals, toileting, dressing and other activities of daily living. Evidence from the south west and the north east of England, from a variety of provider units (voluntary, not for profit, local authority and private), suggests this situation is still a reality for some residents (Thompson, 1994). A recent Department of Health report evaluating the first full year of the Community Care reforms found that many users and carers had 'experienced little change' and:

> . . . there had inevitably been an emphasis on plans, systems and structures leaving less time, energy or resources for developing the real agenda: independent living opportunities and community based services. (DOH, 1993)

So while the structures for service delivery have changed (ostensibly for the better) it appears that the experience of using services has not followed suit, at least not uniformly. If the analytical policy model developed earlier is adopted then the reasons for the delay in actualizing the spirit of the reforms become more alarming. It could be that the multitude of competing agendas, at every level of the reforms, act to distort the values assigned to the Act at the highest level and favour the professional groups involved more heavily than the users. The problem is that while the structures and language of service delivery have changed (local authorities as lead agencies, explicit assessments, Community Care plans, the use of terms such as 'customers' not patients) the broader structures involving professionals have remained static, so the power base remains unaltered. As Oliver (1990) points out:

> Economic structures determine the roles of professionals as gatekeepers of scarce resources, legal structures determine their controlling functions as administrators of services, career structures determine their decisions about whose side they are actually on and cognitive structures determine their practice with individual disabled people who need help – otherwise, why would they be employed to help them?

If this argument is accepted as valid then it follows that the only way in which it is possible to combat this anomaly is to fundamentally alter the structures outlined in ways which encourage user participation and control on an equal footing. The emerging model of care in the community does not do this.

Proponents of professional involvement may suggest that their role in promoting client independence negates some of these criticisms; but even here there are problems. Professionals often view independence as a composite entity, made up of social and self-care skills, for example, ease of communication, dressing, feeding and cooking – a view not always held by disabled people themselves. This difference is encapsulated nicely by the disabled sociologist Zola:

> We must expand the notion of independence from physical achievements to sociopsychologic decision-making. Independent living must include not only the quality of physical tasks we can do but the quality of life we can lead. Our notion of human integrity must take into account the notion of taking risks. Rehabilitation personnel must change the model of service from doing something to someone to planning and creating services with someone. In short we must free ourselves from some of the culture-bound and time-limited standards and philosophy that currently exist. (Zola, 1982).

At the level of local services it appears that such messages derived from disabled people themselves are being listened to, given the evidence of community-based advocacy organizations and the importance given to the notion of empowerment in purchasing by some local authorities. A similar gap between the professional and the client exists in the use of specialist language and the development of discourse and ideology. The shift from a medical to an educational approach to learning disability in the 1970s and early 1980s has been accused of perpetuating the

> enshrining of the professional in a world of exclusive and privileged knowledge, [which] consequently entombs the individual with learning difficulties in a fundamentally dependent role. (Oliver, 1990)

However, similar criticisms can be laid at the door of the 'dominant ideologies' (Cullen, 1991) of the late 1980s and 1990s; namely, normalization and the ideology that has superseded it, social role valorization (SRV).

Normalization has been summarized as:

- the use of culturally valued means to enable people to lead culturally valued lives
- the use of culturally normative means to provide life conditions that are at least as good as those of the average citizen
- the enhancement of the behaviour, appearance, experience and status of the devalued person
- the use of culturally normative means to support behaviour, appearance, experience and status that are themselves culturally normative (Chappell, 1992).

The theory which has superseded normalization – SRV – posits:

- that people are highly apt to be accorded the good things in life if they are seen in positive, valued social roles in society
- that devalued people tend to be cast, even forced into, and kept, in very devalued social roles
- therefore, people who are societally devalued, or at risk of such devaluation, need to be

helped to obtain and maintain valued social roles (Wolfsenburger and Thomas, 1994).

The development of normalization in British services for people with a learning disability occurred in parallel with the development of the 'new' community model of care which has its roots in the hospital scandals of the 1960s and the reintroduction of learning disability on to the policy and research agenda after the 1971 White Paper *Better Services for the Mentally Handicapped* (Cmnd 4683). Recently the principles have been absorbed into the debate about the quality of service provided in the form of standards or guidance (Hoyes, 1990). While the development of a concept which is ostensibly concerned with maximizing the quality of lives for people with a learning disability is prima facie positive, there are some criticisms of the ideology which fit into a discussion of the politics of learning disability. Because the axioms or 'truths' upon which SRV is based are derived from normalization, the criticisms can also be levelled at this new player in political arenas.

First, the absorption of normalization into the quality literature represents a means of shaping the agenda for what constitutes 'quality' in favour of the professional opinion. By using normalization principles as opposed to service user's views then their views are more often assumed than canvassed (Chappell, 1992).

Second, normalization in this context is about improving services which are dominated by professionals. The deinstitutionalization of people with a learning disability that has been occurring since the mid-1980s has been accompanied by the rise of normalization and more latterly SRV as a means of sanctioning the role of the professional in the face of changing service contexts. Alternatively, this means that if we (as professionals) can prove what we do is based on a *good* set of principles and values then that role will be retained. What normalization neglects is a recognition of the essential material paradox attached to using services:

... how meaningful is it to talk about achieving quality through normalisation in a day centre or residential home, when, in order to receive that service, users are poor and segregated. (Chapell, 1992)

Reader Activity 11.3
What set of principles do we hold as professionals and how can we assess that they are 'good'?

Normalization does not address the socially constructed nature of the experience of being a person with a learning disability in Britain; it lacks a political location. The assignment of values and worth both inside *and* outside services are part of a disabled person's life. Therefore, truly empowering services should play their part in changing the socially constructing (or constricting) factors which negatively value the person with a disability. The principles of normalization are based on the view of the person's life as a mix of provider–user interactions as opposed to the more challenging, and hence difficult to resolve, issues of relationships between people with a learning disability and the rest of society. Normalization encourages reliance on professionalized services:

Its starting point is the supposition that people with learning difficulties *need* professionals. The question is then *how* can professionals organise services in a way that achieves normalisation's goals. (Chappell, 1992)

It is interesting to note that Wolfsenburger, himself the prime advocate of normalization over the past 20 years, has attempted to move away from the vision of normalization (or SRV) as a feature of human services and towards a vision of SRV based firmly on the premise of 'trainers' who are drawn from the non-professional ranks of the community. The basic argument behind such a shift is that professional identity actively hinders the actualization of the principles of SRV (Wolfsenburger and

Thomas, 1994). If there is any validity attached to the theory of normalization (and more latterly SRV) at all, then it falls upon professionals in services to question their roles and to embrace some of the wider political issues put forward by users and their carers themselves.

11.6 What Does All This Mean for the Person with a Learning Disability?

So what do these models, constructs, hypotheses and discourses mean for the person with a learning disability? One way, indeed the conventional way, of examining the effects of such analyses and patterns of thought is to look at the nature of legislation relating to the person with a learning disability. However, justice cannot be done to the myriad of clauses and text which affect the lives of those people with learning disabilities in Great Britain in just 10 000 words. There are at least 42 Acts of Parliament which have a direct or potential impact on the person with a learning disability and many more which have indirect consequences.

An alternative to studying legislation, and one which is more enlightening given this chapter's political context, is to examine the degree to which people with learning disabilities achieve their proper and fair allocation of universal 'goods' such as citizenship, rights, participation and access. Such an analysis places the emphasis on the effects of legislation on the lives of people with a disability as a whole instead of merely examining the value shifts that occur between each piece of policy legislation. Citizenship, and the rights that accompany the concept, provides an appropriate framework for this examination.

11.7 The Nature of Citizenship and the Person with a Learning Disability

Citizenship is a fashionable concept in relation to learning disability and society as a whole. There are numerous emerging ideologies and projects based around the notion of extending the benefits of citizenship to 'disadvantaged' groups in society. The aim here is to show why the concept is so useful as a means of improving the lot of the person with a learning disability.

Discussions of citizenship in its modern context often take as their starting point the tenets identified by Marshall in his seminal work *Citizenship and Social Class* (Marshall, 1950). In this influential work, Marshall asserts that there are three necessary prerequisites for citizenship:

- **Civil rights** – such as the right to own property, and equality in the eyes of the law.
- **Political rights** – including the right to vote.
- **Social rights** – these are more difficult to define, but have been described as those that enable people to make use of political and civil rights. These might include the right not to fall below a certain level of income, the right to an education and perhaps most pertinently, in relation to people with a learning disability, the right to exercise one's own choice between the available options.

The Contribution of Citizens with a Learning Disability

The concept of citizenship also implies that citizens contribute to society in various ways in order to receive the economic, social and political rights described above. Given the over-riding dominance of economic rationality and capitalism in western societies, these contributions usually take the form of work or training for work. This notion of the citizen as contributor is one which appears attractive to theorists and proponents of the 'new-right' and neo-liberalism such as Charles Murray, Lawrence Mead and Michael Novak. Citizenship is, therefore, a highly influential idea in politics and one that dovetails well with the ideas of the present govern-

ment. Plant (1991) summarizes this relationship thus:

> Citizenship is a matter of duties as well as rights and entitlements. The obligations in question, to undertake work or training, will break the cycle of dependence and link the recipient of benefits much more to the disciplines and obligations of work, which the employed have to accept and which form a dominant part of the values of society.

It would be easy to argue that as people with a learning disability are by and large steered into the needs-based as opposed to the work-based systems (Stone, 1985) by policy, then they should not be entitled to make claims for full citizenship. Or, more importantly, they should not grumble when decisions are made on their behalf by fully 'paid up' contributor–citizens. However, there is a flip-side to the notion of contribution as a prerequisite for citizenship; for when a broader conceptualization of the 'citizen' is employed then the nature of the contribution made by people with a learning disability becomes clearer. Walmsley (1991) identifies four areas where the contributions of people with a learning disability amount to a very definite giving to, as opposed to taking from, society:

- Many women with learning difficulties have informal roles as carers, for elderly parents, for brothers, for peers in group homes (though rarely for children).
- People with learning difficulties work in hostels at domestic tasks which in other situations would be classed as paid work, and historically hospital residents have undertaken unpaid hard manual labour, in laundries, hospital kitchens, gardens and hospital workshops, or, indeed, caring for other residents/patients.
- Some people with learning difficulties undertake voluntary work in the community (e.g. at old peoples' lunch clubs, day centres for stroke victims, etc.).

- People with learning difficulties undertake low-paid jobs, which are not easy to fill by non-labelled people, in day centres, horticulture, and as home helps (Walmsley, 1991).

Cheap or unpaid labour is, of course, not the only way in which people with disabilities contribute to the greater social good. Citizen advocacy, for example (which involves non-disabled and disabled people forming mutually supportive alliances in key policy arenas such as community care and education) fits neatly into the present government's conceptualization of the active citizen, the beginnings of which can be traced back to the late 1980s and were expressed by a former cabinet minister:

> ... tax cannot remain the only way in which citizens discharge their obligations, time and commitment have to be added to money. (John Patten, 1988)

Taylor and Bogdan (1989) examine the sociology of acceptance between non-disabled people and persons with a learning disability and highlight the most essential contribution which people with a learning disability make to the greater social good; namely, friendship. Most importantly from a citizenship perspective, many of the respondents in Taylor and Bogdan's qualitative study described their friendships with people with a learning disability as reciprocal in that the disabled 'gave' as well as 'took' in the relationships.

If one accepts that people with a learning disability do actually contribute to society in both economic and non-economic ways, then it logically follows that they should enjoy the same entitlements and rights as the rest of society. However, the evidence suggests that this is not the case.

Civil Rights and People with a Learning Disability

There are a number of areas where the civil rights of people with a learning disability are undermined. These include:

- The lack of legislation to protect people with learning disabilities from discrimination in the same ways as legislation exists to protect rights on the basis of gender or race.
- The Mental Health Act 1983 makes provision for Courts to sanction almost any legal or financial transaction (investments, the making of gifts and settlements and sale and purchase of property) if the person is deemed to be 'incapable by reason of mental disorder of managing his property and affairs' (Mental Health Act 1983, sec. 94(2) and the Public Trustee and Administration of Funds Act 1986).
- The ways in which disabled people cannot easily exercise the legal rights which in theory they enjoy because of the broader social constraints of poverty, public attitude, delayed policy implementation, and negative public attitudes.

In latter years there have been some moves towards a recognition of civil rights in relation to those with a learning disability. The Disabled Person's (Services, Consultation and Representation) Act 1986 recognized the inadequacies of previous legislation and gave disabled people the right to be assessed, consulted and represented in areas related to their disabilities, although consequently the implementation of parts of the Act were delayed, due partly to the recalcitrance of underfunded local authorities. While undoubtedly a significant step forward in terms of the growing political importance attached to the issue of disability, the Act continued to foster images of the 'dependent' disabled (Oliver, 1990), and the lack of desire for full implementation was disheartening.

Over the past 40 years the civil rights agenda for the disabled has both developed and gained a tentative foothold in the political mainstream. Few will doubt the worth of measures such as the Mental Health Acts of 1959 and 1983, which, while far from perfect and often subject to abuse, did offer a chance to:

reduce the scope and use of compulsory powers and to promote the provision of services without legal formalities (Thompson and Mathias, 1992).

The recent governmental scuppering (through abuses of Parliamentary procedure) of several Private Members Bills aimed at full antidiscriminatory rights for the disabled (primarily on the grounds of affordability) says much in terms of the negative values attached to this section of the population. Moreover, it does not bode well for prospects of real, meaningful, reform – particularly as upwards of nine previous attempts have also been scuppered.

Political Rights and People with a Learning Disability

There are a number of areas where having a learning disability is a barrier to political involvement:

- The electoral register itself acts as a barrier to participation. There are many reasons why people with a learning disability do not appear on registers. These include:

  (1) The complexity of the 'Patients Declaration' form used to allow people in long-stay institutions to vote under the Representation of the People Act 1983. These forms are written in formal language and residents must complete them unaided unless visual or physical impairment makes it impossible, they are countersigned by staff and the resident must sign the form him/herself. In reality this means, unlike everyone else in Britain, the disabled must prove that they are worthy of voting.

  (2) Patients have to fill in their home address as the hospital does not qualify as a residence. Therefore they often cannot get to their own district to vote and have no access to local political literature and can-

didates. This problem is compounded by the apparent lack of will on the part of political parties to visit residential accommodation in election campaigns.

(3) Obviously as the numbers of residents in institutions further declines these situations will improve. However, there is evidence (Barnes, 1991) to suggest that the situation is little better in the community.

- Professional discretionary power can act as a means of preventing participation in the political process. People with a disability living in the community are as entitled as the rest of us to vote providing that their name appears on the electoral register each year. The mechanism for inclusion on the register involves the head of household (or home) filling in a declaration of the names of people entitled to vote in the residence. However, Barnes (1991) found that many people living in the community were denied this right by the mistaken belief on the part of staff that residents were not entitled to vote. Moreover, they were also denied the opportunity by the ways in which the professional carers made arbitrary decisions regarding the eligibility and capability of the residents.

- Even in families, such ignorance of the rights of disabled people to participate has been seen to be present. Barnes (1991) suggests that low expectations on the part of other family members and lack of information may be partly to blame.

- For those people with both learning and physical disabilities the electoral process presents particular difficulties. The poor physical access arrangements, and the dependency this incudes, are a real problem in some polling districts. Furthermore, there is no statutory obligation on the part of the presiding officers to provide anything other than assistance with marking the ballot paper for those people who are illiterate or prevented from voting in the usual way (Barnes, 1991).

- Logically it would appear that postal or proxy votes are the solution to these problems; however, the arrangements for voting in this way are far from ideal. To register such a vote the person must be either registered as blind, in receipt of mobility allowance, or unable 'reasonably' to be expected to go to the polling station in person or vote there unaided due to physical impairment. Apart from applications from those persons with a visual impairment, the forms have to be verified by either a doctor, first-level nurse or Christian Science practitioner. These measures effectively amount to professional's deciding how, or if, the person with a disability will vote. Aside from the practical problems which the postal or proxy systems present, many disabled people find the idea of voting before everyone else and prior to the finish of political campaigns objectionable.
- The political party system does not offer much opportunity for inclusion and as a means of getting the perceptions of disabled people on to the mainstream agenda the party system is seriously flawed. Elected politicians are neither expected or allowed to represent overtly one specific section of the community or their interests. While disabled and non-disabled politicians do comment on issues related to disability (e.g. Jack Ashley and David Blunkett) they do not purport to represent specifically the disabled or disability organizations (Barnes, 1991).

Social Rights and the Person with a Disability

Social rights are perhaps the most important of the components of citizenship. Social rights enable the citizen to make use of his or her political and civil rights and are therefore central to the experience of disability. It may appear futile to talk of social rights when the image presented thus far in this chapter represents a somewhat bleak map of the political and civil rights enjoyed (or not) by people with learning disabilities. However, as Walmsley (1991) points out, people with learning disabilities do enjoy some social rights (notably, income support and special education) – although it is the nature of these social rights which can contribute to the creation of the traditional picture of the 'dependent' disabled individual:

> Crucially for people with learning difficulties, the 'social rights' to which they are entitled within the Welfare State create a powerful and often controlling, bureaucratic and professional layer to administer them . . . to obtain mobility allowance, for example, disabled people are subject to a medical examination to judge whether they are sufficiently immobile to warrant the allowance. Any improvement in their capacity to walk jeopardises their entitlement. 'Rights' are dependent on incapacity, and this incapacity is the subject of a medical judgement. (Walmsley, 1991)

Reader Activity 11.4

Walmsley wrote before the effects of NHS and Social Service reforms were felt in the UK. Are his comments still pertinent after those reforms?

The ways in which policy decisions can negatively affect the lives of people with learning disabilities can be seen in the field of education. The 1981 Education Act made provision for local education authorities (LEAs) to offer non-educational services such as speech therapy in 'statements', produced by the authority as a means of obtaining special educational provision for children with special educational needs. The process of 'statementing', and the spirit of the Act in general, were broadly welcomed by commentators, people with a disability and their carers. However, the 1988 Education Act altered funding arrangements for schools and introduced, what was in effect, a quasi-market in schooling. The

Act also removed the *duty* for the LEA to arrange for non-educational provision, although it did allow them to do so if they wished. These two policy/structural factors, and the perceived effects which enroling people with learning disabilities might have on school numbers (and therefore funding), has led to fears that the integration of people with a learning disability into mainstream education, which the 1981 Act had encouraged, was now compromised.

The social rights of citizens are not always easily identified and dealt with by policy. In some cases the rights of citizens are discriminated against in more pernicious ways by the communities in which they live; for example, the withholding of information by local services such as general practitioners or local authorities. At other times 'social' rights to the most fundamental values and institutions, over which non-disabled people exercise considerable choice, such as friendship, marriage, childbirth, and life itself, may be decided by the state. This often occurs in ways that neglect the experiences of disabled people themselves. Hudson (1988) offers a framework for understanding such rights with reference to two categories:

- **Claim-rights** – these recognize that 'having a claim to X is not (yet) the same as having a right to X, but it is rather having a case of at least minimal plausibility that one has a right to X. A claim-right is a right to consideration. Obviously in situations where people have competing claims then some claims will be stronger than others; but it is important to note that such claims are not static and, in time, the weaker claims will be strengthened and possibly developed into full rights (Hudson, 1988). The challenge for politicians and policy makers (at all levels) is to balance these competing claims. The concept of claim-rights is associated with the phenomenon of routine discrimination: discrimination on a regular basis and in a wide range of social groups. An example of the negative weighting

assigned to the claim-rights of people with a learning disability can be seen in the ways in which the process of deinstitutionalization was accompanied by a National Health ombudsman ruling that health authorities had a duty to consult neighbours before housing people with a learning disability in residential areas based on '... the views of neighbours', who were, 'concerned about the effect on them and, frankly, the values of their own houses'. The ombudsman suggested that health authorities 'balance the interests of the community and mentally handicapped people' (Hudson, 1988), although the degree to which this 'balance' should favour the disabled was patently clear.

- **Moral-rights.** The basic premise of this approach to the rights of people with a learning disability can be summed up as one in which all people are created equal in that all human beings are seen as ends in themselves. Harris defines the principle more succinctly:

> The ultimate aim of the whole social way of life is the fullest possible development of the capacities of the individuals who make up the society concerned, giving the fullest possible satisfaction of the complete personality. This 'end for man' can only be realised in persons, and it follows that each and every person is himself of ultimate worth as the final source and vehicle of value ... The most important values can be enjoyed by any persons only if, and to the extent, that they are enjoyed by all. (Harris, 1968)

Moral-rights are applied to areas where the granting of the right will not impinge on, or conflict with, another individual's rights, and where everyone has an equal claim. Moral-rights can be negative, in that they include the right *not* to have something (i.e. the right not to be subjected to discrimination). Feinburg (1973) identifies three areas where moral rights might apply:

(1) positive rights to 'goods' that cannot be in scarce supply, such as the right to a fair trial or the right to equal protection of the law

(2) the negative right *not* to be treated inhumanely

(3) the right *not* to be subjected to exploitation or degradation, even when this is physically painless.

It is possible to identify many areas where the moral rights of people with a learning disability are infringed but two of the most fundamental are the right to life and the right to procreation and parenting.

In the early 1980s, two trials involving babies born with Down's syndrome took place. The first, in which the baby (Alexandra) also had an intestinal block, upheld the decisions of the parents and the doctors not to operate on the child. A later appeal court ruling overturned this decision and the baby underwent surgery. The baby subsequently recovered and was returned to the natural parents after a year. In the second case, the parents rejected the child and the consultant prescribed nursing care only and sedation at very high levels. The baby subsequently died and the consequent manslaughter trial found the doctor not guilty. The issues here are not the decisions made by the courts *per se*, but the roles played by the courts in effectively deciding or sanctioning the devaluation of the lives of people with a learning disability. In baby Alexandra's case, the status of her moral-right to life was further diluted to a claim-right by the media, who used headlines such as 'Council faces £100 000 bill for mongol child' as a basis for reporting the case (Hudson, 1988).

Hudson (1988) also points to the ways in which the moral-rights to procreate and to parent have been undermined by the courts. In particular, he uses two examples:

- 'Jeanette' a 17-year-old woman who was subject to a Law Lords ruling that the compulsory sterilization which was proposed for her was legal on the basis of the girl's best interests and that 'the right to reproduce would mean nothing to her'.

- Gerald and Mandy Morgan, both of whom had learning disabilities, and who had recently produced a child. Despite vigorous protests from the new parents, the new baby was made a ward of court and removed from the parents at birth. The local director of social services felt that the moral-rights involved concerned the rights of the baby not the parents. The issue of training and support systems for the parents made little or no impact on the debate surrounding the case.

The implication of these two cases, but especially in the 'Jeanette' ruling, is that people with a learning disability lack an appreciation of these rights and therefore the undermining of them is no great loss. Such a view does not equate with the notion of 'rights', which by definition are inviolable – they are not dependent on whether a potential user appreciates them or not (Hudson, 1988).

11.8 Why Politicize Learning Disability?

This chapter so far has ostensibly been concerned with the notion of politics as the allocation of values and the promotion of an individual's worth at different levels in policy – the national, local and individual service levels. It has highlighted the ways in which discourses are deployed which reinforce negative images of people with disabilities. The chapter has also given a flavour of the lack of progress made towards full 'citizen-status', and all the rights that the term infers, by people with a learning disability. Many of the problems associated with being a person with a learning disability have been shown to arise from those current political, economic and social structures that act to devalue the citizen labelled as 'disabled'. However, it is these structural factors that represent the operational contexts that must be addressed and worked within by campaigners and professionals who support the promotion of the full worth of people with a learning disability. The next two sections outline the available options at national and (perhaps more usefully) specific local/service levels.

11.9 Promoting a Positive Agenda on Learning Disability: the 'Political' Options

The current Westminster-based political system, with all its flaws, remains the primary mode of legislative policy formation at the national level. Given this operational context, there appear to be two choices for disabled people and their advocates. First, whether to continue to try and make in-roads into political machinery from the top-down (i.e. from Westminster) using pressure-group lobbying techniques. Or second, to shift the energies of campaigners into developing policy from the bottom-up, creating public opinion shifts (and by default, pressure on Parliament) by initiating changes at the lower levels of policy.

Pressure Groups

Pressure groups are a useful, indeed essential, part of the political process as long as they are all seen as effective as means of advancing and advocating their representative group's interests, and they all have equal access to the key 'players' in government. However, these assumptions can be questioned (Barnes, 1991).

Pressure groups can be divided into two kinds:

- **the competitive groups** – the members of which come from a variety of economic and social backgrounds but share a particular interest (e.g. Royal Society for Mentally Handicapped Children and Adults (MENCAP))
- **the corporate groups** – the members of which share a common social and economic status

within society (e.g. the Confederation of British Industry and the British Medical Association).

Quite evidently it is clear that because of the high levels of social and economic power attached to the latter group it is their influence which exerts the greater pressure on government.

The legacy of tradition in pressure groups has also played a part in diluting any claims to influence that they may have. Traditionally many pressure goups have been registered as charities, which while useful in terms of increasing fundraising capacity has a down-side in that it bars them from direct and overt political activity. Over time many organizations have established good links with policy makers (Barnes, 1991), although these links are often based on credibility through tradition rather than claims to power, or more importantly, claims to be representative of disabled people. Within these organizations the decision makers are often salaried professionals who put forward *their* perceptions of the needs of those with a disability rather than the perceptions of the people with the disability themselves.

The success of the civil rights and women's movements in the US and the similar, though less successful, achievements of the race and gender lobbies in this country, might suggest that people with a learning disability should make similar claims to the rights of citizenship based on their position as a minority or oppressed group. By doing this they could enter the macropolitical arena as one of the many competing special interest pressure groups. Barnes (1991) suggests that this would involve disabled people accepting the distinction between disabled and non-disabled people and therefore the notion of the 'normalizing' society. More importantly, as Oliver and Zarb (1989) point out, it would involve:

special pleading and . . . moves away from the strategies disabled people have chosen for themselves, that is the personal and public affirmation of disabled identities and the demands that disabled people can be accepted by and integrated into society as they are; that is, as disabled people.

There is also little evidence that either conventional or minority-interest disability pressure groups have much effect on policy makers. While they have had some success in introducing certain issues (such as the need for antidiscriminatory legislation based on citizenship rights) on to the mainstream political agenda, their influence on the outcomes of the parliamentary process has not been great.

Given the relatively low social and economic status of people with a learning disability as a collective group, the over-riding ideological contexts of capitalism and economic rationality, and the ways in which legislation shapes the experience of disability, opting out of mainstream political agendas and processes is not really an option. As Topliss (1982) argues, the meta-principle of economic rationality, as a core value behind policies, probably offers the best hope of an increased quality of life for those people with a learning disability. An assertion made on the basis that moral approaches to the maximization of welfare have, in the past, all failed. Moreover, economic-rational (macro-political) approaches, with their emphasis on facts and statistics, have led to a 'readier and more embracing perception of collective responsibility for welfare' and will lead to the 'best hope for peaceful piecemeal improvements in the lives of the majority of the people, including handicapped people'. Economic rationality has also, however, been the focus for many of the criticisms of the approaches to disability in the post-war welfare state.

The essential question concerning the quality of life and the influence of politics on those people with a learning disability is one of expectation: how soon do people with disabilities hope to see real tangible improvements in their lives as citizens via involvement in national level politics? On the evidence delivered since the development of the modern welfare state it would appear that patience

is the primary virtue for those seeking change through mainstream Westminster-based national political processes.

11.10 Change at a Lower Level?

The British welfare state, in common with other welfare states, places great reliance on the involvement of professional and bureaucratic structures to 'deliver' policy to citizens. Given this reliance, and the ways in which professionals contribute to policy and disability, then it is feasible to argue that the disabled person's best hope for 'political' change is at the micro (or service) level.

Reader Activity 11.5
What 'politically' motivated actions have you encountered at the micro (service) level?

Politics, as we have seen, involves the allocation of values in different 'arenas'. It can be argued that this allocation of values has already favoured the person with a learning disability at service level via the rise of the dominant ideologies of normalization and deinstitutionalization. In recent years the growth in service-based concepts of empowerment, advocacy and SRV is often claimed to have played a part in improving the lives of those with a learning disability. Coupled to these service-based philosophies, the broader welfare trends towards more accountable management functions, the rise of 'quality' as a lever in internal and free markets, and the move towards consumerism at both macro and micro policy levels, mean that service-values are more explicit than at any time since the Second World War. It would be easy to assume that because values are explicit and the facilities to 'prove' raised levels of quality exist, that all is rosy in the service-based arena. However, the negative side of the application of such 'service-technologies and crazes' is that they often lack any form of tested validity (Wolfsenburger and Thomas, 1994). Despite Wolfsenburger's criticism, there does appear to be some hope for the politicized service organization as a means of improving the lives of clients.

Newness (1994) points to the politicized practices and natures of organizations such as Values in Action:

> Some organisations in the UK (e.g. Values in Action, People First, and Skills for People) appear to have recognised the abilities, expertise and potential for working alongside people with learning disabilities in order to further their aims.

More importantly he goes on to argue that such recognition of the worth of the individual with a learning disability has the potential for broader effects on society:

> ... recognition and integration within these agencies may, or may not, be followed through into integration in friendships, social or community activities outside the activities of the agency. (Newnes, 1994)

There are, however, dangers attached to the politicization (involving concepts such as empowerment) of service organizations:

> attempts to politicise or personalise service agencies may be seen as patronising or paternalistic rather than as humanitarian and laudable. Such empowerment efforts, whether they seek to integrate traditional service users into the task group of the agency or, via personal friendship, into socially valued communities outside the agency, can be viewed with scepticism by both the traditional user group and the established professional culture. (Newnes, 1994)

The idea that professionals might resist the 'political' re-examination and allocation of values is taken up by Wolfsenburger and Thomas (1994), who highlight six barriers to the successful implementation of SRV (itself explicitly concerned with the allocation of worth and value):

- Professionals are deeply distrustful of ordinary citizens, sceptical and pessimistic as to what citizens can and will do, and very unrealistically mindful of their own capacities, their supposedly specialized knowledge, education and training and the expertise with human service technology they believe they possess.
- Professionals are themselves often relatively poorly integrated into society. Professionals seem to have fewer contacts outside of human service circles and belong to fewer non-service based organizations when compared to other citizens of similar social and economic status.
- Professionals often live away from the communities in which they work. This cuts down the contact with community groups and consequently the contacts available to facilitate integration.
- Professional socialization means that there is often a 'discourse-gap' between ordinary citizens (including clients) and the professionals. This means that professionals often have a poorer grasp of SRV, and therefore ways to promote valued roles, than the non-professional staff they supervise.
- The technologies and 'crazes' employed by professionals (does this include SRV?) are often lacking in validity or are naively subscribed to and implemented.
- Because 'common-sense' is often trained out of the professional and because they are often out of touch with what is currently normatively valued, professional service workers often end up meddling in, rather than contributing to, the lives of clients.

The remedies to all of these barriers are entirely within the 'political' capabilities of professionals:

- Acknowledging the methods and knowledge employed by ordinary citizens, who after all have been the largest group of carers long before the current trends in community care, and carers in professional training would go some way in combating the cynicism with which some professionals view lay-input into services.

- Recognizing the worth of good links between professionals and local communities and promoting such links will enhance the nature of the experience of integration for people with a learning disability. If done with respect for, and building upon, existing opinion, some of the stigma attached to the notion of disability can be overcome. Similarly, opportunities for integration of the non-disabled community into learning disability services will also be reinforced.

- Encouraging professionals and clients to become members of the communities in which they work, including participation in local party politics, might provide a means of getting the views of disabled people into the mainstream political system. The involvement of professionals and service users could also provide a means of bringing politics to those clients never previously aware of their potential role in the system.

11.11 Conclusion

This chapter has outlined a broad theoretical framework for understanding what might be called the 'politics' of learning disability. The notion of politics employed is one concerned with the allocation of worth, values and, as a consequence, status. Politics is seen as both the fundamental challenge to the person with a learning disability and also as one of the most feasible routes for the liberation of people with a disability through true political 'empowerment' by way of proper recognition of their rights and worth as citizens – the most basic of political units.

A model for understanding policy development, which acknowledges the gaps between rhetoric and reality, the different 'levels' of policy, the role of discourse, and the contribution of the professional has also been put forward. The resulting discussion demonstrated that the processes of worth and value allocation do not just occur at governmental level but extend right down the policy chain. Professionals, therefore, are not absolved of responsibility for promoting positive values in services along 'political' lines. Part of this responsibility means acknowledging the contribution of the professionalized service to the development of dependency in people with a learning disability. Particularly as the 'political' barriers to full citizenship (at both macro and micro levels) for people with a learning disability are closer to being recognized and overcome than at any time since the First World War.

Politics affects most, if not all, the elements of 'health' used as the basis for this book. Education, family environment, financial resources, and medical care, to name just a few, are all directly or indirectly shaped and influenced by politics and its associated processes. As such, the link between politics and the health of the person with a learning disability is too important to be ignored by those concerned with improving the quality of the lives of this group of citizens. Politics as the conceptual framework for action at the national and local policy levels could yet prove to be 'the art of the possible'.

Discussion Questions

1 How can I utilize my knowledge of the politics of learning disability in ways which increase the quality of life for the people that I work with?

2 In what ways does the service I work in neglect the politics of learning disability?

3 How can I encourage the people I work with to become more political?

4 Does my local community have any arrangements for citizen advocacy or active empowerment in formats which are not just based on rhetoric? Do I know how to access them?

5 Do I really know how the machinery of politics (central and local government, legislation) works and how can I use it to clients' best interests?

6 Are our service's values explicit and do they recognize the rights of clients as citizens?

References

Albrecht, G. and Levy, J. (1981) Constructing disabilities as social problems. *In* Albrecht, G. (Ed.) *Cross National Rehabilitation Policies: A Sociological Perspective*, p. 14. London: Sage.

Audit Commission (1986) *Making a Reality of Community Care*. London: HMSO.

Audit Commission (1992) *Community Care: Managing the Cascade of Change*. London: HMSO.

Barnes, C. (1991) *Disabled People in Britain and Discrimination*. London: Hurst Calgary.

Borsay, A. (1986) Personal trouble or public issue? Towards a model of policy for people with physical and mental disabilities. *Disability, Handicap and Society* 1(2): 179–197.

Chappell, A.L. (1992) Towards a sociological critique of the normalisation principle. *Disability, Handicap and Society* 7(1): 35–54.

Cullen, C. (1991) Experimentation and planning in community care. *Disability, Handicap and Society* 6(21): 115–128.

Department of Health (1993) *Monitoring and Development: First Impressions April–September 1993*. London: HMSO.

Deutsch, K.W. (1974) *Politics and Government*. Boston: Houghton Miffin.

Eayres, J. (1961) *The Art of The Possible: Government and Foreign Policy in Canada*. Toronto: University of Toronto Press.

Feinburg, J. (1973) *Social Policy*. London: Prentice Hall.

Finklestein, V. (1980) *Attitudes and Disabled People: Issues for Discussion*. New York: World Rehabilitation Fund.

Fulcher, G. (1989) *Disabling Policies? A Comparative Approach to Education Policy and Disability*. London: Falmer Press.

Hoyes, L. (1990) *Promoting an Ordinary Life: A Checklist for Assessing Residential Care for People With Learning Difficulties*. Bristol: School for Advanced Urban Studies.

Hudson, B. (1988) Do people with mental handicap have rights? *Disability, Handicap and Society* 3(3): 227–239.

Hugman, R. (1991) *Power in Caring Professions*. London: Macmillan.

Lipsky, M. (1980) *Street Level Bureaucracy: Dilemmas of the Individual in Public Services*. Beverly Hills: Sage.

Newness, C. (1994) A commentary on 'Obstacles in the professional human service culture to implementation of social role valorisation and community integration of clients'. *Care in Place* 1(1): 57–64.

Oliver, M. (1986) Social policy and disability: Some theoretical issues. *Disability, Handicap and Society* 1(1): 5–17.

Oliver, M. (1990) *The Politics of Disablement*. London: Macmillan.

Oliver, M. and Zarb, G. (1989) The politics of disability: A new approach. *Disability, Handicap and Society* 2(2): 221–240.

Plant, R. (1991) Welfare and the enterprise society. *In* Wilson, T. and Wilson, D. (Eds) *The State and Social Welfare: The Objectives of Policy*, pp. 73–88. Harlow: Longman.

Potter, J. and Collie, F. (1989) Community care as persuasive rhetoric: A study of discourse. *Disability, Handicap and Society* 4(1): 57–64.

Stone, D. (1984) *The Disabled State*. London: Macmillan.

Taylor, S.J. and Bogdan, R. (1989) On accepting relationships between people with mental retardation and non-disabled people: Towards and understanding of acceptance. *Disability, Handicap and Society* 4(1): 21–37.

Thompson, C. (1994) The Transition from Voluntary to Non-Profit Organisation. Report to two provider organizations (unpublished).

Thompson, T. and Mathias, P. (Eds) (1992) *Standards and Mental Handicap: Keys to Competence*. London: Baillière Tindall.

Topliss, E. (1982) *Social Responses to Handicap*. Harlow: Longman.

Walmsley, J. (1991) Talking to top people: Some issues relating to the citizenship of people with learning difficulties. *Disability, Handicap and Society* **6**(3): 219–233.

Wolfsenburger, W. and Thomas, S. (1994) Obstacles in the professional human service culture to implementation of social role valorisation and community integration of clients. *Care in Place* **1**(1): 53–56.

Wright Mills, C. (1970) *The Sociological Imagination.* Harmondsworth: Penguin.

Zola, I. (1982) Social and cultural disincentives to independent living. *Archives of Physical Medicine and Rehabilitation* **63**: 396.

Further Reading

Mead, L. (1986) *Beyond Entitlement: The Social Obligations of Citizenship.* New York: Macmillan.

Murray, C. (1984) *Losing Ground, American Social Policy 1950–1980.* New York: Schuster.

Novak, M. (1987) *The New Consensus on Family and Welfare.* Wisconsin: Marquette University.

Chapter 12: Economic dimension of learning disability
Colin Beacock and Tom Tait

12.1 Introduction

This chapter briefly considers how economic theories have influenced services for people with a learning disability. The focus for the chapter is services in the UK although the principles involved have been applied to similar services throughout Europe and the USA.

The UK has a history of investing part of its national resources to provide a service for people with a learning disability. Shiell and Wright (1988) describe how:

> ... This investment is intended to improve the welfare of people with a mental handicap (*sic*) but it is apparent that other client groups also have legitimate and competing demands for these resources. Faced with the responsibility of reconciling these demands, statutory authorities must ensure that resources are used in the best possible way. The efficient use of resources means obtaining maximum beneficial impact on client welfare for a given cost ... The evaluation of efficiency requires an assessment of both the costs and outcomes associated with different methods of service delivery.

From this perspective of analysing how national investment is efficiently used in respect of services for people with a learning disability, the study of economics has considerable application.

Mooney *et al.* (1986) defined the study of economics as:

> ... How men and society end up choosing, with or without the use of money, to employ scarce resources that could have alternative uses, to produce various commodities and distribute them for consumption, now or in the future, among various people and groups in society.

This definition gives rise to one of the basic principles of economics: that supply and demand are inextricably linked.

The first 30 years of health and social-care provision by the 'Welfare State' in the UK were characterized by central allocation of budgets. Management of the financial and economic consequences of running such a service was the responsibility of individuals who were distant from the point of service delivery. Decisions on what was required within the service was left to planners rather than practitioners and the views of service users were seldom considered in the evaluation of services. With the arrival of the 1980s came a new means of

evaluating the effectiveness and efficiency of service provision throughout welfare provision in the UK.

In considering change in the management of welfare provision in the UK, Barry (1987) described how:

> ... One of the most striking features of the development of social science during the last decade has been the re-establishment of the intellectual respectability of the decentralized market exchange system as a social institution. There has been a growing recognition of the freedom-enhancing properties of market society.

The limited availability of resources thereby leads to the development of a market price for any commodity. In the case of services for people with a learning disability this could be any aspect of service provision: housing; educational opportunities; day care. With limited resources to spend and the availability of services regulated by their price, what emerges is a 'market economy' for care. Barry (1987) goes on to state that:

> ... A market is in essence a self-regulating, self-controlling system in which supply and demand and profit and loss are said to allocate resources more efficiently.

It is against the emergence of the logic of 'market forces' having an ever-increasing role to play in the management of welfare services that this chapter considers how economic principles have influenced the lives of people with a learning disability.

12.2 The Economic Analysis of Health

In pursuing an economic analysis of services for people with a learning disability this chapter focuses in particular upon the provision of health service facilities. This allows for the application of the principles of health economics in a market-led service.

Health economics considers the costs and benefits of changing patterns of resource allocation within health service provision. The main issues which are addressed within the study of health economics are listed in Box 12.1.

Box 12.1 Health economics: key issues

- **What services to provide, when and at what level?**
- **How and where to provide such services?**
- **Who should receive such services?**

Whilst market forces may influence planning and decision making in the National Health Service (NHS), the fact that the great majority of individual health-care consumers are not charged for the service at the point of delivery means that the NHS does not function in the same way as a supermarket or retail outlet. The cost of any hip replacement, coronary bypass or Spitz–Holster valve that is supplied is charged directly to very few individual patients. It is therefore 'zero-priced' to NHS consumers. When people shop in a supermarket they consider the price they must pay for an article. The price they are willing to pay depends heavily on the degree to which they need the commodity on offer.

The degree to which that need is satisfied by the purchased article is described by economists as 'utility'. Given that every shopper only has a finite amount of money with which to make their purchases, they will try to gain as much satisfaction as possible from the resources they have at their disposal. When they have achieved this, economists would consider that they have achieved 'optimum utility' from the resources available to them. As extra units of a commodity are consumed by an individual the satisfaction gained from each extra unit will fall. This is termed 'diminishing marginal utility'. Both of these concepts are common to many economic models.

Early economic models of welfare considered redistribution from rich to poor would increase total welfare. Such models assume that everyone is fundamentally alike in preferences and that every additional unit of money earned yields less utility than the previous unit. More recent economic models of welfare are based around the concept of 'ordinal utility'. This term reflects a measure of consumer satisfaction in terms of ranking of preferred combinations of commodities rather than through the assignment of some absolute utility measure. By establishing what individual consumers would prefer to purchase from a given amount of money, a model of analysis emerges which does not require us to calculate the exact relationship between utility from different goods. No matter which model is used, the presumption is that money and individual value judgements are essential in determining the utility of goods and services.

Reader Activity 12.1

How do you decide what to buy from your limited resources?

Are you aware of the value judgements that you make in doing so?

12.3 Issues of Demand

Without a charge being made to individual patients, optimum utility must be achieved by those managers responsible for the purchasing of health care. In today's NHS that responsibility falls to general practitioner (GP) fundholders and the commissioning authorities. In principle, each of these bodies has an allocation of monies with which to purchase health-care products and services to meet the needs of their patient population. In reality, the transactions take place on paper and the ability of each to generate increased levels of resources through the raising of revenue is restricted by legislation. The system is internally regulated by a form of contracting which restricts the choice of individual patients but which sets funding on a 'per capita' basis with increased levels of funding for patients with special needs. In these circumstances, although a form of 'market' for health care is established it is highly regulated and could not be described as 'free'. Value judgements are applied on behalf of individual consumers rather than by them.

Following the government's reforms of health and social services, similar principles apply in the provision of social care.

In seeking to achieve optimum utility, the value judgements of each individual shopper will vary considerably. Personal choice and taste would reveal a wide variety of preferences. Techniques of marketing and the influence of social processes result in fashions and trends in purchasing behaviours. Given the complex issues involved in the economic planning in health care and the fact that the funding of the NHS is open to public rather than individual scrutiny, the relevance of factors such as fashion and personal value judgements should be kept to a minimum. In keeping with the principles of optimum utility, individual purchasers will value a commodity more highly, dependent upon the levels of satisfaction derived from it. The decisions of health and social service planners need to be based upon more objective data if they are to utilize scarce resources to achieve high levels of utility for the greatest number of consumers.

12.4 Issues of Supply

Although the episode of care which any given patient receives is not directly charged to them, the inputs and interventions they receive carry a cost. This could be made up of the price of medications; the cost of equipment used in therapy; the training costs for the preparation of practitioners; and the expenses incurred in maintaining the fabric and buildings of the service. In considering the management of these production costs and the products which the service achieves, health-care planners must examine the 'technical efficiency' of their service. This requires the examination of resources and the means by which they are combined to produce maximum output. Technical progress occurs when a given output can be produced from fewer inputs. Given the amount of modification applied to the 'market' for health and social care, purchasers of such services might consider the

economic principles of 'production function' as a means of analysis of efficiency. This approach specifies the maximum output that can be produced from any given amount of inputs. In this approach, inputs in the form of costs are more readily identified than outputs. Combinations of inputs can be considered as a means of maximizing output by minimizing costs.

There are a number of different types of cost and terms which apply in this form of analysis:

- **fixed costs** – costs that do not vary with the level of production
- **variable costs** – costs that do not vary with the level of production
- **average costs** – costs divided by the total level of output
- **marginal costs** – the costs associated with the next run of production
- **short run** – the period in which the organization can only make partial adjustment of its inputs to changes in trading conditions
- **long run** – the period long enough for the organization to adjust all its inputs to changes in trading conditions
- **economies of scale** – occur when the long-run average costs decrease as output rises.

12.5 Issues of Cost and Benefit

As a result of an episode of care, the patient's condition should improve and the outcome may lead to a number of benefits. These may relate to the individual themselves or their family and be in the form of increased independence and decreased need for support. There may be benefits for society as a whole in that the incumbent patient may be able to return to a role or job which offers other essential services to the community. Equally, the benefit may be felt in that the patient is able to revert from a situation of being a cost-burden to society to becoming a productive taxpayer who will make a financial contribution to meeting personal and societal costs. Whilst the procedures applied to the patient have costs, they in turn produce bene-fits. Economists utilize this phenomenon to produce a 'cost:benefit analysis'. This is one means by which planners can gain a more objective analysis of the economic performance of health-care and social-care systems.

Reader Activity 12.2
Do you think taxpayers should meet the health-care costs of non-taxpayers in modern society?

A further economic derivative of cost:benefit analysis is 'opportunity costing'. This approach requires that an analyst should ask what alternatives exist for the spending of each and every unit of cost. The presumption is that greater utility and increased benefit could be gained if existing resources were used for alternative purposes. It is this approach which has led to the re-evaluation of many health-care operations in the NHS, resulting in a reductionist approach towards non-clinical services and the franchising of operations such as laundry, cleaning and catering services. In learning disability services, opportunity costing has acceler-ated the closure programmes of former hospital sites so that capital which was tied up in property could be sold off and the subsequent revenue used to develop community-based services in partnership with a variety of agencies. The imperatives to close institutions were not all philosophical. The very practical reality of economic planning exerted con-siderable influence upon politicians and service planners.

12.6 Economic Measurement of Health

When considering the measurement of health-related interventions and services, the issues involved in determining both cost and benefit are complex. Economic and societal factors mean that we still cannot give every sick or disabled person the fullest possible form of treatment to meet their needs. Gudex (1986) suggested that, given the

limited availability of health-care resources, any decision on priorities for expenditure in the NHS should be based upon the costs of treatment and the health outcomes of those being treated. To define 'health' is, in itself, a challenging task. When attempting to define health 'outcomes' to assist in economic analysis the task becomes further compli-cated.

In attempting to quantify health outcomes the work of McGuire *et al.* (1988) indicated two main aspects of health; namely, the duration of life, and the quality of life. Duration of life is readily quantifi-able in terms of life expectancy. Quality is a more complex concept. The World Health Organization (1961) defined health as:

> . . . A state of complete physical and mental well-being and not merely the absence of disease and infirmity.

Although this definition raises the question as to whether or not such a state could ever be achieved, it does hold two implications that influence health outcome measures, as perceived in cost:benefit analysis. These are:

- **health includes the absence of disease and infirmity**
- **health takes account of subjective feelings.**

In evaluating health states from the patient's perspective, Drummond (1980) suggested that the two features most frequently specified were pain and degree of restriction of activity. Whilst both of these features may be objectively measurable, they are each subject to interpretation by the individual patient, giving rise to wide variations in perception as to the relative value of interventions.

Kind *et al.* (1982) recognized the influence that individual patient perceptions can have when attempting to achieve an objective evaluation of the comparative worth of health states. An alternative scale of measurement was compiled by asking healthy non-professionals and health-care practi-tioners to rate varying degrees of health and distress along a continuum from health to death. One outcome from the study was that two states, long-term unconsciousness and bedfast with severe distress, were rated as being worse than death. In undertaking an economic evaluation of health-care priorities, using a cost:benefit or opportunity-costing model, such objective outcome measures are essential if personal value judgement and social influences are to be minimized. Whereas costs may be calculated more simply across a range of measures determined by the 'input and output' of the organization or upon a 'cost per case' basis, the measurement and evaluation of benefits is far more difficult to achieve.

12.7 Developments in the Theory of Health Economics

As a means of enabling decisions on health-care priorities to be made, one particular model has gained favour in recent years. Arising from economic analysis 'Quality Adjusted Life Years' (QALY) were described by Williams (1985) as a model which takes a year of healthy life to be worth a value of one, but which attributes a value of less than one to a year of life in which the individual is less than healthy. The QALY's precise value is given to be lower as the quality of life for the unhealthy person diminishes. On this basis, specific conditions can be ascribed comparative values and, indeed, some conditions may be considered to be worse than death and therefore score a negative value. In economic terms, priority would be given to activity where the given cost of an intervention achieved the maximum outcome in terms of QALYs.

Reader Activity 12.3
This economical approach to evaluating health-care activity creates dilemmas for practitioners and service users. By the use of QALYs, for instance, it is implied that suffering a disabling illness for 2 years is twice as bad as suffering the same condition for 1 year. Consider the implications of such a simplistic

analysis of disability. Most contracts of employment in the NHS offer no sick pay after 1 year. The consequent lack of income would make the second year of any disability far more uncomfortable than the first. You may wish to consider what such a prognosis might mean for yourself and your employment status. Most contracts of employment do not offer protection of earnings and sick pay for more than 6 months.

12.8 The Ethical Debate on QALYs

Seedhouse (1988) argued that the QALY was a crude measurement in that it assumes that a healthy life is one in which there is good life expectancy, no pain and no disability. He considered the notion of someone becoming less healthy as their life expectancy diminished or as their degree of disability increased to be too simplistic.

McGuire *et al.* (1988) suggested that the measurement of QALYs should involve a number of value judgements as well as technical judgements. They argued that health outcomes should reflect the physical, social and psychological consequences of diagnoses and prognosis. In their crudest form, simple economic analyses give rise to certain anomalies. Given that life expectancy in women is greater than that in men, any priority decision which involved the need to prioritize between male and female patients would always favour the woman, given the pure application of QALYs.

12.9 Further Application of Cost:Benefit Analysis

Whereas most health economists consider products to be costed in monetary terms, the definition offered by Mooney *et al.* (1986) offers scope for interpretation. The fact that Mooney acknowledges that such analyses can be undertaken with or without the use of money and that resources are in themselves scarce, allows for a further application of cost:benefit analysis. This takes the form of a consideration of the nature of interaction between people with a learning disability and their carers.

An indication of how this theory might be applied is offered by Rushing (1964) who considered the characteristic behaviours of nurses who were caring for mentally ill patients in institutional care in the USA. He considered that every interaction between the nurse and patient had a cost and benefit value for both parties. Rushing (1964) suggested that the main cost factor in this process, from the perspective of the nurse, derived from their status and authority. The outcome of interactions would either add to, or detract from, that status. The skills of the nurse could hold benefit to the patient but to actively offer them held a cost to the nurse in terms of the effort expended. In this study many nurses chose not to interact with patients, preferring to retain their social distance and thereby incur no cost in terms of effort or threat to their status. The institutional care patterns meant that patients were generally obliged to seek the attentions of the nursing staff. Admonition and ridicule were common features of the nurses' response patterns and the patients clearly incurred the risk of a cost should they seek benefit of attention from nursing staff.

It is now some 30 years since the completion of these studies. The principles and philosophies of contemporary services for people with a learning disability would prevent such blatant abuse of power on the part of practitioners and carers. None the less, there is value in reconsidering the relevance of cost:benefit principles in respect of the informal culture of service provision.

12.10 Service User's Perspective

Central to the successful application of any form of cost:benefit analysis are the service user's perceptions of the quality of life which results from the utilization of resources. Choice is an essential component of optimum utility. Equally, choice is an essential component of care systems which empha-size quality of life measures. In services for people with learning disabilities the concept of quality of life offers an opportunity to measure outcomes (benefits) from the service user's perspective. Such an approach presents problems for the person who has disabilities which inhibit their capacity to communicate their needs and preferences effectively.

When considering the implications of the use of a quality of life model for the planning of care, Kohnke (1982) suggested that to enable personal growth for the client the relationship between themselves and the cover must be equitable. Furthermore, Malin and Teasdale (1991) argued that practitioners should be aware of their own power base. If the deficiencies of former systems of care are to be overcome and the cost:benefit analysis of service provision is to reflect positive gain for both carer and client then a shift in the acknowledged power base is essential. The imbalance identified by Rushing (1964) in terms of beneficial outcomes towards staff and carers can only be redirected towards the service user if there is a genuine attempt to empower that party in the relationship.

Service planners and practitioners need to recognize that empowerment should be a pivotal process to be embraced alongside other service accomplishments. However, Brown (1988) argued that recognition of consumer choice is more challenging and satisfying from the practitioner's perspective but is also very challenging to service planners. If cost:benefit analysis can be applied to measure inputs and outcomes then quality of life is an eminent means by which to evaluate outcomes. The complexity of the relationship between carer and client indicates that benefits must accrue to both parties. What appears, then, is an opportunity to introduce a more systematic approach to evaluation of services which recognizes the implications of cost:benefit analysis from the perspective of both carers and service users.

Mansell (1986) suggested that quality initiatives are really about the development of an environment in which staff feel motivated to critically appraise the service they are offering and try to improve it and their contributions within it. Dale (1990) suggested that the benefits of a quality-enhancement system are:

- **A clear agenda for action which produces a more precise identification of problems.**
- **Focus upon the present and immediate client need thereby giving direction for future services.**
- **It legitimized constructive criticism and provided a process for identifying areas of life for quality improvement.**

If the cost of establishing such systems is borne by the resources of the service and the requisite changes in status of carers within their relationships with clients, then the benefits to both parties may well be a more secure and focused future. This results in staff viewing the outcome of their efforts (costs) as producing a mutually attractive outcome (benefits).

Sines (1987) suggested that the fundamental objective of a high-quality service for people with a learning disability and their families should be that each consumer has access to a personal plan detailing their needs and wants. Practitioners should have the guidelines that define the criteria of a high-quality service. Each discipline of the organization should formulate client-centred objectives which should aim to increase the skills and competence of clients and actively encourage community integration. It is apparent that quality initiatives can be a major catalyst in focusing care away from traditional overt and covert systems of control to a regime which truly empowers people with learning disabilities to take back control of their lives and concentrate on areas of quality of life that matter to the individual client. In economic terms, this would enable greater opportunity for consumers to exercise their own value judgements. In achieving the characteristics of a high-quality service and in auditing that service through a system of quality enhancement, practitioners and providers would be utilizing a form of ordinal utility where service users were able to exercise personal choice.

12.11 Economics and the 'Market' for Health/Social Care

In seeking to reform the systems of health and social care in the UK the government introduced legislation which fundamentally altered the way in which such services were organized and managed.

The foreword to the White Paper *Caring for People* (DOH, 1989) felt that the system of community care which it was proposing would provide service users with:

... a much better opportunity to secure the services they need and will stimulate public agencies to tailor services to individual's needs. This offers the prospect of a better deal for people who need care and for those who provide care. Our aim is to promote choice as well as independence.

This fundamental concept, therefore, is in keeping with the principles of ordinal utility; that is, that choice and independence would be maximized. In order for ordinal utility to be achieved, however, control of expenditure by the individual would need to be in keeping with their right of choice. *Caring for People* (DOH, 1989) went on to state that, in terms of services for people with learning disabilities:

... The Government wishes to promote further progress within available resources and is exploring how best this can be done.

Given that it is the government that controls the vast majority of available resources, the principles of ordinal utility would appear to be immediately compromised and the concept of individual choice corrupted. Whilst the overall principles of community care as portrayed by the government may have an apparent economic dimension, those principles were further controlled by the role that was designated to social services authorities in respect of services for people with learning disabilities. *Caring for People* (DOH, 1989) indicated that these authorities would have responsibility for:

- **appropriate assessment of individual need for social care**
- **designing packages of care**
- **securing delivery of services**
- **monitoring quality and cost effectiveness of services**
- **establishing arrangements for assessing clients' ability to contribute to the full economic cost of care**
- **establishing procedures for receiving comments and complaints from service users.**

The overall outcome, therefore, is a system in which there is a dearth of individual choice. The controlling authority is responsible and accountable for the level of service but has no control over the funding which supports it. Far from being a 'free market' for care, the outcome is a highly controlled model in which the individual consumer has little opportunity to exercise choice because he or she does not have the capacity to decide how each unit of resource will be spent. The potential for a full economic analysis of the achievements of care in the community in respect of people with a learning disability is therefore limited.

If an economic analysis of these services were to be undertaken there would need to be established criteria and data against which such an analysis could be undertaken. In support of reforms within the NHS, the government established a strategy for health resulting in the publication of *The Health of the Nation* (DOH, 1992) a Green Paper in which targets for national health gain are identified. In seeking to achieve an economic analysis of the targets set by the Green Paper, Akehurst *et al.* (1991) identified problems in achieving costing methodologies where the system of accounting is still heavily weighted in favour of average unit costs. Without more appropriate systems which provide for a more accurate analysis of cost and volume, the

authors felt that local and national prioritizing of health-care provision would continue to be extremely difficult. Furthermore, Akehurst *et al.* (1991) considered that:

> ... Any strategy formulated around objectives and targets which can be monitored using only existing data sources will necessarily be compromised by the dearth of suitable information available from a health service traditionally geared to provide process measures rather than outcomes and benefits.

Whereas the government produced the targets for health care, they did not do likewise for social care. None of the targets of *Health of the Nation* is specific to the needs of people with learning disabilities.

Reader Activity 12.4
Should the health-care needs of people with learning disabilities be separately identified if we are seeking 'normality'?

One aspect of services for people with learning disabilities which has been subjected to an economic evaluation is that of community care, as opposed to institutional care. Shiell and Wright (1988) considered the economic costs of the expansion in community-based residential facilities for people with a learning disability. They advised that economic appraisal is principally an aid to decision making and that in undertaking such an exercise five features should be considered. These were:

- **Alternative options.** The planners should consider the size, location and staffing of any proposed unit to ensure efficient use of resources.
- **Opportunity costs.** This feature assumes that costs are equivalent to foregone benefits because resources have alternative uses. Planners should therefore compare the benefits of doing one thing as opposed to another.

- **The margin.** The nature of economic costs makes them context-specific and planners should consider that changing the scale of a service usually produces average costs which are greater than those associated with maintaining the service at its current level.
- **Discounting.** As costs and benefits cannot be considered to be equal in value, despite the fact that they may have the same nominal value, planners should consider the time duration over which costs are incurred so as to achieve a more balanced view of accruing benefits.
- **Sensitivity.** Whilst economic appraisals in respect of services for people with a learning disability may be affected by value judgements and uncertainty, policy options should be evaluated by a system of risk analysis that is sensitive to the factors involved.

12.12 Summary

The economical dimension of learning disability is complex. Economic theory can assist in decision making and in establishing priorities for care. It can be of significant assistance in service management and planning of developments. What is also evident is that economic analysis on its own is insufficient as a means for evaluating policy decisions in respect of such a vulnerable client group. If concepts of empowerment and advocacy are to be fully tested in respect of their value to disenfranchised consumers, then the economic analysis of services for people with a learning disability offers opportunity to consider the real achievements of policy, philosophy and rhetoric in terms of their influence over resource allocation and the measurement of efficiency.

Discussion Questions

1 **The principles of health care on demand and a service which is free at the point of delivery are fundamental to the NHS. Can such principles be sustained in a society which is faced with the economic burdens of a health service which was bankrupted by its consumers within 10 years of its establishment?**

2 **Can the UK afford its NHS?**

3 **Is the argument for sustaining our current level of NHS provision economically valid given the principles of cost and benefit?**

4 **Can economic principles alone reflect the value of people with learning disabilities in a consumer society?**

References

Akehurst, R., Godfrey, C., Hutton, J. and Robertson, E. (1991) *The Health of the Nation: An Economic Perspective of Target Setting. Discussion Paper* **92**, University of York.

Barry, N. (1987) Understanding the market. *In* Bocock, R., Clarke, J., Cochrane, A., Graham, P. and Wilson, M. (1987) *The State of the Market.* London: Sage.

Brown, I. (1988) *Quality of Life for Handicapped People.* New York: Croom Helm.

Dale, C. (1990) Introducing quality assurance. *Nursing* **4**(21)

Department of Health (DOH) (1989) *Caring for People: Community Care in the Next Decade and Beyond,* Cm 849. London: HMSO.

Department of Health (DOH) (1992) *Health of the Nation: Strategy for people with learning disabilities.* London: HMSO.

Drummond, M. (1980) *Principles of Economic Appraisal of Health Care.* London: Oxford University Press.

Gudex, C. (1986) *Quality Adjusted Life Years and Their Use by the Health Service. Discussion Paper* **20**, University of York.

Kind, P., Rosser, R. and Williams, A. (1982) Valuation of quality of life: some psychometric evidence. In Jones-Lee, M.W. (Ed.) *The Value of Life and Safety.* North Holland Publishing Company.

Kohnke, M. (1982) *Advocacy, Risk and Reality.* St Louis: C.V. Mosby.

Malin, N. and Teasdale, K. (1991) Caring versus empowerment: considerations of nursing practice. *Journal of Advanced Nursing* **16**.

Mansell, J. (1986) The nature of quality assurance. *In* Beswick, D. and Felce, D. (Eds) *Evaluating Quality of Care.* Kidderminster: British Institute for Mental Handicap.

Mooney, G., Russell, E. and Weir, R. (1986) *Choices for Health Care: A practical introduction to the economics of health care provision.* London: Macmillan.

McGuire, A., Henderson, J. and Mooney, G. (1988) *The Economics of Health Care.* London: Routledge.

Rushing, W. (1964) *The Psychiatric Professions.* Raleigh: University of North Carolina.

Seedhouse, D. (1988) *Ethics, The Heart of Health Care.* Oxford: Alden Press.

Shiell, A. and Wright, K. (1988) *Counting the Costs of Community Care.* York: University of York.

Sines, D. (1987) *Towards Integration; Comprehensive Services for People With a Mental Handicap.* London: Harper & Row.

Williams, A. (1985) Economics of coronary artery bypass grafting. *British Medical Journal* **291**.

World Health Organization (1961) *Constitution of the World Health Organization,* Basic Documents (15 edn). Geneva: WHO.

Further Reading

Baldwin, S., Godfrey, C. and Propper, C. (1990) *Quality of Life: Perspectives and Policy.* London: Routledge.

Barr, N. (1987) *The Economics of the Welfare State.* London: Weidenfeld & Nicholson.

Begg, D., Fischer, S. and Dornbusch, R. (1987) *Economics.* New York: McGraw-Hill.

Gordon, A. (1982) *Economics and Social Policy.* Bristol: Martin Robertson.

Keynes, M. (1988) *The Political Economy of Health and Welfare.* London: Macmillan.

Knapp, M. (1984) *Economics of Social Care.* London: Macmillan.

Part Eight: National and International Dimensions of Learning Disability

Part Eight of *Dimensions of Learning Disability* considers how services for people with a learning disability are organized in a variety of European countries. Services in three countries have been examined: the UK, Sweden and Romania. This allows the reader to reflect upon issues which arise in countries with an established history of service provision but with varying philosophical perspectives and to contrast these issues against a country with no similar history of philosophy.

In Chapter 13, Sam Ayer examines service provision in the UK. He provides an overview of policies that have influenced service provision since the Second World War and shows how this has led to a variety of structures and processes of care throughout the nations of the UK. The emerging trends are considered and matters of reality and practicality are addressed in the summary to the chapter.

In Chapter 14, David Lewis examines services in Sweden as a case history of a country with mature services for people with a learning disability. David offers a brief history of Sweden and introduces the reader to some of the geographical, economic and political factors that have shaped services in Sweden. The chapter is principally made up of an analysis of the philosophical perspectives and a description of how reality does not always match up to the stated intent of managers and politicians. David Lewis is able to offer personal perspectives on the issues raised as a means of summary.

Whereas Chapters 13 and 14 have a wide range of published references, Chapter 15 has only one. This reflects the situation of services in the country of Romania where the plight of people with learning disabilities emerged following the revolution of 1989/90. Norman Daniels and Colin Beacock, and the volunteers of the Poplars Church (Romania) Appeal, offer anecdotal evidence of how they strive to meet the needs of the client group in a country whose social and economic infrastructure is in turmoil. To provide a means of contrast between the countries described, Chapter 15 has an introduction into the features and history of a country about which few western Europeans had any insights until 1990.

The outcome is a work of contrasts in which the reader can examine the competing nature of philosophy and reality in countries of varying economic wealth and sociopolitical stability.

Chapter 13: Services for people with learning disabilities in the UK
Sam Ayer

13.1 Introduction

The current population of the UK of Great Britain, England and Wales, Scotland and Northern Ireland is estimated at 58 million. The UK covers an area of 240 000 km^2. Three languages that are spoken in the UK are English, Welsh and Gaelic; clearly these are the native languages and it must be said that within our pluralistic society a number of other languages are also spoken. While Wales, Scotland and Northern Ireland are directly represented in Parliament; each has a Secretary of State, a member of the Cabinet, who is responsible for administrating their affairs, including responsibility for people with a learning disability. Since the Second World War, primary and secondary education for all children from age 5 to 16 years has been free and compulsory. Social security is a comprehensive national system that covers maternity, unemployment, industrial accidents, old age, family support and housing costs. Since 1948, the National Health Service (NHS) has provided free medical and nursing care. The NHS is also responsible for residential institutions (hospitals) for people with a learning disability. Provision of local education, housing and social services is largely the responsibility of elected local authorities. Since the early 1960s there has been a gradual shift away from hospital to community and family care. As a consequence, the need for team work and co-operation, locally and regionally between statutory, the voluntary sector and the private sector, has become an important feature in the provision of services for people with a learning disability in all the countries of the UK.

In each of the four countries of the UK developments in the services for people with a learning disability have taken different forms. However, similarities exist in some areas which have been increasingly involved in the development of services for these client groups. Notable areas are research and developments and the contribution of voluntary bodies in service development.

In recent years, universities and other organizations have established research centres that carry out research and development work in various aspects of learning disability including the development of services. Voluntary organizations aim to provide direct services for people with a learning disability and their families. They endeavour to enhance the quality of life of families and to pioneer new areas of service provision.

The Impact of Official Policies

Government directions in the 1940s and the 1960s transformed services for people with learning disabilities. The National Health Service Act of 1946 was an important landmark; the colonies and institutions that had developed in the previous decades were now to be managed by the NHS and not the local authorities.

When the NHS Act came into operation in 1948, the existing institutions were transferred to the new hospital authorities. Local authorities continued to provide services such as training and occupation for people with learning disabilities who lived at home. The new 'hospitals' continued to admit people with a learning disability who required residential care on either social or health grounds. Segregation continued within the local authority service, as well as within the new hospital service. In spite of the fact that local authorities provided for the welfare and social needs of other clients, the needs of people with a learning disability were provided by the Department of Health. Medical services for people with learning disabilities were provided outside the new hospital service. Each hospital for people with learning disabilities had separate hospital management committees.

A Royal Commission was established in 1954 and reported in 1957. It recommended radical changes in mental health legislation. It promoted the breaking down of segregation and placed new emphasis on community care. The Commission's general approach was very similar to our current thinking. It recommended that all general social services should be available to people with learning disabilities, and that mental health services should be fully integrated with other health and welfare services. Hospitals, it recommended, should be responsible only for those who required specialist medical treatment or training, or continued nursing supervision. It was further stated that automatic admission to hospital should be discontinued and more out-patient services should be provided. Small residential homes or hostels should be provided by local authorities for adults and children who could not be cared for at home, but did not need to be in hospital. These homes and hostels should not be segregated, but rather should be integrated into communities so that residents could take part in the life of the local community. The Royal Commission recommended the provision of more training centres for children and adults to be built in the community. It also recommended the provision of extra places in sheltered workshops to provide activity and occupation as well as increased social support for people with learning disabilities and their families.

The recommendations of the Royal Commission were accepted by the government. Subsequent actions heralded a sea change in the operation of social policies toward people with learning disabilities and their families. The local authorities and health authorities were required to act upon the Commission's recommendations. Those recommendations that required legislation were embodied in the Mental Health Act of 1959. In August 1959 the Minister of Health, by a directive under the National Health Service Act of 1946 and the new Act, laid a

duty on the local authorities to provide a full range of community services for all people with a learning disability. This directive replaced their previous duties under the pre-war Mental Deficiency Acts that required them to provide supervision, training and occupation for people with learning disabilities who lived at home.

In the 1960s local authorities were faced with a task not only of building residential homes from scratch, but also of greatly expanding day-care services which had formerly been provided only on a relatively small scale. Faced with financial constraints, most local authorities had to make a choice. There was a large expansion in the provision of training centres, later to be named social education centres (and more latterly as resource centres), and purpose-built residential homes.

Until 1 April 1971, when local education authorities became responsible for the education of children with learning disabilities, children with more severe learning disabilities were excluded from the educational system. The training of those living at home was the responsibility of the local authority's health department, and hospital authorities were responsible for those in hospital. This change in responsibility was a natural consequence of the considerable advances made by health and hospital authorities in meeting the educational needs of children with learning disabilities.

By the end of the 1960s, services for this client group were being improved out of all recognition of the previous decades. However, an emergent problem was that of shortage of provision and its effect. The main effect of the shortage of residential places was that people with a learning disability living at home continued under unbearable stress and many hospital authorities felt duty bound to admit more people to already overcrowded wards.

Government Direction in the 1970s and 1980s

In the midst of a spate of scandals (see e.g. Howe Reports, 1969) concerning the way in which people with learning disabilities were treated in hospitals, the White Paper, *Better Services for the Mentally Handicapped* was published (DHSS, 1971). The White Paper announced changes in policy towards the provision of care for people with learning disabilities. For the first time changes in official policy were underpinned by clearly set out principles that reflected current thinking about people with learning disabilities.

These principles incorporated the values and behavioural patterns of everyday life into their models of service delivery. The main principles are summarized in Box 13.1.

The Jay Report (Jay, 1979) reinforced this new emphasis placed on the social aspects of care in nurse education and training (Briggs, 1972) and proposed a new model of care with an emphasis on normal patterns of life for people with learning disabilities. The recommendations gave guidelines on the formation of new categories of carers and their associated needs, and a redefinition of the roles and responsibilities of staff in the design, management and delivery of services.

The central direction, during the 1980s, in implementing a policy of community care was concerned with hospital closures, and the rapid acceleration of developments to reinforce the community as a main locus of care.

In 1980, the Department of Health and Social Security reviewed the 1971 White Paper (DHSS, 1980). As a result the government encouraged a joint approach to planning and working between all the agencies involved in the development and delivery of services to people with learning disabilities and their families. Three years later the government provided further opportunities for transferring funds from the Health Service to both local authorities and the voluntary and independent sectors (DHSS, 1983).

The policy of rapid hospital closure and the transition of care to the community was reaffirmed in the government's response to the Social Services Committee Report (DHSS, 1985).

The Griffith's Report, *Community Care: Agenda for Action* (Griffiths, 1988) took its essential values from the 1971 White Paper, and spelt out the new approach to the value and purpose of community care, and the role of the state in its provision. Griffiths stated that publicly provided services constitute only a small part of the total care provided to people in need. Families, friends, neighbours and other local people provided the majority of care in response to needs which they were uniquely well placed to identify and respond to. It was envisaged that this would be the primary means by which people were enabled to live normal lives in community settings. Griffiths' starting point was that the first task of publicly provided services was to support and, wherever possible, strengthen networks of carers. Public services could help by identifying actual and potential carers, consulting them about their needs and those of the people they were caring for, and then tailor the provision of extra services accordingly. The second task for publicly provided services was to identify where these caring networks had broken down, or could not meet required needs, and decide what public services were desirable to fill the gap. The primary function of public services was to design and arrange the provision of care and support in line with people's needs. The care and support could be provided from a variety of sources. There was value in the multiplicity of providers of care, because this would ensure flexibility and innovation. The proposals were, therefore, aimed at stimulating the further development of a mixed economy of care. It was vital that social services authorities should see themselves as the arrangers and purchasers of the care services – not as monopolistic providers. The resources available for public services would always be finite. As well as assessing needs and arranging suitable services, managers of public services were therefore bound to apply priorities.

A fundamental purpose of the proposals was to ensure that someone was in a position to apply priorities in a way that maximized the chances that those most in need would receive due care and attention, and that eliminated the possibility of low

---

Box 13.1 Principles of the 1971 White Paper: *Better Services for the Mentally Handicapped*

- A family with a person who has a learning disability has the same needs for general social services as all other families. The family and the disabled person need special additional help, which varies according to the severity of the disability whether there are associated physical handicaps or behaviour problems, the age of the disabled person and his or her family situation.
- People with learning disabilities should not be segregated unnecessarily from other people of similar age, nor from the general life of the local community.
- Full use should be made of available knowledge which can help to prevent disability or to reduce the severity of its effects.
- There should be a comprehensive initial assessment and periodic reassessment of the needs of each disabled person and his or her family.
- Each disabled person needs stimulation, social training and education and purposeful occupation or employment in order to develop his or her maximum capacity and to exercise all the skills he or she acquires, however limited they may be.
- Each disabled person should live with his or her own family as long as this does not impose an undue burden on them and his or her family should receive full advice and support. If he or she has to leave home for a foster home, residential home or hospital, temporarily or permanently, links with the family should normally be maintained.
- The range of services in every area should be such that the family can be sure that their disabled member will be properly cared for when it becomes necessary for him or her to leave the family home.
- When a disabled person has to leave his or her family home, temporarily or permanently, the substitute home should be as homelike as possible, even if it is also a hospital. It should provide sympathetic and constant human relationships.
- There should be proper co-ordination in the application of relevant professional skills for the benefit of individual disabled people and their families, and in the planning and administration of relevant services, whether or not these cross administrative frontiers.
- Local authority personal social services for people with learning disabilities should develop as an integral part of the services recently brought together under the Local Authority Social Services Act, 1970.
- There should be close collaboration between these services and those provided by other Local Authority departments (i.e. child health services and education), and with general practitioners, hospitals and other services for the disabled.
- Hospital services for people with learning disabilities should be easily accessible to the population they serve. They should be associated with other hospital services, so that a full range of specialist skills is easily available when needed for assessment or treatment.
- Hospital and local authority services should be planned and operated in partnership.
- Voluntary service can make a contribution to the welfare of people with learning disabilities and their families at all stages of their lives and wherever they are living.
- Understanding and help from friends and neighbours and from the community at large is needed to help the family to maintain a normal social life and to give the disabled member as nearly normal a life as his or her disability permits.

---

priority needs being met, while higher priorities were neglected.

Earlier in the decade the DHSS (DHSS, 1985) in its official statement to the House of Commons Committee on Social Services (HC 13 1984–85) identified the principles and objectives of community care that could be used to guide the development of appropriate services. The principles and

---

Box 13.2 Principles and objectives of community care

- To enable an individual to remain in his or her home whenever possible, rather than being cared for in a hospital or residential home.
- To give support and relief to informal carers (family, friends and neighbours) coping with the stress of caring for a dependent person.
- To deliver appropriate help, by means which cause the least possible disruption to ordinary living.
- To relieve the stress and strain contributing to or arising from physical or emotional disorder.
- To provide the most cost-effective package of services to meet the needs and wishes of those being helped.
- To integrate all the resources of a geographical area in order to support the individuals within it. The resources might include informal carers, NHS and personal social services and organized voluntary effort, but also sheltered housing, the local social security office, the church, local clubs, and so on.

Box 13.3 *Caring for People*: underlying principles

- Services that are based upon responding to individual need, rather than ones that attempt to fit people into existing provision.
- Services that adopt an equal opportunities approach and that, in particular, are ethnically sensitive.
- Services that actively seek (and act upon) the advice of users and carers concerning the planning, implementation and monitoring of provision.
- Services that respond to local circumstances and requirements, and ensure that access to and availability of provision are tailored to the needs of the local population. Appropriateness, access and availability are vital aspects of an equal opportunities approach to service delivery.
- Services that are integrated in such a way that users experience them as coherent, consistent and well planned, despite the fact that a number of agencies will be involved.
- Services that provide value for money, are capable of being adjusted to meet new requirements and are open to being monitored.

---

objectives of community care are reproduced in Box 13.2.

These two documents (DHSS, 1985 and Griffiths, 1988) formed the basis of a new approach to service planning, development and delivery that was spelt out in the 1989 White Paper, *Caring for People* (DHSS, 1989). Central to the successful implementation of *Caring for People* was the assumption that local authorities, health authorities, the voluntary, private and not-for-profit sectors would work together to achieve the necessary changes.

The changes envisaged were significant. In a speech to directors of social services and senior health services managers, the Secretary of State underlined the three key areas where progress needed to be made above all others. These were:

- **To promote the development of domiciliary day and respite services to enable people to**

live in their own homes wherever feasible and sensible.
- **To ensure that service providers make practical support to carers a high priority.**
- **To make proper assessment of need and good care management the cornerstone of high-quality care.**

Making a reality of these objectives, it was anticipated, would require staff from all levels of relevant organizations to train together so that community care services could be developed to meet the needs of users and carers, and to secure better value for money. The government, therefore, wished to promote joint approaches to training as a realistic way of achieving its objectives.

The fundamental objective of *Caring for People* was to achieve an improvement in community services by making them more sensitive to individual users and carers and ensuring better value for money. The underlying principles are reproduced in Box 13.3.

In order to ensure that these principles were implemented, a number of key ingredients needed to be built into existing community care systems. The details of how they were built in and what 'shape' they took would depend on local circumstances. Local agencies were required to develop the following community care systems:

- A system that would produce an integrated community care plan.
- A system that actively involved users and carers in key processes.
- An assessment system, agreed between agencies, that could make the best use of demographic ('top down') data and individual need ('bottom up' information). This system would include an assessment method that could be used by all relevant parties.
- A care management system, agreed between agencies, that acted effectively as a bridge between purchasers, providers and service users.
- A purchasing and contracting system that was explicit about:
  - involvement of users and carers
  - quality standards
  - money flows and the respective responsibilities of purchasers and providers.

This section provides an extension of some aspects covered in Chapter 1 by further exploring central policies that have had a major impact on the provision, delivery and development of services since the Second World War. In the main, these policies have impacted on the trend of service provision, delivery and development throughout the UK. The reader should refer to Chapter 11 for a more in-depth analysis of social policy in the area of learning disability.

The broad similarities between the countries in the UK are an important feature of the history of service development for people with learning disabilities and their families.

The remainder of this chapter explores the provision of services for people with a learning disability and their families. This exploration includes England, Northern Ireland, Scotland and Wales.

Reader Activity 13.1
The reader might find it interesting to make comparisons between provision of services in the UK with provision in Romania and Sweden as outlined in Chapters 14 and 15.

13.2 England: Introduction

The population of England, according to the 1993 estimate, is 48.5 million. England covers an area of 129 000 km^2.

Until 1988, the government department with major responsibility for people with a learning disability was the Department of Health and Social Security (DHSS). This department was directly responsible for social security benefits, and indirectly for social services and health services in England. It held responsibility for strategic planning of the NHS which provided hospital and community medical services. The DHSS also had a responsibility for the social services provided by local authorities including training, housing and domiciliary support. In the summer of 1988 the DHSS was divided. Matters relating to people with learning disability are now mainly with the Department of Health. There were 14 regional health authorities and 192 district health authorities; as from April 1995 in England the number of regional health authorities has been reduced to eight. Other government departments, with some responsibility for people with a learning disability, are the Department of Education and Science, the Department of Employment and the Manpower Services Commission.

13.3 Current Developments in England

In England, the White Paper (DHSS, 1971) was an important landmark in the thinking about what pattern of services would be most appropriate to meet the needs of people with learning disabilities and their families. Following this paper, service providers throughout the country began to apply themselves to working out the elements of a new model of service delivery. To develop better services for people with learning disabilities and their families, service planners and developers had to translate the underlying principles and philosophy of the White Paper into specific plans for the provision required in a particular community.

Two issues preoccupied the minds of service developers. First was the need to develop needs-led services. This would allow for change and flexibility so that a service could be needs-led and could cater for individuals, rather than expecting people with learning disabilities to be a homogeneous group who fitted into whatever service statutory and other bodies chose to provide.

Second, there was the need to plan, manage and provide co-ordinated services that would meet the needs of people with learning disabilities throughout their life cycle. During the 1970s, local communities took the initiative to explore the elements of a model service. Several innovative health and local authorities published comprehensive proposals. These outlined the principles guiding their ideas about planning for specific services (for notable examples see Wessex Regional Health Authority, 1979; Kent Area Health Authority and Kent County Council, 1981; Newcastle City Council and Newcastle Area Health Authority, 1981; Sheffield Area Health Authority and Sheffield Metropolitan District Council, 1981; The Bloomsbury Project Report – University College London, Department of Community Medicine, 1982; North Western Regional Health Authority, 1982). These authorities were amongst the first to see the need to overcome the problem created by the division of responsibility between health and social services, and other agencies such as education, housing, voluntary and the private sectors.

The government of the day perceived that some local initiatives were too drastic and ambitious in their aims, in terms of their scope and the degree of integration that was implied. The Department of Health and Social Security review of the White Paper (DHSS, 1980) argued that the disruption entailed by revolutionary changes of the magnitude envisaged in, for example, some of the above-mentioned local plans, would have to be balanced against any benefits that might be gained at times of resource constraints. A more piecemeal approach to service integration was advocated by the DHSS. In the review of services for people with learning disabilities in England the DHSS set out its position. The DHSS suggested that consideration should be given to less radical changes. They argued that the aim of the service should be to reduce the areas of confusion and overlap between the responsibilities of authorities, and to improve and encourage joint working by health, social services and other agencies, including the private and voluntary sectors. This approach involved the establishment of a comprehensive service that met the assessed needs of people with a learning disability and their families. It was essential that all agencies collaborated to ensure the best use of limited financial and manpower resources.

Following the Report of the Committee on Local Authority and Allied Personal Social Services (the Seebohm Report, 1968), and the previously mentioned 1971 White Paper (DHSS, 1971), the principle of taking services to people with learning disabilities and their families and providing local facilities in the community in which they live, became firmly ingrained in the thinking of service planners and providers in England.

Unfortunately, these reports provided few guidelines on how the principle should be put into practice. No detailed recommendations on how progress could be achieved were spelt out by official policy. Lack of central direction accounted for the 'local revolutions' that took place during the 1970s.

Locally based comprehensive services for people with learning disabilities became the way forward for service development during the 1980s. This was mainly due to the detailed work of three expert groups that were set up by the government. These were the National Development Group for the Mentally Handicapped; Development Team for the Mentally Handicapped; and Independent Development Council for People with Mental Handicap. These three groups spelt out their views on how community-oriented services should be organized in England. The Independent Development Council spelt out its principles of a local service (IDC, 1981). A local service was one which fulfilled the roles set out in Box. 13.4.

The National Development Group for the Mentally Handicapped, in its pamphlet *Mental Handicap Children: A Plan for Action* (NDG, 1977), recommended the setting up of community mental handicap teams (CMHTs) throughout the country. The overall purpose of CMHT was to provide a support service for people with learning disabilities, their families and their carers from the cradle to grave within their local community. Three specific functions were spelt out:

- **to act as the first point of contact and to provide advice and help**
- **to co-ordinate access to services**
- **to establish close working relationships with relevant local voluntary organizations.**

Community teams worked at local level and within a small population unit of approximately 60 000–80 000 people. Originally, they consisted of a core membership of only two – a specialist nurse and specialist social worker. These two full-time workers would be backed up by a range of other specialists, such as clinical and educational psychologists; consultants in mental handicap; family doctors; speech, occupational, art and drama therapists; as well as special teachers and staff of social education centres.

Box 13.4 The role of a local service

- Valued the client as a full citizen with rights and responsibilities, entitled to be consulted about his or her needs and had a say about plans that were being made to meet those needs, no matter how severe his or her handicap might appear at first sight.
- Aimed to promote the independence and to develop and maintain the skills and abilities of both clients and their families.
- Aimed to design, implement and evaluate a programme of help which was based on the unique needs of each individual and responded to changes in those needs.
- Aimed to help the client to use ordinary services and resources of the local community, e.g. primary care, education, health, social, employment, housing, welfare and recreational services.
- Aimed to meet special need arising from disabilities by means of local, fully co-ordinated, multidisciplinary, specialist services delivered by appropriately trained staff.
- Was easily accessible.
- Was delivered dependent upon assessed need to the client's home, school, adult training centre (ATC) or place of work.
- Was delivered regardless of age or severity of disability.
- Was planned actively for people who lived in residential institutions to return to the locality and use its services.
- Was staffed by locally based small teams who were available to visit families in their own homes and clients in their places of study and work.

Reader Activity 13.2
Reflect on the structure of community teams in your area. Are the nurse and social worker both 'specialists in their field'?

Community teams worked at two levels. They worked at first hand with families in their own homes, concentrating on problems of behaviour and management that called for additional expertise – for example, people with challenging behaviour, the multiple disabled and those with communication difficulties. There were also on hand at special periods of difficulty at times of transition between services – such as entry to school, preparation for school leaving, or entry into alternate forms of residential care. Community teams also acted as a mobile task force to help staff tackle difficult problems presented by certain clients in schools, social education centres, residential group homes, or any other setting. Thus, the two basic components of local services for people with learning disabilities were the community learning disability team and the community unit. Figure 13.1 shows how these

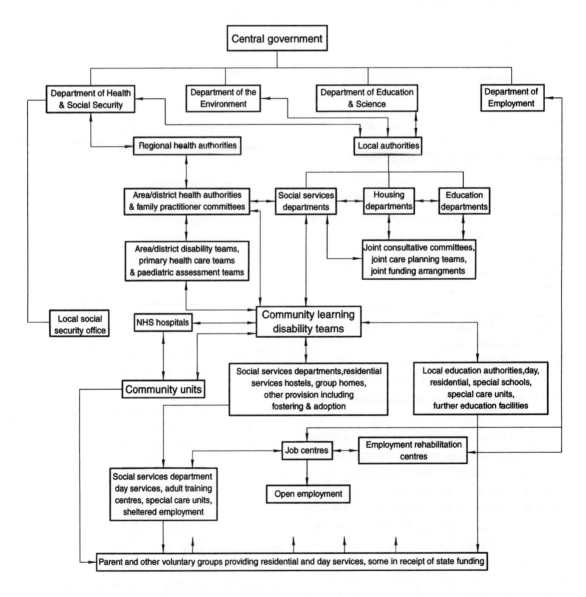

Figure 13.1 How community mental handicap teams (CMHTs) and community units fitted into services for people with learning disabilities in England in the 1980s (adapted from Simon, 1983).

Box 13.5 The services provided by community mental handicap teams (CMHTs)

- Establishing and maintaining a register of people with learning disabilities in their area. The register should be co-ordinated by the CMHT administrator and all CMHT members should add to it the information they collected about the people with learning disabilities known to them. The register should be regularly reviewed.
- Arranging a 'sitting in' service to allow parents an evening out of the home and a 'shopping' service, providing a few hours of care during the day either at home or in a community unit, nursing group or other setting so that parents could go shopping.
- Establishing toy library services where these did not already exist and enabling families to use them; for example, by arranging appointments when convenient for the family and transport if needed.
- Ensuring that people with learning disabilities took full advantage of community facilities, such as swimming, adventure playgrounds, groups and clubs.
- Organizing social skills training groups for young people with social inadequacies.
- Organizing workshops to provide parents (and others involved with people with learning disability) with guidance on management of their child and information about learning disability and the benefits and services available.
- Offering an on-demand home intervention service when needed, offering advice and support in times of stress, supervision or help with the giving of medication, the management of status epilepticus and immediate care to clients and their families in times of crisis, such as during an acute behaviour disturbance or where there was sudden parental incapacity.
- Supervising and operating behaviour modification or other training programmes in the home.
- Befriending and explaining to brothers/sisters of normal intelligence the needs of their relative with learning disability.
- Organizing holidays for people with learning disability, separate from or together with their families.
- Supervising people living in the community away from their own family home and assisting in their placement.
- Providing a 24-h 'on call' service for crisis intervention.
- Organizing short-term and day-care when required.
- Providing a domiciliary venepuncture service and supervising the collection of other specimens when necessary.
- Assisting in the organization and supervision of fostering arrangements.
- Supervising the routine of giving medication and notifying any adverse reactions requiring a doctor's attention.
- Serving on planning teams which could decide a future service provision by bringing first-hand knowledge of the local needs of people and their families, and their likely future needs as indicated by the register maintained by the team.

---

two elements fitted into the overall picture of service provision in England.

As Simon (1983) and Cheseldine (1991) pointed out, community teams differed from district to district, depending on the size of the geographical area covered; whether there was a mental handicap hospital within the district; whether health, social services and education had the same boundaries within an area; whether there was one building to house all the members of the CMHT; and whether

there was a policy for joint planning and funding between health and social services.

In a detailed examination of the activities of CMHTs by the British Institute of Mental Handicap, Simon (Simon, 1983, pp. 84–85) identified a number of examples of the services provided by CMHTs in various parts of England in the 1980s; these are reproduced in Box 13.5.

Recent years have shown great commitment to change in the context of service provision to people with a learning disability in England. The emphasis has been on creating better residential services and developing locally based projects. The way forward is not easy. There is a need for constant and sensitive support systems for staff, especially new staff who have been created by the mixed economy and the internal market ethos and who work with clients in new and untried ways in ordinary housing in the community. There is also the need for increased commitment to the participation of people with learning disabilities themselves in the services that affect their lives – through self-advocacy groups or the involvement of families or volunteer advocates speaking on their behalf. In England, a key restraint to current development is the financial one. Any future progress could prove vulnerable to the imposition of additional resource constraints in areas such as local authority and social security provision. In this regard, there is a need to recognize that community care does not necessarily mean cheaper care since that has too often in the past been obtained at the expense of intolerable burdens on the families with a person with a learning disability, and in particular on the women members of these families.

Reader Activity 13.3
Given that the *Better Services for the Mentally Handicapped* White Paper was published in 1971, why do you think there was such a long period of time identified for the inevitable closure of the large learning disability hospitals in England?

13.4 Northern Ireland: Introduction

Northern Ireland has an estimated population of 1.6 million. It covers an area of $76\,800\ km^2$. It is part of the UK and it elects 17 members of Parliament to the House of Commons. The administrative capital is Belfast. As in England, the education of children between the ages of 5 and 16 years is compulsory

and free education, health and social security provisions are generally similar to that of England. The introduction of the Mental Health Acts (Northern Ireland 1948 and 1961) laid the legislative base for services for people with mental illness and learning disability who had been ascertained as requiring special care. Until the 1961 Act, a person requiring special care was defined as 'a person suffering from arrested or incomplete development of mind (whether arising from inherent causes or induced by disease or injury) which renders him socially inefficient to such an extent that he requires supervision, training or control in his own interest or in the interests of other persons. Under the Health and Personal Social Services (Northern Ireland) Order 1972, the Department of Health and Social Services has a duty to promote the physical mental health and social welfare of the people of Northern Ireland. The day-to-day provision and delivery of health and personal social services, including services for people with a learning disability, is the responsibility of four health and social services boards.

Children with a learning disability who are capable of being taught in special schools or classes, but not in need of special care, are provided with education by five education and library boards (the Education Libraries Order 1972) under the control of the Department of Education. Since 1987 this responsibility has included all children with a learning disability. Children with a learning disability may be referred to the health and social services boards at the age of 16 if they are found, after comprehensive assessment, to need further supervision and training.

13.5 Current Developments in Northern Ireland

The provision of services for people with learning disabilities in Northern Ireland is based upon a unique partnership between health and social services departments. This partnership includes a strong involvement and interest by many voluntary and private organizations that have always been historically active in health and social-care issues. The partnership was given formal recognition when the 1973 statutory reorganization united health and social services together under a single management framework.

This single management framework received a block grant from central government that was then allocated to four health and social services boards within Northern Ireland.

A clear statement of values, shared vision of the services that would meet the needs of people with learning disabilities in each of the four boards, provided a common starting point for effective community care. Each board existed to facilitate the provision of optimum quality health and social care in the community, and for the community. In striving to achieve this aim, within available resources the boards sought to ensure the priorities listed in Box 13.6.

Box 13.6 Optimum quality health and social care: priorities

- Rights and choices are respected.
- Planning and management of services are determined by the needs of clients.
- Clients are assured of care with dignity.
- Services are flexible and responsive to needs.
- Participation of all providers is sought in planning and determining health and social care provision.
- Priority is given to those in greatest need.
- Carers are supported in their endeavour to care for their relatives and friends.
- Standards of care are tested to ensure acceptability.
- Staff are enabled to maintain their expertise and to develop their potential.
- Staff work collaboratively, have opportunities to share ideas, pool resources and develop integrated approaches to providing the best possible health and social care in the community.

The Policy Context

The current debate in Northern Ireland about the provision of community care services took place within the context of the government's community care policy as outlined in *People First* (DHSS, 1989). *People First* proposed the strengthening of family support networks, the promotion of personal independence for all, and the extension of a range of choices open to service users. In Northern Ireland, health and social services boards were being encouraged to stimulate a mixed economy of care services and increasingly to become the purchasers rather than primarily the providers of services. Through this strategy lay the potential to generate a wider range of service options.

Concern about the future of day services in the province had not been confined to issues of supply and demand, but extended to the debate about the nature of day services and the role of social education centres (SECs) in particular. The transition from adult training centres (ATCs) to SECs became a topical issue in the 1970s. In 1977 the National Development Group produced *Day Services for Mentally Handicapped People* in which it was suggested that the title 'adult training centre' should be changed to 'social education centre' to reflect the change in purpose and orientation to a pattern of social and development services (NDG, 1977). The National Development Group perceived the SEC as a much more developed mental and educationally based facility than had previously been imagined, but saw most of the services being provided within a centre. At the time services were still seen as being group organized and usually in large centres with 125 places being considered the optimum size.

In 1978, the Department of Health and Social Services issued its policy, *Day Services for People with a Mental Handicap in Northern Ireland* (DHSS, 1978). The policy was aimed at providing an infrastructure of services and family support capable of maintaining people in their own homes, where that was their wish. It acknowledged the need for assessment and review and for programmes of educational and social training, stimulation, purposeful occupation or employment to develop to the maximum capacity the skills and abilities of individuals. This policy became part of the strategy for Northern Ireland. It reiterated the general principles and objectives aimed at helping people with learning disability to lead their lives as normal as possible and to keep to a minimum the need for long-stay hospital care.

In 1985, the Independent Development Council (IDC) issued *Living Like Other People*. The IDC provided a guide as to what it saw as the next steps in developing day services for people with a learning disability. This report recommended much greater involvement of service users in planning and delivery of day services, a philosophy which recognized that people with a learning disability, regardless of their degree of disability, had the same values and rights as those who were not disabled. It was argued that service users should be enabled to experience different kinds of service so that they could make informed choices as to which they wanted to access.

In 1985, the National Association of Teachers of the Mentally Handicapped issued a policy statement *Towards Tomorrow* (NATMH, 1985). The document stated that, instead of being the sole centre for activities for people with learning disabilities in defined areas, in future the SEC should become part of a network of community services that also included, for example further education colleges, vocational training schemes, pathway schemes, community/leisure services, etc. In practice this meant that the programme of education and other activities and the range of facilities offered within the SEC buildings would gradually change in character and decrease in number and range as people with learning disabilities increasingly began to use community services. It also meant that the SECs would gradually develop into resource centres, carrying out assessment, individual programming and practical research of varying types. Additionally, it would run a wide range of

courses on learning disability for SEC staff, parents and staff in further education colleges. The role of centre staff would focus in particular on designing and applying individual programme plans and how to ensure that multidisciplinary activity became interdisciplinary action.

In Northern Ireland this thinking led to a reappraisal of the proposal to adopt a 5-day-a-week attendance at a particular building. SECs found it valuable to use the whole range of community services. They offered their clients a wider range of experience, as well as an opportunity to learn to use ordinary services with appropriate additional help, only relying on special and separate provision where their particular educational, health and social needs demanded it.

The 1989 document, *People First* (DHSS, 1989) expanded a number of concepts that were introduced in the 1978 policy paper. It emphasized the need for the right services to be provided. It ensured that those who used services had a greater say in and a wider choice of what was provided. *People First* also acknowledged the right of people to remain in their own homes for as long as possible. The 1978 policy paper perceived the provision of 'day-care' services within the context of 'adult training centres'. *People First* acknowledged that a wider range of day services, which were not based in centres, should be made available. This broader concept of day services was aimed at assisting people to use the full range of community services including leisure centres, colleges of further education and work training placements and therefore reinforced the earlier policy statement by the National Association of Teachers for the Mentally Handicapped.

As has already been pointed out, one distinctive feature of recent developments of service in Northern Ireland was the way in which the country adopted a common stance in relation to policy, values and philosophies that underpinned service provision. Another distinctive feature was the existence in each health and social service board of different approaches and emphasized the ways in which each

Board applied common policies, values and philosophies to the planning and delivery of services.

A close scrutiny of health and social service boards in their respective area strategic plans for the same period indicated this trend. The Northern Board in its 1988/89 operational plan emphasized the role of the voluntary sector and subsequent negotiations with the Bridge Association, Antrim, led to the creation of 36 places for vocational training. In its 1990/91 operational plan, the board acknowledged that no one agency could expect to provide for the full range of services needed by individuals and their families. It relied on collaboration and partnership as the best way to provide a comprehensive range of services.

The Southern Board announced in its operational plans 1989/90 that it would endeavour to provide a social educational centre in each of its units of management. In its plan for 1990/91, an undertaking was given to examine the day services currently provided in order to determine future requirements.

The Eastern Board, in its operational plan 1989/90, stated that the success of sustaining and developing community care strategies was critically related to the provision of day services. It recognized a continuing need to invest in day care to support individuals living within a range of residential settings.

The Western Board's operational plan 1989/90 identified as a major requirement the need to increase provision in social educational centres to provide industrial therapy and improve staffing levels.

The regional strategy 1992/97 was based on an agenda of challenge and change. It drew together a number of recent policy developments and emphasized the separation of purchaser and provider functions in the provision of a seamless service. This strategy envisaged the development of a wide range of community service provision in the voluntary and the private sectors. The ultimate objective was to ensure that services were brought more closely into line with assessed need.

In Northern Ireland, long-stay hospitals currently provide an important setting for the care of people with learning disabilities. Recent developments have enabled these hospitals to adopt service philosophies that ensure a high degree of quality individual care. The independent and voluntary sectors are collaborating with the health and social services boards to provide a comprehensive range of community based care and support for clients and their families.

13.6 Scotland: Introduction

The population of Scotland is estimated to be 5.1 million. Scotland covers an area of 76 800 km². Its administrative capital is Edinburgh. The country is represented in the House of Commons by 71 Members of Parliament, but has separate government departments and local government legislation.

The British Cabinet has a Secretary of State for Scotland. However, it should be noted that there are historically based unique differences in its system of law, judiciary, education, local government and national church. Official languages are English and Gaelic.

As from April 1995, the 18 area health boards that provided health and community services have been replaced by 15 health boards. In Scotland education and social work are the responsibility of 11 regional and island authorities. Scottish legislation lays down principles for these services, but there is considerable local variation.

13.7 Current Developments in Scotland

In the 1950s and 1960s the policies contained in the Royal Commission on the Law Relating to Mental Illness and Mental Deficiency provided the framework for the provision of services for people with learning disabilities in Scotland. In 1958, the Dunlop Committee showed how the major recommendations of the Royal Commission could be applied to Scotland. In 1961 the Allan Committee on Local Authority Services performed a similar exercise. Both committees reached a similar conclusion that:

The object of every Local Authority must be to expand its services to the point at which no person need be resident in hospital who would not benefit from or did not require specialist medical treatment or training, or continual nursing supervision. (Scottish Office, 1992).

Other important points made were that local authorities should provide small residential homes or hostels for adults and children who could not remain at home, but did not need to be in hospital. There should be more support for people with learning disabilities and their families. There should be more training centres for children and adults in the community and more sheltered workshops.

In other words, like the rest of the UK, Scotland embraced the concept of community care. In 1972, the Department of Health in Scotland published a document, *The Blue Book* (DHS, 1972) that provided a thorough analysis of the state of service provision and development in Scotland. It pointed out that 'in national terms there was still a short fall'. In particular, there was substantial regional variation in provision. There was a shortage of qualified social work staff. In education services, implementation of the changes required by the Education (Mentally Handicapped Children) (Scotland) Act 1974, had been less speedy than the authorities concerned would wish. Many hospitals accommodated patients who did not need to be there if alternative community facilities were available and this meant that hospitals remained under pressure to admit clients. Many hospital staff had grave doubts that the provision of community-care facilities would have any effect on the present number of patients in hospital and were sceptical of seeing any reduction in the number referred for admission to hospital. Where standards of accommodation and staffing in hospital were particularly

---

Box 13.7 The *Blue Book*: objectives

- To continue the implementation of government policy which was that there should be an increasing emphasis on care in the community.
- To make available through the medium of local authorities an increasing proportion of residential care in the community.
- To phase out redundant hospital accommodation when local authority accommodation became available.
- To develop comprehensive assessment as an integral part of the process of ascertaining the needs of people with learning disabilities.
- To increase the provision of day-care services specifically for preschool children and also for children of school age.
- To provide education and training for children.
- To ensure that hospital services for children were provided only where the children were seriously impaired or where their disability was accompaniod by severe physical handicap or persistent emotional or behavioural disorder to such a degree as would require hospital treatment and care regardless of their disability.
- To provide support to the families of people with learning disabilities.
- To enable as many people with learning disabilities as were capable of doing so to work in paid employment.

---

poor, continuing pressure on the health services led to cynicism and despair (DHS, 1972, p. 13). In reference to the principles set out in the White Paper (DHSS, 1971) the *Blue Book* spelt out the main objectives of the services for people with learning disabilities in Scotland. These are reproduced in Box 13.7.

The position in 1972 was that there had been little change in government policy regarding an increasing emphasis on care in the community. Steps so far taken by all statutory agencies to achieve this desirable end had been inadequate. Almost without exception, there had been little effect on the transfer of patients from hospital to community care (Scottish Office, 1992).

Since the mid 1970s, the Scottish approach to service provision and development had been to formulate and spell out views as to what the policy should be. Policy had been based on three elements. First, there was a recognition that collaborative effort based on effective communication and co-ordination between the various statutory and non-statutory agencies was a prerequisite of effective action. Second, there was a move away from the concept of a national service. Third, and most important, 'a wind of change' in the form of a broad international movement concerned with care in the community has swept away a lot of ideas and practices and is beginning to provide some of the answers to the questions that have been raised. These questions have been mainly in terms of pioneering projects here and there rather than in terms of standard practice. In essence, Scotland had embarked upon specific 'pathways to progress' (DHS, 1992, p. 14) whereby an innovative approach was adopted towards the development of an aspect of care. The service was then rigorously evaluated 'to test the extent to which innovation can be repli-cated and become incorporated in general practice' (Seed, 1988, p. 2).

In the rest of this overview, brief mention is made with respect to three services where research has identified marked progress in service provision and development. These are day-care services, respite-care services and social support for children with learning disabilities and their families.

During the 1980s there was an enormous expan-sion in the scale of provision of day-care services in Scotland (Seed, 1988). As the Scottish Home and Health Department and Scottish Education Depart-ment Report (SHHD/SED) pointed out there was an urgent need to clarify the aims and objectives of Adult Training Centres (SHHD and SED, 1979). Consequently, various studies and projects were initiated by the SHHD and SED in the 1980s (see

> **Box 13.8 Seven models of practice in day-care service**
>
> - **The work model.** To provide work experience and where possible, preparation for employment.
> - **The social-care model.** To provide social education; that is, to develop normal living potential and social skills needed in a family and community context.
> - **The further education model.** To provide continuing education to develop adult potential.
> - **The throughput model.** To channel people to more appropriate (more normal) placements including preparation for employment.
> - **The recreational model.** To provide opportunities to develop the individual through a range of interests and activities.
> - **The shared-living experience.** To provide opportunities for shared learning.
> - **The resource centre model.** To meet a variety of clients and community needs, as a resource centre.
>
> For a fuller account of these analyses see Seed *et al.* (1984).

e.g. Seed *et al.*, 1984; Britten, 1985; Baker and Urquart, 1987; Seed, 1988). Together these studies identified seven models of practice in day-care ser-vices (i.e. ATCs or SECs). The seven models, and aims associated with them, are reproduced in Box 13.8.

In a later project by Philip Seed (Seed, 1988) these original seven models of practice in adult training/social education centres were used to ascertain the perspectives of management, staff, parents and clients in order to answer the crucial question 'what are centres for?' The answers to this question can be summarized as follows.

First, centres had a broad aim to develop the client's potential. This implied that clients attended in order to learn something. It was a general educa-tional aim that different models of practice would interpret with particular slants. In the case of the work model, the emphasis was on the potential for work. In the case of the recreational model, the emphasis is on sport and leisure pursuits.

A second aim was a specific application of the first in terms of preparation for more independent forms of living. All models of practice subscribed to this, tending to see their particular slant as the means to its attainment. Thus work was a means to a greater independence because being at work offered more independent status. Developing the capacity for recreational activities also enhanced status and in general gave confidence. Preparation for independent forms of living was central to the social care, further education, resource centre and throughput models.

A third aim was the specific one of a positive throughput. It regarded attendance at centres as temporary, and a specific preparation either for work or for some other positive purpose outside the centre. This had particular significance for the work, further education, throughput and resource centre models. It was considered as appropriate, perhaps, for only a minority of clients in the social-care model. It was not necessarily an aim at all in the recreational model.

A fourth aim, which was a general one, could be described as the enrichment of clients' patterns of living at home. This applied particularly to the social-care and resource centre models and it applied least, if at all, to the work model.

Seed identified a fifth aim, which was to provide social activities and opportunities for mixing amongst clients at centres. This aim was given high priority by parents and clients.

The sixth aim was to provide respite for parents or other carers at home. Seed and his colleagues found it difficult in considering how this fitted into other aims but was convinced that it was an important aim, not only for centres closest to the social care model but also (in some cases) for most other models except the work model.

A seventh aim, also controversial, but nevertheless widely acknowledged, was simply to provide constructive forms of occupation.

Finally, there was a specific aim associated with the resource centre model – namely to be a resource to clients, their families and to the wider commu-nity, including those in the community who were helping to support people with learning disabilities to live more normal lives.

This pioneering work provided a means of considering the various outcomes in relation to each model of practice in day centres.

Reader Activity 13.4
What constitutes 'constructive forms of occupation' for you?

Respite Care Services

In Scotland, as in other parts of the UK, the focus of care is shifting from settings in hospitals, purpose-built residential establishments and hostels to community settings for family-based care.

There is also a shift away from care by trained professionals to care by untrained, informal and voluntary people. Respite care has become a key community service in Scotland. The Scottish Social Work Services Inspectorate recently commissioned a study in order to establish the current position as regards respite care (Lindsay *et al.*, 1993). Lindsay *et al.* have described the definitive character of respite care services in Scotland as services that are intended to assist two different types of service users simultaneously. These two types of service users were carers and people with dependency needs who were assisted by the former. It was this interchange between the carer and the person with the dependency, and a recognition of their need for external assistance in maintaining a quality of life within the two roles that was the distinctive aspect of any respite care service (Lindsay *et al.*, 1993).

The provision of services that shared responsibility of caring both at home and away from home was seen as central to preserving the carers well being and also resolving some of the inevitable stresses in the relationship between carer and cared for person. In Scotland, the development of respite care was intended to have four main aims. These are reproduced in Box 13.9.

There are two distinctive characteristics about the provision of respite care in Scotland for people with learning disabilities. They are no longer regarded as a homogenous group for whom exclusive services should be provided. The quality of respite care for these client groups is measured alongside the quality of respite care for other community care groups such as elderly people, people who have dementia, people who have mental health problems and adults and children with physical disabilities.

Social Support for Disabled Children and Their Families

The Curtis Report (Curtis Committee, 1946) was a landmark in child-care policy in the UK. It identified the need to keep children out of long-stay institutions. Its recommendations were enacted in the 1948 Children's Act. In spite of its original brief to look at the conditions of all children not living in their own homes, the report drew its boundaries to exclude those who had significant disabilities (Shearer, 1980). The Curtis Committee pointed out that:

the mentally or physically handicapped child presented different problems, most of which . . . were outside the committee's terms of reference. (Curtis Committee, 1946, p. 508).

The Thalidomide affair (see Bradshaw *et al.*, 1981) caused a refocusing on the needs of disabled children and their families. In the 1970s and the 1980s there was a spate of studies and official reports highlighting public awareness of the problems of families caring for disabled children (see, e.g. Young Husband *et al.*, 1970; Voysey, 1975; Wilkin, 1979; Peters, 1978; Ayer, 1982; Glendinning, 1983; Ayer, 1984; Ayer and Alaszewski, 1984; Wright, 1986; Stalker, 1988; Meltzer *et al.*, 1989). Together these publications helped to provide a mass of information on the needs of families and the level of public support for them.

Both Ayer (1982) and Glendinning (1983) for example, described in detail the 'daily grind' that constituted the experience of mothers and drew parallels between this and the repetitive, largely unrewarding nature of housework. Caring for children whose disabilities 'in many reports represent a prolonging of the dependencies of early childhood . . . gives rise to an essentially repetitive set of servicing functions which can be physically taxing, mentally exhausting and dispiritingly monotonous' (Glendinning, 1983, p. 41). It included help with feeding, washing, bathing and dressing the child, carrying them up and down stairs, in and out of bed. (Ayer, 1982; Glendinning, 1983).

Gough *et al.*'s recent (1993) study could be used as a 'tracer' to identify the views and aspirations of a sample of contemporary Scottish mothers with disabled children. Basically, this study echoed the findings of those mentioned above. Gough *et al.* made the case for a better model of service covering more sensitive disclosure of the child's disability to parents; the need to improve quality of service provision; improvements in management information; service co-ordination and communication; greater power for parents; and the need to improve policies for case management (Gough *et al.*, 1993, summary, pp. iv–v).

As Baldwin and Carlisle (1994, p. 54) point out, 'it is very clear what parents want is care management: an individually designed and co-ordinated package of service to help them support the child at home'. Implementation of the Children Act, 1989 could make this a real possibility in England and Wales. The White Paper, *Scotland's Children* (Scottish Office, 1993) on services for children should equally create possibilities for improving the situation in Scotland, with its commitment to assessment of social care needs and improving information for parents.

As in Northern Ireland, Scotland still currently relies on long-stay residential institutions (hospitals) that are dispersed throughout the country as the main setting for the provision of care for adults with learning disabilities. The introduction of the Government's National Health Service and Community Care Act 1990 has provided the impetus for co-operation and partnership between agencies. The Act has provided a co-ordinated approach and is enabling services to transfer from long-stay hospital to the community. Current developments include increased provision for day-care services, respite-care services and social support for children with learning disabilities and their families.

Reader Activity 13.5
Compare and contrast the similarities and differences between Northern Ireland and Scotland in the services they offer to people with learning disabilities and their families.

13.8 Wales: Introduction

Wales has an estimated population of 2.9 million and covers an area of 20 540 km^2. The capital of Wales is Cardiff. Before April 1995, health services

were provided by nine area health authorities. Although England and Wales are generally considered as one unit for most administrative purposes, the Welsh Office have some autonomy in policy development. This is demonstrated by the initiation in 1983 of the All Wales Strategy for the development of services for people with a learning disability. This document provided the initiative and leadership towards the development of progressive community-based services in Wales. The cohesive and collaborative approach to service development in Wales is demonstrated by the success of a pioneering model of community services based on individual needs. Ideas for the care of Mentally Retarded People in Ordinary Dwellings (NIMROD) commenced in 1977 in Cardiff. This venture was supported by the Welsh Office, the Mental Handicap in Wales Applied Research Unit; the health authority, the South Glamorgan County Council and Cardiff City Council.

13.9 Current Developments in Wales

The unique features of the Welsh approach to the current development of services for people with learning disabilities were based on four clearly defined approaches to future development:

- First, the approach was based on a clear set of strategies that would create new patterns of comprehensive and integrated community based services throughout Wales.
- Second, the approach was based on a vision that set out general principles, philosophy and objectives that provided a touchstone to underpin the development and delivery of new patterns of health and social care services for this client group in Wales.
- Third, the approach was based on a commitment from central government, local authorities, people with learning disabilities, their families and others to work together for a common cause.

- Fourth, planning and management arrangements were inter-related in a cohesive approach that embraced the All-Wales level, the county level and the local level.

The All-Wales Strategy for the development of services for people with learning disabilities commenced in April 1983 (Welsh Office, 1983). It played an important part in ensuring those with professional or consumer interest as well as the general public had the opportunity to play their full part in the development of a new pattern of services in Wales. The strategy was underpinned by three general principles that provided the philosophy and objectives for current and future developments.

The first principle stated that people with learning disabilities should have a right to normal patterns of life within the community in which they lived. They should enjoy as full a range of life opportunities and choices that their families, friends and the community could provide. They should be enabled to become respected members of their communities and should not be devalued because of their intellectual impairment. They should enjoy equal right of access to normal services and be obliged to rely on special services only where they had a special need that could not be met by services available to the general public. This principle also meant that help in making opportunities and following the kind of choices that made for a full life was not solely the concern and responsibility of professionals but was rather one for society as a whole.

The second principle stated that people with learning disabilities should have a right to be treated as individuals. There was the recognition that each individual had different needs, capacities and aspirations that needed to be identified and that must guide the efforts of service providers. This principle also meant that people with learning disabilities and their families had to play a full part in decisions that were intended to help them. This approach to meet their needs emphasized personal development, quality of life and enabled people with

a learning disability to encounter the ordinary hazards of life without being overprotected.

The third principle stated that people with learning disabilities required additional help from the communities in which they lived and from professional services, if they were to develop to their maximum potential as individuals. Great emphasis was placed on the need to support the caring efforts of the families of people with learning disabilities, as well as those who would enable them to live as independently as possible, when they wished to leave home or when their families were no longer able to care for them.

The Policy Context

The innovatory approach adopted by the All-Wales Strategy included a deliberate policy to move away from the disjointed, piecemeal, *ad hoc* nature in which services had developed in the past. The new pattern of services was designed to be comprehensive and fully integrated. Great emphasis was placed on the development of collaboration between formal and informal carers, and to ensure that future services were given sympathetically and sensitively. It was recognized that the large majority of people with learning disabilities in Wales were maintained in the community, with the support mainly of informal systems of voluntary care and support from parents, relatives, friends, neighbours and acquaintances.

Historically, the voluntary organizations in Wales that were concerned with people with learning disabilities had developed a high degree of co-ordination in their approach to service provision and development; they spoke with one voice. The voluntary sector had three main roles. The first was in representing the interests of people with learning disabilities and their families in the planning and management of services. It was especially well placed to provide advice to the families of people with learning disabilities and to bring people together in schemes of mutual assistance and social activity.

Box 13.10 Functions of the All-Wales advisory panel

- To advise the Welsh Office.
- To act as a consultancy (either as individual members or collectively) to assist service planners and providers as well as voluntary organizations in the drawing up of plans and in the development of services throughout Wales.
- To act as a catalyst for the pooling of ideas and information and the dissemination of good practice throughout Wales.
- To advise on the monitoring and evaluation of the strategy.

Box 13.11 Functions to be fulfilled at All-Wales level

- To provide a mechanism by which the strategy would be financed.
- To assess the compatibility of locally prepared plans with the strategy.
- To provide guidance on the preparation and implementation of local plans for the implementation of the strategy.
- To encourage the pooling of ideas and information and to disseminate good practice.
- To monitor and evaluate the development of services and ensure that they were provided successfully in accordance with the strategy, that value for money was secured and that lessons learnt were applied to successive phases of development throughout Wales.

Box 13.12 Functions to be fulfilled at the county level

- The preparation of plans for comprehensive services which, in so far as they were to be centrally funded, would be submitted to the Welsh Office for approval.
- Responsibility for the provision of services under approved plans.
- Co-ordination of the efforts of individual service providers.
- Monitoring the quality of service provision at the local level and ensuring the maintenance and improvement of standards where necessary.
- Ensuring that lessons learned nationally in the implementation of the strategy were made known and applied to the development of services at the local level and generally the dissemination of good practice.

The second was in the direct provision of a range of services developed in co-operation with, and complementary to formal and statutory services.

Third, the voluntary sector in Wales made a unique contribution in promoting the acceptance of people with learning disabilities in the community and in encouraging others to live and work alongside people with learning disabilities so that they developed opportunities in their lives.

Recognizing their history and record of innovation, the strategy gave the voluntary sector two specific roles in the development of the new patterns of comprehensive services. The first was to establish advocacy schemes for people with learning disabilities. Advocacy should be available to those in existing, as well as in newly established services. It should also be organized so as to be completely independent of the service-providing agencies. The second was to include the voluntary sector in the All-Wales advisory panel. The panel's functions are reproduced in Box 13.10.

Co-ordination between formal, statutory and informal service delivery was matched by co-ordination and compatibility at the All-Wales level, the county level and at the local level.

The All-Wales Strategy provided specific functions at each level of planning and service delivery in an attempt to ensure desired outcomes. Box 13.11 lists the essential functions that had to be met at the All-Wales level. The functions that had to be carried out at the county level are reproduced in Box 13.12.

The principal goal at the local level was to enable people with learning disabilities and their families to achieve as independent a life as possible. It was recognized that clients and their families might need access at different times to a wide range of individuals within many organizations. These would include doctors, nurses, psychologists, occupational therapists, speech therapists, dentists, teachers, social workers, residential staff, day-care staff, home helps, housing officers and social security officers.

In spite of the wide range of professionals, clients and their families in the past faced a variety of problems. Problems commonly faced by clients and their families in relation to these services included the following:

- Help was not available or not easily accessible when required.
- Inappropriate or inadequate help was given.
- Conflicting advice or help was given, sometimes by different professionals in touch with the client at the same time.
- There was not always a sensitive response to individual needs.

In the new pattern of services, local services needed to be organized to ensure that:

- Clients and their families had ready access to the help they required, when they required it.
- The help provided was of an adequate quality.
- The effort of professionals took on a multi-disciplinary approach and were co-ordinated so that the number of separate interventions by professionals was kept to a minimum and conflicting advice was avoided as far as possible.

Review of the Strategy

The 1983 All-Wales Strategy document envisaged that money from the Revenue Support Grant would be transferred to the local authorities. This was proposed because a crucial objective of the strategy was to remedy the historic anomaly that enabled the bulk of services and resources (as much as 80%, see evidence and references in *Better Services for Mental Handicap Services* (DHSS,

1971)) to be spent on providing health-care services, largely in traditional hospitals, for the care of some 2200 people with severe learning disabilities. By contrast, only 20% of the resources were being spent on social care in support of some 8000 people with equally severe disabilities, living with their families. It was, therefore, necessary to build up the provision and delivery of new patterns of social care, and supportive contributions from community, health- and social-care services, until such time as sufficient confidence had developed in the new pattern of services' ability to sustain the full weight of care.

The evidence from the strategy confirmed this analysis and showed that the transfer of resources from institutional forms of care to more flexible forms of community care had been gradual and consistent; significant progress has now been achieved.

In 1989/90 in Wales as a whole some 29% of social services authorities' budgets and nearly 13% of district health authorities' budgets for people with learning disabilities were being spent on new patterns of services, compared with only 3% and 0.6% respectively in 1982/83 (Welsh Office, 1992). The evidence shows that the unique All-Wales Strategy had made a significant impact on the funding arrangements and arguably the lives of people with learning disabilities and their families.

The additional resources under the strategy had been used to build up new patterns of community services for people with learning disabilities, so as to prevent the breakdowns in networks of care that led in the past to admissions to institutional care. This transfer of resource paved the way for the carefully planned resettlement of people from hospital and hostels into ordinary homes of their own. Bennett (1992) noted:

When the strategy was launched in 1983 only 41 families received support in their own homes; today well over 3000 do so; in 1983 only 166 people with severe learning disabilities had homes of their own now over 1000 do so. These are just two examples of the great strides we have made in Wales because of the Strategy. (Bennett, 1992)

Equally positive of the advances made by this strategy, Hunt (1992) was encouraged to say:

The All-Wales Mental Handicap Strategy has blazed a trail in providing more local and more flexible forms of care in the community. I see its future development as a crucial contribution, for some of the vulnerable members of our society and their family carers, to our objectives under the Citizens' Charter of there being clear local standards of services and equally clear systems of representation and complaint where these standards are not being met.

The All-Wales Strategy from April 1993

It was important that developments for people with learning disabilities should be fully compatible with the comprehensive programme to improve social and community care for all client groups that was being introduced in the light of the White Paper *Caring for People* (DHSS, 1989) and that came fully into effect from April 1993. These arrangements gave local authority social services the lead role and required them to devise, with health authorities, the voluntary sector, the independent sector, the family health services and families plans for social and community care that provided the basis for assessing the needs of individuals, and to provide services to meet identified needs within available resources.

The objectives set out in the current White Paper were compatible with the visions of the All-Wales Strategy. The Strategy had not been replaced by *Caring for People*. It provided a fresh impetus for developments in the field of learning disabilities. The publication of the All-Wales Strategy marked a unique approach to service development, in the UK. The most important aspect of this initiative was that it laid down a philosophy and objectives to be followed and set new patterns for comprehensive services to be developed for this

client group in Wales. Unlike England, where the policy of community care lacked adequate financial commitment, in Wales the Welsh Office appreciated that major savings from the transfer of patients from hospital to the community could not be expected for some years. As a result, the Welsh Office provided the necessary funding to finance those new services that were in accordance with the strategy. The impetus provided by the Welsh Office, with its Strategy and the provision of finance, brought about two significant developments in Wales. Firstly it brought about the closure of all mental handicap hospitals in Wales. Second, it encouraged the development of good practice that influenced the progress of community-based services in Wales. With respect to Wales, it could be argued that the success that was achieved in service development was due to the existence of an active policy that had government support and special funding.

13.10 Discussion of UK Learning Disability Services

Community care underpins the approach for service provision and development in all the countries of the UK. There is some evidence of a determined attempt throughout the UK to achieve integrated service delivery for people with learning disabilities. The culture of community care has embraced a set of ideas and perspectives that are strange bedfellows. The community-care agenda has brought about different paradigms concerning the nature of care for people with learning disabilities. As Kuhn (1970) has pointed out, the concept of a paradigm is used to describe the way a set of beliefs shapes what people believe, and also puts limits on the questions that can and cannot be asked. There is a shift from the traditional caring – professional paradigm to a market- and business-oriented paradigm. Relevant questions such as Who will pay for this service? How much does it cost? Am I value for money? Are we value for money?, are in currency (Ayer, 1994a).

There is also a shift from rigid, fragmented, single-agency, service-led institutional provision to flexible, multi-agency, seamless, demand-led community provision. The paradigm shift is marked by a period of conflict, tension and confusion. At the same time there is still great expectation that the reforms will bring about joint-planning, joint-financing, joint-training and joint-working.

Reader Activity 13.6
Reflect on this idea of agencies and professions working jointly. How easy is this to achieve and what, from your experience, are the prerequisites for such an idea to be translated into practice?

Indeed the need for close collaboration and co-operation by care agencies in the delivery of health- and social-care provision is at the heart of the community-care reforms. Current community-care policies abound with terms that convey powerful messages that much of what community-care workers and care agencies do, require them to operate in an interagency and multidisciplinary context.

Figure 13.2 portrays current community-care vocabulary that brings this powerful message home. So, from the official policy angle, the objectives of the new agenda for care are comprehensively articulated. These are understood and accepted by both service users and care agencies as well as other stake holders. A more complex issue emerges when one tries to address the question 'can we trust the new system?'. This question evokes a mixture of anxiety, threat and optimism on the part of managers and practitioners (Ayer, 1994b).

A commitment to community care has been central government policy since the early 1960s. The old community care was traditionally associated with slotting people into existing services. The new community-care agenda is intended to be needs-led rather than service-led. Through the new community-care agenda a fresh attempt to convert rhetoric

Figure 13.2 Collaboration in community care: working together.

into reality is now being made (Hunter and Wistow, 1987; Higgins *et al.*, 1993).

A number of writers have made statements that articulate the current tensions, conflicts and confusion referred to above. For example, Leedham and Wistow (1992) point out that the extension of GP fundholding to the purchasing of community health services and the setting up of community-care trusts have made the system more not less complex. The increasingly complex system of purchasing in community care only adds to the confusion.

Reader Activity 13.7
Who is the lead purchaser for services to people with learning disabilities in your area? Can you name the purchasing organization or describe its contracting process?

There is an inevitable tension in achieving user-led assessment whilst at the same time managing scarce resources in a cost-effective manner (Richardson and Higgins, 1992). Numerous research studies, official reports and enquiries have concluded that effective collaboration remains largely an elusive goal (Audit Commission, 1986; Hunter and Wistow, 1987, 1991; National Audit Office, 1987; Griffiths, 1988). Hunter and Wistow have argued that:

> One reading of the recent history of most, if not all, categories of joint activity would suggest it to be a chimera: a self defeating illusion. In practice, it might be argued that inter-agency and inter-professional relationships have been more generally marked by conflict or stand-off rather than productive co-operation. (Hunter and Wistow, 1991, p. 9).

An obstacle to the seamless service concept is user costs. Health care is still largely free at the point of use, whilst social care increasingly has a price on it. There have been fears that health authorities are subject to perverse incentives to convert health problems into social problems that then become the responsibility of local authorities. People are shunted from free services to means-tested social care (Higgins *et al.*, 1993). Thus Ong (1992) has commented that the logic of allocation in relation to need follows different paths, making the possibility of unifying a budget across the full spectrum of community care remote.

Reader Activity 13.8
What does the term 'a seamless service' mean in practice?

13.11 Conclusion

This overview of the services delivery and development in the countries of the UK since the Second World War has revealed a mixture of failure and relative success. Searching questions still remain to be asked and addressed. Efforts are being made through the new community-care agenda to create a kind of culture in the service which offers dignity, quality, respect, privacy, autonomy, innovation and choice.

Discussion Questions

1 **How have services for people with a learning disability changed since the Second World War?**

2 **What are the principal differences between services offered to people with a learning disability in the different countries of the UK?**

3 **How realistic is the idea of collaborative working, training in learning disability between the various key players; that is, social services, health, private and the voluntary sector, for example?**

References

Audit Commission (1986) *Making a Reality of Community Care*. London: Audit Commission.

Ayer, S. (1982) *Family Care for Severely Mentally Handicapped School Children*, unpublished PhD thesis, The University of Hull.

Ayer, S. (1984) Community care: failure of professionals to meet family needs. *Child: Care, Health and Development* **10**: 127–140.

Ayer, S. (1994a) *The Culture of Community Care, Programme Bulletin: Developing Managers for Community Care*, NHS Executive, (May).

Ayer, S. (1994b) Training for community care, a joint approach: survey of staff attitudes. *Nursing Research Abstract* **16**(3): 43.

Ayer, S. and Alaszewski, A. (1984) *Community Care and the Mentally Handicapped: Services for mothers and their Mentally Handicapped Children*. London: Croom Helm.

Baker, N. and Urquart, J. (1987) *The Balance of Care for Adults with a Mental Handicap in Scotland*. Edinburgh: ISD Publications.

Baldwin, S. and Carlisle, J. (1994) *Social Support for Disabled Children and their families: A review of the literature*. Edinburgh: HMSO.

Bennet, N. (1992) Quoted in *'David Hunt Announces Re-Launch of All-Wales Mental Handicap Strategy'*, News Release – Information Division. Cardiff: Welsh Office.

Bradshaw, J.R., Piachaud, D. and Weale, J. (1981) The income effect of a disabled child. *Journal of Epidemiology and Community Health* **35**: 123–127.

Briggs Report (1972) *The Report for the Committee on Nursing*. London: HMSO.

Britten, J. (1985) *Putting People First*. Glasgow: the Mental Health Foundation and the Scottish Council for Community and Voluntary organisations.

Cheseldine, S. (1991) Community mental handicap teams. *In:* Fraser, W.I., MacGillivray, R.C. and Green, A.M. (Eds) *Caring for Mentally Handicapped People*, pp. 215–224. London: Butterworth Heinemann.

Curtis Committee (1946) *Report of the Care of Children Committee*. Cmnd 6922, London: HMSO (Curtis Report).

Department of Health for Scotland and Scottish Health Services Council (1958) *Mental Health Legislation, Report by a Committee appointed by then Council*. Edinburgh: HMSO (Chairman: J. Dunlop).

Department of Health for Scotland and Scottish Health Services Council (1961) *Mental Health Services of Local Health Authorities, Report by the Standing Advisory Committee on Local Authority Services*. Edinburgh: HMSO (Chairman: Mrs T.M. Allan).

Department of Health for Scotland (DHS) (1992) *Services for Mental Handicap: Memorandum from the Scottish Home and Health Department and Scottish Education Department*. Edinburgh: HMSO (The Blue Book).

Department of Health and Social Security (DHSS) (1971) *Better Services for the Mentally Handicapped*. London: HMSO.

Department of Health and Social Security (DHSS) (1978) *Day Services for People with a Mental Handicap in Northern Ireland*. Belfast: HMSO.

Department of Health and Social Security (DHSS) (1980) *Mental Handicap: progress, problems and priorities. A review of mental handicap services in England since the 1971 White Paper – 'Better Services for the Mentally Handicapped'*. London: DHSS.

Department of Health and Social Security (DHSS) (1983) *Health Services Development: Care in the Community Joint Finance*. London: HMSO.

Department of Health and Social Security (DHSS) (1985). *Government Response to the Second Report from Social Services Committee 1984–5 session*. London: HMSO.

Department of Health and Social Security (DHSS) (1989) *White Paper: Caring for People*. London: HMSO.

DHSS (1989) *People First: Community Care in Northern Ireland for the 1990s*. Belfast: HMSO.

Glendinning, C. (1983) *Unshared Care: Parents and their disabled children*. London: Routledge and Kegan Paul.

Gough, D., Li, L. and Wroblewska, A. (1993) *Services for Children with a Motor Impairment and their Families in Scotland*. University of Glasgow: Public Health Research Unit.

Griffiths, R. (1988) *Community Care: An agenda for action*. London: HMSO.

Higgins, R., Oldham, C. and Hunter, D.J. (1993) *'Let's Work Together'; Lessons for Collaboration between Health and*

Social Services. Working Paper **7**. Leeds: Nuffield Institute for Health.

Howe Report (1969) *Report of the Committee of Enquiry into Allegations of Ill-treatment of Patients and Other Irregularities at the Ely Hospital.* London: HMSO.

Hunt, D. (1992) *Relaunch of All-Wales Mental Handicap Strategy.* News Release, Information Division. Cardiff: Welsh Office.

Hunter, D.J. and Wistow, G. (1987) *Community Care in Britain: Variations on a theme.* London: King's Fund.

Hunter, D.J. and Wistow, G. (1991) *Elderly People's Integrated Care System (EPICS): An organisation, policy and practice review.* Leeds: Nuffield Institute for Health Service Studies.

Independent Development Council (IDC) (1985) *Living Like Other People.* Belfast: IDC.

Independent Development Council (IDC) for people with Mental Handicap (1981) *Statement of General Principles.* London: IDC.

Jay, P. (1979) *Report of the Committee of Enquiry into Mental Handicap Nursing and Care.* London: HMSO.

Kent Area Health Authority and Kent County Council (1981) *Mental Handicap – A 'single service partnership'.* Kent Area Health Authority and Kent County Council.

Kuhn, T.S. (1970) *The Structure of Scientific Revolutions.* Chicago: University of Chicago Press.

Leedham, I. and Wistow, G. (1992) *Community Care and General Practitioners: Working Paper No 6* Nuffield Inst for Health Studies, University of Leeds.

Lindsay, M., Kohls, M. and Collins, J. (1993) *The Patchwork Quilt: A Study of Respite Care in Scotland.* Edinburgh: Scottish Office.

Meltzer, H., Smyth, M. and Robus, N. (1989) *Disabled Children: Services, transport and education, Report* **6**. London. HMSO.

National Association of Teachers of the Mentally Handicapped (NATMH) (1985) *Towards Tomorrow.* Belfast: NASTMH.

National Audit Office (1987) *Community Care Development: Report to the controller and auditor general.* London: HMSO.

National Development Group (NDG) (1977a) *Day Services for Mentally Handicapped Adults: Pamphlet* **5**. London: HMSO.

National Development Group (NDG) (1977b) *Mentally Handicapped Children – A plan for action.* London: HMSO.

Newcastle City Council and Area Health Authority (Teaching) (1981) *Mentally Handicapped People and Their Families: A blue print for a local service.* Newcastle CC and AHA.

North Western Regional Health Authority (1982) Services for people who are mentally handicapped: A model district service. Unpublished report.

Ong, B.N. (1992) Job sharing. *Health Service Journal* **12 November:** 24–25.

Peters, A. (1978) *A Better Life: Report on services for the mentally handicapped in Scotland.* Edinburgh: Scottish Office (The Peters Report).

Richardson, A. and Higgins, R. (1992) *The Limits of Case Management: Lessons from the Wakefield Case Management Project, Working Paper* **5**. Leeds: Nuffield Institute for Health Services Studies.

Royal Commission on the Law Relating to Mental Illness and Mental Deficiency 1954–1957 (1957) London: HMSO (cmnd 169).

Scottish Home and Health Department and Scottish Education Department (SHHD/SED) (1979) *A Better Life.* Edinburgh: HMSO.

Scottish Office (1992) *Services for the Mentally Handicapped Memorandum from the SHHD and the SED.* Edinburgh: Scottish Office.

Scottish Office (1993) *Scotland's Children – Proposals for child care policy and law.* Edinburgh: HMSO.

Seebohm, G. (1968) *The Seebohm Report.* London: HMSO.

Seed, P. (1988) *Day Care at the Cross-roads.* Tunbridge Wells: D.J. Costello.

Seed, P. (1984) *Which Best Way?* Tunbridge Wells: D.J. Costello.

Shearer, A. (1980) *Handicapped Children in Residential Care – A study of policy failure.* London: Bedford Square Press.

Sheffield Area Health Authority (Teaching) and Sheffield Metropolitan District Council (1981) *Report on Strategic Planning of Services for the Mentally Handicapped.* Sheffield: AHA (Teaching) and Sheffield Metropolitan District Council.

Simon, G.B. (Ed.) (1983) *Local Services for Mentally Handicapped People.* Kidderminster: British Institute of Mental Handicap.

Stalker, K. (1988) *Family Based Respite Care for Children with Severe Learning Difficulties: An Evaluation of the Lothian Scheme.* Report No. 1. Edinburgh: Social Services Research.

University College, Department of Community Medicine (1982) *The Bloomsbury Project Report.* London: UC Department – Community Medicine.

Voysey, M. (1975) *A Constant Burden: The reconstruction's of family life.* London: Routledge and Kegan Paul.

Welsh Office (1983) *The All-Wales Strategy for Mental Handicap.* Cardiff: Welsh Office.

Welsh Office (1992) *The All-Wales Strategy for Mental Handicap: Framework for development from April 1993.* Cardiff: Welsh Office.

Wessex Regional Health Authority (1979) *Review of Health Services Policy for the Mentally Handicapped in Wessex.* Wessex Regional Health Authority.

Wilkin, D. (1979) *Caring for the Mentally Handicapped Child.* London: Croom Helm.

Wright, F.B. (1986) *Left to Care Alone.* Aldershot: Gower.

Young Husband, E., Burchall, D., Davi, R. and Kellmer Pringle, M.L. (1970) *Living with Handicap.* London: National Children's Bureau.

Further Reading

Ayer, S. and Alaszewski, A. (1984) *Community Care and the Mentally Handicapped: Services for Mothers and their Mentally Handicapped Children.* London: Croom Helm.

Department of Health and Social Security (DHSS) (1980) *Mental Handicap: Progress, Problems and Priorities.* London: HMSO.

Department of Health and Social Security (DHSS) (1985) *Government Response to the Second Report from the Social Services Committee 1984–5 Session.* London: HMSO.

Flynn, M. and Hirst, M.A. (1992) *This Year, Next Year Sometime? Learning Disability and Adulthood.* London: National Development Team/SPRU.

Griffiths, R. (1988) *Community Care: An Agenda for Action – a report to the Secretary of State for Social Services.* London: HMSO.

Hirst, M.A., Baldwin, S.M, Glendinning, C., Graham, B and Parker, G.M. (1991) *After 16 – What Next? Services and Benefits for Young Disabled People 8th edition.* York: The Family Fund.

Smith, M., Robinson, P. and Duffy, B. (1992) *The Prevalence of Disability Among Children in Northern Ireland. PPRU, Surveys of Disability Report 2.* Belfast: Policy Planning and Research Unit.

Social Services Inspectorate (1991) *Organisation of Social Services for Children with a Disability.* Cardiff: SS1/Welsh Office.

Stalker, K. (1988) *Family Based Respite Care for Children with Severe Learning Difficulties: An Evaluation of the Lothian Scheme No. 1.* Edinburgh: Social Services Research.

Chapter 14: Mature services: a case history of Sweden
David Lewis and Andrew Ferguson

- ■ FUB aims

- ■ FUB principles

- ■ Activities

14.1 An Introduction to Sweden

History

Sweden has been inhabited since about 8000 BC (Armitage, 1990), its peoples developing to what were known to the rest of Europe as the Vikings.

The Vikings had an organized system of government (Thing), which was an assembly of freemen,

representing the nation (Althing) or a small community (Husthing). Between AD 800 and 1060 they sailed mainly east establishing cities such as Novgorod in the USSR which, until destroyed by Ivan the Terrible in 1570, was the original capital of the Russian state.

In the twelfth century the Swedish people were united with the Goths (Teutonic tribes) and accepted Christianity. From 1397 to 1502 Sweden was part of the Danish Dynasty after which they revolted, Gustavas Vasa being crowned king and establishing Lutheranism as the state religion.

The Vasa line ruled until 1818, when Napoleon Bonaparte established a French Marshal Bernadotte on to the throne as King Karl XIV Johan, and this dynasty is still in power.

Involvement in warfare throughout the sixteenth, seventeenth and eighteenth centuries resulted in a collapse of the Swedish Baltic Empire. This led directly to the adoption of a Parliamentary Constitution (1723) under which the Riksdag came to exercise greater authority than that of the crown.

In 1865 the old four-chamber Riksdag (nobility, clergy, burgher and peasants) was replaced by a parliament of two houses with equal rights. However, franchise qualifications ensured that the first chamber was dominated by wealthy landowners

---

Box 14.1 An introduction to Sweden

● **Status**	Kingdom (constitutional)
● **Area**	449 790 km^2
● **Population**	8.6 million
● **Capital**	Stockholm
● **Other major towns**	Gothenburg (Göteborg), Malmö, Norrköping
● **Chief language**	Swedish
● **Religion**	95% Evangelical Lutheran
● **Currency**	Swedish Krona (SEK)
● **Membership**	The UN, Council of Europe, EFTA, OECD, EU
● **System of government**	349-member chamber (Riksdag) elected by proportional representation

and industrialists and the second by the more affluent farmers.

In the late nineteenth century Sweden was still predominantly agricultural, and had endemic rural poverty. This instigated large-scale emigration to North America.

As industrialization gathered pace, so too did the organized labour movement, emerging as the Social Democratic Labour Party (1889) which united with the Liberal Party in 1900, to pursue full democracy, in opposition to the Conservatives who defended the *status quo* and maintenance of crown prerogative.

In 1907 there was Adult Male Franchise, and proportional representation was introduced for second-chamber elections. The result of this was the Liberals gaining victory in 1911, and a Liberal prime minister (Karl Staaff) being appointed.

1914–1918 saw an economic boom, owing to the demand for industrial products by the German war machine. This selling of goods to Germany resulted in the League of Nations (1921) handing over the Swedish populated Aaland Islands to the newly independent Finland.

Universal adult suffrage was introduced by the 1919 Liberal Government.

During the Second World War Sweden, although neutral once more, once again came under criticism for continuing to trade with Nazi Germany, and for granting 'transit rights' to German forces (up till 1943).

The Social Democrats dominated post-war Swedish politics, governing alone since 1976. During this period legislation was enacted establishing Sweden as the world's most advanced welfare state, while economic progress made it one of the world's most affluent countries.

Sweden was a founder member of the Nordic Council (1953) and the European Free Trade Association (1959). In 1972 they signed an Industrial Free Trade Agreement with the European Community.

Major constitutional reform (fully implemented in 1975) created a Unicameral Riksdag with a 3-year term and reduced the monarch to purely ceremonial functions. Unicameral being a 'one-chamber' parliament, unlike the UK with the House of Lords and House of Commons, and the USA with the House of Representatives and the Senate.

Administration

The country is divided into 24 national regional counties responsible for regional administration and advising the municipalities. Local government is the responsibility of the municipal councils (municipalities) of which there are 286. These councils are vested with broad powers and maintain a wide range of services, including social welfare facilities, schools, libraries, recreational activities, water and power supplies, sewage and waste management. They have a considerable degree of autonomy; however, there is still a need to comply with the requirements and minimum 'norms' laid down in legislation and ordinance by parliaments and central government.

The main source of revenue for the municipalities is the direct local income tax, which all residents have to pay. This is assessed on a fixed rate and is directly proportional to income. The rate is determined by the municipalities, but in 1991–92 it was frozen by parliamentary decision.

The Local Government Act (1992) established county councils, and like their municipal counterparts, these are elected bodies with the power to levy taxation from within their jurisdictional areas, which generally coincide geographically with the areas of the county administrative boards.

Each county council area comprises within its boundaries a number of municipalities and these two levels of local government work in close collaboration. The county councils are responsible for tasks affecting a large population base. Their principal concern is the provision of health and medical care. Other concerns are the national dental service, certain types of care of the disabled and mentally retarded persons, and in certain cases, local public transport.

Terminology

The primary term used in Sweden with reference to people with learning disabilities is that of mental retardation, which is an internationally accepted term, being utilized in the USA and by the United Nations.

However, there appears in Sweden to be moves to adopt more appropriate and less devaluing terms. The Swedish National Society (FUB) uses the term mental handicap within its full title, but still uses mentally retarded in its literature, although the person is 'seen' first rather than the ascribed label.

14.2 Historical Development of Services

As with the UK, care and education commenced in the late 1800s and for many years the developments were extremely slow. Not until the post-war years did a systematic service begin to emerge.

The services initially concentrated on the child, perhaps symbolizing the child as representative of future progress. As with most countries at this time it was only those children deemed 'educable' where investment was made. The more severely retarded continued to wait.

> It would appear that only those with a 'voice' that could be heard were listened to. Bed patients and others unable to make their voices heard had to wait until last. (Grunewald, K., 1974, p. 8)

Denmark was the first of the Scandinavian countries to implement some form of provision for its mentally retarded population, initially building large psychiatric hospitals within the early decades of this century. Sweden opened its first specialist hospital in 1930.

Initially it was down to private individuals and foundations to create institutions and educational establishments, but county councils, followed eventually by the state, gradually assumed the responsi-

bility for mental retardation care. 'Idiot schools' were the initial creation, but when it came to leaving school and returning to community life, this created problems regarding adequate housing provision, and so residential homes were added to the schools. This congregation of retarded individuals unfortunately led to special children's asylums being built. In 1895 there existed in Sweden 19 idiot schools, six boarding homes and eight asylums for children or adults (Grunewald, 1974).

Grunewald (1974) describes the development of Swedish care services as passing through four specific phases:

- The first stage, commencing around 1870, involved the identification of problems encountered by a specific group of individuals and was therefore described as the 'diagnostic stage'.
- The second stage was one of 'specialization' as the specific needs were dealt with by specific solutions. This specificity led to a centralization of services, with a single institution taking responsibility for the county or region in which it was sited. The result of this 'central' theme was the domination of the 'specialists' themselves over the subordinate retarded individual. With 'specialists' only concerned with providing solutions and treatment for the problem area, the holistic needs, especially aspects such as social and emotional aspects, did not feature as a priority.
- The third stage is described as the 'differentiation' stage, where there was a realization that a particular service could not be standardized to meet the needs of all individuals. It was during the 1970s that this stage was predominant and a major feature was that the individuals needs demanded far greater co-ordination from the multidisciplinary agencies, in particular medical, educational and social specialists.
- The fourth stage, and the current one, is characterized by a decentralization of services, creation of integrative services which utilize

the facilities available to all members of the community. Key features of this stage, and essential to its success, are improved training for care staff, greater resource availability, research and development and public education, which would create an accepting open-minded population able to receive with warmth their retarded community members.

One agency responsible for promoting the development of care through certainly the second, third and fourth phases, is the Swedish National Association for Mentally Retarded (FUB) which was originally known as the Swedish National Society for Retarded Children (Riksfvrbundet fvr Utvecklings stvrda Barn) and formed in 1956. Its development and changes are similar to those of Mencap in the UK; however, it has been perceived as one of the most powerful parent pressure groups in Europe, and was able to apply tremendous political pressure with regard to service provision during the post-war years, and is still today a very activist group.

The 1960s

Most other countries, including the UK, were continuing to segregate and thus stigmatize their learning disability population; however, Sweden, along with Denmark, were developing their 'normalization' philosophy, which recognized the human value of the retarded individual, and identified a need to adapt the existing facilities to the needs of the handicapped, rather than the other way around.

This view is reflected in the way in which conscription was applied to the mentally retarded, who were included in the process, albeit only affecting about one-third of the retarded population, but whose roles within the services conscripted into centre mainly around the carrying out of manual work. Where facilities were non-existent in relation to the abilities of individuals, these were judged to be unacceptable and were rejected. This principle, although embryonic in its development, perceived 'integration' as the ultimate aim, despite the difficulties this initially posed.

It was during this decade that there was great emphasis placed on the development of technical aids, special education and training, medical and vocational rehabilitation and organized leisure-time activities. The adaptation programme involved the necessity of reorganizing cities, public and residential buildings, shops, traffic systems, schools and leisure facilities so that they were suitable for use by disabled and retarded people. Even today, special adaptations exist on buses and trains to allow easy access to disabled people.

In 1967, the Swedish National Board of Urban Planning published *Regulations for Access for Disabled to Buildings* (Larsson, 1992). This document made it obligatory for at least one means of approach to public buildings to be designed and constructed so that it can be utilized by the disabled. It also states other necessary adaptations and provisions, such as lifts in school buildings, free provision for educational aids, making available personal assistants and state grants for municipalities.

The 1960s placed considerable emphasis on the need for both specialist and multidisciplinary research, as the services emerging were quite new and untested. Also noted were the inequity of service provision, and the necessity to make available those services already available to the 'more able' retarded person, to those people with more severe and serious disabilities.

The principles still reflected, in part, a medical model with stress being placed upon aspects such as early rehabilitation and prevention, and, as in the past, it was children who seemed to be the major focus. Apparently, Sweden seemed to be planning its services for the future.

The integration of retarded children into mainstream schooling received particular energy at this time. It was hoped to replace the special school with 'special classes' in ordinary schools and technical aids and equipment were made available to facilitate this process. The result of this practice was that numbers in the 'boarding schools' decreased, diminishing the isolationist approach, and many remained within their own home, attending school on a daily basis, or being 'boarded' in town for the weekdays if they happened to come from rural settings.

The Education Act of 1968 saw the implementation of compulsory education for all children, including those deemed 'ineducable' (i.e. with IQs below 40) with this education lasting 10 years as opposed to 9 years for 'normal' children. Upon completion of their schooling there was free retarded 'compulsory' vocational education usually until the age of 21 years, but with some students this was extended until 23 years. Also, to attract teachers within the field of special education, higher salaries were offered than for those teachers teaching normal children, but these specialist teachers were required to undergo specialized studies and training resulting in a specialized certificate. Considerable financial investment was made to ensure integrative opportunities were available for retarded and disabled children, and this was supported by a humanistic stance which involved creating a greater awareness of disability amongst ordinary children.

Anderson (1971) noted a headmaster who commenced the new term for all new children with a special assembly involving all the school. Once this was over the disabled children would leave and this headmaster would give a talk to the remaining pupils regarding the nature of disabilities and retardation. Also, at the end of the first year children were shown films about aspects of disability such as cerebral palsy, the disabled children having been consulted and asked if they would wish to attend, which Anderson notes 'they have always chosen to do' (Anderson, 1971, p. 32). The results of these approaches were that the problem of teasing had not arisen and that greater understanding and acceptance were shown by the normal pupils.

It was apparent that considerable efforts were placed upon development of awareness in ordinary children, which involved a variety of resources and explanations on aids to disabilities, however Anderson (1971) also notes the distinct lack of integration between the handicapped and non-handicapped children despite the greater understanding, but

suggests this was due to administrative mismanagement and the poor planning of class arrangements.

Sterner (1969) recognizes the commitment to the development of services in Sweden during this period. He highlights the fact that taxation in Sweden was high, but public expenditure on the handicapped and their rehabilitation was growing rapidly, with 22% of contributions going directly to these aspects. Although philosophies in the UK at this time were similar, their basis being the Scandinavian model, there was not the same commitment towards financial investment which in Sweden would result during the 1970s in many fine new residential and day-care establishments being established.

With adults the progress was much slower, even with unemployment low in Sweden it was repeatedly documented that 'handicapped persons are among those likely to remain unemployed once they have lost their jobs' (Sterner, 1969, p. 9). Certainly, despite figures showing a reasonably high percentage of handicapped in employment (10% of the work-force), people with 'mental retardation' were under-represented.

It was noted that individuals required not only compensation for their loss of or lack of income, but also for such extra costs and services necessary through their disabilities, for example transport, and therefore the Swedish social security system made provisions for this. Sterner (1969) notes, however, that such stringent eligibility requirements were created and only 1% of the handicapped succeeded in obtaining these provisions. On the surface these improvements seemed to be available, but in reality this was not so clear cut.

Also in the area of care delivery itself, many improvements were highlighted but Sterner (1969) noted that only a proportion of the staff were adequately trained and some institutions, in particular the 'special hospitals' which housed the multiply handicapped and 'other' complications, were below standard. Criticism was offered by Sterner (1969) in other aspects, such as the shortage of integrated community facilities, too little systematic collaboration between various welfare agencies and the families of handicapped, and that there was only meagre pioneering work undertaken with adult education.

Patient care in hospital was free, but in many cases the sponsoring public agency withheld disability pensions in order to cover part of the cost of care, the patient being entitled to some pocket money only. In the case of those patients unable to spend it themselves, this small amount was spent on their behalf to provide extra benefits for them. A similar approach was used in the UK (unfortunately throughout the 1970s), and it reflects a failure to recognize the individuality and autonomy of the retarded person's life style.

It seemed that although many disabled people benefited during this period of growth, for those with 'mental retardation' in the institutions this remained their place of residence despite philosophies addressing 'valued social roles'.

> Some of the most severely handicapped, particularly some of the severely or profoundly mentally retarded, have to live in special hospitals or in other residential institutions for long periods or indefinitely. (Sterner, 1969, p. 23).

The Act of 1968 regarding services for the mentally retarded heralded a new dawning of the reality for care practice change, and a new momentum commenced. Emphasis was placed upon the training and preparation relating to moves from these residencies and institutions, to be relocated in major residential areas and integrated into a more normal community life. It was recognized that the institutions had become segregated 'islands' of retardation, with many housing around 700 people. The new move was to create environments with a maximum of 200 beds, which at the time was seen as a massive improvement.

Reader Activity 14.1
What is the largest population of people with a learning disability that you have encountered in a single facility/service?

The 1970s

This decade saw the fruition of the 'normalization principle', which was applied to the development and handling routine of the retarded individual, to the functions of institutions and to the actual organization of services. The differences in an individual's capacity to adjust to society was seen as purely quantitative, and even the most profoundly affected individual was seen as being able to have some aspects of their life 'normalized'. The term 'normalization' was applied to the 'striving' in various ways towards what was regarded as normal. Its actualities included ensuring that the retarded person was accorded the same rights and obligations as other citizens. However, those people with severe retardation were not going to be forced into society for humanitarian reasons.

Integration was the most important feature as Swedish services moved towards its fourth phase. It was necessary to co-ordinate the services for the mentally retarded with other social services to ensure they received their particular assistance among other people and not in isolation from them. Integration was seen as a means 'towards normalization' and not an end in itself. The major fear being that overdoing the process would result in further isolation with respect to friendships and social contacts.

The purpose of the service was to create an individual who was both harmonious and socially adjusted, able to interact and having been trained and assisted towards emotional maturity despite their retardation. Social adjustment related to having a worthwhile job, and sufficient money which would enable greater freedom and an ability to utilize more fully their leisure time, thus offering greater control over their own daily life.

Integration was explained in three steps (Grunewald, 1977):

- First, 'physical integration', which involved living in smaller units. However, the concept of small at this time was between 40- and 200-

bedded units as opposed to the large numbers found in special hospitals.

- The second step was 'functional integration', which was about the individual utilizing the services within the community.
- The third step was 'social integration' which centred upon interaction with others and being a valued member of a social group.

The 1970s saw a need for a less rigorous care regime, but now under one authority, with the efforts of the private and voluntary sectors acknowledged but subordinate to and co-ordinated with the public sector. Clarke (1984) recognized the existence of the single authority, the Mental Retardation Care Services, who were part of the Swedish Board of Health and Welfare.

Services were seen as needing to be planned on the basis of normal communities. The increasing comprehensive network was seen as comprising of services of equal importance, and it was felt the philosophy reflected the terms 'from without the institution to within', and not 'from within and out towards society' (Grunewald, 1974, p. 24).

It was felt that the specialist services should not be tied to the institutions. Clarke (1984) highlighted that a major difference between Sweden and the UK at the time was that services were based upon a social rather than a medical model, the facilities being much smaller, more numerous, organized and administered upon social lines. 'The social model of care has been developed from the principle of normalisation' (Clarke, 1984, p. 225).

Key features of this service were the small, heterogeneous groups, with individuals having both a personal and sexual identity, far greater privacy, a range of personal possessions and far more opportunity to utilize services and facilities outside of their residential establishment. The individual's legal capacity and self determination were perceived as fundamental rights, and the right to self-expression, participation and acceptance were given high priority and importance. Local and national conferences, in the main organized by the Swedish National Society for Mental Retardation, took place and their main theme was that of self-advocacy.

The development of the smaller residential units was a further innovation. At the time, 37% lived in residential homes, a figure which represents around 11 000 people. Clarke (1984) cites the number of people with mental retardation in the 1970s in Sweden as being approximately 30 000.

This 37% enjoyed the smaller units; however, these could have as many as 200 beds. Figures show approximately 21 units with 100–200 beds at this time (1978), and 104 smaller local residential units, generally of around 40–50 beds. There were only six special hospitals still being utilized, and these catered for around 4–6% of the mentally retarded population, under 1800 in numbers, and these included people requiring 24-hour care, individuals who presented 'antisocial' behaviour and others who were dangerous and difficult to control.

The hospitals functioned on a regional basis, and often acted as the 'core' within the service network, accepting individuals on short-term care when necessary. The total responsibility for the 'patients', legally and financially, lay within the region, and although the opportunity was there to return to the proximity of their own home community, this system was reversible.

The hospitals were not seen as part of the 'way forward'. They were awkwardly situated, often isolated, and were under review as to their continued utilization. The Swedish view at the time was that 'the group home principle is the best approach in integrating the Mentally Handicapped with the community' (Clarke, 1984, p. 226).

An extension of this approach was the purchasing of flats within tower blocks for small family sized groups of three to six people to utilize. The major reason flats were chosen as opposed to houses is that the public response at the time was still far from accepting, the retarded person being viewed as a 'disturbing element' within the environment, affecting property prices and the safety of the locality. The house owner was viewed as far more 'territorial', and more likely to put up opposition to the location of this small group, therefore flats were seen as the best way to create a more accepting public sector.

Those people living in smaller residential units were taught skills which would enable independent community living. The focus was the activities of daily living model (ADL), and although there was a move away from behavioural approaches, the ADL methods consisted of considerable recorded development and teaching similar to those used in behavioural techniques.

Sensitivity was accorded to the fact that these homes could become like small institutions if collective rules appeared, and the privacy and respect of the individual was ignored, and these aspects were addressed with great importance.

The role of the staff was to facilitate this actualization of the small group home approach based on normalization philosophies, and included facilitating leisure activities and social contacts. The training for the 'care assistants', as staff were known, became far more structured and specialist, and consisted of both theoretical and practical skill development throughout the training course, which lasted 2 years. The first year involved a common foundation programme and included other specialisms. The final year specialized in mental retardation.

Once trained, staff tended to work far more as a collective team within residential settings, the manager or director usually being based external to the residential unit. One interesting feature at the time was that despite the emphasis placed upon actualization of rights,

a person of 15 or over can be committed to a residential home or special hospital without his own consent, or that of his parents or guardian.
(Grunewald, 1974, p. 49)

It was not clear at the time who could make this committal, although a court of law could enact this, but the 'rules' surrounding this were similar to those of the UK's Mental Health Act (1959).

Grunewald (1974) recalls the 'decisions committee' who could enforce enrolment to a special school or other establishment at 15 years, and even override the parents' wishes. However, the process involved medical certificates, and psychological, pedagogical (paediatric) and social investigations of each case.

Important improvements at this time included features such as the recognition of being legally competent and the removal of legislation of the general impediments to marriage. Grunewald (1974) sadly notes that laws relating to sterilization still existed and 'since the early 50's, only very few retarded persons have been sterilized – in the last ten years only about 30 persons per year ...' (Grunewald, 1974, p. 56).

The building programme of the 1970s was one of the major features reflecting the more positive side of the development of Swedish care services. Day centres, such as the Sodertarps Day Centre (built in 1977, Malmö) were well resourced, innovative and highly therapeutic. Supported well with specialized agencies, utilizing shared facilities for staff and clients, such as the gymnasium and canteen, and with a ratio that reflected the intention that clients received appropriate contact (25:65 staff/student ratio). The residential units were built with single and double bedrooms (Lindangens, Malmö) and residents enjoyed the use of saunas, showers and modern swimming pools (Pilangen, Malmö, built 1971).

The developments of the 1970s, Grunewald (1974) notes, saw the fourth phase being implemented, with emphasis on decentralization and far greater integration, but, as in the UK, the programme still met with resistance from both the public themselves and the municipalities reluctance to provide fully the funding necessary to implement this programme.

Current Care Services (1980 to the Present)

Background to Normalization Principle in Scandinavia

Bank-Mikkelson, head of Danish services, had the normalization principle included within the

1959 Danish law. Wolfensberger (Clarke, 1984) notes that despite its adoption into Danish mental retardation practices, the principle was not systematically stated and elaborated in literature until 1969, when Bengt Nirje wrote a chapter in English as a contribution to *Changing Patterns in Residential Services for the Mentally Retarded* (Kugel and Wolfensberger, 1969), which was commissioned by the President's Committee on Mental Retardation in the USA. Grunewald (1974) notes that it then had to be translated back into Swedish in order to become the first major written treatise on this topic in the entire Scandinavian literature. (The parallel Danish translation did not appear until 1972.)

Wolfensberger cites Nirje explaining the principle in 1969 as 'making available to the mentally retarded, patterns and conditions of everyday life which are as close as possible to the norms and patterns of the mainstream of society' (Flynn and Nitsch, 1980). Despite the normalization principle not being systematically presented before Nirje did this in 1971, its significance had been noted in earlier legislation affecting provisions and services. The 1968 Swedish Code of Statutes at least alluded to important aspects covered by the principle, and included the provision of homes 'as close to normal as possible'.

Bengt Nirje differed from other exponents of the principle in that he placed primary emphasis on normalization as a means and process, rather than as an end in itself. Nirje saw integration as an important corollary of the normalization principle, and in 1976 he further defined this through six modes; physical, functional, social, personal, societal and organizational.

In 1969 Nirje saw normalization as sharing:

- **a normal rhythm of the day, with privacy, activities and mutual responsibilities**
- **a normal rhythm of the week, with a home to live in, a school or work to go to, leisure time with a modicum of social interaction**
- **a normal rhythm of the year, changing modes and ways of life and of family and community**

customs as experienced in different seasons of the year.

Nirje's work centred not upon normalization of a person, but on the services and life conditions, and was more concerned with the image and representation that people presented, which would be enhanced and improved upon through striving to create a better adjustment to society, and living a life that resembles the lives of other community members.

The developments undertaken during the 1970s continued to strive towards implementation of the normalization principles. However, the rapid building programme of the 1970s slowed down as a realization hit home that even the 40–50-bedded units were too large and still reflected an 'abnormal' style of daily living.

In order to illustrate the existing services the author has considered them in six different ways:

- **legal developments/current legislation**
- **education services**
- **vocational opportunities**
- **culture and leisure**
- **housing and social welfare**
- **personal perspectives.**

14.3 Legal Developments/Current Legislation

Sweden in post-war years experienced exceptionally good economic growth and this, coupled with a relatively small population, enabled a number of radical social reforms to be implemented. These reforms enacted into law have either directly or indirectly affected the disabled members of Swedish society.

Sweden has a strong central government administration combined with an extensive local government network. In order for services to be developed appropriately at local level, the government applied a process of decentralization in relation to the decision-making bodies, in order to reduce the gap between the general populace and their elected representatives.

Taxes are levied at local level through the municipalities and county councils, which in the main are redistributed locally to service providers, the figure being approximately 70%. In Sweden the majority of service providers are run and controlled by the local government agencies. One main reason behind this is historically based; social welfare and medical care has been 'public care' since the sixteenth century.

Charitable organizations with social objectives are therefore less developed with regards to the provision of service, but they created an influential role in relation to this provision. An example of this is the political lobbying undertaken by the Swedish National Society for Mentally Handicapped (FUB). A characteristic of the Swedish people, which can be traced back for 100 years, and is that of the tradition of popular movements. There is a strong disabled movement with approximately 460 000 members (Swedish Institute, 1994), who at national level have about 40 associations representing a variety of disability groups. The majority of these are co-ordinated by the National Society for Associations of the Disabled, which has county committees in all of the 24 counties and local committees within many of the municipalities. This representation adds considerable pressure to ensure the services developed by local government are both appropriate and user led.

In connection with the International Year of the Disabled in 1981, a Swedish action programme was created to address issues surrounding disability. This response was presented to the Swedish Parliament in 1983, and the National Council for the Disabled implemented a follow-up study to determine the effectiveness of the programme. Politically, the Swedish goal for the disabled is that they should be part of the community and live like others. The opportunities should be there to ensure an adequate income, comfortable home, to be mobile and to be usefully employed, enjoying free time to the fullest also.

To promote this goal, handicap is defined as a 'problem in the interface between individuals and the environment they find themselves in, not as a characteristic of the individuals themselves' (Swedish Institute, January 1994). It is the intention of Swedish policy to avoid 'special solutions' for the disabled and, instead, to make community life accessible to all.

The Social Services Act (1982) ensures regulation of the local authorities' responsibilities, and emphasizes the need for disabled people to live in a way which corresponds to their needs, and to have an active role in society. The local authorities are obliged to ensure that assistance is offered and readily available.

This was further supported by the Special Services for Intellectually Handicapped Persons Act (1986) which also addressed the principles governing the care and services for the mentally retarded, in particular the integration and normalization of services. This Act recognizes the entitlement of specialist services, including support and assistance, in order to facilitate normal daily living. The Act's primary ideology was that services should be tailored towards the needs of the individual, be accessible, and that decisions should involve both the client and their family.

The person with mental retardation is entitled to social services, administered by the municipal authorities, which includes financial assistance, transport services, home-help services and preschool and leisure centre placements. They are entitled to the health and medical care on the same terms as the rest of the population and additional special health-care services in relation to their impairments.

The Act also continued the phasing out programme of institutional care, in particular the special hospitals and larger residential units, and admissions were ceased (except for extraordinary reasons).

However, despite the rapid building programme which occurred after the 1986 Act, there are still approximately 30% of the mentally retarded population awaiting appropriate placement in group homes. In 1989, a Commission on Policies for the Disabled was established, its remit to include general measures to give people with functional impairments parity of status with other community members, and individual measures to improve personal capabilities and achieve greater independence. In its final report of 1992, the Commission recommended a number of additions to existing legislation as well as entirely new enactments affecting persons with functional impairments.

The report noted

considerable inequalities of welfare between the disabled and others, and also between different categories of disabled persons, between different parts of the country, between different input fields and so on. (Larsson, 1992, p. 5)

This disparity in service availability was addressed by the Commission, attempts being made to devise measures for reducing these inequalities.

Perhaps the most interesting philosophy utilized by the committee is one of self-determination and influence, echoing the popular movement system so prevalent in Sweden. The thinking, however, is double-edged; first, empowering the individual through self-determination (an example of this is the personal assistance scheme discussed later); and second, through joint responsibility:

Every sector of society must assume its share of responsibility for enabling persons with functional impairments to participate in sectorial services on a basis of parity with others. (Larsson, 1992, p. 6)

It can be seen that the process of integration is firmly reiterated in that recognition is given to the valued role of the disabled person and emphasis is placed upon ensuring adequate service provision to support the self-determination of the individual.

The Commission recognized that in order to reduce inequalities, the municipalities (local authorities) should be legally required to assert in all their activities the parity of the disabled, a report of this being included in their annual reports. The Commis-

sion also reiterated the 1967 publication *Regulations for Access for Disabled to Buildings* from the Swedish National Board of Urban Planning (Larsson, 1992), in recommending that environments and activities should be designed and conducted so as to make them accessible to everyone.

Recommendation was made to include within the Swedish constitution a ban on discrimination, by law or statutory instrument, on the grounds of functional impairment, and the inclusion of a Bill of Rights to supplement existing legislation. As a response, an Act was passed in 1993, the Support and Services for Persons with Certain Functional Impairments and the Assistance Benefit Act, which identified measures to be implemented with regard to special support and special service, and which would promote equality in living conditions and full participation in community life for people with disabilities.

The major features of this legislation include:

- Advice and personal support entitlement from someone with expertise and experience of the problems of living with someone with severe disabilities, and includes a number of specialist professionals.
- Personal assistance or financial support, in order to maximize daily activities and facilitate pursuance of a career or area of study.
- Escort service, for people not entitled to the personal assistants, but who need support in going out.
- A contact person who can act as a friend, provide advice on everyday situations, help participation in leisure activities and help to reduce loneliness and isolation.
- Relief service in the home, providing respite periods for parents in particular.
- Short-term stays away from the home.
- Short-term minding (supervision) for school-children over 12 years outside their own home.
- Special arrangements for children living away from the parental home, to include fostering and boarding.

- Residential arrangements and adaptations for adults.
- Daily activities for adults who have no gainful employment nor are doing any training.

On initial viewing this Act seems to encourage personal freedom and growth. However:

Organizations for the handicapped have both expectations and misgivings regarding the new Act and the reforms which are being introduced at the same time. Many members hope that the entitlement support and services will mean a more normal and worthwhile life for them and their relations. But the Act comes at a time of cutbacks. Just when people with severe functional impairments have been given new legal rights, many community services have become more expensive (Sjoberg, 1994, p. 5)

It is clear from the concerns expressed by professionals and organizations that meeting the legal requirements is going to be a problem, and when cutbacks are required it is generally those with disabilities who suffer more than others.

The earlier inequalities highlighted by the Commission (Larsson, 1992) suggest that the awareness and knowledge of the different municipalities would mean that interpretation of the legal requirements would be varied and at times insufficient. It is estimated (Swedish Institute, 1994) that some 100 000 people with lasting long-term support requirements are entitled to some kind of assistance and provision in relation to this Act.

Swedish law regarding people with mental retardation is particularly powerful when compared to British law. The bill of rights within the Functional Impairments Act (1994) is especially dominant in ensuring the status of people with disabilities. It is important to ensure that the ideals ensuring parity of status are rigorously enforced, and that the process of actualizing the ideals takes place.

Unfortunately, as with any area of interest, other parties will seek to utilize methods in overcoming statute if sufficiently motivated. Money is still the over-riding feature of Western culture, and this means that the disabled are often victimized due to their low or non-existent returns that investment would yield, despite morally and justly being entitled to financial support and costly services. To this end, as with other non-productive societal members, budget holders tend to deprioritize expenditure in these areas. This leads to ideals, once indoctrinated into law, becoming useless. The personal assistance scheme, for example, is reported by Lindelhof (Sjoberg, 1994) to have run out of funds after only 6 months.

It is possible that to implement the services laid down by legislation would be costlier for the municipalities (local authorities) than to pay the fines acquired through their non-implementation. This may account for a continued disparity in service provision.

In conclusion, it is important to note that with any new legislation the process of enactment and implementation requires time for the change to take effect, and the impact of this legislation has only recently been felt.

14.4 Education Services

Responsibility

On 1st July 1991, the National Board of Education was replaced by the National Agency for Education (Skolverket), a smaller authority, which included a field organization.

The responsibility, following legislation in 1991, for the application of national curriculum, was transferred to the municipalities (local authorities) who ensure that activities materialize. The 24 county education committees were abolished; however, despite this decentralization, the municipal local committees still have to maintain their uniformity and ensure that equivalent standards are upheld all over the country.

At the same time the National Swedish Agency for Special Education (SIH) was established in order to aid municipalities in making schooling more readily accessible to all. The appointment of consultants guarantees the availability of expertise to the school authorities, school management, teachers, pupils and parents. Resource centres enable practical help for problems related to all aspects of disability, and there is also the development of remedial teaching material at these centres. There are consultants now in nearly every county, and SIH resource centres in Stockholm, Örebro, Göteberg and Umee.

Compulsory Schooling

Schooling for young people in Sweden is for 9 years, between the ages of 7 and 16 years, although following legislation in 1968 an extra year of schooling, totalling 10, was made available to young, intellectually handicapped children.

The compulsory school systems incorporate basic school, Lapp Nomad school, special schools for children with sensory impairment and special schools for the intellectually handicapped.

Schooling after the age of 16 years is generally extended for a further 4 years, and in exceptional cases for the mentally retarded, up until age 23 years. This period of education is called voluntary schooling. The voluntary school system includes upper secondary school, upper secondary school for the mentally disabled, municipal adult education, the national school for adults, and adult education for the mentally disabled.

Skolverket (National Agency for Education, 1994) highlights the major aim of schooling as laid down in the Education Act, as giving knowledge and skills, and in partnership with the home, promoting a balanced development towards becoming a responsible member of society.

In 1994, a new national curriculum was developed for all compulsory schooling, which came into effect in July 1995. This replaced the 1980 curriculum for basic school and the 1980 curriculum for special education for the mentally disabled. On July 1st 1996, the municipalities adopted the complete responsibility for all education (including adults) relating to the intellectually handicapped. All public

sector schooling is free of charge, nor as a rule do pupils or their parents incur any expenditure, for example, on teaching material, school meals, health care and school transport (National Agency for Education (Skolverket), 1994).

It is apparent that there is great emphasis being placed upon the education of all young people in Sweden and both financial and time investment in the processes and resources which will benefit the country's future.

Reader Activity 14.2
What part of your educational needs were covered free of charge? Did you have to provide your own exercise or textbooks? Did the same apply to your parents?

1994 Curriculum

It is the responsibility of each municipality to develop an educational plan. This plan defines the scope within which the head teacher, teachers and pupils of the school adapt the syllabus and curriculum to local conditions.

There is a time schedule that guarantees the duration of teacher-supervised instruction for pupils in the various subject areas. The subject areas are similar to those on the National Curriculum in the UK, but both Swedish and English are compulsory languages, and the curriculum includes 470 hours for pupil options.

The total hours of teacher contact are 6665 hours of which 1490 hours are devoted to Swedish studies.

Curriculum for the Mentally Disabled

The Swedish Ministry of Education determines the overall goals and guidelines for school activity, the municipalities being responsible for the implementation processes.

The 1994 Curriculum for Compulsory School has stated the goals, which in accordance with their own individual circumstances, mentally disabled students should achieve upon completion of their schooling.

The school is responsible for ensuring that all pupils leaving the compulsory school for the mentally disabled:

- Have increased their awareness of their own circumstances.
- Be able to, in accordance with individual ability, listen, read and communicate.
- Have developed such skills in mathematics that they can solve problems in everyday life.
- Know about and have a basic understanding of the world around them, and as far as possible gain insight into the knowledge areas and general perspectives of the compulsory school.
- Have improved their ability to search for knowledge and know where they can get help to do this.
- Have increased knowledge within one or more subject areas that develops them as individuals and may enrich their leisure time.
- Can understand and use simple words and expressions in English.
- Have developed their ability to express themselves creatively and have become more interested in participating in the range of cultural activities society has to offer.
- Know the fundamental principles for good health.
- Have improved their ability to compensate for the effects of their handicap in daily life.

The school is responsible for ensuring that all pupils leaving training school for the mentally disabled have developed their ability:

- to interact socially
- to communicate by means of language, symbols, signs or signals
- to handle time, space, quality, quantity and causality in the world around them
- to get to know their bodies and their locomotive power
- to be physically active for health and well being
- to be curious and take initiatives

- to react to their own feelings and be receptive to impressions
- to use different ways of expressing their experiences and also when expressing themselves creatively
- to participate in and try to take responsibility for the recurring activities of their daily life
- to use skills and be aware of rules that make it easier to function in daily life
- to understand themselves as individuals and have an understanding of others
- to actively interest themselves in areas that can enrich them as individuals in and outside of school. (Hultinger, 1994, p. 13)

These goals and objectives reflect a very positive attitude towards the person with a mental retardation, and although they seem fanciful, they represent ideologies to be strived for in a positive sense, although one must ask questions related to whether these aims incorporate all children with mental disabilities or whether they are aimed at the more able and only slightly retarded child.

Reader Activity 14.3
Reflect on your own experiences of striving for an ideal outcome? How often have you achieved it?

Schooling for the Mentally Retarded

Children unable to attend regular compulsory basic school and upper secondary school because of their intellectual handicap have three major options available to them:

- The compulsory basic schools for mentally disabled offer a schooling similar to that of the compulsory basic school except there is a 10th year of schooling available. The subjects taught are the same, as this school takes pupils with only a slight retardation.
- The second option is that of the training school (Soderskola) which takes pupils whose

disabilities prevent them from assimilating instruction in the same way as normal or slightly retarded children. The Sdrskola system concentrates on social training and practical skills, still relating them to curricular areas, the content and scope of the subjects being adapted to each pupil's aptitudes, resulting in every child receiving an individual teaching plan. As from July 1st 1995, Sdrskola has had to follow the new curriculum legislation. However, its intentions are to facilitate good holistic development through a syllabus with five main teaching areas: communication and social interaction; motor skills; perception of reality and knowledge of the surrounding world; everyday activities; and creative activities. The curriculum is integrated into these five main areas.

- The third option is voluntary, in that it is outside of the Swedish period of compulsory education. This takes place in the upper secondary school for the mentally disabled. Here students are offered a programme which centres upon vocational development, the same emphasis as the upper secondary school for normal students. The course, run for 3600 hours, offers a range of core areas, coupled with areas of specialism. The course includes placements in work settings and vocational preparation.

Adult Education

The curriculum for non-compulsory schooling, which includes the upper secondary schooling system and the adult educational network, also came into being in 1994 and replaced the 1970 curriculum for upper secondary school, 1982 curriculum for adult education and the 1973 curriculum for the school for the disabled. Once again the state determines the overall goals and guidelines with the municipalities being responsible for their implementation.

Adult education was intended to bridge the education gaps and in doing so increase equality and social justice. It aimed to enhance the individual's ability to participate in a full social, political and cultural life style and contribute to the development of a democratic society. It intended to focus upon a range of work tasks, making the individual adaptable and able to access full employment. It was hoped it would be able to supplement their upper secondary school education, and satisfy the individual's desires for broader study and education opportunities.

Hjorth (1994) points out that the head teacher has a responsibility to ensure that the education is offered in a way that enables the individual to access courses in their own time, either part-time or full-time, and that the level of entry could suit their ability, especially where the individual has missed out on opportunities earlier in their life.

The most common type of supplementary education school available to adults is the Sarvux school. It has the same curriculum as the upper secondary schools but with a specially adapted syllabus and time schedules. Its task is to supplement previous education according to the student's previous studies, experience and aptitudes, and is able to confer qualifications both in individual subjects and in the equivalent of compulsory schools and non-compulsory schools for the mentally disabled.

These services constitute a well-organized but differential educational system which, although adopting an integrative philosophy, is almost realistic in relation to the realities of learning potential and capability found in many people with mental retardation.

Vocational Opportunities

'Work for all' has been the aim for many years of the Swedish employment policies; however, for the functionally disabled, and in particular the mentally retarded this is not yet a reality. Some of the background to unemployment in Sweden can be seen in

Box 14.2 Background to unemployment in Sweden

Swedish unemployment was low in the 1970s and 1980s, and has risen steeply through the recession period, trebling in number, and in June 1993 unemployment was at 10% (G. Lardsson in Swedish National Labour Market Administration, 1994a). This high number of unemployed is likely to affect the resources and funding available to develop services for the disabled. However, in 1992 Sweden gave priority to employment training measures for young persons and the disabled, and the positive approaches adopted have resulted in their long-term unemployment figures being comparatively lower than other European countries. A large proportion of the labour market policy funding goes towards active rather than passive measures.

Box 14.2. Despite considerable state support and enthusiasm, much of it directed towards obtaining meaningful employment for the disabled, a great many individuals face lengthy periods of unemployment or sheltered activities.

Perhaps a drawback to the employability of disabled people is the requirement identified within the Work Environment Act prescribing adaptations to the physical environment and work organization so that it suits the needs of the disabled employee.

However, one major cause as to the present situation is the recession, which has affected much of western Europe, and its subsequent effect upon unemployment in Sweden.

Never before in modern times have so many jobseekers been registered with our employment offices . . . Competition for an insufficient number of jobs has stiffened considerably, which means greater difficulties for disadvantaged groups in the employment sector, for example for young persons looking for their first job, for the disabled and for non-Nordic citizens. (Swedish National Labour Market Administration, 1994a, p. 1)

The county labour boards bear overall responsibility for Labour Market policy in each county, totalling 24 boards in Sweden. The executive head of each is a county labour director who manages the organizations at local level. These are employment offices (AF), the employability institutes (AMIs) and the working life services (ALT). There is representation from each of these on the local employment advisory board. These bodies are responsible for the distribution of resources allocated to the county between the various areas of activity, defining local targets and planning the necessary action.

The employability institutes (AMIs) provide support for functionally disabled job seekers and others who need particular help in finding, obtaining and retaining employment. The activities are mainly vocational preparation and intensified guidance. There are about 100 in Sweden and with the employment offices (AF) and the working life services (ALT) they constitute the 'field organization' of the labour market administration.

The internal organization of the institutes varies according to their size, activities and local needs. Each institute has professionals on hand, such as psychologists, to assist in their functioning. Only about one-third cater for people with intellectual handicaps, having specialist resources to assist with the role.

The AMIs engage in close co-operation with the public authorities in order to ensure there are effective medical and social support measures. One subgroup of the AMIs are the employability institutes for the intellectually handicapped (AMIs-1A) who channel people with mental retardation into working life. Their perceptions of the client group highlight the difference: 'characterised limitations in ability to think abstractly, take an overall view and to solve problems' (Swedish National Labour Market Administration, 1994c). They also add 'the handicap may be hard to identify and is often successfully concealed by the job applicant' (Swedish National Labour Market Administration, 1994c). The result of these characteristic features is that the mentally retarded will have difficulties in obtaining and holding down employment.

Their job applicants come mainly from the employment services, but direct applicants also come from rehabilitation clinics in the health service, direct from schools, or even from social insurance offices. The main aim is to help the applicant perceive their own resource limitations and opportunities within the work market, through regular discussion, placements in employment and assessments undertaken by specialists which focus upon the individual's career potential. Occasionally, work is undertaken outside in employment settings, assisting induction and discussing problems with managers and even other employees.

It is possible for employers to purchase rehabilitation services via the working life services (ALT) whose main role is to assist those people currently in a job to be able to retain it, through assessment and discussion regarding possible alternatives to their present role at work.

Employers are able to gain financial contributions from the state to support the employment of disabled people. This is available where adaptations are necessary, and also where employees are taken on at full rates of pay.

However, the numbers of mentally retarded people in open employment are small, and many disabled people face long periods of unemployment. One successful initiative developed to combat this was the formation of an organization that undertook responsibility for all sheltered employment. Initially state run, Samhall AB is now a limited company, whose role is to develop meaningful work and skills in disabled people. It is run as a business, acquiring finance through the sale of goods and also through a state remuneration which is set annually by Parliament (Riksdag). Although successful, this organization caters for clients other than the mentally retarded, though nearly half of its 28 000 clients were either intellectually handicapped, mentally ill, or persons with more than one disability, exact figures being unavailable.

Box 14.3 Adults in daily occupations in Sweden (from Zetzell et al., 1994, with permission)		
Activity	Numbers	Percentage
School	319	1.4
Day-time activity	17 204	77.4
Regular work	507	2.3
Sheltered work	794	3.6
Other activity	471	2.1
No activity/or less than 15 h a week	2938	13.2
Total	22 233	100.0

The figures in Box 14.3 perhaps offer a clearer picture of the distribution of adults with regard to daily occupation. There are over three-quarters in day-time activities, which are usually the municipal day centres, where the activities are mainly educational, although some paid work is available. Of the large percentage of people without any form of employment, many are elderly; however, a large proportion are young people between the ages of 21 and 24 years, who have even been offered early retirement pensions when they are young.

The labour market policy programmes have seen an increase in the number of disabled persons admitted to them, testifying to the impact of distributive prioritizations. The concrete targets set by the government for work with the disabled have been achieved, but the person with an intellectual handicap still finds themselves both resigned to long-term placement in the day centres and under represented on the AMs advisory council (Council for Employment Offices).

In principle the approach to vocational provision is without fault, especially over aspects such as wages, employment benefits and the working environment, but the reality can be seen as quite different. Finding jobs in a recession is difficult for any individual, but the extra problems presented by immigrants along with the retarded have seen them placed as a priority by employment offices (AF).

Where supported work settings exist, Pedlor (1990) notes that the retarded tended to fare badly when competing with individuals who have varying disabilities or debilitating conditions, particularly where industrial work was involved. The result was that the 'pecking order' that invariably developed placed the retarded person in the lowest position and this in turn resulted in them undertaking the most menial of tasks, giving them little real preparation for gaining real employment in an open market.

Even if fortunate enough to acquire a job in the open market, the technological advances so rapidly occurring these days tended to leave the retarded person 'standing', unable to progress alongside other workers. To compensate, innovative schemes, in particular enclaves, have been established to create meaningful images of employment to all concerned, which although 'sheltered', have a strong emphasis on work-skill development and self-sufficiency.

These small schemes are a result of the reluctance of Swedish service provision to return to the creation of a service within a community which Ericsson and colleagues (1992) note failed to integrate with that community. Ericsson further notes that day-centre buildings would fail to comply with the development of services which facilitated community integration, instead they would merely provide activities which promoted community participation whilst being perceived by that community as different.

Day centres still exist, such as the Sodertorps Centre in Malmö, but these cater primarily for the more severely disabled, following the 1994 reorganization of day care services.

14.5 Culture and Leisure

1974 saw a Parliamentary resolution passed in the Riksdag which stated

> . . . the functionally handicapped should have the same access as others to the range of cultural activities on offer. (Swedish Institute, January 1994)

yet the Swedish Institute (1994) also point out that cultural life is barely accessible to the disabled, and by this they mean aspects such as mass media, literature, educational material, access to cultural institutions and recreational arrangements.

There have been improvements in the co-operation between study organizations and various organizations for disabled people. This has enhanced opportunities for disabled people to engage in cultural and leisure activities. Government grants are making the developments far more of a reality.

This inability to utilize the opportunities is perceived as an anomaly in that Sweden offers ample opportunities on the whole due to a large range of leisure facilities coupled with extensive natural areas, many of which are close to the major towns and cities.

The state does finance considerable literature, on both tape and in Braille, which through the Swedish Library of Talking Books and Braille (TPB) is distributed to all the libraries throughout the country. These libraries also provide sign language video programmes. Swedish Television broadcasts the news in sign language, and the state produces literature in an easy to read form for the mentally retarded. One large-scale project being undertaken is the creation of an electronic version of the *Swedish National Encyclopaedia*.

So it would seem that, despite a philosophy which advocates freedom to utilize one's own leisure time, the social life of the person with mental retardation still seems to focus around opportunities organized by organizations such as the Swedish National Society for Persons with a Mental Handicap (FUB), who run along similar lines to the National Federation of Gateway Clubs in Britain. Yet Dybwad (1978) points out that this is insufficient, particularly for those who are severely retarded, multiply handicapped or living in rural areas.

One important cultural difference between Sweden and the UK, with regards to social life in the evenings, is that the familiar 'public house' found all over Britain, is not so familiar as part of Sweden's evening activities. Drinking alcohol in Sweden usually accompanies a meal or is undertaken within one's home, as the supermarket is a much cheaper option to a drink purchased in a bar.

Leisure activities are similar to those enjoyed throughout much of the western world. TV has a prominent role, as does enjoyment of music and dancing.

Unfortunately, as with most countries, people with mental retardation congregate together for most social functions, perhaps because it is safer and there is little chance of rejection, and maybe also

> Because in the FUB you make friends and you feel a sense of belonging. You gather at meetings, parties and at dances. You have fun together. (Arvidsson, 1994, p. 3)

The FUB is responsible for establishing a huge number of clubs which provide a range of activities throughout the entire week. This powerful organization is very influential within service development, but there is a danger of it serving to perpetuate the 'difference' in its control over the lives of so many people with mental retardation. Although it encourages self-advocacy through meetings and conferences, one is hardly likely to criticize the one providing the opportunity to speak out; does one bite the hand that feeds it?

An example of this control could be the arrangement of holidays away, which are organized more often in the autumn during a time when normal society is engaged in work. The retarded persons themselves would prefer to go away in the summer, but as of yet this aspect has not been addressed.

The Work of the FUB

The role of the FUB might be compared to that of Mencap in the UK, who also have a recreational responsibility. They play a major part in the provision of leisure activities through their clubs, which create programmes that offer a wide and varied range of opportunities. Volunteers are encouraged to assist, especially the young people, in the clubs' evening activities. This is one way of raising public awareness of disability, which is another role undertaken by the FUB who publish many informative leaflets and documents offering the unknowing citizen insight into the nature of mental retardation.

One such document *When You Meet Mentally Handicapped Persons* (Swedish National Society for Persons with a Mental Handicap, 1994e) explains the varying degrees of handicap, provides facts and statistics relating to recent legislation, and highlights the personhood of the handicapped individual, emphasizing the need to recognize the

The FUB-sign

The two circles that you see on the cover of Steget is the sign of FUB.

As you can see the inner circle is marked by a small cut. The two circles are all of us human beings. The outer circle represents all of those who are not handicapped. The inner circle with the cut is those who are mentally retarded. The small cut shows that they find it more difficult in society. But, as you can see, there is not much difference.

Figure 14.1 The FUB symbol.

difficulties that people with handicaps have in their everyday social interaction.

The FUB Symbol (Figure 14.1)

Their symbol is two red circles, an outer complete one and an inner one with a slight cut. The whole circle represents non-handicapped persons, and the inner circle represents the mentally handicapped, its intention to indicate that they find it more difficult to cope, but emphasize 'there is not much of a difference'. It might be said that it does not emphasize enough of the similarities, serving only to strengthen the image of differentness. There is a danger in representing the difference through such a clear distinction of dissimilarity, especially through disproportionate-sized circles.

FUB Aims

The overall aims are organized on two levels: the human viewpoint and the social viewpoint.

The human viewpoint emphasizes:

All human beings should be regarded as equal, independently of talent. Therefore, all human beings should be met with the same respect and consideration – every human being has the right to make his own decisions and to lead his life accordingly. (The Swedish National Society for Persons with Mental Handicap, 1994, p. 4)

The interesting slant on this is that the philosophies are not written from a 'retarded perspective' but serve to remind everyone of the rights ascribed to all human beings.

The social viewpoint emphasizes:

All human beings should be regarded as equal independently of talent. Therefore, every mentally handicapped person should have the same rights and obligations as everyone else. Every mentally handicapped person should be given the care and support he/she is in need of without extra charges. Every mentally handicapped person has the right to

be an active member of society on his own terms. We also wish to accomplish this on an International level. (The Swedish National Society for Persons with Mental Handicap, 1994c, p. 4).

Once again this points to the right to have services available, to enhance the individual's life style, and it stresses the responsibilities of society to effect this pro-rights enactment.

FUB Principles

The FUB identifies a number of care features which it considers important. Their basis can be found in the Principles of Normalization stated and updated by Wolfensberger in 1972, Nirje in 1969, and Bank-Mikkelson in 1959, and are articulated as:

The FUB wants:

- All mentally handicapped children to grow up in a safe and loving environment, where the family is given all the support and help it needs.
- Every mentally handicapped person to lead as normal a life as possible.
- All mentally handicapped persons to have
    - their own places to live in and a high standard of living
    - access to services and care, which is individually adjusted
    - a good education
    - work or meaningful day-time activities
    - leisure-time activities
    - access to culture and information
    - the support they need to become active members of society.
- All those working with mentally handicapped people to have a qualified vocational training.

(The Swedish National Society for Persons with Mental Handicap, 1994c, p. 5)

These statements reflect the development of Swedish services in post-war years and encompass philosophies found in normalization theories. Yet their inclusion in recent documents seems to suggest that there is still a struggle to achieve services which adequately meet the user's needs, and that the FUB is still advocating on behalf of this realization.

Reader Activity 14.4
Do you hold a vocational qualification? Do you believe that you should?

To summarize the FUB, they are campaigners for the rights of the mentally retarded, influencing politicians to ensure the interests of the mentally retarded are high on the political agendas of Parliament, local authorities (municipalities), county councils and the executive authorities.

The FUB provides information, supports the mentally retarded through advocacy groups and by pursuing research through an offshoot of the FUB, the ALA Research Foundation. In a more direct role they arrange activities for their members such as youth and camp activities, parent counselling, courses and conferences.

They publish two news magazines: *FUB-Kontakt* for a wider audience and *Steget* (the Step), which is written in simple Swedish, for readership by the mentally retarded.

The FUB encourages membership from both handicapped and non-handicapped people, and is one of the most influential organizations in the field of disability.

Activities

It would appear that the role, originally undertaken in the 1970s by sociotherapists, which involved co-ordinating leisure activities for the mentally retarded, has left its legacy in that independent utilization of leisure facilities still seems limited, despite the integrative philosophy prevalent in most documentation. The individual still relies heavily upon preordained leisure activities provided for them. There is access to all the facilities enjoyed by normal community members, but there is a tendency for them to be utilized in a collective fashion.

It is difficult to ascertain why, in the area of leisure, there has not been giant leaps, especially with all care based upon a social model, but perhaps the original intentions of Swedish services, which concentrated on the development of appropriate day care, higher standards of daily living and housing, and educational changes, has meant this aspect not becoming a major priority.

One major concern, earlier highlighted by Dybwad (1978) is the needs of the more profoundly handicapped. The ideologies seem to avoid definitive statements relating to this particular group's needs, tending to concentrate mainly on principles that are generalized and non-specific, resulting in a vague, rather than clear, picture of service provision in this area. The FUB are evolving in a similar way to other strong parental groups in Europe, and are likely to eventually join service providers through establishing residential units, along with the many other beneficial services currently provided. One hopes that this will not inhibit the independent thoughts and decisions of the very group that they were originally formed to encourage.

14.6 Housing and Social Welfare

By 1978, most retarded children and adolescents and approximately 25% of adults with mental retardation (Dybwad, 1978) lived with their parents or in the family home. A very small minority of children and less than 33% of adults remained in the larger residential units (Dybwad, 1978). Most of these residential units had less than 75 beds, the smaller group approach being implemented, with the ideal being a group home for three to six people.

In 1992, the National Board of Health and Welfare instructed the municipalities to assist in providing specially adapted housing:

> Only in exceptional circumstances should a disabled person have to live in an institution. (National Board of Health and Welfare, 1992a, p. 33)

There are still institutions in operation, and the social policy continues in its efforts to close them finally and implement small group home residences for all. 1992 figures (Box 14.4) do not identify the exact percentage still living in hospital residence, preferring to couple it with the numbers living in residential units, which can be anything from 20- to 200-bedded establishments. However, these figures do show a large proportion still living in larger units, and this shows the government legislation regarding housing provision is still not an actualization, this affecting the overall philosophy of care.

Another significant percentile figure of concern is that of the high numbers of adults still living in the parental home. These two figures combined represent over one-third of the adult mentally retarded population are still not enjoying an independent life style in keeping with the ideologies of care.

Zetzell *et al.* (1994) highlight the objective as being for all mentally retarded to be able to live as others do. This is perceived as children living with their parents and adults moving to homes of their own. Where this is not possible, there is legislation to ensure the person is accommodated either in family homes for children and young people that are not their own but private, student or communal accommodation that is homely, or group dwellings for adults that may involve common living areas but should have private apartments.

Although the figures in Box 14.4 reflect perhaps some concern for the numbers still waiting for suitable accommodation, the progress over recent years has been significant, 90 residential units being closed in the last 10–15 years (Zetzell *et al.*, 1994). In 1979, only 11% lived in communal units compared to a figure of 44% in 1992.

The major characteristics of the group home is that they are located within communities and furnished to a high standard, and they are not part of a community network of care (i.e. combined with elderly homes or homes for the mentally ill).

Many of those living in residential homes are elderly and on humanitarian grounds are not

Box 14.4 Adults aged 21 and over (accommodation available in 1992) (from Zetzell *et al.*, 1994, with permission)

Type of accommodation	Numbers	Percentage
Parental home	4106	18.5
Other family home	355	1.6
Own home	3562	16.0
Group dwellings	9852	44.3
Student home	314	1.4
Residential home, special hospital	3610	16.2
Other accommodation	434	2.0
Total	22 233	100.0

pushed into independent life. However, it is estimated that by the end of 1998 there will only be 800 people still living in residential homes.

The 1989 Disability Commission reported that many people with mental retardation are still in these institutions and do not have their own home, and that others, as adults, are still living with their parents when they would prefer not to be. The Commission also reported that nursing homes for the intellectually handicapped should be abolished, the deadline being 1 January 1998, a move that would be somewhat controversial in the UK.

It must be noted that the 1994 Care Act (LSS) (Act on Support and Service for the Disabled) has included within its legislation the right to accommodation in group dwellings for adults and that the municipalities had until 31 December 1995 to incorporate these reforms into their normal activities. This will allow those people still living in residential homes and specialized hospitals to be able to appeal to a court of law if they are dissatisfied with care aspects.

Social Welfare Policy

The Swedish social welfare policy is provided through both central and local government. Hedlund (1992) describes the aim as being to reduce inequalities in the life styles, not only of the varying groups and different classes, but also with the alternative periods and circumstances that occur throughout the life cycle.

This century has seen Sweden develop a welfare system that has maximized equality between different population groups. The basis for this has been a series of allowances that benefit those groups hardest hit, which includes the sick and injured, pensioners and the disabled. Hedlund (1992) identifies the four major cornerstones to the social welfare policy as being:

- **national social insurance**
- **family welfare**
- **social services**
- **health and medical care.**

National Social Insurance

The Swedish National Social Insurance Scheme, financed from government subsidies, covers health and parental insurance, pensions, work injury insurance and unemployment, guaranteeing basic financial security against hardship. A mentally retarded person over the age of 16 years is able to obtain a disability pension, if the ability to work is permanently reduced, and/or a disability allowance if specialist support for daily living is required.

The 1982 Social Services Act allowed the municipalities the funds in order to prioritize their own needs and services. The result of this is that over 40 municipalities have introduced 'buyer and supplier' systems. This parallels the 'purchaser and provider' services currently at the forefront of UK care services today. This approach has enabled services such as the day centre to function more autonomously in their everyday management.

One drawback has been that certain municipalities have been able to avoid fulfilling legislative requirements and

> ... the authorities often blame the poor economic situation. (Zetzell *et al.*, 1994, p. 6)

The decentralization of the social services leading to self-administration at local authority (municipal) level can be seen as a positive step, enabling a flexible service, and local client-need prioritization, but if there is a failure to prioritize correctly, and disparity in service provision, certain groups in need, particularly the disabled, will find the struggle to actualize services being perpetuated. Therefore one can see that the legislation and the ideologies do not always equate with the realities.

14.7 Personal Perspectives

Although services in Sweden have shown tremendous advances in the application of philosophies through appropriate service provision, the reality shows a service that has in many ways lost an identity of its own, through its varied couplings and integrative approaches with other services provided for other areas of social need. An example is that of the organization of services for the mentally retarded in Malmö which are shared with the service provision for the elderly – who are all seen as citizens in need, and requiring a service which enables them to 'live like others'. A further example from Uppsala, which reflects this, is the lack of communication that exists between the employment services for disabled people and the existing service provision for mentally retarded people, especially that which caters for severe disabilities.

It is difficult to provide the reader with anything other than an example of expressed views, as this area alone would warrant a chapter in itself. What is possible is for the reader to reflect upon some of the views expressed and consider them in relation to the detailed account of service provision earlier.

The advances in Swedish care services have been at such a pace that in some respects the client and carer have not kept up with them and are no longer in a position to offer any comments other than to support the 'wonders' of environmental change that have occurred in recent years. Generally the responses to the changes are favourable, with very few being prepared to challenge developments or criticize service provision, and if they do so it is 'tempered' towards comments that tend to offer alternative options, although from personal perspectives there are areas of concern.

The clients themselves, without 'models' upon which to base their challenges, have adopted stances that are reflective of the submissiveness associated with historical care provision. One such example was that in one residential flat visited by us; a client who smoked, had to utilize the balcony in winter to do this, instead of being able to use their own living room.

Service users have become so disseminated that their collective power is no longer felt, and this has resulted in an acceptance that 'everything is really incredible' as one individual cited, despite the fact this person also related to us a recent story of abuse experienced in his local community.

The environments visited all reflect considerable financial investment yet each lacked an atmosphere that reflected control by its occupants. The orderliness encountered may be part of Swedish culture, or it may also be the result of the need for the care staff to be doing 'something' during the day, now that their intervention with clients has been minimized to 'only when necessary'.

The organization of the 'independent living' arrangements, all tended to have a communal area which acted as a focus, which in some environments was used regularly, and in others remained barren but neat.

In some areas care staff expressed concern as to their role, which tended to be vague, especially as there were no obvious expectations on them in relation to the client's development. It was always the environmental adaptations that were shown to

us, as if this was what they were used to showing visitors.

Experienced staff, who have been in service throughout the years of change, were more open in their concerns regarding the lack of expertise in staff being currently employed, and also with regards to the specialist knowledge disappearing gradually as services are further integrated into a generic service provision. However, despite our own perceived apprehensions, the staff and client perspectives regarding service provision concur. 'We are happy, well supported and feel the service reflects the correct philosophies' stated one care manager. But the total lack of challenge from those staff and clients encountered, in a range of visits to care settings in Uppsala, Sandviken and Malmö, have created some doubts as to the readiness of service providers to consider other aspects pertaining to care delivery.

There is a feeling that there is greater public awareness of the needs of, and services for people with mental retardation, yet despite this we found that the organization which had taken over the occupancy of areas of the Pilangen residential home in Malmö as it decreased in numbers, were not even aware of the existence of the remaining mentally retarded people still living in parts of Pilangen.

Despite advances, evidence remains of practices which reflect Gilbertsson's (Ericsson *et al*, 1992, p. 6) view that the 'self-determination', so crucial to the philosophy supporting independent living, was gradually being eroded by the care staff. The 'time-out' practices adopted in respite periods were openly evident at a number of visits, and, apart from meal times, little actual interaction was visible to us between staff and client, which, as Pedlor (1990) notes following interviews with staff, may result in the already overpowering role adopted by staff, completely overwhelming and segregating the mentally retarded person from mainstream society. Pedlor (1992) further notes that subconscious adoption of protective or custodial roles by staff, who are used to being 'all things' to their clients and consequently limit outside interaction. Most certainly all initial interviews upon our arrival were held with the staff always present, either with or without clients.

In Pilangen, Malmö, the residential unit of only five clients openly paraded an activities programme on the wall of the living unit, and the care practices described for their physically disabled and severely learning disabled clients, was comparative to care practices in the UK, with an acknowledgement that they may even be below UK standard.

But by far the most disturbing evidence of this limited client involvement was where staff have opened new homes, and they have chosen the internal decor prior to clients moving in. So it would seem that true independence continues to remain elusive, and the clients, through their acceptance and limited knowledge of alternative options, perpetuate the subtle control exercised over their lives, despite the service being of such a high standard. The protective stance, which ensures 'a good life', fails to recognize that 'good' is only truly appreciated in relation to 'bad', and that after a year or so of the life styles on offer, 'good' might easily be replaced by 'mundane', and even eventually by more outrageous terms.

Can one imagine a life without problems, stresses, losses and trauma? If so this idyllic life could only take on the monotony which Homer (1000 BC) describes when Odysseus and his crew partake of the lotus and forget their perilous journey home.

The heavy emphasis upon the actualization of earlier social policies, and perhaps the role ascribed to Sweden as the 'standard setter' in care delivery, have resulted in an almost rigid application of policies, with little or no deviation from targets established over 30 years ago. But these have not taken into account the changes in culture and life style that have taken place in both Swedish and European life styles, and the many global influences which have also had impact.

So strong is the influence of the policy-makers, that staff have tended to ignore care philosophies in their desire to apply them, which is because independent thought and action, coupled with flexibility, are not essential requisites for the care practitioner. Hence there are now individuals, such as Pedlor (1990) and Gilbertsson (Ericsson *et al*, 1992, p. 6), who are beginning to question the actualities of care in the 1990s.

The hope that smaller residential units would create greater opportunities for more meaningful interaction between clients and carers, as opposed to the larger establishments (institutions) which tended to be carer/carer dialogues, has not been realized due to the almost 'isolated' outposts they seem to have become. Staff, from our view, tending to see their 'duty' as would the 'nightwatch' on board ship – important, but glad when it's over. The interactions expected are dependent on much more than the creation of such environments, and hinge around a life involving leisure and recreation, which is one major area of deficit in Swedish care provision, especially if this aspect requires facilitation by the carer.

The question as to whether the person with a learning disability has a valued social role is an arguable one. Their living environments would certainly reflect this as being so, especially as these have resulted in considerable personal contentment for the client themselves.

Certainly, public attitude seems to reflect a greater awareness, understanding and tolerance of this particular group of people, but their identities have been disseminated within a range of other services. In some sense they seem to have disappeared, and therefore the public are unlikely to be disturbed by their presence, which continues to be on the periphery of everyday life.

The danger perceived is that the singular life style offered to people in their own apartments may result in loneliness and decreased interaction, as this is now dependent in total upon the 'carer' on duty, whose role is to be available rather than to intervene.

The approaches in both Sweden and the UK have almost ignored the development of the individual, the need being to create 'model' citizens, able to satisfy public expectations and the critics of their value as human citizens. To some degree, the poor organization and communication of the differing care services actually serves to promote a practice that truly does reflect a reduction in control over the client's life style. The poor communication between residential and day-care services allows the client privacy from intrusion by carers, which is reflective of how ordinary people live, but this has not been consciously strived for.

The same could be said for the lack of personal care plans and individual documentation, which in the UK have become standardized to such an extent that behaviours throughout life can almost be predicted from the person's birth – the same life style and patterns of living to be adopted by everyone, 24 hours a day. In Sweden these were discontinued with service dissemination, which has resulted in greater emphasis upon the individual's identity, but the lack of continuity and consistency, especially with staff turnover, quite often has led to a move towards their reintroduction, which may in turn affect the way in which client independence was originally envisaged. They can represent a form of disempowerment, as the completion of these documents is always the responsibility of a 'carer', someone who is ultimately in a position of 'power' over the client.

Sweden continues to set an example with regards to providing appropriate living conditions for people with mental retardation, and these in some ways are as ambitious as they are costly. The recession has resulted in a decrease in developments recently, but this will allow for the opportunity to evaluate other aspects of service provision.

The move to total integration throughout Sweden, the UK and other leading countries has always appeared to ignore the fact that the clients, are ill-equipped to compete with ordinary members of the public, and will need to rely on legislation and policies which enforce the equality sought for in well-meaning philosophies.

The real need, which is to 'celebrate the differences' and thus provide care settings appropriate to need, desire and ability, has been lost in a dogma that emphasizes the intention not to make people 'normal', yet in its application almost certainly tends to target this 'normality'.

Discussion Question

Compare this chapter's treatment of the situation as regards learning disability in Sweden to Chapters 13 and 15. What conclusions can be drawn?

References

Anderson, E. (1971) *Guidelines for Teachers No. 10: Making ordinary schools special.* London: National Council for Special Education.

Armitage, H. (Ed.) (1990) *ITN Factbook*, p. 488, London.

Arvidsson, K. (1994) *Steget:* FUB's easy-to-read magazine (Special English Edition). Stockholm, Sweden: Swedish National Society for Persons with Mental Handicap (FUB).

Asberg, K. (1989) The need for medical care among mentally retarded adults. A 5-year follow-up and comparison with a general population of the same age. *British Journal of Mental Subnormality* 35(1): 68.

Clarke, D. (1984) *Mentally Handicapped People: Living and learning.* London: Baillière Tindall.

Dybwad, R. (Ed.) (1978) *Sweden. An International Directory of Mental Retardation Resources.* London: International League of Societies for Persons with Mental Handicap.

Box 14.5 The 24 counties		
Stockholm	Blekinge	Örebro
Uppsala	Kristianstad	Västmanland
Södermanland	Malmöhus	Kopparberg
Östergötland	Holland	Gälveborg
Jönköping	Göteborg och Bohur	Västernorrland
Kronoberg	Älvsborg	Jämtland
Kalmar	Skaraborg	Västerbotten
Gotlands	Värmland	Norbotten

Ericsson, K., Gilbertsson, S., Norden, R., Tuvesson, B., Wendelholt, A.-M. and Ohman, I. (1992) When all residential institutions are closed (on community alternatives and the lives they offer persons with handicap). *IASSMD 9th World Congress in Brisbane, Australia.* Skaraborg, Sweden: Landstringet.

Flynn, R. and Nitsch, K. (Eds) (1980) *Normalisation, Social Integration and Community Services.* Baltimore: University Park Press.

Grunewald, K. (1974) *The Mentally Retarded in Sweden.* Stockholm: Swedish Institute.

Grunewald, K. (1977) *Community Living for Mentally Retarded Adults in Sweden.* Nyköping, Sweden: Current Sweden.

Hedlund, M.-B. (1992) *Social Services in Sweden.* Stockholm: National Board of Health and Welfare.

Hultinger, E. (1994) *Curriculum for Compulsory Schools.* Stockholm: Swedish Ministry of Education and Science.

Hjorth, S. (1994) *Curriculum for Non-Compulsory schools.* Stockholm: Swedish Ministry of Education and Science.

Intra (1993) *Utvecklingsstordan i Kultur och samhalle.* Stockholm: Liber Utbildning, No. 2.

Kent, P. (1976) *International Aspects of the Provision of Medical Care.* London: Oriel Press.

Larsson, G. (1991) *Report of the 1989 Disability Commission: Disability Welfare Justice: Summary.* Stockholm: Allmanna Forlaget.

Larsson, G. (1992) *Final Report of the 1989 Commission on Policies for the Disabled: A society for all: Summary.* Stockholm: Allmanna Forlaget.

Lewis, D., Ramjean, R., Soopen, V. and Aaron, D. (1979) A Study on the Service and Care Provided for the Mentally Retarded in Sweden and Denmark. Unpublished.

Malmo (1978) Omsorgsstyrelse Lindangen: En anlaggning inom omsorgsverksamgheten. Stockholm: Dratselkontords Tryeker.

Ministry of Education and Science (1994) *A New Curriculum for the Compulsory School.* Stockholm: Ministry of Education and Science.

Ministry of Health and Social Affairs (1986) *International Secretariat Special Services and Intellectually Handi-capped Persons Act and The Act Concerning Implementation of Special Services for Intellectually Handicapped Persons Act.* Stockholm: Regeringskansliets Offsetcentral.

Ministry of Health and Social Affairs (1993) *International Secretariat The Compulsory Mental Care Act and the Forensic Mental Care Act.* Stockholm: Regeringskansliets Offsetcentral.

Ministry of Health and Social Affairs (1994) *Social Welfare in Transition: A presentation of Swedish welfare policies.* Stockholm: Ministry of Health and Social Affairs.

Ministry of Health and Social Affairs (1994) *International Secretariat Act Concerning Support and Service for Persons with Certain Functional Impairments and The Assistance Benefit Act.* Stockholm: Regeringskansliets Offsetcentral.

National Agency for Education (Skolverket) (1994) *The Swedish Schools System.* Stockholm: Ekblad.

National Board of Health and Welfare (1992a) *Social Services in Sweden: A Part of the Social Welfare System.* Stockholm: Modin-Tryck.

National Board of Health and Welfare (1992b) *Your Right to Old Age Care and Disability Care.* Stockholm: Modin-Tryck.

National Board of Health and Welfare (1993) *Today.* Stockholm: Modin-Tryck.

National Council for the Disabled (1993) *Disability Politics in Sweden.* Stockholm: National Council for the Disabled.

National Social Insurance Board (1993) *Annual Report 1992/93. Social Insurance in Sweden.* Stockholm: Dala Offset Sweden AB.

National Swedish Agency for Special Education (1994) SIH Stockholm: National Swedish Agency for Special Education.

Pedlor (1990) *Alternative Services and Economic Aspects.* Stockholm: Swedish Institute.

Sjoberg, M. (1994) *Current Sweden: New rights for persons with functional impairment.* Stockholm: Swedish Institute.

Statistics Sweden Education in Sweden (1994) Stockholm: SCB-Tryck.

Sterner, R. (1969) *Services for the Handicapped.* Stockholm: Kugelbergs.

Swedish Institute (March 1992) *Fact Sheets on Sweden: Primary and Secondary education.* Stockholm: Swedish Institute.

Swedish Institute (May 1992) *Fact Sheets on Sweden: Child care in Sweden.* Stockholm: Swedish Institute.

Swedish Institute (March 1993) *Fact Sheets on Sweden: Support for the disabled.* Stockholm: Swedish Institute.

Swedish Institute (April 1993) *Fact Sheets on Sweden: The health care system in Sweden.* Stockholm: Swedish Institute.

Swedish Institute (December 1993) *Fact Sheets on Sweden: Social insurance in Sweden.* Stockholm: Swedish Institute.

Swedish Institute (January 1994) *Fact Sheets on Sweden: Swedish handicap policy.* Stockholm: Swedish Institute.

Swedish National Labour Market Administration (1994a) *Annual Report of Activities.* Stockholm: Arbetsmarknadsinstitutet.

Swedish National Labour Market Administration (1994b) *Vocational Rehabilitation in Sweden: County labour boards.* Stockholm: Arbetsmarknadsinstitutet.

Swedish National Labour Market Administration (1994c) *Vocational Rehabilitation in Sweden: The employability institute for the intellectually handicapped* (AMI-IA). Stockholm: Arbetsmarknadsinstitutet.

Swedish National Labour Market Administration (1994d) *Vocational Rehabilitation in Sweden: Employability institutes (AMIs).* Stockholm: Arbetsmarknadsinstitutet.

Swedish National Society for Persons with Mental Handicap (1994a) *LSS: Enny lag far Susanna.* Stockholm: Gnesta Tryck.

Swedish National Society for Persons with Mental Handicap (1994b) *On Mental Handicap.* Stockholm: Swedish National Society for Persons with Mental Handicap.

Swedish National Society for Persons with Mental Handicap (1994c) *This is the FUB.* Stockholm: Swedish National Society for Persons with Mental Handicap.

Swedish National Society for Persons with Mental Handicap (1994d) *What is the FUB?* Stockholm: Swedish National Society for Persons with Mental Handicap.

Swedish National Society for Persons with Mental Handicap (1994e) *When you Meet Mentally Handicapped Persons.* Stockholm: Swedish National Society for Persons with Mental Handicap.

Weyler, K. (1993) *Current Sweden: Big changes in Swedish education.* Stockholm: Swedish Institute.

Wolfensberger, W. (1972) *The Principle of Normalization in Human Services.* Toronto: National Institute on Mental Retardation.

Zetzell, I., Begler, A.M. and Illborg, H. (Eds) (1994) *The Social Services and Care in Sweden 1993.* Stockholm: National Board of Health and Welfare, Modin-Tryck.

Chapter 15: Establishing services: a case history of Romania
Norman Daniels, Jan Brown, David Hall, Marilyn Robinson, Rachel Jacklin and Colin Beacock

15.1 An Introduction to Romania

Box 15.1 An introduction to Romania	
• **Status**	Republic
• **Area**	237 500 km^2
• **Population**	23 490 000
• **Capital**	Bucharest (Bucureşti)
• **Other major towns**	Timişoara, Craiova, Cluj-Napoca
• **Languages**	Romanian, Hungarian
• **Religion**	65% Orthodox, 8% Roman Catholic although religion was discouraged until recently
• **Currency**	leu (ROL)
• **Membership**	The UN, OIEC
• **System of government**	Emerging democracy

Situated on the eastern extremity of Europe, Romania is a country of contrasts. Inhabited since prehistoric times, its evolution as a state is relatively recent. Romania's boundaries have altered frequently over the centuries, the annexation of Transylvania for example, was not confirmed until 1920 and the territory still remains a matter of sensitivity with neighbouring Hungary.

Reader Activity 15.1

Before reading this text, could you place Romania on a map of Europe?

The decision of the King of Romania to support the cause of Nazi Germany in the Second World War was to prove a turning point in the country's recent history. Previously, Romania had, either in part or total, been conquered and influenced by a succession of other nations and states. The Magyars of Hungary, the Ottoman Turks and the Romans shaped the culture and personality of this volatile Balkan state. In its language based on Latin roots,

Romania also differs from its Slavic neighbours yet the native tongue is not the universal first choice throughout the nation. In Transylvania, Hungarian and German are noticeable as the preferred or second language. English and French are studied widely and spoken amongst the younger generations.

The modern boundaries of Romania were reaffirmed at the end of the Second World War. The northern boundary is the border with the former Soviet Union; to the west the River Danube divides Romania from Hungary and also acts as the southerly border with Bulgaria. To the east, Romania has a coastline along the shores of the Black Sea. The Danube delta forms a substantial part of that boundary.

At the same time that the boundaries of the country were reaffirmed, oversight for the future development of the country passed to the Soviet Union. Consequently, a communist government was formed in Romania in 1947 and the country became part of the eastern bloc with Moscow as the focal point for all policy development and trade. The 'liberation' of the country by the Russians thereby led Romania into the centralized political bankruptcy of the communist system.

The capital of Romania, Bucharest, is home to 2.1 million of the country's acknowledged population of 23.5 million people. In terms of surface area, Romania is approximately 50% larger than the UK. As with most Balkan countries, the ethnic mix of the inhabitants is derived from a number of significant sources. The indigenous peoples of Romania were known as the Dacian people and were a well-organized civilization in the times of the Roman empire. Indeed, a Dacian legion served in the Roman army during battles in Gaul and in Palestine. The legacy of this Roman influence is the Romanian language with its Latin structures and script. The peoples of Transylvania however draw their inheritances from Hungary and the influence of German settlers upon that central part of Romania is pronounced. In the north of the country, many of the Moldovan people have been separated from their families since the end of the Second World War by the effects of the redrawn boundaries with the Soviet Union. The culture and traditions of these more Caucasian peoples have remained intact throughout that period, however, and the instinctive wish of the people of former Soviet and Romanian Moldova is that they should become one regional administration within the state of Romania. Whilst these are the predominating racial and ethnic elements of Romanian society one of the most significant groups in the country are its gypsy population of approximately 3 million people. This group is mainly outwith mainstream society and is generally the brunt of most people's discontent throughout the country. The gypsies have their own, very separate, history and culture and whilst Romania is their country of origin, they tend not to be governed by many of its conventions. They have separate political parties within the modern constitution of Romania and form a significant lobby within government but tend to focus their attentions upon the parochial interests of their own social group.

Set against this background of complex social and ethnic mix the Romanian people have sought to establish a democratic means of government following the revolution of 1989. The first free democratic elections took place in May 1990.

The Romanian Government is in two houses. The Senate (elected elder statesmen) and the House of Deputies, together comprising 420 seats. The Cabinet led by a Prime Minister has executive authority whilst the President, theoretically, has limited powers. The judiciary form the remaining law-making sector of government. Forty-one districts form the administrative structure of the country based on the French system with a Prefect for each district. Each city, town and village has its own mayor, system of funding and areas of responsibility. Taxes, though collected locally, are allocated by the government departments and the individual districts further allocate priority expenditure, but learning disability has never had any historical priority or acceptance.

Bucharest was formally known as the 'Paris of the East' and is the country's seat of government. It is a mixture of the elegance of the old, French-inspired architecture and the mundane of the new. Successive communist governments sought to destroy the decadence of former administrations and to replace it with more utilitarian structures. Consequently, the visual policies of centralization are evident in the wide boulevards, vast squares and nondescript architecture of row upon row of sterile, multistorey tenement blocks based upon structured street plans. Such was the communist bloc obsession with equality and uniformity, this policy was repeated throughout the country so that other major centres of population and production are similarly bland and lacking in comfort. These centres include the major cities of Cluj, Iaşi, Ploeşti, Craiova and Timişoara. None the less, the demise of the communist regime came in time to save substantial parts of these and other cities from redevelopment and areas of more traditional architecture remain.

At the same time, the economic base of the country remains agrarian rather than industrial. The agricultural systems are largely focused upon subsistence farming and cash cropping, which means that local, rather than national, markets flourish. A peasant life style has evolved and the privations of city dwellers are not felt to the same degree by their contemporaries in the countryside. Where the communist party imposed collective farming systems on the peasant populations they were largely unsuccessful. The independent mentality of the rural populations was despised by centralist planners and it was when these planners attempted to clear large areas of the peasant agricultural areas that their tenure of power began to fail.

Reader Activity 15.2
When did you first become aware of Romania and its needs?

15.2 Communism and its Impact upon Romania

With communist rule in 1947 came the emergence of a new form of logic in Romania. The objective of government was to produce a state system which would promote individual excellence in pursuit of common good. Central to this theory was the emergence of a 'new man' within the nation. There was to be no acknowledgement of racial or ethnic difference. The 'new man' and the new nation would have no time for historical facts; history, as is so often the case in totalitarian states, began on the date that the new regime acceded to power. Imperfection was not to be tolerated and the guideline for quality was to be the ideology of the one-party state.

None the less, by communist standards, Romania did well during the immediate post-war years; but at significant cost. The Romanian Communist Party had come to power in a nation with considerable physical and natural assets. Despite the intensive bombing campaigns of the USA Air Force, the oil fields of Ploeşti had emerged from the war relatively unscathed. The coal fields of the Jiu Valley had never been properly exploited by capitalist predecessors and there was a ready supply of labour upon which to base a highly intensive, low-technology industrial base. Although the internal infrastructure of the country was dominated by mountain ranges such as the Carpathians and the Dacian Alps, the rail and road networks had sustained only minimal damage during the war and the advantages of being able to export and import to and from the hinterland along the Danube set Romania at a considerable advantage in comparison with its eastern bloc neighbours. In Constanta, Romania also had the most southerly of all communist-bloc sea ports with immediate access to the eastern Mediterranean.

Within the communist bloc, however, Romania remained relatively non-aligned and never signed the Warsaw pact, much to the annoyance of the Russians. Much of this apparent indifference to the Soviet Union was little more than bravado. In reality,

the USSR had first call upon all of Romania's exports and fully exploited the country's resources by importing their produce at enormously discounted prices with little material or goods of any value being received by Romania in return. As a government, therefore, the Romanian Communist Party was seeking to impose ill-fitting industrial, social and economic policies upon a nation whose natural wealth was being exploited to the detriment rather than the benefit of its people.

Against such an economic and political background people with a learning disability and their families had no role to play in an idealistic society. They simply did not exist.

Reader Activity 15.3
The UK has no formal constitution. What ensures your rights as a citizen and those of the people in your care?

15.3 The Rise and Fall of Nicolae Ceauscescu

In totalitarian regimes the power and influence of the leader can be all-pervading. With no direct internal opposition and the requirement to appease the will of only one dominant supporter on the international stage, a politician might exert their influence in all areas of national policy. Such was the case with Nicolae Ceauscescu.

Having made steady but unspectacular progress through the ranks of the Romanian Communist Party, Nicolae Ceauscescu became the country's leader in 1967. He remained in power, along with his wife Elena, until the revolution of December 1989. Presiding over a country of outstanding natural beauty and wealth, Ceauscescu's mismanagement and unworkable industrial programmes thrust the population into declining living standards and poverty. The families of peasant workers and industrial labourers were equal in their suffering. Lack of food and resources became a way of life. Indeed, it was a policy decision of the government that workers should have minimal calorific intake per day; a hungry work-force was seen as a compliant work-force. The role of women was particularly difficult. The government supported a policy which required that fertile women were to have a minimum of four children. With larger families came greater social security benefits. The prospect of rearing children in cold, damp tenement blocks where electricity and gas supplies were strictly rationed was a severe disincentive and many women had illegal abortions which were often administered after 24 weeks of pregnancy. The only alternative to rearing a child in such circumstances was to have the child placed into a state orphanage for which a substantial levy was charged upon the family. Many new-born infants were therefore abandoned to their fate. 'Orphanages' were, therefore, home to many thousands of children with learning disabilities although they did not officially exist.

In the state of the 'new man' there was no such terminology as 'mental handicap'; these children were simply 'orphans'. If the privations of the labour force were severe, then the privations which these non-productive members of society were to suffer were far greater. For those few children with learning disabilities whose parents could cope with their continued presence at home, only one specialized centre existed in the whole of Romania for their assessment and treatment. That centre, Centrul de Recuparare Handicapati Copii (Centre for the Recuperation of Handicapped Children) was established and funded by the World Health Organization. There was no formal recognition of such people by the government and, therefore, no formal policy in respect of their care, treatment or education.

For the people of Romania, simply to exist was itself a struggle. They cared little for their fellow members of society and knew very little about the world around them. This arose from a governmental policy of controlling information and active disinformation on the part of government agents throughout society. Gatherings of more than four people were strictly forbidden unless they were

overseen by an approved 'commissar'; no-one was allowed to speak to foreigners; to listen to foreign radio stations was a crime which carried a compulsory prison sentence. Television in the country was limited to 2 hours per night and the only programmes featured reports on the achievements of the state or deferential programmes hailing the Ceauscescu family. The most dreaded forces of all were the Secret Police; the Securitate. It was their role and that of similar forces throughout eastern Europe, to control access to information and to limit freedom of the individual.

In common with the rest of the world, Romanian people were shocked to disbelief when the Revolution erupted and the new-found freedom exposed the facts. Forced evictions and relocations; the pressure of low wages plus the emphasis upon large families and the denial of means of contraception had led to the abandonment of thousands of children who were to become sentenced to one of the country's orphanages or institutions. The first to be abandoned were those with the greatest needs; those with disabilities and illnesses whose families could not cope.

Nicolae Ceauscescu had very few policies by which he governed Romania. His industrial policy was simply to produce as much as possible for the least cost. His economic policy highlighted the illogical and obsessional thinking that characterized his regime. He sought only to ensure that Romania never suffered a balance of trade deficit. To this end he exported almost all of Romania's gross national product and imported inferior products and materials for consumption by his own people. This he took to be sound economic policy. His only social policies were aimed at controlling his population by keeping them poor in material and intellectual terms. In the matter of international relationships he was honoured by the UK through the award of an honorary knighthood for his apparent resistance to the USSR. It soon become evident, however, that Ceauscescu was acting as an agent of the Kremlin and was obtaining technology from the western powers which the Soviet bloc was then copying. The international stature of Ceauscescu reached its lowest point in 1987 when, having stayed at the Elysee Palace as a guest of the French President, he and his wife were ordered to return the crockery, cutlery and linen they had stolen.

However comical the antics of Ceauscescu may have appeared to those of us in western Europe, the legacy of his regime registered most upon the lives of the most fragile and needy in society. People with a learning disability were the most affected of all. The lessons learned from this experience of the effects of no policies of positive discrimination in favour of people with a learning disability were registered with frightening effect through the footage of western newsreel cameras during the immediate post-revolutionary period. By February 1990 the whole world was aware of the effect Ceauscescu had had upon the children of Romania.

These revelations resulted in a genuine and overwhelming desire to help from every conceivable type of individual across the whole of western Europe. The larger aid agencies, along with a plethora of smaller ones, soon flocked to the country and met the immediate needs for food, medicines, equipment and appropriate clothing. What follows are accounts of the involvement of one such small group, Poplars Church, and the strategies they have sought to develop in assisting people to come to terms with the needs of people with a learning disability in a society where few, if any, positive policies exist to protect and promote the interests of such a vulnerable group of people.

15.4 The Involvement of Poplars Church

Poplars Church, one of the many smaller volunteer groups, moved into Brasov within weeks of December 1989 immediately targeting the sick children of the orphanages and the paediatric wards of the city's hospitals. This soon developed into an active input into the less publicized but equally desperate needs of those with learning disabilities.

Some of these people were in institutions but the majority were found to be living at home with parents who had refused to give in to pressure for their admission to institutions. There they received no formal education or professional care.

No particular strategy was identified for overcoming the problems that presented. The situations which emerged on a day to day basis meant that constant reprioritizing was essential. The overall intention of Poplars Church was to help the Romanian people to help themselves. That commitment led to the establishment of a number of projects. Each of the projects had a primary objective; either to promote self-help amongst the people of Brasov or to co-ordinate and focus the efforts of volunteers so that programmes could be maintained and their benefits evaluated.

Promoting Self-help in Brasov

Personal contact was made with a number of families of children with Down's syndrome and we were introduced to the Brasov Parents' Association for Mentally Handicapped Children. This group was inaugurated by parents and professionals in March 1990 and was the first group of its kind to be established in the province of Brasov. Most of the families lived in a two- or three-roomed apartment in a tower block with little or no play facilities. Water supplies were limited and mains gas pressure was sometimes only available between midnight and 2 a.m. It was government policy before 1990 that mothers should return to work when their baby was 4 months old. These families had fought hard to keep their child at home despite the stressful life style and the lack of support, services and relief facilities.

Reader Activity 15.4
How valuable are support services to the parents and lay carers who provide for people with learning disabilities in the UK? What do they achieve?

The determination of these parents and their request for help encouraged the Poplars Church personnel to seek advice in the UK. It was decided to link with Colin Beacock, a nurse educator with experience of working in Romania, to arrange schemes of training for parents in the UK. The purpose of those schemes would be to assist parents in meeting the needs of their own children more effectively and to establish networking skills so that the group could become a more powerful lobby in seeking services and facilities for their families. The needs of professionals who had an interest in services for people with learning disabilities also gave rise to problems. Their lack of contemporary information meant that the development of their knowledge and skills base had been severely restricted.

Informal training courses for parents and professionals were arranged in Romania and after a succession of these, two parents and one teacher were invited to Britain to participate in a formal programme. The programme lasted 4 weeks and addressed matters of theory and practice with the primary focus being upon developmental day services and parent-support schemes. Their ability to organize and lead a developmental session and to arrange a programme of developmental exercises was assessed through a series of practical assessments and the group was able to return to Romania and to begin a cascade through other members of their Association so that they might begin to provide for the long-term needs of children by self-sufficient means. The process was repeated several times over the next 2 years.

Since that time and the initial attempts to resolve problems which had emerged over 40 years of neglect, the professionals involved in the programmes have continued to give of their skills in Brasov. Their input varies according to availability but the results of their commitment and the determination of the Parents' Association have given rise to many changes in service delivery.

Volunteer Work and its Co-ordination

By developing relationships and sharing confidences with Romanian professionals, it soon became evident that there were areas of need that could not be met by the meagre resources available to the Romanians themselves. An educational psychologist at a local orphanage and a paediatrician from one of the several polyclinics each reluctantly shared concerns regarding the needs of children in their care and of families whom they knew to be under intense pressure. Following up these contacts led to the realization that a programme of community visiting and home-based support was essential.

Many of the deficiencies found could undoubtedly be met by the provision of medicines, food and educational materials, but beyond these the skills and knowledge of professional helpers would provide the encouragement needed to enhance the commitment of the Romanian parents.

A number of larger charities stipulated that their prospective voluntary aid workers should show a commitment of at least 6 months to their placements. Poplars Church recognized that criteria were restrictive both to the willing and the capable who, in time of recession and unemployment, were unable to give such a commitment. Initially, therefore, volunteers became short-term workers giving periods from 1 week to 3 months.

Inevitably the language and communications barrier had to be overcome by the use of translators, since skills in this area could not be learned in so short a timescale. Emphasis was placed on building long-term relationships whereas placements generated a continued enthusiasm amongst volunteers such that repeated visits became the norm, thereby strengthening the relationships even further and similarly support from UK quarters mushroomed.

Reader Activity 15.5
Have you ever undertaken voluntary work? What were the most demanding and rewarding aspects of that experience?

Training of Volunteers

It soon became evident that mere enthusiasm and compassion were not enough. Long-term goals and accountable management practices were essential for both efficiency and effectiveness. Induction and training days became a necessary feature for volunteers being introduced to the work of Poplars Church. The education and training of field workers from the UK had to be given equal status with the input given to our Romanian counterparts. The programmes included sessions on the culture of Romania and its language; scope of placements and areas of need; health issues and health education; practical and administrative details and group interviews. From these programmes have emerged standards and criteria for selection of volunteers and the maintenance and monitoring of activities and projects in Romania.

Each volunteer is self-funding. The charity makes available accommodation and some transport for volunteers as well as the services of a project co-ordinator and use of an international telephone. In such circumstances, the need to maintain standards of behaviour and professional input is of paramount importance. Whilst the Romanian temperament is generous and warm it is also very Latin and the impetus to maintain relationships must come from the volunteers who are guests in a foreign land with a very different culture and values system.

Volunteer Placements

The initial input by Poplars Church into the needs of people with a learning disability arose not only from the publicity generated by appalling conditions prevailing in the institutions but also from community visits and a programme of home-based support. Rapidly this input developed into more direct support and expertise for Romanian

professionals practitioners and carers. Opportunities arose for input from occupational and speech therapy specialists through consistent liaison with the local special-needs orphanage and input to the Parents' Association. This culminated in regular summer schools providing play and learning facilities and an opportunity to refresh and update professionals and families.

Meanwhile, projects based in the local institutions, schools and in home-based support became the mainstay of the Poplars Church input. Longer-term plans, which are nearing fruition, included the commissioning of a children's hospice and phase care centre for the families of Brasov.

15.5 Case Studies

By working on the Poplars Church projects over a number of years, professional volunteers have been able to reflect upon the effects those projects have had, both upon the client group they have been assisting, and upon themselves. In the following descriptions of their experiences, volunteers attempt to portray the realities of trying to establish services in a country with little or no central policy in services for people with a learning disability. At the same time, the authors give an insight into the life styles of the people they have encountered and the problems that everyday people face after 40 years of living under a single-party state.

Reader Activity 15.6
You are about to read personal perspectives from practitioners and volunteers who have faced considerable adversity in providing services to people in Romania. Have you considered the value of keeping a reflective diary in your own role as a provider? If so, consider how you would present its very personal content.

Case Study 15.1 Jan Brown – preschool special needs teacher

As a preschool special needs teacher in England, I first became involved with community work in Brasov during my first visit to Romania in February 1991. I had undertaken a placement as a volunteer with Poplars Church.

During my work in the local paediatric hospital I met some of the parents of the children in the various wards and I also encountered a paediatrician who was most concerned about the welfare of her patients in the community at large. I was shocked to discover that professionals were working with totally outdated equipment and with information that was drawn from Russian text books which were 30 years out of date. The commitment of the paediatrician and the intense pleading of the parents subsequently led me to make visits to their homes in the local community.

Some of the parents I had first met had formed themselves into an Association and it was these parents who asked me to consider their home circumstances and what they could do to help their children. What aid there was arriving in Brasov was being targeted towards the hospitals and orphanages but there was a specific need for help and expertise in the families of children with special needs in the community.

Visits to families on subsequent trips to Brasov proved to be both uplifting and despairing. I found the families in differing home circumstances; from professional to gypsy families. The vast majority were in poor housing in blocks of apartments which dominate the suburbs of Brasov.

The families were all desperate for any kind of guidance, help or support. Many were living in very difficult circumstances with no specialist equipment, no wheelchairs, no incontinence aids or bathing facilities to meet the most basic needs of their children. There was nothing of the equipment that we consider vital to support the care and independence of children with severe physical problems and learning disabilities. No support was offered to the families from any professional personnel. There was no physiotherapy, occupational therapy or health advice. There was no form of education or even basic stimulation for the children. Many of the children were quite able and appeared to have considerable personal assets.

The ignorance of parents with regard to the condition of their children caused me great concern. Often they had been given a diagnosis but precious little else. They were simply sent away with the option of coping with the needs of their child or being excessively taxed if they became a burden of the state in institutional care. No medical treatment was offered even for conditions such as hydrocephalus which would have proved so amenable to surgical intervention.

Volunteer help in the community from a variety of charities has gradually expanded over the past 4 years. Professionals including teachers, occupational therapists, physiotherapists, nurses and speech therapists have been actively involved in supporting home-based care programmes. More suitable types of aid has entered the country including specialist seating, mobility aids and educational toys. These have been targeted at individual families in need.

Special emphasis has been placed upon encouraging and motivating the parents of special-needs children so that they might become more self-supporting. The simple belief that someone else was interested in the welfare of their child has proved to be of enormous benefit to parents and families. After years of neglect and being told that their child was 'irrecuperable', they have found others who believe that their child is worth bothering about.

Training sessions for parents and professionals have proved to be highly beneficial. Simple feeding methods and up to date literature on overcoming disabilities have helped countless families to cope. Conditions such as autism are finally being recognized. I found that there was no information at all available for parents of these children and no assistance whatsoever in coping with the difficulties of their complex and demanding behaviours.

Long-term volunteers have been able to target children with special needs for home tuition. This has motivated parents to maintain programmes between visits. Some children have achieved well beyond their anticipated targets, given consistent input. This has led us to speculate as to their true potential given more appropriate learning environments.

Although community-based volunteer work has expanded, it has led to an ever-increasing demand. I meet people in despair whenever I visit Brasov and there is still no improvement in the nature and level of input from the Romanian authorities. Whatever progress has been made has resulted from the unified efforts of parents with help from outside agencies and charities. They are combining to put added pressure upon the relevant authorities to provide for the educational needs of these children but it remains available to only a few of the many thousands of children who require it and none of that service is available to non-ambulant children in their own home.

In a recent survey undertaken by the Parents' Association, none of the sample group identified any state services that were available to them in Brasov. Each of them was aware of services of a voluntary nature. They stated that they all felt isolated from society because of their childrens' condition and needed much more advice and support at the time of diagnosis of that condition. Some parents have gained from the new-found freedoms in Romania and have paid for private speech therapy but such measures are rare in a society where hardship and deprivation are still rife. Inflation is still soaring and basic needs for clothing, food and shelter are becoming increasingly difficult to meet.

When asked about their future the respondents said that they placed their hope upon their families and their faith in God. They all had hope for a brighter future but had little hope for any immediate change.

My own feelings of frustration about the plight of the families of Brasov increase with every visit. Despite the promises of politicians, there is no real improvement in their lot. I would like to think that as things begin to change within Romanian society, pressure from parents and the governments of other European nations could create a brighter future. A school for children with Down's syndrome has been established by a British charity; the Swiss have set up a centre for physiotherapy and in each case their maintenance and management has now passed to local professionals in Brasov. As an interim measure this model has some credibility and is further reinforced if representatives of the founding charity and service users continue as members of the relevant board of management.

Romania is a fascinating and charming country. Its people are warm and generous and, despite their years of isolation and exposure to propaganda, they are beginning to see themselves as possible partners in a new world order. If they are to fulfil that ambition, it is essential that they are assisted to develop services for the most needy members of their society.

Case Study 15.2 David Hall – nurse for people with learning disabilities

Health Care and Learning Disabilities

Within the Romanian health services there are very few facilities that cater specifically for the needs of people with a learning disability. Such people appear to be scattered throughout the various establishments that exist in Romanian society, from schools to prisons. Many of them, therefore, find themselves in psychiatric hospitals. One such hospital is in the town of Zarnesti, near Brasov.

As a volunteer with Poplars Church I have undertaken regular placements in the Zarnesti Neurological/ Psychiatric Hospital.

Health Care in Zarnesti

Box 15.2 illustrates the sort of place Zarnesti is. The factories control three or four dispensaries which cater for the basic health-care needs of the workers. There is a small general hospital within the town where a small and devoted team tries very hard to meet the enormous needs of the local population with very limited resources.

In theory, health care in Romania is free for all, though prescriptions provided by the dispensaries have to be paid for. In practice, money paves the way for better treatment and corruption is common. The young, the old and the poor do not always get the health care they require.

Box 15.2 The town of Zarnesti

Zarnesti is a town of some 5000 inhabitants, about 25 km from the city of Brasov. The surrounding scenery within the Carpathian mountains, with peaks rising to 3648 m, is stunningly beautiful throughout the year. Wild flowers and animal life abound in the local coniferous forests; the brown bear and the wolf roam free and relatively undisturbed in the nearby mountains.

Zarnesti itself is no beauty spot, however. The main local industry is paper pulping and manufacture and 10 000 workers a day travel into the three main factories in Zarnesti. The effects of this industry can be seen throughout the area with raw waste being discharged into streams and rivers without control. The town has a very poor and disadvantaged population. The inhabitants mostly live in apartment blocks which are typically two or three rooms with outdated and minimal sanitary and cooking facilities. The supply of electricity and water is irregular. Whilst there are some more traditional buildings which house the local farming community, they are mainly dishevelled and add to the overall appearance of urban decay and dilapidation.

Zarnesti Neurological/Psychiatric Hospital

There is a hospital within Zarnesti which caters for patients with neurological and psychiatric disorders. From the outside it resembles all of the other residential blocks that surround it. It is virtually indistinguishable from these buildings except for the fact that there is a large, blue 'H' on the wall facing the road. The windows all have bars and there are people in pyjamas entering and leaving the building. Many more people, similarly clad, are to be seen around the immediate vicinity. The large, blue 'H' denotes a hospital in Romania; the wearing of pyjamas when one is a hospital in-patient appears to be culturally derived but is commonplace throughout Romania.

The hospital has three floors each with small rooms or 'salons'. There are communal toilets with baths and showers and an office on each floor. The hospital is an annexe of a similar facility in Brasov which is accessible by car, bus or train; a journey that takes around 1 hour by any method.

The bars at the windows denote the type of hospital it is and how the needs of its patients are viewed. The people who are admitted to Zarnesti have varying diagnoses that would require their admission. These diagnoses would include uncomplicated learning disability as well as mental illnesses, epilepsy, physical disability, old age and specific neurological problems. Any diagnosis, from physical disability following amputation to severe learning disabilities, would be sufficient to warrant admission to the hospital.

Male and female patients live in separate dormitories with three to five people per room. Relationships between residents are closely monitored and any fraternizing is severely discouraged. The priority is to keep the building quiet and interaction is not encouraged. The hospital has no garden but more-able residents are encouraged to go shopping, to take walks and to visit Brasov by train. The pyjamas are the property of the hospital and the patients must wear them beneath their outdoor clothes. These act as a form of message to the local community as does the 'Bulletin de Identitate' which each patient must carry indicating their diagnosis, any specific information and to which hospital they should be sent in the result of any emergency.

Life in the Neuro/Psychiatric Hospital Zarnesti

The Staff

The staff of the hospital comprise of medical assistants, who function as nurses, and ancillary staff. The staff work a simple but arduous shift pattern and their hours of duty are 0700–1500 h and 1500–0700 h. There are normally five medical assistants plus one senior assistant per early shift. They are expected to care for the 200 resident patients whose wards are spread across three floors within the building. On a late shift there are usually three or four staff to provide the same. The medical assistants do not make beds, empty bed pans or help any residents with feeding problems. These tasks fall to the domestic staff who also clean the hospital and give out meals. The medical assistants tend to spend their time on administrative duties and remain in their respective offices keeping records. They do assist in medical procedures such as administration of medicines, taking blood samples and administration of intravenous substances.

Two doctors are assigned to the hospital. One is a medical specialist, the other a psychiatrist. Each doctor visits at least once per week. Their main role is to authorize documents and to oversee the regimes of the hospital. The psychiatrist offers electroconvulsive therapy and has a resident office in the hospital. Whilst medications are theoretically free, they tend to be in limited supply and the role of the doctors as prescribers of medication is therefore somewhat limited.

The Patients

I will try to describe the hospital from the patient's or visitor's perspective. A series of six steps leads up to the door of the hospital. As you pass into the building you are confronted by a stone staircase with corridors to either side of it. The first impression that assails you is the indescribable smell of the place which appears to be a mixture of damp, urine, vomit, food remains and bad drainage with other unknown smells mixed in. The second realization that strikes you is the poor state of repair of the building and the general uncleanliness of the fabric of the building.

On the ground floor are the kitchens and store rooms. The kitchens are in an especially poor condition. Food debris litters the floor and the cookers appear to be on their last legs. There are no refrigerators and the food is generally stored in the open. When the food is cooked it is transported around the hospital in old enamel buckets from which the domestic staff ladle it directly to the patients. Whilst there are some offices and rooms on the ground floor they are there primarily for the use of medical staff and their senior assistants.

The remaining two floors are used for patient accommodation. On the first floor are those people with neurological problems, elderly confused people and people with varying degrees of need associated with their learning disability. On the top floor live people whose mental illness or learning disability makes them more difficult to manage.

On both floors, rooms range off a dimly-lit corridor. Most of these rooms measure approximately 3.5 m × 2 m. They accommodate three people and all of their worldly possessions. The beds have metal frames and the bedding consists of worn sheets and blankets. The poverty of the surroundings is striking.

Life is very difficult for the patients at Zarnesti. They suffer appalling poverty. Whilst the state provides them with the facilities of the hospital, very few of them receive any form of pension, however meagre. The patients must rely upon their families for support. There is no money for the few luxuries that exist in Romanian life. Food is expensive in Romania. Food in the hospitals is meagre, unappetizing and nutritionally poor. Fruit, vegetables, milk and dairy products are rare commodities and seldom, if ever, appear on the hospital menu.

The patients' rooms are barely large enough to accommodate the beds. The layout of the hospital makes it extremely difficult to mobilize anyone with a physical disability and immobile patients are turned and repositioned only when the beds are made or their clothes are changed. Many have no opportunity to leave their beds. The hospital has no garden and even the more able-bodied patients have limited opportunity for recreation because of lack of facility. The residents of the top floor are frequently locked into that floor to limit their movements.

There are few facilities and little choice for patients. The winters are long and intensely cold. There are no newspapers or books; no television other than in the medical staff's office. A few patients possess radios and tape recorders but cannot obtain batteries to operate them.

Although the medical assistants and domestic staff create a caring atmosphere, the overall impression is that life in the hospital is generally governed by the survival of the fittest. With so few facilities and resources, this is much the same as Romanian life in general. In a hospital such as that at Zarnesti, however, a physical or intellectual impairment can lead to a very isolated life style with little or no stimulation.

Romania does not have specialist facilities for people with a learning disability, nor does it have specialist doctors or practitioners to cater for their needs. As in any society, when resources are scarce it is those people who cannot help themselves or who have no voice that tend to be forgotten or who are deliberately missed. Romania is changing rapidly and Its health-care systems improve constantly. The needs of a person with a learning disability are slowly being recognized but, as yet, this has not penetrated into the realms of adult hospital services such as that in Zarnesti.

Case Study 15.3 Marilyn Robinson and Rachel Jacklin – occupational therapist, and community worker

Marilyn and Rachel pioneered the community-visits programme. As an occupational therapist and a special-needs care assistant they were supported by a number of qualified personnel who came to Romania as volunteers to support and further develop the programmes they had established. Regularly visiting a case load of 10 children with learning disabilities, they have seen progress and benefit for both the children and their families as a result of their specialist input.

Supporting the programme are other initiatives. The toy library is a low-cost but highly valued facility. Parents appreciate the new ideas and approaches of the western toy manufacturers and recognize the educational value of play. The library is most valued during the winter months when severe frosts and heavy snow fall restrict movements. With regular summer daytime temperatures around 30°C, outdoor activities are predominant in the summer months.

The summer school and playscheme was introduced in 1990 and a 2-week programme is offered in conjunction with the Parents' Association. Experienced and trainee nursery nurses are recruited as volunteers from the UK to assist the parents and professionals in providing a range of practical activities. These vary from creative art projects to sports activities and educational visits. Whereas the overall aim is to help parents understand and value the educational potential available through play and in their surrounding environment, an important product of these schemes has been their undoubted social value.

In Romanian society, both the parent and their child with learning disabilities have become victims of social isolation. Partnerships have emerged from the summer school enabling parents to offer and receive mutual support. The respite afforded by the scheme allows parents to relax and the therapeutic atmosphere of the occasion is beneficial to carers and volunteers alike.

The main support for the community programme continues to be the Parents' Association itself. This group has proved to be effective in co-ordinating resources and as a source of expertise for its members. It also provides a focus for political campaigning on behalf of people with learning disabilities. Having proved to be the means by which the Poplars Church accessed services for people with learning disabilities in Brasov, the Parents' Association has been the agency through which the volunteers have been able to sustain their support and input.

Outcomes of the Community Support Programme

Sister and brother, Lydia (aged 16 years) and Cyprian (aged 10 years) are typical of Marilyn and Rachel's client group. Both suffer from amiotrophic neural spinal degeneration (Werdnig Hoffman syndrome). Their physical needs have led to restrictions in their educational provision. They receive no schooling whatsoever because they live in a first-floor flat and are thereby effectively immobilized. Their mother is a single parent working to meet the needs of the family, fortunately assisted by a sister and her husband. Family pressures and limited funding have further restricted their potential learning and life-style opportunities.

The main objective for volunteers on the community support programme has been to enhance the quality of life for Lydia, Cyprian and their family whilst providing stimulation and learning opportunities. The visits alone have provided the family with opportunities for communication and the simple expression of care has reduced their social isolation. Consistency and commitment to the maintenance of simple programmes of stimulation have led to increased confidence in both the children and their mother. They even speak a few words of English. The gift of electric wheelchairs has enabled Lydia and Cyprian to move around their home more freely and in overcoming this physical barrier their developmental programmes have been extended to provide greater incentive for educational dis-coveries. The children and their family have been enabled to enjoy social encounter and to identify learning opportunities within their home environment. The further benefit of mobility aids has been to reduce their social isolation and to provide opportunities for developmental programmes based outwith the limitations of their home. Perhaps the greatest achievement of all has been that the family now has hope for its future.

15.6 Summary

This chapter illustrates how a volunteer organiza-tion has sought to address the problems of providing a service for people with learning disabilities in a country where the fabric of daily life has been drastically affected over a 40-year period. The effect of that 40-year period has been to render Romania deficient in almost every area of societal need. The need to develop services for people with a learning disability must be viewed within the context of the need to develop services in all areas of Romanian life.

When considering social policy development in postcolonial countries of the Third World, MacPherson (1982) said that:

> In the development of appropriate policies two features stand out – the enormous gap between rhetoric and reality, and the variation between different sectors. In health, for example, far more progress has been made in the direction of a 'basic needs approach' than in housing and social services. But even in health, the patterns of resource distribution and the nature of health services continue to reflect the imperatives of underdevelopment. It is only recently that discussion of social policies has begun to focus on the relationship between these policies and overall patterns of development, rather than being concerned with more effective implementation of inappropriate programmes derived from external sources.

In contrasting the chapters in Part Eight the reader might reflect upon this statement. Sweden has a history of generating policies and programmes in areas of social need. Romania has no comparable history. Whilst the response of the international community to the plight of Romania may be one that is fuelled by moral outrage, reality decrees that the imperatives of underdevelopment require their social planners to prioritize economic and industrial policy. By utilizing a 'basic needs approach' Poplars Church has achieved tangible outcomes for the people it is seeking to assist.

Discussion Questions

1 **To what degree has the pursuit of philosophical ideals developed into a form of rhetoric which is distant from reality in our own societies?**

2 **By what model or means should planners approach the needs of people with a learning disability on the scale revealed in Romania?**

3 **Examine Sweden and the UK's response to the needs of its citizens in comparison to Romania. By what means can we compare the relative quality of services in each of these countries?**

Reference

MacPherson, S. (1982) *Social Policy in the Third World,* p. 183. Brighton: Wheatsheaf.

Further Reading

Whilst there is no Further Reading suggested for this chapter the reader may wish to consider literature searches under the headings: 'Ceauscescu' and 'Romania'. The lack of further publications illustrates how little we know of Romania before the 1980–90 revolution. For further enquiries please contact 'Poplars Church Romania Project'.

Part Nine: New Dimensions of Learning Disability

16	Contemporary and New Horizons in Learning Disability Research	343

Janet Allen

In the final part of this book, Janet Allen presents a scholarly yet accessible account of research from the field of learning disabilities. The various dimensions of learning disability that have formed the structure of this book direct the wide research base that have been drawn and reported on. Research that encompasses mental health, medication, challenging behaviour, sexual abuse, biological, psychosocial and educational issues are all portrayed. The chapter clearly demonstrates a richness of research that nurse practitioners should incorporate into their work with people with learning disabilities. The chapter concludes with an acknowledgement of the differing epistemological bases of research, and questions whether research is conducted for the advancement of life opportunities for people with learning disabilities or the advancement of researchers. Also questioned is the manner in which people with learning disabilities have been involved in studies. It is regrettable that issues of consent, or how people with learning disabilities were informed about research, have been largely ignored. The final section of the chapter outlines a vision for the future of research in the field.

Chapter 16: Contemporary and new horizons in learning disability research
Janet Allen

16.1 Introduction

This chapter presents an overview of research relevant to the dimensions of learning disability that have been explored in this book. This comprises an overview of educational, biological, psychosocial and health research in the field of learning disabilities. It is suggested that one of the main purposes of research in this field is to change practice, through informing, educating and adding to the body of knowledge that people working with people with a learning disability have. The aim of this review is to highlight recent areas of research concerning people with learning disability, research that will be useful to students, professionals, and others who may wish to explore present-day research in this field. Research on, and with, people with a learning disability is proliferate throughout the health and social-service disciplines. The quality, method,

subject matter and generalizability of the research varies greatly, therefore it is not the intention of this review to cover all research published recently. Rather, the research presented is intended to provide a representative overview of the range and subject matter of the most recent research.

Within these areas, the research reviewed has been selected with the following criteria in mind:

- **the usefulness of the research findings**
- **the accessibility of the research**
- **the relevance of the research**
- **the representativeness of the research.**

The Usefulness of the Research

At some level all research is useful; for example the researcher gains insight into the subject, and learns about the success or otherwise of applying certain methods to answer questions. Additionally, the participants may learn about aspects of themselves that have been under study; and the readers of published research can appraise the usefulness of the information in terms of the contribution to a body of knowledge and evidence. This selection is useful because it highlights a number of issues in learning disability. Issues such as, why do people with a learning disability living in the community suffer with more remediable health problems than the general population? Why is there a higher incidence of mental health problems in the learning disability group than in the general population? Does the simple addition of zinc and vitamin C in the diet really reduce the risk of infection? This review also highlights areas in need of further research, and a number of suggestions are made concerning this at the end of this chapter.

Accessibility of the Research

There are at least two meanings to the word 'access'. One relates to the quality of the information that is accessed through context and understanding, when a reader is reading the research. For example, the information in a research article written in Chinese will not be easily accessed by a person who cannot read Chinese. At another level, if the context and explanation of a piece of research is esoteric, and not related to the everyday practice of the reader in terms of literacy and experience, then access to the information is narrow and the research is inaccessible to a wider audience. With this in mind, the research selected for this review is accessible in terms of the context, subject matter and the resultant information from the research, which can be used to inform the local practice of the reader.

The most accessible research is that which is published in journals or books that are widely available. The research selected for this review,

therefore, has been selected from journals that can be accessed in most university or health college libraries and to which the reader can easily refer if they wish to investigate a piece of research or subject in further depth.

Relevance of the Research

Clearly, whether the research is relevant depends on the subject matter, the cultural context, the date of the research, and the validity and reliability of the findings. It may be the case that research conducted in the 1970s may be interesting, but not of immediate relevance to the present day. This review concentrates on British research, published in British journals, as the cultural context makes the research more relevant than American and European research. However, where pertinent some European and American studies are identified. The majority of the research presented in this overview was published between 1993 and 1995, although research from earlier years that supports and/or is pertinent to the findings is included. The research has been chosen from journals which have an editorial board that scrutinizes the submitted papers; one may therefore place some confidence in the quality of the research, in that the published papers have been subjected to peer review.

Representativeness of the Research

In constructing this review of research in learning disability, over 200 articles in various journals and books have been reviewed. The selection here is not meant to be an annotated bibliography, nor a substitute for reading the original material. Rather it is meant to give the reader a flavour of the quality and quantity of recent research that is available, provide references for further study, and raise the profile of research literature in the reader's experience, thereby encouraging the assimilation of research to inform knowledge and practice in the field of learning disability. The research selected is merely representative of the main body of published research, and it is anticipated that this will inspire the reader to search for further research.

16.2 Research into the Health of People with a Learning Disability

The term 'health' has wide connotation and various definitions (see Chapter 3). For the purpose of this review health includes the mental and physical well being of people with a learning disability.

Mental health problems relate to depression, anxiety, neurosis and psychosis in people with a learning disability, and the research reflects not only descriptions of these conditions, but also relates to the social context in which mental illness may arise.

An important aspect for people working in the field of learning disability is also legal terminology, and the use of diagnostic tests that define mental illness and thereby influence the subsequent courses of intervention and treatment through the forensic system. For this reason, research around definitions and the use of diagnostic tests has also been included.

The research around physical health includes the results of recent surveys into the health of people with a learning disability, as well as description and prevalences of illnesses that people with a learning disability may encounter.

Mental Health in People with a Learning Disability

Although this is an increasingly popular area for researchers, the quality of research varies in accordance with sample and population size, and ranges from large-scale surveys from aggregated client register data to isolated studies of specific diseases.

Definition of Mental Health

The actual definitions of mental health, mental disorder and mental illness are directed by the International Classification of Diseases (ICD-10) (WHO, 1994), of which the diagnostic criteria for

research (DCR) is concerned with mental and behavioural disorders. The use of these diagnostic tools has implications for the people upon whom they are used. Results are often used as part of the legal system to determine treatment and intervention, and contribute to labelling and classification of people, thereby reducing their individuality to a medical term and influencing the pattern of their lives, in terms of how they are treated and seen by others. Not surprisingly then, concerns about the use of these measures have led to research that investigates some of the issues that arise from the use of these diagnostic tools.

Clarke *et al.* (1994) undertook a study to investigate the use of the DCR published with ICD-10, asking clinicians to look at the limitations of the DCR, in terms of applying it to people with a learning disability. Other studies have looked at the use of the psychiatric assessment schedule for adults with a learning disability (Moss *et al.*, 1993; Patel *et al.*, 1993). Both Clarke and Moss in these studies have revealed problems in using these diagnostic and classification systems, and urge the need for further work in this area, to avoid the overgeneralization of labelling people with mental disorder, and to identify other factors and needs in the original presenting problem.

A recent term arising from the literature is that of dual diagnosis, and this refers to people with a learning disability who have mental health problems. Sturmey and Sevin (1993) have provided a useful annotated bibliography of current American and British research, based on the DSM-III-R classification.

Prevalence

There are conflicting reports of the prevalence of mental health problems in people with a learning disability, but there is general agreement that the incidence is higher than that for the general population, which is thought to be around 25–35% (Naylor and Clifton, 1993).

Day and Jancar (1994) has provided a useful overview of research in the area of elderly people with a learning disability, and it is the most recent findings from this review that are included here. Prevalence rates vary from 12.9% for dementia (Sansom *et al.*, 1994), while Moss *et al.* (1993) found prevalence rates of 11.4% for mental and depressive illnesses, and a combined prevalence for all mental health problems of 21% in a population of people aged 50 years and over. Day (1994) suggested that mental health problems in people with a learning disability are three to five times greater than in a comparative normal population. The majority of research has, however, been undertaken on populations within hospitals, where the effects of institutionalization may account for the mental illness, rather than it being related to the learning disability. Overall, Day (1994) claimed that the mental health problems of elderly people with a learning disability are similar to those of the elderly population as a whole. Owing to the variety in the quality of the research, and the increased longevity of this population, it is clear that there is a need for further research, especially in light of the requirements for information for service planners and/or commissioners of health and social care.

While there is evidence of discrepancies between the figures from different sources, the research does highlight the need for staff to be cognizant of the fact that a person presenting antisocial or withdrawn behaviour may actually have a mental health problem. Appropriate assessments can then inform treatment and interventions. Without such an understanding staff may neglect to find the true cause of problems, as found by Patel *et al.* (1993), who claimed that 75% of mental illness was underreported and unrecognized by staff, with symptoms and behaviour ascribed to old age rather than mental health problems, and that this may result in the problems being untreated.

Research on people with a learning disability living in the community indicates that there is a similar pattern of increased prevalence of mental illness to that found in the general population, but a better detection rate by staff, and more chance of the mental illness being treated (Patel *et al.*, 1993).

This evidence has implications for staff training to gain skills in detecting and treating mental illness, and also for professionals from nursing, clinical psychology and psychiatry to promote good mental health.

Finally, various studies, including that of Bouras *et al.* (1993), have reported on the effects of relocation, either within a hospital, or when moving from hospital to the community. Often such moves produce symptoms of trauma, depression and anxiety in people with a learning disability, even when the relocation is planned and the resident prepared as much as possible. Staff should be alerted to the symptoms of depression and anxiety, which may develop into more serious mental illnesses if not attended to.

Down's Syndrome and Mental Health

Recent research has suggested that people with Down's syndrome are less prone to psychotic disorders but more prone to depressive illnesses (Collacott, 1993), with the occurrence and severity of recurring depression increasing with age. This population is also prone to Alzheimer's disease (Fraser, 1988). These findings have been confirmed by Prasher *et al.* (1994) who have suggested an approach for the early detection of Alzheimer's disease. Symptoms that may be early warning signs of Alzheimer's disease are onset of epileptic seizures, depression, emotional disorders and cognitive confusion.

One further study worthy of mention was undertaken by Reid (1994) who revealed the difficulties in diagnosing schizophrenia, using ICD-10, in people with an intelligence quotient (IQ) of less than 45, because of language difficulties. One conclusion was that schizophrenia in this population is possibly under-reported, and therefore remains untreated. The problem of detecting illnesses in people with a profound learning disability, for whom most diagnostic tests (designed for the general population) are unsuitable, is an area worthy of trial and investigation. If different ways of recognizing symptoms could be found, then treatment and interventions may be more accurate in relieving symptoms and improving the quality of life for people with a learning disability who have a mental illness.

Physical Health

Research within this area is varied, and the selection below originates from studies on specific diseases, to several useful overviews of the uptake of health care by people with a learning disability living in the community.

Using Primary Health Services

Access to, and uptake of, primary health-care services has been a cause of concern to those working with people with a learning disability. The research below reflects that for a variety of reasons, people with a learning disability suffer from physical ailments that go undetected, because they do not access primary-care services, such as their general practitioner (GP). Wilson and Haire (1990) undertook a study of 65 people in a day centre who were given a physical examination, which revealed that 57 people had a health problem that was not being treated. Other studies (Howells, 1986; Beange and Baumann, 1990; Langan et al., 1993) have revealed corroborating evidence, concluding that people with a learning disability living in the community do not access primary health-care services as often as the general population. Possible reasons are that the people with learning disabilities may have problems communicating their symptoms, and difficulties accessing GP surgeries or clinics.

With regard to hospitals, Gannesh et al. (1994) undertook an audit of hospital residents and concluded that GP consultations by residents were similar to those of the normal population, mainly because the GP visited the hospital wards. A similar picture of physical needs being missed is presented in a study by Yeates (1992) who investigated 1048 people in hospitals, community homes and adult training centres to ascertain their hearing needs. The published report covered 300 people, of whom 119 were discovered to have a hearing loss sufficient to require amplification, yet they were not being treated. However, the methods of such studies, including non-random selection of subjects and the lack of control groups in the normal population, reveal a need for further research into the factors that result in people with a learning disability attending and using primary health-care facilities.

Further evidence of the need for physical assessment of people in the community comes from Stewart et al. (1994) who conducted a study in Australia on diet and nutrition and found that the frequency of overweight was twice that in the normal population, with a subsequent rise in the numbers of people with learning disability who had hypertension and other diet-related problems.

With regard to physical health in the elderly, it has been suggested by Moss et al. (1993) that health problems are similar for people with a learning disability as for the general elderly population, although this conclusion is limited to a study of the causes of death in residents in one hospital from 1930 to 1980. Physical health problems often relate to loss of mobility, increased incontinence, deterioration in vision and hearing, and proneness to falls and injury. This is supported by Maaskant and Havemann (1990), who provided useful indicators for assessing the health needs of the elderly population.

An interesting note of caution is provided by Rodgers (1993) who indicated that in the literature around health-care needs of people with learning disability, there are suggestions that health needs are better met in institutions, under the medical model of health care, because of the ease of access to GPs and consultants. This should not be seen as an argument for institutionalized living, but rather should urge further research into why people are unable to access normal community primary health-care services, and find ways to enable them to do so.

Evidently, research appears to indicate a need for people with a learning disability to be helped to access a range of primary health-care services, a function that community teams for people with a learning disability could develop to strengthen their role in increasing health in this section of the population. The primary function of such multi-professional health-care teams is to support people with a learning disability living in the community, and a core role should be in promoting optimum physical health. The above studies have provided evidence that this may be a role that needs strengthening.

Medication

Studies concerning medication are included because of the implications for health-care workers, and because of the role that medication plays in terms of treatment for mental illness behaviour disorders and epilepsy, the side effects of which affect the lives of people with learning disabilities.

Clarke (1994) undertook an investigation into the hazards and benefits of lithium treatment for people with depression and mania. One of the conclusions was that people who had more knowledge of the effects of their medication responded better to treatment.

Two studies regarding the prescribing of medication for people with a learning disability highlighted the differences between hospital and community. Branford and Kollacott (1993) surveyed the prescribing of medicines on the population with a learning disability in Leicestershire (2,300 people) in National Health Service (NHS) settings and living in the community. This paper provided a useful overview of the research in this area, and the conclusions revealed that people in NHS settings received more controlling drugs for

behavioural difficulties than those living in the community. Several suggested reasons for this are that people living in a hospital are more likely to be seen by a doctor or consultant, and to be treated with medication for their behaviour difficulties rather than with other forms of treatment, such as behaviour therapy. Also, people with a learning disability living in the community may be less likely to see their GP or consultant, and more likely to receive other forms of intervention and treatment.

A further study of the prescribing of antiepileptic drugs in NHS settings and community settings (Branford, 1993) suggested that specialist consultants were more likely to prescribe more accurately using newer drug therapies, than were GPs. A study by Nichols and colleagues using a case note survey found that 55% of people with epilepsy were on multiple drugs, and other findings have indicated the need for further research into the control of epilepsy.

Finally, a small-scale study was conducted into the potential harm of administering sugar-coated medication to children. In 143 subjects, 68% taking anticonvulsant medication were suffering from excessive damage to their teeth. The recommendations included a reminder that health-care workers should encourage mothers to use medication with the least sugar in it; that is tablets and capsules rather than sugary syrup (Sheiham and Eadsforth, 1993).

Reader Activity 16.1
Does the research presented thus far reflect the difficulties that were outlined in Chapter 3 concerning the health of people with a learning disability?

16.3 Psychosocial Research

This section presents research that relates to the psychological and social aspects of the lives of people with a learning disability. Psychological research on people with a learning disability covers all the psychological therapies, cognitive behaviour therapy, behaviour modification, treatments for anxiety and phobias, anger management and relaxation therapies, and people who exhibit challenging behaviour, sexual disturbances, depression, anxiety and phobias.

Challenging Behaviour

The term 'challenging behaviour' in this chapter refers to any prolonged behaviours that place the person with a learning disability at risk of harm to themselves or others. This includes aggressive behaviour, self-injurious behaviours, and harm to property. Hastings and Remington (1993) looked at the connotations of the label 'challenging behaviour' and found that within a population of university students, the label had more positive connotations than that of learning disability. Although this was a limited study in terms of the sample, it reveals some useful information around the use and abuse of labels.

Interventions

Mansell (1994) reviewed the research on challenging behaviour, especially regarding the understanding and response of people to challenging behaviour. He also discussed current issues in learning disability services for adults, and priorities for service development were considered; this focused on how the contracting process could be used to help improve services.

Most responses regarding treatment are through behaviourist therapy techniques, an approach discussed by Hastings and Remington (1994) who, while describing the advantages of behaviourist approaches, suggested that such techniques fail in achieving their goals because of the inadequate skills in the people, including nursing staff who used such techniques. They advocated increased support for staff, and also suggested that in the absence of adequate training

---

Box 16.1 Prevalence of challenging behaviour

An epidemiological survey in 1992 (Qureshi and Alborz) identified rates of prevalence for people with challenging behaviour, and revealed that incidence of challenging behaviour rose in health districts which included cities, as opposed to rural and urban areas. Emerson (1992) reported that between 4 and 10% of people with a learning disability living in hospitals inflict injuries upon themselves, half of whom are also destructive to property and other people. The figures for people living at home and in group homes were considerably lower (8% and 2.7% respectively), supporting other evidence about the impact of the environment on the development of challenging behaviour within individuals. Harris (1993), however, in a survey of the whole South Western Health Region found 17.6% of aggressive behaviour in adults with a learning disability, and 12.6% for children with a learning disability. These differences may be accounted for by different perceptions of verbal and physical aggressive behaviour, and would be enhanced by looking at similar levels of physical aggression in the general population.

A study in Hampshire (Norgate, 1994) identified the rate for children exhibiting self-injurious behaviour and aggression to others to be 7% and 24% respectively of the school's population, with a ratio of male to female of 2:1. However, caution should be exercised in generalizing the findings to the population of people with a learning disability as a whole, but the study gives some indication of the level of the problems of challenging behaviour.

---

for staff, it might be useful to look at the way that behaviour can be improved by building on the therapeutic social relationships between staff and people with learning difficulties, rather than aversive interventions that do not necessarily result in long-term improvements. Certainly, in the meta-analysis undertaken by Scotti et al. (1991) no clear evidence was found to support the view that structured behaviourist interventions, by themselves, eliminated challenging behaviours over a long period of time. This was supported by the results of the overview by Emerson (1992) cited earlier.

Reader Activity 16.2
Given that we have no empirical evidence to suggest that structured behaviourist interventions, on their own, necessarily eliminate challenging behaviours, why do such approaches remain the most consistently used by professional care staff?

Clegg (1994) challenged the behavioural interventionist view, seeing it as limited and impoverished in dealing with the complex reasons and causes of challenging behaviour, which, it is argued, reside as much in the environment as in the individual. Clegg (1994) called for a more sympathetic approach, looking at the way that staff and caregivers deal with such behaviours within the environment, building on the strengths of more general interactions, and supportive relationships rather than imposed interventions.

Evidence of the success of a treatment and structured interventionist approach is provided by Matthews who undertook a record analysis and interviews of 44 people who were attending a crisis intervention unit because of their behaviour. He concluded that people with challenging behaviour respond more favourably within a treatment unit, using behaviourist techniques, than in their own environment. This conclusion has also been reached by other researchers, but mainly by those connected with or working in a treatment unit.

Butterfield (1990) discussed the ethical implications concerning the use of non-aversive and aversive techniques of treating challenging behaviours, and described the research undertaken, from medication to behaviourist approaches. A new approach, that of gentle teaching, is a non-aversive approach, building on the resources within people and the environment, which reflects many of the suggestions regarding using non-aversive interventions. Gentle teaching is a relatively new approach, and apart from brief case studies and anecdotal accounts, there is little reported research of value.

The issues in the debate surrounding interventions with people with challenging behaviour are clearly unresolved, and the research alone does not provide enough valid or reliable evidence for supporting either non-aversive or aversive techniques. More published research is needed into the effectiveness or otherwise of carrying out interventions with people with challenging behaviour in their own homes, in order to provide a comparison with the above studies. It would seem that, until further research is undertaken, using the controlled-trial method of investigation, approaches to interventions with people with challenging behaviour should be based on the unique needs of clients, and the skills of staff.

Sexual Abuse of People with a Learning Disability

The formerly hidden population of people with a learning disability who have, or are being, sexually abused, is slowly emerging through the literature of the late 1980s (Brown and Craft, 1989; Craft, 1987) which has highlighted the need for further investigation into this area.

Recent figures for prevalence and incidence varies across American and British studies. Cooke (1990) estimated that 4–5%, of adults with a learning disability have suffered sexual abuse (from information from consultants in the psychiatry of mental handicap), while Buchanan and Wilkins (1992) reported 18% and Finkelhor *et al.* (1990) reported 25–58%. The discrepancies may be accounted for by the different methods of investigation (self-report by interview, staff reporting, and allegations). However, when compared to figures for abuse in the general population (10%) for children under 16 years (Baker and Duncan, 1985) it would seem that people and children with a learning disability have a higher risk of being sexually abused.

Turk and Brown (1993) have reported on the largest survey to date of the sexual abuse of adults with a learning disability. The research, funded by the Joseph Rowntree Foundation, and undertaken across South East Thames Health Authority, aimed to investigate all the new cases of reported allegations and cases of sexual abuse since 1989, and to increase staff confidence in recognizing and dealing with abuse. The report contained a useful and thorough definition of sexual abuse. The results of Turk and Brown's survey (1993), if extrapolated to the rest of the population, suggest that 830 new cases of sexual abuse occur each year, with the ratio between men and women being 1:3 respectively. In almost 50% of reported cases, no action is taken against the perpetrator, 98% of whom are men.

One of the reasons that sexual abuse is to a large extent still submerged may be because of the difficulties that staff working with people with a learning disability have in confronting and coping with the issue. This survey involved staff teams across the region, and found that confidence in their abilities to acknowledge, recognize and deal with sexual abuse varied. The level of confidence appears to be related to gender differences and the amount of training and education that staff had received.

These findings were similar to research undertaken by Allington (1992) who undertook a survey of 107 day and residential staff, and found that over one-third never discuss the issue, even though all staff thought that people with learning disabilities were at risk of sexual abuse. Over 80% of staff thought that further information regarding what to do about suspicions of sexual abuse would assist them with dealing with the issue. One of the issues to arise from this research is that staff do need training in recognizing and dealing with sexual abuse.

Further research on gender differences and staff experience and attitude in this area is recommended.

Bereavement

The effects of a bereavement on children and people with a learning disability have been highlighted, with the recognition that an unresolved grieving process can precipitate disturbed behaviours and depression (Oswin, 1994). Cathcart (1995) looked at the effects of different interventions to assist the grieving process, and Lindsay *et al.* (1993) described the application of cognitive therapy for people with a learning disability who may be depressed as a result of bereavement.

16.4 Social Research

Six areas are reviewed under this heading: community homes, hospitals, parents with a learning disability, social support networks, leisure and recreation, and social education centres (resource centres).

Community Homes

A useful piece of cost analysis was undertaken by Shiell *et al.* (1992) who summarized that the cost of residential facilities for people with a learning disability averaged £38 per day, ranging from £16 to £90. Higher dependent residents in smaller homes were more expensive to maintain, voluntary and private sectors were the least expensive, and health authorities the most expensive. The research did not pursue the question of the quality of peoples' lives in the different residential homes, and clearly further research in this area should look at quality as well as cost.

Research and evaluation of the benefits or otherwise of the transition of people with a learning disability from hospital to community has virtually dominated the social research world, with endless reports describing the lives and activities of staff and people with learning disabilities in terms of community presence, activities and other benefits. The few studies reported here represent the most recent, and possibly the most useful.

With regard to community living, recent research by Ballinger (1993) studied residents in four community homes, ranging from 8 to 19 residents, with the quality of life indicated by community contacts and presence. There was a significant difference between the smaller homes, and the 19-bedded unit, and the findings from this study were corroborated by Joyce (1994) who, whilst looking at how the individual characteristics of people with a learning disability would affect the outcome of a move to residential care, found that smaller group homes were more likely to result in an improved quality of life.

More recent research has focused on the concept of 'first generation' housing, people with learning disabilities who moved into the community in the 1980s supported by detailed planning and development and research, and 'second generation' housing, people who have since been moved out, with perhaps less money, planning and support. Research on the first generation of people with learning disabilities moving into the community (Felce et al., 1986; Lowe and de Pavia, 1991) reported the benefits in terms of quality of life, community presence, improved environment and staffing ratios. Perry and Felce (1994) have since reported on the second generation, looking at indicators such as skill acquisition and the use of community facilities. The implications are that further energy needs to be put into people with a learning disability being actually integrated into the community in terms of participation and social integration. To achieve this in the first instance, people with a learning disability rely on the skills and energy and willingness of staff to help them achieve integration into community activities. This research recognized the fact that simply living in the community does not result in the full benefits of community life as the general population may experience. Community presence is not simply living in the community, but living with the community, and future research needs to explore the constraints on community participation.

Hospitals

With a number of people still living in hospitals, and enduring relocation within the hospital as a result of policies, a useful study by Firth *et al.* (1990) compared groups of hospital residents who had been relocated, with a group who had not and a third group that suffered disturbances but were not relocated. Findings were similar to earlier research, in that symptoms from relocation were weight loss, anxiety, depression and behavioural problems, and advocated thorough assessments before and after relocation, with follow-up support, especially for the more profoundly handicapped residents. Although this research was undertaken in hospitals, it is often the case that people in the community have to be moved between residential settings.

Whilst hospitals are slowly closing, specialist assessment and treatment services for people with a learning disability who offend, or have severe challenging behaviour and mental illness, are being developed. Research from two such units includes a follow-up study of six residents from a mental impairment evaluation and treatment service by Clare and Murphy (1993) who found that all residents, who initially had severe problems, had made gains in skills and social functioning. This study followed a previous study (Murphy and Clare, 1991) which analysed the benefits of such a treatment centre. Without a comparative treatment group within the community, it is difficult to determine whether such a unit is better than treatment in the client's home or community. Certainly, when Cumella and Sansom (1994) looked at the need for a medium-secure unit and low-level secure unit, they recommended that local community mental impairment services should be developed, rather than medium-secure units.

Parents with a Learning Disability

This small but needy population has been well researched in America through the 1970s and 1980s, but has only recently caught the attention of researchers in Britain. While policies and attitudes changed, resulting in more people with a learning disability marrying and/or having children, little concerted action has been taken to support these people and their families, a conclusion reached by Allen (1991) in an early study of four parents with a learning disability. As a consequence, children are disadvantaged environmentally, socially and educationally. More recent reviews (Booth and Booth, 1993; Dowdney and Skuse, 1993) point to the methodological difficulties in identifying the population, and researching parental skills in a sympathetic and non-judgemental manner. Sample sizes have tended to be small, and checklists for adequate parenting have not defined minimum parenting requirements. Booth and Booth (1994) undertook an in-depth study of 20 parents with a learning disability which highlighted the risk of this population having children taken into care. Also, that there was insufficient support from professionals and this has implications for services to provide more support to keep the families together. In America, training and support programmes have been initiated for parents with a learning disability (Tymchuk and Andron, 1992).

Reader Activity 16.3

Given the extreme sensitivities over the ability of parents wtih a learning disability to care appropriately for their children, do you think it likely that research in this area will ever be able to change practice of professional carers, as they may fear public opinion?

Social Support Networks

Support for people with a learning disability and their carers has been researched mainly in the area of respite care services. A study by Grant (1993) elicited information from carers of 79 people with a learning disability over a period of 2 years, and showed that support networks can change and vary.

The over-protective nature of some carers resulted in restriction of the lives of their sons and daughters. This highlighted a need for full and careful information for carers on the rights and choices of people with a learning disability, and the need for support to the carers in promoting independent living for their children.

Leisure and Recreation

Most people in the general population are able to organize their leisure time and pursue recreational activities that enhance their physical and mental well being. The increased interest in outdoor pursuits, and the development of sports centres are testimony to this. People with a learning disability may need help accessing sport and leisure opportunities, and Brown and Chamov (1993) have described the benefits that such activities produce. Further evidence of the positive results of outdoor activity is described by Rose and Massey (1993), who introduced a group of people with learning disabilities to outdoor pursuits, with benefits outlined in the research-based evaluation of their endeavours. In this research the views of people with a learning disability are reflected, and the information should provide encouragement to others in helping people with a learning disability access experiences that develop their confidence and physical skills.

Social Education Centres (Resource Centres)

For many people with a learning disability, access to structured activity and leisure is obtained through attending a day centre. Social education centres provide social, educational and vocational opportunites, and assist people with a learning disability to access and use general community facilities. Most research into day centres has reflected concerns around the range and quality of provision offered by day centres, using an evaluative approach to investigate the benefits (or otherwise) of day centres to the people who use their services.

One example is a study by Lowe *et al.* (1992) of two Welsh day centres. Findings were that internal organization of activities resulted in a high level of activity for the students, but work placements and outside trips did not automatically result in more engagement with the community. The researchers did not consult the clients as to their views. A more recent study by Beyer *et al.* (1994) of all the day centres in Wales led to several conclusions, including that not all activities within the centres resulted in benefits for the clients, and that there needs to be more consultation with consumers. An observational study by Pettipher and Mansell (1993) revealed that clients were disengaged from activities from between 1 and 2 h in a 5-h day, sitting around waiting for various reasons. Another observational study by Rose *et al.* (1993) looked at the difference between provision for clients with special needs in two day centres, finding that those who were integrated into the centre had less contact with staff and meaningful activities than those who had their own unit with the centre. Their research advocated the use of separate units, suggesting that one of the benefits is the increased integration with the general community. These findings are controversial, in that they contradict the movement towards integration of people with special needs into the mainstream of a centre, rather than segregating them in special units. Research into consumer satisfaction with a day centre for older people with a learning disability was conducted through interviews of 15 clients by Foote and Rose (1993). Results revealed the major sources of satisfaction were the social contact and the activities facilitated by the centre. Areas of dissatisfaction included the desire to go out of the centre more.

The research methods used in the above studies limit the application of the findings to those areas where the investigations took place, although some of the conclusions can be used to inform service providers. There appears to be a need for research that investigates and explains the cause of some of the problems experienced by people attending day centres, especially more research which invites the views and experiences of day centres from people with a learning disability.

16.5 Biological Research

Research into the biological aspects of learning disability has traditionally reflected the more medical and physiological elements, including research into identified causation and syndromes. This research is providing more specific reasons for the causation of learning disability, which is important to parents who are often unhappy with vague explanations of handicap such as birth trauma. Such research is also significant for helping to identify new preventive measures, more specific prognosis, and areas for further research. Published biological research is wide-ranging, and to a large extent has focused on minute and remote aspects of learning disability. Presenting all such research undertaken over the last 2 years would resemble little more than an annotated bibliography. For the purpose of this review, the research in the two most prolific areas is presented, namely recent developments in autism and Down's syndrome.

Down's Syndrome

This is the commonest cause of learning disability, and historically has been a well-researched area. Some of the more recent research in the area has included the uptake of prenatal investigations to detect Down's syndrome in the womb, the aetiology of Down's syndrome and Alzheimer's disease, and research into the immune system.

Steele (1993) has surveyed the uptake of amniocentesis and has estimated it at between 20 and 40% of eligible women. What effect this has had on the birth rate of babies with Down's syndrome is unknown, and one proposal is that biochemical methods of detection may lead to more frequent prenatal diagnosis, as women may be reluctant to

Box 16.2 Autism

This umbrella term refers to a wide range of infantile and childhood disorders listed under DSM-111 as pervasive developmental disorders (Fraser, 1995). Recent developments have included the use of the up-dated American Diagnostic and Statistic Manual of Mental Disorders (DSM-111 R 1987), that has resulted in three subdivisions, infantile autism, atypical autism and childhood onset of pervasive developmental disorder. Use of this diagnostic tool has resulted in more accurate diagnosis of children, with implications for improvement in attending to the complex needs of these children. Children with autism often have accompanying syndromes, for example epilepsy, fragile X and tuberous sclerosis.

A recent study by Deb and Prasad (1994) of 634 children with a learning disability in the Grampian region of northeast Scotland sought to identify prevalence. Using DSM-111 R for a diagnosis of autistic disorder, supplemented with information from questionnaires, findings revealed that 14.3% of the children fulfilled some of the diagnostic criteria for autistic disorder, with a male:female ratio of 3:1. Figures from the research overall, revealed a 9 per 10 000 minimum prevalence of autistic disorder among all school-age children in the region. There was a higher prevalence of autistic disorder in the cities compared with the rural areas, the prevalence increasing with decreasing IQ.

On a broader scale, Gillberg (1991) undertook a multinational survey and found a prevalence rate of 17 per 10 000, with little difference in rural and urban areas, but the same male to female ratio.

A further development with regards to autism and Down's syndrome by Ghaziuddin *et al.* (1992) has suggested that 4–5% of people with Down's syndrome may have autism, a finding that is corroborated by Gillberg (1991) in his study. As the symptoms of autism may at present be masked by the Down's syndrome diagnosis, this research again has implications for people working with people with Down's syndrome.

A syndrome related to autism, Asperger's syndrome, has also received attention, with new findings reporting a higher incidence than autism (36 per 10 000). Ehler and Gillberg (1993) suggested that previously many children with Asperger's syndrome have been misdiagnosed as autistic. Three case studies by Simblett and Wilson (1993) have highlighted the social difficulties that people with this syndrome experience, failing to meet the criteria for autistic services and sometimes not intellectually impaired enough to benefit fully from learning disabled services, thus falling through the gaps in service provision.

undergo amniocentesis because of the risks. Nicholson and Alberman (1992) predict that the live birth rate of babies with Down's syndrome will be higher in the year 2000 than ever before, from an average of 1.7/1000 to 1.5/1000, with factors such as the rising population of women of child-bearing age, the low rate of uptake of screening and abortion, and the higher age of women giving birth. These findings correspond to studies in other countries (Goodwin and Huether, 1987; Stefalaar and Evenhuis, 1989) and this has implications for the planning of services.

Recent research has supported the hypothesis that there is a link between ionizing radiation and Down's syndrome, with Bound *et al.* (1995) reporting on the Fylde district of England, where maximum birth rates of babies with Down's syndrome coincided with maximum doses of ionizing radiation across the whole population.

Further biological research that may be of interest was the finding by Nespoli and colleagues in 1993 that children and people with Down's syndrome are prone to infection because of a greater reduction in the T cells of the immunization system compared with the general population. Following this, Licastro *et al.* (1994) undertook a clinical trial giving children with Down's syndrome oral zinc supplementation over 4 months to boost their resistance to infections. This resulted in a significantly reduced incidence of infection.

Collacott (1993) has reported on evidence that suggests that changes in behaviour in ageing people with Down's syndrome may be related to late-onset epileptic seizures, which are themselves associated with the onset of Alzheimer's disease. This concords with findings mentioned earlier in this chapter.

Hepatitis B

Devlin *et al.* (1993) in a study of 307 people with a learning disability attending various day centres in Ireland, found an incidence rate of 4% for hepatitis B, compared with less than 1% for the general population, suggesting that populations in residential centres should be routinely tested. Similarly, Arulajan *et al.* (1992) found that 5.7% of a hospital population in Southampton showed hepatitis B surface antigen, with 7.9% of the population carriers. Their research advocates the cost benefits of screening before immunization, rather than blanket immunization.

Tardive Dyskinesia

A general cluster of abnormal physical movements known as tardive dyskinesia has been the subject of research for a number of years, with attempts to find associations between age, degree of handicap, and the use of neuroleptics. The most recent report, which summarizes the previous evidence and looked for factors associated with tardive dyskinesia, was undertaken by Branford *et al.* (1995) on a hospital population of 213 residents. Their results supported an association between tardive dyskinesia and the use of neuroleptics, although no particular drug was uniquely responsible. People with profound disabilities who were not on neuroleptic medication were also susceptible to tardive dyskinesia, and these findings correspond to the findings of a previous study by Rogers *et al.* (1991), who suggested that motor disorders in general have a cerebral rather than drug-induced basis.

Gingell and Nadarajeh (1994) looked at the range of movement disorders in general, in relation to antipsychotic medication. Using a control group of non-medication, matched with a group who used medication, they did not find a significant difference in movement disorders between the two groups. Further research is necessary in this area to clarify some of the issues raised.

16.6 Education

Three main issues in current research in education have been the integration of children with learning disabilities into mainstream education and the provision of education for these children; the use of conductive education; and research into children who present challenging behaviours.

Provision of Education for Children with Special Needs

Recent interest in the educational system has been driven by the need to demonstrate value for money, which has become more pertinent since the emphasis on local management of resources.

School effectiveness studies, looking at performance indicators (Raudenbush and Williams, 1991) and postschool outcome indicators (Thompson *al.*, 1993) have both influenced policy and pr More recently, Thompson and Ward (1⁰ applied a cost/benefit analysis to seco provision for children with learr undertaking a national survey o looking at the results of ed variables which included r and society, employment, ciency. While the ben described, there is a cauti sion regarding measuring tion solely in terms of econ

Integration of Pupils with Special Needs into Mainstream Schooling

Under the Education Act of 1981, education authorities were encouraged to integrate children with special educational needs into mainstream schooling, a movement that at the time was already being addressed in other western countries. Research has, through the years, identified a wide range of barriers: political, resources, parental and teachers attitudes. The introduction of the Education Reform Act (1988) emphasized league tables of performance. As a result, integration varies widely across the country.

Reader Activity 16.4
Construct arguments both for and against the integration of children with a learning dissibility into ordinary schools. Use research obtained from this chapter to support your arguments.

Conductive education

This method of intense education for children was developed by the Peto Institute of Hungary, and was introduced to Britain in the early 1980s. Recent research has attempted to evaluate and determine the benefits of conductive education, as opposed to more usual special education programmes. One study by Hur and Cochrane (1995) studied children with cerebral palsy, one group undertaking conductive education and one group a special education programme. Both groups were matched for IQ, age and social class. The researchers found no significant difference in attainment levels in terms of education and physical abilities between the two groups, who both performed and achieved as expected.

s with Challenging Behaviours

ren who present at school with challenging
r harm their chances of successful educa-
an be a danger to themselves and others.

With the advent of community care, such children are no longer admitted to long-stay hospitals and removed from the education system. Schools now have to learn to cope with these children, and it is in the light of these changes that research has been undertaken.

Kiernan and Kiernan (1994) undertook a survey of one in six schools in England and Wales, to determine the prevalence of perceived challenging behaviour in the schools, and the training needs of teachers. Approximately 18% of children exhibited severe challenging behaviour, while overall 26% exhibited some form of mild to severe challenging behaviour, with 9% being prescribed medication. Concern expressed by the teachers was around lack of staff to assist with disruptive behaviour, and lack of experience in dealing with the children. Most felt that they, and other children, suffered as a result of the behaviours. It is recognized that intensive assessment treatment is necessary, in partnership between professionals and parents. In a study that looked at the topography of challenging behaviours displayed at home and school, Cromby et al. (1994) found that there were similarities in behaviour at home and school, and differences, with more pupils expressing challenging behaviours at their schools than in their homes. In their study of one special school, one of the conclusions emphasized the need for partnership between home and school, especially in terms of interventions to reduce the behaviours.

16.7 Conclusions

- It is clear from this overview that research emerges from a variety of epistemological standpoints, with a tenuous relationship between the needs of the researcher and the needs of people with a learning disability. Research has looked at evaluating policy changes and investigating various aspects of the lives of people with a learning disability, based on observation of local populations. This has resulted in research of varying quality, with findings that can seldom be generalized. Exceptions to this are national research funded by agencies such as the Joseph Rowntree Fund. These and other factors make it difficult for the results of research to influence policy and practice, although it is beyond the remit of this chapter to explore the relationship between research and policy.

- In the description of the research, there has been little mention of the procedures adopted to gain the permission of people with a learning disability to be research subjects. Following careful analysis of all the studies presented in this chapter no researcher has explained or mentioned how consent for the research was obtained from the people with a learning disability, who were the subjects of such research, how the subjects were informed about the research, or how any of the information derived from their participation was fed back to them. It is also disappointingly rare to find research that has been undertaken that includes the views of people with a learning disability.

  To further strengthen the case for people with a learning disability to be accorded the same rights as the general population, the research community could make explicit how the rights of their subjects were recognized and respected during the process of the research, and how ethical considerations influenced the research. For example, where possible all research should be explained fully in a way that can be understood, either to the person with a learning disability, their advocate or carer, and permission obtained. Furthermore, it is good practice to feed back the results of research to the participants; no mention has been made of any procedures relating to dissemination to the subjects of the research.

- In presenting this overview, three types of research have emerged:

(1) Local investigations or evaluations, based on small populations and with results that can be used to monitor or change practice locally. These reinforce the use of research as an evaluative tool that should be used as a matter of practice to monitor and evaluate aspects of the quality of life for people with a learning disability.

(2) Epidemiological research, to find out prevalence and indicators of conditions and syndromes. Such studies are useful for planning, but they appear to be undertaken on an *ad hoc* basis, originating from the skills and interest of the researcher rather than the overall needs of this population. The result is that there is a wealth of information on certain syndromes, such as Down's syndrome or autism, while other groups of people for whom the need of information is just as relevant for planning and policy purposes are neglected.

(3) Large-scale investigations into issues that relate to the whole of the population of people with learning disability, such as research on sexual abuse, mentioned earlier in the chapter. These to some extent provide valid generalizable findings that can inform policy makers and planners across the whole of the community.

While all of the above are relevant, it is evident that there is an element of duplication, with researchers covering similar themes in isolation. While some areas of the lives of people with a learning disability receive a lot of attention from the research community, for example evaluation of various aspects of the quality of life of people in residential homes, many other areas receive little attention with a consequent dearth of information. It should be noted that duplication should not be conflated with replication; replication is a valid scientific process that is important in the field of research.

16.8 The Future for Research

Given that this review has presented research from the recent past and present, and that this chapter is also concerned with new horizons for people with a learning disability, below is a suggested approach to the future direction of research in the field.

Areas for Research

- **Bereavement.** The needs of people with a learning disability who have been bereaved, the skills of staff in coping with bereavement.
- **Advocacy.** There are numerous advocacy schemes, and a need for advocacy to assist people with a learning disability to achieve their rights. Research into evaluating different types of advocacy schemes and the outcomes and results of such schemes, would assist in developing effective advocacy schemes. A national survey of people with a learning difficulty, to assess their views on their lives and how they wish to live them.
- **Annual surveys and assessments** on the influences, both economical and social, on carers and people with a learning disability, undertaken on a national scale and feeding annually into an evaluation of how their lives are being affected by government and local policies.

It has appeared that research into learning disability is by and large not co-ordinated, work is disparate and therefore often fails to address the immediate health needs in the lives of people with a learning disability in a focused way. Research can be one source of information upon which strategies, policies and plans can be developed. While there are centres that are committed to a research programme into learning disability, for example the Hester Adrian Centre Manchester, the Norah Fry Unit, Bristol (see Box 16.3 for a useful list) it might be useful if the efforts of such centres were co-ordinated in a unified approach.

A national council for learning disability research could be set up, with the remit to:

- Advise on priorities for research into learning disability, based on the needs of people with a learning disability, national policy issues and government health priorities.
- Develop a strategy for research, that would drive a co-ordinated approach to research into learning disability, thereby developing information that can be used to advise planning, locally and nationally.
- Develop an ethical code for research into learning disability, taking into account the rights of people with a learning disability, codes of good practice for research, and advise researchers on how to develop these codes into practice when undertaking research.

Part of the role of such a council would be to generate funding for research, both by acting as a pressure group to lobby for funds from national funding agencies such as the NHS research and development directorate, and to publicize access to funding, and to attract funding for research. In addition the council could provide standards for research into learning disabilities that include methodological guidelines on selection criteria of subjects, ethics, and encourage quality research.

Reader Activity 16.5
Reflect on the learning disability journals that you read. How often are research papers included and what are the themes of research that are reported on?

Discussion Questions

1 **How relevant is the research surveyed in this chapter to the development of evidenced practice?**

2 **What specific examples of research can be identified that have had an impact, either on the practice of professional carers or the development of services?**

3 How feasible or even desirable is it for people with a learning disability to give their permission for research to be conducted in this area, as has been suggested in this chapter?

References

Allen, J. (1991) What support do parents with a learning disability need? Dissertation. University of Hull.

Allington, C. (1992) Sexual abuse within services for people with learning disabilities. *Mental Handicap* **20**: 59–63.

Arulajan, A., Tyrie, C., Phillips, K. and O'Connell, S. (1992) Hepatitis B screening and immunisation for people with a mental handicap in Southampton: costs and benefits. *Journal of Intellectual Disability Research* **36**: 259–264.

Baker, A. and Duncan, S. (1985) Child sexual abuse: A study of prevalence in Great Britain. *Child Sexual Abuse and Neglect* **9**: 457–467.

Ballinger, C. (1993) Do smaller homes result in increased integration? *Mental Handicap Research* **6**(4): 303–311.

Beange, H. and Baumann, A. (1990) Health care for the developmentally disabled. Is it necessary? *In* Fraser, W. (Ed.) *Key Issues in Mental Retardation Research.* London: Routledge.

Beyer, S., Kilsby, M. and Lowe, K. (1994) What do ATCs offer in Wales? A survey of Welsh day services. *Mental Handicap Research* **1**(1): 16–22.

Booth, T. and Booth, W. (1993) Parenting with learning difficulties: lessons for practitioners. *British Journal of Social Work* **23**: 459–480.

Booth, T. and Booth, W. (1994) Parental adequacy, parenting failure and parents with learning difficulties. *Health and Social Care* **2**: 161–172.

Bound, J., Francis, B. and Harvey, P. (1995) Down's syndrome: prevalence and ionising radiation in an area of north west England. *Journal of Epidemiology and Community Health* **49**: 164–170.

Bouras, N., Kon, Y. and Drummond, C. (1993) Medical and psychiatric needs of adults with a mental handicap. *Journal of Intellectual Disability Research* **37**: 177–182.

Branford. D. and Kollacott, R. (1993) Comparison of community and institutional prescription of antiepileptic drugs for individuals with learning disabilities. *Journal of Intellectual Disability Research* **36**: 115–129.

Branford, D., Bhaumik, S., Collacott, R. and Mohamed, W. (1995) Dyskinetic movements in a population of people with learning disabilities. *British Journal of Developmental Disabilities* **XLI**(Part 1) No.80: 23–32.

Brown, H. and Craft, A. (Eds) (1989) *Thinking the Unthinkable.* London: FPA Unit.

Brown, H., Hunt, N. and Stein, J. (1994) Alarming but very necessary: working with staff groups around the sexual abuse of adults with learning disability. *Journal of Intellectual Disability Research* **38**: 393–412.

Brown, J. and Chamove, A. (1993) Mental and physical activity benefits in adults with mental handicap. *Mental Handicap Research* **6**(2): 155–168.

Buchanan and Wilkins (1992) Sexual abuse of the mentally handicapped: difficulties in establishing prevalence. *Psychiatric Bulletin* **15**: 601–605.

Butterfield, E. (1990) Serious self-injury, the ethics and treatment of research. *In* Repp, A.C. and Singh, N.N. (Eds) *Perspectives on the Use of Non-aversive Intervention for Persons with Developmental Disabilities.* Sycamore IL: Sycamore.

Cathcart, F. (1995) Death and people with learning disability: interventions to support clients and carers. *British Journal of Clinical Psychology* **34**: 165–175.

Clare, I. and Murphy, G. (1993) MIETS (Mental impairment evaluation and treatment service) a service option for people with mild mental handicaps and challenging behaviours and/or psychiatric problems. *Mental Handicap Research* **6**(1): 70–78.

Clarke, D. and Pickles, K. (1994) Lithium treatment for people with a learning disability. *Journal of Intellectual Disability* **38**(2): 187–194.

Clarke, D., Cumella, S., Corbett, J. *et al.* (1994) Use of ICD-10 Research Diagnostic Criteria to categorise psychiatric and behavioural abnormalities among people with learning difficulties. *Mental Handicap Research* **7**(4): 273–295.

Clegg, J. (1994) Epistemology and learning disability. *British Journal of Clinical Psychology* **33**: 439–444.

Collacott, R. (1993) Epilepsy, dementia and adaptive behaviour in Down's syndrome. *Journal of Intellectual Disability Research* **37**: 153–160.

Cooke, L. (1990) Abuse of mentally handicapped adults. *British Medical Journal* **300**: 193.

Craft, A. (1987) *Mental Handicap and Sexuality: Issues and perspectives.* Tunbridge Wells: Costello.

Cromby, J., Sheard, C., Bennet, B., McConville, R., Richardson, M. and Stewart, D. (1994) Challenging behaviour amongst SLD students: a social constructionist analysis. *British Journal of Special Education* **21**(3): 128–135.

Cumella, S. and Sansom, D. (1994) A regional mental impairment service. *Mental Handicap Research* **7**(3): 257–268.

Day, K. and Jancar, J. (1994) Mental and physical health and ageing in mental handicap: a review. *Journal of Intellectual Disability Research* **38**: 241–256.

Deb, S. and Prasad, K. (1994) The prevalence of autistic disorder among children with learning disability. *British Journal of Psychiatry* **165**(3): 395–399.

Devlin, J., Mulcahy, M., Corcoran, R., Ramsay, L., Tyndall, P. and Shattock, A. (1993) Hepatitis B in the non-residential mentally handicapped population. *Journal of Intellectual Disabilities* **37**: 553–560.

Dowdney, L. and Skuse, D. (1993) Parenting provided by adults with mental retardation. *Journal of Child Psychology and Psychiatry* **34**: 25–47.

Ehler, S. and Gillberg, C. (1993) The epidemiology of Asperger syndrome. A total population study. *Journal of Child Psychology and Psychiatry,* (in press).

Emerson, E. (1992) Self-injurious behaviour: an overview of recent trends in epidemiological and behavioural research. *Mental Handicap Research* **5**(1): 49–81.

Felce, D., de Kock, U., Thomas, M. and Saxby, H. (1986) An eco-behavioural comparison of small home and institutional settings. *Applied Research in Mental Retardation* **7**: 393–408.

Finkelhor, D., Hotaling, G., Lewis, I. and Smith, C. (1990) Sexual abuse in a national survey of adult men and women. *Child Abuse and Neglect* **14**: 19–28.

Firth, H., Holtom, R., Mayor, J. and Wood, A. (1990) An evaluation of the effects of relocation within institutions. *Mental Handicap* **18**: 145–149.

Foote, K. and Rose, J. (1993) A day centre for elderly persons with learning disabilities, the consumers views. *Journal of Developmental and Physical Disabilities* **5**(2): 153–166.

Fraser, B. (1995) Psychiatry. *In* Fraser, W., McGillivray, R. and Green, A. (Eds) *Hallas's Caring for People with Mental Handicaps,* 8th edn. Butterworth Heinnemann.

Fraser, H. (1988) *Dementia: Its Nature and Management.* Wiley.

Gannesh, S., Potter, J. and Fraser, W. (1994) An audit of physical health needs of adults with profound learning disabilities in a hospital population. *Mental Handicap Research* **7**(3): 228.

Ghaziuddin, M., Tsai, L. and Ghaziuddin, N. (1992) Autism in Down's syndrome: presentation and diagnosis. *Journal of Intellectual Disability Research* **36**: 449–456.

Gillberg, C. (1991) Autism and related behaviours. *Journal of Intellectual Disability Research* **37**: 343–372.

Gingell, K. and Nadarajeh, J. (1994) A controlled community study of movement disorder in people with learning difficulties on anti-psychotic medication. *British Journal of Intellectual Disabilities Research* **37**: 53–59.

Goodwin, B. and Huether, C. (1987) Revised estimates and projections of Down's syndrome births in the United States, and the effects on pre-natal diagnosis utilisation, 1970–2002. *Prenatal Diagnosis* **7**: 261–271.

Grant, G. (1993) Support networks and transitions over two years among adults with a mental handicap. *Mental Handicap Research* **6**(1): 36–55.

Harris, P. (1993) The nature and extent of aggressive behaviour amongst people with learning difficulties in a single health district. *Journal of Learning Disabilities* **37**: 221–242.

Hastings, R. and Remington, B. (1993) Connotations of labels for mental handicap and challenging behaviour: a review and research evaluation. *Mental Handicap Research* **6**(3): 237–253.

Hastings, R. and Remington, B. (1994) Staff behaviour and challenging behaviour. *British Journal of Clinical Psychology* **33**: 445–450.

Howells, G. (1986) Are the medical needs of mentally handicapped adults being met? *Journal of the Royal College of Practitioners* **36**: 449–456.

Hur, J. and Cochrane, R. (1995) Academic performance of children with cerebral palsy: a comparative study of conductive education and British special education programmes. *British Journal of Developmental Disabilities* **XLI** (Part 1) No. 80: 33–41.

Joyce, T. (1994) The effect of individual and environmental characteristics on outcomes in residential services. *Mental Handicap Research* **7**(2): 134–142.

Kiernan, C. and Kiernan, D. (1994) Challenging behaviour in schools for pupils with learning difficulties. *Mental Handicap Research* **7**(3): 177–203.

Langan, J., Russel, O. and Whitfield, M. (1993) *Community Care and the General Practitioner. Primary health care for people with learning disabilities.* Bristol: Norah Fry Research Centre.

Licastro, F., Chiricolo, M., Mocchegiani, E., Fabris, N., Zannoti, M., Beltrandi, E. *et al.* (1994) Oral zinc supplementation in Down's syndrome subjects decreased infections and generalised some humoral and cellular immune parameters. *Journal of Intellectual Disability Research* **38**: 149–162.

Lowe, K. and DePavia, S. (1991) *NIMROD: an overview.* London: HMSO.

Lowe, K., Beyer, M., Kilsby, M. and Felce, D. (1992) Activities and engagement in day services for people with a mental handicap. *Journal of Intellectual Disability Research* **36**: 489–503.

Lyndsay, W., Howells, L. and Pitcaithly, D. (1993) Cognitive therapy for depression with individuals with intellectual disabilities. *British Journal of Medical Psychology* **66**: 135–141.

Maaskant, M. and Havemann, M. (1990) Elderly residents in Dutch mental deficiency institutions. *Journal of Mental Deficiency Research* **34**: 475–482.

Mansell, J. (1994) Challenging behaviour: the prospect for change. A Keynote review. *British Journal of Learning Disability* **22**(1): 2–5.

Moss, S., Patel, P., Prosser, H., Goldberg, D., Simpson, N., Rowe, S. and Lucchino, K. (1993) Psychiatric morbidity in older people with moderate and severe learning disability. *British Journal of Psychiatry* **163**: 471–480.

Murphy, G. (1993) Epidemiology of self-injury, characteristics of people with severe self-injury and initial treatment outcome. *In* Kiernan, C. (Ed.) *Research to Practice?*

Implications of research on the challenging behaviour of people with learning disability. Kidderminster: BILD.

Murphy, G. and Clare, I. (1991) MIETS: A service option for people with mild mental handicaps and challenging behaviour of psychiatric problems. *Mental Handicap Research* **4**: 180–206.

Naylor, V. and Clifton, M. (1993) People with learning disabilities – meeting complex needs. *Health and Social Care* **1**: 343–353.

Nicholson, A. and Alberman, E. (1992) Prediction of the number of Down's syndrome infants to be born in England and Wales up to the year 2000 and their likely survival rates. *Journal of Intellectual Disability Research* **36**: 505–517.

Norgate, R. (1994) Responding to the challenge. *Educational Psychology in Practice* **9**(4): 201–206.

Oswin, M. (1994) Don't ask us to dance. *Clinical Psychology Forum* **44**: 16–21.

Patel, P., Goldberg, D. and Moss, S. (1993) Psychiatric morbidity in older people with moderate and severe learning disability. *British Journal of Psychiatry* **163**: 481–491.

Perry, J. and Felce, D. (1994) Outcomes of ordinary housing services in Wales: objective indicators. *Mental Handicap Research* **7** (9): 286–311.

Pettipher, C. and Mansell, J. (1993) Engagement in meaningful activity in day centres: an exploratory study. *Mental Handicap Research* **6**(3): 263–274.

Prasher, V., Krishnan, V., Clarke, D. and Corbett, J. (1994) The assessment of dementia in people with learning disabilities. *Journal of Developmental Disability* **XL** (Part 2) No. 79.

Qureshi, H. and Alborz, A. (1992) Epidemiology of challenging behaviour. *Mental Handicap Research* **5**(2): 130–139.

Raudenbush, S. and Williams, J. (Eds) (1991) *Schools, Classrooms and Pupils: International studies of schooling from a multi-lateral perspective.* London: Academic Press.

Reid, A. (1994) Psychiatry and learning disabilities. *British Journal of Psychiatry* **164**(5): 613–618.

Rodgers, J. (1993) Primary health care provision for people with learning difficulties. *Health and Social Care* **2**: 11–17.

Rogers, D., Kirki, C., Bartlett, C. and Procock, P. (1991) The motor disorders of mental handicap. An overlap with motor disorders of severe psychiatric illness. *British Journal of Psychiatry* **158**: 97–102.

Rose, S. and Massey, P. (1993) Adventurous outdoor activities: an investigation into the benefits of adventure for seven people with learning disabilities. *Mental Handicap Research* **6**(4): 287–298.

Rose, J., Davis, C. and Gotch, L. (1993) A comparison of the services provided to people with profound and multiple disabilities in two different day centres. *British Journal of Developmental Disabilities* **39** (Part 2) No. 77: 83–94.

Sansom, D., Singh, I., Jawed, S. and Mukherjee, T. (1994) Elderly people with learning disabilities in hospital: a psychiatric study. *Journal of Intellectual Disability Research* **38**: 45–52.

Scotti, J., Evans, I., Meyer, L. and Walker, P. (1991) A meta-analysis of intervention research with problem behaviour: Treatment, validity and standards of practice. *American Journal of Mental Retardation* **96**: 233–256.

Sheiham, A. and Eadsforth, W. (1993) Sugar coated care. *Nursing Times* **90**(7): 34–35.

Shiell, A., Pettifer, C., Raynes, N. and Wright, K. (1992) The costs of community residential facilities for adults with a mental handicap in England. *Mental Handicap Research* **5**(2): 115–128.

Simblett, G. and Wilson, D. (1993) Asperger's syndrome: three cases and a discussion. *Journal of Intellectual Disabilities Research* **37**: 85–94.

Steele, J. (1993) Prenatal diagnosis and Down's syndrome: Part 2 Possible effects. *Mental Handicap Research* **6**(1): 56–68.

Stefelaar, J. and Evenhuis, H. (1989) Epidemiological onderzoeknaar de te verwachten aantallen oudered patients with Down's syndrome in de jaren 1990–2025. *Nederlandsch Tijdschrift voor Geneeskunde* **133**: 1121–1125.

Stewart, L., Beange, H. and Mackerras, D. (1994) A survey of dietary problems of adults with learning disabilities in the community. *Mental Handicap Research* **1**(1): 41–50.

Sturmey, P. and Sevin, J. (1993) Dual diagnosis: an annotated bibliography of recent research. *Journal of Intellectual Disability Research* **37**: 437–448.

Thompson, G. and Ward, K. (1994) Cost effectiveness and provision for special educational needs. *Mental Handicap Research* **7**(1): 78–95.

Thompson, G., Ward, K., Riddell, S. and Dyer, M. (1993) Pathways to adulthood for young people with special educational needs. *Issues in Special Education and Rehabilitation* **8**(1): 51–61.

Turk, V. and Brown, H. (1993) The sexual abuse of adults with learning disabilities: results of a two year incidence survey. *Mental Handicap Research* **6**(3): 193–215.

Tymchuk, A. and Andron, L. (1992) Project parenting: child interactional training with mothers who are mentally handicapped. *Mental Handicap Research* **5**(1): 4–15.

WHO (1994) *The ICD 10 Classification of Mental and Behavioural Disorders: Diagnostic Criteria for Research.* Geneva: World Health Organization.

Wilson, D. and Haire, A. (1990) Health care screening for people with mental handicap living in the community. *British Medical Journal* **301**: 1379–1381.

Yeates, S. (1992) Have they got a hearing loss? *Mental Handicap* **20 Dec.**: 126–132.

Box 16.3 Research centres in learning disability

British Institute of Learning Disabilities, Wolverhampton Road, Kidderminster, Worcs DY10 3PP, UK.

Centre for Research and Information into Mental Disability, Department of Psychiatry, University of Birmingham, Mindelshon Way, Birmingham B15 2QZ, UK.

Centre for Social Policy, Research and Development, University of Wales Bangor, Gwynedd LL57 2DG, UK.

Hester Adrian Research Centre, University of Manchester, Oxford Road, Manchester M13 9PT, UK.

Norah Fry Research Centre, University of Bristol, 32 Tindalls Park Road, Bristol BS8 1PY, UK.

Tizard Centre, Beverley Farm, University of Kent, Canterbury, Kent, UK.

Welsh Centre for Learning Disabilities, Applied Research Unit, University of Wales College of Medicine, 55 Park Place, Cardiff CF1 3AT, UK.

Appendix: Learning disability policy development
Sue Merrylees

Learning disability services and provision have undergone many changes in the 20th century, with key milestones at every stage. The aim of this checklist is to enable the reader quickly to reference key events in service development.

The checklist has been structured to demonstrate some of the relationships between issues in society and the development of policy. For example the idea of 'rights' of the disabled person comes from both national and international movements and resulted in some key policy changes. This is why the antecedent → policy → consequence structure has been used. One important point to note is that the consequences of many policies form the antecedents to others.

The checklist is not intended to be exhaustive and the issues raised are of particular relevance to health care agencies. Social and educational trends follow their own patterns of development.

The checklist is intended to provide a guide for further reading.

Antecedents	■ Recognition of rights of people with disability
	■ Hospital enquiries: Ely, Cardiff **1969**, Farleigh **1971**
	■ Publication of *Put Away* Pauline Morris (**1968**), Sociological study of hospitals
	■ Education Act (Handicapped Children) **1970**. Responsibility for children in hospital transferred to local authority
Milestone	■ CMND 4683 *Better Services for the Mentally Handicapped* (**1971**)
	Advocated – drop in hospital places from 52 000 to 27 000
	Recognized need for continued hospital care for some individuals
Consequences	■ Long-standing consequences in numbers. Attitudes to hospitalized care, admission patterns in particular, have been affected
	■ Establishment of specialist social service teams to meet needs of community care
	■ Establishment of campaign for mental handicap (CMH), now called Campaign for People with Mental Handicap
Antecedents	■ Briggs Report on Nursing (**1972**)
	■ Restructuring of NHS. Area health authorities established new local government boundaries (**1974**)
	■ Joint Care Planning Teams (JCPT) set up for client groups
	■ **1975** – Barbara Castle took Briggs recommendations and addressed annual NSMCH (National Society for Mentally Handicapped Children – which became MENCAP) conference *which*: (1) set up committee to explore Briggs recommendations (The Jay Committee); (2) set up National Development Group to advise Secretary of State; (3) set up National Development Team (NDT) to examine standards in care.
	■ **1976** – Priorities published by Labour government – mental handicap seen as priority
	■ **1978** – Warnock report – Education and services for children

- EXODUS campaign launched for speeding up hospital closures
- Normansfield hospital enquiry published
- Court Report – Fit for the Future – advocated community mental handicap teams. CMND 7468

Milestone
- The Jay Report **1979**
  Advocated
  – principles of Normalization
  – individualized care
  – local care
  – training changes: RNMH and social work together under CCETSW

Consequences
- Opening of debate on ordinary life principles
- Rethink on training – **1982** syllabus – emphasis on social care and community provision

Antecedents
- **1980** – publication of review of progress, problems and priorities since *Better Services for the Mentally Handicapped* – mental handicap – showed: under 16s major beneficiaries; local authority expansion slow; hospital beds not reducing as quickly as expected
- **1981** – Education Act adopted many Warnock proposals
- Introduction of initial ideas about marked influences into statutory sectors
- People not patients – Mittler estimates 2% population with learning disabilities
- NHS restructured area health authorities replaced by district health authorities
- End of NDG in abandonment of quangos by Conservative government
- Exploration of shared training ENB/CCETSW
- Report of a study on Community Care
- Mental Health Act **1983** changes in terminology – mental impairment and severe mental impairment
- Economic factors such as land price rises

Milestone
- **1984** Griffiths Report
  Advocated
  – changes in NHS management services
  – performance indicators for managers

Consequences
- Introduction of general management and performance indicators which allow for rapid closure and selling off of land
- The establishment of a thriving independent residential sector
- The introduction of clinical grading and resource management initiatives

Antecedents
- Increasing introduction of principles of internal market
- **1985** – House of Commons Select Committee Report on Community Care with special reference to adult mentally ill and mentally handicapped people. The Short Report CMND 9674. Changes views on replacement services and future role of community nurse
- Establishment of National Society for Mentally Handicapped People in Residential Care (RESCARE) – a reactionary group against rundown and closure of hospitals
- **1986** – Project 2000 published by the UKCC advocates common foundation studies followed by specialist training branch

- Audit Commission publish *Making a Reality of Community Care*
- Disabled Persons Act which had many points that facilitated development of community care initiatives
- **1987** Review of Community Care under Sir Roy Griffiths
- **1988** – Published *Community Care – An Agenda for Action*
- **1989** – Publishing of *Care for People – Community Care in the Next Decade Beyond* CM849
- Discussion on health service reforms

Milestones
- **1993** – Community Care Act
- **1992** – Working for Patients
  Advocated – The implementation of purchaser and provider systems

Consequences
- Services based on health and social care models
- Establishment of NHS trusts as health providers
- Social services responsible for purchasing community care
- Establishment of care management role
- Greater use of independent sector
- Greater role for GP fundholders in purchasing of community health services

Antecedents
- **1990** onwards
- NHS and Community Care reforms
- Further hospital enquiries at Ashworth and Stallington
- Evaluation of Project 2000 – national and local responses
- Nurse education moves into higher education
- 'Cost' of the RNMH as a part of the NHS budget
- Steven Dorrell's letter
- The Cullen Report
- The Mansell Report

Milestone
Consequences
- The **1993** debate on the future of the RNMH
- John Brown's analysis of responses to DOH
- Establishment of learning disability nurses project and publication of *Continuing the Commitment* highlighting eight key areas for nurses to address
- Re-establishment of dialogue on shared training

Index

Note: page numbers in *italics* refer to figures